CENSUS OF INDIA 1931

CENSUS OF INDIA, 1931

BOOK - 46: VOLUME - XXVII

RAJPUTANA AGENCY

AND

AJMER-MERWARA

PART I, II: REPORT AND TABLES AND ADMINISTRATIVE

LIEUT. COLONEL B. L. COLE

GYAN

Published by

Gyan Publishing House
5, Ansari Road
Daryaganj, New Delhi-110002
Phone: 011-47034999, 9811692060
E-mail: books@gyanbooks.com

Distribution Network
gyanbooks.com
India, USA, Canada, UK, Australia

ISBN: 978-81-212-7124-0 (Set) 28 Vols. In 52 Bindings

ISBN: 978-81-212-7510-1 (HB) Vol. XXVII, Pt. I, II

First Published, 1932

2nd Impression 2024

Printed at: Gyan Press, Delhi.

CENSUS OF INDIA 1931

Published by

Gyan Publishing House
5, Ansari Road
Daryaganj, New Delhi-110002
Phone: 011-47034999, 9811692060
E-mail: books@gyanbooks.com

Distribution Network
gyanbooks.com
India, USA, Canada, UK, Australia

ISBN: 978-81-212-7123-3 (Set) 28 Vols. In 52 Bindings

ISBN: 978-81-212-7509-5 (PB) Vol. XXVII, Pt. I, II

First Published, 1932

2nd Impression 2024

Printed at: Gyan Press, Delhi.

CENSUS OF INDIA 1931

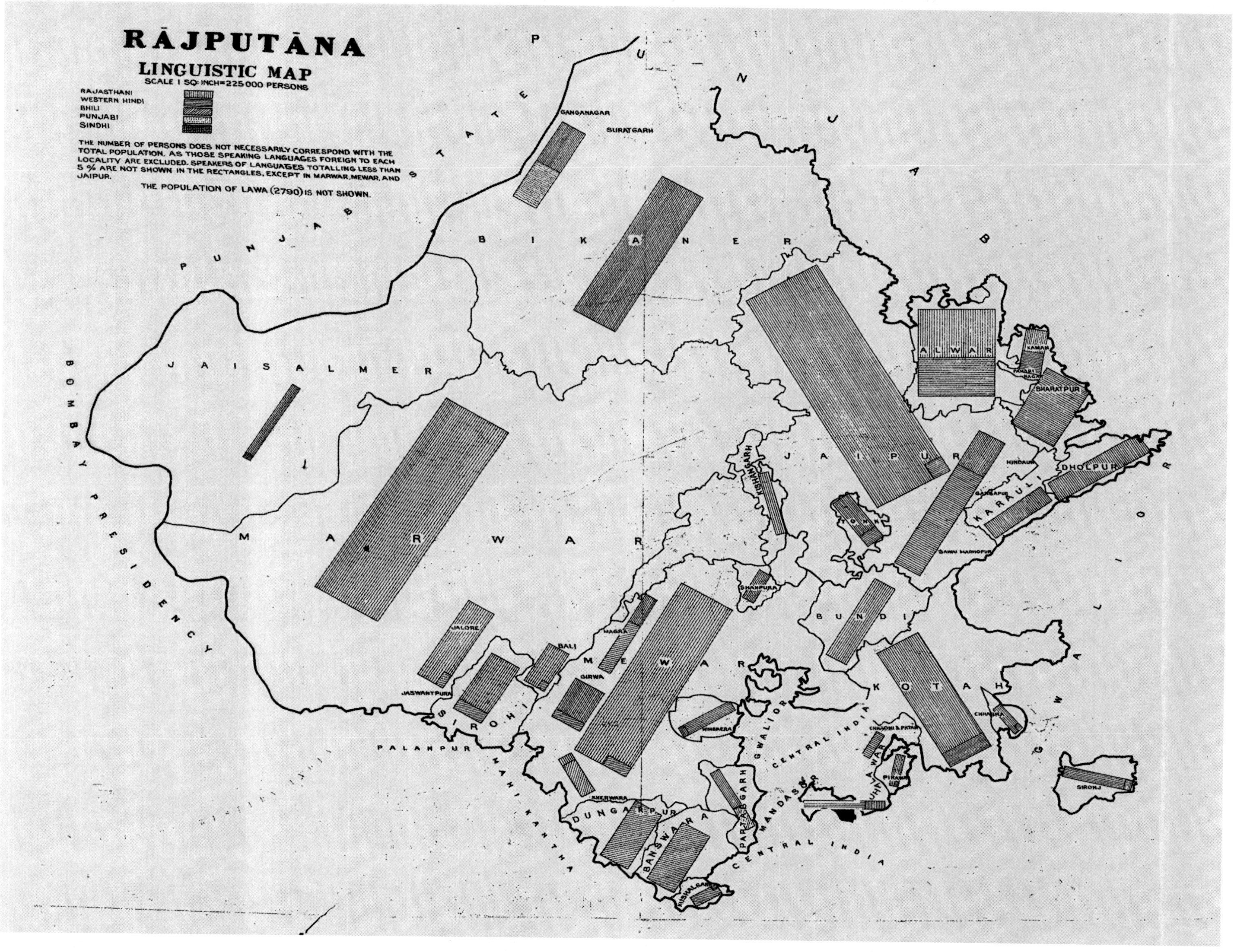
RĀJPUTĀNA
LINGUISTIC MAP
SCALE 1 SQ: INCH=225 000 PERSONS
RAJASTHANI
WESTERN HINDI
BHILI
PUNJABI
SINDHI
THE NUMBER OF PERSONS DOES NOT NECESSARILY CORRESPOND WITH THE TOTAL POPULATION, AS THOSE SPEAKING LANGUAGES FOREIGN TO EACH LOCALITY ARE EXCLUDED. SPEAKERS OF LANGUAGES TOTALLING LESS THAN 5 % ARE NOT SHOWN IN THE RECTANGLES, EXCEPT IN MARWAR, MEWAR, AND JAIPUR.
THE POPULATION OF LAWA (2790) IS NOT SHOWN.
PUNJAB STATE
PUNJAB
GANGANAGAR
SURATGARH
BIKANER
JAISALMER
MARWAR
JALORE
JASWANTPURA
SIROHI
BALI
MEWAR
MAGRA
GIRWA
KISHANGARH
SHAHPURA
JAIPUR
ALWAR
KAMAN
BHARATPUR
HINDAUN
DHOLPUR
KARAULI
GANGAPUR
SAWAI MADHOPUR
TONK
BUNDI
KOTAH
CHHABRA
SIRONJ
PIRAWA
JHALAWAR
MANDASOR
PARTABGARH
GWALIOR
CENTRAL INDIA
NIMBAHERA
KHERWARA
DUNGARPUR
BANSWARA
KUSHALGARH
PALANPUR
MAHI KANTHA
BOMBAY PRESIDENCY

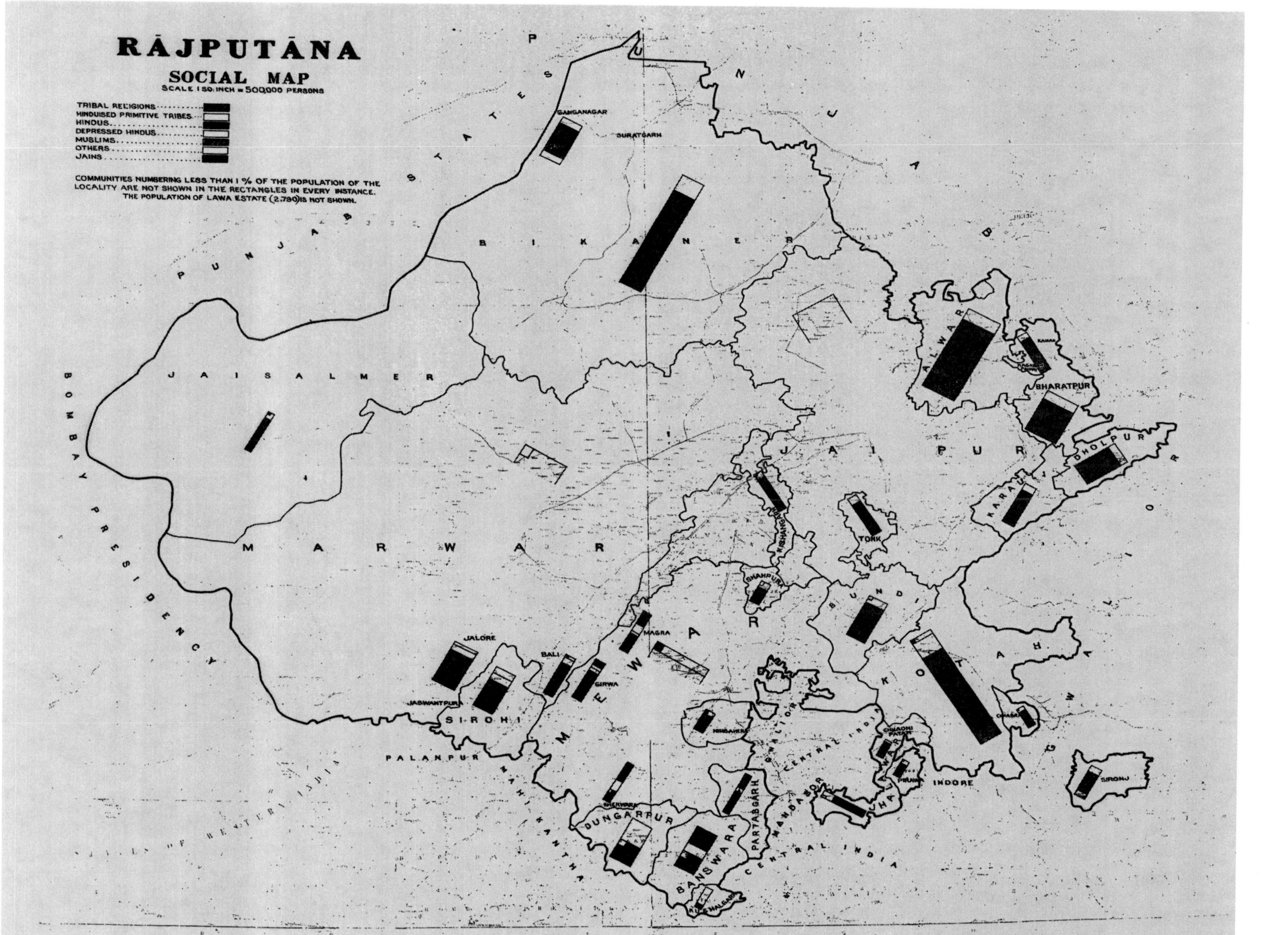
RĀJPUTĀNA
SOCIAL MAP
SCALE 1 SQ. INCH = 500,000 PERSONS
TRIBAL RELIGIONS
HINDUISED PRIMITIVE TRIBES
HINDUS
DEPRESSED HINDUS
MUSLIMS
OTHERS
JAINS
COMMUNITIES NUMBERING LESS THAN 1 % OF THE POPULATION OF THE LOCALITY ARE NOT SHOWN IN THE RECTANGLES IN EVERY INSTANCE.
THE POPULATION OF LAWA ESTATE (2,790) IS NOT SHOWN.
PUNJAB STATES
PUNJAB
BOMBAY PRESIDENCY
GANGANAGAR
SURATGARH
BIKANER
JAISALMER
MARWAR
ALWAR
BHARATPUR
DHOLPUR
JAIPUR
KARAULI
TONK
KISHANGARH
SHAHPURA
BUNDI
KOTAH
MEWAR
MAGRA
GIRWA
BALI
JALORE
JASWANTPURA
SIROHI
PALANPUR
MAHI KANTHA
DUNGARPUR
BANSWARA
PARTABGARH
KUSHALGARH
NIMBAHERA
GWALIOR
CENTRAL INDIA
MANDASOR
JHALAWAR
PIRAWA
CHHABRA
INDORE
SIRONJ
GWALIOR

CENSUS OF INDIA, 1931.

VOLUME XXVII

RAJPUTANA AGENCY

REPORT AND TABLES.

Government of India Publications are obtainable from the Government of India Central Publication Branch, 3, Government Place, West, Calcutta, and from the following Agents:—

EUROPE

OFFICE OF THE HIGH COMMISSIONER FOR INDIA, India House, Aldwych, LONDON, W. C. 2

And at all Booksellers.

INDIA AND CEYLON: Provincial Book Depots.

MADRAS :—Superintendent, Government Press, Mount Road, Madras.

BOMBAY :—Superintendent Government Printing and Stationery, Queen's Road, Bombay.

SIND :—Library attached to the Office of the Commissioner in Sind, Karachi.

BENGAL :—Bengal Secretariat Book Depôt, Writers' Buildings, Room No 1, Ground Floor, Calcutta

UNITED PROVINCES OF AGRA AND OUDH :—Superintendent of Government Press, United Provinces of Agra and Oudh, Allahabad.

PUNJAB :—Superintendent, Government Printing, Punjab, Lahore.

BURMA :—Superintendent, Government Printing, Burma, Rangoon.

CENTRAL PROVINCES AND BERAR :—Superintendent, Government Printing, Central Provinces, Nagpur.

ASSAM :—Superintendent, Assam Secretariat Press, Shillong.

BIHAR AND ORISSA :—Superintendent, Government Printing, Bihar and Orissa, P. O. Gulzarbagh, Patna

NORTH-WEST FRONTIER PROVINCE :—Manager, Government Printing and Stationery, Peshawar.

Thacker Spink & Co., Ltd., Calcutta and Simla.
W. Newman & Co., Ltd., Calcutta.
S. K. Lahiri & Co., Calcutta.
The Indian School Supply Depôt, 309, Bow Bazar Street, Calcutta.
Butterworth & Co., (India), Ltd., Calcutta
M. C. Sarcar & Sons, 15, College Square, Calcutta.
Standard Literature Company, Limited, Calcutta.
Association Press, Calcutta.
Chukervertty, Chatterjee & Co., Ltd., 13, College Square, Calcutta.
The Book Company, Calcutta.
James Murray & Co., 12, Government Place, Calcutta. (For Meteorological Publications only.)
Ray Chaudhury & Co., 68-5, Ashutosh Mukherji Road, Calcutta.
Scientific Publishing Co., 9, Taltola Lane, Calcutta.
Chatterjee & Co., 3-1, Bacharam Chatterjee Lane, Calcutta.
Standard Law Book Society, 8-2, Hastings Street, Calcutta
The Hindu Library, 3, Nandalal Mullick Lane, Calcutta
Kamala Book Depôt, Ltd., 15, College Square, Calcutta.
*Bengal Flying Club, Dum Dum Cantt.
Kali Charan & Co., Municipal Market, Calcutta.
N. M. Roy Chowdhury & Co., 11, College Sqr., Calcutta.
B. C. Basak, Esq, Proprietor, Albert Library, Dacca.
Higginbothams, Madras.
Rochouse and Sons, Madras.
G. A. Nateson & Co., Publishers, George Town, Madras.
P. Varadachary & Co., Madras.
City Book Co., Madras.
Law Publishing Co., Mylapore, Madras.
The Booklover's Resort, Taikad Trivandrum, South India.
E. M. Gopalakrishna Kone, Pudumandapam, Madura.
Central Book Depôt, Madura.
Vijapur & Co., Vizagapatam.
Thacker & Co., Ltd., Bombay.
D. B. Taraporevala, Sons & Co., Bombay.
Ram Chandra Govind & Sons, Kalbadevi Road, Bombay
N. M. Tripathi & Co., Booksellers, Princess Street, Kalbadevi Road, Bombay.
New and Secondhand Bookshop, Kalbadevi Road, Bombay.
J. M. Pandia & Co., Bombay.
A. H. Wheeler & Co., Allahabad, Calcutta and Bombay.
Bombay Book Depôt, Girgaon, Bombay.
Bennett, Coleman & Co., Ltd, The Times of India Press, Bombay.
The Popular Book Depôt, Bombay.
The Manager, Oriental Book Supplying Agency, 15, Shukrawar, Poona City.
Rama Krishna Bros., Opposite Bishrambag, Poona City.
S. P. Bookstall, 21, Budhwar, Poona.
Mangaldas and Sons, Booksellers and Publishers, Bhaga Talao, Surat
The Standard Book and Stationery Co., 32-33, Arbab Road, Peshawar.
The Students Own Book Depôt, Dharwar.
Shri Shankar Karnataka Pustaka Bhandara, Malamuddi, Dharwar.
The Standard Bookstall, Karachi, Quetta, Delhi, Murree and Rawalpindi.
Frontier Book and Stationery Co., Rawalpindi.
*Hossenbhoy Karimji and Sons, Karachi.
The English Bookstall, Karachi.
Rose & Co., Karachi.
The Standard Bookstall, Quetta.
U. P. Malhotra & Co., Quetta.
J. Ray and Sons, 43, K and L, Edwardes Road Rawalpindi, Murree and Lahore.
The Standard Book Depôt, Lahore, Nainital, Mussoorie Dalhousie, Ambala Cantonment and Delhi.
The North India Christian Tract and Book Society, 18, Clive Road, Allahabad.
Ram Narain Lal, Katra, Allahabad.
"The Leader," Allahabad
The Indian Army Book Depôt, Dayalbagh, Agra
The English Book Depôt, Taj Road, Agra
Gaya Prasad & Sons, Agra.
Narain & Co., Meston Road, Cawnpore
The Indian Army Book Depôt, Jullunder City, Daryaganj, Delhi.
Manager, Newal Kishore Press, Lucknow.
The Upper India Publishing House, Ltd., Literature Palace, Aminuddaula Park, Lucknow.
Rai Sahib M. Gulab Singh & Sons, Mufid-i-Am Press, Lahore and Allahabad.
Rama Krishna & Sons, Booksellers, Anarkali, Lahore
Student's Popular Depôt, Anarkali, Lahore.
The Standard Bookstall, Lahore
The Proprietor, Punjab Sanskrit Book Depôt, Saidmitha Street, Lahore.
The Insurance Publicity Co., Ltd., Lahore
The Punjab Religious Book Society, Lahore
The Commercial Book Co., Lahore
The University Book Agency, Kachari Road, Lahore
Manager of the Imperial Book Depôt, 63, Chandni Chowk Street, Delhi.
J. M. Jaina & Bros., Delhi.
Fono Book Agency, New Delhi and Simla.
Oxford Book and Stationery Company, Delhi, Lahore, Simla, Meerut and Calcutta.
Supdt., American Baptist Mission Press, Rangoon.
Burma Book Club, Ltd., Rangoon.
S. C. Talukdar, Proprietor, Students & Co., Cooch Behar.
The Manager, The Indian Book Shop, Benares City
Nandkishore & Bros., Chowk, Benares City
The Srivilliputtur Co-operative Trading Union, Ltd., Srivilliputtur, (S. I. R.)
Raghunath Prasad & Sons, Patna City.
The Students' Emporium, Patna.
K. L. Mathur & Bros., Guzri, Patna City.
Kamala Book Stores, Bankipore, Patna.
G. Banerjea and Bros., Ranchi.
M. C. Kothari, Raipura Road, Baroda.
B. Parikh & Co., Baroda.
The Hyderabad Book Depôt, Chaderghat, Hyderabad (Deccan).
S. Krishnaswamy & Co., Teppakulam P. O. Trichinopoly Fort.
Karnataka Publishing House, Bangalore City.
Bheema Sons, Fort, Bangalore City.
Superintendent, Bangalore Press, Lake View, Mysore Road, Bangalore City.

AGENT IN PALESTINE:—Steimatzky, Jerusalem.

*Agents for publications on aviation only.

CENSUS OF INDIA, 1931.

VOLUME XXVII

RAJPUTANA AGENCY

REPORT AND TABLES

BY

Lieut. Colonel B. L. COLE

of the Indian Army.

1932

PRINTED FOR THE GOVERNMENT OF INDIA BY THE SARASWATI PRESS,

MEERUT, U.P. (INDIA).

ADDENDA AND CORRIGENDA.

Introduction.

Page v In the penultimate line of paragraph 3, *for* 'final' *read* 'preliminary'.

Report.

Page 2. In the 13th. line from the bottom, *for* 'Countries' *read* 'Counties'.
Page 3. In column 3 of the marginal statement *for* '+20·6' *and* '−20·5' *read* '+20·3' *and* '−19·0' respectively.
Page 13. In column 2 of the heading *for* '1930' *read* '1931'.
Page 18. In column 8 *against* 'Partabgarh' *for* '8·4' *read* '18·4'.
Page 20. In the 5th. line from the bottom, *for* 'ot' *read* 'to'.
Page 28. In column 4 *against* 'Tonk', *for* '966' *read* '967'.
Page 28. In column 1 *for* 'Kushalgarh (Chiefship)' *read* 'Kushalgarh'.
Page 34. In column 9 of Subsidiary Table 1 (a) *against* 'Jaisalmer', *for* '237,832' *read* '37,832'.
Page 35. In column 4 of Subsidiary Table 2 (a) *against* 'Jaisalmer' *for* '33,903' *read* '33,913'.
In column 13 of Subsidiary Table 2 (a) *against* 'Dholpur' and 'Dungarpur' *for* '72,62' *and* '3,041' *read* '7,261' *and* '3,042' respectively.
Page 45. In the diagram *against* 'Tonk' *for* '512' *and* '488' *read* '513' *and* '482' respectively.
Page 56. In column 5 of the first marginal statement in paragraph 5 *against* 'age-group 0–5', *for* '19' *read* '18'.
In the last but one line of paragraph 5 *for* 'particulary' *read* 'particularly'.
Page 57. In the last line in column 2 of the second statement, *for* '137' *read* '37'.
Page 69. In the 9th. line from the bottom, *for* 'latter' *read* 'later'.
Page 89. In column 3 *against* 'Group No. 172' *for* '1,29' *read* '1,296'.
Page 101. In column 15 of Subsidiary Table 1, *against* 'Sikh', *for* '...' *read* '1'.
In column 1 of Subsidiary Table 2, *for* 'hahpura' *read* 'Shahpura'.
Page 107. In column 2 of the marginal Table against 'Merwari', for '10,016' *read* '10,046'.
Page 109 In the 14th. line from the top, *for* 'these' *read* 'those'.
Page 116. In column 10 against 'Jain', *for* '−1' *read* '−15·8'.
Page 120. In the heading *for* ' Appendix A ' *read* ' Appendix '.
Page 134. In the 4th. line of paragraph 2 *for* ' outnumberd ' *read* ' outnumbered '.

Tables.

Page 1. Delete the reference to British Administration so far as it concerns Kherwara, Kotra, Erinpura and Deoli Agency.
Page 4. In column 4 *against* ' Bharatpur ' *for* ' 588, 785' *read* ' 558, 785 '.
In column 7 *against* ' Partabgarh, ' *for* ' 79, 29 ' *read* ' 79, 298 '.
Page 50 In column 9 *against* ' age-period 5-10 ' *under* ' Kotah-Hindu, ' *for* ' 1,402 ' *read* ' 1,042 '.
Page 63. In column 15 *against* ' Rajput Females ' *in* ' Jaipur ' and *against* 'Rebari Males' *in* 'Sirohi,' *for* '2,919' *and* ' 321 ' *read* ' 2,199' *and* '312' respectively.
In column 24 *against* ' Mina Females ' *in* ' Alwar, ' *for* '1,314 ' *read* '1,134'.
In column 25 *against* ' Bhil Females ' *in* ' Dungarpur ' and 'Khati Females' *in* ' Mewar, ' *for* ' 3,218 ' *and* ' 0,431 ' *read* ' 3,128 ' *and* ' 1,431 ' respectively.
Page 67. In column 6 *against* ' Tonk, ' *for* ' 70 ' *read* ' 71 '.
Page 129. In column 11 *against* ' age-period 5—10' *under* ' Dholpur Muslim, ' *for* ' . ' *read* ' 1 '.
Page 167. In the last column *under* ' Marwar ' *against* ' Bambhi ', *for* ' 76,006 ' *read* ' 76,066.'
Page 168. In column 3 *under* ' Mewar ' *against* ' Rajput, ' *for* ' 17,829 ' *read* '57,829 '.
In column 3 *under* ' Tonk ' *against* ' Others ' *for* ' 31,780 ' *read* ' 31,781 '.

TABLE OF CONTENTS.

IMPERIAL SERIES—VOLUME XXVII.

REPORT.

MAPS AND DIAGRAMS.

IMPERIAL TABLES.

INTRODUCTION.

1. This Report deals with the sixth Census which was taken in the several States, etc., of the Rajputana Agency on the night of the 26th. February, 1931. The figures in the margin show the population as recorded at each Census since the first one in 1881. The Census of 1901 was the first at which any degree of accuracy was attained, since at the two preceding ones the Bhil population was estimated and not enumerated.

1881	...	10,102,105
1891	...	12,153,631
1901	...	9,842,482
1911	...	10,518,345
1921	...	9,831,755
1931	...	11,225,712

2. Since the last Census in 1921 the only change has been that the population of the two isolated *parganas* of Nandwai and Gangapur—situated within the boundaries of Mewar—has been included in those of Indore and Gwalior to which States they respectively belong, and not in that of this Agency. For a proper understanding of what is involved by a Census, it is necessary to describe briefly the various stages that finally lead up to a publication of the figures. The willing cooperation of the Darbars having been obtained by the Political authorities, the first step was the preparation of a General Village Register for each Tehsil or other administrative unit. In this Register is shown the names of villages and dependent hamlets and the number of houses in each. From this and with the aid of Maps, Census units are formed. The smallest unit is a Block consisting of from 30 to 50 houses in charge of an Enumerator. A Circle is a compact group containing 10 to 15 Blocks under a Supervisor, and finally a Charge which is usually the Tehsil or other administrative unit, is under a Charge Superintendent, generally the Tehsildar himself. In each State a Census Superintendent was appointed who corresponded with me direct on all matters pertaining to the Census Operations. There were thus in the whole Agency 408 Charges, 6,064 Circles and 76,351 Blocks. After these divisions had been clearly demarcated and entered in the Charge Registers, the next step was to number the houses and write up the House Lists. With a preliminary issue of Schedules, for training purposes, the instruction of the staff was undertaken, followed by a final distribution of all necessary forms.

3. With the exception of 625 Bhil villages in Mewar, the Census was taken in the usual manner by a house to house visitation. In the villages referred to which contained a population of 98,539 persons, the Census was non-synchronous in so far that it was taken by summoning the headmen and obtaining from them the requisite information concerning the population of each village. A preliminary enumeration started early in January when particulars of the bulk of the resident population were entered on the Schedules and subjected to the scrutiny of Supervisors and Charge Superintendents. The final count was taken between sunset and midnight on the 26th. February in all except the more inaccessible areas where it was taken during the afternoon. At this count the record of the final enumeration was checked, new entries being made as required.

4. Special arrangements were made for the enumeration of passengers at Railway Stations and in trains. The latter were stopped at convenient wayside stations early on the morning of the 27th. February for this purpose. Each Railway Station constituted a Census Circle in the adjacent Charge of the State concerned.

5. As soon as possible after the count had been taken, Enumerators were required to enter their totals and take them to their Supervisors, who in their turn communicated the figures to their Charge Superintendents. The totals for each Charge were communicated with all despatch to the State Superintendent and the State totals were then telegraphed to me and to the Census Commissioner. The first figures to be received were from Banswara at 05·45 on the 27th. February and the last from Jaisalmer at 0·55 on the 3rd. March. The provisional totals for the whole Agency were thus known 90 hours and 55 minutes after the last train enumeration and only varied by 1,501 persons or ·01 per cent. from the final totals as subsequently compiled in the Abstraction Offices.

6. The post enumeration stages of a Census fall into 3 heads (1) Copying details from the schedules on to a slip for each individual. These slips were of different colours for the various Religions and had easily recognised symbols to denote sex and civil condition; (2) Tabulation, or successive sortings of these slips in order to obtain materials for the various Imperial Tables; (3) Compilation or the posting and addition of the results of the several sortings. An innovation was tried at this Census whereby the whole of the post enumeration work was done in each State and not at certain fixed Centres as heretofore. Three touring Inspectors, or rather Advisers, were appointed by Government to co-ordinate the work of abstraction and the system was a complete success proving satisfactory both to Government and the Darbars. The last Table necessary for incorporation in this Volume was received on 14th. August, 1931. The maximum staff necessary for the Central Office at its busiest time when State Tables were checked and co-ordinated for the preparation of Agency Tables, was 1 Deputy Superintendent, 1 Head Clerk and 7 Assistant Clerks. This staff also dealt with matters of general office routine and the preparation of the Report and Tables for Ajmer-Merwara which for the first time since the Census of 1901 were published in a separate Volume. The first Table was ready for the Press on the 25th. May, 1931, and the last on 15th. December, 1931, though several months elapsed before they emerged in their final form. The writing of this Report commenced in September, 1931, and continued side by side with that of Ajmer-Merwara till June, 1932. By that time the Press had dropped behind and the proofs of several Chapters and Tables were outstanding.

7. The cost of the Census to the States from the commencement of operations to the completion of the final Table works out on the average to Rs. 25—2—10 per 1,000 of population, as against Rs 26-11-3 in 1921 in spite of higher wages now prevailing. The total cost to Government, States and British Indian Municipalities for the Census in Ajmer-Merwara and the Agency was approximately Rs. 35-1-0 per 1,000 of population. At previous Censuses this was Rs. 36-6-11 in 1921 and Rs. 29-2-8 in 1911.

8. It would be almost impossible to specify by name all those who have so materially assisted in bringing this Census to a successful and expeditious close. My warmest thanks are due to the undermentioned gentlemen who were in charge of the operations in each State, etc :—

- Mount Abu ...Captain D. R. Smith, I. A., District Magistrate.
- Alwar ... Rai Sahib Shyam Singh. / Rai Bahadur Pandit Nand Lal Tikku.
- Banswara ...Babu Nand Lal Banerjee.
- Bharatpur ...Babu Hari Dutt.
- Bikaner ...Rai Bahadur Mr. D. M. Nanawati.
- Bundi ... Munshi Jagat Narain Lal. / Munshi Prabhu Dayal.
- Dholpur ... Pandit M. C. Sharma. / Rai Sahib Munshi Din Dayal.
- Dungarpur ...Pandit Niranjan Das Dutt.
- Jaipur ...Munshi Ram Pratap Khuteta.
- Jaisalmer ...Mr. V. U. Dave.
- Jhalawar ...Pandit Dhani Ram Sharma.
- **Karauli** Lala Kistur Chand.
- **Kishangarh** ...Mehta Amar Singh.
- **Kotah** ...Babu Man Mohan Gupta.
- **Kushalgarh** ...Mr. Amar Singh.
- **Lawa** ...Lala Chuttan Lal Saksena.
- **Marwar** ...Pandit Bishambar Nath Kaul.
- **Mewar** ... Mr. Ajodhya Prasad Phatkiwala. / Pandit Yamuna Lal Dashora.
- **Partabgarh** ...Munshi Fateh Lal Khasgiwala.
- **Shahpura** ...Shah Amar Singh.
- **Sirohi** ...Khan Sahib Munshi Ekramullah.
- **Tonk** ...Sahibzada Khalil-ur-Rahman Khan.

The work in the larger States of Jaipur, Marwar, Mewar and Bikaner was particularly onerous and an extra meed of praise is due to the gentlemen concerned who shouldered their responsibilities so cheerfully and efficiently.

I would also tender my best thanks to all the Ruling Princes, Chiefs and Political Officers in Rajputana; to the heads of State administrations and to all officials for their ready and unfailing help and to all Railway Census Officers for their ungrudging and valuable cooperation.

Coming to my own staff, the work of Babu Debi Dayal as Deputy Superintendent was invaluable throughout, while my Head Clerk, Lala Lachman Das Gupta by his industry, initiative and energy proved himself to be a man of more than average ability. The three gentlemen named in the margin filled the experimental appointments of Touring Tabulation Inspectors very satisfactorily and justified such appointments being made at each Census in the future. I owe a personal debt of thanks to Mr. F. A. Leslie Jones, C. B. E., (late Principal of the Mayo College) for advice when writing the Report and to Rao Bahadur Raja Hari Singhji of Mahajan, C. I. E., and Rai Bahadur Pandit Gauri Shankar Ojha for their kind assistance in the preparation of the Appendix on the Rajput clans.

1 Lala Kanahaiya Lal Varma.
2. Pandit Bishamber Nath.
3. Mr. Kanwar Bahadur.

I cannot bring this brief review of the Census of Rajputana to a close without recording my sense of obligation to the Hon'ble Sir Leonard W. Reynolds, K. C. I. E., C. S. I., M. C., who, as Agent to the Governor General, readily gave me the benefit of his experience and advice at all stages of my endeavours and to Dr. J. H. Hutton, C. I. E., Census Commissioner for India for the patience and sympathy with which he treated my many references to him.

2-7-32. B. L. C.

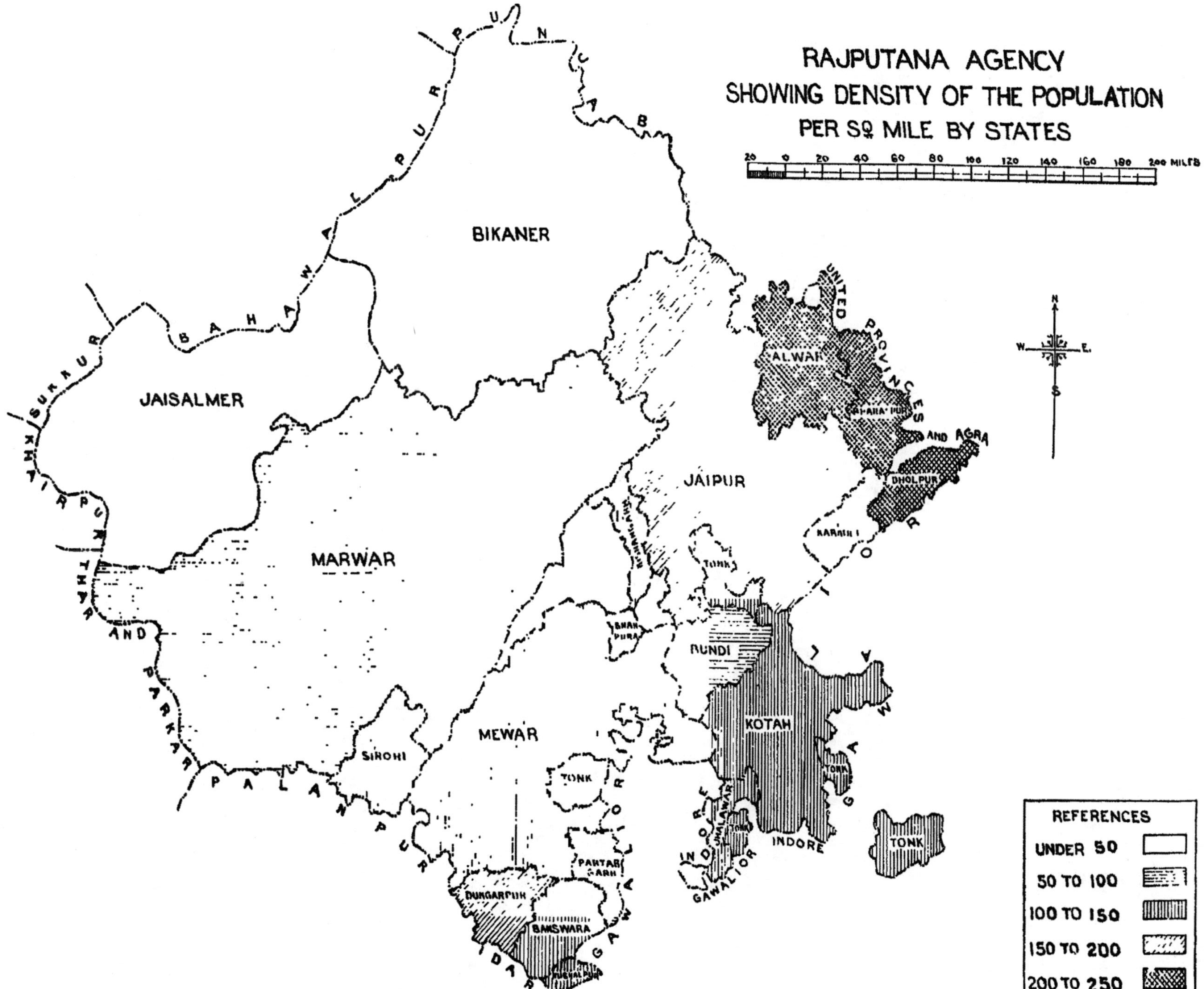

RAJPUTANA AGENCY
SHOWING DENSITY OF THE POPULATION
PER SQ MILE BY STATES
20 0 20 40 60 80 100 120 140 160 180 200 MILES
N
S
W
E
BIKANER
JAISALMER
MARWAR
JAIPUR
ALWAR
DHOLPUR
KARAULI
TONK
BUNDI
KOTAH
SIROHI
MEWAR
DUNGARPUR
BANSWARA
PARTABGARH
INDORE
GWALIOR
JHALAWAR
UNITED PROVINCES AND AGRA
PUNJAB
BAHAWALPUR
SUKKUR
KHAIRPUR
THAR AND PARKAR
PALANPUR
IDAR
REFERENCES
UNDER 50
50 TO 100
100 TO 150
150 TO 200
200 TO 250

REPORT

ON THE

CENSUS

OF THE

RAJPUTANA AGENCY, 1931.

CHAPTER I.

Distribution and Movement of the Population.

PART I.—The Rajputana Agency.

Reference to Statistics.

1. The figures with which this Chapter deals are found in Imperial Tables I and II and Provincial Table 1, while at the end of the Chapter will be found five Subsidiary Tables showing comparative figures.

Area dealt with.

2. The territory dealt with in this Report is known as the Rajputana Agency, and comprises 19 independent States, 1 Chiefship and 1 Estate grouped together for their political relations with the Government of India through the Agent to the Governor General in Rajputana. A small area of 6 square miles known as the Abu District is leased from the Sirohi Darbar and its population is shown separately throughout this Report. There have been no changes in the external boundaries since the last Census, except for the addition of 2 uninhabited square miles to Bikaner from the Punjab. In the centre of Mewar lie the isolated *parganas* of Gangapur and Nandwai belonging respectively to the States of Gwalior and Indore. At former Censuses their population was included in that of this Agency but such is not now the case. For these reasons and also on account of recent and more accurate surveys in Alwar, Bharatpur, Dholpur and Marwar the total area is now 129,059 square miles as against 128,987 in 1921.

Natural Divisions.

3. In a presentation of Census statistics it is usual to partition a Province into areas which possess more or less homogeneous physical features and these are styled Natural Divisions. At previous Censuses it has been the practice to divide the Agency into 3 such Divisions, the Western, Southern and Eastern. The Western Division comprised the sparsely populated States of Bikaner, Jaisalmer and Marwar, the Southern included Banswara, Dungarpur, Kushalgarh, Mewar, Sirohi and Partabgarh, while the rest of the Agency formed the Eastern Division. Now this scheme had many anomalies and to mention only a few, Tonk has one pargana, Nimbahera which is almost surrounded by Mewar and the same applies to Shahpura. A considerable portion of Marwar has a more copious rainfall and a greater density than the

Northern tracts of Jaipur, and the Eastern Division included such diversities as Bharatpur, with a density figure of nearly 250, and Bundi with one of under 100. For these reasons, and also for the reason that each State is entirely independent of any other, it was held that any scheme for a presentation of figures by Natural Divisions would only produce a result of small academic interest and very little value. In this Report therefore, the former Western Division, now described as the North-West Dry Area, has been retained for figures of density, variation in population, and migration only, the rest of the Agency being shown for the same purposes as Rajputana East.

Before proceeding to discuss in detail questions of area and population, the marginal statement may be considered as it emphasises the contribution that each Natural Division makes to these two subjects. It may also be stated that the normal annual rainfall in the North-West Dry Area is 10·40 inches whereas in the rest of Rajputana it is 29·64.

NATURAL DIVISION.	PERCENTAGE OF AGENCY AREA.	PERCENTAGE OF POPULATION.
North-West Dry Area.	57·64	27·95
Rajputana East.	42·36	72·05
Total.	100	100

Meaning of Population.

4. Figures for population as obtained at a Census represent a *de facto* population. That is to say, it is the population as enumerated in a given area on a specific date. In certain areas of Mewar inhabited by Bhils, the final enumeration was achieved, not by ordinary enumeration, but by summoning the headman of each *Pal* to give an accurate record of the population concerned, which numbered 98,539. The *de jure* population is the sum of those ordinarily resident in a given area and is liable to be disturbed by such occurrences as large fairs, waves of migration and so forth. No such disturbances occurred at this Census and the population that was going about its lawful occasions was both *de facto* and *de jure*.

Accuracy.

5. The accuracy of an Indian Census is almost impossible to assess. Previous experience has however taught the controlling staff where omissions are liable to occur, and, as a result, foresight and adequate arrangements combine to make the enumeration as accurate as it is humanly possible to be. However, what may seem a small omission to an individual enumerator of, say, 1 in 100, amounts in the total to a very large figure and in this Agency would represent about half of the entire population of Banswara State. With these explanations and qualifications, an examination of the figures may be commenced.

Summary of figures for population and area.

6. Within its 129,059 square miles the Agency contains 11,225,712 persons. Density is the correlation of these two figures and is, for the whole Agency, 87 persons per square mile. In size, it is larger than the British Isles or Norway, but its population only approximates to that of the Countries of Yorkshire, Lancashire, Durham and Northumberland combined. For comparison with other parts of India, it may be stated that the population of Rajputana is a million and a half less than that of Oudh, while in size it is over five times as large. The mean density figure of 87 conveys little for it is calculated on two such extremes as Jaipur City and Jaisalmer State. In the latter, the proximity in yards of the population is 888 or in other words if the people were spread evenly over its surface, each person would be half a mile from his nearest neighbour or practically out of earshot. When a large area consists of Indian States grouped together for political convenience, it is inevitable that the States should vary considerably in size and population. The extent to which this is so is shown in the diagram opposite while the Map prefacing this Chapter shows the density of the population in each State.

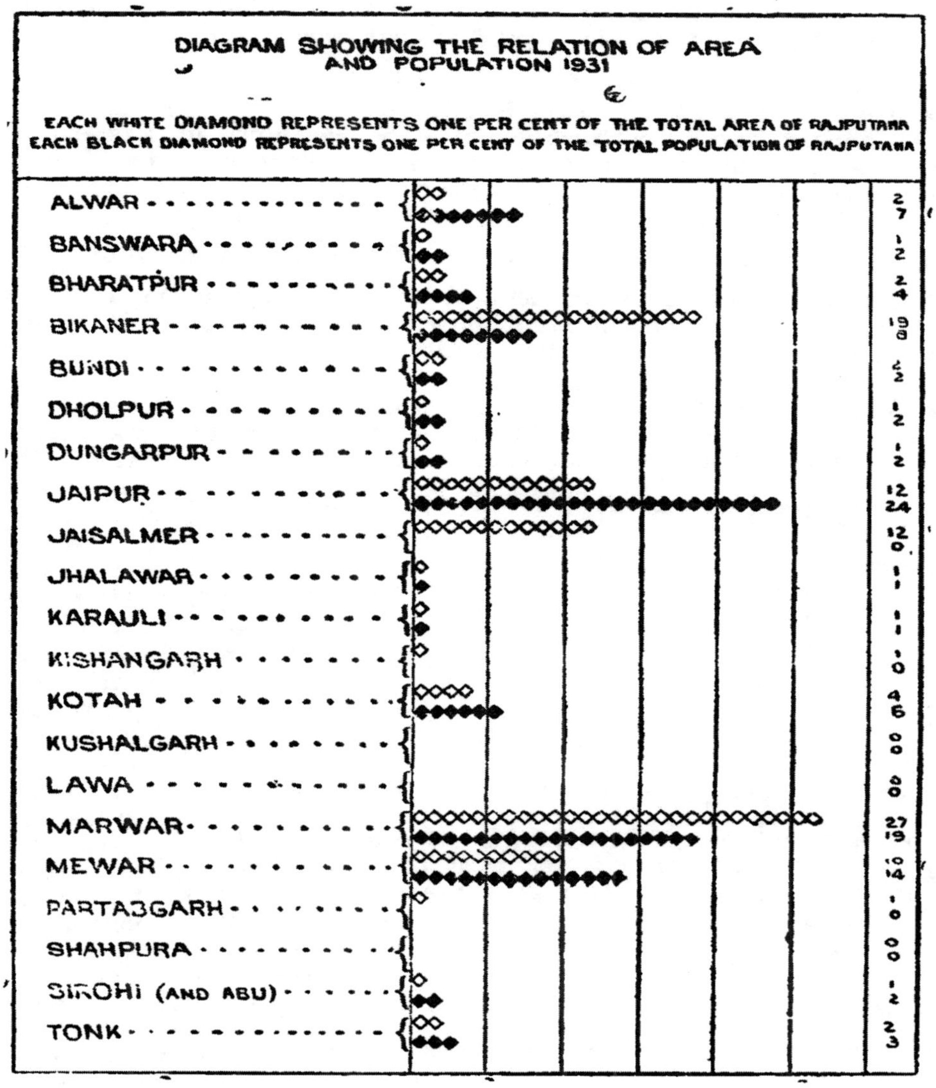

Variation in the population at previous Censuses.

7. The population now recorded is the highest since the Census of 1891 when a considerable portion of the Bhil population was estimated and not enumerated. The figures in the margin show in a succinct form the population at each Census since 1881 and its variation from the preceding one. It is unfortunate that the first really accurate Census was that of 1901 as the population was then considerably reduced on account of a series of years of scanty rainfall, culminating in the severe famine of 1899-1900 with its attendant lower birth-rate and increased emigration. The power of recovery among Indian people is however shown by the figures for 1911, which would have been higher, had it not been for an epidemic of plague and, in some parts, of cholera and small pox. The decade ending in 1921 saw the population at its lowest recorded limit as a result of a very severe outbreak of influenza in 1918. The variations from Census to Census resemble mighty swings of Nature's pendulum and the present population is only 613,374 more than the average in the past fifty years.

Census Year.	Population.	Variation per cent.
1881	10,102,105	...
1891	12,158,681	+20·6
1901	9,842,482	−20·5
1911	10,518,845	+ 6·9
1921	9,881,755	− 6·5
1931	11,225,712	+14·2

Conditions of the past decade.

8. The particular features during the past decade that have led to this increase in the population may be summarised as, freedom from epidemics, absence of famine conditions, and increased immigration into Bikaner State. Should Nature repeat the history of the past 50 years and, by the next Census, swing the pendulum back at the rate shown by her previous vagaries, it will

require all the efforts of man and Administrations to combat the loss of over a million and a half persons which would in that case occur.

Variations in Natural Divisions.

9. Subsidiary Table 3 at the end of this Chapter shows that the population of the North-West Dry Area has increased by 22·2 per cent. This high figure is chiefly due to an increase of 41·9 per cent. in Bikaner State on account of an increase in irrigated land and a consequent flow of immigrants. In Rajputana East, the increase is 11·3 per cent. and in its component parts ranges from + 23·3 in the Lawa Estate, to − 1·9 in Bharatpur.

Vital Statistics.

10. No vital statistics are available for the Agency as a whole.

Variations in Natural Population.

11. Subsidiary Table 4 shows that the Natural population, i. e. those born in the Agency wherever enumerated, now stands at 11,741,489 which is an increase of 12·1 per cent. during the decade.

Population in relation to density.

12. The natural features and variations in rainfall are such that the population is by no means evenly distributed over the whole area. The number of persons per square mile varies from 5 in Jaisalmer to 247 in Bharatpur. The statement in the margin which has been compiled from figures for the smaller units, e.g., Tehsils, etc., in each State, shows the distribution, for the Agency and each of the two Natural Divisions, of the population and area according to density.

NATURAL DIVISION.	DENSITY UNDER 150.		150—300.		300—450.	
	PERCENTAGE.		PERCENTAGE.		PERCENTAGE.	
	Area.	Population	Area.	Population.	Area.	Population.
North-West Dry Area	100	100	...	...	...	...
Rajputana East	74	61	25	36	1	3
Total Rajputana	**89**	**72**	**11**	**26**	...	**2**

It will be seen that 28 per cent. of the population reside in areas where the density is over 150 persons per square mile. The highest proportionate contributors to the population in these areas are Alwar with 96, Bharatpur 100 and Dholpur 94 per cent. of their populations. All three are contiguous States in the extreme East of the Agency. In these three States combined, the population has only increased during the decade by 4·5 per cent. while the figure for the rest of the Agency is 15·8 per cent. To take the case of Jaipur, we find that in the three most congested Nizamats the increase in the population has been materially less than in the three where the population is least dense. Other factors being equal, there would appear from a perusal of these figures to be some connection between variation and density.

Nizamat.	Density.	Variation 1921-1931 per cent.
Kot Kasim	247	+ 3·1
Hindaun	229	+ 9·8
Dausa	223	+ 7·7
Malpura	88	+15·4
Sawai Madhopur	91	+11·7
Shekhawati	88	+14·6

Houses and families.

13. In rural areas, for Census purposes, a house is defined as a building or part of a building occupied by one commensal family, but in towns, a somewhat different definition was adopted. Some towns are notoriously overcrowded and therefore, to obtain figures where such a condition was prevalent, a house was treated as a structural and not as a commensal unit. According to this definition one frequently came across a 'House' in which eight or more families were residing. However, for various reasons the distinction was not justified as the average number of persons per urban 'House' worked out at 5·05 as against 4·64 persons in a rural one. Since the 'House' is the only clue available for the number and size of families, it is really preferable to have the same definition in rural and urban areas. Subsidiary Table 5 shows the average number of persons per house in each State, etc. at each Census since 1881 and very little change is observed. For the whole Agency, the average is now 4·7 or 4,700 persons per 1,000 houses. Now we know from Imperial Table VII the distribution of the population by Sex, Age and Civil Condition and can assess

Unmarried Males	1,208
Unmarried Females	780
Married Males	1,081
Married Females	1,109
Widowed Males	174
Widowed Females	348
Total	4,700

4,700 persons to be as shown in the margin. It may be assumed that 81 married males and 109 married females are too young to have set up house. That would make in addition to a married man and woman in each house, 1,289 sons, 889 daughters and 522 widowed persons of both sexes in 1,000 houses.

PART II.—The States, etc., of the Rajputana Agency.

Abu District:—The population of this small area of 6 square miles leased by Government from the Sirohi Darbar, fluctuates according to the time of year. It is at its fullest in May and June when the population was 5,405 in 1921. At the time of the Census it is usually at its lowest but now shows an increase of 25·7 per cent. since the last Census. No Summer Census was taken on this occasion.

Alwar:—The population of Alwar has only increased by 6·9 per cent. during the decade and on the whole compares unfavourably with increases observed in contiguous States and Districts i.e. Nabha 9·2, Patiala 8·4, Gurgaon 8·5, Jaipur 12·5. The greatest increase of 18·9 is recorded in the Govindgarh Tehsil, whilst an actual decrease of 10·5 per cent. is shown for the Partabgarh Tehsil. The all round increase is attributed to the absence of scarcity and epidemics and to the reclamation of waste lands which has attracted immigrants from neighbouring States. The increased number of immigrants during the decade was 11,375. Rainfall varied between an annual average of 27·9 inches at Rajgarh in the south of the State to 20·3 inches at Bahror in the north. The 1921 Census Report foreboded an inauspicious future for the progress of the population, and based the gloomy prediction on the loss occasioned by a decrease in immigration and a greater number of emigrants, combined with a reduced proportion of married females of child-bearing ages. Although it is not possible on this occasion to quote the number of emigrants, it has already been seen that immigration increased during the past decade.

Banswara:—The population of this State with an area of 1,606 square miles has increased from 190,362, in 1921 to 225,106, or 18·3 per cent. Bhils form 64 per cent. of the population and by reason of their being short lived but prolific people, it is not possible to compare, accurately, the figures for this State with those of any other. As an instance of this, the age distribution for 100 persons in the whole Agency is 0-15, 41; 15-50, 49; and 50 and over, 10; while for Banswara it is 47, 45 and 8 respectively. The increase recorded is the highest since the first accurate Census taken in 1901 but it is curious to note that the increase in the *Khalsa* villages has been only 7·7 per cent. while in the *Jagir* and other villages it is 26·5. At the preceding Census the increase was 15 per cent. for both. No part of this well wooded State has a density of more than 140 persons per square mile. The annual rainfall varied from 20·37 inches in 1925 to 41·96 in 1928. The increase in population is attributed by the Darbar to an absence of epidemics and scarcity and, in some measure, to industrial developments though immigrants have only increased by 1,084 persons of whom females number 1,025.

Bharatpur:—The decrease by 1·9 per cent. in the population continues the tale of woe so adequately narrated in previous Census Reports. This is the only State in Rajputana and, possibly the whole of India, which has never, since the first Census of 1881, recorded an increase in its population. The losses in the several decades are shown in the margin and represent a net loss since 1881 of 24·6 per cent. The urban and rural populations have decreased since 1921 by 4·4 and 1·5 per cent. respectively. Bharatpur city has sustained a loss of 9·9 per cent., while in the rural areas the northern Tehsils of Nagar and Pahari show increases of 8·9 and 2·3 respectively.

Years.	Decrease per cent.
1881—91	0·8
1891—01	2·1
1901—11	10·8
1911—21	11·2
1921—31	1·9

The rural areas to lose most were the Tehsils of Bharatpur 7·8, Rupbas 7·0 and Uchain 7·5. These are the central parts of the State which suffered severely from the floods of 1924. Rainfall varied from 37·54 inches in 1926 to 12·72 in 1929 giving an average of 25·2 for the decade. Compared with the number of immigrants in 1921, there were, at this Census, 3,000 fewer males and 7,715 more females who returned birthplaces outside the State leaving a balance of 4,715 more immigrants since the last Census. No figures are now available for emigrants but in 1921 they numbered 40,152. The Darbar consider that the loss in population is due to the floods, meagre rainfall in the last years of the decade, reduction in the Army and other State departments and the stagnant condition of industry and trade. All these adverse features have undoubtedly led to increased emigration.

Bikaner:— During the past ten years, the population of this State has risen from 659,685 to 936,218 — an increase of 41·9 per cent. which is the highest recorded for any State or District in India. Various factors have contributed to this unparallelled increase and may be quoted as follows:—

(1) An absence of epidemics. (2) Normal rainfall. (3) The opening of the Gang Canal and an increase of more than 300,000 acres of irrigated land. (4) The extension of Railway Mileage from 509 to 796. (5) The separation of the State Railway from joint working with the Jodhpur State Railway and consequent erection of workshops at the Capital. (6) The opening of new *Mandis* especially in the Gang Canal area. (7) The impetus given to industry by irrigation and extension of Railways, and lastly (8) the return to their homes of persons who had emigrated especially from the northern Tehsils on account of scarcity prior to the Census of 1921. Rainfall during the years 1921-30 varied between a yearly average of 7·57 at Lunkaransar to 15·37 at Churu. The lowest recorded in any one year was 1·54 at Anupgarh and the highest 31·68 at Churu in 1926. The latter was a very exceptional years rainfall for this part of Rajputana. On the whole, the Eastern Tehsils, such as Churu and Ratangarh, are the most favoured and in good years appear to get a combination of the Arabian Sea and Bay Monsoons. During the decade the urban population increased by 31·3 and the rural by 45·7 per cent. Highest individual increases were returned from Rajgarh Town 74·8 and Ganganagar Nizamat 453 per cent. Immigrants increased from 53,287 in 1921 to 161,303 and to this latter figure the Punjab contributed 98,289 and the other States in the Agency 57,415 persons.

Religions.	Year.	Persons.	Males.	Females.
Hindu.	1921 1931	552,952 725,084	293,294 388,017	259,658 337,067
Jain.	1921 1931	23,555 28,773	9,840 12,479	13,715 16,294
Muslim.	1921 1931	74,748 141,578	39,656 76,471	35,092 65,107
Sikh.	1921 1931	8,218 40,469	4,774 24,017	3,444 16,452

The marginal statement shows the population by main religions in 1921 and at this Census. Hindus have increased by 31·1, Jains by 22·2, Muslims by 89·4 and Sikhs by 392·4 per cent. An attempt may now be made to explain this phenomenal expansion in the population. The statement in the margin shows the main figures compared with those for 1921. Now of all the emigrants from Rajputana in 1921, 90,207 returned no particular State as their Birthplace. Supposing that 10,000 of these had migrated from Bikaner this would, in addition to the 126,615 who definitely returned the State as their birthplace, give a total of 136,615 emigrants in 1921. The Natural population may therefore be assumed to have been 743,013 at the last Census. Supposing that this Natural population had increased by 14 per cent. the figure would now be

Detail.	1931.	1921.	Variation.
Born and enumerated in the State. Immigrants.	774,915 161,303	606,398 53,287	+168,517 +108,016
Total Population.	936,218	659,685	+276,533

847,034. But of these, 774,915 have at this Census been enumerated in the State leaving 72,119 to be classed as emigrants. If the number of emigrants in 1921 was 136,615, it means that over 60,000 of them have returned to their parent State since 1921. The actual figures for those born and enumerated in the State show the marginal variations per cent. during the decade in Bikaner and the two neighbouring States. Now, if the wave of immigration had started soon after the Census of 1921, the progeny aged under 10 of the immigrants would doubtless help to account for the abnormal increase observed. The number of children aged 0-10 in Bikaner is 404 per mille of the total 1921 population whereas in Marwar (where there was no variation in immigration) the ratio was 343. Had this been the ratio in Bikaner there would have been about 40,000 children less. In other words those born and enumerated in the State would have been 734,915. Even this figure shows an increase of 21·1 per cent. which is abnormal. Supposing that a normal increase were 14 per cent., that would have given 691,293 as an approximate figure for those born and enumerated in the State. Allowing for the increase in this category caused by increased immigration, there would still be a balance of 43,322 who could only be emigrants who had returned to the State.

Bikaner	+27·8
Marwar	+15·7
Jaipur	+13·9

Now emigrants to the Punjab in 1921 numbered 79,161 whereas the figure is now 33,819, or 45,342 less. In the absence of detailed figures for emigration to other Provinces, it is impossible to assess with accuracy the total numbers that have returned to the State. It is, however, natural that they should have been attracted to do so. Their parent State was embarking on an era of unprecedented prosperity in which they had a desire to share. What their numbers are it is not possible to know but the arguments put forward assess the figure at anything from 40,000 to 60,000. It is usual to discuss variations in caste in the Chapter devoted to the subject, but the changes that have occurred in this State since the last Census present problems that are not observed in any other and are therefore unique. For this reason the marginal statement is of interest. The phenomenal increase of Bhangis is doubtless due to the greater need for conservancy arrangements among the growing population. Naiks are in demand as labourers on earthworks for canals and railways, while Raths are Muslim cultivators found in the north of the State and contiguous Districts and States of the Punjab. Due allowance should be made for possible changes in nomenclature among the more obscure castes. It is, however, interesting to observe how increased facilities for trade, agriculture, etc., have affected every section of the population. Though strictly within the sphere of the Chapter which deals with Age it is not out of place or devoid of interest to assess the ages of the increased population. The statement overleaf shows the number in each decennial age-period per mille of what should ordinarily be the surviving population of periods ten years younger as recorded at the last Census. For the sake of comparison similar figures for the neighbouring State of Marwar (where there was no variation in the amount of immigration) are also shown.

Variation in certain Castes in Bikaner.

Caste.	1931.	1921.	Increase actual.	Increase per cent.
Agarwal	19,904	15,401	4,503	29·2
Bhangi	15,087	5,845	9,242	158·1
Bishnoi	16,415	10,921	5,494	50·3
Brahman	81,685	68,239	13,446	29·2
Chamar	75,574	59,416	16,158	27·2
Jat	215,947	158,413	57,534	36·3
Kaimkhani	9,426	7,195	2,231	31·0
Kumhar	37,901	22,639	15,262	67·4
Mahesri	16,801	12,694	4,107	32·4
Nai	20,260	16,084	4,176	26·0
Naik	23,882	9,589	14,293	149·1
Oswal	27,568	24,551	3,017	12·3
Rajput	55,512	48,279	7,233	14·9
Rath	52,671	13,474	39,197	290·9
Others	267,585	191,945	75,640	39·4
Total ...	936,218	659,685	276,533	41·9

STATE AND RELIGION	PER 1,000 OF 1921 POPULATION / Number of children in 1931 aged 0-10		PER 1,000 OF 1921 MALE AND FEMALE POPULATION RESPECTIVELY.												VARIATION PER CENT. 1921-31
			1921 Aged 0-10 / 1931 Aged 10-20		10-20 / 20-30		20-30 / 30-40		30-40 / 40-50		40-50 / 50-60		50-60 / 60 & over		
	M	F	M	F	M	F	M	F	M	F	M	F	M	F	
Bikaner															
Hindu ...	190	177	1136	1019	1071	1116	1100	1023	891	853	825	786	821	979	+ 31·1
Jain ...	179	175	804	1018	946	1134	1035	972	920	856	874	736	851	780	+ 22·2
Muslim ...	302	284	1542	1381	1620	1572	1438	1313	1199	1129	1144	1022	1197	1086	+ 89·4
Sikh ...	747	661	4128	3255	4816	4213	4244	3745	3666	2851	2909	2298	2813	2337	+ 392·4
Total ...	209	195	1215	1090	1177	1204	1183	1086	957	902	887	820	888	992	+ 41·9
Marwar															
Hindu and Tribal	178	167	954	839	824	1008	955	999	774	769	660	659	653	795	+ 15·9
Jain ...	151	147	809	894	843	946	968	968	842	819	703	696	698	737	+ 10·2
Muslim ...	182	173	905	815	868	963	881	902	743	691	659	649	673	823	+ 14·5
Total ...	177	166	943	839	828	1000	949	988	774	766	662	661	656	791	+ 15·4

Assuming, therefore, that the increase in population had been normal and similar to that shown in Marwar, we can roughly assess, as in the margin, the approximate ages of those whose presence in the State is due to the abnormal conditions. These 175,000 persons represent the difference between a normal increase of say, 15 per cent., and that actually recorded which was 41·9 per cent. The high proportion of young persons is an encouraging factor for the future growth and prosperity of the population in Bikaner.

Age.	Numbers.
0—10	39,000
10—20	46,000
20—30	38,000
30—40	16,000
40—50	15,000
50—60	12,000
60 and over	9,000
Total	175,000

Bundi:—The population of this State has increased from 187,068 to 216,722 which is a variation of +15·9 per cent. as against a loss of 14·5 during the preceding decade. In spite of this the net variation since 1881 is −14·9 per cent. A large portion of its 2,220 square miles is uncultivable, being a mass of low hills and scrub jungle, and the density of the population varies from 109 in Gaindoli Tehsil to 49 persons per square mile in Talwas. Conditions during the decade were good and the annual rainfall as recorded at the Capital averaged 28·0 inches, extremes being 41·3 in 1924 and 14·8 in 1930. Among the various Tehsils, Baroondhan with a variation of + 23·6 per cent. showed the greatest increase in population, while Talwas recorded an increase of only 1·1. The number of immigrants increased from 12,500 to 14,003 during the decade.

Dholpur:—The increase of 10·8 per cent. during the decade on the whole compares favourably with the following variations observed in contiguous States and Districts:—Bharatpur −1·9, Karauli +5·1, Gwalior +10·3 and Agra +13·4. The population is now 254,986 and shows a net increase of 2·1 per cent. since 1881. The physical features of the State are such that 6 per cent.

of the population are found in areas which have a density of under 150 persons per square mile, while 77 per cent. are found on 75 per cent. of the area which has a density ratio of 150-300. 10 per cent. of the State area has a density of 300-450 and is occupied by 17 per cent. of the population, the mean density of the whole State being 209* persons per square mile. Conditions during the decade were uniformly good. Irrigation has been extended and means of communication by road and rail improved. The stone quarrying industry for which the State is well known has in consequence received an impetus. Rainfall averaged 26·5 inches there being little difference in the amounts recorded at the six recording stations. The best year was 1924 with an average of 36·8, and the worst 1929 with an average fall of 17·2 inches. Among the various Tehsils, Gird records the highest increase of 17·1 per cent. while the lowest, 5·3 is shown by Baseri. The proportion of immigrants is 110 per mille of the population of whom 81 are females. The number of children under 10 years of age per 100 persons aged from 15 to 40 is 66 and was also the proportion at the last Census.

Dungarpur:—In the 3 towns and 749 villages which comprise this State in the South of the Agency, the population has increased by 20·2 per cent., or in other words from 189,272 to 227,544 persons. At the Censuses of 1881 and 1891 the large Bhil population was estimated and not enumerated and the figures were therefore unreliable. Since 1901 however, when famine was abroad in the land, the population has increased steadily from 100,103 to its present dimensions—an increase of 127·3 per cent. The State has a mean density of 158 persons per square mile though 58 per cent. of the population are found in areas where the density is below 150. There were no epidemics during the decade and conditions were favourable. The average annual rainfall varied from 46·93 inches in 1926 to 16·35 in 1923. The number of immigrants recorded fell from 10,431 in 1921 to 9,606.

Jaipur:—This State has the largest population in the Agency. The inhabitants now number 2,631,775 as against 2,338,802 in 1921—an increase of 12·5 per cent. The population is, however, not so great as in 1891 and 1901 and since 1881 the variation is only + 4·1 per cent. Although the mean density is 169 persons per square mile, the physical features are so varied that the density ratio ranges from 247 in the isolated Nizamat of Kot Kasim, and 229 in Hindaun, to 88 in Shekhawati and Malpura. The population in urban areas has increased by 18·2 and in rural areas by 11·4 per cent. The conditions during the decade were good and the increase in population is partially ascribed to the many improvements in the condition of the people brought about by the Minority Administration in the shape of increased facilities for employment, improved communications, and a stimulus to trade and industry. The average rainfall for the whole State was 23·8 inches but varied from 16·7 in the area covered by Sambhar and Shekhawati Nizamats to 24·6 inches in the rest of the State. Immigrants have decreased by 21,119 persons and although complete figures for emigration are not available this is partially set off by a decrease of 18,760 emigrants to the Punjab.

Religion as shown in the margin has played a curious part in the increase of the population. Immigration has definitely decreased while the surmise is that emigration has done so as well. The abnormal increase in Muslims in both urban and rural areas can only be due to returned emigrants. The increase in Jains is markedly small and probably means more emigration than was the case in 1921.

VARIATION IN 1921-31.			
Religion.	State.	Urban.	Rural.
Hindu.	+ 12·1	+ 16·7	+ 11·4
Muslim.	+ 19·5	+ 28·8	+ 14·8
Jain.	+ ·01	+ 8·6	− 5·3

The increase in the various Nizamats is fairly uniform except that Dausa 7·7, Hindaun 9·8, Kot Kasim 3·1 per cent. where the density is comparatively high show increases below the average. A satisfactory feature of the figures showing the ages of the population is that the number of children per 100 persons aged 15-40 has risen from 67 to 70.

*According to the latest survey the area is 1,178 square miles and the density is therefore 218 persons per square mile.

Jaisalmer:— This State presents problems of population unequalled by any other State in Rajputana. Its area is 12 per cent. but its population is only ·7 per cent. of that of the whole Agency. Despite the disadvantages of a density of only 5 persons per square mile, the population has increased by 12·7 per cent. The average annual rainfall was 5·9 inches at the Capital and immigrants increased by 1,422. The barren nature of the country and the precarious rainfall are factors that affect emigration and although figures are not now available, 19,144 emigrants were recorded in 1921 and 20,910 in 1911.

Jhalawar :—The population has increased from 96,182 persons to 107,890 during the decade—a variation of +12·2 per cent. A marked feature is the large proportion of immigrants who show an increase of 16·4 per cent. whereas those born and enumerated in the State only show an increase of 10·9 per cent. No part of the State has a density of more than 135 persons per square mile. The greatest increase is 19·9 per cent. recorded for the Pachpahar Tehsil and the smallest is +4·6 in the Capital. The conditions during the decade were uniformly good and the average annual rainfall varied between 41·3 inches at the Capital to 28·2 at Pachpahar. The prospects of a further increase in the population are not improved by the small ratio of 286 children aged 0 to 10 years per mille of the 1921 population. Moreover the proportion of such children to 100 married females aged 15-40 is only 150 which is the lowest figure recorded by any State in the Agency.

Karauli:—The physical features of this State vary to such an extent that 34 per cent. of the population occupy 763 square miles and the remaining 66 per cent. are found in the denser area of 479 square miles. The total population has increased from 133,730 to 140,525—a variation of only +5·1 per cent. The number of immigrants who form 12·8 per cent. of the population, has remained practically unchanged. Conditions during the decade are reported to have been good and the rainfall satisfactory. Population increases in the Tehsils vary between 13·2 in Mandrail to 3·2 per cent. in Sapotra. Now the increase in the Jaipur State Nizamat of Gangapur which adjoins Sapotra is 14·5 per cent; as the proportion of children in Karauli is normal, it is possible that the relatively small increase recorded during the decade is due to increased emigration.

Kishangarh:—The population has increased from 77,734 to 85,744 during the decade but is still 23·9 per cent. less than it was at the 1881 Census. The area of the State is 858 square miles and the rainfall recorded at the Capital averaged 20 inches and varied from 11·43 inches in 1923 to 30·80 in 1929. The Darbar consider that the present recorded increase of 10·3 per cent. in the population is due to an absence of epidemics and that it would have been higher still but for the fact that nearly 5,000 persons had recently left the State with their cattle on account of a scarcity of fodder. A perusal of the actual figures in Imperial Table II shows that the State has never completely recovered from the heavy loss occasioned by emigration and mortality during the decade of 1891-01. The proportion of children aged under 10 per 100 persons aged 15-40 has risen from 67 to 71.

Kotah:—The small increase of 8·8 per cent. recorded at this Census now brings the population of Kotah to 685,804 which is the highest since the total of 718,771 recorded in 1891. Although the mean density is 121 persons per square mile, 43 per cent. of the population are found in areas where the density exceeds 150. Conditions during the decade were uniformly good. The average annual rainfall throughout the intercensal period varied from 41·32 inches at Manohar Thana in the south of the State, to 27·19 at Ladpura close to the Capital. Out of 21 recording Stations, 16 reported an annual average of over 30 inches. Among the individual administrative units of the State the variation in population has ranged from +25·6 per cent. in Chechat to −·1 in Digod. The urban population has increased by 16·1 per cent. while the total number of immigrants to the State has decreased by 1,858 persons since 1921.

Kushalgarh:—The population of this small Chiefship in the extreme south of the Agency has increased by 22·0 per cent. since 1921 and the total now stands at 35,564 of whom 29,985 are Bhils. Factors which favoured such an increase were the absence of epidemics and any scarcity; the annual rainfall averaging 36·4 inches.

Lawa:—This small Estate has a population of only 2,790 persons within its 19 square miles. The increase recorded since 1921 is 23·3 per cent.

Marwar:—In size, Marwar with its 35,016 square miles, is by far the largest State in Rajputana and in population it stands second. The recorded total of 2,125,982 persons is the highest since 1901 and shows an increase of 15·4 per cent. since the last Census. No portion of the State has a density of over 150 persons per square mile. A ratio of 135 is found in the pargana of Sambhar-Marwar in the east while in Sheo in the west the ratio is only 10. The Darbar considered that the decade 1921-1930 was an exceptionally fortunate one for the State, there being no epidemics or scarcity. The rainfall as recorded at 29 stations—mostly the headquarters of parganas—showed an annual average of 14·8 inches for the whole State. For the four 'Sub-Aravallian' parganas of Bali, Desuri, Jaswantpura and Sojat, the average was 22·1 while for the remainder of the State it was 13·6 inches, ranging from 7·1 at Phalodi to 19·9 at Nawan. Although the whole State is considered as being in the North-West Dry Area of India, the four 'Sub-Aravallian' parganas have little claim for inclusion in it. All the parganas except the ill favoured one of Sheo have contributed to the marked increase in the population. Sheo shows an actual decrease of 13·9 per cent. and Phalodi an increase of only 1·3. If we take all the parganas and classify them into (a) those with a density ratio greater than 61, the mean for the whole State, and (b) those with a density ratio less than 61, we find that in (a) the population has increased by 16·5 per cent. and in (b) by 12·5. The number of immigrants has decreased from 26,744 to 26,105. The prospects for a further increase in the population are very bright, for the number of children aged under 10 years per mille of the 1921 population is 343—a figure which is only exceeded in Bikaner.

Mewar:—Mewar stands third as regards population among the States in the Agency and the present total of 1,566,910 persons shows an increase of 14·6 per cent. since 1921. No figures for the area of Tehsils, etc., are available but the mean density for the whole State with its area of 12,694 square miles is 124. Conditions during the decade were good and there was no scarcity or epidemic. The annual rainfall between 1921 and 1930 averaged 25·0 inches and varied from 33·5 at Sadri to 23·1 at Rajnagar. The number of immigrants fell from 26,491 in 1921 to 24,443. The number of children under 10 years of age is 328 per mille of the 1921 population so that prospects for a further increase are good.

Partabgarh:—The population has increased during the decade by 14·1 per cent. and now stands at 76,539. Although the mean density is 87 persons per square mile, the Magra Tehsil of 274 square miles or 31 per cent. of the whole State area, is jungle and hills and has a density figure of only 36. Conditions during the decade were favourable to an increase in the population and immigrants increased by 2,068 and now number 13,507 persons. Rainfall averaged 33·7 inches and although the fall in 1925 was as small as 16·4 inches, 1928 and 1929 both recorded falls of over 40 inches.

Shahpura:— The population of 54,233 persons represents an increase of 12·7 per cent. since 1921. The mean density is 134 persons per square mile and ranges between 77 in Kanechan Tehsil and 301 in Shahpura Tehsil which includes Shahpura Town. The average annual rainfall as recorded at the Capital was 27·8 inches and other conditions during the decade were also good. The number of immigrants now stands at 9,847 and was 7,995 at the last Census.

Sirohi:—The population now recorded is 216,528 and is the largest shown at any Census. The increase since 1921 is 16·0 per cent. although immigrants have only increased by 386 persons. Conditions during the decade were good, the annual rainfall averaging 31·8 inches at Abu Road in the south, 20·2 at Sheoganj in the north and 22·9 at the Capital.

Tonk:—The total area is 2,553 square miles but a reference to the Map will show that the component parganas lie at a distance from each other. Sironj and Chhabra are geographically in Central India, Nimbahera is almost surrounded by Mewar and Pirawa by Jhalawar. Despite its scattered nature, density per square mile in the individual parganas only varies between 99 in Tonk proper and 145 in Nimbahera. The population is 317,360 which, though representing an increase of 10·2 per cent. since 1921, is not so large as the population recorded in 1881 (338,029) and 1891 (380,069). Conditions during the decade were good and the average annual rainfall was 32·7 inches—fluctuating between 40·5 at Sironj and 26·9 at Aligarh. Immigrants numbered 40,804 and 45,662 at the preceding Census.

PART III.—A forecast of the future trend of Population.

It has been usual in the past to base a forecast of the future trend of the population in each State, on a comparison of the proportion of children under 10 years of age to adults aged 15-40, with reference to any variation noticed during the decade. The decade 1921-31 was one of the most prosperous experienced in this part of India and one would expect to find a higher ratio of children to adults than in 1921.

The marginal statement shows that this is not so and that in the whole of Rajputana the ratio of children to 100 adults has dropped from 74 to 72 and to 100 females of child-bearing ages from 189 to 175. Apart from variations due to the system of adjusting ages now in force and which is described in Chapter IV, a smaller proportion of children to adults either means that fewer were born or that the proportion at the previous Census was unduly high on account of excessive mortality among adults. A feature of the 1921 Census was a relatively small proportion of adults due to mortality from influenza in 1918 and considering the conditions of the decade 1921-30 it is reasonably safe to assume that the decreased proportion of children to adults now observed is due, not to fewer births during the decade but to fewer adults in 1921. To call a forecast gloomy merely because the proportion of children has now dropped would therefore be fallacious. It is thought therefore that a better clue to the future trend of population in each State, exists in the proportion of children now aged under 10 to the total population at the previous Census. This is shown in column 3 of the statement above. It will therefore be interesting to see in 1941 whether the variations in population then observed have any connection with this proportion.

STATEMENT SHOWING THE PROPORTION OF CHILDREN IN THE POPULATION.

STATE, ETC.	VARIATION 1921-31	NUMBER OF CHILDREN 0—10 in 1931 PER MILLE OF 1921 POPULATION	PROPORTION OF CHILDREN 0-10			
			Per 100 persons aged 15-40		Per 100 married females aged 15-40	
			1931	1921	1931	1921
Rajputana	**+ 14·2**	**326**	**72**	**74**	**175**	**189**
Alwar	+ 6·9	290	65	71	161	182
Banswara	+ 18·3	397	93	107	220	253
Bharatpur	− 1·9	274	67	63	165	168
Bikaner	+ 41·9	404	72	75	182	200
Bundi	+ 15·9	328	68	77	165	197
Dholpur	+ 10·8	307	66	66	170	178
Dungarpur	+ 20·2	393	90	98	204	230
Jaipur	+ 12·5	314	70	67	167	168
Jaisalmer	+ 12·7	314	68	71	198	248
Jhalawar	+ 12·2	286	61	68	150	177
Karauli	+ 5·1	294	69	70	174	187
Kishangarh	+ 10·3	318	71	67	168	172
Kotah	+ 8·8	292	64	73	151	180
Kushalgarh	+ 22·0	435	100	110	237	267
Marwar	+ 15·4	343	77	75	246	202
Mewar	+ 14·6	328	74	81	237	203
Partabgarh	+ 14·1	338	74	83	179	202
Shahpura	+ 12·7	314	69	75	230	181
Sirohi	+ 16·0	349	79	84	183	211
Tonk	+ 10·2	311	70	75	167	183

PART IV.—Vital Statistics.

No record is maintained of births and deaths in the Rajputana Agency as a whole, although a record is kept by some of the individual States. It is, however, of interest to attempt an assessment of the number of casualties that have occurred between this and the last Census. The best known method is that of Sir George Hardy. After making an allowance for immigration during the decade, it is, in brief, to deduct the population aged 10 and over from the total population at the previous Census and to assume the difference to be the deaths among the previous population aged, on an average 5 years and over. By this method the statement opposite shows the result for the Agency and each State.

STATEMENT SHOWING THE APPROXIMATE WASTAGE IN EACH STATE DURING THE DECADE.

CATEGORY	RAJPUTANA.	ALWAR.	BANSWARA.	BHARATPUR.	BIKANER.	BUNDI.	DHOLPUR.	DUNGARPUR.	JAIPUR.	JAISALMER.	JHALAWAR.
1	2	3	4	5	6	7	8	9	10	11	12
Present population. Aged 0—10 ...	11,225,712 3,208,334	749,751 203,060	225,106 75,491	486,954 186,262	936,218 266,571	216,722 60,360	254,986 70,647	227,544 74,417	2,631,775 733,801	76,255 21,246	107,890 27,525
Balance of 1921 Population ...	8,017,378	546,691	149,615	350,692	669,647	156,362	184,339	153,127	1,897,974	55,009	80,365
Add decrease / Deduct increase } in immigrants.	87,937	11,375	1,084	4,715	108,016	1,503	6,831	825	21,119	1,422	3,538
Balance now living. 1921 Population. Balance now living.	7,929,441 9,831,755 7,929,441	535,316 701,154 535,316	148,531 190,362 148,531	345,977 496,437 345,977	561,631 659,685 561,631	154,859 187,068 154,859	177,508 230,188 177,508	153,952 189,272 153,952	1,919,093 2,338,802 1,919,093	53,587 67,652 53,587	76,827 96,182 76,827
Casualties during the decade ...	1,902,314	165,838	41,831	150,460	98,054	32,209	52,680	35,320	419,709	14,065	19,355
Casualty rate per mille per annum.	19·4	23·6	22·0	30·3	14·8	17·2	22·9	18·7	17·9	20·8	20·1
Variation per cent. 1921—31 ...	+ 14·2	+ 6·9	+ 18·3	− 1·9	+ 41·9	+ 15·9	+ 10·8	+ 20·2	+ 12·5	+ 12·7	+ 12·2

CATEGORY.	KARAULI.	KISHANGARH.	KOTAH.	KUSHALGARH.	MARWAR.	MEWAR.	PARTABGARH.	SHAHPURA.	SIROHI.	TONK.
1	13	14	15	16	17	18	19	20	21	22
Present Population. Aged 0—10.	140,525 39,349	85,744 24,293	685,804 183,880	35,564 12,682	2,125,982 631,339	1,566,910 453,123	76,539 22,660	54,233 15,107	216,528 65,140	317,360 89,519
Balance of 1921 Population ...	101,176	61,451	501,924	22,882	1,494,643	1,113,787	53,879	39,126	151,388	227,841
Add decrease / Deduct increase } in immigrants.	173	1,609	1,858	985	639	2,048	2,068	1,852	386	4,858
Balance now living. 1921 Population. Balance now living.	101,349 133,730 101,349	59,842 77,734 59,842	503,782 630,060 503,782	21,897 29,162 21,897	1,495,282 1,841,642 1,495,282	1,115,835 1,366,980 1,115,835	51,811 67,110 51,811	37,274 48,130 37,274	151,002 186,639 151,002	232,699 287,898 232,699
Casualties during the decade.	32,881	17,892	126,278	7,265	346,360	251,145	15,299	10,856	35,637	55,199
Casualty rate per mille per annum.	24·2	23·0	20·0	24·9	18·8	18·1	22·8	22·6	19·1	19·2
Variation per cent. 1921—31 ...	+ 5·1	+ 10·3	+ 8·8	+ 22·0	+ 15·4	+ 14·6	+ 14·1	+ 12·7	+ 16·0	+ 10·2

To test the approximate accuracy a comparison can be made with the figures for Ajmer-Merwara wherein Vital Statistics are maintained. In this latter province the number of deaths among persons aged 5 and over was 66,684 which gives a death-rate of 15·2 per mille per annum among the 1921 population similarly aged. By Sir George Hardy's method the ratio is 17·2 per mille—or practically the same allowing for omissions in the registered number. The difference of 2 per mille between the ratios for Rajputana and Ajmer-Merwara is undoubtedly due to greater facilities for medical treatment enjoyed in the latter. The figures for some States present curious features. The high ratio of 30 3 in Bharatpur is partially due to increased emigration. It is known that emigrants to the United Provinces have increased by some 30,000 and if allowance is made for these, the ratio is then 24·3, which is more in keeping with the ratios of 23·6 and 22·9 shown by the neighbouring States of Alwar and Dholpur respectively. Similarly the ratio of 14·8 for Bikaner is unduly low and if allowance is made for an estimated number of 40,000 returned emigrants, the ratio becomes 20·9 as compared with 20·8 in Jaisalmer and 18·8 in Marwar. For the rest, it may be noted that as a general rule, a higher death-rate explains a lower increase in the population. An exception to this is however seen in the Bhil States in the south of the Agency. Here the comparatively short lived but prolific population presents a high casualty rate combined with a high percentage of increase in the population.

A comparison of the healthiness of the past decade may be gauged by the fact that a similarly assessed ratio for Rajputana during the period 1911-21 is 32·1 per mille per annum.

1.—DENSITY, WATER-SUPPLY AND CROPS.

AGENCY, NATURAL DIVISION AND STATE OR DISTRICT.	MEAN DENSITY PER SQUARE MILE IN 1931.	NORMAL RAINFALL IN INCHES.	REMARKS.
1	2	3	4
RAJPUTANA	***87***	***27·02***	
North-West Dry Area	***43***	***10·40***	
Bikaner	41	10·44	
Jaisalmer	5	5·94	
Marwar	61	14·84	
Rajputana East	***148***	***29·64***	
Abu District	756	69·79	
Alwar	238	21·65	Including Nimrana.
Banswara	141	38·8	
Bharatpur	247	25·2	
Bundi	98	27·96	
Dholpur	*209	26·49	
Dungarpur	158	29·80	
Jaipur	169	23·8	
Jhalawar	134	33·63	
Karauli	¶ 114	28·48	
Kishangarh	100	20·03	
Kotah	121	33·42	
Kushalgarh (Chiefship)	105	36·44	
Lawa (Estate)	147	19·42	Average only for 5 years beginning from 1926.
Mewar	124	24·96	
Partabgarh	87	38·71	
Shahpura	134	27·82	
Sirohi	111	24·95	
Tonk	125	32·67	

NOTE.—Statistics for Crops and Cultivated area have been omitted as no reliable figures are available in Rajputana as a whole.
* According to the latest survey the area is 1,173 square miles and the density is therefore 218 persons per square mile.
¶ According to the latest survey the area is 1,227 square miles and the density is therefore 115 persons per square mile.

2.—DISTRIBUTION OF POPULATION CLASSIFIED ACCORDING TO DENSITY.

AGENCY, NATURAL DIVISION, STATE, ETC.	TEHSILS OR SUB-DIVISIONS WITH A POPULATION PER SQUARE MILE OF—							
	Under 150.		150—300.		300—450.		450 and over.	
	Area.	(Population) (000's omitted).	Area.	Population (000's omitted).	Area.	Population (000's omitted).	Area.	Population (000's omitted).
1	2	3	4	5	6	7	8	9
RAJPUTANA ...	115,514·5 *89*	8,047 *72*	14,029·5 *11*	2,958 *26*	665 ...	216 *2*	6 ...	4 ...
North-West Dry Area ...	74,395 *100*	3,138 *100*	...	...	...	...	...	...
Bikaner ...	23,317 *100*	936 *100*	...	...	...	...	...	...
Jaisalmer ...	16,062 *100*	76 *100*	...	...	...	...	...	...
Marwar ...	35,016 *100*	2,126 *100*	...	...	...	...	...	...
Rajputana East ...	41,119·5 *74*	4,909 *61*	14,029·5 *25*	2,958 *36*	665 *1*	216 *3*	6 ...	4 ...
Abu ...	...	...	...	...	...	...	6 *100*	4 *100*
Alwar ...	409·5 *13*	33 *4*	2,463·5 *76*	610 *82*	344 *11*	107 *14*	...	...
Banswara ...	1,606 *100*	225 *100*	...	...	...	...	...	...
Bharatpur ...	...	...	1,776 *90*	421 *86*	196 *10*	66 *14*	...	...
Bundi ...	2,220 *100*	217 *100*	...	...	...	...	...	...
Dholpur * ...	191 *15*	15 *6*	905 *75*	196 *77*	125 *10*	48 *17*	...	...
Dungarpur ...	970 *68*	132 *58*	477 *32*	95 *42*	...	...	...	...
Jaipur ...	11,459 *69*	1,539 *58*	5,223 *31*	1,098 *42*	...	...	...	...
Jhalawar ...	810 *100*	108 *100*	...	...	...	...	...	...
Karauli ¶ ...	763 *61*	47 *34*	479 *39*	94 *66*	...	...	...	...
Kishangarh ...	858 *100*	86 *100*	...	...	...	...	...	...
Kotah ...	3,827 *67*	388 *57*	1,857 *33*	298 *43*	...	...	...	...
Kushalgarh (Chiefship).	287 *84*	26 *74*	53 *16*	9 *26*	...	...	...	...
Lawa (Estate) ...	19 *100*	3 *100*	...	...	...	...	...	...
Mewar ...	12,694 *100*	1,567 *100*	...	...	...	...	...	...
Partabgarh ...	886 *100*	77 *100*	...	...	...	...	...	...
Shahpura ...	361 *89*	41 *76*	44 *11*	13 *24*	...	...	...	...
Sirohi ...	1,782 *91*	179 *83*	176 *9*	38 *17*	...	...	...	...
Tonk ...	1,977 *78*	226 *71*	576 *22*	91 *29*	...	...	...	...

NOTE.—Figures in Italics shown below the absolute figures represent proportions per cent. of each density group to the area and population of each State, Natural Division and the Agency as a whole.

* Area as furnished by the Survey of India is 1,173 square miles.

¶ Area as furnished by the Survey of India is 1,227 square miles.

3.—VARIATION IN RELATION TO DENSITY SINCE 1881.

AGENCY, NATURAL DIVISION, STATE OR DISTRICT.	PERCENTAGE OF VARIATION. INCREASE (+), DECREASE (—).					NET VARIATION PER CENT. 1881 to 1931.	MEAN DENSITY PER SQUARE MILE.					
	1921—31.	1911—21.	1901—11.	1891—1901.	1881—91.		1931.	1921.	1911.	1901.	1891.	1881.
1	2	3	4	5	6	7	8	9	10	11	12	13
RAJPUTANA ...	***+ 14·2***	***— 6·5***	***+ 6·9***	***— 20·5***	***+ 20·6***	***+ 9·3***	***87***	***77***	***82***	***77***	***96***	***80***
North-West Dry Area ...	***+ 22·2***	***— 9·8***	***+ 9·8***	***— 25·4***	***+ 46·4***	***+ 32·2***	***43***	***35***	***39***	***35***	***47***	***32***
Bikaner ...	+ 41·9	— 5·9	+ 19 9	— 29·7	+ 63·4	+ 83·9	41	29	31	26	36	22
Jaisalmer ...	+ 12·7	— 23 4	+ 20 4	— 36 6	+ 7·0	— 29·5	5	5	6	5	8	7
Marwar ...	+ 15·4	— 10·5	+ 6·3	— 23 4	+ 43·8	+ 21·0	61	53	59	56	73	51
Rajputana East.	***+ 11·3***	***— 5·3***	***+ 5·8***	***— 18·6***	***+ 12·8***	***+ 2·5***	***148***	***133***	***141***	***133***	***163***	***145***
Abu District ...	+ 25·7	— 16·0	+ 5·5	+ 32·2	...	...	756	601	716	678	513	...
Alwar ...	+ 6·9	— 11·4	— 4·4	+ 7·9	+ 12·4	+ 9·8	238	223	251	263	244	217
Banswara ...	+ 18·3	+ 15·0	+ 11·0	— 17·3	+ 39·2	+ 48·1	141	119	104	98	113	79
Bharatpur ...	— 1·9	— 11·2	— 10·8	— 2·1	— 0·8	— 24·6	247	251	283	317	324	327
Bundi ...	+ 15·9	— 14·5	+ 27 7	— 42·1	+ 16·1	— 14·9	98	85	99	78	134	115
Dholpur ...	+ 10·8	— 12·7	— 2·9	— 3·0	+ 12·1	+ 2·1	209	189	216	223	230	205
Dungarpur ...	+ 20·2	+ 18·9	+ 59·02	— 39·5	+ 7·8	+ 48·4	158	131	111	70	115	106
Jaipur ...	+ 12·5	— 11·3	— 0·8	— 5·9	+ 11·7	+ 4·1	169	151	170	171	182	163
Jhalawar ...	+ 12·2	— 0 1	+ 6·8	— 40·3	+ 0·5	— 28·2	134	119	119	112	187	186
Karauli ...	+ 5·1	— 8·8	— 6·5	+ 0·1	+ 5·3	— 5·5	114	108	119	127	127	120
Kishangarh ...	+ 10·3	— 10·8	— 4·2	— 27·5	+ 11·4	— 23·9	100	91	102	107	146	132
Kotah ...	+ 8·8	— 1·4	+ 17·3	— 24·2	+ 1·6	— 3·05	121	111	113	96	127	125
Kushalgarh (Chiefship).	+ 22·0	+ 32 5	+ 35·6	— 48·3	...	...	105	86	65	48	93	...
Lawa (Estate) ...	+ 23·3	— 11·8	— 4·00	— 20·5	+ 25·3	+ 4·0	147	120	135	141	177	142
Mewar ...	+ 14·6	+ 6·7	+ 25·8	— 44·8	+ 23·5	+ 4·9	124	108	101	81	146	118
Partabgarh ...	+ 14·1	+ 7·0	+ 20·5	— 40·9	+ 10·6	— 3·8	87	76	71	59	100	90
Shahpura ...	+ 12·7	+ 1·5	+ 11·1	— 32·9	+ 23·0	+ 4·8	134	119	118	106	158	123
Sirohi ...	+ 16 0	+ 1·0	+ 22·8	— 19·9	+ 33·5	+ 51·5	111	96	95	77	96	73
Tonk ...	+ 10 2	— 5 0	+ 10·9	— 28·1	+ 12·4	— 6·1	125	113	119	108	149	133

NOTE:—The figures in this Table are based on the adjusted figures of Area and Population contained in Imperial Tables I and II, but columns 5, 6, 7, 12 and 13 take into account also the estimated and unenumerated Bhil and Grassia Population of 1881 and 1891 which is excluded from the Imperial Table figures for those years.

4.—VARIATION IN NATURAL POPULATION.

POPULATION 1931.				POPULATION 1921.				VARIATION IN NATURAL POPULATION 1921—31.	
Actual Population.	Immigrants.	Emigrants.	Natural Population	Actual Population.	Immigrants.	Emigrants.	Natural Population.	Net.	Percentage
1	2	3	4	5	6	7	8	9	10
11,225,712	330,939	846,716	11,741,489	9,844,384	243,002	869,110	10,470,492	+ 1,270,997	+ 12·1

5.—PERSONS PER HOUSE AND HOUSES PER SQUARE MILE.

AGENCY, NATURAL DIVISION AND STATE OR DISTRICT.	AVERAGE NUMBER OF PERSONS PER HOUSE.						AVERAGE NUMBER OF HOUSES PER SQUARE MILE.					
	1930.	1921.	1911.	1901.	1891.	1881.	1931.	1921.	1911.	1901.	1891.	1881.
1	2	3	4	5	6	7	8	9	10	11	12	13
RAJPUTANA ...	***4·7***	***4·33***	***4·32***	***5·09***	***5·47***	***4·82***	***18·5***	***17·6***	***18·9***	***15·0***	***17·2***	***16·3***
North-West Dry area ...	***4·8***	***4·36***	***4·48***	***4·46***	***5·23***	***4·55***	***8·8***	***7·9***	***8·5***	***7·8***	***8·9***	***7·0***
Bikaner ...	5·0	4·54	4·59	5·02	6·13	4·73	8·0	6·2	6·6	5·0	5·8	4·6
Jaisalmer ...	4·2	3·84	4·22	4·13	4·58	4·12	1·1	1·1	1·3	1·1	1·6	1·6
Marwar ...	4·7	4·32	4·46	4·33	5·02	4·53	12·8	12·2	13·2	12·8	14·4	11·1
Rajputana East...	***4·7***	***4·32***	***4·26***	***5·36***	***5·77***	***4·87***	***31·8***	***30·8***	***33·0***	***25·0***	***28·4***	***25·8***
Abu District* ...	3·8	3·60	...	...	...	...	197·7	166·5	...	...	...	...
Alwar ...	4·9	4·43	4·49	6·41	5·63	6·74	48·9	50·4	56·2	41·1	43·4	32·3
Banswara ...	5·0	4·76	4·39	5·66	3·91	2·90	28·1	24·9	23·4	16·4	24·5	22·3
Bharatpur ...	4·7	4·20	4·16	6·84	7·32	7·38	52·7	59·6	67·7	47·6	44·1	44·5
Bundi ...	4·5	4·23	4·30	4·77	5·67	4·21	21·8	19·9	22·9	16·2	23·5	27·3
Dholpur ...	4·6	4·46	4·64	4·72	4·64	5·16	45·0	44·6	49·1	49·7	52·2	41·9
Dungarpur ...	4·9	4·53	4·18	3·58	4·34	4·44	32·3	28·9	26·3	19·3	15·7	13·5
Jaipur ...	4·6	4·36	4·41	6·71	7·23	4·99	36·4	34·4	38·4	25·4	24·9	32·5
Jhalawar ...	4·6	4·17	4·05	5·16	5·63	5·40	29·1	28·5	29·3	21·6	33·1	34·4
Karauli ...	4·5	4·08	4·07	4·85	4·49	5·73	24·9	26·4	29·0	26·0	28·1	20·9
Kishangarh ...	4·7	4·30	4·09	4·07	6·53	4·52	21·4	18·9	24·9	26·0	22·2	29·1
Kotah ...	4·5	4·24	4·07	4·67	4·98	3·96	27·0	26·1	27·6	20·5	25·7	31·4
Kushalgarh (Chiefship) ...	5·5	5·09	4·75	4·41	...	...	19·0	16·9	13·6	10·8	...	...
Lawa (Estate) ...	4·6	4·02	3·96	5·54	6·82	4·54	32·0	29·6	34·1	25·4	25·9	31·1
Mewar ...	4·7	4·23	4·02	3·71	4·61	4·45	26·4	25·6	25·3	21·8	29·4	25·7
Partabgarh ...	4·7	4·30	3·90	3·52	4·15	4·26	6·4	17·6	18·2	16·7	23·9	21·0
Shahpura ...	4·7	4·88	4·20	3·98	4·66	4·77	28·8	27·2	27·9	26·5	33·7	26·8
Sirohi ...	4·4	4·16	¶ 4·08	¶ 3·90	¶ 4·36	¶ 4·68	25·3	22·9	¶ 23·6	¶ 20·2	¶ 22·0	¶ 15·5
Tonk ...	4·4	4·20	4·24	5·25	4·52	4·60	28·0	26·9	28·0	20·4	33·0	28·8

* Area leased in 1917 and formed into a separate unit.
¶ Includes Mount Abu.

APPENDIX.

A Note on different kinds of Population.

It has already been seen that, generally speaking, the population in the north and west of the Agency shows a tendency to increase at a rate higher than that observed in the south and east. For further enquiry into this phenomenon the figures of certain States will be analysed in greater detail. In the first place, it is as well to bear in mind the variations during the past 20 years shown by the populations of the States concerned.

State	Variation 1911—21	Variation 1921—31
Bikaner	− 5·9	+ 41·9
Marwar	− 10·5	+ 15·4
Mewar	+ 6·7	+ 14·6
Jaipur	− 11·3	+ 12·5
Jhalawar	− 0·1	+ 12·2
Tonk	− 5·0	+ 10·2
Kotah	− 1·4	+ 8·8
Alwar	− 11·4	+ 6·9
Bharatpur	− 11·2	− 1·9

The States are shown in the margin in the order of their variation during the past decade. The causes that led to a general decrease in the population during the decade of 1911—21 were few really good agricultural years, recurring epidemics of plague and cholera and finally in 1918 a very severe epidemic of influenza. Mewar was comparatively free from plague and suffered less from influenza than the other States mentioned. The decade 1921-1931 has been uniformly healthy and agricultural conditions have on the whole been good. Severe floods in 1924 in Bharatpur and bad economic conditions in that State are the principal causes for the only minus variation observed in the Agency. The abnormal increase observed in Bikaner is due to an influx of colonists to the newly irrigated lands in the north of the State. The manner in which conditions prevailing in previous decades leave their mark on the present population is shown by the following statement:—

Statement showing the variation in the population by decennial age-groups as now recorded, compared with those of similar ages in 1921.

State.	Age-periods. 0—10		10—20		20—30		30—40		40—50		50—60		60 and over	
	Males	Females	Males	Females	Males	Females	Males	Females	Males	Females	Males	Females	Males	Females
Bikaner	+ 46	+ 45	+ 55	+ 55	+ 66	+ 62	+ 25	+ 20	+ 38	+ 22	+ 26	+ 22	+ 15	+ 2
Marwar	+ 22	+ 28	+ 15	+ 24	+ 25	+ 28	− 5	+ 2	+ 14	+ 7	+ 11	+ 9	− 3	− 5
Mewar	+ 12	+ 9	+ 22	+ 41	+ 48	+ 35	− 13	− 9	+ 5	+ 3	+ 12	+ 3	− 7	− 4
Jaipur	+ 21	+ 20	+ 15	+ 31	+ 20	+ 21	+ 3	+ 4	+ 4	...	− 3	− 1	− 13	− 16
Jhalawar	+ 12	+ 7	+ 21	+ 37	+ 41	+ 31	− 6	− 2	+ 6	...	+ 6	− 2	− 11	− 16
Tonk	+ 11	+ 8	+ 16	+ 34	+ 30	+ 20	− 6	− 3	+ 3	+ 2	+ 10	− 1	− 9	− 16
Kotah	+ 6	+ 3	+ 16	+ 35	+ 36	+ 25	− 7	− 4	+ 3	+ 3	+ 3	− 2	− 20	− 27
Alwar	+ 6	+ 4	+ 7	+ 18	+ 14	+ 20	+ 12	+ 9	+ 11	...	− 6	− 7	− 17	− 25
Bharatpur	+ 6	+ 4	+ 3	+ 15	− 8	+ 1	− 2	+ 1	− 7	− 13	− 21	− 21	− 29	− 31

The influenza epidemic of 1918 has left its mark by the proportionately high increase among those aged 20-30 since the decrease was particularly selective to those similarly aged and left a reduced number at the Census of 1921. Likewise the reduced proportions of those now aged 30-40 are the survivors of that epidemic, those aged 30-40 ten years ago being not so severely attacked as those just younger. They are also the result of the low birth-rate after the famine of 1900; those aged 30-40 ten years ago were 10-20 at the time of that famine. Again the markedly reduced proportions now aged 60 and over and 50-60 in Alwar and Bharatpur may be traced back to mortality among children at the widespread famines in 1868—69 and in a lesser degree to the famine in 1877-78 which was severe in Eastern Rajputana.

To turn now to the conditions of the past decade. The marginal statement gives for each State four sets of figures which are germane to the subject of variation. Leaving aside the figures for Bikaner where conditions were abnormal, one is struck by the low proportion of children born in the Eastern States in spite of a higher ratio than in the West of females aged 15-35. With the highest proportionate increase in immigrants, and of females of child-bearing ages, Jhalawar shows, excepting Bharatpur, the lowest increase in children born since the last Census. Its population was practically stationary between 1911 and 1921, as has already been observed and in all the Eastern States the mortality from influenza was not quite so great as in the West. A further examination of certain comparative figures may lead to a better appreciation of the subject. The following statement shows the survival of the 1921 population by decennial age-periods at this Census:—

STATE	PER 1,000 OF 1921 POPULATION					
	Variation 1921-31		Variation in immigrants 1921-31		Number of children in 1931 aged 0-10	Number of females in 1931 aged 15-35
Bikaner	+	419	+	164	404	222
Marwar	+	154		...	343	178
Mewar	+	146	—	1	328	178
Jaipur	+	125	—	9	314	179
Jhalawar	+	122	+	37	286	188
Tonk	+	102	—	17	311	180
Kotah	+	88	—	3	292	185
Alwar	+	69	+	16	290	184
Bharatpur	—	19	+	9	274	164

STATE.	PER 1,000 OF 1921 POPULATION OF EACH SEX—											
	Aged in 1921 } 0—10.		10—20.		20—30.		30—40.		40—50.		50—60.	
	Aged in 1931 } 10-20.		20—30.		30—40.		40—50.		50—60.		60 and over.	
	Males.	Females.	Males.	Females.	Males.	Females.	Males.	Females.	Males.	Females.	Males.	Females.
Bikaner ...	1,215	1,090	1,177	1,204	1,183	1,086	957	902	887	820	888	992
Marwar ...	943	889	828	1,000	949	988	774	766	662	661	656	791
Mewar ...	920	800	903	1,073	1,049	1,025	714	746	607	608	519	610
Jaipur ...	943	846	891	1,142	965	922	788	748	651	644	633	714
Jhalawar ...	958	891	907	1,113	1,115	1,044	748	728	659	542	721	679
Tonk ...	856	789	948	1,118	990	892	742	716	592	602	639	656
Kotah ...	869	796	1,002	1,147	1,031	950	721	703	572	575	572	568
Alwar ...	872	780	891	1,092	875	832	755	711	720	649	698	668
Bharatpur ...	840	741	848	1,075	753	731	646	629	553	522	512	514

We may now consider the survival rate for each age-period in turn :—

0-10 in 1921. Now 10-20.

In the first place we observe a generally higher rate of survival among males in the west than in the east although Jhalawar shows the highest individual rate. The lower survival rate among females can be attributed to high mortality due ot early marriage and also to neglect. "A son is the care of his parents but a daughter is cared for by God" who is distant. The wilful understatement of ages of unmarried females is also a factor. Here again is observed a lower survival rate among females in the east than in the west—Jhalawar again excepted.

For males the interesting point to note is that in this group the survival rate for western Males is lower than the preceding group and that shown by their eastern contemporaries. These latter show a higher survival rate than those in the group now aged 10-20. The perils of early childhood are past and their ranks have been augmented by immigrants to a greater degree than is observed in the Western States. Among females, this is the only group in which all the States show the survivors to have exceeded the original numbers ten years previously. Here again understatement of ages in the group 10-20 leaves its mark tempered by immigration for social purposes and again the east shows, on the whole higher survival ratios than the west.

10-20 in 1921. Now 20-30.

In no other group are such diverse survival ratios shown. Marriage is past for both sexes and the only movement that should normally occur is migration. One point of interest is the comparatively low rates observed in Alwar and particularly in Bharatpur. This can only mean excessive mortality or migration or both.

20-30 in 1921. Now 30-40.

30-40 in 1921. Now 40-50.

Except in Bharatpur where hardship, sickness and migration have obviously taken their toll, this group shows very uniform survival ratios for both sexes in all the States with a slight advantage to the west.

40-50 in 1921. Now 50-60.

The toll levied by sickness, etc., in Bharatpur is now very marked. Except for an inexplicably high male ratio in Alwar, all the Eastern States have suffered more than the Western.

The greater longevity of females now begins to show itself in the Western States and to a lesser extent in Tonk and Bharatpur. Mortality in Bharatpur is very marked among both sexes and the low ratio observed in Mewar may be attributed to a large number of Bhils in the population who, though prolific, are not long lived.

50-60 in 1921. Now 60 and over.

The salient features in this comparative statement are (a) an apparently lower survival rate in the Eastern States among children from 0 to 10 and, except in Jhalawar, among persons aged from 10 to 20, (b) marked mortality or loss by emigration in Bharatpur after the age of 20, and (c) except in Alwar, higher mortality rates in the east after the age of 40.

Can density be a contributing factor? The following statement shows the distribution of the population of each State according to density:—

STATE.	PERCENTAGES OF THE AREA OF EACH STATE AND OF THE POPULATION FOUND THEREIN.					
	Under 150.		150—300.		300—450.	
	Area.	Population.	Area.	Population.	Area.	Population.
Bikaner	100	100	...	...	...	...
Marwar	100	100	...	...	...	...
Mewar	100	100	...	...	...	...
Jaipur	69	58	31	42	...	...
Jhalawar	100	100	...	...	...	...
Tonk	78	71	22	29	...	...
Kotah	67	57	33	43	...	...
Alwar	13	4	76	82	11	14
Bharatpur	...	...	90	86	10	14

The similarity of the distribution in Kotah and Jaipur is noticeable as is the greater density in Alwar and Bharatpur.

Statisticians have enunciated a theory that the population can be classified in five types according to the age distribution. *Progressive* where the proportion aged below 15 is high and the proportion above 50 low. *Regressive* where the proportions are the other way round and *Stationary* where the proportions are between the two extremes. To these are added two types to cover cases where the distribution is disturbed by migration. *Secessive* where a proportion much below 50 between ages 15 and 50 indicates large losses by emigration and *Accessive* where a proportion much above 50 between the same ages indicates gains by immigration. We thus have five types which are illustrated below:—

Theoretical types of Population according to age distribution.

Age-groups.	Progressive.	Stationary.	Regressive.	Secessive.	Accessive.
0—15	40	33	20	40	25
15—50	50	50	50	40	60
50 and over	10	17	30	20	15

If we apply this grouping by ages to the States concerned we get the following result:—

AGE DISTRIBUTION PER CENT. OF THE POPULATION.

Age-group.	Bikaner.	Marwar.	Mewar.	Jaipur.	Jhalawar.	Tonk.	Kotah.	Alwar.	Bharatpur.
0—15	41	42	42	40	37	40	39	39	40
15—50	49	48	49	49	52	50	52	51	51
50 and over	10	10	9	11	11	10	9	10	9

It will be seen that the population of each State comes within the progressive category though in varying degrees. The immigrants to Bikaner have obviously been accompanied by their families and all the States of the west show a more progressive character than those of the east. We may return to the purport of this enquiry which is to determine why the populations of certain States show a bigger increase than others during the decade under review. Without a technical knowledge of questions relating to public health the following suggestions are tentatively made:—

(a) In the absence of disease in a severe epidemic form the west of Rajputana is more healthy than the east.

(b) A low density figure in seasons of average rainfall is favourable to an increase in the population where land exists for cultivation.

(c) Assuming that fecundity is equal, infant mortality is higher in the east than in the west.

(d) A reduction in the population tends, in areas where there is not undue pressure on the land, to increase the potential food supply for the survivors and therefore leads to better nourished children.

(e) The number of children aged 0—10 per mille of the population at the previous Census is the most important factor favouring an increase. For instance survival rates in Alwar, at later ages compare very favourably with those shown by the Western States and had Alwar been able to show a 0—10 ratio equal to that of Marwar the increase would have been 12·2 per cent. instead of 6·9.

(f) Lastly—and this is only a theory put forward for what it is worth—after a considerable loss through famine or epidemics in any one decade, Nature will, if the seasons are favourable, assist a high infant survival rate during the succeeding one.

THE URBAN POPULATION PER 1000

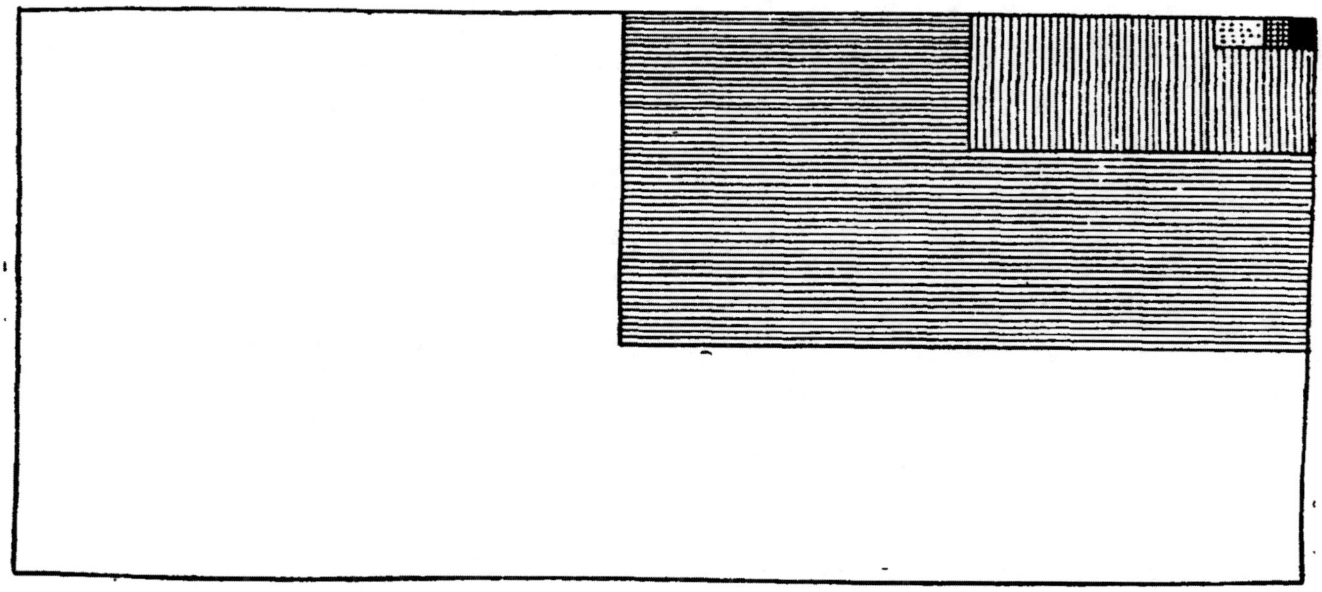

THE RURAL POPULATION PER 1000

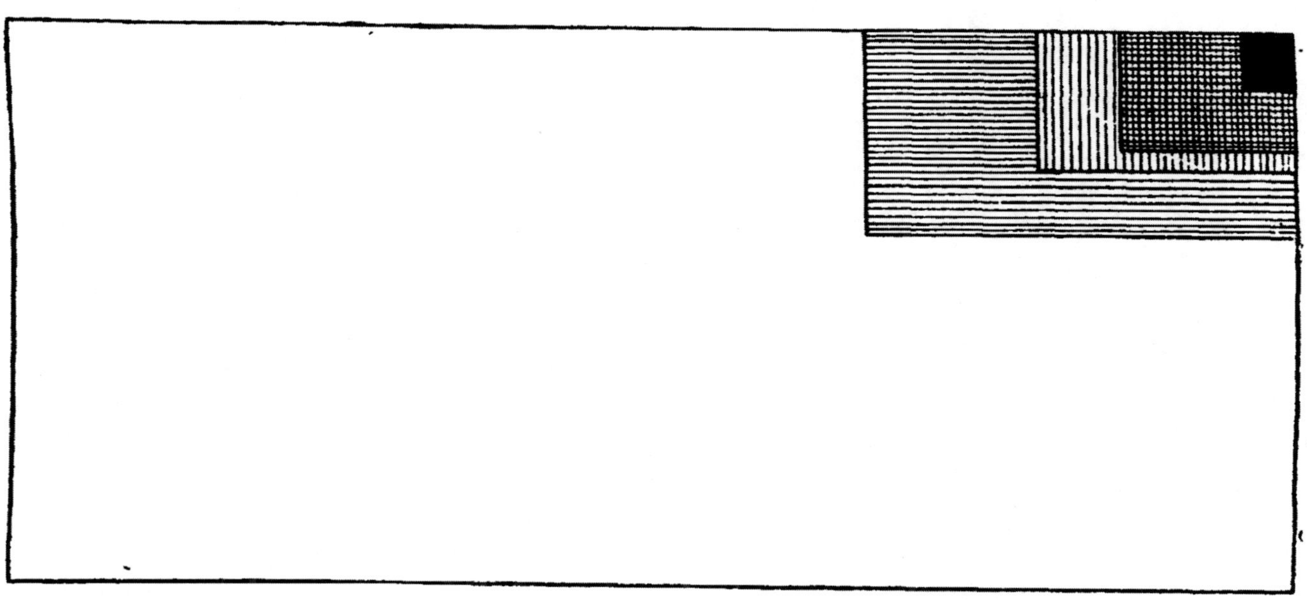

FOR URBAN	
HINDUS	690
MUSLIMS	246
JAINS	60
CHRISTIAN	2
TRIBAL	1
OTHERS	1

FOR RURAL	
HINDUS	879
MUSLIMS	71
JAINS	22
TRIBAL	24
SIKHS	4

CHAPTER II.

The Population of Cities, Towns and Villages.

1. Imperial Table I gives particulars of the Urban and Rural population. Imperial Table III shows towns and villages classified by population. Imperial Table IV gives the list of towns classified by population with variations since 1881, and Imperial Table V shows the population of each town classified by Religion. **Reference to Statistics.**

At the end of this Chapter there are four Subsidiary Tables which show—

(1) the distribution of the population between towns and villages,
(2) the number per mille of each religion who live in towns,
(3) the towns classified by population with variations since 1881, and
(4) miscellaneous information regarding each city and important town of each State.

The diagrams at the beginning of this Chapter illustrate the proportions by religions of the population in Urban and Rural areas.

2. The usual definition of a 'City' is a town with a population of 100,000 and over, but Local Governments and Administrations have discretion to treat other large towns as 'Cities' also. Certain Tables are prepared for Cities as well as for each State and District, and in the Rajputana Agency, 10 towns—all Capitals of the larger States—have been treated as Cities, although only one of them, Jaipur, has a population of over 100,000 persons. **Definitions.**

A 'Town' includes every Municipality, and Cantonment and every other continuous collection of houses with a population of not less than 5,000. The Provincial Superintendent has discretion however to treat any place, not coming within these categories, as a town provided it has urban characteristics.

A 'Village' varies in nature according to the revenue system prevailing in each State. In some it is the residential village, while in others it is a collection of hamlets.

3. Of every 1,000 persons in the Agency, 139 live in urban areas. Similar figures through the decades are 134 in 1921, 131 in 1911, 148 in 1901, 130 in 1891 and 135 in 1881. It cannot therefore be said that the march of time is appreciably affecting the comparative size of the urban population. Among the larger States the greatest ratio of 241 is in Bikaner, while the lowest figure of 75 is found in Mewar. At the Census of 1921, the urban population of England and Wales constituted 793 per mille of the total population. **The Population of Towns.**

4. The statement overleaf is a summary of all information concerning the urban population of each State:— **Detail by States.**

STATE, ETC.	NUMBER OF TOWNS.	NUMBER OF TOWNS BY CLASSES.						NUMBER PER MILLE OF TOTAL POPULATION WHO RESIDE IN TOWNS		VARIATION IN URBAN POPULATION SINCE 1921.	STATE VARIATION.
		100,000 and over. I.	50,000 and over. II.	20,000 and over. III.	10,000 and over. IV.	5,000 and over. V.	Under 5,000. VI.	1931.	1921.		
1	2	3	4	5	6	7	8	9	10	11	12
Abu ...	1	...	...	...	...	...	1	919	778	+ 48·5	+ 25·7
Alwar ...	7	...	...	1	...	2	4	100	103	+ 5·1	+ 6·9
Banswara ...	1	...	...	...	1	...	...	46	45	+ 21·6	+ 18·3
Bharatpur ...	7	...	...	1	1	3	2	147	151	— 4·4	— 1·9
Bikaner ...	15	...	1	1	3	7	3	241	255	+ 26·0	+ 41·9
Bundi ...	4	...	...	...	1	1	2	148	140	+ 22·0	+ 15·9
Dholpur ...	3	...	...	...	2	1	...	141	137	+ 14·9	+ 10·8
Dungarpur ...	3	...	...	...	...	2	1	77	91	+ 2·7	+ 20·2
Jaipur ...	38½	1	...	1	6½	19	11	170	162	+ 18·2	+ 12·5
Jaisalmer ...	1	...	...	...	...	1	...	93	71	+ 47·3	+ 12·7
Jhalawar ...	2	...	...	...	1	1	...	155	167	+ 4·3	+ 12·2
Karauli ...	3	...	...	...	1	...	2	172	176	+ 2·9	+ 5·1
Kishangarh ...	3	...	...	...	1	...	2	215	198	+ 19·1	+ 10·3
Kotah ...	4	...	...	1	1	...	2	86	81	+ 16·1	+ 8·8
Kushalgarh ...	1	...	...	...	...	...	1	86	94	+ 12·4	+ 22·0
Marwar ...	25½	...	1	...	5½	15	4	133	126	+ 21·9	+ 15·4
Mewar ...	15	...	...	1	1	6	7	75	71	+ 14·7	+ 14·6
Partabgarh ...	1	...	...	...	1	...	...	141	137	+ 18·1	+ 14·1
Shahpura ...	1	...	...	...	...	1	...	171	172	+ 12·1	+ 12·7
Sirohi ...	4	...	...	...	...	2	2	107	110	+ 11·9	+ 16·0
Tonk ...	5	...	...	1	1	2	1	201	198	+ 12·3	+ 10·2
Total	**145**	**1**	**2**	**7**	**27**	**63**	**45**	**139**	**134**	**+ 16·7**	**+ 14·2**

The variation in column 11 excludes the population of the three towns included as such for the first time at this Census. These are Sri Ganganagar and Hanumangarh in Bikaner and Kapasin in Mewar.

It will be seen that among the States that have 5 or more towns, the urban population has increased at a rate higher than that for the whole population in Jaipur, Marwar, Mewar and Tonk, while the converse prevails in Alwar, Bharatpur and Bikaner. In the latter the influx of colonists to the Canal areas has disproportionately increased the rural population.

Of the 145 towns, only 10 have a population of more than 20,000 persons, while among the individual larger towns the following increases per cent. in population during the decade are notable:—

Jaipur State.		*Marwar State.*		*Bikaner State.*	
Sikar.	24·7	Jodhpur.	28·9	Bikaner.	23·8
Nawalgarh.	34·5	Ladnun.	30·4	Churu.	29·7
Gangapur.	35·8	Nagaur.	35·3	Sardarshahr.	35·3
				Sujangarh.	37·0
				Rajgarh.	74·8

Other increases such as Jaisalmer 47·3, Udaipur 26·6 and Lakheri (Bundi) 56·4 are above the average. A reduced population is observed in 4 out of the 7 towns in Bharatpur and may be ascribed to the economic depression that prevailed in that State during the greater part of the decade. It is interesting to note that the majority of the towns which have recorded a large increase are the homes of wealthy persons who in all parts of India are known by the comprehensive appellation of 'Marwaris'. Their business concerns lead them to every corner of the Indian Empire, and the success of their enterprise is reflected in the stimulation of local trade and such beneficent undertakings as the building of palatial residences, sinking of wells for drinking water and the maintenance of schools and dispensaries in their native towns.

Small Towns.

5. Towns that have a population of under 5,000 are 45 in number and in them reside 109 per mille of the total urban population. Twenty nine of them have had at one time or another in the past fifty years, a population of over 5,000 and it is these small towns that are, on the whole, losing their urban characteristics situated as they are for the most part off the Railway. The increase in the population of towns of this class since 1921 is only 11·9 per cent. which is below the total increase of 14·2 per cent. in the whole population.

Religious distribution in urban areas.

6. The statement below shows for urban areas the distribution of the population by religions:—

Per mille of-	Tribal.	Christian.	Hindu.	Jain.	Muslim.	Sikh.	Others.
Each religion	7	572	112	308	358	34	...
Urban population	1	2	690	60	246	...	1

Average urban population.

7. The average population of a town is now 10,734 and was 9,279 in 1921. The average is notably exceeded in Bikaner (15,010), Kotah (14,762), Tonk (12,784) and Dholpur (12,028).

Sex proportions.

8. The number of females per 1,000 males in towns is 913 as against 907 in rural areas. The excess may be explained by the more or less permanent nature of the urban population unaffected by an excess of males attracted by temporary employment, and, among trading castes, by the absence of many males at their places of business in other parts of India.

The population of villages.

9. The Agency contains 33,688 villages with an average population of 287 in each. In every thousand of the rural population 910 reside in villages with a population of under 2,000 while villages with a population of under 500 account for 494 of these 910. It has already been explained that the nature of a 'village' varies in the different States according to the revenue system in force. The small village is however the rule as the marginal statement shows. The greater part of the Agency consists of infertile tracts lacking the means of irrigation, and agriculturists eke out a somewhat precarious existence by cultivating scattered and extensive holdings, producing crops dependent on the uncertain rainfall. These conditions of cultivation tend to prevent the concentration of the agricultural population in large villages, as cultivators prefer to settle in hamlets adjacent to their holdings.

PERCENTAGE OF VILLAGES WITH A POPULATION OF UNDER 500.

Alwar	78	Jaipur	80	Marwar	72
Banswara	93	Jaisalmer	95	Mewar	93
Bharatpur	82	Jhalawar	93	Partabgarh	95
Bikaner	87	Karauli	82	Shahpura	74
Bundi	91	Kishangarh	86	Sirohi	69
Dholpur	72	Kotah	91	Tonk.	92
Dungarpur	85	Kushalgarh	99		

Religious distribution in rural areas.

10. The statement below shows the distribution of the rural population by religions: —

Per mille of—	Tribal.	Christian.	Hindu.	Jain.	Muslim	Sikh.
Each religion	993	428	888	692	642	966
Rural population	24	...	879	22	71	4

1.—DISTRIBUTION OF THE POPULATION BETWEEN TOWNS AND VILLAGES.

AGENCY, NATURAL DIVISION AND STATE OR DISTRICT.	AVERAGE POPULATION PER		NUMBER PER MILLE RESIDING IN		NUMBER PER MILLE OF URBAN POPULATION RESIDING IN TOWNS WITH A POPULATION OF				NUMBER PER MILLE OF RURAL POPULATION RESIDING IN VILLAGES WITH A POPULATION OF			
	Town.	Village.	Towns.	Villages.	20,000 and over.	10,000 to 20,000	5,000 to 10,000.	Under 5,000.	5,000 and over.	2,000 to 5,000.	500 to 2,000.	Under 500.
1	2	3	4	5	6	7	8	9	10	11	12	13
RAJPUTANA ...	***10,734***	***287***	***139***	***861***	***366***	***231***	***294***	***109***	***3***	***87***	***416***	***494***
North-West Dry Area...	***12,428***	***356***	***164***	***836***	***393***	***225***	***334***	***48***	...	***111***	***467***	***422***
Bikaner ...	15,010	259	241	759	479	235	238	48	...	42	391	567
Jaisalmer ...	7,120	140	93	907	...	...	1,000	...	...	...	262	738
Marwar ...	11,116	447	133	867	336	223	393	49	...	142	503	355
Rajputana East ...	***10,054***	***268***	***129***	***871***	***352***	***234***	***275***	***139***	***4***	***78***	***396***	***522***
Abu ...	4,165	92	919	81	...	...	...	1,000	...	...	...	1,000
Alwar ...	10,799	331	100	900	633	...	185	182	8	70	472	450
Banswara ...	10,444	196	46	954	...	1,000	...	...	...	41	275	684
Bharatpur ...	10,211	316	147	853	422	156	292	130	...	39	461	500
Bundi ...	8,015	229	148	852	...	561	204	235	...	36	329	635
Dholpur ...	12,028	417	141	859	...	821	179	...	...	67	546	387
Dungarpur ...	5,867	281	77	923	...	...	802	198	...	10	446	544
Jaipur ...	11,602	373	170	830	382	195	319	104	10	124	440	426
Jhalawar ...	8,379	211	155	845	...	623	377	...	...	118	186	696
Karauli ...	8,054	312	172	828	...	814	...	186	...	20	507	473
Kishangarh ...	6,127	295	215	785	...	649	...	351	...	31	390	579
Kotah ...	14,762	249	86	914	641	194	...	165	...	89	305	606
Kushalgarh (Chiefship).	3,069	116	86	914	...	...	...	1,000	...	...	942	58
Lawa (Estate) ...	...	254	...	1,000	...	...	...	...	...	778	...	222
Mewar ...	7,863	180	75	925	373	88	325	214	4	55	323	618
Partabgarh ...	10,845	140	141	859	...	1,000	...	...	...	...	261	739
Shahpura ...	9,298	388	171	829	...	...	1,000	...	...	55	556	389
Sirohi ...	5,766	473	107	893	...	...	745	255	...	136	560	304
Tonk ...	12,784	199	201	799	560	192	179	69	...	21	306	673

2.—NUMBER PER MILLE OF THE TOTAL POPULATION AND OF EACH MAIN RELIGION WHO LIVE IN TOWNS.

AGENCY AND STATE OR DISTRICT.	NUMBER PER MILLE WHO LIVE IN TOWNS.						
	Total Population.	Tribal.	Christian.	Hindu.	Jain.	Muslim.	Sikh.
1	2	3	4	5	6	7	8
Rajputana ...	**139**	**7**	**572**	**112**	**308**	**358**	**34**
Abu District ...	919	...	1,000	907	1,000	967	741
Alwar ...	100	...	810	95	434	111	973
Banswara ...	46	...	405	56	80	454	1,000
Bharatpur ...	147	...	962	132	502	193	325
Bikaner ...	241	...	597	216	747	327	21
Bundi ...	148	1,000	1,000	129	340	605	156
Dholpur ...	141	...	1,000	110	267	559	390
Dungarpur ...	77	...	1,000	41	236	761	889
Jaipur ...	170	5	422	133	415	546	947
Jaisalmer ...	93	59	...	115	180	42	222
Jhalawar ...	155	...	100	116	273	562	278
Karauli ...	172	...	1,000	146	817	611	...
Kishangarh ...	215	159	1,000	178	471	608	1,000
Kotah ...	86	42	128	66	298	389	271
Kushalgarh (Chiefship).	86	...	...	60	976	522	...
Lawa (Estate) ...	...	...	...	...	...	...	...
Marwar ...	133	35	908	104	246	359	588
Mewar ...	75	10	336	60	175	441	348
Partabgarh ...	141	3	328	146	584	530	667
Shahpura ...	171	...	1,000	143	352	631	...
Sirohi ...	107	...	974	83	177	542	900
Tonk ...	201	20	907	121	378	665	700

3.—TOWNS CLASSIFIED BY POPULATION.

CLASS OF TOWNS.	NUMBER OF TOWNS OF EACH CLASS IN 1931.	PROPORTION PER CENT. TO TOTAL URBAN POPULATION.	NUMBER OF FEMALES PER 1,000 MALES.	VARIATION PER CENT. IN THE POPULATION OF TOWNS AS CLASSED AT PREVIOUS CENSUSES.					VARIATION PER CENT. IN URBAN POPULATION OF EACH CLASS FROM 1881—1931.	
				1921 to 1931.	1911 to 1921.	1901 to 1911.	1891 to 1901.	1881 to 1891.	In towns as classed in 1881.	In total of each class in 1931 as compared with the corresponding total in 1881.
1	2	3	4	5	6	7	8	9	10	11
Rajputana ...	**145**	**100**	**913**	**+ 16·7**	**− 5·1**	**− 6·7**	**− 8·5**	**+ 13·5**	**+ 4·4**	**+ 7·4**
I. 100,000 and over ...	1	9	850	+ 19·9	− 12·3	− 14·4	+ 0·9	+ 11·4	+ 1·1	+ 1·1
II. 50,000 to 100,000 ...	2	12	844	+ 26·4	+ 5·4	− 8·9	− 7·2	− 25·2	+ 1·1	+ 79·8
III. 20,000 to 50,000 ...	7	16	891	+ 14·5	− 0·6	− 14·4	− 12·4	+ 38·3	+ 7·4	− 7·4
IV. 10,000 to 20,000 ...	27	24	955	+ 17·5	− 9·3	− 1·0	− 9·1	+ 8·5	+ 2·3	+ 15·0
V. 5,000 to 10,000 ...	63	28	989	+ 15·4	− 5·8	+ 6·1	− 9·8	+ 15·1	+ 7·5	+ 7·2
VI. Under 5,000 ...	45	11	917	+ 11·9	− 3·0	+ 1·3	− 10·9	+ 36·5	...	− 20·7

4.—CITIES AND PRINCIPAL TOWNS.

CITIES AND PRINCIPAL TOWNS.	POPULATION IN 1931.	NUMBER OF PERSONS PER SQUARE MILE.	NUMBER OF FEMALES TO 1,000 MALES.	PROPORTION OF FOREIGN BORN PER MILLE.	PERCENTAGE OF VARIATION.					
					1921—31.	1911—21.	1901—11.	1891—1901	1881—1891.	1881—1931.
1	2	3	4	5	6	7	8	9	10	11
Cities.										
Alwar ...	47,900	10,912	872	64	+ 7·0	+ 8·4	− 28·9	+ 11·5	+ 3·2	− 3·9
Bharatpur ...	30,178	3,017	803	161	− 9·9	− 1·2	− 22·2	− 35·5	+ 2·1	− 54·4
Bikaner ...	85,927	2,772	875	116	+ 23·8	+ 24·3	+ 5·2	+ 5·1	+ 52·4	+ 159·1
Bundi ...	17,991	1,799	960	80	+ 11·7	− 17·3	+ 1·5	− 14·3	+ 8·7	− 13 3
Dholpur ...	19,586	3,917	859	186	+ 20·8	− 18·7	+ 3·2	+ 13·4	+ 7·5	+ 23·7
Jaipur ...	144,179	48,060	850	45	+ 19·9	− 12·3	− 14·4	+ 0·9	+ 11·4	+ 1·1
Jodhpur ...	94,736	3,644	816	64	+ 28·9	− 7·9	+ 0·8	− 1·6	+ 27·0	+ 49·6
Kotah ...	37,876	9,469	870	283	+ 19·4	− 3·2	+ 1·9	− 12·9	− 4·1	− 5·9
Tonk ...	35,798	1,884	966	92	+ 17·8	− 10·3	− 12·6	− 15·6	+ 12·8	− 12·1
Udaipur ...	44,035	*	852	42	+ 26·6	+ 4·7	− 27·5	− 1·5	+ 22·2	+ 15·2
Principal Towns.										
Abu ...	4,165	*	640	Not available.	+ 48·5	− 14·7	− 5·8	+ 34·9	...	...
Banswara ...	10,444	1,305	1,032		+ 21·6	+ 12·0	+ 8·9	− 14·5	+ 4·1	+ 32·1
Dungarpur ...	8,560	21,400	938		+ 16·8	+ 13·2	+ 6·2	− 5·2	− 0·3	+ 32·7.
Jaisalmer ...	7,120	7,120	921		+ 47·2	− 34·8	+ 3·9	− 32·1	− 4·2	− 35·1
Jhalrapatan (Chhaoni) ...	10,442	11,602	986		+ 4·6	− 13·0	− 19·9	− 38·7	+ 15·1	− 48·5
Karauli ...	19,671	6,557	816		+ 0·5	− 1·1	− 15·7	+ 1·5	− 9·7	− 23·2
Kishangarh ...	11,929	5,964	866		+ 26·2	− 9·3	− 17·3	− 18·1	+ 4·3	− 19·5
Kushalgarh (Chiefship)	3,069	3,611	979		+ 12·4	+ 5·3	− 8·6	+ 0·7	− 5·7	+ 2·7
Partabgarh ...	10,845	1,807	936		+ 18·1	+ 10·2	− 15·2	− 38·7	+ 19·2	− 12·4
Shahpura ...	9,298	516	943		+ 12·1	+ 4·6	− 11·6	− 23·4	+ 10·1	− 12·7
Sirohi ...	7,463	*	954		+ 20·4	− 6·3	+ 17·0	− 9·0	+ 8·9	+ 31·0

* Figures of area not available.

DIAGRAM SHOWING STATES IN ORDER OF POPULATION WITH THE NUMBER OF THOSE BORN OUTSIDE PER MILLE OF THE POPULATION.

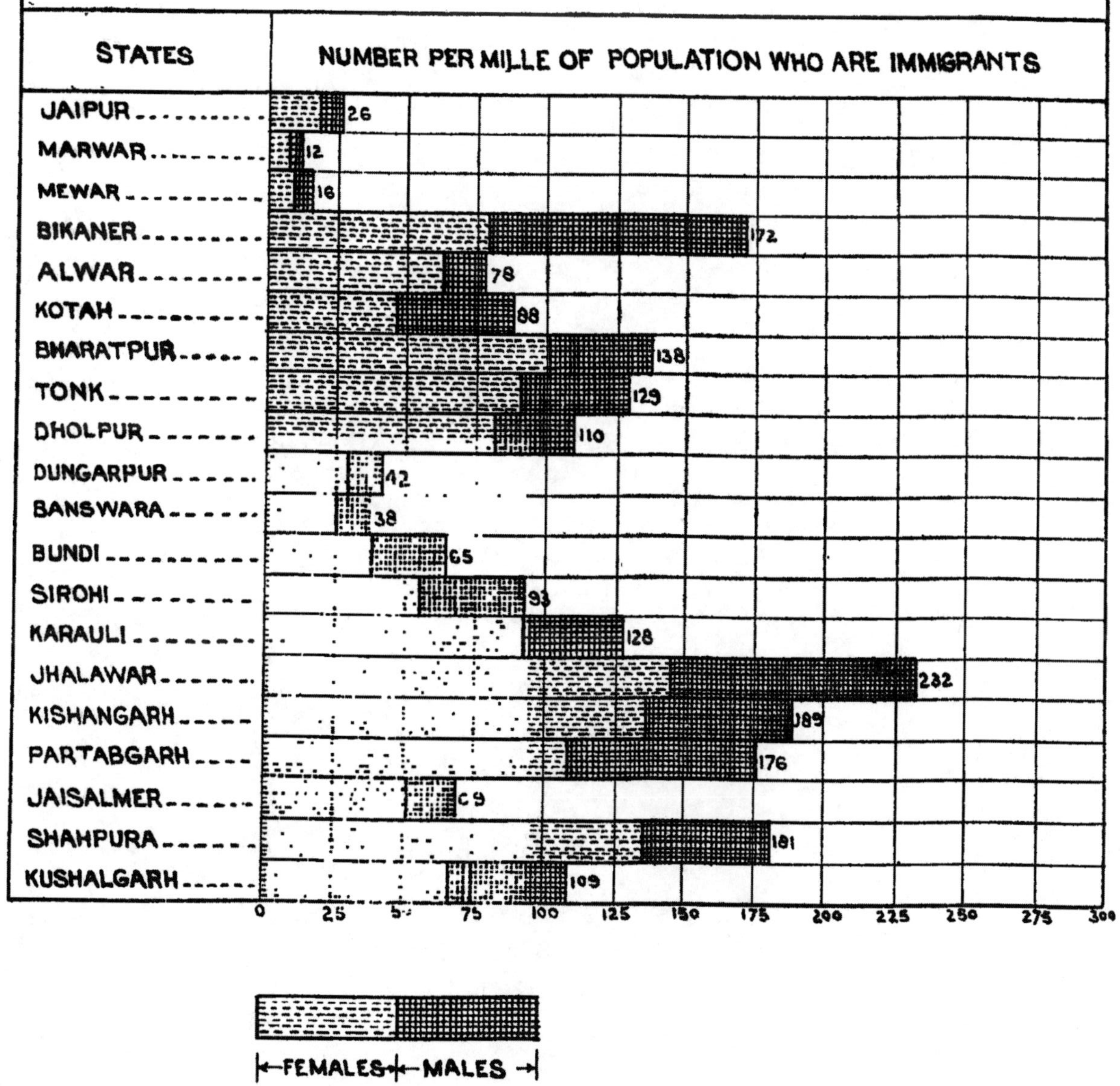

CHAPTER III.

Birthplace and Migration.

1. Every person was required to record on the schedule the District or State and Province or Agency of his or her birth, and the results for each State and City are recorded in Imperial Table VI. Information relative to the birthplaces of persons born in but enumerated outside the Agency, was communicated by other Superintendents, but for reasons of economy it was decided that such figures should be for the Agency as a whole and not for each State. The enquiry has therefore been deprived of much of the interest that has at previous Censuses been a feature of this subject. At the end of this Chapter will be found three Subsidiary Tables dealing with the figures in greater detail. **Reference to statistics.**

2. An immigrant is a person who was born outside the State wherein he or she was enumerated, while an emigrant is one who was enumerated outside the State wherein he or she was born. It will therefore be understood that migration can be Casual, Temporary, Periodic, Semi-permanent or Permanent. They can be distinguished by the following descriptions:— **The nature of migration.**

(*a*) *Casual.*—Minor movements between villages lying in different States or Districts in or out of the Agency. Females generally predominate on account of the practice of obtaining wives from other villages. Such females often return to their parents' villages for their first confinement.

(*b*) *Temporary.*—Due to journeys on business, pilgrimages and the temporary demand for labour, etc.

(*c*) *Periodic.*—Such as the annual migration which takes place in different tracts at harvest time and the seasonal movements of pastoral nomads.

(*d*) *Semi-permanent.*—When the natives of one place reside and earn their living in other, leaving their families at their homes to which they return at intervals.

(*e*) *Permanent.*—When overcrowding drives people away or the superior attractions of some other locality induce people to settle there.

3. The absence of industrialism on any large scale, a scanty rainfall and a lack of irrigation are all factors that combine to prevent immigration to any large extent of a Periodic, Semi-permanent or Permanent nature to the Agency from Provinces and States beyond its borders. The Casual or Temporary nature of such immigration as occurs is shown by the marginal figures and subsequent remarks. Of the 682,499 persons returned as having birthplaces outside the States of enumeration, no less than 424,697 are females, which is conclusive proof that immigration is largely due to marriage and other social reasons. Immigrants from other States in Rajputana outnumber those from all other parts of India and elsewhere, and among them females are in excess of males by 93 per cent. Even among those from outside the Agency excluding Ajmer-Merwara, there are 1,384 females for every 1,000 males. The diagram prefacing this Chapter shows that on the whole, immigration varies inversely with the size of the State and its population. The larger the State, the more it can rely on its own population for marriages. The three largest States, Jaipur, Marwar **Immigration.**

Birthplace.	Persons.	Males.	Females.
The State of enumeration ...	10,543,213	5,627,226	4,915,987
Other States of Rajputana ...	351,560	120,161	231,399
Ajmer-Merwara ...	21,522	7,875	13,647
Outside Rajputana ...	309,417	129,766	179,651
Total enumerated population.	11,225,712	5,885,028	5,340,684

and Mewar only show ratios for immigrants of 26, 12 and 16 respectively per mille of their populations, while the highest ratios of 232 and 189 are shown by Jhalawar and Kishangarh respectively. The case of Bikaner is of course different. Due to the opening of Canal Colonies, its ratio is 172 in which females are only 45 per cent. In 1921 the ratio was 81 per mille with a female proportion of 58 per cent.

Immigration within Rajputana.

4. The part that Casual migration for social reasons between various parts of Rajputana plays in the life of the people is shown by the marginal statement. As might be expected, the geographical position of each State is the factor that determines the proportion of immigration from other parts of Rajputana, and the detailed figures in Imperial Table VI show that females in every case predominate in such migration.

State, etc.	Proportion who returned birthplaces in other States in the Agency and in Ajmer-Merwara per mille of all immigrants.
Lawa ...	995
Shahpura ...	986
Kishangarh ...	969
Bundi ...	856
Jaisalmer ...	851
Karauli ...	800
Jaipur ...	789
Marwar ...	713
Sirohi ...	712
Abu ...	643
Dungarpur ...	640
Tonk ...	631
Banswara ...	597
Kotah ...	593
Alwar ...	591
Mewar ...	590
Partabgarh ...	453
Bharatpur ...	435
Jhalawar ...	410
Bikaner ...	360
Kushalgarh ...	350
Dholpur ...	133

Immigration from outside.

5. It remains therefore to consider whence the remaining 309,417 immigrants from outside have come and the reason for their coming. The marginal statement shows the large part that contiguity plays in such migration. Excepting Bikaner where there is a definite attraction for immigrants apart from those of a Casual type, in every other instance, females exceed males and this clearly brings out that such immigration is on the whole for social purposes connected with marriage, etc. Sufficient has been quoted to show that the genuine immigration of persons on any large scale for economic reasons is, except in Bikaner, practically non-existent in the Agency.

Statement showing the number of Immigrants from places outside Rajputana and the States in which chiefly found. (*ooo's omitted*).

Province, etc.	Persons.	Males.	Females.
Bombay Presidency and Western India States.	**18**	**8**	**10**
Banswara ...	2	1	1
Dungarpur ...	3	1	2
Marwar ...	2	1	1
Mewar ...	3	1	2
Sirohi ...	4	2	2
Punjab and States and Delhi ...	**142**	**69**	**73**
Alwar ...	21	3	18
Bharatpur ...	9	3	6
Bikaner ...	99	58	41
Jaipur ...	9	3	6
United Provinces ...	**68**	**24**	**44**
Bharatpur ...	28	7	21
Dholpur ...	17	4	13
Central India Agency ...	**26**	**9**	**17**
Jhalawar ...	8	3	5
Kotah ...	5	2	3
Partabgarh ...	3	1	2
Tonk ...	3	1	2
Gwalior ...	**47**	**15**	**32**
Dholpur ...	6	1	5
Jhalawar ...	6	2	4
Kotah ...	11	4	7
Mewar ...	3	1	2
Partabgarh ...	4	1	3
Tonk ...	11	4	7
Elsewhere ...	**8**	**4**	**4**
Total ...	***309***	***129***	***180***

Immigration in cities.

6. No figures are available for emigration from the 10 cities of the Agency. Imperial Table VI Part II, however gives for each city the birth-places of the population found therein. Of 51,356 persons whose birthplaces were not located in the State concerned, 23,227 (11,700 males and 11,527 females) had come from other Rajputana States and 13,107 (6,551 males and 6,556 females) from the United Provinces. The equality in the numbers of the

sexes suggests a permanent nature of migration. The marginal statement shows the city immigration figures in detail. The large proportion of immigrants in the population of Kotah has always been a feature of that city and was ascribed 20 years ago to railway development. It may not have been entirely unconnected with the former trade in opium and 70 per cent. of its immigrants are from other States in the Agency. Notable increases in the proportion of immigrants have occurred in Bikaner and Jodhpur and point to trading and industrial developments. On the whole, however, immigration plays a small part in the existence of these cities and the only remarkable feature is the large proportion of immigrants from the United Provinces.

CITY.	NUMBERS BORN OUTSIDE THE STATE.			IMMIGRANTS PER MILLE OF POPULATION.			RATIO IN 1921.
	Persons.	Males.	Females.	Persons.	Males.	Females.	Persons
Kotah ...	10,710	5,810	4,900	282	153	129	311
Dholpur ...	3,646	1,365	2,281	186	70	116	165
Bharatpur ...	4,854	1,982	2,872	161	66	95	202
Bikaner ...	9,928	6,128	3,800	115	71	44	77
Tonk ...	3,303	1,176	2,127	92	33	59	98
Bundi ...	1,432	670	762	79	37	42	134
Jodhpur ...	6,079	3,554	2,525	64	37	27	50
Alwar ...	3,055	1,249	1 806	64	26	38	74
Jaipur ...	6,479	3,602	2,877	45	25	20	64
Udaipur ...	1,870	1,084	786	42	24	18	52
Total ...	51,356	26,620	24,736	92	48	44	98

Emigration.

7. It has already been seen that 351,560 persons, of whom 120,161 were males and 231,399 females, may be styled intra-Agency emigrants. That is to say they were persons who were born in some State of the Agency and enumerated in another. Detailed figures for the States of birth are not available but the proportion of 1,926 females per 1,000 males amongst such emigrants is conclusive proof of the nature of such migration and need not be considered further. What is of greater interest is the fact that 846,716 persons who were born in the Agency were, at this Census, enumerated elsewhere. This flow of emigration can better be judged by the fact that of 1,000 persons born in the Agency, 72 were enumerated elsewhere, 37 being males and 35 females. The statement in the margin shows whither these persons have gone and compares the figures with those obtained at the last Census.

RETURN OF EMIGRANTS FROM RAJPUTANA.
(000's omitted).

PROVINCE.	1931.			1921.		
	Persons.	Males	Females.	Persons.	Males.	Females.
Assam ...	22	16	6	16	12	4
Bengal ...	33	24	9	48	34	14
Bihar & Orissa ...	21	13	8	19	12	7
Hyderabad ...	7	4	3	8	5	3
Central Provinces.	52	32	20	49	30	19
Bombay including Western India States but excluding Sind.	82	50	32	103	65	38
Sind ...	38	22	16	53	30	23
Central India Agency ...	106	54	52	86	45	41
Gwalior ...	76	35	41	76	35	41
United Provinces.	82	34	48	68	28	40
Punjab and Delhi less States.	167	80	87	185	92	93
Punjab States ...	69	25	44	71	29	42
Ajmer-Merwara ...	76	33	43	69	31	38
Elsewhere ...	16	11	5	18	14	4
Total Emigrants.	847	433	414	869	462	407

Emigration in 1921 and comparison with present figures.

8. In the absence of detailed figures by States it is not possible to show whence these people have emigrated but some clue is afforded by the 1921 figures in which details by States are available. In the first place, out of 613,948 emigrants for whom details were available at that Census, no less than 42 per cent. hailed from the three States of Bikaner, Jaisalmer and Marwar in the North-West Dry Area whose population was only 26 per cent. of the whole Agency. A poor soil and a dependence on a scanty rainfall are factors which are favourable to emigration but that these are not the only ones that prevail in Western Rajputana will be shown in the succeeding paragraphs.

Apart from details regarding some 90,000 emigrants who were returned from various parts of India as having birthplaces in Rajputana without the particular State being specified, the marginal statement gives some indication of the origin of those for whom such information was known. A reference to the various Provincial Reports for 1921 shows that in Assam and Bengal these emigrants were described as chiefly Marwari traders whose activities extended to every corner. The same may be assumed to have been the case in the distant areas of Bihar and Orissa and the Central Provinces. As regards Bombay, the emigrants were described as persons in search of work in the larger cities, though the preponderance of females in the numbers from Mewar suggests social reasons. The contiguity of Sind to Marwar and Jaisalmer would seem to imply that emigration from these States was probably due in part to agricultural and pastoral reasons. Emigration to the United Provinces and the Central India Agency, particularly from the many contiguous States, showed a preponderance of females and was therefore largely social in character. The amount of emigration that was due to trade ten years ago, may be gauged by the fact that among all Mahajans enumerated in the Agency, the ratio of females to 1,000 males was 1,004. Now this could but mean that many males were away from the Agency at the time of the Census. Not all leave their wives and families at home, and considering that this community numbered nearly 600,000 in the various States and that the so-called 'Marwari' often accompanied by a male Rajput protector, penetrates to all parts of India in pursuit of his calling, it cannot but be assumed that a very large number of emigrants from Rajputana are of this description, and that those who are genuinely driven from their homes in search of a livelihood form but a comparatively small proportion of all emigrants. The decrease in the number of emigrants at this Census to such parts as Sind, Bombay and the Punjab points in some degree to a better standard of prosperity in the Agency, while the increase observed to Assam, Bihar and Orissa and the Central Provinces would seem to indicate an increase in trade. A greater number of emigrants to the United Provinces probably accounts for the decrease in the population of Bharatpur while the increase in the population of the contiguous States is sufficient to account for migration in larger numbers for social reasons to the Central India Agency and to Ajmer-Merwara.

Province wherein enumerated in 1921.	Principal States of birth.	Persons.	Males.	Females.
Assam		15,770	11,443	4,327
	Bikaner	5,954	4,464	1,490
	Jaipur	5,660	3.855	1,805
	Marwar	2,078	1,489	589
Bengal		47,865	33,473	14,392
	Bikaner	20,105	14,532	5,573
	Jaipur	17,018	11,345	5,673
	Marwar	4,581	3,491	1,090
Bihar and Orissa ...		18,812	11,449	7,363
	Jaipur	12,440	7,475	4,965
	Bikaner	1,733	1,257	476
	Marwar	1,711	986	725
Central Provinces ...		49,207	29,609	19,598
	Jaipur	18,516	11,154	7,362
	Marwar	18,783	11,366	7,417
Bombay including Western India States and excluding Sind.		103,473	65,458	38,015
	Marwar	32,705	21,922	10,783
	Jaipur	5,908	4,843	1,065
	Mewar	4,080	1,651	2,429
	Rajputana unspecified	54,949	33,831	21,118
Sind		52.884	30,405	22,479
	Marwar	42,688	24,336	18,352
	Jaisalmer	6,844	3,891	2,953

The extent to which emigration deprives the larger States of their home born population is best shown by the marginal statement of proportionate figures obtained at the 1921 Census. The exodus from Jaisalmer was certainly great and in view of the present reduced number of emigrants to the Punjab and Sind from the whole Agency, the assumption can be made that the emigrant ratio in Jaisalmer is now not so great as it was ten years ago. The next highest emigrant ratio of 158 from Bikaner can also now be considered as less, for the increase since 1921 in the population born and enumerated in the State is 27·8 per cent. and the conjecture is that many of the 1921 emigrants to the Punjab and else where have now returned to their homes on account of the greater agricultural prosperity prevailing in the State.

STATE.	NUMBER OF EMIGRANTS TO OUTSIDE THE AGENCY AND AJMER-MERWARA PER MILLE OF HOME BORN POPULATION.	PROVINCES, ETC. WHEREIN CHIEFLY FOUND.										
		Assam.	Bengal.	Bihar and Orissa.	Hyderabad.	Central Provinces.	Bombay.	Sind.	United Provinces.	Punjab and Delhi.	Gwalior.	Central India Agency.
Alwar ...	98	...	...	1	...	1	1	...	18	73	1	2
Bharatpur ...	51	...	...	...	...	1	...	...	16	26	2	3
Jaipur ...	79	2	7	5	...	7	2	...	9	32	5	8
Kotah ...	30	...	...	...	...	...	...	...	2	...	12	15
Mewar ...	26	...	2	...	...	...	3	...	2	...	10	8
Tonk ...	74	...	...	...	...	1	...	...	3	1	47	21
Bikaner ...	158	8	27	2	...	3	...	...	4	109	...	1
Jaisalmer ...	208	...	...	...	...	10	...	83	31	76	3	3
Marwar ...	74	1	2	1	3	9	16	21	8	6	1	8

The balance of migration.

9. Subsidiary Table 3 shows that emigrants to other parts of India exceed immigrants by 516,790. The excess in 1921 was 626,663. Except for a favourable balance of 40 from Kashmir, there is no part of India from which this Agency receives more than it gives. The greatest loss of 94,127 is to the Bombay Presidency, closely followed by 93,821 to the Punjab and Delhi, 79,070 to the Central India Agency and 54,852 to Ajmer-Merwara. The marginal statements show a comparison of the balance of migration to and from certain parts of India at this and at the last Census. In spite of the population being the highest recorded for the last 30 years the balance of migration has never been so favourable as it is now. Improved communications and a series of favourable seasons have undoubtedly contributed to the ability of the Agency to maintain, to an increasing extent, the comparatively small proportion of the population born within its borders that is liable to emigrate in search of a livelihood.

EXCESS OF EMIGRANTS OVER IMMIGRANTS.

Province, etc.	1931.	1921.
Bombay including Western India States Agency	102,999	141,595
Punjab and Delhi ...	93,821	190,378
Central India Agency.	79,070	58,434
Ajmer-Merwara ...	54,852	48,994
Assam ...	21,656	15,724
Bengal ...	31,899	47,091
Bihar and Orissa ...	20,304	18,479

Year.	Population born in Rajputana wherever enumerated.	Excess of emigrants over immigrants.
1931	11,741,489	515,777
1921	10,470,492	626,108
1911	11,032,304	552,372
1901	10,531,101	677,735

1.—IMMIGRATION.—ACTUAL FIGURES.

AGENCY WHERE ENUMERATED.	BORN IN—											
	AGENCY WHERE ENUMERATED.			CONTIGUOUS PROVINCES, ETC.			NON-CONTIGUOUS PROVINCES, ETC.			OUTSIDE INDIA.		
	Total.	Males.	Females.	Total.	Males.	Females.	Total.	Males.	Females.	Total.	Males.	Females.
1	2	3	4	5	6	7	8	9	10	11	12	13
Rajputana ...	10,894,773	5,747,387	5,147,386	322,270	133,324	188,946	7,643	3,635	4,008	1,026	682	344

1 (a).—IMMIGRATION BY STATES, ETC.—ACTUAL FIGURES.

AGENCY AND STATE, ETC.	1931.						1921.					
	ACTUAL POPULATION.			IMMIGRANTS.			ACTUAL POPULATION.			IMMIGRANTS.		
	Persons	Males.	Females.	Persons.	Males	Females.	Persons.	Males.	Females.	Persons.	Males.	Females.
1	2	3	4	5	6	7	8	9	10	11	12	13
Rajputana	*11,225,712*	*5,885,028*	*5,340,684*	*330,939*	*137,641*	*193,298*	*9,844,384*	*5,184,891*	*4,659,493*	*243,002*	*92,798*	*150,204*
Abu District.	4,532	2,753	1,779	3,062	1,924	1,138	3,606	2,147	1,459	2,325	1,400	925
Alwar ...	749,751	396,261	353,490	58,272	11,185	47,087	701,154	371,975	329,179	46,897	9,410	37,487
Banswara...	225,106	111,983	113,123	8,374	2,715	5,659	190,362	94,562	95,800	7,290	2,656	4,634
Bharatpur.	486,954	263,325	223,629	67,326	18,093	49,233	496,437	272,345	224,092	62,611	21,093	41,518
Bikaner ...	936,218	501,153	435,065	161,303	88,545	72,758	659,685	347,690	311,995	53,287	22,615	30,672
Bundi ...	216,722	113,101	103,621	14,003	6,191	7,812	187,068	97,635	89,433	12,500	4,834	7,666
Dholpur ...	254,986	140,497	114,489	28,063	7,295	20,768	229,734	126,837	102,897	21,232	5,316	15,916
Dungarpur.	227,544	114,480	113,064	9,606	2,882	6,724	189,272	95,233	94,039	10,431	3,437	6,994
Jaipur ...	2,631,775	1,387,067	1,244,708	68,191	20,553	47,638	2,338,802	1,242,742	1,096,060	89,310	26,742	62,568
Jaisalmer...	76,255	42,342	33,913	5,257	1,394	3,863	67,652	237,882	29,770	3,835	1,001	2,834
Jhalawar ...	107,890	56,518	51,372	25,072	9,247	15,825	96,182	50,318	45,864	21,534	7,985	13,549
Karauli ...	140,525	76,729	63,796	17,954	5,119	12,835	133,730	73,647	60,033	18,127	5,317	12,810
Kishangarh.	85,744	44,494	41,250	16,217	4,499	11,718	77,734	40,859	36,875	14,608	4,492	10,116
Kotah ...	685,804	355,056	330,748	60,144	28,417	31,727	630,060	327,015	303,045	62,002	28,851	33,151
Kushalgarh (Chiefship)	35,564	17,754	17,810	3,891	1,520	2,371	29,162	14,575	14,587	2,906	1,270	1,636
Lawa(Estate)	2,790	1,445	1,345	940	188	752	2,262	1,199	1,063	838	251	587
Marwar ...	2,125,982	1,109,912	1,016,070	26,105	9,213	16,892	1,841,642	971,115	870,527	26,744	9,440	17,304
Mewar ...	1,566,910	807,184	759,726	24,443	10,509	13,934	1,380,063	712,100	667,963	26,491	13,505	12,986
Partabgarh.	76,539	38,991	37,548	13,507	5,223	8,284	67,110	34,090	33,020	11,439	4,559	6,880
Shahpura...	54,233	27,907	26,326	9,847	2,515	7,332	48,130	24,819	23,311	7,995	1,867	6,128
Sirohi ...	216,528	111,675	104,853	20,118	8,313	11,805	186,639	96,938	89,701	19,732	10,076	9,656
Tonk ...	317,360	164,401	152,959	40,804	12,262	28,542	287,898	149,168	138,730	45,662	15,843	29,819

2.—IMMIGRATION.—ACTUAL FIGURES.

AGENCY WHERE BORN.	ENUMERATED IN—												NATURAL POPULATION OF THE AGENCY (THAT IS, THE TOTAL NUMBER OF PERSONS BORN IN THE AGENCY AND ENUMERATED ANYWHERE).		
	AGENCY WHERE BORN			CONTIGUOUS PROVINCES, ETC.			NON-CONTIGUOUS PROVINCES, ETC.			OUTSIDE INDIA.					
	Total.	Males.	Females.	Total	Males.	Females.	Total.	Males.	Females.	Total.	Males.	Females.	Total.	Males.	Females.
1	2	3	4	5	6	7	8	9	10	11	12	13	14	15	16
Rajputana	10,894,773	5,747,387	5,147,386	647,720	305,833	341,887	198,977	127,185	71,792	13	12	1	11,741,489	6,180,423	5,561,066

2 (a).—EMIGRATION BY STATES.—ACTUAL FIGURES.

AGENCY AND STATE, ETC.	1931.						1921.					
	ACTUAL POPULATION.			EMIGRANTS.			ACTUAL POPULATION.			EMIGRANTS.		
	Persons.	Males.	Females.	Persons	Males.	Females.	Persons.	Males.	Females.	Persons.	Males.	Females.
1	2	3	4	5	6	7	8	9	10	11	12	13
Rajputana	***11,225,712***	***5,885,028***	***5,340,684***	***846,716***	***433,036***	***413,680***	***9,844,384***	***5,184,891***	***4,659,493***	***869,110****	***461,766***	***407,344***
Abu District	4,532	2,758	1,779	Not available	Not available	Not available	3,606	2,147	1,459	50	34	16
Alwar ...	749,751	396,261	353,490				701,154	371,975	329,179	108,246	39,805	68,441
Banswara.	225,106	111,983	113,123				190,362	94,562	95,800	6,350	2,481	3,869
Bharatpur.	486,954	263,325	223,629				496,437	272,345	224,092	40,152	14,910	25,242
Bikaner ...	936,218	501,153	435,065				659,685	347,690	311,995	126,615	66,741	59,874
Bundi ...	216,722	118,101	108,621				187,068	97,635	89,433	19,700	7,883	11,817
Dholpur.	254,986	140,497	114,489				229,734	126,837	102,897	•14,115	6,854	7,262
Dungarpur.	227,544	114,480	113,064				189,272	95,233	94,039	4,533	1,491	3,041
Jaipur ...	2,631,775	1,387,067	1,244,708				2,338.802	1,242,742	1,096,060	380,770	159,590	171,180
Jaisalmer.	76,255	42,342	33,903				67,652	37,882	29,770	19,144	9,652	9,492
Jhalawar.	107,890	56,518	51,372				96,182	50,318	45,864	19,522	7,730	11,792
Karauli ...	140,525	76,729	63,796				133,730	73,647	60,083	16,106	5,683	10,423
Kishangarh.	85,744	44,494	41,250				77,734	40,859	36,875	10,942	3,914	7,028
Kotah ...	685,804	355,056	330,748				630,060	327,015	303,045	31,257	13,731	17,526
Kushalgarh (Chiefship).	35,564	17,754	17,810				29,162	14,575	14,587	1,371	623	748
Lawa (Estate).	2,790	1,445	1,345				2,262	1,199	1,063	249	83	166
Marwar ...	2,125,982	1,109,912	1,016,070				1,841,642	971,115	870,527	214,915	116,872	98,043
Mewar ...	1,566,910	807,184	759,726				1,380,068	712,100	667,968	80,166	31,510	48,656
Partabgarh.	76,539	38,991	37,548				67,110	34,090	33,020	12,750	6,698	6,052
Shahpura	54,233	27,907	26,326				48,130	24,819	23,311	1,854	578	1,276
Sirohi ...	216,528	111,675	104,853				186,639	96,938	89,701	6,734	3,124	3,610
Tonk ...	317,360	164,401	152,959				287,808	149,168	138,730	37,376	15,443	21,933

* Includes 90,207 persons—55,009 males and 35,198 females—returned under Rajputana unspecified and 204 persons—143 males and 61 females—enumerated outside India who are not included in any State figures.

3.—MIGRATION BETWEEN RAJPUTANA AGENCY AND OTHER PARTS OF INDIA.

PROVINCE, ETC.	IMMIGRANTS TO RAJPUTANA.			EMIGRANTS FROM RAJPUTANA.			EXCESS OR DEFICIENCY OF IMMIGRATION OVER EMIGRATION.	
	1931.	1921.	Variation.	1931.	1921.	Variation.	1931.	1921.
1	2	3	4	5	6	7	8	9
GRAND TOTAL ...	***329,913***	***242,243***	***+ 87,670***	***846,703***	***868,906***	***− 22,203***	***− 516,790***	***− 626,663***
Total British Territory ...	***219,935***	***135,961***	***+ 83,974***	***547,092***	***648,977***	***− 101,885***	***− 327,157***	***− 513,016***
Ajmer-Merwara ...	21,522	19,616	+ 1,906	76,374	68,610	+ 7,764	− 54,852	− 48,994
Andamans and Nicobars ...	...	...	...	85	175	− 90	− 85	− 175
Assam ...	83	38	+ 45	21,780	15,770	+ 6,010	− 21,697	− 15,732
Baluchistan ...	44	55	− 11	914	1,913	− 999	− 870	− 1,858
Bengal ...	1,003	774	+ 229	32,011	46,850	− 14,839	− 31,008	− 46,076
Bihar and Orissa ...	436	330	+ 106	18,987	17,059	+ 1,928	− 18,551	− 16,729
Bombay ...	9,970	9,157	+ 813	96,524	126,176	− 29,652	− 86,554	− 117,019
Burma ...	70	27	+ 43	1,909	3,418	− 1,509	− 1,839	− 3,391
Central Provinces and Berar ...	2,914	628	+ 2,286	48,184	43,417	+ 4,767	− 45,270	− 42,789
Coorg ...	2	1	+ 1	Not available	Not available	Not available	+ 2	+ 1
Madras ...	258	203	+ 55	Not available	1,415	− 1,415	+ 258	− 1,212
North-West Frontier Province ...	277	328	− 51	1,545	292	+ 1,253	− 1,268	+ 36
Punjab including Delhi ...	115,817	48,758	+ 67,059	167,105	255,902	− 88,797	− 51,288	− 207,144
United Provinces of Agra and Oudh ...	67,539	56,046	+ 11,493	81,674	67,980	+ 13,694	− 14,135	− 11,934
Total Indian States ...	***108,932***	***104,997***	***+ 3,935***	***299,611***	***219,929***	***+ 79,682***	***− 190,679***	***− 114,932***
Baroda State ...	745	862	− 117	8,973	7,473	+ 1,500	− 8,228	− 6,611
Central India Agency ...	26,335	27,465	− 1,130	105,405	85,899	+ 19,506	− 79,070	− 58,434
Gwalior State ...	46,601	53,045	− 6,444	76,480	76,063	+ 417	− 29,879	− 23,018
Hyderabad State ...	200	396	− 196	6,608	8,046	− 1,438	− 6,408	− 7,650
Kashmir State ...	104	133	− 29	64	113	− 49	+ 40	+ 20
Madras States including Cochin and Travancore ...	4	9	− 5	48	21	+ 27	− 44	− 12
Mysore State ...	72	163	− 91	2,348	2,971	− 623	− 2,276	− 2,808
Punjab States Agency ...	26,527	16,766	+ 9,761	69,060	...	+ 69,060	− 42,533	+ 16,766
Western India States Agency ...	3,597	*	+ 3,597	12,469	...	+ 12,469	− 8,872	...
In Relation with Local Governments.								
Assam States ...	41	8	+ 33	...	...	...	+ 41	+ 8
Baluchistan States ...	7	...	+ 7	...	21	− 21	+ 7	− 21
Bengal States ...	4	...	+ 4	895	1,015	− 120	− 891	− 1,015
Bihar and Orissa States ...	16	3	+ 13	1,769	1,753	+ 16	− 1,753	− 1,750
Bombay States ...	4,362	¶ 5,605	− 1,243	11,935	30,181	− 18,246	− 7,573	− 24,576
Central Provinces States ...	81	1	+ 80	3,437	5,790	− 2,353	− 3,356	− 5,789
North-West Frontier Province Agencies and Tribal areas ...	2	...	+ 2	...	451	− 451	+ 2	− 451
United Provinces States ...	234	541	− 307	120	132	− 12	+ 114	+ 409
India Unspecified ...	***883***	***1,140***	***− 257***	...	...	...	***+ 883***	***+ 1,140***
French and Portuguese Settlements ...	***163***	***145***	***+ 18***	...	...	...	***+ 163***	***+ 145***

*Figures included in Bombay States.
¶ Includes figures of Western India States.

DIAGRAM SHOWING PER 10,000 THE NUMBERS
IN EACH QUINQUENNIAL AGE GROUP

MALES

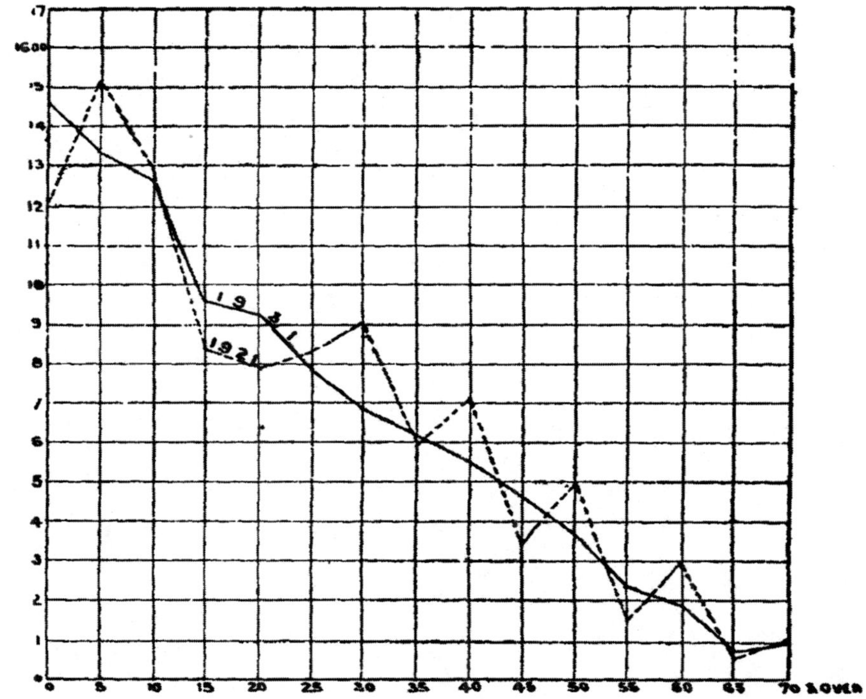

FEMALES

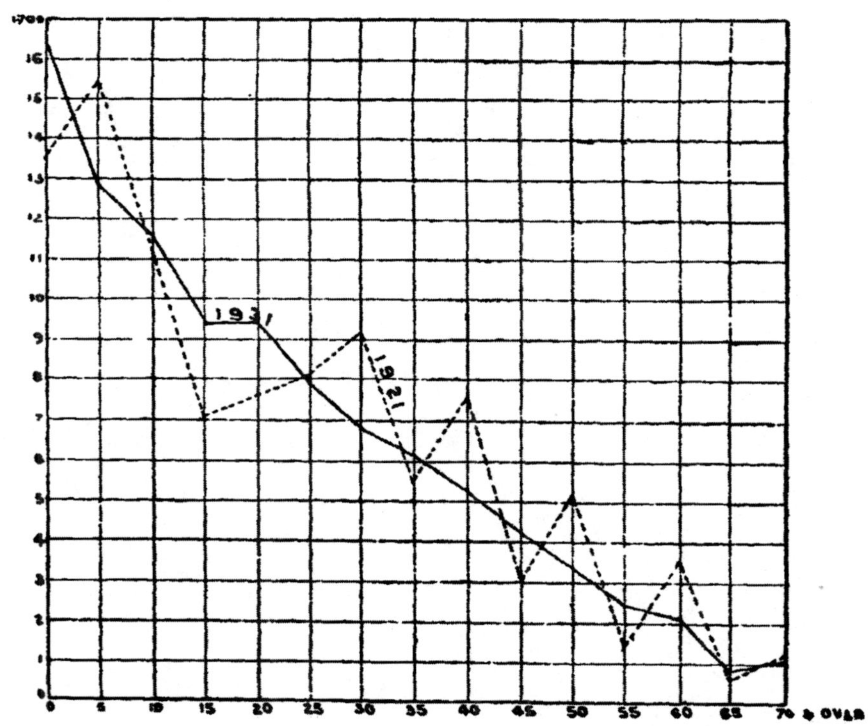

CHAPTER IV.

Age.

1. The age of each person to the nearest birthday was entered in column 7 of the Schedule, but if this was not known with accuracy, as it was not by the bulk of the population, the age as given to the enumerator was accepted and entered. If the answer given was manifestly absurd, the enumerator was instructed to use his discretion and to try and fix the age with reference to some well known occurrence. The age of infants under 6 months old was entered as zero.

Instructions to enumerators.

2. The results of this enquiry are found in Imperial Table VII and, for certain selected castes, in Imperial Table VIII. Appended to this Chapter will be found six Subsidiary Tables dealing with the figures in comparative and analytical detail.

Reference to statistics.

3. It is a well known fact that the ignorance of the majority of Indians concerning their true ages is one of the most unsatisfactory features of every Census. A reference to previous Census Reports will reveal that in the mind of the average person, there are few ages except those that end with the digits of 0 or 5 — preferably the former. Such inaccuracy greatly detracts from the value of the enquiry, but at this Census an attempt has been made, by a method of adjustment, to arrive at more correct figures for the ages of the population as a whole. Wilful mis-statement is not however a common failing. Among males there is a tendency to exaggerate ages on reaching puberty, while among unmarried females at the same period, the tendency is towards understatement. However, comparatively few nubile females are unmarried, and the young married ones, immature as they often are, seem prone to make themselves out as being older than is really the case. Exaggeration is undoubtedly rife among the very aged, for no less than 437 persons returned their ages as 100 or over. Of this band of veterans, 150 were males and 235 were females. The special enquiry failed to reveal the sex of the remaining 52. The highest age of 125 was returned from a female in Kotah State, and the age of the very large majority of the others was exactly 100. It would be interesting to know what ages they returned at the Census of 1881 and whether for them the progress of time has been in accordance with the calendar.

Value of statistics.

4. The predilection of the population for ages ending in the digits of 0 and 5 has led to an attempt being made at this Census to adjust the recorded figures so as to bring about a representation of ages that would show a greater semblance of probability. The preference for digits ending with 0 over those ending in 5 and for either over any others, has been dealt with by dividing the population into 3 year and 5 year groups alternately. Ages with a digit ending in 0 were placed in the centre of a 5 year group and those such as 5, 15, 25, etc., in the centre of a 3 year group. Thus 7 to 13 is one group, 14 to 16 the next, followed by 17 to 23 and so on. In order to present the figures in groups of 5 as are shown in the Tables, half the population in each group is added to half the population in the two adjacent groups. The result of this adjustment is that those who are shown in the Tables as, say 20-25, are really half of those returned as 17, 18, 19, 20, 21, 22 or 23, plus half of those returned as 24, 25 or 26, the other halves of these groups going to the 5 year groups of 15 to 20 and 25 to 30 respectively.

Adjustment of age-groups.

A reference to the diagram prefacing this Chapter shows that the method has been amply justified. The curves for the present Census are approximately, gently descending ones, while those of the last Census, at which the ages were unadjusted, resemble a range of mountains more than anything else, emphasising as they do the partiality for ages which are multiples of 10 and 5 alternately.

With regard to the adjustment refered to above, the Government Actuary pointed out that the method introduced a small error due to no allowance being made for the continuous decrement which deaths cause in the numbers living in the successive age-periods of every normal population, and suggested a corrective formula based on All India mortality rates. This formula is shown in the margin; one fifth part of the first transfer going to each of the five annual groups under 5 years of age. The changes effected by this formula have not been shown in Imperial Table VII, since this shows figures for each religion and civil condition as well, nor are they quoted elsewhere. The following statement however shows the population in quinary age-groups as exhibited in Imperial Table VII and after the decremental allowance referred to above has been applied:—

TRANSFER FROM ONE GROUP TO ANOTHER.

·84 per cent. of group	5—10	to group 0— 5
1·24 „ „ „ „	10—15	„ „ 5—10
1·55 „ „ „ „	20—25	„ „ 15—20
2·38 „ „ „ „	30—35	„ „ 25—30
3·66 „ „ „ „	40—45	„ „ 35—40
5·09 „ „ „ „	50—55	„ „ 45—50
6·87 „ „ „ „	60—65	„ „ 55—60
7 43 „ „ „ „	70 and over	„ „ 65—70

THE POPULATION AS SHOWN IN IMPERIAL TABLE VII AND AFTER APPLYING THE DECREMENTAL ALLOWANCE FORMULA.

AGE-GROUP.	PERSONS.		MALES.		FEMALES.	
	Table VII.	After applying formula.	Table VII.	After applying formula.	Table VII.	After applying formula.
1	2	3	4	5	6	7
0— 1 ...	346,766	*349,241*	172,374	*173,691*	174,392	*175,550*
1— 2 ...	343,154	*345,629*	169,005	*170,322*	174,149	*175,307*
2— 3 ...	359,065	*361,540*	175,296	*176,613*	183,769	*184,927*
3— 4 ...	349,990	*352,465*	174,235	*175,552*	175,755	*176,913*
4— 5 ...	336,364	*338,837*	172,187	*173,503*	164,177	*165,334*
5—10 ...	1,472,995	*1,477,547*	783,824	*786,482*	689,171	*691,065*
10—15 ...	1,364,988	*1,348,063*	745,362	*736,120*	619,626	*611,943*
15—20 ...	1,064,302	*1,080,574*	563,456	*571,896*	500,846	*508,678*
20—25 ...	1,049,804	*1,033,532*	544,510	*536,070*	505,294	*497,462*
25—30 ...	881,282	*899,566*	460,573	*470,174*	420,709	*429,392*
30—35 ...	768,253	*749,969*	403,402	*393,801*	364,851	*356,168*
35—40 ...	691,035	*713,215*	362,456	*374,220*	328,579	*338,995*
40—45 ...	606,013	*583,833*	321,423	*309,659*	284,590	*274,174*
45—50 ...	494,616	*514,762*	269,231	*280,129*	225,385	*234,633*
50—55 ...	395,814	*375,668*	214,115	*203,217*	181,699	*172,451*
55—60 ...	272,038	*287,604*	139,756	*147,510*	132,282	*140,094*
60—65 ...	226,578	*211,012*	112,872	*105,118*	113,706	*105,894*
65—70 ...	89,276	*97,700*	45,521	*49,639*	43,755	*48,061*
70 and over.	113,379	*104,955*	55,430	*51,312*	57,949	*53,643*
All ages.	***11,225,712***	***11,225,712***	***5,885,028***	***5,885,028***	***5,340,684***	***5,340,684***

It will be seen that the general effect is to increase the numbers in the second half of each decennial age-period and to decrease them in the first half. The consequences of the allowance are barely perceptible when applied to a graph such as prefaces this chapter.

Comparisons with previous Censuses.

5. It will be readily understood that this method of adjustment precludes a close comparison being made with figures for ages recorded at previous Censuses. For instance, 24,658 males out of a population of 100,000 males shown in 1921 as being from 0-10 would, as adjusted for this Census, become 26,298. The marginal statement explains these divergences in greater detail. 100,000 males of the 1921 population are shown grouped according to the ages actually returned and recorded at that Census. The last column shows exactly the same population grouped according to the method of adjustment in force at this Census.

Age-group.	By 1921 method.	By 1931 method.
0—10	24,658	26,298
10—20	21,256	21,459
20—30	15,876	17,589
30—40	15,112	14,827
40—50	11,107	10,158
50—60	6,873	6,023
60 and over	5,118	3,646
Total	**100,000**	**100,000**

Conditions of the decade.

6. On the whole the Agency was very free from any epidemic or famine during the years from 1921-30, and there were no factors that would tend to

disturb the proportions of the population at the various age-periods. It is interesting therefore to examine the figures in the light of a theory enunciated by the Swedish Statistician Sündbürg. According to him, in Western countries at any rate, the number of persons aged 15-50 is uniformly about half the population, and any variations which occur in the age constitution, take place in the other two age-groups 0-15 and 50 and over. Where the population is growing, the number in the former group is much greater than in the latter, but where it is stationary the numbers in the two groups approach equality.

The following statement shows that this theory to some extent holds good in India. A little less than half the population is aged between 15 and 50, and those aged under 15 are considerably more numerous than those over 50:—

Age-period.	PER 1,000 PERSONS.								
	Rajputana, 1931.	Rajputana North West Dry Area, 1931.	Rajputana East, 1931.	Hindus, 1931.	Muslims, 1931.	Tribal Religions, 1931.	India, 1921.	Rajputana, 1921.	England and Wales, 1921.
0—15 ...	407	415	404	406	414	494	391	400	277
15—50 ...	495	485	499	496	491	436	495	485	533
50 and over.	98	100	97	98	95	70	114	115	190

Comparison with the figures for England and Wales emphasises the great difference that exists in the age constitution in the East and the West. The figures for the Primitive tribes are also of interest, showing as they do, that their marriages are fruitful and that they are not long-lived people. It is not possible to quote entirely similar figures for individual castes since they are only available, after adjustment, for the age-periods 0-15 and 15 and over.

Age-period	Rajputs	Minas	Bhils
0-15 ...	359	405	505
15 and over	641	595	495

The marginal figures, however, disclose a very marked difference in the age constitution of Rajputs, Minas and Bhils of certain localities—peoples on different storeys of the social structure. It should be explained that some Bhil of these localities have been returned as Hindus and others as followers of Tribal religions.

General distribution by ages.

7. The statement in the margin shows the age distribution per 1,000 persons in this Agency with similar figures for England and Wales in 1921. The proportions between the sexes at all ages are the reverse of what they are in England and Wales. At the age-period 20-40, numbers are approximately equal but the shorter duration of life in the East is shown by the comparatively greater number of children in the Agency and the larger number of old persons in the Western World.

AGE-PERIOD.	RAJPUTANA, 1931.		ENGLAND & WALES. 1921.	
	Males.	Females.	Males.	Females.
All ages.	**524**	**476**	**477**	**523**
0- 5	77	78	44	43
5-10	70	61	47	46
10-20	117	100	94	95
20-40	157	145	142	168
40-60	84	73	109	119
60 and over	19	19	41	52

Detailed distribution by ages and in religions.

8. Subsidiary Tables 1 and 2 show the age distribution of 10,000 persons of each sex at the last four Censuses. If the former is studied in conjunction with the diagram at the beginning of this Chapter, it will be noticed that the curves for both males and females tend to drop abnormally in the age-period 15-20 and then to flatten out in the period 20-25. This is probably due to a smaller number of births during the Influenza epidemic of 1918 and also to a

tendency to exaggerate ages on reaching puberty. The group 20-25 contains half of those who returned their ages as 17 to 23, many of whom would probably be more accurately 14 to 16 in age. In age distribution, the proportions in each sex are approximately equal at 25-30-35-40. In Subsidiary Table 2 the comparatively small proportion of children among Jains and the high proportions of them among those of Tribal religions are very noticeable. The figures are summarised in the following statement:—

Age-Period.	Hindu.		Jain.		Muslim.		Tribal.	
	Males.	Females.	Males.	Females.	Males.	Females.	Males.	Females.
0-5	1,456	1,625	1,439	1,358	1,499	1,692	1,831	2,007
5-10	1,327	1,283	1,249	1,124	1,339	1,331	1,655	1,580
10-15	1,269	1,157	1,143	1,019	1,241	1,181	1,452	1,348
15-20	961	937	893	906	944	952	915	939
20-40	3,013	3,036	2,994	3,187	3,047	3,064	2,638	2,615
40-60	1,613	1,555	1,881	1,933	1,531	1,396	1,275	1,251
60 and over.	361	407	401	473	399	384	234	260
Total	10,000	10,000	10,000	10,000	10,000	10,000	10,000	10,000

Mean age.

9. The mean age of the population should not be confused with the average expectation of life. It merely represents the average age of all persons enumerated at the Census. It is shown for each sex of the various religions in Subsidiary Tables 1 and 2. The lowest figure of 20·3 years is shown by females of Tribal religions, and the highest 25·8 by Jain females. The figures merely serve to emphasise the high proportion of young persons in the former and the comparatively low proportion in the latter religion.

The age distribution in selected castes.

10. Subsidiary Table 3 shows the age distribution per 1,000 of each sex in certain castes of certain localities. The absolute figures are taken from Imperial Table VIII. The large proportion of children among Bhils, Grassias, Bhangis and Chamars is noticeable, while the comparative paucity of them among Rajputs and Sondhias raises the proportion of persons over the age of 24 in those two communities.

Proportion of children, aged persons and married females.

11. Subsidiary Table 5 shows for the Agency and for each State the proportion of children under 10 years of age to 100 persons aged 15-40, and to 100 females aged 15-40: also the proportion of persons aged 60 and over to 100 aged 15-40: and lastly, the number of married females aged 15-40 per 100 females of all ages. The only point of interest is the high proportion of children in Banswara, Dungarpur and Kushalgarh in which States the bulk of the population are Bhils. The Table shows similar figures for the Censuses of 1921 and 1911, but comparisons are unreliable on account of the system of adjusting ages now in force.

Vital statistics.

12. Some States record births and deaths while others do not, and for this reason vital statistics for the whole Agency are not available.

General conclusions.

13. From the information available the following general conclusions can be drawn:—

(a) The system of adjusting ages described in paragraph 4 is entirely satisfactory and the results so obtained furnish a sound basis from which to make comparisons at future Censuses.

(b) The heavy mortality from Influenza in 1918 which was supposed to be selective to those in the prime of life, has not left its mark on the present age constitution of the population, except possibly by reducing the number of births in that year.

1.—AGE DISTRIBUTION OF 10,000 OF EACH SEX.

AGE.	1931.		1921.		1911.		1901.	
	Males.	Females.	Males.	Females.	Males.	Females.	Males.	Females.
1	2	3	4	5	6	7	8	9
0— 1 ...	293	327	295	326	372	405	131	144
1— 2 ...	287	326	140	157	141	159	122	138
2— 3 ...	298	344	224	260	276	313	192	210
3— 4 ...	296	329	261	309	314	355	204	223
4— 5 ...	293	307	268	301	273	290	228	240
Total 0— 5 ...	**1,467**	**1,633**	**1,188**	**1,353**	**1,376**	**1,522**	**877**	**955**
5—10 ...	1,332	1,290	1,517	1,541	1,212	1,186	1,204	1,223
10—15 ...	1,267	1,160	1,290	1,109	972	798	1,339	1,172
15—20 ...	957	938	841	708	923	789	1,111	992
20—25 ...	925	946	689	766	899	995	903	973
25—30 ...	783	788	825	807	957	942	907	871
30—35 ...	685	688	901	915	947	965	906	915
35—40 ...	616	615	588	550	569	524	570	548
40—45 ...	546	533	710	756	718	779	741	813
45—50 ...	458	422	341	302	335	305	350	332
50—55 ...	364	340	501	524	584	563	491	541
55—60 ...	237	248	153	135	147	128	190	176
60—65 ...	192	213	202	354	273	347		
65—70 ...	77	82	59	57	50	47	411	489
70 and over ...	94	109	105	123	88	110		
Mean age ...	**23·5**	**23·4**	**24·6**	**24·8**	**24·8**	**25·2**	**25·4**	**25·9**

2.—AGE DISTRIBUTION OF 10,000 OF EACH SEX IN EACH MAIN RELIGION.

AGE.	1931.		1921.		1911.		1901.	
	Males.	Females.	Males.	Females.	Males.	Females.	Males.	Females.
1	2	3	4	5	6	7	8	9
CHRISTIAN.								
0— 5 ...	1,432	1,715	1,489	1,557	1,204	1,727	764	1,104
5—10 ...	1,316	1,329	1,585	1,779	1,038	996	1,167	1,604
10—15 ...	1,249	1,157	1,024	859	1,121	617	1,925	1,553
15—20 ...	969	1,026	554	602	938	1,110	1,065	1,036
20—40 ...	3,087	3,321	3,499	3,668	4,109	4,110	3,165	3,192
40—60 ...	1,728	1,288	1,535	1,269	1,420	1,148	1,703	1,307
60 and over ...	219	164	321	266	170	292	211	204
Mean age ...	**23·4**	**21·4**	**23·9**	**22·4**	**23·8**	**22·8**	**24·1**	**21·9**
HINDU.								
0— 5 ...	1,456	1,625	1,164	1,331	1,349	1,499	869	941
5—10 ...	1,327	1,283	1,496	1,528	1,196	1,173	1,188	1,216
10—15 ...	1,269	1,157	1,290	1,102	970	790	1,334	1,158
15—20 ...	961	937	851	707	931	789	1,112	982
20—40 ...	3,013	3,036	3,020	3,043	3,389	3,433	3,288	3,813
40—60 ...	1,613	1,555	1,720	1,744	1,753	1,803	1,796	1,395
60 and over ...	361	407	459	545	412	513	418	495
Mean age ...	**23·6**	**23·5**	**24·6**	**24·8**	**24·9**	**25·4**	**25·5**	**26·1**
JAIN.								
0— 5 ...	1,439	1,358	1,157	1,100	1,319	1,248	864	894
5—10 ...	1,249	1,124	1,378	1,251	1,235	1,124	1,105	1,022
10—15 ...	1,143	1,019	1,268	1,128	923	813	1,405	1,285
15—20 ...	893	906	775	737	838	793	1,228	1,168
20—40 ...	2,994	3,187	3,076	3,221	3,404	3,503	3,137	3,206
40—60 ...	1,881	1,933	1,877	1,982	1,871	1,987	1,883	1,939
60 and over ...	401	473	469	581	410	532	378	486
Mean age ...	**24·8**	**25·8**	**25·5**	**26·6**	**25·5**	**26·6**	**25·2**	**26·4**
MUSLIM.								
0— 5 ...	1,499	1,692	1,203	1,394	1,317	1,469	1,034	1,147
5—10 ...	1,339	1,331	1,442	1,483	1,233	1,236	1,321	1,296
10—15 ...	1,241	1,181	1,286	1,155	1,112	963	1,311	1,202
15—20 ...	944	952	845	756	958	851	1,019	967
20—40 ...	3,047	3,064	3,045	3,066	3,157	3,256	3,127	3,081
40—60 ...	1,531	1,396	1,655	1,606	1,725	1,689	1,722	1,760
60 and over ...	399	384	524	540	498	536	466	547
Mean age ...	**23·5**	**22·7**	**24·6**	**24·2**	**24·9**	**24·8**	**25·0**	**24·8**
TRIBAL.								
0— 5 ...	1,831	2,007	1,594	1,801	2,105	2,273	670	836
5—10 ...	1,655	1,580	2,108	2,021	1,485	1,373	1,386	1,372
10—15 ...	1,452	1,348	1,309	1,120	720	584	1,466	1,277
15—20 ...	915	939	701	609	736	657	1,220	1,092
20—40 ...	2,638	2,615	2,579	2,805	3,489	3,602	3,923	3,837
40—60 ...	1,275	1,251	1,446	1,325	1,285	1,261	1,189	1,365
60 and over ...	234	260	263	319	180	250	146	221
Mean age ...	**20·4**	**20·3**	**21·1**	**21·0**	**21·3**	**21·4**	**23·3**	**23·6**

3.—AGE DISTRIBUTION OF 1,000 OF EACH SEX IN CERTAIN CASTES.

CASTES.	LOCALITY.	MALES—NUMBER PER MILLE AGED—						FEMALES—NUMBER PER MILLE AGED—					
		0—6	7—13	14—16	17—23	24—43	44 and over.	0—6	7—13	14—16	17—23	24—43	44 and over.
1	2	3	4	5	6	7	8	9	10	11	12	13	14
Brahman ...	Marwar and Mewar ...	171	166	73	120	274	196	176	150	65	135	278	196
Rajput ...	Jaipur, Marwar and Mewar ...	160	167	79	126	282	186	169	149	63	123	294	202
Sondhia ...	Jhalawar ...	152	153	74	127	303	191	163	156	69	145	301	166
Agarwal ...	Jaipur ...	180	171	67	119	269	194	187	152	58	127	287	189
Oswal ...	Marwar and Mewar ...	187	173	62	124	274	180	171	155	57	133	290	194
Ahir	Alwar ...	166	172	73	125	293	171	203	174	62	122	283	156
Gujar ...	Bharatpur and Jaipur ...	186	185	77	105	290	157	204	168	64	111	300	153
Jat ...	Bikaner, Jaipur and Marwar ...	188	175	83	126	262	166	216	172	72	125	256	159
Khati ...	Jaipur and Mewar ...	191	181	75	112	274	167	203	160	67	122	278	170
Kumhar ...	Jaipur ...	199	181	75	110	279	156	216	164	70	113	286	151
Rebari ...	Marwar and Sirohi ...	190	187	91	118	259	155	208	168	69	123	262	170
Bhil ...	Banswara and Dungarpur ...	247	219	77	106	231	120	261	208	75	115	226	115
Grassia ...	Sirohi ...	261	203	70	89	235	142	259	188	70	116	247	120
Mina ...	Alwar, Jaipur and Kotah ...	187	183	74	107	291	158	206	167	61	117	300	149
Bhangi ...	Jaipur and Marwar ...	216	190	78	115	267	134	231	169	77	128	271	124
Chamar ...	Bharatpur, Jaipur and Kotah.	204	188	77	104	286	141	222	169	72	117	289	131
Khanzada ...	Alwar ...	168	177	70	134	271	180	188	163	62	128	290	169
Meo ...	Alwar and Bharatpur ...	189	183	73	117	299	139	215	167	62	130	300	126

4.—PROPORTION OF CHILDREN UNDER 14 AND OF PERSONS OVER 43 TO THOSE AGED 14—43 IN CERTAIN CASTES; ALSO OF MARRIED FEMALES AGED 14—43 PER 100 FEMALES.

CASTES.	PROPORTION OF CHILDREN BOTH SEXES PER 100		PROPORTION OF PERSONS OVER 43 PER 100 AGED 14—43.		NUMBER OF MARRIED FEMALES AGED 14—43 PER 100 FEMALES OF ALL AGES.
	Persons aged 14—43.	Married females aged 14—43.	Males.	Females.	
1	2	3	4	5	6
Brahman ...	70	190	42	41	36
Rajput ...	67	199	38	42	37
Sondhia ...	61	167	38	32	40
Agarwal ...	74	182	43	40	33
Oswal ...	73	189	39	40	35
Ahir ...	74	204	35	33	38
Gujar ...	78	190	33	32	42
Jat ...	81	209	35	35	39
Khati ...	79	185	36	36	41
Kumhar ...	81	185	34	32	42
Rebari ...	82	212	33	37	37
Bhil ...	112	267	29	28	35
Grassia ...	110	248	36	28	38
Mina ...	78	190	33	31	41
Bhangi ...	86	200	29	26	42
Chamar ...	88	190	30	28	42
Khanzada ...	73	189	38	35	37
Meo ...	77	198	28	26	41

5.—PROPORTION OF CHILDREN UNDER 10 AND OF PERSONS OVER 60 TO THOSE AGED 15—40; ALSO OF MARRIED FEMALES AGED 15—40 PER 100 FEMALES.

AGENCY, STATE OR DISTRICT.	PROPORTION OF CHILDREN, BOTH SEXES, UNDER 10. Per 100 Persons aged 15—40.			Per 100 Married Females aged 15-40.			PROPORTION OF PERSONS AGED 60 AND OVER PER 100 AGED 15—40. 1931.		1921.		1911.		NUMBER OF MARRIED FEMALES AGED 15-40 PER 100 FEMALES OF ALL AGES.		
	1931.	1921.	1911.	1931.	1921.	1911.	Males.	Females.	Males.	Females.	Males.	Females.	1931.	1921.	1911.
1	2	3	4	5	6	7	8	9	10	11	12	13	14	15	16
Rajputana ...	**72**	**74**	**62**	**175**	**189**	**151**	**9**	**10**	**12**	**14**	**10**	**12**	**34**	**31**	**37**
Abu District * ...	46	46	...	140	139	...	3	4	5	6	...	...	40	39	...
Alwar ...	65	71	64	161	182	152	11	10	15	15	14	14	36	32	35
Banswara ...	93	107	70	220	253	185	7	9	8	13	4	7	30	28	36
Bharatpur ...	67	63	54	165	168	137	9	8	12	12	10	11	37	34	36
Bikaner ...	72	75	61	182	200	156	11	12	14	18	10	14	34	29	35
Bundi ...	68	77	68	165	197	159	7	8	10	13	8	10	35	30	38
Dholpur ...	66	86	58	170	178	148	8	9	13	15	11	13	36	33	36
Dungarpur ...	90	98	72	204	230	171	7	8	7	11	8	6	32	30	38
Jaipur ...	70	67	58	167	168	139	11	11	14	16	12	14	35	33	37
Jaisalmer ...	68	71	62	198	245	174	7	8	9	14	8	11	32	25	38
Jhālawar ...	61	68	57	150	177	142	11	9	15	14	9	9	36	31	38
Karauli ...	69	70	57	174	187	146	9	9	12	14	10	11	35	33	37
Kishangarh ...	71	67	55	163	172	139	7	9	8	11	7	10	35	33	38
Kotah ...	64	73	62	151	180	145	8	8	12	13	9	9	37	32	39
Kushalgarh (Chiefship) ...	100	110	84	237	267	205	8	10	9	15	4	8	30	28	34
Lawa (Estate) ...	70	68	55	156	170	132	8	8	10	11	10	8	33	25	38
Marwar ...	77	75	68	246	202	153	9	11	11	15	9	13	33	29	36
Mewar ...	71	81	67	237	203	163	7	9	9	12	5	8	34	30	38
Partabgarh ...	74	83	65	179	202	156	6	8	9	11	4	6	34	31	39
Shahpura ...	69	75	63	230	181	152	8	6	9	14	6	10	36	32	39
Sirohi ...	79	84	73	183	211	171	9	10	11	14	9	12	30	30	37
Tonk ...	70	75	64	167	183	153	9	9	11	13	9	11	35	32	38

* Figures not available for 1911 when they were included in Sirohi.

5 (a).—PROPORTION OF CHILDREN UNDER 10 AND OF PERSONS OVER 60 TO THOSE AGED 15—40 IN CERTAIN RELIGIONS; ALSO OF MARRIED FEMALES AGED 15—40 PER 100 FEMALES.

RELIGION.	PROPORTION OF CHILDREN, BOTH SEXES, PER 100.						PROPORTION OF PERSONS AGED 60 AND OVER PER 100 AGED 15—40.						NUMBER OF MARRIED FEMALES AGED 15-40 PER 100 FEMALES OF ALL AGES.		
	Persons aged 15—40.			Married Females aged 15—40.			1931.		1921.		1911.				
	1931.	1921.	1911.	1931.	1921.	1911.	Males.	Females.	Males	Females.	Males.	Females.	1931.	1921.	1911.
1	2	3	4	5	6	7	8	9	10	11	12	13	14	15	16
Hindu ...	72	72	61	173	187	149	9	10	11	14	9	12	34	31	37
Muslim ...	73	71	64	177	179	153	10	10	13	14	12	13	35	33	36
Tribal ...	99	112	85	231	254	190	7	7	8	9	4	6	31	30	39

Figures of 1931 against Hindus include those of Aryas, Brahmos and Deo Samajists.

6.—VARIATION IN POPULATION AT CERTAIN AGE-PERIODS.

Period.	Variation per cent. in Population.					
	All ages.	0—10.	10—15.	15—40.	40—60.	60 and over*
1	2	3	4	5	6	7
1901—1910	+6·9	+32·5	−24·5	+4·4	+3·2	+8·5
1911—1920	−6·5	−1·2	+26·6	−16·6	−8·8	+1·2
1921—1930	¶ +14·0	+16·6	+15·1	+19·2	+5·0	−11·5

*Includes figures for unspecified age-periods.
¶Based on the unadjusted population figures for 1921.

CHAPTER V.

Sex.

Reference to statistics.

1. In all the Imperial Tables and Provincial Tables I and II, the figures for the population have been shown by Sexes. Imperial Table VII shows the population by sexes at the various age-periods, while Imperial Table VIII gives similar information for selected castes. At the end of this Chapter are three Subsidiary Tables setting forth the proportions of the sexes in greater detail. No vital statistics are obtainable for the Agency as a whole, and for this reason no reference is possible to sex ratios at birth and death.

Accuracy

2. There is no reason to doubt the general accuracy of this enquiry. The enumerators were all local men who had intimate knowledge of the population resident in their blocks, and wilful concealment of persons of either sex would not have been possible on any large scale.

General proportions of the sexes.

3. Of the 11,225,712 persons enumerated, 5,885,028 were males and 5,340,684 were females. There was thus an excess of 544,344 males, or in other words, the number of females per 1,000 males is 908. The following diagram illustrates the number of males and females per 1,000 persons in each of the States, etc., and Subsidiary Table 1 shows the sex ratio at this and the two previous Censuses.

SEX PROPORTIONS IN STATES PER 1000 PERSONS
(THE DOTTED LINE REPRESENTS EQUAL PROPORTIONS)

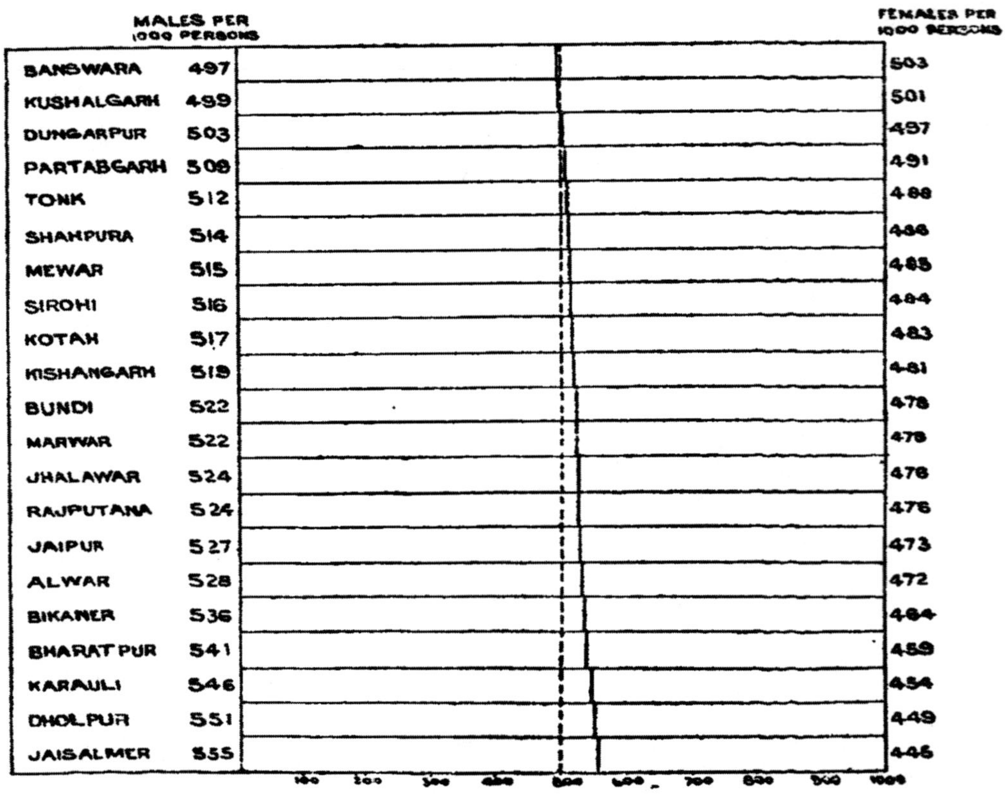

For the whole of Rajputana the proportion is 524 males and 476 females per 1,000 of the population. A scrutiny of the diagram shows that the female proportion is, on the whole, exceeded in the South and West and that a lesser proportion of females prevails in the North and East. An exception to this is found in Jaisalmer where conditions are peculiar and proportions are somewhat vitiated by the presence of nomad herdsmen in search of a precarious pasture for their flocks. Since 1921, males have markedly increased more than females in Bikaner only, and this can be attributed to recent immigration into the Canal Colonies. In other States comparatively large female increases are shown in the marginal statement. The reverse was the case during the decade 1911-21 due to the particularly heavy mortality from influenza in 1918 among the female population in most parts of the Agency.

State.	Percentage of increase.	
	Males.	Females.
Jaipur.	11·6	13·5
Karauli.	4·1	6·2
Kishangarh.	8·9	11·9
Marwar.	14·3	16·7

Sex proportions in various parts of India reveal a deficiency in females in the North and North-West, and a gradually increasing proportion as one goes South, culminating in an actual excess in Bihar and Orissa and the Madras Presidency. The marginal statement shows this in greater detail and reveals the fact that on the whole the tide of femininity seems to be setting Northward. In one respect Rajputana stands alone in that there are comparatively more females in the towns than in the villages. For every 1,000 males, the female ratio is 913 in urban and 907 in rural areas. This can only be explained by the absence of urban industrialism on a scale large enough to attract male immigrants. Possible contributory factors are the facilities for medical treatment, a higher standard of living and the less exacting work demanded of females in urban areas.

Province, etc.		Number of females per 1,000 males.	
		1931.	1921.
Baluchistan	...	778	731
Sind	...	782	786
Punjab and Delhi	...	829	826
Ajmer-Merwara	...	892	837
United Provinces	...	904	909
Rajputana Agency	...	908	899
INDIA	...	**940**	**945**
Central India Agency	...	948	954
Central Provinces	...	1,000	1,002
Bihar and Orissa	...	1,008	1,029
Madras	...	1,022	1,023

The Sex ratio in cities.

4. The number of females per 1,000 males in the 10 towns that are classed as cities varies from 803 in Bharatpur to 967 in Tonk. The marginal statement shows that in all, save Tonk and Bundi, where the inaccessibility by rail precludes casual fluctuation of the male population to any large extent, the proportion of females is less than obtains in the Agency as a whole, whether collectively or in the urban and rural areas separately.

City.		Number of females per 1,000 males.
Tonk	...	967
Bundi	...	960
Bikaner	...	875
Alwar	...	872
Kotah	...	870
Dholpur	...	859
Udaipur	...	852
Jaipur	...	850
Jodhpur	...	816
Bharatpur	...	803

Sex ratios in relation to density.

5. We may now examine how far the deficiency of females is affected by the density of the population. Going from West to East we find that in the North-West Dry Area of Bikaner, Jaisalmer and Marwar which has a density of 43 persons per square mile, there are 898 females per 1,000 males. In the rest of Rajputana, excluding the States in which Bhils form a large proportion of the population, the density is 161 and the female ratio is 895. So far it would appear as if a low density was favourable to females. On the other hand, those portions of Alwar State in which the density is over 300 per square mile, the ratio of females is 916 as compared with 892 in the whole State. In Marwar where the density figure in the several parganas varies from 10 to 137 we find that in those where the density is over 100, the ratio is 942, and where it is under 50, the number of females per 1,000 males is only 893. Even if we exclude the urban population from these two divisions of the State, the ratio of females is 937 and 885 respectively. The statement overleaf shows similar

State.	Number of Females per 1,000 Males.		
	Density under 100.	Density 100-200.	Density over 200.
Bharatpur ...	...	884	857
Jaipur ...	886	907	892

figures for various parts of Bharatpur and Jaipur States. Those parts of Rajputana in which Bhils form a large element of the population have not been taken into consideration in this investigation, for it is known that among these tribes, females are in a far greater proportion than obtains in the remainder of the population. Taking the Agency as a whole, there is little to show that the ratio of females is affected by density. There are indications however, in some of the States for which figures are shown, especially Marwar, that females are in a greater proportion where the density is highest. The discrepancies however are not sufficiently large for an adequate reason to be assigned.

The sex ratio at various ages.

6. Subsidiary Table 2 and the diagram below show the number of females per 1,000 males at each age up to 5 and thereafter by quinquennial age-periods.

DIAGRAM SHOWING THE NUMBER OF FEMALES PER 1000 MALES BY MAIN AGE PERIODS 1931

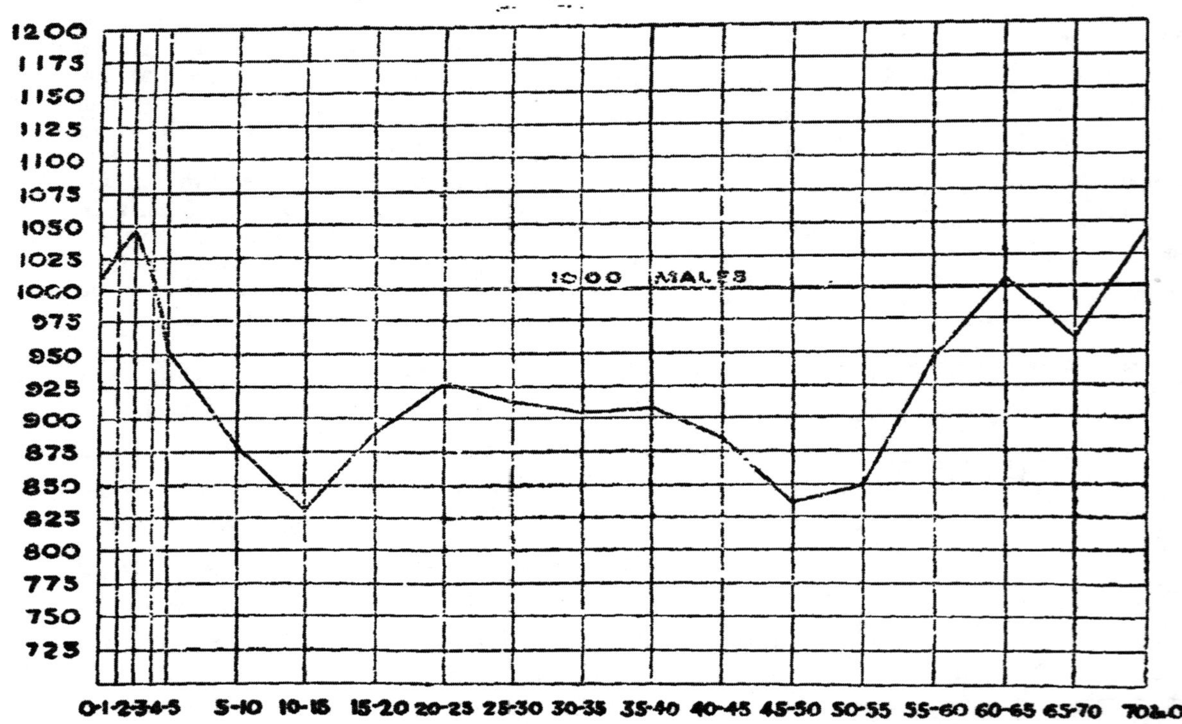

Despite the well known fact that in all parts of the world, more males are born than females, the excess of living females at ages up to 4 points to their better capacity for surviving the vicissitudes of infancy. At all subsequent ages till senility is reached, the masculinity of the population is very marked. Neglect of female children, so common in India, begins to show its effect at the age of 5 and those that survive have still to undergo the perils of early marriage and premature child-bearing. The nadir reached by females at the age-period 10-15 bears eloquent testimony to this. The low ratios at the age-periods 45-50 and 50-55 are possibly the effect of heavy adult female mortality from influenza in 1918.

The Sex ratio by religions.

7. Subsidiary Table 2 shows the sex ratio at various ages in each of the main religions. For the population at all ages the highest proportion of females is 1,060 and is recorded by Jains. The lowest is 889 among Muslims. The

Religion.	Number of Females per 1,000 males.	
	1931.	1921.
Hindu ...	904	891
Jain ...	1,060	1,078
Muslim ...	889	889
Tribal ...	985	966

marginal statement compares the ratios at this Census with those obtained in 1921. The excess of females in the Jain community is due to the absence on business in other parts of India of many males. The 'Marwari' trader is a common feature everywhere but he is seldom accompanied by his family. The low female ratio among Muslims is shown in greater detail by the following figures for the States in which they are more numerous:—

Alwar—887, Bharatpur—870, Bikaner—851, Jaipur—910 and Marwar—897. In Jaipur and Marwar combined where more than a third of the Muslim population of the Agency is found, the ratio is 904. In Bikaner the deficiency of Muslim females is caused by the marked excess of males in the Canal Colonies. In Alwar and Bharatpur the Muslim female ratio is higher than in the adjoining provinces of the Punjab and Agra. The highest female ratio at the various ages is 1,129 among those of Tribal Religions and 1,280 among Jains at ages of 70 and over. The lowest female ratio is 780 among Muslims aged from 45 to 50, a period at which females are prone to understate their ages. For the ages at which females are subjected to the risks attendant on early marriage, unskilful midwifery and premature motherhood, the marginal statement demonstrates an increase in the proportions during the decade among all save Jains aged from 10 to 15.

Age-period.	Number of females per 1,000 males.							
	Hindu.		Jain.		Muslim.		Tribal.	
	1931.	1921.	1931.	1921.	1931.	1921.	1931.	1921.
10—15	825	761	945	955	846	798	914	826
15—20	882	741	1,075	1,021	896	795	1,010	840

Apart from epidemics like the Influenza in 1918 which caused heavy mortality among young females, the system of adjusting ages now in force renders a strict comparison with the figures for 1921 more or less unreliable, though not entirely devoid of interest.

Sex by caste.

8. The following statement shows the sex proportions among numerous and representative castes which comprise 75 per cent. of the total population. The figures provide ample material for discussion as to the effect that occupation and customs have on this subject:—

Caste.	Number of females per 1,000 males.	Caste.	Number of females per 1,000 males.
Brahman	**933**	Kumhar	928
Rajput	**796**	Khati	924
Jat	845	Lohar	930
Gujar	841	Teli	913
Ahir	851	Sonar	929
Dhakar	896	**Total Artisans** ...	**926**
Dangi	973	Daroga	998
Meo	865	Nai	918
Mali	917	**Total Domestic Servants**	**958**
Total Agriculturist s...	**861**	Mina	891
		Bhil	971
		Grassia	922
Agarwal	947		
Oswal	1,085		
Mahesri	960	**Total Semi-Primitive Tribes** ...	**931**
Saraogi	909	**Depressed Castes** ...	**944**
Total Traders, etc. ...	**1,000**	**Grand Total**	**907**

Bearing in mind the female sex ratio in the total population of the Agency, one is at once struck by the fact that the people appear to fall into two categories—one in which the ratio is considerably above, and the other in which it is considerably below the average. In the former group we find Brahmans, Traders, Artisans and Domestic Servants among whom females, as a rule, do not perform duties involving manual labour; Semi-primitive Tribes and Depressed Castes whose females work as hard as males, but among whom difficulties connected with the marriage or re-marriage of females are practically non-existent. In the latter group are the land-owning Rajputs whose females are secluded, and the purely agricultural classes among whom females lead lives of unremitting toil and questions of marriage are matters of financial anxiety. Leaving aside for the moment the low female ratio among Rajputs, the inference to be drawn from these figures is that factors favourable to females are, (1) non-participation in manual labour, and (2) lack of restriction connected with marriage and re-marriage, though combined with manual labour.

A remarkably low female ratio among Hindu Rajputs is a subject of comment in every Census Report for this Agency. The present ratio of 796 is an improvement on the figures of 774 in 1921 and 778 in 1911. Cases are not unknown of the omission to record females especially among the nobility and landed gentry and this probably affects the figures to some small extent. It is a matter of interest to examine the ratios for various clans.

The clans shown in the margin in order of numerical importance vary in numbers from 163,288 Rathors, 96,429 Kachwahas and 88,694 Chauhans to 5,307 Gaurs, 5,068 Jhalas and 3,147 Bargujars. Each is an exogamous clan, Bhatti being a sub-division of Jadon. The female retains the name of her clan after marriage and throughout her life. Thus, if a Kachwaha female marries a Rathor male she remains a Kachwaha but her children are all Rathors. There is therefore no question of a clan dying out on account of a diminished number of females. In considering these figures one is at once struck by the very low female ratio among Kachwahas. It is this that brings the ratio for all Rajputs as low as 796. If they are excluded the ratio is 841 which approximates to those for the closely akin Indo-Aryan races such as Jats, Gujars and Ahirs. The reason for the paucity of females must therefore be sought for among conditions that are peculiar to the Kachwahas. This large, important and numerous clan acknowledges as its head the Ruler of Jaipur, a State the geographical position of which, renders the Rajput matrimonial adage of '*Pachcham ka beta aur Purab ki beti*' difficult of fulfilment. A bridegroom from the West can only suitably be sought from the Rathors of Bikaner and Marwar among whom the laws of hypergamy and the advantages of propinquity render easy the obtaining of brides from the Parihars, Sesodias and Bhattis. The most numerous by far of the Kachwaha clan are the Shekhawats, inhabitants of the Northern and, by Nature most ill-favoured portion of the State. Poverty precludes the payment of the substantial wedding dowry that is usually demanded, and the family is traditionally haunted by the prospect of unmarried girls. There has thus grown up such a studied neglect of female infant life, both actual and potential, as results in a recorded ratio of 530 female Shekhawats for every 1,000 males.

Clan	Number of females per 1,000 males.
Rathor ...	799
Kachwaha	584
Chauhan ...	899
Sesodia ...	799
Bhatti ...	846
Ponwar ...	709
Parihar ...	969
Tonwar ...	863
Solanki ...	866
Jadon ...	908
Gaur ...	734
Jhala ...	841
Bargujar ...	880

The Sex ratio at various ages for selected castes.

9. Subsidiary Table 3 shows the number of females per 1,000 males of 18 selected castes in various localities at the ages of 0-6, 7-13, 14-16, 17-23, 24-43 and 44 and over. During the earliest age-period of 0-6 the highest proportion of 1,042 females is shown by the Bhils. For these ages Rajputs can only show 842. At the crucial ages of 7 to 16, no caste can show a higher proportion of females than Oswals (950) and Bhils (943), while at these ages the proportion of Rajput females is as low as 688. The diagram opposite is of interest showing as it does the vicissitudes of female life at the various ages among the Rajputs, Jats and Bhils.

DIAGRAM SHOWING THE NUMBER OF FEMALES PER 1000 MALES AMONG RAJPUTS, JATS AND BHILS AT CERTAIN AGE PERIODS 1931

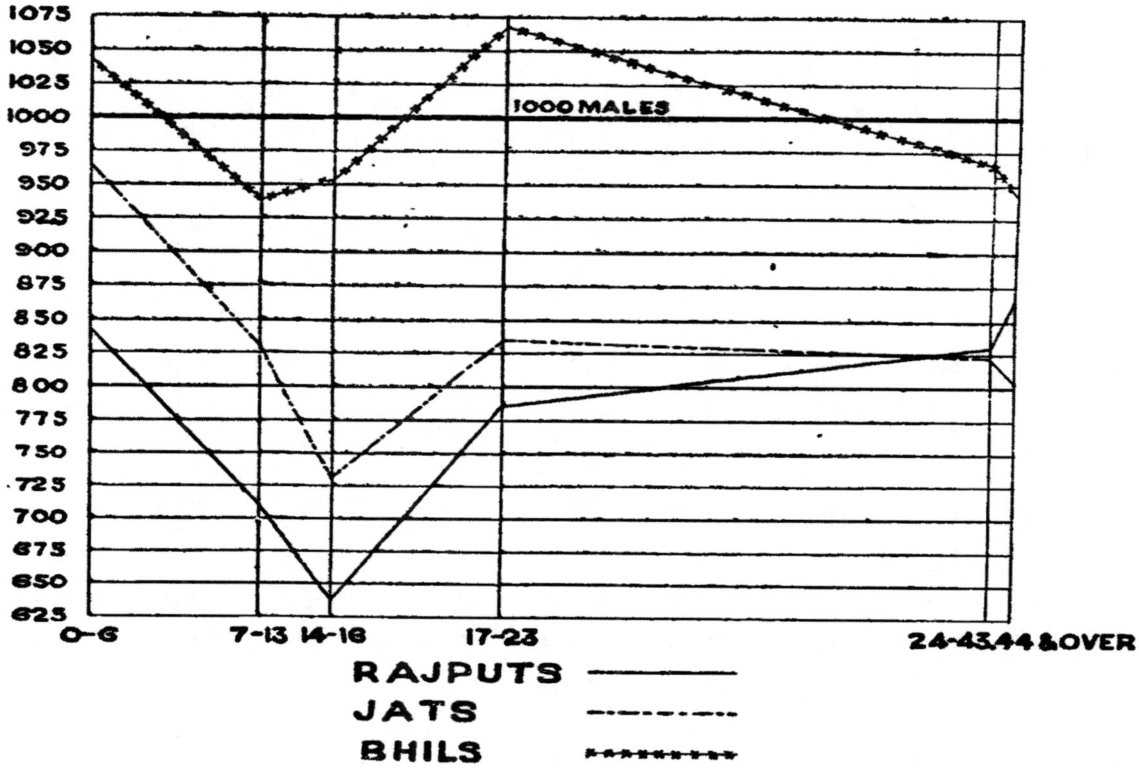

The excess of Bhil females in the age-period of 17-23 may be influenced by exaggeration of age among those below 17 and by understatement on the part of those actually over 23. The continuance of the upward course of the curve for Rajput females after the age of 23 shows that those who have escaped the perils of infancy and early married life, profit by avoiding the result of manual labour and exposure that is undergone by Bhil and Jat women.

10. The reasons usually ascribed to a deficiency of females in the censused population are (a) faulty enumeration, (b) female infanticide, (c) neglect of female child life, and (d) early marriage and premature child-bearing. Of these four there is no reason to think that the enumeration has been faulty on a large scale. Omission to record females was possible and probable in some families among the Rajput aristocracy. Deliberate infanticide seldom comes to light, but there is no doubt that unwanted female infants are often so neglected, especially in some clans of Rajputs, that death is the result. In Jaipur State for 1,000 little Rajput boys aged from 0 to 6, there are only 659 little girls while similar figures for Marwar and Mewar are 856 and 982 respectively. The diagram in paragraph 6 for the whole population shows that in childhood, boys thrive at the expense of girls and the sudden drop in the proportion of females after the age of four bears testimony to this and the very low proportion at the ages of 10 to 15 is undoubtedly caused by early marriage and its attendant evils. General conclusions.

1.—GENERAL PROPORTIONS OF THE SEXES.

State or District.	Number of females to 1,000 males in actual population.			Percentage of variation in actual population.					
	1931.	1921.	1911.	1921-31.		1911-21.		1901-11.	
				Males.	Females.	Males.	Females.	Males.	Females.
1	2	3	4	5	6	7	8	9	10
Abu District ...	646	680	636	+ 28·2	+ 21·9	− 18·1	− 12·6	+ 10·2	− 1·1
Alwar ...	892	885	914	+ 6·5	+ 7·4	− 10·1	− 12·9	− 4·0	− 4·9
Banswara ...	1,010	1,013	1,027	+ 18·4	+ 18·1	+ 15·9	+ 14·3	+ 11·0	+ 10·9
Bharatpur ...	849	828	849	− 8·3	− ·2	− 9·9	− 12·7	− 9·8	− 12·0
Bikaner ...	868	897	887	+ 44·1	+ 39·4	− 6·4	− 5·8	+ 21·2	+ 18·4
Bundi ...	916	916	932	+ 15·8	+ 15·9	− 13·8	− 15·2	+ 27·6	+ 27·9
Dholpur ...	815	811	825	+ 10·8	+ 11·2	− 12·1	− 14·4	− 2·3	− 3·6
Dungarpur ...	988	988	1,012	+ 20·2	+ 20·2	+ 20·4	+ 17·4	+ 58·1	+ 60·0
Jaipur ...	897	882	908	+ 11·6	+ 13·5	− 10·4	− 12·4	− 1·4	− 0·2
Jaisalmer ...	801	786	821	+ 11·8	+ 13·9	− 21·9	− 25·2	+ 23·1	+ 17·2
Jhalawar ...	909	912	924	+ 12·3	+ 12·0	+ 0·6	− 0·8	+ 7·1	+ 6·4
Karauli ...	831	816	831	+ 4·1	+ 6·2	− 8·0	− 9·7	− 6·2	− 6·9
Kishangarh ...	927	903	907	+ 8·9	+ 11·9	− 10·6	− 11·1	− 3·7	− 4·6
Kotah ...	932	927	935	+ 8·6	+ 9·1	− 1·2	− 2·0	+ 17·6	+ 17·0
Kushalgarh (Chiefship)...	1,003	1,001	1,009	+ 21·8	+ 22·1	+ 33·0	+ 32·0	+ 33·1	+ 38·2
Lawa (Estate) ...	931	887	960	+ 20·5	+ 26·5	− 7·9	− 15·8	− 1·8	− 6·2
Marwar ...	915	896	914	+ 14·3	+ 16·7	− 9·7	− 11·4	+ 5·9	+ 6·8
Mewar ...	941	938	929	+ 13·4	+ 13·7	+ 6·2	+ 7·2	+ 24·7	+ 26·6
Partabgarh ...	963	969	976	+ 14·4	+ 18·7	+ 7·4	+ 6·6	+ 21·9	+ 19·2
Shahpura ...	943	931	927	+ 12·4	+ 12·9	+ 0·9	+ 2·2	+ 10·7	+ 11·5
Sirohi ...	939	925	932	+ 15·2	+ 16·9	+ 1·3	+ 0·6	+ 21·0	− 24·8
Tonk ...	930	930	939	+ 10·2	+ 10·3	− 4·6	− 5·5	+ 11·0	+ 10·9

	1931.	1921.	1911.
Number of females to 1,000 males in the Natural Population of Rajputana Agency.	**900**	**885**	**898**

2.—NUMBER OF FEMALES PER 1,000 MALES AT DIFFERENT AGE-PERIODS BY RELIGIONS AT EACH OF THE LAST 3 CENSUSES.

AGE.	ALL RELIGIONS.			HINDU.			JAIN.			MUSLIM.			TRIBAL.		
	1931.	1921.	1911.	1931.	1921*.	1911*.	1931.	1921.	1911.	1931.	1921.	1911.	1931.	1921.	1911.
1	2	3	4	5	6	7	8	9	10	11	12	13	14	15	16
Total all ages (Actual Population) ...	**908**	**899**	**909**	**904**	**891**	**921**	**1,060**	**1,073**	**1,054**	**889**	**889**	**905**	**985**	**966**	**963**
0— 1 ...	1,012	991	989	1,018	986	988	964	986	983	1,008	906	984	1,082	1,069	1,025
1— 2 ...	1,030	1,008	1,022	1,033	1,004	1,017	1,006	1,052	1,055	1,000	1,014	1,097	1,116	1,044	1,061
2— 3 ...	1,048	1,041	1,029	1,048	1,034	1,026	1,035	1,012	987	1,097	1,047	1,031	1,117	1,149	1,080
3— 4 ...	1,009	1,165	1,030	1,006	1,062	1,028	1,014	1,044	1,008	1,019	1,063	1,028	1,074	1,119	1,070
4— 5 ...	953	1,018	967	950	1,007	964	984	1,032	992	959	1,085	987	1,014	1,055	962
Total 0—5 ...	*1,011*	*1,024*	*1,006*	*1,010*	*1,018*	*1,003*	*999*	*1,020*	*996*	*1,004*	*1,030*	*1,009*	*1,079*	*1,091*	*1,040*
5—10 ...	879	912	889	875	910	885	954	978	960	884	915	907	941	926	890
10—15 ...	831	772	747	825	761	735	945	955	928	846	798	783	914	826	782
15—20 ...	889	756	778	882	741	765	1,075	1,021	997	896	795	808	1,010	840	860
20—25 ...	928	999	1,006	923	985	993	1,131	1,221	1,169	925	983	1,014	979	1,259	1,168
25—30 ...	913	879	896	909	864	883	1,128	1,071	1,071	910	862	895	946	1,117	1,025
Total 0—30 ...	*911*	*889*	*894*	*906*	*879*	*885*	*1,025*	*1,026*	*1,016*	*914*	*899*	*904*	*989*	*978*	*975*
30—35 ...	904	913	927	902	903	919	1,112	1,174	1,099	870	916	950	988	958	902
35—40 ...	907	841	838	905	835	834	1,141	1,025	967	855	785	818	999	935	860
40—45 ...	885	957	985	883	955	983	1,108	1,222	1,237	833	932	978	981	890	909
45—50 ...	837	797	829	835	792	828	1,059	982	969	780	762	764	929	826	1,892
50—55 ...	849	940	959	848	939	956	1,059	1,221	1,193	788	885	896	953	903	1,038
55—60 ...	947	790	786	951	789	787	1,152	969	902	852	702	696	1,027	9	999
60—65 ...	1,007	1,090	1,157	1,014	1,091	1,158	1,263	1,431	1,466	884	980	1,034	1,105	1,152	1,383
65—70 ...	961	874	860	977	886	874	1,190	1,078	987	792	651	667	1,020	1,250	1,234
70 and over ...	1,045	1,050	1,139	1,067	1,063	1,156	1,280	1,247	1,433	859	911	976	1,129	1,211	1,208
Total 30 and over ...	*901*	*915*	*936*	*901*	*901*	*933*	*1,121*	*1,146*	*1,115*	*838*	*872*	*906*	*983*	*938*	*938*

*Brahmanic Hindus only.

3.—NUMBER OF FEMALES PER 1,000 MALES FOR CERTAIN SELECTED CASTES

CASTES.	NUMBER OF FEMALES PER 1,000 MALES.							
	Locality.	All ages.	0—6.	7—13.	14—16.	17—23.	24—43.	44 and over.
1	2	3	4	5	6	7	8	9
Brahman ...	Marwar and Mewar ...	959	989	869	857	1,085	971	953
Rajput ...	Jaipur, Marwar and Mewar ...	798	842	711	638	784	830	864
Sondhia ...	Jhalawar ...	872	937	889	809	998	865	757
Agarwal ...	Jaipur ...	1,001	1,036	891	866	1,063	1,071	975
Oswal ...	Mewar and Marwar ...	1,054	966	943	970	1,124	1,118	1,136
Ahir ...	Alwar ...	836	1,022	844	706	815	808	767
Gujar ...	Bharatpur and Jaipur ...	835	914	758	695	878	864	817
Jat ...	Bikaner, Jaipur and Marwar. ...	842	966	830	731	884	823	804
Khati ...	Jaipur and Mewar. ...	950	1,008	842	857	1,042	968	962
Kumhar ...	Jaipur. ...	943	1,024	857	872	971	965	912
Rebari ...	Marwar and Sirohi ...	935	1,025	840	713	975	947	1,020
Bhil ...	Banswara and Dungarpur.	985	1,042	939	954	1,067	965	941
Grassia ...	Sirohi ...	940	932	872	941	1,225	991	791
Mina ...	Alwar, Jaipur and Kotah.	900	900	813	743	977	930	854
Bhangi ...	Jaipur and Marwar ...	934	1,000	829	921	1,045	946	865
Chamar ...	Bharatpur, Jaipur and Kotah. ...	948	1,031	852	887	1,068	956	882
Khanzada ...	Alwar ...	985	1,102	903	870	944	1,056	925
Meo ...	Alwar and Bharatpur ...	865	984	789	738	954	868	788

PROPORTION OF UNMARRIED, MARRIED AND WIDOWED PERSONS PER 1000 OF EACH AGE GROUP

MALES

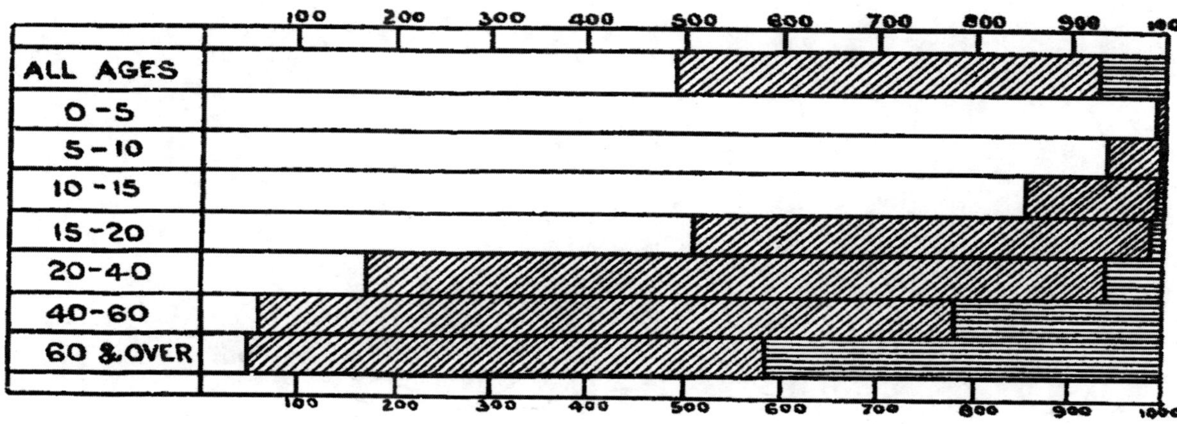

FEMALE

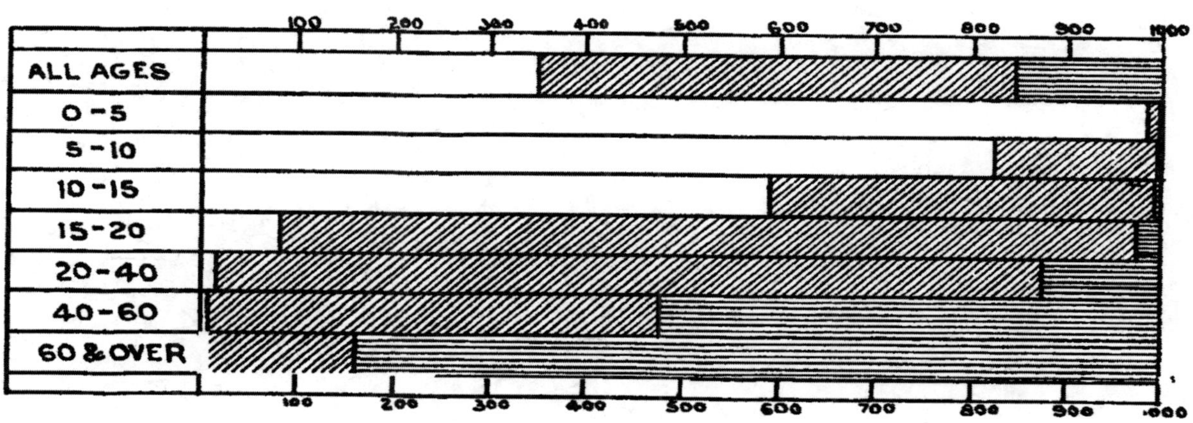

	MALES			FEMALES		
	UNMARRIED	MARRIED	WIDOWED.	UNMARRIED	MARRIED	WIDOWED
ALL AGES	491	438	71	348	496	156
0-5	990	10	-	981	18	1
5-10	938	60	2	824	173	3
10-15	852	144	4	592	401	7
15-20	510	474	16	85	888	27
20-40	173	767	60	13	860	127
40-60	63	717	220	4	476	520
60 & OVER	48	538	414	3	161	836

CHAPTER VI.

Civil Condition.

1. The fact that a person was *unmarried*, *married*, or *widowed* was recorded in column 6 of the Enumeration Schedule. Instructions were issued that persons who were recognised by custom as married were to be entered as such, even though they had not gone through the proper ceremony, e. g. widows who had taken a second husband by the rite variously known as *Karao* or *Nata*, etc., or persons living together whose religious or social tenets enjoin or allow cohabitation without preliminary formalities. Divorced persons were to be entered as widowed. So far as the enumerated population is concerned these simple instructions made it almost impossible for inaccuracies on any large scale to arise. Any omission to record females, whatever their civil condition, would of course tend to disturb the proportionate figures as discussed in this Chapter. Imperial Table VII shows for the whole population and for each religion the number of unmarried, married and widowed persons at various ages, while for certain castes in selected localities similar information is found in Imperial Table VIII. The five Subsidiary Tables at the end of this Chapter show the information in an analysed form.

Reference to statistics.

2. Of a total population of 11,225,712 persons, 4,746,017 are unmarried, 5,227,694 are married while 1,252,001 are widowed. The marginal statement summarises the marital condition of every 1,000 persons at this Census and the two preceding ones. The mortality from influenza tended to disturb the normal balance between the three marital conditions as recorded in 1921, so that a comparison of existing conditions with those obtaining 20 years ago, is a more interesting one, especially as the proportion of the sexes in 1,000 persons is the same now as it was then.

General summary.

CIVIL CONDITION.	1931.		1921.		1911.	
	Males.	Females.	Males.	Females.	Males.	Females.
Unmarried ...	257	166	269	167	259	151
Married ...	230	236	208	216	230	239
Widowed ...	37	74	50	90	35	86
Total ...	524	476	527	473	524	476

3. The diagram at the beginning of this Chapter shows for 1,000 of each sex the number of unmarried, married and widowed at certain ages. Among males and females the numbers per mille of each who are unmarried are 491 and 348 respectively. A comparison of these figures with those for some Western countries, as shown in the margin, at once brings to light the greater prevalence of marriage in the East. Another point that is brought out by these figures is that a very large number of the unmarried males in this Agency will eventually marry females who are yet unborn.

Main statistics.

COUNTRY.	NUMBER PER MILLE OF UNMARRIED.	
	Males.	Females.
Rajputana ...	491	348
England ...	592	571
Italy ...	598	545
Russia ...	571	530
France ...	515	454
United States ...	580	527

4. In the East marriage is a duty incumbent on all regardless of the fitness of the contracting parties. So striking is the result that, in this Agency, there are only 85 girls per mille of those aged from 15 to 20 who have remained unmarried. At these ages 490 per 1,000 males or slightly less than half, have already been married, while between the ages of 25 and 30 only 14 per cent. are unmarried.

The Universality of marriage.

The early age of marriage.

5. The custom of infant marriage is not peculiar to India and numerous instances of its existence can be found among primitive people in Australia, Africa and elsewhere. Nor is it correct to assume that it originated with high caste Hindus and spread gradually from them to the lower castes. Figures for the whole of India show that it is least common in the North-West where the Aryan element is strongest and that it chiefly prevails in the central tracts. Its evil effects lie in premature cohabitation and, among certain castes, in the creation of a number of child-widows who are precluded from re-marriage. The system of age adjustment in use at this Census renders the figures by ages not strictly comparable with the figures obtained at other Censuses, but in Rajputana the number of little boys and girls who have been married before the age of 10 shows a material increase in the past ten years as disclosed by the marginal statement. Figures for All India in 1921 were, for boys, 6 in the group 0-5 and 34 in the group 5-10. For girls the corresponding figures were 12 and 93 respectively. The maximum proportions of early marriages and the parts of India wherein recorded in 1921 are shown in the margin. The increase in such marriages cannot but be disturbing to all reformers who have the welfare of the population at heart. When the proposed provisions of the Sarda Act became known, the effect in the neighbouring British Province of Ajmer-Merwara was to hasten on the marriages of many little boys and girls who were far below the proposed minimum ages of 18 and 14. Although the Act was not to apply to the Indian States, the same haste appears to have been noticeable among the parents of many immature boys and girls in this Agency. Whatever may be the real cause, there are now 36,336 more boys and 74,883 more girls under 10 years of age who have been married than was the case ten years ago. We may now examine the relevant figures for certain localities in an endeavour to discover whether the increase has been more marked in the south and east which are contiguous to the central tracts of India than in the north and west of the Agency. Apart from the inexplicable increased ratio in Marwar, the marginal statement is not altogether conclusive, but leaving aside the low ratios in Kotah, where the marriages of boys and girls below 16 and 12 years of age respectively have been prohibited since 1927, the prevalence of early marriage is particulary indicated by the figures for Tonk and Jhalawar which adjoin the Central India Agency.

AGE-GROUP.	NUMBERS WHO HAVE BEEN MARRIED PER 1,000 OF EACH AGE-GROUP.					
	Boys.			Girls.		
	1931.	1921.	1911.	1931.	1921.	1911.
0—5	10	4	2	19	9	6
5—10	62	23	20	176	80	66

LOCALITY.	NUMBERS WHO HAD BEEN MARRIED PER 1,000 OF EACH AGE-GROUP.			
	Boys.		Girls.	
	0—5	5—10	0—5	5—10
Central India...	16	53	26	134
Gwalior ...	25	47	29	121
Hyderabad ...	15	51	30	212

LOCALITY.	NUMBER OF FEMALES PER MILLE AGED 0—10 WHO HAVE BEEN MARRIED.	
	1931.	1921.
Bikaner ...	61	42
Jaisalmer ...	53	33
Marwar ...	108	55
Jhalawar ...	140	110
Kotah ...	47	29
Tonk ...	113	61

The number of widows.

6. While widowers are only 7 per cent. of the male population, the number of widows per 1,000 females is 156. Subsidiary Table 1 shows that this figure is considerably less than that recorded at previous Censuses and is probably due to the absence of any abnormal mortality among males during the decade. In 1921 the ratio in England was only 82 in spite of male losses in the War.

Civil Condition by religion.

7. Subsidiary Table 2 shows by civil condition and by certain ages the proportions per mille of each sex. The principal points of interest are the numbers of each sex that are married in the earlier stages of life. The marginal statement shows how the figures for the whole population are affected by those for the Hindus

RELIGION.	NUMBER OF MARRIED PER 1,000 IN EACH AGE-PERIOD.					
	MALES.			FEMALES.		
	0—5	5—10	10—15	0—5	5—10	10—15
Hindu ...	9	62	150	18	184	420
Jain ...	11	33	68	16	78	265
Muslim ...	11	59	119	20	186	320
Tribal ...	4	28	93	6	63	216

who are in the large majority. The later age for marriage among Jains and those of Tribal religions is very noticeable.

The marginal statement compares the marital condition of 1,000 persons of each religion at this and the two preceding Censuses. In every case the proportion of the married has increased during the decade and noticeably so among Hindus and Jains. The smaller numbers of the widowed are due to the absence of epidemics during the past ten years. The high proportion of widows among Jains is due to the prohibition of re-marriage. The figure for Hindu widows is also affected by a similar prohibition among higher castes. For a more detailed scrutiny of the figures the statement below shows the distribution of 1,000 persons by civil condition at certain ages and enables an idea to be formed of the balance between the sexes at various stages of their lives. In the first place one looks for and finds, except among Jains and Christians an approximate equality in the number of married males and females. The excess of married females among Jains is due to the absence on business in other parts of India of many husbands, while the excess of married Christian males is due to the absence of their wives in England, etc. An excess of wives among Hindus and Tribals is partly due to polygamy and partly to male emigration.

Religion.	Civil Condition.	Males.			Females.		
		1931.	1921.	1911.	1931.	1921.	1911.
Hindus ...	Unmarried	256	269	258	162	162	147
	Married	232	209	231	238	217	240
	Widowed	37	51	.36	·75	92	88
Muslims.	Unmarried	263	255	258	179	175	165
	Married	231	217	233	232	222	238
	Widowed	36	48	84	59	73	72
Jains ...	Unmarried	251	261	251	165	171	155
	Married	189	167	190	223	198	218
	Widowed	45	55	45	127	148	141
Tribals ...	Unmarried	288	289	272	240	238	210
	Married	204	200	222	214	206	232
	Widowed	17	20	15	42	47	49
Christians.	Unmarried	290	291	330	234	230	205
	Married	222	216	219	195	200	194
	Widowed	26	26	17	33	37	35

CIVIL CONDITION OF 1,000 PERSONS OF ALL RELIGIONS AND EACH MAIN RELIGION.

Civil Condition.	All Religions.		Hindu.		Muslim.		Jain.		Tribal.		Christian.	
	Males.	Females.	Males.	Females.	Males.	Females.	Males.	Females.	Males.	Females.	Males.	Females.
Unmarried. ...	**257**	**166**	**256**	**162**	**263**	**179**	**251**	**165**	**288**	**240**	**290**	**234**
Aged 0-10 ...	142	127	141	125	145	132	127	122	178	173	145	136
10-15 ...	56	33	56	32	58	37	52	38	66	52	60	46
Over 15 ...	59	6	59	5	60	10	72	5	44	15	85	52
Married. ...	**230**	**236**	**232**	**238**	**231**	**232**	**189**	**223**	**204**	**214**	**222**	**195**
Aged 0-10 ...	5	12	5	13	5	10	3	6	3	5	3	4
10-15 ...	10	22	10	23	8	18	4	14	7	15	6	7
Over 15 ...	215	202	217	202	218	204	182	203	194	194	213	184
Widowed. ...	**37**	**74**	**37**	**75**	**36**	**59**	**45**	**127**	**17**	**42**	**26**	**33**
Aged 0-10 ...	...	...	...	...	...	...	...	...	...	...	...	...
10-15 ...	...	...	...	...	...	...	...	...	...	...	1	1
Over 15 ...	137	74	37	75	36	59	45	127	17	42	25	32

The chief point of interest is however, the disparity in the numbers of the unmarried. Among Hindus who are in a large majority there are only 162 potential brides for 256 prospective bridegrooms, and it appears that if marriage for the female is postponed till she is in the neighbourhood of 15 years of age, the effect will be, at any rate for some years to come, to postpone the age of marriage for many males till they are over 20. The marginal statement explains this surmise with more detail. From 15 to 30, ages at which males contemplate or achieve marriage, there are 46 unmarried males per 1,000 persons while there are only 4 unmarried females at similar ages. It therefore follows that these 46 males must arrange marriages with girls who are aged from 5 to 10 and from 10 to 15 of whom there are 82. Observing these proportionate figures the approximate number of girls that have reached the age of 14 is 11 while boys of 18, 19 and 20 may be assessed as 30. It looks therefore as if the discrepancy of 4 years fixed by the Sarda Act of 14 for females and 18 for males is for the present, insufficient in practice, and that if the provisions of the Act are rigidly complied with, the age of marriage for males will automatically rise to 21-23 for some years to come for want of sufficient girls who have reached the age of at least 14.

DISTRIBUTION OF 1,000 HINDUS IRRPESECTIVE OF CIVIL CONDITION.			DISTRIBUTION OF 1,000 HINDUS BY CIVIL CONDITION.		
Ages.	Males.	Females.	Civil Condition and Ages.	Males.	Females.
All ages.	**525**	**475**	**Unmarried.**	**256**	**162**
0— 5	76	77	0— 5	76	76
5—10	70	61	5—10	65	50
10—15	67	55	10—15	56	32
15—20	50	45	15—20	25	3
20—25	49	45	20—25	15 }	1
25—30	41	37	25—30	6 }	
Over 30.	172	155	Over 30	13	...
			Married.	**232**	**238**
			0—10	5	13
			10—15	10	23
			Over 15.	217	202
			Widowed.	**37**	**75**
			0—10	...	...
			10—15	...	...
			Over 15	37	75

Civil condition by selected castes and localities.

8. The castes selected are 18 in number and represent every stratum of society. Subsidiary Table 4 shows their distribution by civil condition at certain unadjusted age-periods. The diagram below illustrates the proportions in certain of these castes.

DISTRIBUTION OF 1,000 OF EACH SEX IN CERTAIN CASTES OF SELECTED LOCALITIES. 1931

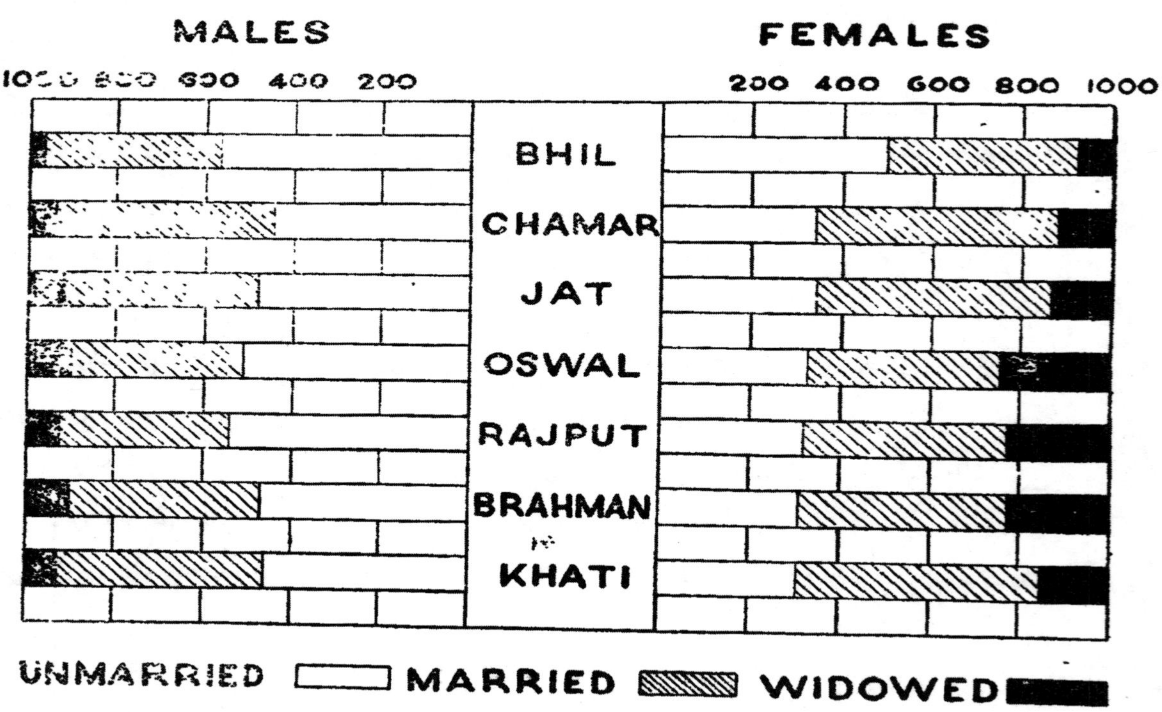

The highest proportion of unmarried males is found among two such extremes as the Rajputs on one hand, and the Bhils and Grassias on the other.

Among the former the reason is partly economic and partly the shortage of women. Among the latter, the preponderance of young persons in the population combined with a later age for marriage, tends to show a high proportion of bachelors and also, the highest proportion of unmarried girls. Ratios for married males range from 492 among the Kumhars, 491 among the Chamars to 365 and 380 among Ahirs and Rajputs respectively. More than half the female population is shown as married among Sondhias, Gujars, Jats, Khatis, Kumhars, Minas, Bhangis and Chamars, while the lowest ratio of 426 is recorded by the Bhils. Ratios of 100 and over for widowers are shown by Brahmans, Oswals and Ahirs, and at the other end of the scale are the prolific but comparatively short-lived Bhils and Grassias with ratios of 32 and 27 respectively per 1,000 of the male populations. Proportions for widows range from 243 among the non-remarrying Oswals to 79 and 53 among Bhils and Grassias respectively, no other caste showing a ratio of under 100, while others of over 200 are recorded for the non-remarrying Brahmans, Rajputs, Sondhias and Agarwals. An examination of the figures in the various age-periods shows in the margin ratios at the two extremes for the three civil conditions among these castes. The Sondhias of Jhalawar whose proverbial immorality no doubt encourages early marriage among the females, show an unenviable ratio of only 48 unmarried girls among a 1,000 of those aged from 14 to 16.

CASTE.	0—6		7—13		14—16		17—23	
	Unmarried.	Married.	Unmarried.	Married.	Unmarried.	Married.	Unmarried.	Married.
				Males.				
Bhil ...	1,000	...	...	...	...	...	...	...
Rebari ...	970	29	...	...	...	...	...	...
Khanzada ...	...	...	991	9	939	57	635	351
Bhangi ...	...	...	849	146	...	...	...	...
Kumhar ...	...	...	...	...	533	460	...	...
Chamar ...	...	...	...	...	...	...	215	762
				Females.				
Bhil ...	999	1	...	...	...	...	...	...
Rebari ...	939	60	...	...	...	...	...	...
Sondhia ...	...	...	531	461	48	872	4	922
Ahir ...	...	...	975	25	631	365	...	...
Meo ...	...	...	...	...	...	...	90	897

Civil condition in cities.

9. The figures for civil condition in the 10 cities of the Agency with a total population of 558,201 persons show but little difference from the figures for the Agency excluding these urban areas. The marginal statement shows the proportions for each sex at the quinquennial age-periods up to 15. Familiarity with modern ideas on the advantages of later marriage for both sexes, which might be expected to have had its effect in the larger towns of the Agency, does not as a matter of fact appear to have had any marked influence.

AGE-PERIOD.	UNMARRIED PER MILLE OF EACH AGE-PERIOD.			
	Cities of Rajputana.		Rajputana excluding Cities.	
	Males	Females.	Males.	Females.
0— 5	992	983	990	981
5—10	946	830	933	824
10—15	870	586	851	592

General conclusions.

10. The foregoing discussion on the civil condition of the people leads one to the conclusion that the efforts of social reformers leave little impression on the population of the Agency as a whole. Recent legislation, although inapplicable to the States, has apparently had the effect of hastening on the marriages of immature persons of both sexes. Should public opinion veer round to the desirability of a later age for marriage among females, the figures show that the result will perforce be a considerably later age for marriage among males than at present obtains. In course of time should the present excessive female mortality between the ages of 10—15 cease on account of later marriage, the numbers of the sexes at a proper marriageable age will tend to approximate.

1.—DISTRIBUTION BY CIVIL CONDITION OF 1,000 OF EACH SEX AND MAIN RELIGION AND MAIN AGE-PERIOD AT EACH OF THE LAST FOUR CENSUSES.

RELIGION.	SEX AND AGE-PERIOD.	UNMARRIED.				MARRIED.				WIDOWED.			
		1931.	1921.	1911.	1901.	1931.	1921.	1911.	1901.	1931.	1921.	1911.	1901.
1	2	3	4	5	6	7	8	9	10	11	12	13	14
All Religions.	**Males—All Ages ...**	**491**	**511**	**494**	**479**	**438**	**395**	**438**	**432**	**71**	**94**	**68**	**89**
	0—5 ...	990	996	998	994	10	4	2	6	...	...	...	...
	5—10 ...	938	977	980	965	60	21	19	31	2	2	1	4
	10—15 ...	852	885	888	854	144	108	108	129	4	7	4	17
	15—20 ...	510	648	677	629	474	331	809	328	16	21	14	43
	20—40 ...	173	205	220	223	767	694	722	681	60	101	58	96
	40—60 ...	63	69	71	90	717	688	752	715	220	243	177	195
	60 and over ...	48	62	62	69	538	515	564	572	414	428	374	359
	Females—All Ages ...	**348**	**353**	**317**	**303**	**496**	**457**	**501**	**499**	**156**	**190**	**182**	**198**
	0—5 ...	981	991	994	987	18	8	6	12	1	1	...	1
	5—10 ...	824	920	934	910	173	76	64	84	3	4	2	6
	10—15 ...	592	589	558	608	401	396	433	374	7	15	9	23
	15—20 ...	85	108	91	197	888	849	878	788	27	43	31	65
	20—40 ...	13	11	8	17	860	832	869	806	127	157	123	177
	40—60 ...	4	6	4	6	476	465	472	497	520	529	524	497
	60 and over ...	3	6	8	6	161	144	141	242	836	850	856	752
Christian.	**Males—All Ages ...**	**539**	**546**	**583**	**635**	**413**	**404**	**387**	**319**	**48**	**50**	**30**	**46**
	0—5 ...	993	995	1,000	1,000	7	3	...	...	...	2	...	...
	5—10 ...	961	988	996	989	39	10	4	11	...	2	...	...
	10—15 ...	900	959	981	978	90	41	19	22	10	...	...	...
	15—20 ...	694	834	934	881	293	152	53	113	13	14	13	6
	20—40 ...	254	239	367	460	682	700	604	494	64	61	29	46
	40—60 ...	69	82	61	85	810	796	842	763	121	122	97	152
	60 and over ...	...	48	98	28	765	702	707	748	285	250	195	229
	Females—All Ages ...	**506**	**491**	**471**	**541**	**421**	**429**	**447**	**373**	**73**	**80**	**82**	**86**
	0—5 ...	987	1,000	1,000	1,000	13	...	...	...	...	...	...	...
	5—10 ...	946	978	984	984	51	20	16	16	3	2	...	...
	10—15 ...	854	929	930	945	126	71	44	44	20	...	26	11
	15—20 ...	507	573	585	607	467	420	405	385	26	7	10	8
	20—40 ...	152	111	165	168	793	842	798	718	55	47	37	114
	40—60 ...	67	45	80	65	645	601	571	675	288	354	349	260
	60 and over ...	46	49	56	83	227	328	129	292	727	623	815	625
Hindu.	**Males—All Ages ...**	**488**	**508**	**491**	**476**	**441**	**395**	**440**	**434**	**71**	**97**	**69**	**90**
	0—5 ...	991	997	998	994	9	3	2	6	...	...	...	...
	5—10 ...	936	976	979	965	62	22	20	31	2	2	1	4
	10—15 ...	846	880	888	851	150	113	113	133	4	7	4	16
	15—20 ...	501	642	672	620	484	336	314	336	15	22	14	44
	20—40 ...	171	208	224	223	769	688	717	681	60	104	59	96
	40—60 ...	65	72	74	93	712	679	747	711	223	249	179	196
	60 and over ...	51	65	66	71	532	506	556	564	417	429	378	365
	Females—All Ages ...	**341**	**344**	**308**	**292**	**500**	**460**	**506**	**507**	**159**	**196**	**186**	**201**
	0—5 ...	981	991	993	985	18	8	7	13	1	1	...	2
	5—10 ...	813	913	923	908	184	83	70	91	3	4	2	6
	10—15 ...	572	562	530	578	420	422	460	398	8	16	10	24
	15—20 ...	74	94	76	174	899	860	891	761	27	46	33	65
	20—40 ...	11	9	7	13	860	828	868	809	129	163	125	178
	40—60 ...	3	6	3	5	472	457	469	496	525	537	528	499
	60 and over ...	3	5	3	5	156	140	139	234	841	855	858	761

1.—DISTRIBUTION BY CIVIL CONDITION OF 1,000 OF EACH SEX AND MAIN RELIGION AND MAIN AGE-PERIOD AT EACH OF THE LAST FOUR CENSUSES.—*Concluded.*

RELIGION.	SEX AND AGE-PERIOD.	UNMARRIED.				MARRIED.				WIDOWED.			
		1931.	1921.	1911.	1901.	1931.	1921.	1911.	1901.	1931.	1921.	1911.	1901.
1	2	3	4	5	6	7	8	9	10	11	12	13	14
Jain.	**Males All Ages ...**	**517**	**540**	**516**	**493**	**390**	**346**	**391**	**396**	**93**	**114**	**93**	**111**
	0—5 ...	988	998	999	994	11	2	1	6	1	...	...	...
	5—10 ...	966	992	995	954	33	7	4	42	1	1	1	4
	10—15 ...	929	959	944	841	68	37	53	134	3	4	3	25
	15—20 ...	575	686	695	604	410	297	296	356	15	17	9	40
	20—40 ...	242	276	262	265	688	616	666	681	70	108	72	104
	40—60 ...	115	124	124	127	612	578	620	599	273	298	256	274
	60 and over ...	71	109	93	71	462	400	446	451	467	491	461	478
	Females All Ages ...	**321**	**330**	**302**	**316**	**432**	**384**	**425**	**442**	**247**	**286**	**273**	**242**
	0—5 ...	982	996	998	993	16	3	2	7	2	1	...	...
	5—10 ...	918	983	987	927	78	12	12	67	4	5	1	6
	10—15 ...	723	774	705	685	265	211	286	281	12	15	9	34
	15—20 ...	78	78	77	284	868	851	869	650	54	76	54	66
	20—40 ...	9	11	6	30	757	690	737	713	234	299	257	257
	40—60 ...	2	3	3	5	356	888	344	424	642	659	658	571
	60 and over ...	3	4	5	7	110	107	96	247	887	889	899	746
Muslim.	**Males All Ages ...**	**496**	**500**	**491**	**494**	**436**	**410**	**444**	**439**	**68**	**90**	**65**	**67**
	0—5 ...	988	989	998	997	11	11	2	3	1	...	...	...
	5—10 ...	939	972	979	961	59	27	20	30	2	1	1	9
	10—15 ...	877	888	899	864	119	106	97	114	4	6	4	22
	15—20 ...	565	680	684	668	418	299	302	301	17	21	14	31
	20—40 ...	178	198	204	223	760	706	739	707	62	96	57	70
	40—60 ...	34	42	43	61	767	736	798	791	199	222	159	148
	60 and over ...	23	33	35	51	580	559	619	670	397	408	346	279
	Females All Ages ...	**381**	**372**	**346**	**361**	**493**	**472**	**502**	**479**	**126**	**156**	**152**	**160**
	0—5 ...	979	987	995	996	20	12	5	4	1	1	...	...
	5—10 ...	861	929	939	947	136	66	60	50	3	5	1	3
	10—15 ...	674	663	655	694	320	326	337	295	6	11	8	11
	15—20 ...	149	165	165	271	830	808	813	676	21	27	22	53
	20—40 ...	21	19	15	35	885	869	892	883	94	112	93	132
	40—60 ...	6	9	8	16	538	532	546	563	456	459	446	421
	60 and over ...	5	8	7	11	210	181	177	298	785	811	816	691
Tribal.	**Males All Ages ...**	**561**	**567**	**535**	**505**	**406**	**393**	**435**	**391**	**33**	**40**	**30**	**104**
	0—5 ...	996	998	999	997	4	2	1	3	...	...	...	...
	5—10 ...	971	990	994	988	28	9	5	10	1	1	1	2
	10—15 ...	904	921	945	916	93	77	53	62	3	2	2	22
	15—20 ...	585	670	753	750	451	320	288	185	14	10	9	65
	20—40 ...	186	108	148	186	824	834	816	662	40	58	36	152
	40—60 ...	12	27	14	48	871	855	898	725	117	118	88	227
	60 and over ...	7	20	10	78	739	741	728	575	254	239	252	347
	Females All Ages ...	**483**	**484**	**428**	**377**	**432**	**420**	**472**	**438**	**85**	**96**	**100**	**185**
	0—5 ...	994	996	998	979	6	4	2	21	...	...	...	...
	5—10 ...	986	971	983	951	63	28	17	47	1	1	...	2
	10—15 ...	781	761	765	802	216	235	232	166	3	4	3	32
	15—20 ...	227	262	217	378	763	726	774	582	10	12	9	90
	20—40 ...	33	18	17	49	904	916	935	756	63	66	48	195
	40—60 ...	5	11	8	11	615	605	513	405	380	384	479	584
	60 and over ...	5	12	8	32	247	179	128	252	748	809	864	716

NOTE.— Hindus in 1931 include Aryas, Brahmos and Deo Samajists.

2.—Distribution by civil condition of 1,000 MALES at certain ages in each main religion.

Religion.	All ages.			0—5.			5—10.			10—15.			15—40.			40 and over.		
	Unmarried.	Married.	Widowed.	Unmarried.	Married.	Widowed.	Unmarried.	Married.	Widowed.	Unmarried.	Married.	Widowed.	Unmarried.	Married.	Widowed.	Unmarried.	Married.	Widowed.
1	2	3	4	5	6	7	8	9	10	11	12	13	14	15	16	17	18	19
All Religions ...	**491**	**438**	**71**	**990**	**10**	...	**938**	**60**	**2**	**852**	**144**	**4**	**255**	**696**	**49**	**60**	**684**	**256**
Christian ...	539	413	48	993	7	...	961	39	...	900	90	10	359	589	52	61	805	134
Hindu ...	488	441	71	991	9	...	936	62	2	846	150	4	250	701	49	62	679	259
Jain ...	517	390	93	988	11	1	966	33	1	929	68	3	319	624	57	107	586	307
Muslim ...	496	436	68	988	11	1	939	59	2	877	119	4	270	679	51	31	729	240
Tribal ...	561	406	33	996	4	...	971	28	1	904	93	3	239	728	33	11	851	138

Distribution by civil condition of 1,000 FEMALES at certain ages in each main religion.

Religion.	All ages.			0—5.			5—10.			10—15.			15—40.			40 and over.		
	Unmarried.	Married.	Widowed.	Unmarried.	Married.	Widowed.	Unmarried.	Married.	Widowed.	Unmarried.	Married.	Widowed.	Unmarried.	Married.	Widowed.	Unmarried.	Married.	Widowed.
1	2	3	4	5	6	7	8	9	10	11	12	13	14	15	16	17	18	19
All Religions ...	**348**	**496**	**156**	**981**	**18**	**1**	**824**	**173**	**3**	**592**	**401**	**7**	**30**	**867**	**103**	**4**	**411**	**585**
Christian ...	506	421	73	987	13	...	946	51	3	854	126	20	236	716	48	64	598	338
Hindu ...	341	500	159	981	18	1	813	184	3	572	420	8	26	869	105	3	407	590
Jain ...	321	432	247	982	16	2	918	78	4	723	265	12	24	782	194	3	307	690
Muslim ...	381	493	126	979	20	1	861	136	3	674	320	6	51	872	77	6	467	527
Tribal ...	483	432	85	994	6	...	936	63	1	781	216	3	84	867	49	5	551	444

3.—DISTRIBUTION BY CIVIL CONDITION OF 10,000 OF EACH SEX AND RELIGION.

RELIGION AND AGE.	MALES.			FEMALES.		
	Unmarried.	Married.	Widowed.	Unmarried.	Married.	Widowed.
1	2	3	4	5	6	7
All Religions.						
0—10 ...	9,658	336	11	9,120	861	19
10—15 ...	8,522	1,436	42	5,918	4,007	75
15—40 ...	2,545	6,962	493	296	8,668	1,036
40 and over ...	602	6,836	2,562	35	4,113	5,852
Christian.						
0—10 ...	9,778	222	...	9,693	295	12
10—15 ...	8,995	902	103	8,544	1,262	194
15—40 ...	3,595	5,889	516	2,360	7,158	482
40 and over ...	611	8,050	1,339	644	5,980	3,376
Hindu.						
0—10 ...	9,644	345	11	9,071	911	18
10—15 ...	8,457	1,501	42	5,719	4,205	76
15—40 ...	2,504	7,004	492	258	8,693	1,049
40 and over ...	625	6,789	2,586	32	4,065	5,903
Jain.						
0—10 ...	9,777	212	11	9,528	444	28
10—15 ...	9,288	684	28	7,231	2,649	130
15—40 ...	3,186	6,238	576	242	7,819	1,939
40 and over ...	1,070	5,857	3,073	26	3,073	6,901
Muslim.						
0—10 ...	9,647	339	14	9,266	711	23
10—15 ...	8,769	1,190	41	6,739	3,196	65
15—40 ...	2,696	6,790	514	513	8,721	766
40 and over ...	315	7,287	2,398	61	4,671	5,268
Tribal.						
0—10 ...	9,840	155	5	9,684	310	6
10—15 ...	9,043	930	27	7,806	2,162	32
15—40 ...	2,385	7,283	332	842	8,667	491
40 and over ...	112	8,504	1,384	49	5,515	4,436

DISTRIBUTION BY CIVIL CONDITION OF 1,000 OF EACH

CASTE.	LOCALITY.	ALL AGES.			0—6.			7—13.		
		Unmarried.	Married.	Widowed.	Unmarried.	Married.	Widowed.	Unmarried.	Married.	Widowed.
1	2	3	4	5	6	7	8	9	10	11
MA (Males)										
Brahman ...	Marwar and Mewar ...	471	429	100	983	16	1	920	77	3
Rajput ...	Jaipur, Marwar and Mewar,	544	380	76	982	18	...	959	40	1
Sondhia ...	Jhalawar	446	472	82	998	2	...	886	114	...
Agarwal ...	Jaipur	499	403	98	995	5	...	951	48	1
Oswal ...	Marwar and Mewar ...	515	385	100	990	9	1	955	43	2
Ahir ...	Alwar	531	365	104	997	3	...	989	11	...
Gujar ...	Bharatpur and Jaipur ...	481	442	77	993	7	...	905	93	2
Jat ...	Bikaner, Jaipur and Marwar.	481	436	83	979	21	...	884	114	2
Khati ...	Jaipur and Mewar ...	464	463	73	986	14	...	900	97	3
Kumhar ...	Jaipur	444	492	64	993	7	...	892	105	3
Rebari ...	Marwar and Sirohi ...	471	458	71	970	29	1	862	134	4
Bhil ...	Banswara and Dungarpur ...	566	402	32	1,000	...	...	962	37	1
Grassia ...	Sirohi	558	415	27	988	12	...	968	30	2
Mina ...	Alwar, Jaipur and Kotah ...	491	439	70	995	5	...	948	51	1
Bhangi ...	Jaipur and Marwar ...	469	463	68	979	20	1	849	146	5
Chamar ...	Bharatpur, Jaipur and Kotah.	447	491	62	994	6	...	890	107	3
Khanzada ...	Alwar	532	383	85	998	2	...	991	9	...
Meo ...	Alwar and Bharatpur ...	525	396	79	998	2	...	977	22	1
FEMA (Females)										
Brahman ...	Marwar and Mewar ...	313	458	229	975	23	2	748	242	10
Rajput ...	Jaipur, Marwar and Mewar.	320	452	228	973	23	4	850	145	5
Sondhia ...	Jhalawar	243	527	230	953	42	5	531	461	8
Agarwal ...	Jaipur	321	469	210	992	7	1	834	163	3
Oswal ...	Marwar and Mewar ...	323	429	248	987	12	1	885	112	3
Ahir ...	Alwar	424	456	120	997	3	...	975	25	...
Gujar ...	Bharatpur and Jaipur ...	316	544	140	983	17	...	635	360	5
Jat ...	Bikaner, Jaipur and Marwar.	343	521	136	967	32	1	667	328	5
Khati ...	Jaipur and Mewar ...	309	536	155	973	26	1	630	363	7
Kumhar ...	Jaipur	313	551	136	985	14	1	580	417	3
Rebari ...	Marwar and Sirohi ...	340	492	168	939	60	1	694	302	4
Bhil ...	Banswara and Dungarpur ...	495	426	79	999	1	...	914	85	1
Grassia ...	Sirohi	472	475	53	983	15	2	913	86	1
Mina ...	Alwar, Jaipur and Kotah ...	356	503	141	991	8	1	814	184	2
Bhangi ...	Jaipur and Marwar ...	362	524	114	971	28	1	704	292	4
Chamar ...	Bharatpur, Jaipur and Kotah.	344	533	123	988	12	...	678	318	4
Khanzada ...	Alwar	387	431	182	996	4	...	953	44	3
Meo ...	Alwar and Bharatpur ...	422	472	106	998	2	...	949	51	...

SEX AT CERTAIN AGE PERIODS FOR SELECTED CASTES.

14—16.			17—23.			24—43.			44 AND OVER.			CASTE.
Unmarried.	Married.	Widowed.	Unmarried.	Married.	Widowed.	Unmarried.	Married.	Widowed.	Unmarried.	Married.	Widowed.	
12	13	14	15	16	17	18	19	20	21	22	23	24
LES.												
662	306	32	390	560	50	148	752	100	75	600	325	... Brahman
843	148	9	584	388	28	221	707	72	134	591	275	... Rajput
598	394	8	365	645	20	166	773	61	111	574	315	... Sondhia
683	310	7	323	659	18	182	715	103	124	530	346	... Agarwal
793	188	19	437	529	34	167	725	108	88	553	359	... Oswal
931	68	1	631	359	10	144	742	114	38	559	403	... Ahir
665	326	9	384	593	23	105	806	89	42	652	306	... Gujar
640	346	14	368	600	32	127	790	83	57	610	333	... Jat
623	359	18	296	672	32	92	825	83	46	685	269	... Khati
533	460	7	236	749	15	57	881	62	25	694	281	... Kumhar
647	338	15	366	605	29	76	848	76	24	683	293	... Rebari
723	273	4	363	621	16	56	898	46	15	825	160	... Bhil
767	228	5	403	583	14	52	912	36	15	871	114	... Grassia
743	253	4	408	577	15	90	833	77	36	673	291	... Mina
545	432	23	253	683	64	70	851	79	44	681	275	... Bhangi
553	436	11	215	762	23	33	899	68	15	709	276	... Chamar
939	57	4	635	351	14	128	789	88	25	647	328	... Khanzada
893	99	8	518	455	27	98	802	100	17	656	327	... Meo
LES.												
208	743	49	67	851	82	11	694	295	18	315	667	... Brahman
258	700	42	44	885	71	17	721	262	15	299	686	... Rajput
48	872	80	4	922	74	2	685	313	...	288	712	... Sondhia
81	899	20	18	924	58	5	731	264	5	337	658	... Agarwal
260	712	28	35	889	76	6	674	320	5	285	710	... Oswal
631	365	4	86	899	15	7	884	109	2	443	555	... Ahir
83	902	15	18	961	21	4	864	132	2	371	627	... Gujar
159	821	20	33	932	35	11	846	143	5	413	582	... Jat
77	899	24	25	928	47	8	837	155	5	386	609	... Khati
50	940	10	8	973	19	3	863	134	1	379	620	... Kumhar
243	736	21	50	907	43	14	780	206	6	365	629	... Rebari
399	596	5	84	906	10	15	899	86	7	487	506	... Bhil
472	522	6	89	901	10	10	961	29	3	684	363	... Grassia
200	790	10	22	957	21	5	847	148	2	378	620	... Mina
143	842	15	28	944	28	12	852	136	7	418	575	... Bhangi
93	892	15	17	963	20	3	856	141	1	400	599	... Chamar
511	480	9	76	890	34	9	781	210	5	312	683	... Khanzada
555	438	7	90	897	13	8	888	104	4	419	577	... Meo

5.—PROPORTION OF THE SEXES BY CIVIL CONDITION AT CERTAIN AGES FOR MAIN RELIGIONS.

RELIGION.	NUMBER OF FEMALES PER 1,000 MALES.														
	All Ages.			0—10.			10—15.			15—40.			40 and over.		
	Unmarried.	Married.	Widowed	Unmarried.	Married	Widowed.	Unmarried.	Married.	Widowed.	Unmarried.	Married.	Widowed.	Unmarried	Married.	Widowed.
1	2	3	4	5	6	7	8	9	10	11	12	13	14	15	16
All Religion ...	**643**	**1,027**	**2,004**	**896**	**2,430**	**1,659**	**577**	**2,319**	**1,508**	**106**	**1,131**	**1,907**	**52**	**540**	**2,049**
Christian ...	807	878	1,293	944	1,263	...	756	1,114	1,500	605	1,120	862	676	476	1,617
Hindu ...	633	1,026	2,011	890	2,494	1,643	558	2,312	1,487	93	1,122	1,926	47	538	2,051
Jain ...	657	1,175	2,815	954	2,048	2,512	736	3,658	4,130	85	1,399	3,757	27	586	2,510
Muslim ...	683	1,005	1,656	910	1,986	1,608	650	2,273	1,355	170	1,149	1,334	157	596	1,803
Tribal ...	849	1,047	2,525	997	2,029	1,816	789	2,126	1,089	348	1,172	1,460	429	640	3,162

MAP SHOWING THE DISTRIBUTION IN EACH STATE OF THE NUMBER OF BLIND PER 100,000

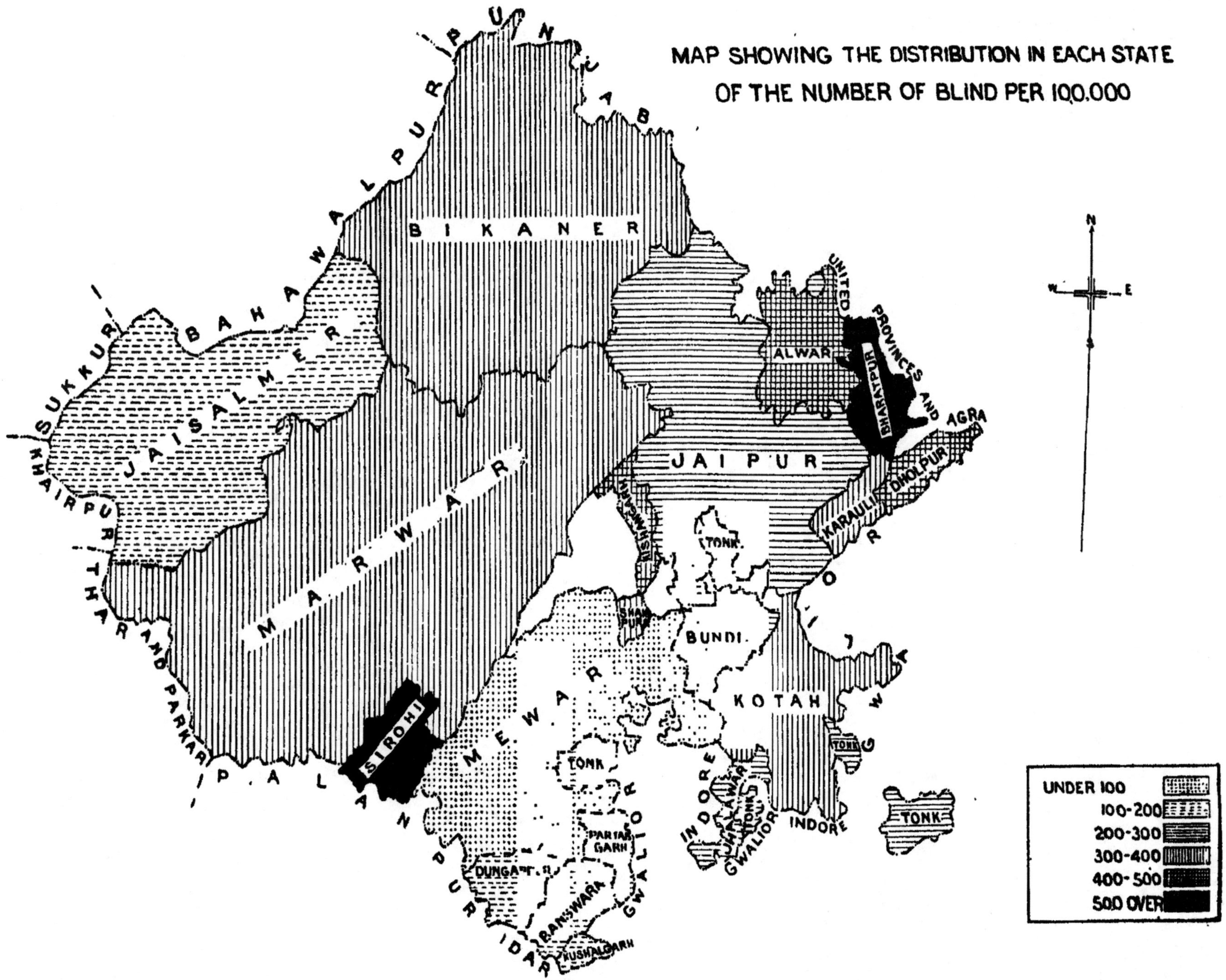

MAP SHOWING THE DISTRIBUTION IN EACH STATE OF THE NUMBER OF DEAF MUTES PER 100,000

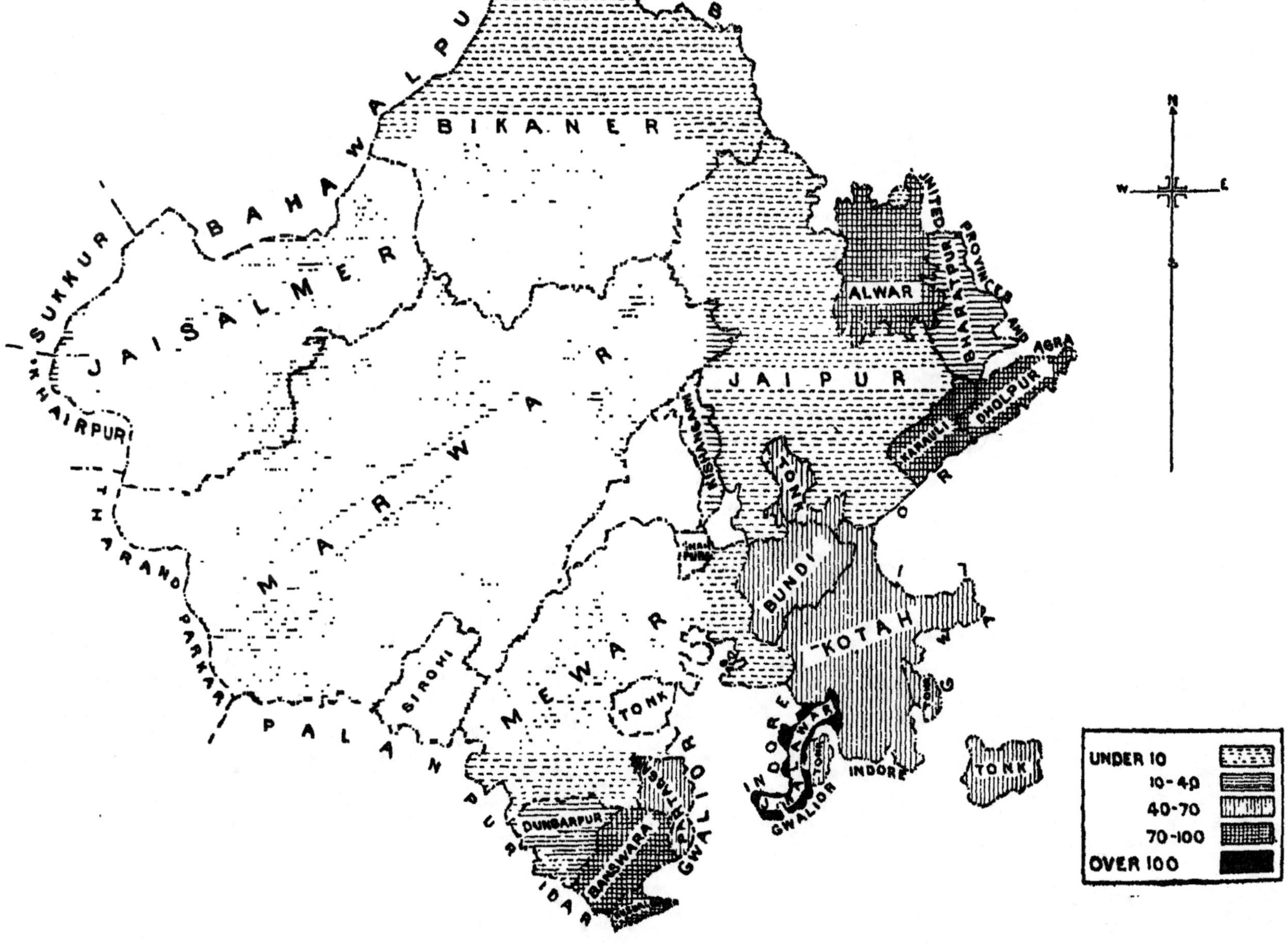

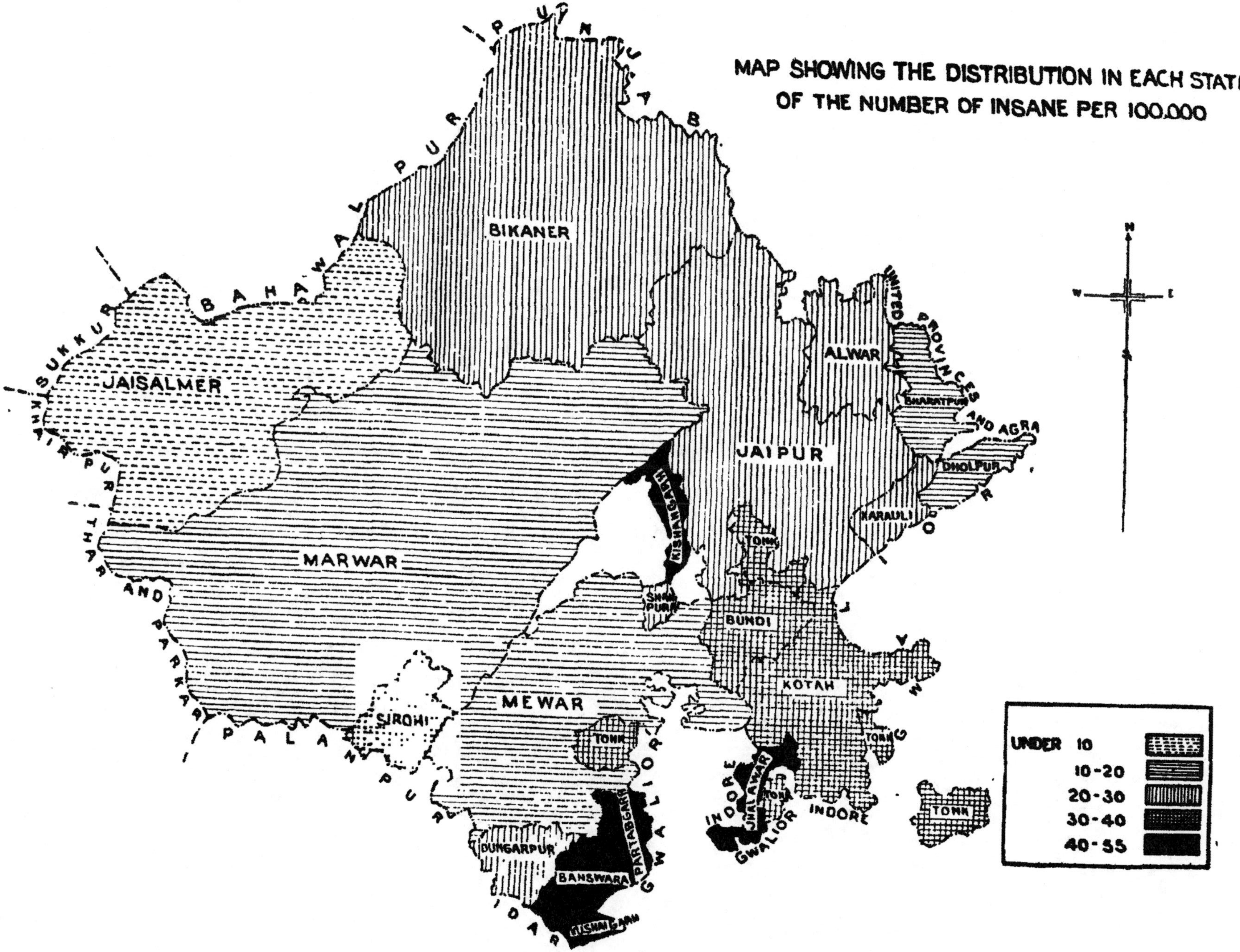
MAP SHOWING THE DISTRIBUTION IN EACH STATE
OF THE NUMBER OF INSANE PER 100.000
PUNJAB
BAHAWALPUR
SUKKUR
KHAIRPUR
THAR AND PARKAR
PALANPUR
IDAR
GWALIOR
UNITED PROVINCES AND AGRA
BIKANER
JAISALMER
MARWAR
JAIPUR
ALWAR
BHARATPUR
DHOLPUR
KARAULI
TONK
KISHANGARH
SHAHPURA
BUNDI
KOTAH
MEWAR
SIROHI
DUNGARPUR
BANSWARA
PARTABGARH
KUSHALGARH
JHALAWAR
INDORE
N
W
E
UNDER 10
10-20
20-30
30-40
40-55

CHAPTER VII.

Infirmities.

1. The Imperial Tables in which are recorded figures for Infirmities are:—Table IX Part I.—Distribution by age, Table IX Part II.—Distribution by States, etc., while at the end of this Chapter will be found three Subsidiary Tables setting forth proportionate figures in detail. Reference to statistics.

1. Number afflicted by each infirmity per 100,000 of the population of each State for the last five Censuses.
2. Distribution of the infirm by quinquennial age-periods per 10,000 afflicted of each sex.
3. Number afflicted per 100,000 persons of each age-period and number of females afflicted per 1,000 males.

2. The instructions given to enumerators were to record in the last column of the schedule whether any person was either insane, blind, deaf and dumb, or a leper. Blindness of one eye was not to constitute blindness and white leprosy and leucoderma were not to be confused with true or corrosive leprosy. Instructions to enumerators.

3. It has long been recognised that the collection of this information is one of the most unsatisfactory and inaccurate features of every Indian Census. Not only is concealment easy, but to the untrained enumerator it is impossible to define the stage at which the feeble-minded come into the category of the insane, or to distinguish leprosy from the diseases which superficially resemble it. There is a reasonable chance however, that errors at each Census are to some extent constant, and therefore the statistics of distribution and variation are of some comparative interest. Accuracy of statistics.

4. The marginal statement shows the number of persons suffering from each infirmity at each of the last three Censuses. The increase in insanity is 112 per cent. and is on the whole general. Marked increases in the larger States during the decade are:—Bharatpur 232 per cent., Bundi 325 per cent. and Tonk 293 per cent. The variation in the number of sufferers from deaf-mutism and leprosy is comparatively small and calls for no comment. The number of blind persons per 100,000 of the population at each of the last three Censuses is 282 in 1931, 200 in 1921 and 212 in 1911. Apart from the possible inclusion of persons blind in one eye only, marked increases per cent. in the decade in actual numbers are found in Alwar 72, Bharatpur 82, Bikaner 54, Jaipur 115 and Kotah 73. Comparison with previous Censuses.

INFIRMITY.	NUMBER AFFLICTED IN		
	1931.	1921.	1911.
Insanity ...	2,590	1,219	1,426
Deaf-Mutism.	3,126	2,577	3,069
Blindness ...	31,627	19,709	22,346
Leprosy ...	543	405	650
Total.	**37,886**	**23,910**	**27,491**

5. The marginal statement compares the ratio of those inflicted per 100,000 of the population of the Agency at this Census with similar figures for India as a whole in 1921. Comparison with figures for India as a whole.

Infirmity.	Rajputana 1931.	India 1921.
Insanity ...	23	28
Deaf-mutism.	28	60
Blindness ...	282	152
Leprosy ...	5	32

It is seen therefore that on the whole, except for the prevalence of blindness, the Agency is singularly well-favoured in the matter of immunity from the more distressing of the infirmities to which humanity is subject. Ratios for blindness in neighbouring parts of India in 1921 were:—Punjab 257, United Provinces 230 and Central India and Gwalior 183.

6. As previously stated in this Chapter the number of people returned as insane has increased by 112 per cent. since 1921. No adequate reason is forthcoming for this phenomenon and the erroneous inclusion of week-minded persons is surmised. The map at the beginning of the Chapter shows the proportion of the insane enumerated in each State. Taken as a whole, the Insanity.

disability appears to be more prevalent in the south and south-east of the Agency, and to be in some relation to the amount of rainfall or to the comparative facility for the consumption of opium cultivated only in those parts.

The following diagram shows that insanity is more prevalent among males than females. Its incidence is high among males aged 30-40 and again at the ages of 60 and over. Excepting generally increased numbers at all age-periods, no marked difference between the figures of this Census and that of 1921 is brought to light. It is difficult however, to feel much confidence in deductions drawn from this diagram and Subsidiary Table 2, which gives the distribution of the infirm by quinquennial age-periods, considering how very uncertain are the statistics both of infirmity and age.

DIAGRAM SHOWING THE NUMBER OF INSANE PER 100000 PERSONS OF EACH AGE PERIOD

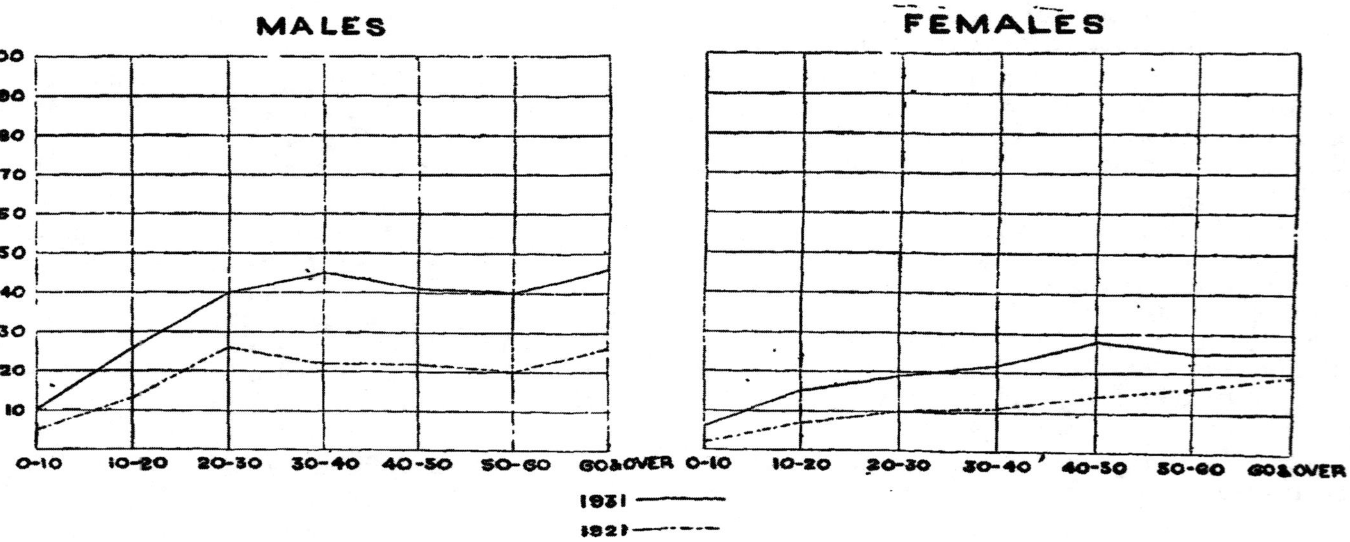

Deaf-mutism. 7. The very small increase in the number of deaf-mutes calls for no particular comment. The map shows the extent to which the infirmity is prevalent in each State. Incidence according to locality is not uniform and no definite conclusions can be drawn that the disability is affected by environment.

The diagram below shows the distribution by age-periods and sexes for each of the last two Censuses. Errors in diagnosis have undoubtedly occurred and as true deaf-mutism is congenital the curves should be descending instead of ascending ones.

DIAGRAM SHOWING THE NUMBER OF DEAF-MUTES PER 100.000 OF EACH AGE-PERIOD

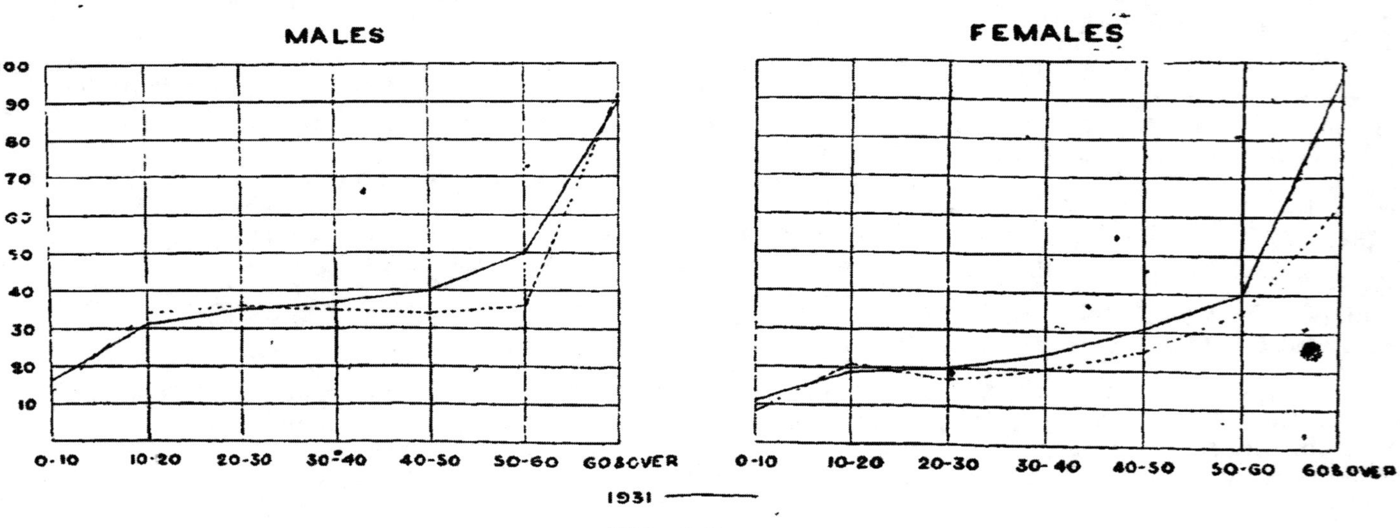

8. Of all the infirmities dealt with, blindness is the only one that is easy to diagnose and there is little temptation to conceal it. In the Census Report for India 1921, Mr. Marten wrote that the infirmity was most prevalent in parts of the country with a hot dry climate and a dusty soil. We should therefore expect a high incidence in Rajputana with its glaring sunshine and dust laden winds of the hot weather which frequently cause ulceration of the eyes and permanent injury. The map shows the distribution in each State per 100,000 persons. Curiously enough Jaisalmer records a comparatively low ratio, while the highest is returned from two such geographical extremes as Bharatpur and Sirohi. Mewar records the lowest ratio of 61 males and 69 females per 100,000 of each. **Blindness.**

The diagram below shows the figures for each sex by decennial age-periods for the last two Censuses. In spite of the well known neglect of children's eyes by their parents, the general increase of 82 blind persons in every 100,000 of the population during the decade is practically confined to age-periods above 40-50. Among aged females, the incidence is very great and, for ages of 60 and over, reaches the high figure of 3,554 per 100,000 females of those ages.

DIAGRAM SHOWING THE NUMBER OF BLIND

PER 100,000 OF EACH AGE-PERIOD

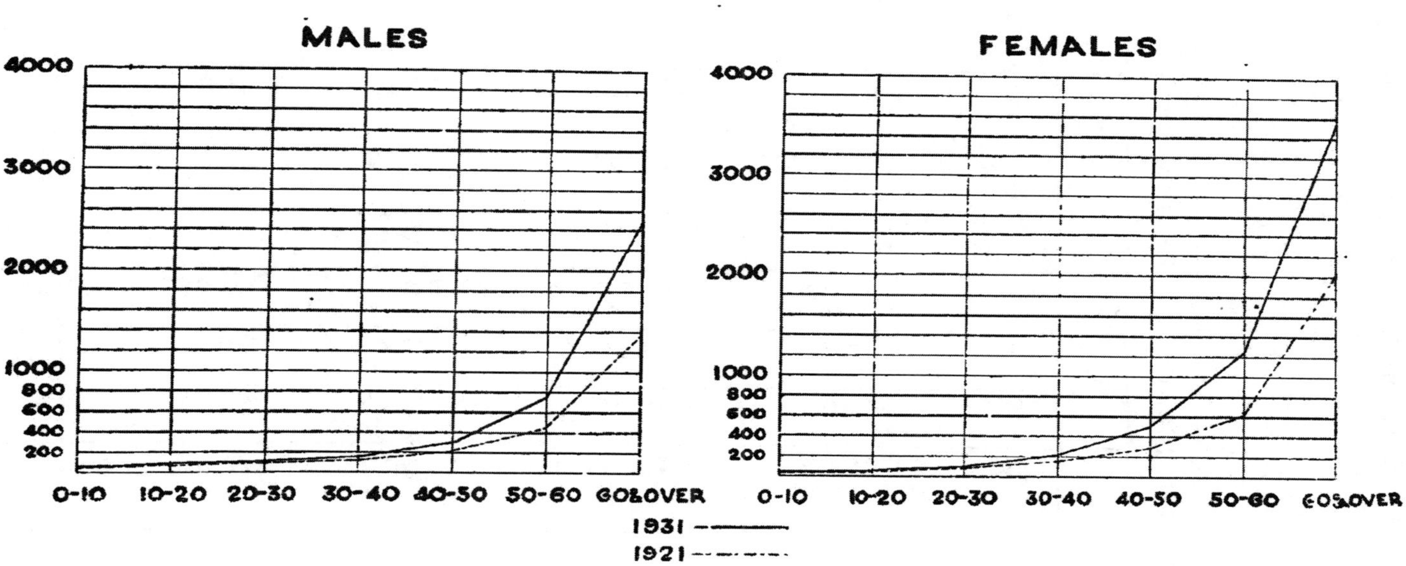

The general conclusions that can be drawn from these figures are that Rajputana continues to share with the rest of north-western India a very large proportion of the number of blind persons in the country; that the infirmity is more prevalent among females than men, especially in the latter age-periods; and that, possibly due to faulty enumeration, blindness is not marked by a high ratio in the hot and dry States in the west of the Agency where it might be expected to prevail.

9. There are only 382 males and 161 females returned as lepers in the whole of the Agency. The highest incidence among males occurs at the age-periods 45-50 and among females at 35-40. The highest ratios per 100,000 of each sex occur in Partabgarh and the figures otherwise call for no particular comment. **Leprosy**

1.—NUMBER AFFLICTED PER 100,000 OF THE POPULATION AT EACH OF THE LAST FIVE CENSUSES.

AGENCY, STATE OR DISTRICT.	INSANE.										DEAF-MUTE.									
	Males.					Females.					Males.					Females.				
	1931.	1921.	1911.	1901.	1891.	1931.	1921.	1911.	1901.	1891.	1931.	1921.	1911.	1901.	1891.	1931.	1921.	1911.	1901.	1891.
1	2	3	4	5	6	7	8	9	10	11	12	13	14	15	16	17	18	19	20	21
Rajputana ...	**29**	**16**	**18**	**12**	**32**	**16**	**8**	**9**	**8**	**19**	**32**	**32**	**36**	**22**	Not available.	**23**	**20**	**22**	**15**	No available.
Abu District ...	36	47	...	...	...	...	69	...	...	...	73	...	...	...		169	69	...	...	
Alwar ...	30	15	15	11	29	19	11	6	6	14	86	44	39	38		61	30	22	21	
Banswara ...	50	29	26	1	8	33	14	17	...	...	72	21	50	...		72	16	37	...	
Bharatpur ...	24	7	11	5	18	13	4	5	3	6	30	19	50	18		18	17	26	14	
Bikaner ...	33	20	29	20	53	17	10	16	9	37	13	63	49	49		6	30	29	30	
Bundi ...	50	14	18	8	49	27	7	10	7	22	48	34	28	7		40	26	24	7	
Dholpur ...	19	17	11	5	19	15	15	8	2	10	85	19	37	33		68	15	20	12	
Dungarpur ...	37	33	20	4	28	18	29	14	8	18	12	26	25	10		11	22	21	6	
Jaipur ...	30	16	20	10	17	12	7	10	4	9	11	26	32	10		5	15	19	7	
Jaisalmer ...	14	32	41	3	53	3	13	18	8	21	33	53	66	33		32	44	50	9	
Jhalawar ...	28	32	22	6	51	70	17	17	...	30	67	26	32	32		134	7	22	12	
Karauli ...	31	12	9	8	23	20	7	6	8	32	111	20	23	39		77	10	14	25	
Kishangarh ...	56	17	35	17	66	32	11	12	16	45	18	20	31	38		15	16	19	34	
Kotah ...	41	17	20	3	35	26	10	14	4	27	46	29	38	14		35	21	29	11	
Kushalgarh (Chiefship) ...	68	...	9	24	34	39	...	...	...	...	96	21	27	24		90	21	9	38	
Lawa (Estate) ...	...	...	...	...	...	...	...	...	...	...	188	...	...	...		149	94	...	...	
Marwar ...	23	15	14	24	40	12	7	7	23	25	84	42	38	34		27	27	22	30	
Mewar ...	18	11	15	3	31	11	6	6	1	17	12	16	26	4		8	12	13	1	
Partabgarh ...	64	26	16	4	59	16	6	3	...	24	72	44	25	12		20	12	23	4	
Shahpura ...	25	16	24	5	30	30	13	22	5	13	11	20	37	9		27	39	4	5	
Sirohi ...	41	30	13	3	51	30	25	7	3	39	28	55	20	42		28	42	6	37	
Tonk ...	43	17	21	12	57	25	2	13	4	23	64	18	47	16		32	5	39	...	

1.—NUMBER AFFLICTED PER 100,000 OF THE POPULATION AT EACH OF THE LAST FIVE CENSUSES.—*Concluded.*

AGENCY, STATE OR DISTRICT.	BLIND.										LEPER.									
	Males.					Females.					Males.					Females.				
	1931.	1921.	1911.	1901.	1891.	1931.	1921.	1911.	1901.	1891.	1931.	1921.	1911.	1901.	1891.	1931.	1921.	1911.	1901.	1891.
1	22	23	24	25	26	27	28	29	30	31	32	33	34	35	36	37	38	39	40	41
Rajputana ...	**234**	**173**	**165**	**78**	**273**	**334**	**230**	**242**	**79**	**372**	**6**	**5**	**9**	**6**	**21**	**3**	**2**	**3**	**3**	**7**
Abu District ...	145	93	...	...	...	169	187	...	...	...	...	...	...	...	...	...	...	...	...	...
Alwar ...	347	237	298	160	310	486	279	311	171	362	10	7	8	11	17	2	3	1	2	3
Banswara ...	133	68	101	5	58	207	112	178	3	87	14	6	11	...	1	3	1	4	...	1
Bharatpur ...	444	235	225	53	192	708	385	363	47	221	8	6	5	4	21	2	...	3	2	6
Bikaner ...	257	248	282	175	468	369	327	418	204	768	5	4	18	7	44	8	2	2	4	16
Bundi ...	215	163	169	37	265	262	201	179	42	329	9	1	8	1	36	5	2	1	...	9
Dholpur ...	301	208	180	109	265	576	375	297	118	368	9	7	9	10	35	3	1	2	2	15
Dungarpur ...	133	133	67	24	99	185	204	94	28	86	3	4	3	...	12	2	...	3	2	8
Jaipur ...	223	128	160	59	219	298	141	187	67	235	3	2	4	2	8	2	...	1	1	2
Jaisalmer ...	135	114	204	61	179	136	151	221	47	240	2	3	4	...	13	3	...	...	...	9
Jhalawar ...	240	181	94	56	391	255	216	121	41	392	7	28	24	13	88	25	11	4	...	30
Karauli ...	283	160	111	83	242	473	240	146	104	379	4	3	8	11	17	3	...	...	7	8
Kishangarh ...	369	235	232	230	529	596	282	338	287	603	...	...	...	2	14	...	...	...	7	5
Kotah ...	219	173	200	48	227	395	249	267	36	288	17	9	20	2	11	6	4	6	3	7
Kushalgarh (Chiefship) ...	130	69	128	49	137	140	171	68	13	210	28	21	...	...	...	...	7	...	...	70
Lawa (Estate) ...	346	167	230	528	232	520	282	475	...	61	...	...	...	...	174	...	...	...	...	...
Marwar ...	237	240	282	91	91	375	336	318	38	626	7	9	15	15	31	4	4	5	11	10
Mewar ...	77	61	81	21	132	91	69	70	5	145	1	2	3	1	7	1	1	...	...	2
Partabgarh ...	167	126	101	35	168	287	200	126	12	152	41	53	44	...	89	56	15	26	...	48
Shahpura ...	244	205	224	27	162	301	360	215	15	220	...	...	...	5	8	...	...	...	...	...
Sirohi ...	452	300	211	93	452	644	580	302	109	301	11	3	6	1	36	3	4	4	...	13
Tonk ...	258	176	216	37	260	326	231	275	39	329	15	15	20	1	38	5	5	12	...	15

2.—DISTRIBUTION OF THE INFIRM BY AGE PER 10,000 AFFLICTED OF EACH SEX.

AGE.	INSANE.										DEAF-MUTE.									
	Males.					Females.					Males.					Females.				
	1931.	1921.	1911.	1901.	1891.	1931.	1921.	1911.	1901.	1891.	1931.	1921.	1911.	1901.	1891.	1931.	1921.	1911.	1901.	1891.
1	2	3	4	5	6	7	8	9	10	11	12	13	14	15	16	17	18	19	20	21
Total.	10,000	10,000	10,000	10,000	10,000	10,000	10,000	10,000	10,000	10,000	10,000	10,000	10,000	10,000	Not available.	10,000	10,000	10,000	10,000	Not available.
0— 5...	197	73	154	457	158	348	127	177	1,091	186	358	104	321	378		480	256	288	591	
5—10...	724	702	524	321	761	811	611	419	266	699	1,028	1,037	1,200	764		959	900	1,105	490	
10—15...	851	944	678	998	1,008	834	636	830	426	792	1,102	1,201	1,175	1,073		1,000	1,174	1,151	720	
15—20...	1,094	739	986	643	889	1,066	763	1,016	852	913	1,034	1,110	1,054	873		715	683	845	706	
20—25...	1,176	956	1,336	1,201	1,057	1,008	916	998	771	1,072	1,002	872	1,215	1,054		748	758	966	634	
25—30...	1,164	1,501	1,285	1,185	1,099	1,008	865	729	691	736	854	835	999	964		748	566	929	778	
30—35...	1,048	1,235	1,326	1,049	1,216	776	1,196	1,170	1,087	960	755	915	1,024	836		659	1,046	993	879	
35—40...	961	799	690	694	697	962	763	662	984	652	755	713	577	700		699	438	455	692	
40—45...	764	1,065	925	1,150	1,028	834	1,247	1,545	957	1,072	622	780	643	827		650	928	929	1,095	
45—50...	631	400	524	643	494	823	483	375	718	457	601	360	271	418		642	895	809	669	
50—55...	475	678	843	491	637	538	1,018	888	372	969	491	549	587	564		537	896	789	562	
55—60...	342	157	206	271	316	383	229	221	532	280	406	201	176	500		480	235	176	605	
60 & over.	573	751	514	897	719	614	1,146	971	1,308	1,212	1,002	1,323	758	1,054		1,683	1,065	975	1,585	

2.—DISTRIBUTION OF THE INFIRM BY AGE PER 10,000 AFFLICTED OF EACH SEX.—*Concluded.*

AGE.	BLIND.									
	Males.					Females.				
	1931.	1921.	1911.	1901.	1891.	1931.	1921.	1911.	1901.	1891.
1	22	23	24	25	26	27	28	29	30	31
Total.	10,000	10,000	10,000	10,000	10,000	10,000	10,000	10,000	10,000	10,000
0— 5...	189	185	286	382	223	180	124	123	238	161
5—10...	862	449	372	475	689	194	229	228	261	366
10—15...	398	487	486	619	565	195	245	180	370	314
15—20...	361	362	446	596	451	198	170	254	318	252
20—25...	985	418	587	601	490	225	240	325	463	321
25—30...	390	492	525	631	487	291	291	386	576	398
30—35...	375	579	649	697	614	330	528	652	686	550
35—40...	474	415	431	464	464	524	438	435	535	407
40—45...	521	779	758	899	772	601	849	961	1,056	840
45—50...	741	537	500	472	495	820	478	498	505	496
50—55...	810	1,155	1,161	891	934	857	1,287	1,358	1,166	1,068
55—60...	1,137	537	484	560	545	1,350	518	488	584	564
60 & over.	3,857	3,605	3,465	2,713	3,331	4,290	4,663	4,117	3,242	4,268

AGE.	LEPER.									
	Males.					Females.				
	1931.	1921.	1911.	1901.	1891.	1931.	1921.	1911.	1901.	1891.
1	32	33	34	35	36	37	38	39	40	41
Total.	10,000	10,000	10,000	10,000	10,000	10,000	10,000	10,000	10,000	10,000
0— 5...	131	33	...	99	76	248	...	...	126	152
5—10...	157	133	78	99	205	248	288	222	189	254
10—15...	286	100	213	431	259	311	...	518	314	457
15—20...	366	133	349	133	304	808	288	518	440	482
20—25...	893	233	447	563	609	745	481	963	755	736
25—30...	811	631	738	629	693	745	865	815	880	787
30—35...	811	963	1,248	960	1,119	808	962	1,630	818	1,091
35—40...	1,257	1,163	796	927	997	1,677	673	667	629	863
40—45...	1,178	1,827	2,078	1,566	1,580	1,304	1,827	1,704	1,321	1,320
45—50...	1,023	997	815	1,192	890	1,118	673	593	1,006	508
50—55...	1,309	1,528	1,700	1,159	1,210	497	2,019	1,259	818	1,294
55—60...	888	432	447	861	510	559	385	74	818	533
60 & over.	800	1,827	1,087	1,391	1,598	932	1,539	1,037	1,886	1,523

3.—NUMBER AFFLICTED PER 100,000 PERSONS OF EACH AGE-PERIOD AND NUMBER OF FEMALES AFFLICTED PER 1,000 MALES.

AGE	NUMBER AFFLICTED PER 100,000.								NUMBER OF FEMALES AFFLICTED PER 1,000 MALES.			
	Insane.		Deaf-mute.		Blind.		Leper.		Insane.	Deaf-mute.	Blind.	Leper.
	Males.	Females.	Males.	Females.	Males.	Females.	Males.	Females.				
1	2	3	4	5	6	7	8	9	10	11	12	13
All ages ...	**29**	**16**	**32**	**23**	**234**	**334**	**6**	**3**	**500**	**649**	**1,295**	**421**
0— 5 ...	4	3	8	7	30	27	1	...	882	881	892	800
5—10 ...	16	10	25	17	64	50	1	1	560	608	698	667
10—15 ...	20	12	28	20	74	56	1	1	490	589	686	556
15—20 ...	34	18	35	18	88	69	2	3	487	449	692	929
20—25 ...	37	17	35	18	98	79	3	2	429	484	755	800
25—30 ...	44	21	35	22	117	123	7	3	433	568	965	387
30—35 ...	45	18	35	22	128	162	8	4	370	566	1,141	419
35—40 ...	46	25	39	26	190	285	13	8	500	601	1,432	563
40—45 ...	41	25	37	28	223	377	14	7	545	678	1,493	467
45—50 ...	40	32	42	35	379	649	23	8	651	693	1,433	290
50—55 ...	38	25	43	36	521	842	28	4	561	710	1,370	160
55—60 ...	42	25	55	45	1,121	1,821	28	7	559	766	1,587	281
60 and over ...	46	25	89	96	2,486	3,554	16	7	535	1,089	1,440	441

CHAPTER VIII.

Occupation.

1. An important but difficult task at every Census is the preparation of an accurate record of the occupation or means of livelihood of the population. The detailed figures are set forth in Imperial Table X for the population as a whole, and Imperial Table XI shows the occupations of Europeans and Anglo-Indians. At the end of this Chapter will be found six Subsidiary Tables dealing with the figures in further detail. **Reference to statistics.**

2. Four columns were provided on the General Schedule wherein to record information on this subject and their purport was as follows:— **Questionnaire.**

Column 9.—Earner or Dependant. " Only those women and children will be shown as earners who help to augment the family income by permanent and regular work for which a return is obtained in cash or in kind. A woman who looks after her house and cooks the food is not an earner but a dependant. But a woman who habitually collects and sells firewood or cowdung is thereby adding to the family income and should be shown as an earner. A boy who sometimes looks after his father's cattle is a dependant, but one who is a regular cowherd and earns pay as such in cash or in kind, is an earner. Boys or girls at school are dependants ".

Column 10.—Principal Occupation of Earner. " This column will be blank for dependants. Stress must be laid on the importance of avoiding vague words like ' labour ' or ' service ' or ' shopkeeping '. The Enumerator must enter the exact kind of labour or service, and the nature of the goods sold. In the case of service, it is necessary not merely to distinguish Government service, Indian State service, Railway service, Municipal service, Village service, service in a shop or office and domestic service, etc., but also to show the exact occupation followed, e. g. in the case of Government service, whether Collector or Army Officer or Civil Court Clerk, or Police Inspector, etc. In the case of clerks, the occupation of their employer must be shown e.g. lawyer's clerk. Persons living on agriculture must be distinguished as owners cultivating or non-cultivating : as cultivating tenants or as agricultural labourers. Gardeners or growers of special products must be shown in detail. Persons whose income is derived from agricultural land should be distinguished from those who derive it from land in towns or from the rent of houses. Coolies employed on earth-work should have the nature of the undertaking entered such as Railway, Roads, etc. "

Column 11.—Subsidiary Occupation of Earners or Occupation of Dependants. " Where an earner has two occupations, enter here the one which is subsidiary to his or her principal occupation. Any kind of occupation followed by dependants should be entered."

Column 12.—Industry in which employed (for organised employees only). Since the Industrial Table was subsequently not compiled for reasons of economy, the detailed instructions for entries in this column are not repeated.

It will thus be seen that the whole population fell into one or other of the following heads:—

1. Earners with one occupation.
2. Earners with Principal and Subsidiary occupations.
3. Working Dependants, and
4. Non-working Dependants.

3. One difficulty encountered concerned the definition of an 'earner' and it was not easy to preserve uniformity in this respect. At previous Censuses it was the custom to classify the population as 'workers' and 'dependants (non-working)' and there was no such fine distinction as exists between the terms ' Earner ' and " Working Dependant. " A grown up son who did most of the work on land owned by his father who also worked, was held by most enumerators to be an 'Earner'. As he did not receive wages in cash or in kind, though he undoubtedly helped to augment the family income, he was in reality a working dependant. A further difficulty was, in the case of agriculture, to **Difficulties encountered.**

enter the correct occupation for working dependants. The son, referred to above, could not rightly be returned as a cultivating owner, as his father, and not he, owned the land. The correct entry in column 11 was " Agricultural labourer ", but, as this apparently offended his susceptibilities, the entry of " Helper in Agriculture " was permitted though subsequently tabulated in the same group (No. 7) as agricultural labourers. No such difficulties were as a rule encountered in other occupations. For instance, the sons of a shopkeeper who assisted their father were entered as 'earners' as a rule, since it was held that they were all joint proprietors and co-workers and therefore, all earners with a common occupation.

Proportion of workers and non-workers.

4. An important feature of the enquiry at this Census was that those who were non-workers and therefore, entirely dependent on others, were not required to return the occupation of those on whom they were dependent. For instance, an infant was shown in column 9 as a dependant with no entries at all in columns 10, 11 and 12. There is thus no material for assessing the total population that is supported by a particular occupation. Figures obtained at previous Censuses revealed however, the almost obvious fact that there were, in proportion far fewer non-workers among the agricultural population than among those who followed any other class of occupation.

The marginal statement shows the proportion of workers and non-workers at this and previous Censuses per mille of the population. At first sight there would appear to be an increase in unemployment, but the difference is really one of definition. In 1921 an "actual worker" was one who helped to augment the family income. This tended to throw into this category a number of women and children who did house work, cooked food and took it to the fields and did other odd jobs. At this Census such persons not having any definite personal occupation, such as could be classified according to the scheme, would be shown as non-working dependants and thus increase the proportion shown in that category. For these reasons the staff found some difficulty in discriminating between working and non-working dependants and decisions arrived at were largely matters of personal opinion.

Category.	1931.	1921.	1911.
Earners and Working Dependants (Actual Workers—1921 and 1911).	528	577	582
Non-working Dependants (Dependants in 1921 and 1911)	472	423	418

The apparent increase in non-workers chiefly affects the female population. The marginal statement shows that among 1,000 persons male workers have only decreased by 10 whereas female non-workers have increased by 42.

It is evident that similar difficulties in discrimination also existed in other parts of India. To take the case of certain other Provinces, Agencies and States, etc., we find that among 1,000 persons in Madras, the Punjab, United Provinces, Central India Agency and Gwalior the proportion

DISTRIBUTION OF 1,000 PERSONS 1921 AND 1931.

Category.	1931.	1921.
Male Earners	308	...
Male Working Dependants	35	...
Male Actual Workers	...	353
Male Non-Working Dependants	181	174
Female Earners	67	...
Female Working Dependants	118	...
Female Actual Workers	...	224
Female Non-Working Dependants	291	249
Total.	1,000	1,000

of earners ranges from 466 in Central India to 299 in the Punjab. The marginal statement shows the proportions in detail and quite apart from differences in the proportions between the sexes prevailing in various parts of India, it is strange to find such divergences in the proportions in the various categories. One would expect to find a certain amount of similarity in contiguous areas but even this does not exist.

Province, etc.	Earners.			Working Dependants.			Non-Working Dependants.		
	Persons.	Males.	Females.	Persons.	Males.	Females.	Persons	Males.	Females.
Madras ...	388	278	110	172	20	152	445	201	244
Punjab ...	299	280	19	69	36	33	632	230	402
United Provinces ...	418	331	87	69	11	58	513	183	330
Central India Agency ...	466	315	151	45	18	27	489	180	309
Gwalior ...	436	343	93	57	20	37	507	167	340

The scheme of classification.

5. All occupations are divided into four Classes which are further subdivided into twelve sub-classes, 55 Orders and 195 Groups.

Class.	Description.	Sub-class.	Description.
A	Production of Raw Materials	I	Exploitation of Animals and Vegetation.
		II	Exploitation of Minerals.
B	Preparation and Supply of Material Substances	III	Industry.
		IV	Transport.
		V	Trade.
C	Public Administration and Liberal Arts	VI	Public Force.
		VII	Public Administration.
		VIII	Professions and Liberal Arts.
D	Miscellaneous	IX	Persons living on their income.
		X	Domestic Service.
		XI	Insufficiently described occupations.
		XII	Unproductive.

Among the Orders, No. 5 (Salt, etc.) has become a group in order No. 4 (Non-metallic Minerals). There are thus only 55 Orders as against 56 in 1921. The number of Occupational Groups now stands at 195 and was 191 in 1921. The increase has been caused by showing some of the 1921 groups in greater detail, a description of which is not necessary. Owing to the need for economy, figures for groups have not, with a few exceptions, been shown in Table X part II against individual States and Cities.

Errors in the return.

6. It is usually the aim of every Census Officer so to instruct his enumerating staff that each entry pertaining to occupation will be so complete that the tabulating offices will have no difficulty in recognising it as belonging to a definite group and thus obviate the necessity for classifying entries in Sub-class XI.—"Insufficiently described occupations." Imperial Table X shows that this Sub-class contains four groups, (188) Manufacturers, etc., (189) Cashiers, Clerks, etc., (190) Mechanics, etc.,—all in unspecified concerns and (191) Labourers and workmen otherwise unspecified. Of the 198,762 persons shown as following these vague occupations, no less than 186,716 were Labourers and workmen in Group 191. Now it may be submitted that there are quite this number of labourers and probably more, whose means of livelihood is of such a general nature that it is quite impossible to describe them in any detail. In one week they will be road mending, in another performing agricultural labour and in a third be found in a ballast train. For this reason an entry of *Am Mazduri* (general labour) was necessary and permitted and should not detract from the value of the record.

The question of Non-working Dependants.

7. It has already been seen that the ratio of non-working dependants among 1,000 persons has increased since 1921 from 423 to 472 on account of changes in definition of the terms 'Worker' and 'Dependant' and the division of the former into 'Earner' and 'Working dependant'. It is therefore interesting to observe as in the marginal statement the part that each sex plays on account of such changes in definition. Among every 1,000 males there are now 15 more non-workers than was the case ten years ago. Among females the ratio has increased from 525 to 612. Such fluctuations in varying degrees are also observed in all except three of the individual States. The exceptions are Banswara, Jaisalmer and Partabgarh where the proportion of non-workers has *decreased* among both sexes. Among males only, it has decreased in Kotah, Mewar and Sirohi. These exceptions demonstrate that differences of opinion as to who was a working or non-working dependant were possible and did occur, though not to any very large extent.

PROPORTION OF NON-WORKING DEPENDANTS PER 1,000 OF EACH SEX.

STATE, ETC.	PERSONS.		MALES.		FEMALES.	
	1931.	1921.	1931.	1921.	1931.	1921.
Rajputana ...	***472***	***423***	***345***	***330***	***612***	***525***
Abu ...	502	428	310	278	800	648
Alwar ...	485	424	338	332	650	529
Banswara ...	418	476	381	449	455	503
Bharatpur ...	548	483	358	334	771	665
Bikaner ...	489	442	349	343	650	554
Bundi ...	465	424	339	338	604	519
Dholpur ...	506	450	321	291	732	646
Dungarpur ...	488	428	392	385	585	472
Jaipur ...	485	416	352	324	635	520
Jaisalmer ...	554	597	328	389	837	862
Jhalawar ...	498	479	312	311	703	662
Karauli ...	427	369	325	294	551	461
Kishangarh.	483	420	345	330	632	520
Kotah ...	429	409	317	326	549	499
Kushalgarh...	470	442	420	405	520	479
Lawa ...	601	425	426	364	788	494
Marwar ...	474	402	360	312	599	504
Mewar ...	432	415	327	338	544	498
Partabgarh ...	421	470	347	412	500	530
Shahpura ...	399	374	323	308	475	444
Sirohi ...	463	445	294	345	644	553
Tonk ...	465	395	349	319	589	477

The effect on the proportion of Earners and Working Dependants.

8. Actual workers who are now styled Earners or Working dependants now form 528 per 1,000 of the population as against 577 in 1921. It is interesting to note how this reduced general ratio affects the proportion in the main classes of occupation. In the Agency as a whole, among every 1,000 workers the proportion in Class A (Production of Raw Materials) has increased from 698 to 721. In Class B (Preparation and Supply of Material Substances) it has decreased from 197 to 174. A decrease from 57 to 47 is observed in Class C (Public Administration and Liberal Arts) while Class D (Miscellaneous) shows an increase from 48 to 58. The statement below shows the variations in each State.

COMPARATIVE STATEMENT OF OCCUPATIONS.

STATE, ETC.	NUMBER OF NON-WORKING DEPENDANTS PER 1,000 OF TOTAL POPULATION.		NUMBER IN EACH CLASS PER 1,000 EARNERS AND WORKING DEPENDANTS. (ACTUAL WORKERS).							
			Class A Production of Raw Materials.		**Class B** Preparation and supply of Material Substances.		**Class C** Public Administration and Liberal Arts.		**Class D** Miscellaneous.	
	1931	1921	1931	1921	1931	1921	1931	1921	1931	1921
Rajputana ...	**472**	**423**	**721**	**698**	**174**	**197**	**47**	**57**	**58**	**48**
Abu	502	428	106	218	894	366	94	105	406	311
Alwar ...	485	424	728	704	172	187	37	58	63	51
Banswara ...	418	476	875	831	88	112	16	39	21	18
Bharatpur ..	548	483	712	705	206	196	35	50	47	49
Bikaner ...	489	442	793	769	117	133	29	41	61	57
Bundi ...	465	424	709	728	174	192	49	52	68	88
Dholpur ...	506	450	805	757	135	167	37	35	23	41
Dungarpur ...	488	428	870	820	93	123	16	29	21	28
Jaipur ...	485	416	641	640	198	227	58	71	103	62
Jaisalmer ...	554	597	632	617	264	278	60	66	44	44
Jhalawar ...	498	479	690	654	179	217	61	87	70	42
Karauli ...	427	369	737	787	171	179	54	46	38	38
Kishangarh ...	483	420	709	662	170	207	63	87	58	44
Kotah ...	429	409	754	700	165	192	41	63	40	45
Kushalgarh ...	470	442	917	891	53	62	22	28	8	19
Lawa ...	601	425	552	688	308	232	73	53	67	27
Marwar ...	474	402	712	695	184	203	54	57	50	45
Mewar ...	432	415	746	722	189	191	49	57	16	30
Partabgarh ...	421	470	803	752	122	149	45	45	30	54
Shahpura ...	399	374	749	750	151	160	43	37	57	53
Sirohi ...	463	445	704	600	182	288	31	56	83	56
Tonk ...	465	395	682	713	145	183	40	38	133	66

It should not be assumed that the changed proportions connote an enthusiasm for Agriculture and miscellaneous pursuits at the expense of Trade, Industry, Public Administration and the Liberal Arts. The principal factor in the case of agricultural pursuits is the scope for the inclusion as working dependants of many males who would not have been considered as actual workers ten years ago. Similarly in Class B (Trade, Industry and Transport) many females are now relegated to the ranks of non-working dependants who would formerly have been classified as actual workers. The reduced proportion in Class C is contributed to by both sexes. The detailed occupations under Public Administration and the Professions leave little scope for the admission of persons of either sex as working dependants and the reduction is due to the omission of some formerly considered as actual workers from the more definitely defined category of earners.

The general results are best shown by a statement of actual figures as in the margin. It should be remembered that the actual increase in the population is 700,137 males and 681,191 females. In spite of this increase the actual numbers show a decrease of female workers in all Occupational Classes except those styled Miscellaneous and a decrease of males in Public Administration and Professions. The large number of working dependants especially females in Class A is most striking and they are practically all returned as Agricultural labourers or helpers in Agriculture

CATEGORY.	MALES.	FEMALES.
All Occupations.		
1931 Earners, Principal Occupations ...	3,457,237	747,473
1931 Working Dependants	396,874	1,323,679
1931 Total Workers	3,854,111	2,071,152
1921 Actual Workers	3,473,466	2,211,112
Variation 1921-31	+ 380,645	− 139,960
Class A. Production of Raw Materials.		
1931 Earners, Principal Occupations ...	2,259,669	406,300
1931 Working Dependants	367,559	1,232,253
1931 Total Workers	2,627,228	1,638,553
1921 Actual Workers	2,306,247	1,661,323
Variation 1921-31	+ 320,981	− 22,770
Class B. Preparation and Supply of Material Substances.		
1931 Earners, Principal Occupations ...	748,004	198,327
1931 Working Dependants	16,989	66,767
1931 Total Workers	764,993	265,094
1921 Actual Workers	731,684	383,919
Variation 1921-31	+ 33,309	− 118,825
Class C. Public Administration and Liberal Arts.		
1931 Earners, Principal Occupations ...	232,450	35,425
1931 Working Dependants	2,632	5,314
1931 Total Workers	235,082	40,739
1921 Actual Workers	271,615	57,115
Variation 1921-31	− 36,533	− 16,376
Class D. Miscellaneous.		
1931 Earners, Principal Occupations ...	217,114	107,421
1931 Working Dependants	9,694	19,345
1931 Total Workers	226,808	126,766
1921 Actual Workers	163,920	108,755
Variation 1921-31	+ 62,888	+ 18,011
1931 Non-Working Dependants	2,030,917	3,269,532
1921 Dependants	1,711,425	2,448,381
Variation 1921-31	+ 319,492	+ 821,151

In a summarised form the variations per mille of each sex in each Class since 1921 are as shown in the margin. With this explanation of the differences between the figures for this and the last Census, we may next proceed to consider in greater detail the occupations as now returned.

Class.	Males.	Females.
A	+62	− 5
B	+ 6	− 25
C	− 7	− 4
D	+12	+ 4
Non-Working Dependants ...	+62	+176
Total ...	+135	+146

General return of occupations.

9. The diagram below shows for each State the proportion per cent of the working population engaged in five main occupational heads.

DIAGRAM SHOWING THE PROPORTIONS OF THE INDUSTRIAL COMMERCIAL, PROFESSIONAL AND AGRICULTURAL POPULATION IN RAJPUTANA AND THE VARIOUS STATES

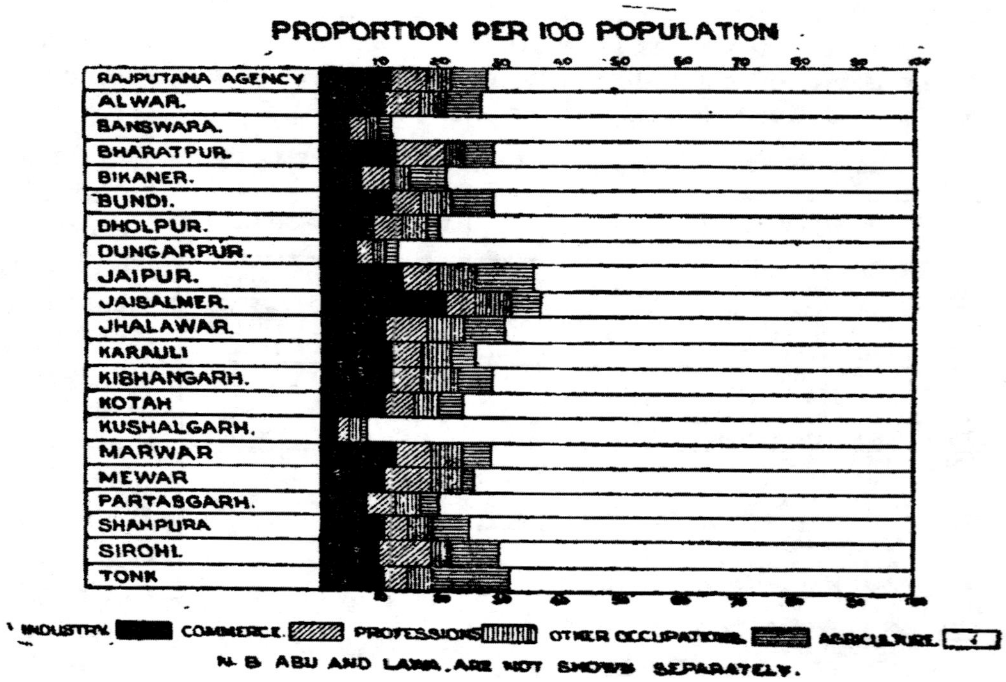

Out of the total population of 11,225,712 persons, 3,854,111 males and 2,071,152 females are earners and working dependants. If we assume that the population under 10 years of age is incapable of either earning or augmenting the family income, it means that of 1,000 persons of each sex over 10 years of age, 909 males and 548 females come within the category of earner or working dependant. The marginal statement shows the actual numbers of each sex that are engaged in one or other of the 12 sub-classes of occupation. Proportional figures per 1,000 workers are shown for each State in Subsidiary Table 2 Part A and having regard to the varied conditions prevailing, they do not call for any particular comment.

DISTRIBUTION OF THE POPULATION ACCORDING TO OCCUPATION.

SUB-CLASS OF OCCUPATION.	EARNERS.		WORKING DEPENDANTS.	
	Males.	Females.	Males.	Females.
I. Exploitation of Animals and Vegetation	2,253,724	404,418	367,550	1,232,109
II. Exploitation of Minerals ...	5,945	1,882	9	144
III. Industry	476,276	135,760	12,073	57,089
IV. Transport	47,127	8,061	441	475
V. Trade	224,601	59,506	4,475	9,208
VI. Public Force	55,376	106	801	262
VII. Public Administration ...	62,088	2,644	209	226
VIII. Professions and Liberal Arts.	114,986	32,675	2,122	4,826
IX. Persons living on their income.	8,888	1,474	124	285
X. Domestic Service	61,061	19,544	889	5,292
XI. Insufficiently described ...	97,535	73,536	2,552	11,015
XII. Unproductive	54,630	12,867	6,129	2,753
Total Workers ...	*3,457,237*	*747,473*	*396,874*	*1,323,679*

Exploitation of Animals and Vegetation.

10. In this Sub-class is found the important Order of Pasture and Agriculture further sub-divided into 5 sub-orders and 24 groups. Of the sub-orders, that of cultivation is of the greatest interest and the principal figures are quoted in the margin. Taking the Sub-class as a whole the proportion engaged in it per 1,000 of all workers is shown below for each State. The four Southern States with their large Bhil population head the list as might be expected.

GROUP.	OCCUPATION.	EARNERS.		WORKING DEPENDANTS.	
		Males.	Females.	Males.	Females.
1	Non-Cultivating proprietors ...	58,144	4,583	...	...
2—4	Estate Agents, Managers, Rent Collectors, etc. ...	18,081	1,508	...	...
5	Cultivating owners ...	258,107	10,333	...	...
6	Tenant Cultivators ...	1,616,712	121,742	...	...
7	Agricultural Labourers and Helpers in Agriculture ...	171,580	247,192	324,864	1,209,695

Kushalgarh	917	Kotah	751	Kishangarh	709	Jaipur	641
Banswara	875	Shahpura	749	Marwar	709	Jaisalmer	632
Dungarpur	870	Mewar	745	Bundi	708	Lawa	552
Partabgarh	803	Karauli	737	Sirohi	703	Abu	105
Dholpur	800	Alwar	728	Jhalawar	689		
Bikaner	793	Bharatpur	711	Tonk	680		

Exploitation of Minerals.

11. The occupations in this Sub-class only provide employment for 7,980 earners and working dependants which is only 2 per mille of all workers. The largest proportions are found in Dholpur (5), Kotah (3) and Marwar (3) due to stone quarries in the two former States and Salt works in Marwar.

Industry.

12. This Sub-class comprises 13 orders and 58 groups and gives employment to 488,349 males and 192,849 females or 115 per mille of all workers. The ratios in the States (excluding Lawa) vary from 215 in Jaisalmer to 63, 54 and 31 in Dungarpur, Banswara and Kushalgarh respectively. This apparently high industrial ratio in the sparsely populated State of Jaisalmer is due to a comparatively large number of persons engaged in the textile industry.

ORDER.	EARNERS.		WORKING DEPENDANTS.	
	Males.	Females.	Males.	Females.
5. Textiles	82,398	47,151	3,640	30,254
6. Hides, skins, etc.	32,922	3,827	608	2,061
7. Wood	49,452	5,696	1,223	2,077
8. Metals	21,006	1,279	428	693
9. Ceramics	46,482	12,842	1,243	5,226
10. Chemical Products, etc. ...	14,033	2,586	281	840
11. Food Industries	13,175	6,929	561	783
12. Industries of Dress and Toilet.	123,134	24,976	2,248	8,909
13. Furniture Industries ...	1,130	59	...	11
14. Building Industries ...	39,882	11,571	370	1,367
15. Construction of means of transport	176	20	...	3
16. Construction and transmission of physical force ...	1,159	5	17	...
17. Miscellaneous	51,327	18,819	1,454	4,865

Transport.

13. This Sub-class includes Transport by Air, Water, Road and Rail and the Post, Telegraph and Telephone Services, and gives employment to 9 persons per thousand workers. There are 16 males concerned with Aerodromes and Aeroplanes, of whom 6 were in Bundi and 10 in Marwar. A disappointing feature of the 27,218 persons employed in Transport by road is that only 244 are shown as owners, managers and employees connected with mechanically driven vehicles. Considering the very marked increase in the number of motors and lorries in all parts of the Agency, there has clearly been some error in tabulating the correct occupations of such persons. The Census returns show 21,404 workers on the various Railways while the figures received from the Departments concerned and exhibited in Subsidiary Table 6 (a) show 23,227 regular employees. Similarly, Subsidiary Table 6 (b) which has been compiled from information received from the Post and Telegraph Department, shows 2,242 workers while the Census figures are 1,964.

Trade.

14. This Sub-class of occupation which is further sub-divided into 17 orders and 38 groups gives employment to 297,785 earners and working dependants or 50 per mille of all workers. The marginal statement shows the actual figures for each of the 17 orders. Now it will be admitted that Trade and Industry are in many instances closely allied. For instance, a man who cures a hide does so to sell it. The curing is an industry and the selling is a trade. For this reason it is of greater interest to treat the two as combined when comparing the extent to which they provide a livelihood among the population in each State.

ORDER.	EARNERS.		WORKING DEPENDANTS.	
	Males.	Females.	Males.	Females.
23. Bank employees and Money lenders, etc.	32,218	2,100	551.	460
24. Brokers and Commission Agents, etc.	2,939	26	48	2
25. Trade in Textiles	15,411	445	250	219
26 Trade in skins, etc.	2,933	93	22	106
27. Trade in wood	874	650	10	70
28. Trade in Metals	680	18	7	3
29. Trade in pottery, bricks, etc. ...	184	100	11	12
30. Trade in Chemical products ...	756	255	5	11
31. Hotels, Cafes, Cook shops, etc. ...	6,029	586	86	422
32 Other Trade in food stuffs ...	101,612	37,915	2,255	5,111
33. Trade in clothing, etc.	9,860	886	218	327
34. Trade in furniture	907	248	9	15
35. Trade in building materials ...	465	257	7	43
36. Trade in means of Transport ...	6,166	208	84	7
37. Trade in fuel	8,038	13,843	149	1,880
38. Trade in articles of luxury ...	7,470	1,074	51	225
39. Trade of other sorts	28,059	1,302	712	290

The statement below shows that in the whole Agency, Industry and Trade provide a livelihood for 165 persons out of every 1,000 workers and that the ratios in the States vary from 305 in the small Lawa Estate to 52 in Kushalgarh with ratios rather above the average in the three largest States of Jaipur, Marwar and Mewar.

Lawa.	305	Marwar.	176	Kishangarh.	163	Partabgarh.	117
Abu.	293	Jhalawar.	170	Karauli.	160	Bikaner.	106
Jaisalmer.	264	Sirohi.	170	Kotah.	150	Dungarpur.	92
Bharatpur.	192	Bundi.	167	Shahpura.	149	Banswara.	87
Jaipur.	188	**Rajputana.**	**165**	Tonk.	142	Kushalgarh.	52
Mewar.	183	Alwar.	165	Dholpur.	126		

Public Force.

15. This Sub-class includes persons employed in the Army, Navy, Air Force and Police. In the aggregate, they number only one per cent. of all earners and working dependants and they include two men of the Navy and one of the Air Force who were presumably birds of passage. It is interesting to compare the average population in each State for each man returned under Public Force showing separately, as in the margin, the figures for the Armies of the Indian States and Policemen who include village watchmen. It will be noticed that in seven States there are more soldiers than policemen. These are Alwar, Bikaner, Dholpur, Karauli, Kishangarh, Mewar and Tonk.

POPULATION PER MAN RETURNED UNDER PUBLIC FORCE—

As a Soldier in an Indian State.		As a Policeman or Village Watchman.	
Kushalgarh		Mewar	792
Lawa		Banswara	724
Sirohi	5,552	Karauli	682
Banswara	4,594	Bikaner	635
Partabgarh	3,062	Alwar	578
Dungarpur	1,431	Kishangarh	479
Marwar	1,286	Dungarpur	464
Shahpura	670	Sirohi	405
Kotah	564	Bharatpur	383
Bikaner	482	Shahpura	366
Bharatpur	398	Dholpur	361
Jaisalmer	397	Jaisalmer	326
Jaipur	388	Jaipur	316
Alwar	310	Marwar	316
Jhalawar	277	Kushalgarh	299
Mewar	274	Tonk	246
Bundi	243	Kotah	219
Dholpur	235	Jhalawar	213
Tonk	162	Lawa	199
Kishangarh	134	Partabgarh	176
Karauli	129		

Public Administration.

16. Sub-class VII (Public Administration) is further sub-divided into five groups which distinguish between Ruling Princes, State, Municipal and Village officials. The total number in this Sub-class is 64,732 earners and 435

working dependants or 11 per mille of all workers. The needs of each State as regards personnel required for its administration are so diverse in character that it is not surprising to find that the ratio per mille of all workers varies from 27 in Kishangarh, 26 in Jhalawar to 5 in Banswara and 4 in Jaisalmer. In the larger States of Jaipur, Marwar, Mewar and Bikaner the ratios are 13, 7, 7 and 9 respectively.

Professions and Liberal Arts.

17. This Sub-class consists of 5 orders and 22 groups and the total number of workers who gain a livelihood therefrom is 154,609 or 26 per mille of all workers. The statement in the margin shows that by far the largest number come into the category of Religion as Priests, Religious Mendicants etc. Of the 7 Portias 6 hail from Mewar and 1 from Partabgarh—localities in which one would not expect to find them. In this Sub-class of Occupation the ratios in each State to all workers vary considerably according to local conditions. In the larger States of Jaipur, Marwar and Mewar the numbers per mille of all workers are 34, 40 and 33 respectively while Jaisalmer shows the unexpectedly highest ratio of 44.

Order.	Earners.		Working Dependants.	
	Males.	Females.	Males.	Females.
45 Religion ...	83,600	18,347	1,630	2,720
46 Law ...	2,127	7	6	...
47 Medicine ...	3,055	4,779	15	484
48 Instruction ...	5,776	437	90	15
49 Letters, Arts and Sciences.	20,428	9,105	381	1,607

Miscellaneous.

18. The remaining four Sub-classes of occupation comprise 6 orders and 11 groups and range in detail from scholarship holders and domestic servants to inmates of Jails and prostitutes. It has already been explained why it is necessary to include in Sub-class XI (Insufficiently described occupations) a large number of labourers who actually come to more than half of all the workers in these four Sub-classes.

This concludes our discussion of the subject of the principal occupations of the people, whether as earners or working dependants. Owing to the omission on this occasion of any record of the occupations on which non-workers are dependent for their existence, it is not possible to quote the proportion of the whole population that is dependent on any calling. The experience of the past, however, has taught us that in Agriculture and allied vocations there are far fewer non-workers than in any other class of occupation. The rise in the proportion of non-working dependants in the population as a whole due to changes in definition, precludes any detailed discussion as to whether a particular calling has attracted more or fewer followers in comparison with the numbers obtained at previous Censuses.

Subsidiary Occupations.

19. When it is well known that many earners have more than one means of livelihood, it is disappointing to find that only 111 males and 75 females out of 1,000 earners of each sex have returned subsidiary occupations.

The marginal statement shows that by far the most favoured subsidiary occupation is that of Agriculture and allied pursuits, but it is not possible to state the principal occupations of those so inclined. So many occupations are inter-connected that a return of only 19 males and 8 females per 1,000 earners with subsidiary occupations of an industrial nature cannot but be defective and the same can be said for the ratios of 10 males and 6 females in the subsidiary pursuits connected with Trade. Weaving is often a subsidiary occupation of persons (chiefly women) engaged in agriculture but as they are generally working dependants in agriculture that occupation being more important was

SUBSIDIARY OCCUPATIONS OF 1,000 EARNERS.

Sub-class or Class.	Males.	Females.
I. Exploitation of Animals and Vegetation ...	66	53
III. Industry	19	8
IV. Transport	2	...
V. Trade	10	6
VI. Public Force	1	...
VII. Public Administration	2	...
VIII. Professions and Liberal Arts	4	2
D. Miscellaneous	7	6
All Occupations	111	75

entered in the Schedule to the exclusion of weaving. As subsidiary occupations can only be recorded for actual earners, a comparison can be made of the occupations when engaged in as principal ones or as subsidiary to others. The general similarity of the proportions is striking. Certain occupations, however, are of such a nature that they more readily lend themselves to being subsidiary to others. This is noticeable in the case of Industry and Trade. On the other hand, occupations such as Public Force and Domestic Service cannot readily be engaged in as subsidiary to any other. The seemingly high ratio of 15 in Public Administration as a subsidiary occupation is due to a number of village officials and servants who have returned this occupation as secondary to another.

Sub-class.	Proportion per 1,000 earners.	
	As Principal Occupation.	As Subsidiary Occupation.
I. Exploitation of Animals and Vegetation	682	607
II. Minerals	2	2
III. Industry	146	159
IV. Transport	12	15
V. Trade	68	90
VI. Public Force ...	13	7
VII. Public Administration ...	15	15
VIII. Professions and Liberal Arts.	85	87
IX. Persons living on their income	1	2
X. Domestic Service ...	19	12
XI. Insufficiently described ...	41	82
XII. Unproductive	16	22

Occupations in Cities.

20. Out of every 1,000 persons in the population 139 reside in urban areas and of 1,000 of the urban population 359 are found in the 10 towns which are classified as Cities. Information regarding the occupations of the entire urban population is not available but Imperial Table X Part II shows the occupations of the population of the Cities. The marginal statement shows that in the Cities the proportion of non-working dependants in 1,000 of the population is 558 while in the remainder of the Agency it is 468. The Cities' ratio consists of 187 males and 371 females while for the rest it is 181 males and 287 females. The statement also shows the proportion of workers in each sub-class per 1,000 earners and working dependants, and calls for no particular comment.

Per 1,000 of Population.		
Category.	Rajputana less Cities.	Cities.
Non-Working Dependants...	468	558
Earners and Working Dependants ...	532	442

Per 1,000 Earners and Working Dependants.	
Sub-class.	Proportion in Cities.
I. Exploitation of Animals and vegetation ...	75
II. Exploitation of Minerals.	1
III. Industry	309
IV. Transport	47
V. Trade	127
VI. Public Force ...	74
VII. Public Administration.	99
VIII. Professions and Liberal Arts	56
IX. Persons living on their income	11
X. Domestic Service ...	84
XI. Insufficiently described.	81
XII. Unproductive ...	86

Occupations of Females.

21. Among every 1,000 females there are 140 earners, 248 working dependants and 612 non-working dependants. Subsidiary Table 3 shows the number of females engaged in various occupations as earners and working dependants combined. As earners pure and simple the only occupations in which females outnumber males are shown in the margin. The female excess is very noticeable in the case of

Occupation.	Males.	Females.
Wood Cutters and Charcoal burners.	1,964	2,538
Rice pounders, huskers and flour grinders	754	5,635
Embroiderers, hat makers and makers of other articles of wear ...	135	982
Trade in barks	81	102
Trade in Thatches and other forest produce	54	112
Dealers in fodder for animals ...	5,752	17,083
Trade in fuel	8,038	13,843
Midwives, Vaccinators, etc. ...	1,292	4,677
Procurers and prostitutes ...	10	187

rice pounding, husking and flour grinding, trade in fodder and fuel and in the essentially female occupations of midwifery and prostitution. If we combine earners and working dependants, the marginal statement shows certain occupations in which the female proportion of workers exceeds the male. In the sphere of working dependants only, we find that in Group No. 7—Agricultural labourers and helpers in Agriculture—there are 1,209.695 females to 324.364 males or 3,729 females per 1,000 males.

Occupation.	Number of females per 1,000 males.
Agricultural labourers and helpers in Agriculture	2,938
Wood cutters and Charcoal burners ...	1,858
Collectors of Forest produce ...	1,038
Cotton Spinning, Sizing and Weaving ...	1,009
Basket making, etc.	1,018
Rice pounders and huskers and flour grinders	7,603
Dealers in dairy products	1,116
Dealers in fodder for animals ...	3,153
Dealers in firewood and charcoal ...	1,920
Midwives, Vaccinators, Compounders, Nurses, etc.	8,971

Occupations of Europeans and Anglo-Indians.

22. Imperial Table XI shows that out of 932 Europeans, earners and working dependants number 346 males and 57 females while the remaining 529 are non-working dependants of both sexes. Anglo-Indians number 224 males and 22 females as earners and working dependants, while 582 are non-workers. Subsidiary Table 5 presents these figures as proportionate numbers per 100 in each sub-class of occupation and shows that the bulk of the male workers both European and Anglo-Indian, are Railway employees.

Unemployment among educated persons.

23. A feature at this Census was a special enquiry into the prevalence of unemployment among educated persons. A separate schedule was provided and the information collected is shown in Imperial Table XII. The definition of 'Educated' was the minimum qualification of having passed the Matriculation examination or the possession of a school leaving certificate. The results show that there were only 128 in all, or 99 aged 20 and over, out of a total English knowing male population of 19,377 similarly aged, who stated that they were out of employment. It is impossible to assess the accuracy of this return. 107 of those stated to be unemployed had no higher qualification than that of passing the Matriculation examination and considering the low standard of literacy in the population as a whole and the amount of administrative work in the States that is conducted in the vernaculars, the problem is not in any way an acute one. Figures for the several States are as shown in the margin and the absence of any figures from Marwar and the large numbers returned from Jaipur compared with the figures for any other State, can but lead one to the conclusion that the record is defective.

State	
Alwar	9
Banswara	1
Bharatpur	9
Bikaner	1
Dholpur	2
Jaipur	72
Jhalawar	2
Kishangarh	1
Kotah	15
Mewar	8
Tonk	8
Total	128

1 (a).—GENERAL DISTRIBUTION OF OCCUPATION—EARNERS (PRINCIPAL OCCUPATION) AND WORKING DEPENDANTS.

CLASS, SUB-CLASS AND ORDER.	NUMBER PER 10,000 OF TOTAL POPULATION.	PERCENTAGE RECORDED	
		In Cities.	In Rural Areas including Towns which are not classified as Cities.
1	2	3	4
NON-WORKING DEPENDANTS ...	*4,722*	6	*94*
ALL OCCUPATIONS. EARNERS (PRINCIPAL OCCUPATION) AND WORKING DEPENDANTS ...	*5,278*	*4*	*96*
A.—Production of Raw Materials.	*3,800*	...	*100*
I.—Exploitation of animals and vegetation	*3,793*	...	*100*
1. Pasture and Agriculture ...	3,793	...	100
(a) Cultivation	3,601	...	100
(b) Cultivation of special crops, fruits, etc. (Planters, managers, clerks, and labourers).	4	32	68
(c) Forestry	11	5	95
(d) Stock raising	177	1	99
(e) Raising of small animals and insects	...	...	100
2. Fishing and hunting ...	...	16	84
II.—Exploitation of minerals ...	7	*3*	*97*
4. Non-metallic minerals ...	7	3	97
B.—Preparation and Supply of Material Substances ...	*917*	*12*	*88*
III.—Industry	*607*	*11*	*89*
5 Textiles	146	10	90
6 Hides, skins and hard materials from the animal kingdom ...	35	5	95
7. Wood	52	7	93
8. Metals	21	11	89
9. Ceramics	59	5	95
10 Chemical products properly so-called and analogous ...	16	7	93
11. Food Industries	19	24	76
12. Industries of dress and the toilet...	142	10	90
13. Furniture Industries... ...	1	53	47
14. Building Industries... ...	47	23	77
15. Construction of means of transport.	...	41	59
16 Production and transmission of physical force	1	82	18
17. Miscellaneous and undefined industries	68	15	85
IV.—Transport	*45*	*23*	*77*
18. Transport by air	...	56	44
19. Transport by water	...	18	82
20. Transport by road	24	22	78
21. Transport by rail	19	24	76
22. Post Office, Telegrah and Telephone Services	2	24	76
V.—Trade	*265*	*11*	*89*
23. Banks, establishments of credit, exchange and insurance ...	31	6	94

CLASS, SUB-CLASS AND ORDER.	NUMBER PER 10,000 OF TOTAL POPULATION.	PERCENTAGE RECORDED.	
		In Cities.	In Rural Areas including Towns which are not classified as Cities.
1	2	3	4
24. Brokerage, commission and export.	3	21	79
25. Trade in textiles	14	19	81
26. Trade in skins, leather and furs ...	3	9	91
27. Trade in wood (not firewood) ...	1	8	92
28. Trade in metals	1	22	78
29. Trade in pottery, bricks and tiles.	...	9	91
30. Trade in chemical products ...	1	16	84
31. Hotels, cafes, restaurants, etc. ...	6	14	86
32. Other trade in food stuffs ...	131	10	90
33. Trade in clothing and toilet articles.	10	15	85
34. Trade in furniture	1	13	87
35. Trade in building materials ...	1	17	83
36. Trade in means of transport ...	6	14	86
37. Trade in fuel	21	8	92
38. Trade in articles of luxury and those pertaining to letters and the arts and sciences ...	8	18	82
39. Trade of other sorts... ...	27	8	92
C.—Public Administration and Liberal Arts	*246*	*20*	*80*
VI.—Public Force	*50*	*33*	*67*
40. Army	25	47	53
41. Navy	...	...	100
42. Air Force	...	...	100
43. Police	25	19	81
VII.—Public Administration ...	*58*	*37*	*63*
VIII.—Professions and Liberal Arts	*138*	*9*	*91*
45. Religion	95	6	94
46. Law	2	48	52
47. Medicine	7	18	82
48. Instruction	6	28	72
49. Letters, arts and sciences (other than 44)	28	11	89
D.—Miscellaneous	*315*	*15*	*85*
IX.—Persons living on their income	*5*	*45*	*55*
X.—Domestic Service ...	*77*	*24*	*76*
XI.—Insufficiently described occupations	*165*	*11*	*89*
XII.—Unproductive ...	*68*	*12*	*88*
53. Inmates of jails, asylums and alms houses	4	80	20
54. Beggars, vagrants, prostitutes ...	63	7	93
55. Other unclassified non-productive industries	1	23	77

1 (b).—GENERAL DISTRIBUTION OF OCCUPATION—EARNERS, AS SUBSIDIARY OCCUPATION.

CLASS, SUB-CLASS AND ORDER.	NUMBER PER 10,000 OF TOTAL POPULATION.	PERCENTAGE RECORDED	
		In Cities.	In Rural Areas, including Towns, which are not classified as Cities.
1	2	3	4
ALL OCCUPATIONS.			
EARNERS—AS SUBSIDIARY OCCUPATION ...	*393*	*2*	*98*
A.—Production of Raw Materials.	*239*	*1*	*99*
I.—Exploitation of animals and vegetation ...	*239*	*1*	*99*
1. Pasture and Agriculture ...	239	1	99
(a) Cultivation ...	202	1	99
(b) Cultivation of special crops, fruits, etc., (Planters, managers, clerks and labourers) ...	...	8	92
(c) Forestry ...	4	1	99
(d) Stock raising ...	33	...	100
2. Fishing and hunting ...	...	...	100
II.—Exploitation of minerals ...	...	...	*100*
4. Non-metallic minerals ...	...	...	100
B.—Preparation and Supply of Material Substances ...	*104*	*2*	*98*
III.—Industry ...	*63*	*2*	*98*
5. Textiles ...	13	2	98
6. Hides, skins and hard materials from the animal kingdom ...	6	...	100
7. Wood ...	10	1	99
8. Metals ...	2	1	99
9. Ceramics ...	5	1	99
10. Chemical products properly so-called and analogous ...	2	1	99
11. Food Industries ...	1	11	89
12. Industries of dress and the toilet...	17	2	98
13. Furniture Industries...	...	13	87
14. Building Industries ...	4	3	97
15. Construction of means of transport.	...	...	100
16. Production and transmission of physical force ...	...	41	59
17. Miscellaneous and undefined industries ...	3	17	83
IV.—Transport ...	*6*	*4*	*96*
18. Transport by air ...	...	...	100
19. Transport by water ...	...	...	100
20. Transport by road ...	5	4	96
21. Transport by rail ...	1	5	95
22. Post Office, Telegraph and Telephone Services ...	...	3	97
V.—Trade ...	*35*	*2*	*98*
23. Banks, establishments of credit, exchange and insurance ...	8	2	98
24. Brokerage, commission and export	...	6	94
25. Trade in textiles ...	1	8	92
26. Trade in skins, leather and furs ...	...	2	98
27. Trade in wood (not fire-wood) ...	...	...	100
28. Trade in metals ...	...	28	72
29. Trade in pottery, bricks and tiles.	...	...	100
30. Trade in chemical products ...	...	2	98
31. Hotels, cafes, restaurants, etc. ...	...	6	94
32. Other trade in food stuffs ...	15	2	98
33. Trade in clothing and toilet articles.	1	2	98
34. Trade in furniture ...	...	...	100
35. Trade in building materials ...	...	8	92
36. Trade in means of transport ...	1	1	99
37. Trade in fuel ...	7	2	98
38. Trade in articles of luxury and those pertaining to letters and the arts and sciences ...	...	7	93
39. Trade of other sorts ...	2	4	96
C.—Public Administration and Liberal Arts ...	*23*	*4*	*96*
VI.—Public Force ...	*3*	*3*	*97*
40. Army ...	1	9	91
43. Police ...	2	1	99
VII.—Public Administration ...	6	6	*94*
VIII.—Professions and Liberal Arts.	*14*	*4*	*96*
45. Religion ...	12	4	96
46. Law ...	...	19	81
47. Medicine ...	...	16	84
48. Instruction ...	...	10	90
49. Letters, arts and sciences (other than 44) ...	2	3	97
D.—Miscellaneous ...	*27*	*4*	*96*
IX.—Persons living on their income.	*1*	*11*	*89*
X.—Domestic Service ...	*4*	*7*	*93*
XI.—Insufficiently described occupations ...	*13*	*3*	*97*
XII.—Unproductive ...	*9*	*2*	*98*
53. Inmates of jails, asylums and alms houses ...	...	7	93
54. Beggars, vagrants, prostitutes ...	9	2	98
55. Other unclassified non-productive industries ...	...	6	94

2.—DISTRIBUTION BY SUB-CLASSES IN STATES AND DISTRICT.

PART A.

Agency, District or State.	Total 1,000. Non-working dependants	Total 1,000. Working dependants	Total 1,000. Earners—(Principal occupation).	Sub-class I.—Exploitation of Animals and Vegetation	Sub-class II.—Exploitation of Minerals.	Sub-class III.—Industry	Sub-class IV.—Transport.	Sub-class V.—Trade.	Sub-class VI.—Public Force.	Sub-class VII.—Public Administration.	Sub-class VIII.—Professions and Liberal Arts.	Sub-class IX.—Persons living on their Income.	Sub-class X.—Domestic Service.	Sub-class XI.—Insufficiently described occupations.	Sub-class XII.—Unproductive.
				Number per mille of the total population occupied as earners (principal occupation) and working dependants in—											
1	2	3	4	5	6	7	8	9	10	11	12	13	14	15	16
RAJPUTANA ...	**472**	**153**	**375**	**719**	**2**	**115**	**9**	**50**	**10**	**11**	**26**	**1**	**15**	**31**	**11**
Abu District ...	502	1	497	105	1	208	101	85	38	28	28	1	125	272	8
Alwar ...	485	143	372	728	...	115	7	50	9	13	15	2	9	32	20
Banswara ...	418	336	246	875	...	54	1	38	2	5	9	1	9	2	9
Bharatpur ...	548	90	362	711	1	127	14	65	10	15	10	4	16	9	18
Bikaner ...	489	228	283	798	...	70	11	36	7	9	13	...	22	25	14
Bundi ...	465	110	425	708	1	122	7	45	10	20	19	1	·10	46	11
Dholpur ...	506	91	403	800	5	87	9	39	14	13	10	2	7	2	12
Dungarpur ...	488	284	228	870	...	63	1	29	4	6	6	...	5	3	13
Jaipur ...	485	172	343	641	...	140	10	48	11	13	34	1	17	72	13
Jaisalmer ...	554	36	410	632	...	215	...	40	12	4	44	...	16	18	10
Jhalawar ...	498	64	438	689	1	108	9	62	15	26	20	7	17	26	20
Karauli ...	427	206	367	737	...	117	11	43	15	21	18	2	8	10	18
Kishangarh ...	483	171	346	709	...	117	7	46	18	27	18	4	9	23	22
Kotah ...	429	94	477	751	3	111	15	39	11	16	14	1	10	14	15
Kushalgarh (Chiefship).	470	256	274	917	...	31	1	21	6	12	4	...	5	...	3
Lawa (Estate) ...	601	49	350	552	...	260	3	45	13	38	22	...	33	13	21
Marwar ...	474	102	424	709	3	130	8	46	7	7	40	...	19	19	12
Mewar ...	432	166	402	745	1	106	6	77	9	7	33	...	9	4	3
Partabgarh ...	421	249	330	803	...	74	5	48	9	11	25	1	16	4	9
Shahpura ...	399	301	300	749	...	108	2	41	7	21	15	...	9	32	16
Sirohi ...	468	172	365	708	1	97	12	73	6	11	14	...	16	45	22
Tonk ...	465	130	405	680	2	103	3	39	19	13	8	2	18	88	25

PART B.

Agency, District or State.	Sub-class I.	Sub-class II.	Sub-class III.	Sub-class IV.	Sub-class V.	Sub-class VI.	Sub-class VII.	Sub-class VIII.	Sub-class IX.	Sub-class X.	Sub-class XI.	Sub-class XII.
	Number per mille of total population of earners having a subsidiary occupation in—											
1	17	18	19	20	21	22	23	24	25	26	27	28
RAJPUTANA ...	**607**	**2**	**159**	**15**	**90**	**7**	**15**	**37**	**2**	**12**	**32**	**22**
Abu District ...	466	...	68	11	58	...	...	5	...	52	314	26
Alwar ...	608	1	102	16	83	9	39	27	9	12	68	26
Banswara ...	704	1	62	24	70	12	33	27	16	17	13	21
Bharatpur ...	643	2	102	39	126	9	8	15	4	17	12	23
Bikaner ...	367	2	339	24	54	5	33	37	4	10	84	41
Bundi ...	454	2	236	18	101	10	20	62	2	14	52	29
Dholpur ...	694	13	117	21	89	6	6	26	2	4	3	19
Dungarpur ...	576	...	199	10	52	20	62	25	...	18	1	37
Jaipur ...	521	1	134	27	89	23	19	65	4	19	79	19
Jaisalmer ...	896	...	38	1	36	1	...	5	...	2	13	8
Jhalawar ...	416	1	228	11	97	12	20	55	4	10	53	93
Karauli ...	682	...	144	24	65	7	24	23	2	5	9	15
Kishangarh ...	560	...	257	3	63	12	20	38	1	10	3	38
Kotah ...	526	...	204	22	102	9	38	30	1	7	9	57
Kushalgarh (Chiefship).	258	...	272	33	207	14	64	51	...	...	...	51
Lawa (Estate) ...	210	...	368	...	316	...	...	53	...	53	...	...
Marwar ...	691	1	178	6	37	1	5	25	1	15	20	20
Mewar ...	573	1	162	8	178	3	3	58	...	6	3	5
Partabgarh ...	787	...	96	8	63	9	15	50	1	7	2	12
Shahpura ...	622	...	186	4	45	4	20	32	...	8	40	39
Sirohi ...	496	1	183	16	137	1	7	28	1	10	71	49
Tonk ...	551	8	125	10	62	7	1	7	...	4	179	46

3.—OCCUPATION OF FEMALES BY SUB-CLASSES AND SELECTED ORDERS AND GROUPS.

Group No.	Occupation.	Number of earners and working dependatns. Males.	Females.	Number of females per 1,000 males.
1	2	3	4	5
	Sub-class I. — Exploitation of animals and vegetation	***2,621,274***	***1,636,527***	***624***
	Order 1.—Pasture and Agriculture	2,621,028	1,636,518	624
7	Agricultural Labourers and helpers in Agriculture ...	495,944	1,456,887	2,938
16	Market gardeners, flower and fruit growers ...	2,389	1,301	545
18	Wood cutters and charcoal burners	2,087	2,835	1,358
19	Collectors of forest produce ...	3,178	3,443	1,083
21	Cattle and buffalo breeders and keepers	51,168	6,553	128
23	Herdsmen, shepherds and breeders of other animals...	109,902	27,079	246
	Sub-class II.—Exploitation of minerals ...	***5,954***	***2,026***	***340***
	Order 4.—Non-metallic minerals.	5,954	2,026	340
37	Building materials (including stone, materials for cement-manufacture and clays) ...	2,207	1,364	618
	Sub-class III.—Industry.	***488,349***	***192,849***	***395***
	Order 5.—Textiles ...	86,038	77,405	900
42	Cotton ginning, cleaning and pressing	9,736	5,115	525
43	Cotton spinning, sizing and weaving	60,541	61,010	1,008
45	Rope, twine, string and other fibres	1,817	1,392	766
46	Wool carding, spinning and weaving	1,277	1,191	933
49	Dyeing, bleaching, printing, preparation and sponging of textiles	11,647	7,979	685
	Order 7.—Wood... ...	50,675	7,778	153
56	Basket makers and other industries of woody materials, including leaves and thatchers and builders working with bamboo, reeds or similar materials	6,520	6,603	1,013
	Order 9.—Ceramics ...	47,725	18,068	379
63	Potters and makers of earthenware	46,529	17,786	382
	Order 10.—Chemical products properly so-called and analogous	14,314	3,426	239
68	Manufacture and refining of vegetable oils ...	13,522	3,350	248
	Order 11.—Food Industries ...	13,736	7,712	561
71	Rice pounders and huskers and flour grinders ...	783	6,024	7,693
	Order 12.—Industries of dress and the toilet ...	125,382	33,835	270
83	Tailors, milliners, dress-makers and darners ...	21,835	10,027	458
85	Washing and cleaning ...	8,106	6,373	786
	Order 14.—Building Industries	40,252	12,938	321
90	Lime burners, cement workers, Excavators and well sinkers, Stone cutters and dressers, Brick layers and masons, Builders (other than buildings made of bamboo or similar materials), painters, decorators of houses, tilers, plumbers, etc. ...	40,252	12,938	321
	Order 17.—Miscellaneous and undefined Industries ...	52,781	23,684	449
100	Scavenging	23,176	20,657	891
	Sub-class IV.—Transport ...	***47,568***	***3,536***	***74***
	Order 20.—Transport by road.	24,368	2,850	117
106	Labourers employed on roads and bridges ...	3,150	1,323	420
	Sub-class V.—Trade ...	***229,076***	***68,709***	***300***
	Order 32.—Other trade in food stuffs. ...	103,867	43,026	414
131	Dealers in dairy products, eggs and poultry ...	3,104	3,465	1,116
133	Dealers in fodder for animals.	5,794	18,268	3,153
134	Dealers in other food stuffs ...	66,833	19,138	286
	Order 37.—Trade in fuel ...	8,187	15,723	1,920
145	Dealers in fire-wood, charcoal, coal, cowdung, etc. ...	8,187	15,723	1,920
	Order 39.—Trade of other sorts.	28,771	1,592	55
150	General store-keepers and shop-keepers otherwise unspecified	26,138	1,442	55
	Sub-class VI.—Public Force.	***55,677***	***368***	***7***
	Sub-class VII.—Public Administration ...	***62,297***	***2,870***	***46***
	Sub-class VIII.—Professions and Liberal Arts ...	***117,108***	***37,501***	***320***
	Order 45.—Religion ...	85,230	21,067	247
164	Monks, nuns, religious mendicants	49,741	16,340	329
	Order 47.—Medicine ...	3,070	5,263	1,714
172	Midwives, Vaccinators, Compounders, Nurses, Masseurs, etc.	1,29[illegible]	5,147	3,971
	Order 49.—Letters, arts and sciences (other than 44) ...	20,809	10,712	515
182	Musicians (composers and performers other than Military), actors, dancers, etc. ...	17,033	10,227	600
	Sub-class IX.—Persons living on their income ...	***4,012***	***1,759***	***438***
	Sub-class X.—Domestic Service	***61,950***	***24,836***	***401***
187	Other domestic service ...	60,516	24,833	410
	Sub-class XI.—Insufficiently described occupations ...	***100,087***	***84,551***	***845***
191	Labourers and workmen otherwise unspecified ...	89,109	83,930	942
	Sub-class XII.—Unproductive	***60,759***	***15,620***	***257***
	Order 54.—Beggars, vagrants, prostitutes	55,156	15,257	277
193	Beggars and vagrants ...	55,140	15,098	274

4.—SELECTED OCCUPATIONS GIVING COMPARATIVE FIGURES FOR 1921 AND 1931.

Order No.	Occupation	1931. Earners—(Principal Occupation) plus Working Dependants.	1931. Earners—Subsidiary Occupation.	1921. Workers—excluding Dependants.
1	2	3	4	5
	A.—Production of Raw Materials ...	*4,265,781*	*268,929*	*3,967,570*
	I.—Exploitation of animals and vegetation ...	*4,257,801*	*268,219*	*3,957,584*
1	Pasture and Agriculture ...	4,257,546	268,188	3,957,480
	(a) Cultivation	4,042,041	226,687	3,787,670
	(b) Cultivation of special crops, fruits, etc. ...	4,313	312	4,518
	(c) Forestry	12,667	4,049	12,629
	(d) Stock raising ...	198,524	37,135	152,663
	(e) Raising of small animals and insects ...	1	...	...
2	Fishing and Hunting ...	255	36	104
	II.—Exploitation of minerals	*7,980*	*710*	*9,986*
3	Metallic minerals ...	...	...	22
4	Non-metallic minerals ...	7,980	710	9,964
	B.—Preparation and Supply of Material Substances ...	*1,030,087*	*116,682*	*1,115,603*
	III.—Industry	*681,198*	*70,074*	*765,400*
5	Textiles	163,443	14,086	241,108
6	Hides, skins and hard materials from the animal kingdom.	39,418	6,881	39,142
7	Wood	58,448	10,994	56,894
8	Metals	23,406	2,324	26,545
9	Ceramics	65,793	5,582	72,076
10	Chemical products properly so-called and analogous ...	17,740	2,541	20,639
11	Food Industries	21,448	1,350	31,289
12	Industries of dress and the toilet	159,267	18,868	164,965
13	Furniture Industries ...	1,200	46	44
14	Building Industries ...	53,190	4,656	33,770
15	Construction of means of transport	199	29	24
16	Production and transmission of physical force ...	1,181	22	301
17	Miscellaneous and undefined Industries	76,465	2,695	79,708
	IV.—Transport... ...	*51,104*	*6,849*	*48,948*
18	Transport by air ...	16	1	...
19	Transport by water ...	502	109	1,042
20	Transport by road ...	27,218	6,066	28,932
21	Transport by rail ...	21,404	635	17,509
22	Post Office, Telegraph and Telephone Services ...	1,964	38	1,465
	V.—Trade	*297,785*	*39,759*	*301,255*
23	Banks, establishments of credit, exchange and insurance ...	25,329	8,627	34,080
24	Brokerage, commission and export	3,015	270	2,710
25	Trade in textiles ...	16,325	758	30,179
26	Trade in skins, leather and furs	3,154	253	3,409
27	Trade in wood (not firewood)	1,604	460	1,493
28	Trade in metals	708	69	316
29	Trade in pottery, bricks and tiles	307	7	192
30	Trade in chemical products ...	1,027	255	205
31	Hotels, cafes, restaurants, etc.	7,128	530	8,351
32	Other trade in food stuffs ...	146,893	16,321	150,088
33	Trade in clothing and toilet articles	10,791	577	2,407
34	Trade in furniture ...	1,179	130	608
35	Trade in building materials ...	772	52	378
36	Trade in means of transport ...	6,465	1,272	8,603
37	Trade in fuel	23,910	8,063	18,988
38	Trade in articles of luxury and those pertaining to letters, and the arts and sciences.	8,820	347	6,321
39	Trade of other sorts ...	30,363	1,768	32,932
	C.—Public Administration and Liberal Arts	*275,821*	*25,850*	*328,730*
	VI.—Public Force ...	*56,045*	*3,244*	*70,525*
40	Army	28,437	609	43,809
41	Navy	2	...	6
42	Air Force	1	...	...
43	Police	27,605	2,635	26,710
	VII.—Public Administration	*65,167*	*6,414*	*64,845*
	VIII.—Professions and Liberal Arts ...	*154,609*	*16,192*	*193,360*
45	Religion	106,297	12,904	145,788
46	Law	2,140	81	1,550
47	Medicine	8,358	399	6,668
48	Instruction	6,318	300	3,969
49	Letters, arts and sciences (other than 44) ...	31,521	2,508	35,385
	D.—Miscellaneous ...	*353,574*	*30,104*	*272,675*
	IX.—Persons living on their income	*5,771*	*1,112*	*20,778*
	X.—Domestic Service ...	*86,786*	*5,090*	*108,243*
	XI.—Insufficiently described occupations ...	*184,638*	*14,124*	*83,652*
	XII.—Unproductive ...	*76,379*	*9,778*	*60,002*
53	Inmates of jails, asylums and alms houses	4,946	27	5,078
54	Beggars, vagrants, prostitutes.	70,443	9,665	54,919
55	Other unclassified non-productive industries ...	990	86	5

5.—OCCUPATIONS OF EUROPEANS AND ANGLO-INDIANS.

Occupation by Sub-classes.	Number per 100 workers engaged on each occupation.	Number of female workers per 100 males.
Europeans.		
Sub-class I. Exploitation of Animals and Vegetation	...	...
Sub-class II. Exploitation of Minerals	1	...
Sub-class III. Industry	4	8
Sub-class IV. Transport	44	...
Sub-class V. Trade	1	25
Sub-class VI. Public Force	16	...
Sub-class VII. Public Administration	9	9
Sub-class VIII. Professions and Liberal Arts	19	130
Sub-class IX. Persons living on their income	2	...
Sub-class X. Domestic Service	3	450
Sub-class XI. Insufficiently described occupations	1	...
Sub-class XII. Unproductive	...	...
Anglo-Indians		
Sub-class I. Exploitation of Animals and Vegetation	1	100
Sub-class II. Exploitation of Minerals	...	...
Sub-class III. Industry	2	...
Sub-class IV. Transport	73	1
Sub-class V. Trade	1	...
Sub-class VI. Public Force	1	...
Sub-class VII. Public Administration	5	...
Sub-class VIII. Professions and Liberal Arts	13	146
Sub-class IX. Persons living on their income	...	...
Sub-class X. Domestic Service	8	14
Sub-class XI. Insufficiently described occupations	1	...
Sub-class XII. Unproductive	...	...

6 (a).—NUMBER OF PERSONS EMPLOYED ON RAILWAYS ON THE 26TH. FEBRUARY, 1931.

PERSONS DIRECTLY EMPLOYED.										PERSONS INDIRECTLY EMPLOYED.								GRAND TOTAL.	
Officers.		Subordinates drawing more than Rs. 75 per mensem.		Subordinates drawing from Rs. 20 to Rs. 75 per mensem		Subordinates drawing under Rs. 20 per mensem		Total.		Contractors		Contractors' regular employees.		Coolies.		Total.			
Europeans and Anglo-Indians.	Indians.	Europeans and Anglo-Indians.	Indians.	Europeans and Anglo-Indians	Indians.	Europeans and Anglo-Indians	Indians.	Europeans and Anglo-Indians	Indians.	Europeans and Anglo-Indians	Indians.	Europeans and Anglo-Indians	Indians.	Europeans and Anglo-Indians.	Indians.	Europeans and Anglo-Indians.	Indians.	Europeans and Anglo-Indians.	Indians.
1	2	3	4	5	6	7	8	9	10	11	12	13	14	15	16	17	18	19	20
42	20	262	1,087	21	5,575	...	16,211	325	22,902	...	77	...	474	...	3,914	...	4,465	325	27,367

6 (b).—NUMBER OF PERSONS EMPLOYED IN THE POST OFFICE AND TELEGRAPH DEPARTMENT ON THE 26TH. FEBRUARY, 1931.

Supervising Officers, (including Probationery Superintendents and Inspectors of Post Offices and Assistants and Deputy Superintendents of Telegraphs and all officers of higher rank than these).				Postmasters, including Deputy, Assistant, Sub and Branch Postmasters.				Signalling establishment, including warrent officers, non-Commissioned officers, military telegraphists and other employees.				Miscellaneous Agents, School masters, Station Masters, etc.				Clerks of all kinds.				Postmen.				Skilled labour establishment, including foremen, instrument makers, carpenters, blacksmiths, mechanics, sub-inspectors, linemen and line-riders and other employees.			
Post Office.		Telegraph Department.		Post Office.		Telegraph Department.		Post Office.		Telegraph Department.		Post Office.		Telegraph Department.		Post Office.		Telegraph Department.		Post Office.		Telegraph Department.		Post Office.		Telegraph Department.	
Europeans and Anglo-Indians.	Indians.	Europeans and Anglo-Indians.	Indians.	Europeans and Anglo-Indians.	Indians.	Europeans and Anglo-Indians.	Indians.	Europeans and Anglo-Indians.	Indians.	Europeans and Anglo-Indians.	Indians.	Europeans and Anglo-Indians.	Indians.	Europeans and Anglo-Indians.	Indians.	Europeans and Anglo-Indians.	Indians.	Europeans and Anglo-Indians.	Indians.	Europeans and Anglo-Indians.	Indians.	Europeans and Anglo-Indians.	Indians.	Europeans and Anglo-Indians.	Indians.	Europeans and Anglo-Indians.	Indians.
1	2	3	4	5	6	7	8	9	10	11	12	13	14	15	16	17	18	19	20	21	22	23	24	25	26	27	28
2	10	...	...	1	240	...	...	...	...	1	5	...	283	...	...	...	238	...	...	...	598	...	...	...	...	...	69

6 (b).—NUMBER OF PERSONS EMPLOYED IN THE POST OFFICE AND TELEGRAPH DEPARTMENT ON THE 26TH. FEBRUARY, 1931.—*Concluded.*

Unskilled labour establishment, including line coolies, cable guards, batterymen, telegraph messengers, peons, and other employees.				Road establishment consisting of overseers, runners, clerks and booking agents, boatmen, syces, coachmen, bearers and others.				Railway Mail Service.												Combined Offices.				Total.	
Post Office.		Telegraph Department.		Post Office.		Telegraph Department.		Supervising officers including Superintendents and Inspectors of Sorting.		Clerks of all kinds.		Sorters.		Mail guards, mail agents, Van peons, Porters, etc.		Messengers.		Other servants.		Signallers.		Messengers and other servants.			
Europeans and Anglo-Indians.	Indians.	Europeans and Anglo-Indians.	Indians.	Europeans and Anglo-Indians.	Indians.	Europeans and Anglo-Indians.	Indians.	Europeans and Anglo-Indians.	Indians.	Europeans and Anglo-Indians.	Indians.	Europeans and Anglo-Indians.	Indians.	Europeans and Anglo-Indians.	Indians.	Europeans and Anglo-Indians.	Indians.	Europeans and Anglo-Indians.	Indians.	Europeans and Anglo-Indians.	Indians.	Europeans and Anglo-Indians.	Indians.	Europeans and Anglo-Indians.	Indians.
29	30	31	32	33	34	35	36	37	38	39	40	41	42	43	44	45	46	47	48	49	50	51	52	53	54
...	173	...	5	...	330	...	...	...	2	...	7	...	76	...	78	...	...	...	...	...	20	...	114	4	2,238

APPENDIX.

A Note on disappearing Industries.

In these days of Railways, Motors and Aeroplanes, it is difficult to imagine what Rajputana must have been like even fifty years ago. In 1881 the only Railway in existence was the main line through Abu Road to Bandikui, Delhi and Agra, with a branch line from Rutlam to Ajmer, a total length of under 600 miles, whereas Main and Branch lines now open to traffic exceed 2,900 miles in length A glance at any map will show the long and weary journeys, usually on camels, that were necessitated to reach such places as Jodhpur, Bikaner, Udaipur and Kotah, to mention only a few. In the North, especially the sandy nature of the country rendered the use of wheeled vehicles almost out of the question. It does not therefore need a very vivid imagination to realise how dependent the people had to be on their own products. Apart from the supply of food which, on account of scanty and varying rainfall, was always precarious, their every day needs such as cloth, utensils, arms, etc., had mostly to be prepared locally. In the course of time railways have extended and there are now few parts (excluding Jaisalmer State) which are much more than 50 miles from a Station. Home woven cloth has been replaced by mill made textiles and other local industries have similarly been ousted by cheaper goods produced by machinery.

The following is a list of local industries that are known to have flourished at one time or another in various States:—

Bharatpur.— Fly whisks and fans of ivory and sandalwood.

Bikaner.— Woollen fabrics, carpets and leathern vessels of camel hide.

Jaipur.— Dyed and stamped cotton cloths, gold enamel work, felt rugs, lacquer work and stone and marble carving.

Jaisalmer.— Blankets of sheeps wool, bags of goat and camel hair and stone cups and platters.

Kishangarh.—Black mineral paint, chintzes, coloured cloths and vessels made from *Khas Khas* grass.

Kotah.— Muslins, silver table ornaments, embroidered elephant and horse trappings and inlaid work on ivory.

Marwar.— Weaving, brass and ivory work, lacquer and marble toys, felt rugs, saddles and bridles, camel trappings and millstones.

Mewar.— Swords, daggers, cotton cloths printed in gold and silver and leathern jars.

Partabgarh.— Metal filigree on glass.

Shahpura.— Weaving and stamping.

Sirohi.— Swords, daggers, spears, knives and bows.

Tonk.— Cotton weaving, felt rugs, saddle cloths, musical instruments and pen cases carved in wood and inlaid with ivory.

A questionnaire was prepared and issued to each State asking for certain definite information concerning the present condition of each industry and the reasons, if any, for its decay. The following paragraphs contain a summary of the replies received.

Weaving.

Reza or homespun cotton weaving is still carried on in most parts of the country but except in very isolated tracts such as Jaisalmer, mill made cloth has largely supplanted it as an article for wear by men. A finer quality of cotton weaving is still found in Tonk State but it only satisfies local needs and is gradually disappearing on account of foreign competition

Chaukhana and *Doria* weaving is carried on by Julahas and Kolis in Kotah City and although finished articles find their way to other parts of India, foreign competition is responsible for the declining state of this industry. Weaving in wool and the production of woollen blankets known as *lohis* was once a thriving industry in parts of Marwar, Bikaner and Jaipur and was carried out by Bambhis, Raigars, Chamars, Khatiks and Kolis. Although there is still a moderate local demand for these articles, mill made blankets are gradually supplanting them.

Goat and Camel hair.

Bags and sacks made from goat and camel hair are still produced in the rural areas of Jaisalmer and Marwar by Kamnigars, Bhils, Jatiyas, Raigars and Bambhis. They were at one time in great demand for carrying grain on camels but the machine made gunny bag now so common all over the country is responsible for a falling off in this industry. Camel hair carpets were made in Marwar by Jatiyas and Bambhis for local use. The industry is however on the decline as cotton carpets or Durries are available at cheaper prices.

Dyeing and Calico Printing.

Dyeing and printing by means of stamps on various kinds of cloth are still to be found in many parts of the Agency notably Shahpura, Sanganer (Jaipur) and Pipar (Marwar). Of these perhaps the best known is the muslin and calico printing of Sanganer. The Aman-i-Shah river which flows by the town is said to have possessed some peculiar properties favourable to the dyeing process which it has now lost. The truth however probably is that cheap foreign imitations have deprived this well known industry of its former prosperity. In Shahpura the finished article is known to Europeans in the form of chair covers and curtains. The stamps are made of wood and the dye is fast. Dyed and stamped cloth is in demand for floor cloths and women's skirts and each caste such as Jats and Gujars appear to have their own distinctive patterns. Here again mill made products have had an unfavourable effect on this industry but lately there is said to have been a slight revival and it now stands at about a quarter of its former prosperity. Another form of this industry is tying and dyeing on silk and cotton and is found in Jodhpur and Jaipur cities and parts of Kotah. The finished articles are sometimes very beautiful and are in demand as shawls, *saris*, scarves, etc.

Stamping on cloth in gold and silver.

This is another form of stamping and was once a prosperous industry in Jaipur City and in some towns in Mewar. It is said to be languishing in Jaipur for want of a market but to be flourishing in Mewar.

Felt.

Felt is made up in the form of rugs and hoods in Tonk and parts of Jaipur and Marwar. A certain amount of trade goes on in rugs but the use of the material as a protection against rain is diminishing.

Leather work.

Vessels of camel hide, often ornamented on the outside, are a production peculiar to Bikaner State. The persons engaged are Dabgars by caste and the industry is a rural one subsidiary to agriculture. The demand for these vessels is now not more than local though some specimens find their way into the hands of tourists. Jars made of leather are also prepared by Dabgars in parts of Mewar but tin vessels from outside are said to be ousting the leather ones and the industry is rapidly diminishing.

Stone.

Utensils such as cups and platters are made in Jaisalmer town and find their way into the hands of pilgrims and travellers. Their extreme weight militates against their exportation as an economic proposition. Mill stones are made in parts of Marwar and in the village of Bhadasar in Jaisalmer both for local use and export. The industry is not prosperous owing to the advent of oil engines for grinding purposes. On the other hand carving in stone is still a prosperous industry in Jaipur and Tonk and purchasers are readily found in distant parts of India. In Jaipur this carving takes the form of busts and images of gods, etc., and it is said that with proper organisation and capital the industry could flourish to a greater extent than it does at present.

Metal filigree on glass.

This peculiar industry deserves mention for it is confined to Partabgarh town and is a secret in the hands of a few families. The work is usually done in gold on blue or green glass and the appearance of the finished article is a fretwork of gold let into the glass.

Saddlery.

At one time the manufacture of saddles was a prosperous industry in parts of Marwar but owing to outside competition and the diminished use of the horse as a means of conveyance, the industry is now practically defunct. Embroidered trappings for elephants and horses were formerly produced in Kotah State but the industry is now said to have died out.

Arms.

The manufactures of swords, daggers, spears, knives, etc., was once a thriving industry in many parts of Rajputana. Tod in his Annals wrote that the "sword blades of Sirohi are as famed among the Rajputs as those of Damascus among the Persians and Turks." The water in a certain locality was said to have wonderful properties for the purpose of tempering. Owing to foreign competition and the increasing demand for modern fire arms, the industry is not flourishing though in Mewar, the demands of tourists assist in keeping the trade alive.

The foregoing remarks conclude a brief survey of industries that at one time flourished in the Agency. In addition, there were and are certain manufactures which more strictly come within the category of Arts such as articles of jewellery, brass work, toys, lacquer, etc. The economic condition of these fluctuates, an important factor being the demand from tourists, etc.

DIAGRAM SHOWING THE PROGRESS OF LITERACY DURING THE PAST DECADE

PER THOUSAND MALES
AGED 5 AND OVER

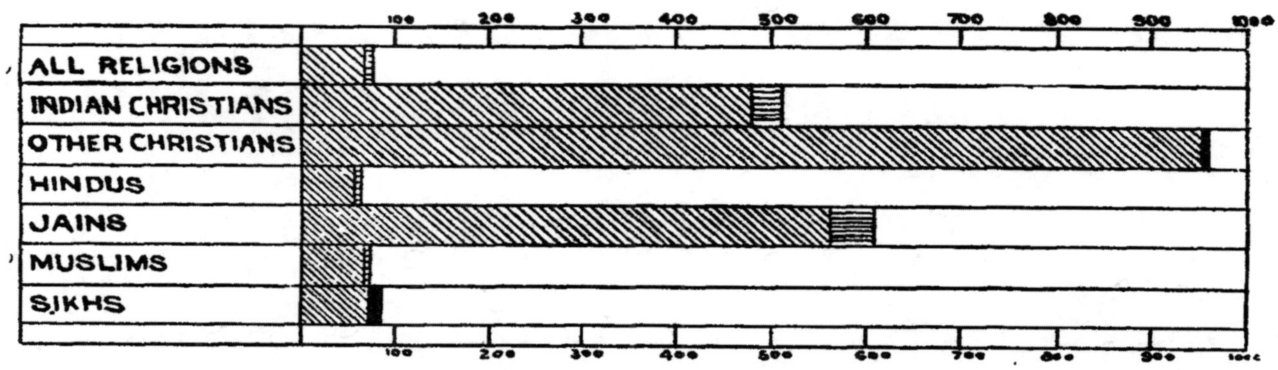

PER THOUSAND FEMALES
AGED 5 AND OVER

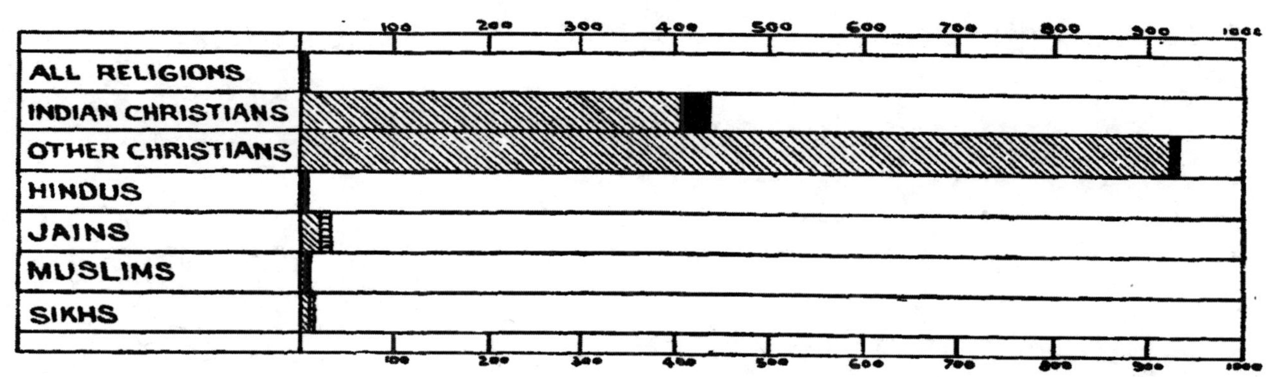

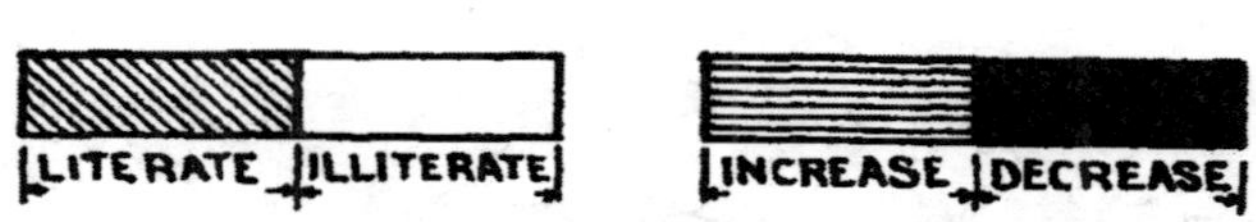

	MALES		FEMALES	
	1931	1921	1931	1921
ALL RELIGIONS	76	68	6	5
INDIAN CHRISTIANS	508	478	403	435
OTHER CHRISTIANS	955	959	927	932
HINDUS	62	56	4	3
JAINS	607	562	32	23
MUSLIMS	71	66	7	9
SIKHS	70	84	14	9

CHAPTER IX.

Literacy.

1. The information concerning literacy was recorded in columns 16 and 17 of the General Schedule. The heading to column 16 was "literate or illiterate" and the definition of literacy was the ability to write a letter and read the answer to it. It was optional for any State to record the language in which each person claimed to be literate, but the results were not compiled for the Agency as a whole. The heading to column 17 was "whether able to read and write English" and as this was also to include an ability to speak and understand it, the instructions to the staff required no further amplification. There was little scope for error in this simple enquiry and the results may be taken as representing the true standard of literacy, or rather of the lack of it, amongst the population as a whole. **The meaning of the statistics.**

The results are set forth in Imperial Tables as follows:—

XIII-A.—By age, sex and each religion in the Agency.

XIII-B.—By age, sex and selected religions in each State.

XIII-C.—By age and sex in each City.

XIV.— Literacy among selected castes of certain localities.

Provincial Table II.—Literacy by sex and religion in Administrative Units in each State. Hindus are further sub-divided into Brahmans, Depressed castes and others.

At the end of this Chapter will be found six Subsidiary Tables dealing with the results in analytical detail.

2. The following statement shows the general standard at present prevailing in the Agency and some comparison with the figures obtained in 1921:— **Summary of the statistics.**

GENERAL SUMMARY OF FIGURES FOR LITERACY.

Population 1931 (000's omitted).		Number of literates (000's omitted).		Increase in population per cent. since 1921.		Increase in literates per cent. since 1921.	
Males.	Females.	Males.	Females.	Males.	Females.	Males.	Females.
5,885	5,341	382	26	13·5	14·6	22·0	35·5

The figures give a general indication that literacy has increased at a rate higher than that for the population. If persons under 5 years of age are excluded, male literates per 1,000 males have risen from 68 to 76 in the decade. Similarly the increase among female literates is from 5 to 6 per 1,000 females. In other words, at ages of 5 and over, one male out of every 13 and one female out of every 167 are literate.

Literacy by religions.

3. The diagram at the commencement of this Chapter shows for each sex aged 5 and over the number of literates per 1,000 of each religion and a comparison with similar figures for 1921. Among the major religions, the Jains easily hold pride of place with a ratio of 607 for males and 32 for females. Next in order are Muslims with 71 males and 7 females and last are Hindus with 62-males and 4 females respectively. Among other and minor religions, Indian Christians have a high ratio of 512 males and 403 females which reflects much credit on the various Missions at work in the Agency.

The following statement shows a comparison between the population by religions, the number of literates in each and the variation since 1921 :—

SUMMARY OF FIGURES FOR LITERACY AT ALL AGES.

RELIGION.	POPULATION IN 1931 (000's OMITTED).		NUMBER OF LITERATES (000's OMITTED).		VARIATION IN POPULATION PER CENT. SINCE 1921.		VARIATION IN NUMBER OF LITERATES SINCE 1921.	
	Males.	Females.	Males.	Females.	Males.	Females.	Males.	Females.
Hindu.	5,030	4,549	268	16	+ 16·4	+ 18·2	+ 23·8	+ 43·8
Muslim.	566	503	34	3	+ 18·7	+ 18·8	+ 25·0	– ·16
Jain	146	155	76	4	+ 8·3	+ 6·9	+ 13·3	+ 46·7
Tribal.	115	114	...	...	– 52·8	– 51·9	– 73·7	+ 100·0
Sikh.	25	17	2	...	+ 389·1	+ 362·7	+ 308·4	+ 600·0
Christian.	3	3	2	1	+ 18·7	+ 16·5	+ 26·9	+ 12·6

The actual figures for literate persons of Tribal religions are 45 males and 2 females! The number of Sikh female literates is 196.

It will have been observed that the standard of literacy among Hindus is lower than that among the population as a whole. But as Hinduism easily predominates every other religion, it is interesting to note how the standard fluctuates when a distinction is drawn between Brahmans, Depressed castes and all other Hindus.

CATEGORY.	POPULATION IN 1931 (000's OMITTED).		NUMBER OF LITERATES (000's OMITTED).		VARIATION IN POPULATION PER CENT. SINCE 1921.		VARIATION IN NUMBER OF LITERATES PER CENT. SINCE 1921.	
	Males.	Females.	Males.	Females.	Males.	Females.	Males.	Females.
Brahmans.	442	413	89	5	+ 10·4	+ 11·5	+ 31·8	+ 47·6
Depressed castes.	805	760	6	...	} Not	ava	ilab	le
Other Hindus.	3,782	3,377	172	11				

The actual number of female literates among Depressed castes is only 292. As this is the first Census at which a distinction has been drawn between Depressed and other Hindus, it is regretted that figures for variations since 1921 are not available. The ratio per mille for male Brahmans is 202 while that for all other Hindu males, excluding Depressed castes, is 46. The number of literates per 1,000 males of Depressed castes is 7.

Literacy among selected castes.

4. Imperial Table XIV shows the figures for literacy among 18 castes selected from certain localities as representing every stratum of society. Ages have been unadjusted and no figures for those under the age of 7 have been included. The marginal statement shows the standard among the various castes selected. If we apply a classification of Advanced (50 per cent. and over), Intermediate (over 10 per cent.) and Illiterate (under 10 per cent.), it will be seen that only the trading castes of Agarwal and Oswal come into the Advanced, Brahmans into the Intermediate and all others into the Illiterate category. With the possible exception of other trading castes and Kayasthas who are usually found in urban areas, it is probable that the large majority of the castes who are most numerous fail to reach a standard higher than 'Illiterate'.

CASTE.	LITERATE PER 1,000.	
	Males.	Females.
Brahman	237	14
Rajput	70	11
Sondhia	11	...
Agarwal	506	19
Oswal	649	26
Jat	12	1
Gujar	8	...
Ahir	14	...
Khati	34	1
Kumhar	11	...
Rebari	6	...
Bhil	1	...
Grassia	8	...
Mina	10	...
Chamar	4	...
Bhangi	11	4
Khanzada	38	2
Meo	5	...

Literacy by age-periods.

5. Subsidiary Table 6 shows the progress per 1,000 of each sex made at each Census since 1901. The figures disclose a steady though slow advance in each decade for both sexes and may be summarised as follows:—

AGE-PERIOD.	MALES.		FEMALES.	
	1901.	1931.	1901.	1931.
10 and over	75	86	2	6
15—20	76	86	3	8
20 and over	83	96	2	6

Literacy in English.

6. The number of persons returned as being literate in English was 28,209 males and 1,686 females as compared with 15,393 males and 1,171 females in 1921. Among males the progress is somewhat marked as the following statement shows:—

AGE-PERIOD.	LITERATE IN ENGLISH PER 10,000.		
	1931.	1921.	1911.
All ages 5 and over	56	34	24
5–10	16	3	2
10–15	35	21	15
15–20	87	56	34
20 and over	66	42	29

Literacy in certain urban areas.

7. The following statement shows the extent to which literacy prevails in those towns and cities which are the Capitals of States when compared with the rest of the Agency:—

Population.	Proportion to total population.	Number of male literates.	Proportion to total male literates.	Number of female literates.	Proportion to total female literates.
661,207	5·9	89,105	23·4	10,587	41·5

It is to be regretted that figures are not available for all urban areas but the population of these Capitals is 42·5 per cent. of the total urban population and therefore it may be deduced that some 55 per cent. and 98 per cent. of all male and female literates respectively are town-dwellers.

Literacy in the States.

7. The acquisition of literacy being a matter of opportunity as well as of inclination and aptitude, it would be invidious to enter upon a detailed discussion of the figures for each State. Not all have equal opportunities for the development of educational programmes while some have large tracts inhabited by primitive tribes to whom education would make no appeal. A perusal however of the figures shown in Subsidiary Table 2 leads to a general conclusion that, other things being equal, a higher standard is usually found in the smaller States with compact boundaries than in larger ones with low density figures. As might be expected, the lowest standard usually prevails in those States in which primitive tribes form a large proportion of the population.

General conclusions.

8. The general conclusions that can be drawn from the facts set forth in this Chapter are, that the prevalence of literacy is markedly small; that the majority of literates are town-dwellers; that the Depressed classes and Primitive tribes are practically entirely illiterate; and that facilities for education appear to be undeveloped in most parts of rural areas in the Agency.

1.—LITERACY BY AGE, SEX AND RELIGION.

RELIGION.	NUMBER PER MILLE WHO ARE LITERATE.											NUMBER PER MILLE WHO ARE LITERATE IN ENGLISH AND ARE AGED 5 AND OVER.		
	All ages 5 and over.			5—10.		10—15.		15—20.		20 and over.				
	Total.	Males.	Females.	Males.	Females.	Males.	Females.	Males.	Females.	Males.	Females.	Total.	Males.	Females.
1	2	3	4	5	6	7	8	9	10	11	12	13	14	15
All Religions ...	**43**	**76**	**6**	**23**	**3**	**43**	**5**	**86**	**8**	**96**	**6**	**3**	**6**	...
Christian ...	610	649	563	462	369	557	492	698	578	711	632	402	424	377
(a) Indian ...	463	512	403	354	254	462	370	605	450	559	450	198	226	168
(b) Others ...	942	955	927	844	747	959	901	962	855	971	979	866	867	864
Hindu ...	35	62	4	19	2	35	4	71	6	79	5	3	5	...
Jain ...	310	607	32	208	20	391	33	708	43	780	32	10	20	...
Muslim ...	42	71	7	20	4	37	7	79	10	92	8	4	7	...
Sikh ...	48	70	14	15	6	29	15	64	26	93	14	9	15	...
Tribal ...	...	...	...	...	...	...	...	...	...	1	...	...	...	...
Zoroastrian ...	834	895	762	538	538	889	417	818	818	948	831	473	608	815

2.—LITERACY BY AGE, SEX AND LOCALITY.

AGENCY, STATE OR DISTRICT.	NUMBER PER MILLE WHO ARE LITERATE.										
	All ages 5 and over.			5—10.		10—15.		15—20.		20 and over.	
	Total.	Males.	Females.	Males.	Females.	Males.	Females.	Males.	Females.	Males.	Females.
1	2	3	4	5	6	7	8	9	10	11	12
Rajputana ...	**43**	**76**	**6**	**23**	**3**	**43**	**5**	**86**	**8**	**96**	**6**
Abu District ...	208	267	110	144	104	209	108	265	97	300	115
Alwar ...	42	74	5	22	3	40	4	81	7	94	5
Banswara ...	27	50	3	12	1	24	2	56	4	71	4
Bharatpur ...	53	91	8	33	5	60	9	106	13	110	7
Bikaner ...	50	85	9	27	4	51	8	95	13	106	9
Bundi ...	30	52	4	13	2	24	3	52	4	69	4
Dholpur ...	41	69	6	19	3	39	5	77	10	86	7
Dungarpur ...	31	59	3	21	2	37	3	72	4	76	3
Jaipur ...	42	74	5	20	3	38	4	83	7	94	6
Jaisalmer ...	31	53	2	8	...	22	1	58	3	73	2
Jhalawar ...	76	128	19	76	20	114	26	149	23	138	16
Karauli ...	45	77	5	18	2	38	4	93	9	100	6
Kishangarh ...	67	120	9	40	5	71	7	132	10	150	11
Kotah ...	52	91	9	42	6	69	11	112	18	103	8
Kushalgarh (Chiefship) ...	26	48	4	16	3	29	5	63	7	64	4
Lawa (Estate) ...	39	65	11	11	...	32	...	75	8	87	16
Marwar ...	45	80	6	24	3	46	5	92	7	102	6
Mewar ...	35	65	3	15	1	31	2	69	3	88	3
Partabgarh ...	70	124	12	39	5	70	8	138	17	168	14
Shahpura ...	59	104	10	46	9	77	13	121	15	123	8
Sirohi ...	54	95	9	38	6	64	9	105	11	118	9
Tonk ...	21	39	2	6	...	13	1	38	2	54	3
Cities ...	**169**	**278**	**39**	**111**	**26**	**204**	**43**	**327**	**53**	**316**	**38**

3.—LITERACY BY RELIGION, SEX AND LOCALITY.

AGENCY, STATE OR DISTRICT.	NUMBER PER MILLE WHO ARE LITERATE.									
	CHRISTIAN.		HINDU.		JAIN.		MUSLIM.		TRIBAL.	
	Males.	Females.	Males.	Females.	Males	Females.	Males.	Females.	Males.	Females.
1	2	3	4	5	6	7	8	9	10	11
Rajputana ...	**649**	**563**	**62**	**4**	**607**	**32**	**71**	**7**	...	...
Abu District ...	892	795	206	81	875	383	367	69	...	...
Alwar ...	...	...	88	5	703	60	23	1	...	...
Banswara ...	192	250	48	4	675	38	285	7	...	...
Bharatpur ...	154	177	97	7	736	90	46	7	...	...
Bikaner ...	514	468	81	8	541	39	41	4	...	...
Bundi ...	...	...	43	3	475	17	48	8	...	...
Dholpur ...	...	...	64	5	313	31	109	16	...	...
Dungarpur ...	...	...	81	2	671	23	336	6	...	...
Jaipur ...	913	730	66	4	621	44	72	9	3	2
Jaisalmer ...	...	...	71	2	375	...	4	1	...	...
Jhalawar ...	...	...	97	13	672	126	303	51	...	...
Karauli ...	...	...	74	4	765	116	102	10	...	...
Kishangarh ...	...	...	100	7	761	74	124	9	...	...
Kotah ...	684	678	79	7	678	95	165	17	1	...
Kushalgarh (Chiefship).	...	...	28	2	777	75	276	12	...	...
Lawa (Estate) ...	...	...	37	11	644	19	20	...	...	...
Marwar ...	555	455	51	4	641	28	62	8	22	...
Mewar ...	613	229	40	2	559	15	171	12	...	...
Partabgarh ...	...	...	127	10	740	101	192	9	...	...
Shahpura ...	...	...	82	8	747	76	159	3	...	...
Sirohi ...	777	777	50	4	676	28	220	41	...	...
Tonk ...	...	...	21	...	320	18	105	7	...	...
Cities ...	**557**	**543**	**266**	**35**	**600**	**73**	**130**	**17**	**41**	...

NOTE.—Christian and Tribal Populations of under 100 persons in any individual State, etc., are excluded, but are included in the Totals for Rajputana and Cities.

The figures in this Table, except as regards Cities, are for persons of 5 years of age and over only. City figures are for the population irrespective of age.

4.—LITERACY IN ENGLISH BY AGE, SEX AND LOCALITY.

LITERATE IN ENGLISH PER 10,000.

Agency, State or District.	1931.										1921.										1911.										1901.	
	All ages 5 and over.		5—10.		10—15.		15—20.		20 and over.		All ages 5 and over.		5—10.		10—15.		15—20.		20 and over.		All ages 5 and over.		5—10.		10—15.		15—20.		20 and over.		All ages 5 and over.	
	Males.	Females.	Males.	Females.	Males.	Females.	Males.	Females.	Males.	Females.	Males.	Females.	Males.	Females.	Males.	Females.	Males.	Females.	Males.	Females.	Males.	Females.	Males.	Females.	Males.	Females.	Males.	Females.	Males.	Females.	Males.	Females.
1	2	3	4	5	6	7	8	9	10	11	12	13	14	15	16	17	18	19	20	21	22	23	24	25	26	27	28	29	30	31	32	33
Rajputana ...	**56**	**4**	**16**	**2**	**35**	**3**	**87**	**5**	**66**	**4**	**34**	**3**	**3**	**2**	**21**	**2**	**56**	**4**	**42**	**3**	**24**	**2**	**2**	**1**	**15**	**2**	**34**	**2**	**29**	**2**	**21**	**2**
Abu District ...	917	364	492	226	498	245	813	278	1,091	451	1,281	664	787	490	2,051	1,125	1,317	588	1,197	627	...	...	...	...	...	...	...	...	...	...	...	...
Alwar ...	54	2	13	...	33	1	88	2	63	2	32	2	5	...	22	2	51	3	38	2	23	1	...	...	4	2	18	1	34	1	20	1
Banswara ...	14	2	1	...	6	...	27	2	19	3	10	2	...	1	4	...	21	...	14	3	7	...	...	...	5	...	8	...	11	1	1	...
Bharatpur ...	54	4	12	1	35	4	80	5	64	4	26	2	2	1	12	2	34	5	34	2	32	2	2	...	22	...	60	3	36	3	22	1
Bikaner ...	93	4	29	2	64	4	138	5	108	4	46	2	2	...	29	2	79	1	57	2	27	1	...	...	17	...	47	...	30	1	12	1
Bundi ...	25	1	5	1	11	2	35	1	[illegible]	2	22	1	1	1	9	...	18	2	33	1	10	...	...	...	8	...	27	2	10	...	8	...
Dholpur ...	40	5	7	1	20	2	66	7	62	6	40	2	1	...	34	...	66	1	47	3	31	1	2	...	17	2	52	3	37	2	6	1
Dungarpur ...	16	1	3	...	8	1	27	3	20	1	10	...	1	...	3	...	12	...	17	...	7	...	...	...	3	...	9	2	10	...	3	...
Jaipur ...	57	6	16	4	31	5	86	7	69	6	39	5	7	4	26	4	54	6	48	5	25	3	4	2	19	3	37	2	29	3	13	2
Jaisalmer ...	20	...	2	...	4	...	26	...	28	...	8	...	...	...	7	...	...	...	11	...	10	...	...	...	8	...	17	3	11	...	5	...
Jhalawar ...	87	3	15	...	49	2	147	4	100	3	79	1	...	...	31	2	344	3	74	1	35	2	...	...	6	...	48	...	44	2	20	1
Karauli ...	21	2	1	1	8	3	28	3	29	1	10	...	...	...	1	...	11	...	15	1	14	...	...	...	9	...	16	...	17	...	6	1
Kishangarh ...	78	2	22	...	50	...	146	...	86	3	36	3	3	2	13	5	40	4	50	3	33	3	...	...	28	4	32	6	41	2	25	1
Kotah ...	59	4	10	1	35	3	105	6	67	4	38	4	3	...	21	1	71	2	47	6	28	1	1	1	12	1	29	1	28	1	9	...
Kushalgarh (Chiefship).	56	...	7	...	41	...	140	...	62	...	29	...	...	...	41	...	108	...	27	...	8	...	...	...	...	...	...	...	13	...	5	...
Lawa (Estate) ...	33	...	...	...	...	...	...	...	57	...	10	...	...	...	...	...	...	...	17	...	9	...	...	...	...	...	...	...	13	...	8	...
Marwar ...	75	3	28	1	59	3	118	6	85	3	41	2	3	1	25	1	81	2	52	2	25	1	1	1	13	1	35	2	31	1	42	1
Mewar ...	23	1	5	...	12	...	38	...	28	1	12	1	...	...	4	1	21	2	17	1	11	1	...	...	4	1	14	1	14	1	16	1
Partabgarh ...	73	2	5	2	27	2	127	5	95	2	30	...	...	...	34	...	111	...	44	...	24	...	...	...	8	...	44	...	29	...	10	...
Shahpura ...	95	5	17	6	108	7	222	4	88	4	78	1	...	...	89	4	187	6	81	1	36	...	...	...	56	...	56	7	39	...	28	1
Sirohi ...	85	19	20	14	50	20	106	24	110	20	59	16	17	15	24	12	66	27	83	15	109	29	41	24	98	48	102	37	129	27	95	30
Tonk ...	16	1	1	...	2	...	15	1	23	1	10	1	...	...	4	...	15	1	13	1	13	1	...	1	6	...	23	2	15	1	15	1

5.—LITERACY BY CASTE.

CASTE.	LOCALITY.	NUMBER PER 1,000 WHO ARE LITERATE. 1931 (7 AND OVER). Total.	Males.	Females.	NUMBER PER 10,000 WHO ARE LITERATE IN ENGLISH. 1931 (7 AND OVER). Total.	Males.	Females.
1	2	3	4	5	6	7	8
Brahman ...	Marwar and Mewar	128	237	14	142	274	4
Rajput ...	Jaipur, Marwar and Mewar	44	70	11	54	95	2
Sondhia ...	Jhalawar	6	11	...	...	...	...
Agarwal ...	Jaipur	263	506	19	104	204	3
Oswal ...	Marwar and Mewar	326	649	26	89	178	6
Ahir ...	Alwar	8	14	...	1	2	...
Gujar ...	Bharatpur and Jaipur	5	8	...	2	3	...
Jat ...	Bikaner, Jaipur and Marwar ...	7	12	1	9	15	...
Khati ...	Jaipur and Marwar	18	34	1	29	57	...
Kumhar ...	Jaipur	6	11	...	4	8	...
Rebari ...	Marwar and Sirohi	3	6	...	3	6	...
Bhil ...	Banswara and Dungarpur	...	1	...	...	...	...
Grassia ...	Sirohi	4	8	...	...	...	...
Mina ...	Alwar, Jaipur and Kotah	5	10	...	1	1	...
Bhangi ...	Jaipur and Marwar	7	11	4	4	7	...
Chamar ...	Bharatpur, Jaipur and Kotah ...	2	4	...	...	...	...
Khanzada ...	Alwar	21	38	2	20	39	...
Meo ...	Alwar and Bharatpur	3	5	...	...	...	...

6.—PROGRESS OF LITERACY SINCE 1901.

AGENCY, STATE OR DISTRICT.	NUMBER OF LITERATES PER MILLE.																							
	ALL AGES 10 AND OVER.								15—20.								20 AND OVER.							
	Males.				Females.				Males.				Females.				Males.				Females.			
	1931.	1921.	1911.	1901.	1931.	1921.	1911.	1901.	1931.	1921.	1911.	1901.	1931.	1921.	1911.	1901.	1931.	1921.	1911.	1901.	1931.	1921.	1911.	1901.
1	2	3	4	5	6	7	8	9	10	11	12	13	14	15	16	17	18	19	20	21	22	23	24	25
Rajputana ...	**86**	**81**	**79**	**75**	**6**	**5**	**3**	**2**	**86**	**80**	**71**	**76**	**8**	**7**	**4**	**3**	**96**	**90**	**88**	**83**	**6**	**5**	**3**	**2**
Abu District ...	282	314	...	...	111	125	...	...	265	311	...	...	97	101	...	...	300	317	...	...	115	120	...	...
Alwar ...	83	78	64	68	5	3	2	2	81	105	46	68	7	4	2	2	94	82	77	76	5	3	2	2
Banswara ...	59	61	70	50	4	4	3	2	56	55	59	46	4	8	3	3	71	69	79	56	4	4	4	2
Bharatpur ...	101	75	72	55	8	5	4	1	106	72	91	48	18	8	6	2	110	81	74	60	7	5	4	1
Bikaner ...	95	87	71	59	9	7	3	2	95	84	62	56	18	10	8	1	106	98	78	67	9	7	4	3
Bundi ...	59	74	61	55	4	5	2	1	52	65	46	52	4	8	2	1	69	87	67	64	4	5	2	1
Dholpur ...	77	61	46	34	7	5	3	1	77	58	43	32	10	8	5	1	86	66	50	39	7	5	3	1
Dungarpur ...	67	79	77	79	3	10	4	1	72	82	60	61	4	11	6	1	76	87	85	99	3	10	4	10
Jaipur ...	83	82	79	59	6	5	3	1	83	72	71	57	7	6	4	2	94	93	89	66	6	5	3	1
Jaisalmer ...	62	59	75	70	2	2	3	2	58	49	65	70	3	6	3	2	73	68	86	88	2	2	4	2
Jhalawar ...	136	137	91	78	19	17	7	2	149	164	90	62	23	31	9	3	138	138	95	91	16	13	7	2
Karauli ...	88	75	61	58	6	4	3	2	93	74	46	47	9	4	3	2	100	83	72	61	6	4	3	2
Kishangarh ...	134	105	107	101	10	6	6	5	132	103	105	91	10	6	9	2	150	116	113	115	11	6	6	7
Kotah ...	99	94	74	85	9	8	3	1	112	102	71	30	13	12	5	1	103	99	79	40	8	8	3	1
Kushalgarh (Chiefship) ...	57	63	65	75	4	5	5	2	63	57	56	76	7	6	4	...	64	67	67	79	4	5	5	3
Lawa (Estate) ...	75	111	89	85	13	16	14	4	75	163	52	38	8	29	9	13	87	121	107	43	16	14	17	3
Marwar ...	91	88	94	118	6	6	4	4	92	86	83	132	7	7	4	5	102	101	103	124	6	6	4	4
Mewar ...	75	65	84	88	3	8	3	3	69	63	66	72	3	5	3	3	88	74	92	105	3	3	3	3
Partabgarh ...	142	149	123	100	13	12	5	1	138	144	115	99	17	15	7	2	163	162	131	114	14	11	5	1
Shahpura ...	115	139	121	115	10	10	5	4	121	142	113	96	15	12	4	4	123	144	128	133	8	10	4	5
Sirohi ...	106	101	129	153	9	9	9	7	105	117	115	130	11	14	12	7	118	110	138	174	9	9	9	7
Tonk * ...	45	52	58	75	2	3	1	3	38	44	60	53	2	4	3	3	54	61	80	89	3	3	2	3

* 1931 Figures include Chhabra, Pirawa and Sironj.

CHAPTER X.

Language.

Reference to statistics.

1. The entries pertaining to the language spoken by each individual were recorded on the General Schedules in column 14—"Mother Tongue"—and column 15—"other language in daily or domestic use", and the results are shown in Imperial Table XV—Parts I and II and in Provincial Table IV. Entries as regards Mother tongue presented no difficulty beyond complete ignorance of its name on the part of the average rustic. Detailed instructions as to the names of dialects found in particular localities had therefore to be issued for the benefit of the enumerating staff. The accuracy of the return was therefore very much in their hands and varied in proportion to the attention that was paid to the instructions issued for their benefit. At the end of this Chapter are three Subsidiary Tables which set forth some of the results in detail and in a folder at the end of this volume will be found a Linguistic map.

Mother tongues.

2. Rajasthani is the Mother tongue of 77 per cent. of the inhabitants of the Agency and it was therefore decided to adopt Sir George Grierson's classification and sub-divide it into four sub-languages—Marwari, Central Eastern Rajasthani, North Eastern Rajasthani and Malvi. With the exception of the first and last named, these terms are unknown to the general public and, for this reason, complete lists of dialects under each head were issued, the names of which were generally recognisable by educated persons. The other two Mother tongues of Western Hindi and Bhili spoken by some 15 and 6 per cent. respectively, presented no difficulty as a rule, although the meeting point of Western Hindi and the most eastern dialects of Rajasthani had, in some localities of Jaipur and Alwar, to be settled arbitrarily.

Distribution of the population by languages.

3. So far as main languages go, the statistics of this Census as shown in the margin disclose some remarkable variations from those of 1921. These are principally due to a better known dividing line between the four sub-languages that comprise Rajasthani. Errors that occurred in 1921 were the non-return of the Mewati dialect from Alwar and the substitution of Western Hindi as the principal Mother tongue of the State: also the classification of Vagdi, a dialect of Bhili in Banswara and Dungarpur, as Bagri of Marwari.

Language.	1931.	1921.
Marwari ...	501	472
Central Eastern Rajasthani ...	192	240
North Eastern Rajasthani ...	43	6
Malvi ...	31	33
Western Hindi ...	153	196
Bhili ...	64	43
	984	**990**
Panjabi ...	11	2
Gipsy ...	1	...
Gujarati ...	2	2
Sindhi ...	1	5
Others ...	1	1
Total speakers ...	**1,000**	**1,000**

Comparison with the Linguistic Survey.

4. The figures obtained at this Census compare on the whole favourably with those of the Linguistic Survey as the marginal statement shows. The Linguistic Survey figures take into insufficient account the extent to which Western Hindi is returned in all urban areas. Since all education is imparted in Hindi or Urdu the tendency is for these two languages to be returned as Mother tongues by those who are literate in them. The Survey assessed the entire population of Alwar State as speakers of Mewati, a dialect of North

Language.	1931 Census.	Linguistic Survey.
Marwari ...	5,618,885	5,663,680
Central Eastern Rajasthani ...	2,157,974	2,707,000
North Eastern Rajasthani ...	478,941	855,654
Malvi ...	350,856	191,584
Western Hindi ...	1,721,186	1,619,419
Bhili ...	719,640	927,800
Total speakers ...	**11,047,482**	**11,965,087**

Eastern Rajasthani, whereas more than 43 per cent. of the population returned Western Hindi as their Mother tongue. A portion of the State to the south and the south east adjoins the Hindi speaking State of Bharatpur and it would perhaps be more accurate to assume that 13 per cent. were properly returned as being speakers of Western Hindi. As regards Malvi, the Survey minimises the extent to which it is spoken in Kotah, Jhalawar and Tonk. The returns on this occasion being 297,625 from those States alone, as against the estimate of 191,534 and in addition, it was returned for more than half the population of Partabgarh which adjoins Malwa in Central India. The difference in the figures for Bhili is probably due to speakers of Malvi in southern Rajputana being reckoned in the Survey as speakers of Bhili. The general excess in the Survey figures may also be ascribed to an over estimate in the population as a whole.

Linguistic map.

5. The map shows the predominance of Rajasthani over the greater part of the Agency and the prevalence of Western Hindi in the east. As a rule, each State was taken as the unit for a rectangle but in those localities where two or more languages appeared to meet, separate rectangles are shown to represent smaller units such as Nizamats, etc. At the end of this Chapter will be found an Appendix amplifying in tabulated detail the information shown on the map.

Dialects.

6. It has been represented that the average Indian State in Rajputana is too large a unit for the purpose of tabulating returns of language. A Provincial Table (No. IV) has therefore been compiled and shows the distribution of dialects in administrative units of the States. It is thus possible to trace the localities in which dialects prevail and their meeting places with other dialects.

Marwari.

7. Including its standard form, Marwari has 19 dialects and is spoken in Marwar, Bikaner, Jaisalmer, Mewar, Sirohi, Shahpura, and northern and western Jaipur by 90 per cent. of the population of those areas. A large number have returned the standard form as their Mother tongue whereas it would in some instances have appeared more correctly among the minor dialects. In the non-Marwari speaking portions of the Agency, such speakers as have returned this Mother tongue, belong as a rule to the mercantile community and make a not inconsiderable addition to the number of speakers of the standard form.

The marginal statement of figures derived from Provincial Table IV shows a comparison with the Linguistic Survey. The variation in the number of speakers of the standard dialect has already been explained. Marwari-Dhundari is a loose term applied to a dialect on the borders of Jaipur and Marwar and the discrepancy is explained by the fact that the Survey recognises its speakers as belonging to Marwar only, while the Census figures disclose it as a prevailing dialect in parts of the Malpura and Sambhar Nizamats of western Jaipur. The dialect known as Gorawati appears to be unknown by that name in Kishangarh, whereas the Survey allots 15,000 speakers to that State and none to the neighbouring Nizamats of Marwar whence the Census derives its figures. Merwari is returned from those parts of Mewar which adjoin Ajmer-Merwara. The discrepancies in Khairari can be ascribed to the large return of Mewari speakers in those areas of Mewar which are really in the 'Kherar', a triangle of country where the four States of Jaipur, Mewar, Bundi and Tonk meet. Speakers of Godwari, Sirohi, Deorawati, Thali and Bikaneri have in most instances been wrongly included in the figures for the standard dialect. The very small locally recognised difference between Marwari-Sindhi

MARWARI.

DIALECT.		CENSUS OF 1931.	LINGUISTIC SURVEY.
Standard	...	2,573,438	1,591,160
Marwari-Dhundhari	...	197,377	49,300
Gorawati	...	7,901	15,000
Mewari	...	1,469,477	1,368,000
Merwari	...	10,016	...
Sarwari	...	19,154	15,000
Khairari	...	90,088	228,264
Godwari	...	17,441	147,000
Sirohi	...	8,719	177,300
Deorawati	...	908	86,000
Marwari-Gujarati	...	20,550	80,270
Thali	...	56,192	480,900
Marwari-Sindhi	...	47,786	131,960
Dhatki	...	121,415	150
Bikaneri	...	81,493	538,000
Shekhawati	...	701,714	483,017
Bagri	...	193,962	327,359
Total speakers	...	**5,617,561**	**5,663,680**

and Dhatki is shown in the totals of the two combined when compared with the corresponding totals of the Survey. Similarly, Shekhawati and Bagri, the dialects of adjoining areas in northern Jaipur and north eastern Bikaner, are correctly estimated when combined for comparison with corresponding totals of the Survey.

Central Eastern Rajasthani.

8. This sub-language is the name given to a group of dialects commonly found in central and southern Jaipur and the adjoining States of Bundi, Kotah, Tonk and Kishangarh. It has, according to the Survey and as shown in the margin, ten dialects but of these, Sipari is ascribed to the Shivpuri *pargana* of Gwalior and the Census only revealed 737 speakers in the adjoining portion of the Agency in Kotah. The Survey states that the Chaurasi dialect is spoken by no fewer than 182,133 persons in southern Jaipur, Lawa and the neighbouring portion of Tonk State. The name has apparently fallen into disuse as the Census returns only show 34 speakers, in spite of instructions as to the localities in which it might be expected to be found. As in the case of Marwari, the standard dialect (Jaipuri) has absorbed many speakers whose Mother tongue would have been more correctly returned as one or other of the minor dialects. The Survey estimated the population on the 1891 Census figures which are greater than those for the present Census. For instance, the Survey allots a population of 123,000 to Kishangarh speaking the three dialects of Kishangarhi, Sarwari (Marwari) and Gorawati (Marwari). The present total population is only 85,744 persons.

CENTRAL EASTERN RAJASTHANI.

DIALECT.	CENSUS OF 1931.	LINGUISTIC SURVEY.
Jaipuri ...	1,021,794	790,231
Torawati ...	264,025	342,554
Kathaira ...	43,943	127,957
Chaurasi ...	34	182,133
Nagarchal ...	51,623	71,675
Rajawati ...	80,771	173,449
Kishangarhi ...	63,614	93,000
Ajmeri ...	8,393	...
Harauti ...	623,011	926,101
Sipari ...	737	...
Total speakers.	**2,157,955**	**2,707,000**

North Eastern Rajasthani.

9. This sub-language with its attendant dialects is confined to Alwar, northern Bharatpur and the north east portion of Jaipur. It represents the Jaipuri dialect merging into the Braj Bhakha and Bangaru forms of Western Hindi and, as in all border languages, correct classification is difficult to obtain. The marginal statement of figures derived from Provincial Table IV shows a comparison with the Linguistic Survey. It has already been explained that the larger figures of the Survey are principally due to an over estimate of the speakers of one or other of the Mewati dialects in Alwar State.

NORTH EASTERN RAJASTHANI.

DIALECT.	CENSUS OF 1931.	LINGUISTIC SURVEY.
Mewati ...	247,293	253,800
Rathi ...	68,135	239,254
Nahera ...	66,377	169,300
Kather ...	63,398	193,300
Ahirwati ...	33,716	...
Total speakers.	**478,919**	**855,654**

Malvi.

10. This sub-language for which figures are shown in the margin represents Rajasthani merging into Bundeli on the one side and Gujarati on the other. It is extensively spoken in Central India and, in this Agency, is found in the adjoining portions of the States of Kotah, Jhalawar, Partabgarh and Tonk (Nimbahera and Chhabra). So far as Rajputana is concerned, only standard Malvi and Sondhwari are found. The discrepancies have already been discussed when dealing with the figures for Malvi as a whole.

MALVI.

DIALECT.	CENSUS OF 1931	LINGUISTIC SURVEY.
Malvi ...	286,894	104,978
Sondhwari ...	63,801	86,556
Total speakers	*** 350,695**	**191,534**

* Excludes a few speakers in Sirohi and Jaipur.

Western Hindi.

11. The dialects of this language that are found in rural areas of the

Agency are Braj Bhakha, Jadobati, Kalimal, Dangbhang and Dangi. The Linguistic Survey describes the four latter as sub-dialects of Braj Bhakha although local opinion denies that the latter has such a wide range. As an instance of this, the Bharatpur Census officials resolutely maintained that the *lingua franca* of the State was Hindi and that Braj Bhakha was only to be found in the Kumher Sub-tehsil which adjoins the Muttra District, the country known as Braj. The figures for dialects as shown in the margin therefore compare unfavourably with these shown in the Linguistic Survey. The figures represent those returned from the States of Dholpur and Bharatpur and from those portions of Jaipur, Alwar and Karauli which may be said to be Hindi speaking. The Linguistic map and Provincial Table IV, however, show quite clearly that the dividing line between Rajasthani and Western Hindi runs through Karauli, eastern Jaipur and Alwar: that Dholpur is entirely Hindi speaking and that, except in the north and north west, Bharatpur is also.

WESTERN HINDI.

DIALECT.	CENSUS OF 1931.	LINGUISTIC SURVEY.
Braj Bhakha (including Jadobati of Karauli)...	340,831	844,638
Kalimal ...	115,160	81,216
Dangbhang ...	140,937	80,363
Hindi ...	682,958	...
Dangi ...	...	108,766
Total speakers ...	**1,279,886**	**1,114,983**

Bhili.

12. The term Bhili is applied to a group of dialects spoken in the Aravalli range and its offshoots, from the south western corner of Ajmer-Merwara to the borders of Gujarat and Central India. So far as this Agency is concerned, the dialects are—Standard (or Bhilodi), Girasia, and Vagdi. The language is a definite link between Mewari and Gujarati and in Partabgarh, the Vagdi dialect appears to be a link between Mewari and Malvi. Bhilodi is an alternative name for the standard dialect and the terms together with Vagdi denote the mother tongue of the Bhil population wherever found except in the Sub-Aravallian portions of Bali (Marwar) and Sirohi where the dialect is known as Girasia. There are also many non-Bhil speakers of Vagdi in Banswara and Dungarpur.

Other Languages.

13. The number of speakers of Panjabi has increased during the past decade from 2 to 11 per mille of the population. This is entirely due to the opening of the Canal Colonies in Bikaner and the consequent flow of immigrants from the Punjab. Speakers of Sindhi have fallen from 5 to 1 per mille since 1921 and the reason is that many speakers of Sindhi in western Marwar and Jaisalmer have now been returned under 'Marwari-Sindhi' a dialect of Rajasthani.

Subsidiary Languages.

14. For the first time, a column was provided in the General Schedule at this Census in which to record "any other language in daily or domestic use". As was to be expected, the result was that the record was full of such entries as Marwari as Mother tongue and Hindi as a Subsidiary language. It was thereupon decided that all entries containing dialects of Rajasthani and Western Hindi as alternatives, were not to be treated as constituting true bilingualism. Similarly, bilingualism due to immigration such as would be shown for a Punjabi motor driver working in Jaipur, was not compiled. The record was therefore reduced to a compilation of entries for combinations of Rajasthani-Bhili-Sindhi-Gujarati-Panjabi in the north west, west and south west of the Agency in border tehsils. The results however were disappointing as will be seen from Imperial Table XV Part II and Subsidiary Table 2. No result was sufficiently large to show on the Linguistic map. The conclusion must therefore be drawn that no genuine bilingualism exists in the Agency. On pages 30 and 31 of Volume I Part I—Introductory—Linguistic Survey of India—Sir George Grierson writes:—

> "The identification of the boundaries of a language, or even of a language itself, is not always an easy matter. As a rule, unless they are separated by great ethnic differences or by some natural obstacle, such as a range of mountains or by a large river, Indian languages gradually merge into each other and are not separated by hard and fast boundary lines......For instance, near Bhatner (Hanumangarh in Bikaner State) there is spoken a mixture of Panjabi and Rajasthani. The Punjabis say that it is Rajasthani but the Rajputs (sic) say that it is Panjabi."

Again on page 87 of Volume IX Part II he writes:—

> "As we follow the southern boundary of Marwar where it marches with Palanpur, the Gujerati element is still stronger........Here the language is so mixed that while the Marwar people call it Gujerati, the Palanpur people (whose native language is Gujerati), call it Marwari. For want of a better name I call it Marwari-Gujerati."

1.—DISTRIBUTION OF TOTAL POPULATION BY MOTHER TONGUE ACCORDING TO CENSUS.

FAMILY AND LANGUAGE.	NUMBER OF SPEAKERS.		PER 100,000 OF POPULATION OF 1931.	WHERE CHIEFLY SPOKEN.
	1931.	1921.		
1	2	3	4	5
A.—Vernaculars of India.	*11,223,676*	*9,842,584*	*99,982*	
Tibeto-Chinese Family.				
Burmese	5	2	...	
Dravidian Family.				
Tamil	181	107	1	
Malayālam	4	7	...	
Kanarese	6	2	...	
Telugu	107	30	1	
Indo-European Family.				
Pashto	585	589	5	
Balochi	191	268	2	
Kashmīrī	11	81	...	
Sanskrit	1	...	...	
Lahndā or Western Panjábī ...	148	812	1	
Sindhi	12,840	55,182	114	Bikaner and Jaisalmer.
Marathī	2,433	1,775	22	
Konkani	11	...	...	
Oriyā	14	4	...	
Bihārī	2,425	2,548	22	
Bengali	818	605	7	
Assamese	3	...	...	
Eastern Hindī	1,715	...	15	
Western Hindī	1,721,186	1,927,796	15,333	Alwar, Bharatpur, Dholpur, Jaipur and Karauli.
Rajasthānī	8,606,659	7,392,689	76,669	Throughout the Agency.
Gujarātī	20,064	18,002	179	Dungarpur, Kotah, Mewar and Sirohi.
Bhilí	719,640	421,487	6,411	Banswara, Dungarpur, Kushalgarh, Mewar, Partabgarh and Sirohi.
Khāndesī	85	2	1	
Panjābī	125,149	19,769	1,115	
Central Pahārī	51	507	...	
Eastern Pahārī or Nepāli ...	245	235	2	
Pahārī Unspecified	383	...	3	
Unclassed Languages.				
Gipsy Languages	8,766	185	78	
B.—Vernaculars of other Asiatic countries and Africa.	**127**	*73*	*1*	
Indo-European Family.				
Persian	99	58	1	
Tibeto-Chinese Family.				
Chinese	...	2	...	
Semitic Family.				
Arabic	16	9	...	
Hebrew	1	8	...	
Mongolian Family.				
Turkish	7	1	...	
Languages not returned.				
Languages not returned ...	4	...	...	
C.—European Languages	*1,909*	*1,727*	*17*	
Indo-European Family.				
English	1,822	1,677	16	
Other European Languages ...	87	50	1	

2.—DISTRIBUTION BY LANGUAGE OF THE POPULATION OF EACH STATE OR DISTRICT.

NUMBER PER 10,000 OF THE POPULATION SPEAKING—

DISTRICT OR STATE.	RAJASTHANI.					WESTERN HINDI.	BHILI.			SINDHI.		GIPSY.	PANJABI.		GUJARATI.			OTHERS.
	As Mother Tongue only.	As Subsidiary to Bhili.	As Subsidiary to Gujarati.	As Subsidiary to Sindhi.	As Subsidiary to Panjabi.	As Mother Tongue only.	As Mother Tongue only.	As Subsidiary to Rajasthani.	As Subsidiary to Gujarati.	As Mother Tongue only.	As Subsidiary to Rajasthani.	As Mother Tongue only.	As Mother Tongue only.	As Subsidiary to Rajasthani.	As Mother Tongue only.	As Subsidiary to Rajasthani.	As Subsidiary to Bhili.	As Mother Tongue only.
1	2	3	4	5	6	7	8	9	10	11	12	13	14	15	16	17	18	19
Abu District ...	2,438	...	...	...	...	4,896	1,999	...	...	...	...	...	...	...	...	...	...	1,167
Alwar ...	5,654	...	...	...	...	4,840	...	...	...	...	...	...	...	...	...	...	...	6
Banswara ...	122	...	...	...	...	28	9,810	4	4	...	...	10	...	...	21	...	...	1
Bharatpur ...	1,837	...	...	...	...	8,650	...	...	...	...	...	...	...	...	...	...	...	13
Bikaner ...	8,414	...	...	...	8	152	...	...	...	94	...	44	1,285	1	3	...	...	4
Bundi ...	9,839	...	...	...	...	63	7	...	...	...	...	...	...	...	...	...	...	91
Dholpur ...	28	...	...	...	...	9,864	...	...	...	...	...	...	...	...	...	...	...	108
Dungarpur ...	143	...	...	...	...	111	9,539	...	...	...	...	...	1	...	96	...	105	5
Jaipur ...	8,533	...	...	...	...	1,447	...	...	...	...	...	...	...	...	...	...	...	20
Jaisalmer ...	9,475	...	...	2	...	1	1	...	...	493	...	...	3	...	9	...	...	16
Jhalawar ...	5,838	...	...	...	...	4,505	21	...	...	...	...	...	...	...	...	...	...	136
Karauli ...	49	...	...	...	...	9,941	...	...	...	...	...	...	...	...	...	...	...	10
Kishangarh ...	9,963	...	...	...	...	20	...	...	...	...	...	...	...	...	...	...	...	17
Kotah ...	8,886	...	...	...	...	1,057	1	...	...	...	...	...	...	...	...	...	...	56
Kushalgarh (Chiefship) ...	700	...	4	...	...	236	8,740	...	...	1	...	204	1	...	111	...	...	3
Lawa (Estate) ...	9,982	...	...	...	...	14	...	...	...	...	...	...	...	...	...	...	...	4
Marwar ...	9,835	...	2	...	...	29	80	...	...	1	46	...	2	...	1	2	...	2
Mewar ...	8,764	2	2	...	...	51	1,101	15	...	...	...	10	4	...	41	...	...	10
Partabgarh ...	5,902	17	...	...	...	176	3,487	...	...	...	...	177	...	...	116	...	...	35
Shahpura ...	9,982	...	...	...	...	13	...	...	...	...	...	...	...	...	...	...	...	5
Sirohi ...	8,200	103	55	...	...	207	1,288	2	8	1	...	...	4	...	89	6	13	29
Tonk ...	8,750	...	...	...	...	1,246	2	...	...	...	...	...	...	...	...	...	...	2

NOTE.—The population speaking Sindhi, Gipsy, Panjābī, and Gujarātī in all the States and Abu District except in Banswara, Bikaner, Dungarpur, Jaisalmer, Kushalgarh, Marwar, Mewar, Partabgarh and Sirohi States being very small their figures have been included in 'others' for the purpose of calculating proportions.

3.—COMPARISON OF TRIBE AND LANGUAGE TABLES.

TRIBE AND LANGUAGE.	STRENGTH OF TRIBE—TABLE XVII.			NUMBER SPEAKING TRIBAL LANGUAGE ONLY.	NUMBER SPEAKING TRIBAL LANGUAGE AND SOME OTHER LANGUAGE.	REMARKS.
	Persons.	Males.	Females.			
1	2	3	4	5	6	7
Bhil (including Grassia)—Bhili.	684,878	347,836	337,042	713,464	5,266	Column 5 includes Non-Bhil speakers of the Bhili language.

APPENDIX TO CHAPTER X.—LANGUAGE.

LEGEND OF DETAIL SHOWN ON THE LINGUISTIC MAP.

(Scale of the Map approximately equals 1" = 24 Miles).

STATE OR SUB-DIVISION.	TOTAL SPEAKERS	SPEAKERS OF—					
		Rajasthani.	Western Hindi.	Bhili.	Sindhi.	Panjabi.	Gujarati.
1	2	3	4	5	6	7	8
Alwar ...	740,301	423,913 *57*	325,388 *43*	...	...	...	...
Banswara ...	223,658	2,837 *1*	...	220,821 *99*	...	...	...
Bharatpur							
(a) Nagar, Pahari and Kaman	120,886	60,627 *50*	60,259 *50*	...	...	...	...
(b) Remainder ...	865,449	4,494 *1*	860,955 *99*	...	...	...	...
Bikaner							
(a) Suratgarh and Ganganagar	241,555	111,749 *46*	6,494 *3*	...	2,785 *1*	120,527 *50*	...
(b) Remainder ...	689,907	676,105 *98*	7,754 *1*	...	6,048 *1*	...	...
Bundi ...	213,225	213,225 *100*	...	...	...	...	...
Dholpur ...	251,520	...	251,520 *100*	...	...	...	...
Dungarpur ...	224,889	3,260 *1·5*	...	219,444 *97·5*	...	...	2,185 *1*
Jaipur							
(a) Sawai Madhopur, Gangapur and Hindaun ...	462,611	117,041 *25*	345,570 *75*	...	...	...	...
(b) Remainder ...	2,163,966	2,128,775 *98 5*	35,191 *1 5*	...	...	...	...
Jaisalmer ...	76,026	72,249 *95*	...	...	3,777 *5*	...	...
Jhalawar							
(a) Chhaoni and Patan ...	29,377	211	29,166 *100*	...	...	...	...
(b) Remainder ...	76,817	57,379 *75*	19,438 *25*	...	...	...	...
Karauli ...	139,700	...	139,700 *100*	...	...	...	...
Kishangarh ...	85,428	85,428 *100*	...	...	...	...	...
Kotah ...	681,907	609,438 *89*	72,469 *11*	...	...	...	...
Kushalgarh ...	33,984	2,489 *7*	...	31,085 *92*	...	...	410 *1*
Marwar							
(a) Bali ...	114,053	106,975 *94*	...	7,078 *6*	...	...	...
(b) Jalore and Jaswantpura	266,214	256,377 *96*	...	9,837 *4*	...	...	...
(c) Remainder ...	1,737,843	1,737,843 *100*	...	...	...	...	...
Mewar							
(a) Girwa ...	121,483	98,112 *81*	...	23,371 *19*	...	...	...
(b) Kherwara ...	72,108	* 10,562 *15*	...	61,546 *85*	...	...	...
(c) Magra ...	96,817	35,516 *37*	...	61,301 *63*	...	...	...
(d) Remainder ...	1,257,908	1,23,1366 *98*	...	26,542 *2*	...	...	...
Partabgarh ...	72,674	45,860 *63*	...	26,814 *37*	...	...	...
Shahpura ...	54,138	54,138 *100*	...	...	...	...	...
Sirohi and Abu ...	213,527	178,826 *84*	...	† 31,303 *15*	...	...	‡ 3,398 *1*
Tonk							
(a) Nimbahera ...	55,884	52,374 *93 7*	3,510 *6 3*	...	...	...	...
(b) Pirawa ...	31,607	29,573 *93 6*	2,034 *6·4*	...	...	...	...
(c) Chhabra ...	34,126	31,475 *92 2*	2,651 *7 8*	...	...	...	...
(d) Sironj ...	88,720	80,961 *91 2*	7,759 *8·8*	...	...	...	...
(e) Tonk and Aligarh ...	106,901	83,299 *77 9*	23,602 *22 1*	...	...	...	...

NOTE.—Figures in italics below absolute figures represent proportions per cent.
* 22 per cent. of whom also speak Bhili.
† 7 per cent of whom also speak Rajasthani.
‡ 35 per cent. of whom also speak Rajasthani.

CHAPTER XI.

Religion.

1. The figures relating to the various religions of the population are set forth in— **Reference to Statistics.**

Imperial Table XVI .... Religion.

Imperial Table V .... The urban population by religions.

The Social map placed in the cover of this Volume shows by means of proportionately coloured rectangles, the religious distribution of the population of each State, Hindus being further sub-divided into Hinduised Primitive Tribes, Depressed Castes and Others. In some States where persons of a particular religion predominate in certain localities, two or more rectangles have been prepared. The key to this Social map with actual figures and percentages in detail forms an Appendix to this Chapter. At the end of this Chapter will be found four Subsidiary Tables dealing with—

1.—Proportions per 10,000 at each Census with variations.

2.—Distribution by States per 10,000 since 1881.

3.—Christians by actual numbers since 1881 and variations, and

4.—Religious distribution of 10,000 (a) urban and (b) rural population.

2. The instructions for the record of each individual's religion to be entered in column 4 of the schedule were that sects of Muslims, Jains and Christians were to be entered, and that Aryas, Brahmos and Deo-Samajists were not to be recorded merely as Hindus, as their numbers were required to be known separately. **Instructions to enumerators.**

An accurate return of those belonging to Tribal religions presented considerable difficulty. As is well known, the dividing line between the lower forms of Hinduism on the one hand and the various forms of Animistic belief on the other, is very slender. For this reason, it was suggested to the State Superintendents that they should pre-determine those localities in which Bhils living under Tribal conditions were not in daily contact with Hindus, and in them to have them all returned as Animists.

3. In every 1,000 of the population 853 are Hindus, 95 Muslims, 27 Jains, 20 of Tribal religions, while the remainder are Sikhs, Christians, Parsis and Jews. There was one Buddhist in Dholpur. **General distribution.**

4. The population as a whole has increased by 14·2 per cent. during the decade and it is interesting to note how each of the major communities has contributed to this— **Main variations since 1921.**

Hindu	+17·2
Muslim	+18·8
Jain	+ 7·5
Tribal	−52·3

These variations are discussed in detail under each head.

5. It has already been pointed out that in localities inhabited largely by primitive people, great difficulty is experienced in discriminating between Tribal religions and the lower forms of Hinduism. The actual number of persons returning the former is 229,092 as against 480,679 in 1921. The difference plus the natural increase has undoubtedly on this occasion gone to swell the number of Hindus. Conversions to Christianity among such people, though few in number, are insignificant in relation to the populations concerned. If Hinduism and Tribal religions are considered together, the combined increase is 13·4 per cent. which is very little below the general **Hindu and Tribal.**

increase of 14·2 per cent. for the Agency as a whole. The principal variation in those of Tribal religions has occurred in Mewar and the Southern Rajputana States whose actual figures have fluctuated to the extent shown in the margin.

State.		1921.	1931.
Mewar	...	199,204	94,544
Banswara	...	117,403	93,830
Dungarpur	...	93,052	...
Partabgarh	...	25,314	26,747
Kushalgarh	...	24,120	...

In Dungarpur and Kushalgarh it was pointed out that considerable social uplift had been effected amongst the Bhils during the decade and that they were now freely recognised as being within the folds of Hinduism, though perhaps only just inside the portals. The States with the highest proportions of Hindus per 10,000 of the total population are Kushalgarh (9,596), Jaipur (9,052), Karauli (9,447), Dungarpur (9,407), Bundi (9,336), Dholpur (9,248) and Kotah (9,166). The lowest proportions occur in Banswara (5,351), Partabgarh (5,402), Jaisalmer (6,789), Alwar (7,322), Bikaner (7,711) and Bharatpur (7,967). Taking Hinduism and Tribal religions together, they are the faiths of 8,737 persons out of every 10,000 of the population.

Muslim.

6. The increase of 18·8 per cent. among Muslims as a whole appears at first sight to mean that Islam had gained more adherents proportionately than the other major communities. The States of Alwar, Bharatpur, Bikaner, Dholpur, Jaipur, Jaisalmer, Kotah, Marwar, Mewar and Tonk contain 94 per cent. of all Muslims in the Agency. In Bikaner alone, the increase during the decade is 89·4 per cent. due to a flow of immigrants from the Punjab and neighbouring areas to the Canal Colonies. If all Bikaner figures are excluded, the increase in the population in the whole Agency is 12·0 per cent. while the increase in Muslims is 12·4 per cent. The increase in this community can therefore be considered as normal. The proportions of Muslims in 10,000 of the total population range from, for instance, 2,900 in Jaisalmer, 2,620 in Alwar, 1,931 in Bharatpur and 1,512 in Bikaner to 344 in Mewar, 661 in Dholpur, 686 in Kotah, 815 in Jaipur and 832 in Marwar. Tonk, the only Muslim State in the Agency, has a proportion of 1,394.

The figures by sects of Islam are as follows:—

Sunni	....	....	....	1,041,361
Shia	....	....	....	21,818
Ahal-i-Hadis	....	....	....	2,004
Unspecified	....	....	....	4,142
Total		....	....	1,069,325

Jain.

7. 79 per cent. of all Jains are found in Marwar (38), Mewar (22), Jaipur (10) and Bikaner (9) and are also returned in comparatively small numbers from other States. Where they are in larger numbers, their variation per cent. in the decade is as in the margin.

Marwar	...	+	10·2
Mewar	...	+	4·5
Jaipur	...		Nil*
Bikaner	...	+	22·2

* Plus 4 persons.

The increase in Bikaner is on account of greater openings for trade in the Canal Colonies, while the relatively small increase of 7·5 per cent. in the Jain population in the whole Agency is due to the absence of many males engaged in trade in all parts of India. The proportion of 1,060 females to 1,000 males, the absence of many married males and the prohibition of widow re-marriage are not factors that are conducive to a high rate of increase. The numbers by sects are as in the margin and show the actual variation in the intercensal period.

Sect.		1931.	1921.
Digambar	...	76,237	71,312
Swetambar	...	134,615	55,969
Baistoia (Dhundia)	...	50,228	48,046
Terapanthi	...	38,563	31,020
Others	...	1,105	73,375

The figures would appear to indicate that in 1921 many of the Swetambar sect were returned under 'Others' (Unspecified).

Arya, Brahmo and Deo Samaj.

8. The number of Arya Samajists has increased from 3,143 to 11,471 during the decade. The increase is most marked in Bharatpur (+1,483), Bikaner (+2,341), Jaipur (+652), Marwar (+1,655) and Shahpura (+1,499) and may be ascribed, with the exception of the last named, to the contiguity of this part of the Agency to the south eastern Punjab, in which this newer form of Hinduism has for a considerable time found so many adherents. In Shahpura the increase is due to local influences. Brahmos have increased in number from 22 to 44

and are returned from Bharatpur, Bikaner and Mewar only. For the first time in this Agency, Deo Samajists appear in the returns to the number of 56, 8 in Bikaner and 48 in Kotah.

9. Persons of the Christian faith are found in all States except Jaisalmer, Kushalgarh and Lawa. They range in numbers from 1 in Shahpura to 1,558 in Jaipur. Of the 5,778 persons in the whole Agency, 4,021 are Indians and the remainder Europeans, Anglo-Indians and Americans, etc. As regards Indian Christians the marginal statement by age-periods comparing the figures of 1921 with the present Census is of interest. The increase being 17·2 per cent., the figures would appear to indicate that such conversions as had been made during the decade were effected in riper years and not in childhood. A full account of the various Missionary Societies in Rajputana was published as an Appendix to Chapter IV of the 1921 Census Report and need not be repeated. It suffices to say that the Presbyterian, Methodist, Baptist, Church Missionary Society and Roman Catholic Missions still continue to do much good work especially in the fields of education, medicine and social uplift. Christian.

Age-period.	1921.	1931.
0—10	1,171	1,232
10—15	307	552
15—20	191	414
20 and over	1,761	1,823
Total ...	3,430	4,021

10. There has been a remarkable increase in the number of Sikhs. Of the 41,605 in the whole Agency, 40,469 have been returned from Bikaner as against 8,218 in 1921 and have been attracted to that State by the new Canal Colonies. Other religions.

Persons of other religions whose figures have not already been discussed are, 319 Zoroastrians, 38 Jews, 1 Buddhist while 1 male in Mewar returned no religion at all.

11. Subsidiary Table 4 shows that of the major communities, Hindus and those of Tribal religions are proportionately more numerous in rural areas and that Muslims and Jains *pro rata* prefer an urban existence. Religion in towns and villages.

1.—GENERAL DISTRIBUTION OF THE POPULATION BY RELIGIONS.

RELIGION.	ACTUAL NUMBER IN 1931.	PROPORTION PER 10,000 of POPULATION IN						VARIATION PER CENT.					PERCENTAGE OF NET VARIATION 1881—1931.
		1931.	1921.	1911.	1901.	1891.	1881.	1921—31.	1911—21.	1901—11.	1891—1901.	1881—91.	
1	2	3	4	5	6	7	8	9	10	11	12	13	14
1. Hindu-Brahmanic ...	9,567,234	8,523	8,296	8,311	8,327	8,351	8,750	+ 17·2	− 6·7	+ 6·7	− 20·8	+ 17·2	+ 8·2
2. Hindu-Arya	11,471	10	3	2	1	...	*	+ 265·0	+ 75·4	+ 188·5	+ 75·7	...	*
3 Muslim	1,069,325	953	915	936	952	811	853	+ 18·8	− 8·7	+ 5·1	− 6·8	+ 16·8	+ 24·1
4 Jain	300,748	268	284	316	349	339	375	+ 7·5	− 1	− 3·4	− 18·0	+ 10·9	− 20·6
5. Tribal	229,092	204	488	422	366	496	*	− 52·3	+ 8·1	− 23·3	− 41·4	...	*
6. Sikh	41,605	37	9	9	2	1	...	+ 378·1	− 2·8	+ 335·9	+ 84·1	+ 12,300·0	+ 462,177·8
7. Christian	5,778	5	5	4	3	2	1	+ 17·7	+ 15·4	+ 49·8	+ 52·6	+ 43·9	+ 346·5

*Figures for 1881 are not known.

2.—DISTRIBUTION OF THE MAIN RELIGIONS BY AGENCY, STATE OR DISTRICT.

AGENCY, STATE OR DISTRICT.	NUMBER PER 10,000 OF THE POPULATION WHO ARE—																	
	Christian.						Hindu (Brahmanic).						Jain.					
	1931.	1921.	1911.	1901.	1891.	1881.	1931.	1921.	1911.	1901.	1891.	1881.	1931.	1921.	1911.	1901.	1891.	1881.
1	2	3	4	5	6	7	8	9	10	11	12	13	14	15	16	17	18	19
Rajputana ...	***5***	***5***	***4***	***3***	***2***	***1***	***8,523***	***8,296***	***8,311***	***8,327***	***8,351***	***8,750***	***268***	***284***	***316***	***349***	***339***	***375***
Abu District ...	309	677	Not	avai	la	ble	7,718	5,194	....	........Not	available....	....	46	92	....	......Not	available	....
Alwar ...	1	1	1	2	2	1	7,322	7,400	7,430	7,464	7,589	7,704	51	48	52	59	59	73
Banswara ...	9	8	...	...	...	...	5,351	8,329	8,647	8,192	8,297	9,564	204	223	266	818	300	...
Bharatpur ...	13	16	10	2	...	...	7,967	8,030	8,102	8,146	8,256	8,293	49	51	49	53	69	70
Bikaner ...	3	3	2	2	...	...	7,711	8,370	8,213	8,442	8,714	8,569	307	357	355	400	316	431
Bundi ...	1	1	...	...	...	...	9,336	9,311	9,003	9,132	9,336	9,506	185	248	302	379	271	122
Dholpur ...	2	1	2	1	...	1	9,248	9,262	9,223	9,214	9,282	9,175	71	73	77	86	95	100
Dungarpur ...	...	1	...	...	...	...	9,407	4,801	4,566	5,602	5,261	8,708	255	237	346	585	430	875
Jaipur ...	6	5	5	4	3	2	9,052	9,093	9,098	9,006	9,121	9,135	112	126	146	168	167	188
Jaisalmer ...	...	...	...	...	...	...	6,789	7,071	6,902	7,086	7,324	5,316	120	106	125	161	181	155
Jhalawar ...	5	4	3	1	...	...	8,944	8,917	8,786	8,652	...	...	244	257	258	347	...	...
Karauli ...	1	1	2	1	1	1	9,447	9,447	9,414	9,395	9,406	9,366	32	30	27	30	23	39
Kishangarh ...	2	2	3	3	2	...	8,887	8,893	8,790	8,758	8,804	8,687	260	281	364	449	442	559
Kotah ...	13	13	8	6	...	...	9,166	9,108	9,140	8,950	...	...	76	87	100	109	...	...
Kushalgarh (Chiefship) ...	...	...	...	...	...	...	9,506	1,317	1,679	2,036	1,353	...	164	174	233	332	180	...
Lawa (Estate) ...	...	...	...	...	...	...	9,108	8,930	8,900	8,798	8,845	9,210	484	557	554	599	679	283
Marwar ...	3	3	2	1	1	1	8,604	8,559	8,311	8,298	8,626	8,123	535	560	642	710	664	985
Mewar ...	3	1	2	2	1	1	8,628	7,746	7,899	7,662	7,127	9,157	421	458	516	635	503	542
Partabgarh ...	9	...	...	1	...	...	5,402	5,085	5,398	6,147	5,707	9,464	581	604	689	914	696	...
Shahpura ...	...	...	...	...	...	1	8,952	8,797	8,703	9,031	9,137	9,340	261	299	342	362	370	124
Sirohi ...	23	23	43	40	26	13	9,949	8,838	8,429	7,272	8,574	8,652	716	793	898	1,115	970	1,129
Tonk ...	1	1	...	1	1	1	8,277	8,383	8,152	8,252	8,596	8,690	216	222	261	242	232	168

2.—DISTRIBUTION OF THE MAIN RELIGIONS BY AGENCY, STATE OR DISTRICT.—*Concluded.*

AGENCY, STATE OR DISTRICT.	NUMBER PER 10,000 OF THE POPULATION WHO ARE— Muslim. 1931.	Muslim. 1921.	Muslim. 1911.	Muslim. 1901.	Muslim. 1891.	Muslim. 1881.	Sikh. 1931.	Sikh. 1921.	Sikh. 1911.	Sikh. 1901.	Sikh. 1891.	Sikh. 1881.	Tribal. 1931.	Tribal. 1921.	Tribal. 1911.	Tribal. 1901.	Tribal. 1891.
1	20	21	22	23	24	25	26	27	28	29	30	31	32	33	34	35	36
Rajputana ...	***953***	***915***	***936***	***952***	***812***	***853***	***37***	***9***	***9***	***2***	***1***	...	***204***	***488***	***422***	***366***	***496***
Abu District ...	1,765	1,688	....	........Not	available...	....	119	19	......	Not av	ailable	......	...	2,205	........Not	available...	....
Alwar ...	2,620	2,550	2,516	2,474	2,350	2,222	...	...	...	1	...	...	...	...	...	...	...
Banswara ...	289	272	295	273	238	436	...	...	...	...	...	...	4,146	6,167	5,792	6,222	6,165
Bharatpur ...	1,931	1,896	1,888	1,707	1,675	1,637	3	2	1	...	...	...	...	...	...	...	...
Bikaner ...	1,512	1,133	1,811	1,130	962	999	432	125	117	25	8	...	...	...	...	...	...
Bundi ...	475	496	487	489	393	372	2	...	...	...	...	...	...	4	207	...	...
Dholpur ...	661	650	694	699	623	725	10	2	4	...	1	...	4	10	...	...	...
Dungarpur ...	338	447	421	427	261	418	...	...	...	...	...	...	...	4,964	4,666	3,385	4,048
Jaipur ...	815	768	743	726	709	674	1	...	1	...	...	...	10	6	7	5	...
Jaisalmer ...	2,900	2,641	2,502	2,542	2,545	2,592	1	1	...	...	...	...	189	182	471	211	...
Jhalawar ...	793	813	896	981	...	...	2	4	6	9	...	...	...	...	44	10	...
Karauli ...	520	521	557	574	571	594	...	...	...	...	...	...	...	...	1	...	...
Kishangarh ...	769	759	778	788	751	754	...	1	1	...	...	...	74	63	61	...	...
Kotah ...	686	692	697	696	...	...	4	3	3	4	...	...	43	92	48	231	...
Kushalgarh (Chiefship) ...	240	236	317	364	168	...	...	...	...	...	...	...	...	8,271	7,771	7,269	8,295
Lawa (Estate) ...	391	518	542	608	476	507	...	...	...	...	...	...	...	...	...	...	...
Marwar ...	832	838	805	772	709	890	...	890	...	...	...	...	15	36	238	218	...
Mewar ...	344	350	354	895	321	300	...	...	...	...	...	...	603	1,443	1,280	1,306	2,048
Partabgarh ...	511	537	571	723	561	585	1	...	...	...	...	...	3,495	3,772	3,338	2,213	3,086
Shahpura ...	469	470	508	591	493	536	...	...	...	...	...	...	...	388	412	...	...
Sirohi ...	302	341	383	384	272	205	...	...	4	7	1	...	...	...	234	1,173	150
Tonk ...	1,394	1,817	1,334	1,504	1,172	1,141	...	...	...	...	...	...	111	77	250	...	...

NOTE.—1. Owing to alteration in the boundaries of Kotah and Jhalawar between 1891 and 1901 details by Religion for the States cannot be given.

2. Sirohi figures for 1891 to 1911 include those of Abu District.

3.—CHRISTIANS.—NUMBER AND VARIATIONS.

STATE OR DISTRICT.	ACTUAL NUMBERS.						VARIATION PER CENT.					
	1931.	1921.	1911.	1901.	1891.	1881.	1921—31.	1911—21.	1901—11.	1891—1901.	1881—91.	1881—1931.
1	2	3	4	5	6	7	8	9	10	11	12	13
Rajputana	**5,778**	**4,911**	**4,256**	**2,841**	**1,862**	**1,294**	**+ 17·7**	**+ 15·4**	**+ 49·8**	**+ 52·6**	**+ 43·9**	**+ 346·5**
Abu District	140	244	*	*	*	*	− 42·6	*	*	*	*	*
Alwar	79	47	92	166	166	90	+ 68·1	− 48·9	− 44·6	...	+ 84·4	− 12·2
Banswara	205	146	...	...	...	2	+ 40·4	...	...	...	− 100·0	+ 10,150·0
Bharatpur	625	794	566	102	6	8	− 21·3	+ 40·3	+ 454·9	+ 1,600·0	− 25·0	+ 7,712·5
Bikaner	298	191	151	95	21	14	+ 56·0	+ 26·5	+ 58·9	+ 352·4	+ 50·0	+ 2,028·6
Bundi	29	20	...	1	...	7	+ 45·0	...	− 100·0	...	− 100·0	+ 314·3
Dholpur	63	33	41	26	6	27	+ 90·9	− 19·5	+ 57·7	+ 333·3	− 77·8	+ 133·3
Dungarpur	7	11	2	3	...	...	− 36·4	+ 450·0	− 33·3	...	...	...
Jaipur	1,558	1,259	1,326	925	706	552	+ 23·7	− 5·1	+ 43·4	+ 31·0	+ 27·9	+ 182·2
Jaisalmer	...	...	...	...	...	1	...	...	...	...	− 100·0	− 100·0
Jhalawar	50	36	26	10	18	13	+ 38·9	+ 38·5	+ 160·0	− 44·4	+ 38·5	+ 284·6
Karauli	16	19	28	22	13	17	− 15·8	− 32·1	+ 27·3	+ 69·2	− 23·5	− 5·9
Kishangarh	15	17	23	31	21	...	− 11·8	− 26·1	− 25·8	+ 47·6	...	...
Kotah	914	830	507	846	55	25	+ 10·1	+ 63·7	− 46·5	+ 529·1	+ 120·0	+ 3,556·0
Kushalgarh (Chiefship) ...	...	1	...	...	...	...	− 100·0	...	...	...	...	...
Lawa (Estate)	...	...	...	...	...	...	...	...	...	...	...	...
Marwar	686	622	440	224	186	207	+ 10·3	+ 41·4	+ 96·4	+ 20·4	− 10·1	+ 231·4
Mewar	479	179	237	243	137	130	+ 167·6	− 24·5	− 2·5	+ 77·4	+ 5·4	+ 268·5
Partabgarh	67	...	...	5	1	1	...	...	− 100·0	+ 400·0	...	+ 6,600·0
Shahpura	1	...	1	...	2	3	...	− 100·0	...	− 100·0	− 33·3	− 66·7
Sirohi	503	434	804	624	504	179	+ 15·9	− ¶ 46·0	+ 28·8	+ 23·8	+ 181·6	+ 181·0
Tonk	43	28	12	18	20	18	+ 53·6	+ 133·3	− 33·3	− 10·0	+ 11·1	+ 138·9

*Not available.
¶1911 figures include figures for Abu also.

4.—RELIGIONS OF URBAN AND RURAL POPULATION.

AGENCY	NUMBER PER 10,000 OF URBAN POPULATION WHO ARE—							NUMBER PER 10,000 OF RURAL POPULATION WHO ARE—						
	Christian	Hindu.	Jain.	Muslim.	Tribal.	Sikh.	Others.	Christian	Hindu.	Jain.	Muslim.	Tribal.	Sikh.	Others.
1	2	3	4	5	6	7	8	9	10	11	12	13	14	15
Rajputana	21	6,902	595	2,461	10	9	2	2	8,796	215	710	235	42	...

NOTE.—Figures for Hindus include Aryas and Brahmos.

APPENDIX A.

LEGEND OF THE DETAIL SHOWN ON THE SOCIAL MAP.

Scale of the map is approximately 1"=24 Miles.

STATE OR SUB-DIVISION.	TOTAL POPULATION.	NUMBERS AND PERCENTAGES OF—						
		TRIBAL RELIGION.	HINDUISED PRIMITIVE TRIBES.	DEPRESSED CLASSES.	OTHER HINDUS.	MUSLIMS.	OTHERS.	JAINS.
ALWAR ...	**749,751**	... ...	... ...	**101,079** *13·5*	**448,287** *59·8*	**196,460** *26·2*	**116** ...	**3,809** *·5*
BANSWARA ...	**225,106**	**93,330** *41·5*	**51,467** *22·9*	**11,365** *5·0*	**57,626** *25·6*	**6,510** *2·9*	**211** ...	**4,597** *2·1*
BHARATPUR ...	**486,954**	... ...	... ...	**98,972** *20·3*	**290,751** *59·9*	**94,054** *19·3*	**787** *·1*	**2,390** *·4*
(*a*) Nagar, Pahari and Kaman.	120,965	... ...	... ...	17,896 *14·8*	43,980 *36·4*	58,388 *48·3*	82 ...	619 *·5*
(*b*) Remainder ...	365,989	... ...	... ...	81,076 *22·1*	246,771 *67·4*	85,666 *9·8*	705 *·2*	1,771 *·5*
BIKANER ...	**936,218**	... ...	... ...	**125,284** *13·4*	**599,800** *64·1*	**141,578** *15·1*	**40,783** *4·3*	**28,773** *3·1*
(*a*) Suratgarh and Ganganagar.	243,488	... ...	... ...	28,040 *11·5*	104,447 *43·0*	70,221 *29·0*	40,205 *16·5*	570 ...
(*b*) Remainder ...	692,735	... ...	... ...	97,244 *14·0*	495,358 *71·5*	71,357 *10·4*	578 ...	28,208 *4·1*
BUNDI ...	**216,722**	**5** ...	**5,495** *2·5*	**32,238** *15·0*	**164,596** *75·9*	**10,292** *4·8*	**77** ...	**4,019** *1·8*
DHOLPUR ...	**254,986**	**98** ...	... ...	**45,309** *17·8*	**190,620** *74·9*	**16,842** *6·6*	**318** ...	**1,799** *·7*
DUNGARPUR ...	**227,544**	... ...	**123,350** *54·2*	**11,165** *4·9*	**79,530** *34·9*	**7,682** *3·4*	**16** ...	**5,801** *2·6*
JAIPUR ...	**2,631,775**	**2,599** ...	**834** ...	**396,791** *15·1*	**1,985,679** *75·5*	**214,581** *8·2*	**1,799** ...	**29,492** *1·2*
JAISALMER ...	**76,255**	**1,444** *1·9*	**504** *·7*	**8,836** *11·6*	**42,429** *55·6*	**22,116** *29·0*	**9** ...	**917** *1·2*
JHALAWAR ...	**107,890**	... ...	**3,250** *3·0*	**18,778** *17·4*	**74,606** *69·1*	**8,558** *8·0*	**68** ...	**2,630** *2·5*
(*a*) Chhaoni and Patan ...	30,299	... ...	217 *·7*	3,417 *11·2*	20,851 *68·8*	5,060 *16·7*	20 ...	784 *2·6*
(*b*) Remainder ...	77,591	... ...	8,083 *3·9*	15,361 *19·9*	53,755 *69·3*	3,498 *4·5*	48 ...	1,896 *2·4*
KARAULI ...	**140,525**	... ...	... ...	**22,481** *16·0*	**110,278** *78·5*	**7,301** *5·2*	**17** ...	**448** *·3*
KISHANGARH ...	**85,744**	**636** *·7*	**306** *·4*	**14,255** *16·6*	**61,702** *72·0*	**6,597** *7·7*	**17** ...	**2,231** *2·6*
KOTAH ...	**685,804**	**2,923** *·4*	**21,290** *3·1*	**102,849** *15·0*	**505,277** *73·7*	**47,068** *6·9*	**1,203** *·2*	**5,194** *·7*
KUSHALGARH ...	**35,564**	... ...	**29,985** *84·4*	**676** *1·9*	**3,466** *9·7*	**854** *2·4*	... ...	**583** *1·6*
LAWA* ...	**2,790**	... ...	... ...	**492** *17·6*	**2,054** *73·7*	**109** *3·9*	... ...	**135** *4·8*
MARWAR ...	**2,125,982**	**3,241** *·1*	**47,929** *2·3*	**301,887** *14·2*	**1,481,625** *69·7*	**176,863** *8·3*	**768** ...	**113,669** *5·4*
(*a*) Bali ...	114,249	3,031 *2·6*	4,374 *3·8*	16,784 *14·7*	73,876 *64·7*	2,370 *2·1*	28 ...	13,791 *12·1*
(*b*) Jalore and Jaswantpura ...	266,294	... ...	18,572 *6·9*	40,001 *15·2*	175,025 *65·7*	6,766 *2·5*	6 ...	25,924 *9·7*
(*c*) Remainder ...	1,745,439	210 ...	24,983 *1·5*	245,102 *14·0*	1,232,724 *70·6*	167,727 *9·6*	739 ...	73,954 *4·3*
MEWAR ...	**1,566,910**	**94,544** *6·0*	**150,272** *9·6*	**169,271** *10·8*	**1,032,486** *65·9*	**53,833** *3·5*	**503** ...	**66,001** *4·2*
(*a*) Girwa ...	121,854	16,791 *13·8*	8,741 *7·2*	10,353 *8·5*	77,653 *63·7*	1,999 *1·6*	... ...	6,317 *5·2*
(*b*) Kherwara ...	73,998	33,241 *45·1*	19,668 *26·6*	2,310 *3·1*	16,010 *21·6*	1,442 *2·0*	100 ...	1,227 *1·6*
(*c*) Magra ...	97,234	30,490 *31·4*	18,988 *19·6*	4,189 *4·3*	37,862 *38·9*	1,047 *1·1*	42 ...	4,616 *4·7*
(*d*) Remainder ...	1,273,824	14,022 *1·1*	102,875 *8·1*	152,419 *11·9*	900,961 *70·8*	49,345 *3·8*	361 ...	53,841 *4·3*
PARTABGARH ...	**76,539**	**26,747** *35·0*	**2,698** *3·5*	**5,350** *7·0*	**33,299** *43·6*	**3,914** *5·1*	**86** ...	**4,445** *5·8*
SHAHPURA ...	**54,233**	... ...	**2,707** *5·0*	**9,088** *16·8*	**38,478** *70·9*	**2,541** *4·7*	**1** ...	**1,418** *2·6*
SIROHI and ABU ...	**221,060**	... ...	**35,877** *16·2*	**33,065** *15·0*	**128,341** *58·1*	**7,338** *3·3*	**910** *·4*	**15,529** *7·0*
TONK ...	**317,360**	**3,525** *1·1*	**2,518** *·8*	**56,178** *17·7*	**203,984** *64·3*	**44,234** *13·9*	**53** ...	**6,868** *2·2*
(*a*) Nimbahera ..	55,390	3,182 *5·6*	496 *·9*	7,311 *13·1*	38,797 *69·4*	3,843 *6·9*	6 ...	2,255 *4·1*
(*b*) Pirawa ...	31,609	80 *·2*	708 *2·2*	5,534 *17·5*	22,307 *70·6*	2,106 *6·7*	2 ...	872 *2·8*
(*c*) Chhabra ...	34,130	36 ...	365 *1·1*	4,929 *14·4*	25,903 *76·0*	2,747 *8·1*	1 ...	149 *·4*
(*d*) Sironj ...	88,782	115 ...	291 *·3*	19,313 *21·8*	55,841 *63·0*	11,977 *13·5*	3 ...	1,242 *1·4*
(*e*) Tonk and Aligarh ...	106,949	112 *·1*	658 *·6*	19,091 *17·9*	61,136 *57·2*	23,561 *22·0*	41 ...	2,350 *2·2*
TOTAL RAJPUTANA ...	**11,225,712**	**229,092** *2·0*	**478,482** *4·3*	**1,565,409** *14·0*	**7,534,914** *67·1*	**1,069,325** *9·5*	**47,742** *·4*	**300,748** *2·7*

Figures in italics below absolute figures represent proportions per cent.

* Not shown on Map.

THE TRIBES AND CASTES
OF RAJPUTANA
PER MILLE OF THE TOTAL POPULATION

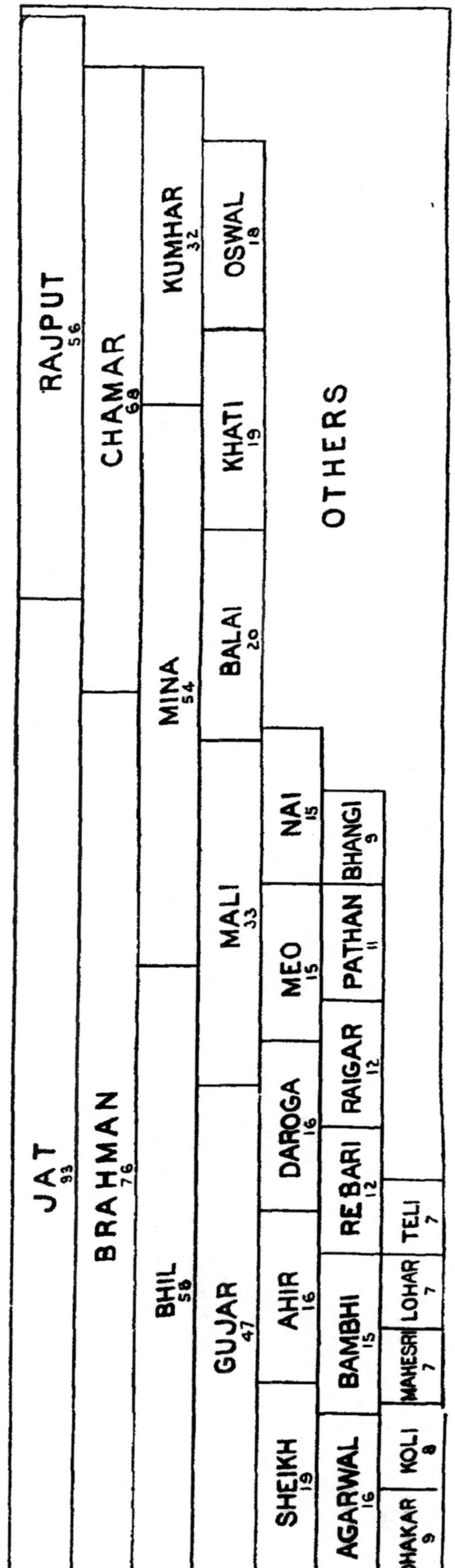

CHAPTER XII.

Race, Tribe and Caste.

PART I.—THE AGENCY.

1. Column 8 of the Census schedule was provided for a record of Race, Tribe or Caste and amplified instructions to enumerators, which were based on those published in the Imperial Code of Census Procedure, were as follows :— **Instructions to enumerators.**

"In the case of all Hindus, except Rajputs and Brahmans, you are only to enter the caste and not the sub-caste. A caste means the biggest group of persons of the same religion (excepting Jains, Sikhs and Hindus of the same caste among themselves), outside which a man cannot marry. Enter the caste of Hindus, Jains, Sikhs, Aryas, Brahmos, and the tribes of Muslims and Primitive tribes and the race of Christians, Buddhists and Parsis, etc. Sikhs and Aryas are not to be pressed into disclosing their caste if they do not wish to do so. Do not enter anyone as Bania or Mahajan, but enter Agarwal, Oswal or whatever caste of Bania the person belongs to. Do not use words which merely indicate the work a person does, such as Mehtar, nor vague words like Bengali, Punjabi or Gujarati which are not names of castes. In the case of Brahmans and Rajputs enter the clan or sub-division *e. g.*, $\frac{\text{Rajput}}{\text{Chauhan}}$, $\frac{\text{Brahman}}{\text{Gaur}}$. As regards Muslims, if they belong to any caste, the members of which will not marry with any other Muslim caste, enter the name of that caste ; for instance Julaha, Pinara, etc.; otherwise enter the tribe they belong to *e. g.*, Sheikh, Saiyad, Pathan or Moghal. In the case of Indian Christians, enter the castes they belonged to before conversion. If they object to telling you this, enter them as Indian Christians. In the case of all married women, except Rajputs, enter their castes as those of their husbands. A married Rajput woman's clan should be that of her father. In the case of all unmarried females enter the caste of their father."

2. Whatever the imperfections of these necessarily elementary instructions, the result of the enquiry is tabulated in Imperial Table XVII which may be summarised as in the margin. At first sight it would seem incredible that such a comparatively small population should contain so many tribes, castes or races as defined in paragraph 1. The statement however shows that 42 large well defined castes, etc., comprise 84 per cent. of the whole population, and that more than half of the castes contain less than 1,000 persons each and only total 44,863 persons. It is this latter category of castes which give the most trouble in the tabulation offices. Many of them are undoubtedly offshoots or **Reference to statistics.**

Category.		No. of castes, etc	Total persons.	Per mille of total population.
Over 300,000	...	9	5,814,611	517·9
100,000 — 300,000	...	13	2,262,064	201·5
50,000 — 100,000	...	20	1,400,641	124·8
10,000 — 50,000	...	54	1,411,775	125·8
1,000 — 10,000	...	72	282,434	25·2
Under 1,000	...	215	44,863	4·0
Not true castes	...	10	4,245	0·4
Caste not returned	...	...	5,079	0·4
Total	...	393	11,225,712	1,000

obscure sub-divisions of larger castes. However it has been found possible to trace all of them except 28, totalling 383 persons; these include such fantastic and meaningless names as Malzada, Hiranbaz and Mahomedi.

The meaning of caste.

3. A caste has been defined as an endogamous group or collection of groups bearing a common name and having a common traditional occupation, who are so linked together by these and other ties, such as the tradition of a common origin and the possession of the same tutelary deity, and of the same social status, ceremonial observances and family priests, that they regard themselves and are regarded by others as forming a single homogeneous community (India Census Report 1911). A distinctive feature of the caste system is that each caste is divided into exogamous patrilineal sub-divisions known as *Gotra* within which marriage is as strictly prohibited as is marriage outside the endogamous caste. An eminent French scientist, M. Senart has shown that similar restrictions existed in ancient Greece and Rome and in the latter there was a long struggle before the plebeians obtained the right of lawful marriage with patrician women. There were similar restrictions in these two countries about commensality and the hearth fire which recall those in force in India. From these and other analogies it has, by some, been inferred that the caste system in India is merely an extension of the ancient Aryan family system. In Europe the family clan and tribe have been absorbed into the nation, in India they have solidified into cast-iron compartments which embrace and lock up the whole population. One theory is that the Aryans were a small and scattered people in the midst of alien races. To preserve themselves as a separate race, they fenced themselves in with high doctrines of descent and purity of blood and in this they were aided by the Brahman priests. Gradually, mixed and impure races began to imitate the custom in a desire to raise their social status.

The people of Rajputana.

4. It was shown in the Ethnographical Survey of India 1901, that the people of Rajputana were predominantly Indo Aryan of whom definite types are the Rajputs and Jats. Except among Minas, where a strain of Bhil blood may be discerned, the type shows no sign of having been modified by contact with the pre-Dravida type. They have not wholly escaped the bonds of caste but they are less rigid than elsewhere in India. The comparative purity of the type is based on the supposition that they originally came into India from the North West and that they probably brought their own women with them and were not reduced to the necessity of capturing Dravidian brides. On no other supposition can the comparative purity of the type be explained. It is thought that some great change had occurred in the climate of Central Asia and Persia and that the people moved in search of arable land. Some think that another wave followed this first one and established itself on the plains of the Ganges and Jumna. Here they came into contact with the Dravidians and here by stress of that contact, caste was evolved and here the *Vedas* were composed and the whole fantastic structure of orthodox ritual and usage was built up. At a later period, spreading over a long time, swarms of nomadic people known by the general term of Scythians poured into India and were gradually driven southward from the western Punjab to the Deccan, possibly leaving some remnants in western Rajputana on their way.

Caste at the present day.

5. The structure of society in the Indian States of the Agency is such that although the Brahmans hold pride of place by reason of their priestly traditions and functions, the Rajputs as rulers are in an unassailable position of temporal power and owners of the soil. Each caste has its definite place in the scheme of things and as elsewhere in India, "the caste system is the main cause of the fundamental stability and contentment by which society has been braced up for centuries against the shocks of politics and the cataclysms of Nature. It provides every man with his place, his career, his occupation and his circle of friends. It makes him at the outset a member of a corporate body: it protects him through life from the canker of social jealousy and unfulfilled aspirations: it ensures him companionship and a sense of community with others in like case with himself. The caste organisation is to the Hindu his club, his trade union, his

benefit and philanthropic society*." Despite the efforts of those who speak of India as if its inhabitants were a homogeneous whole entitled to play their part in the commonwealth of the Empire, an India without caste, as things stand at present, is not easy to imagine.

The value of a record of caste.

6. With this brief sketch of what is involved by a return of caste we may next proceed to discuss its value and accuracy. It has been seriously suggested by some that a return of caste at each Census tends to perpetuate social cleavage and hinders the growth of a national consciousness. It has already been seen what caste means and to ignore it would be to deprive a Census of what, to the majority of Indians, is its most interesting feature. There is moreover no other suitable method of recording the divisions into which the people naturally fall. A return by traditional or general occupations only, would be valueless, for traditions are rapidly changing and in these days a Teli may well be a merchant and a Rajput a mill operative. It is however possible to state that the rigidity of the caste system shows a tendency to weaken. The formerly strict rules for eating and drinking have been relaxed to some extent and it is a popular belief among the common herd that a rich man may override caste while the poor are shackled by an ever present fear of excommunication. The alleged freedom of the rich is fostered by education and the facilities for travel, and in course of time such freedom will tend to spread to others not so well endowed with riches.

As in other parts of the world, the desire for higher social status is also found in India. The desire is perhaps not so prevalent in the Indian States as in British India, for in the former any undue precocity for social recognition outside an accepted sphere, would be as severely dealt with as it was in England up to the end of the nineteenth century. In spite of this, several applications were received from various caste *Sabhas* for a change in a hitherto accepted nomenclature and the desire for Brahman or Kshatriya status was most marked. The marginal statement shows the nature of the requests received. The application of the Darogas was definitely rejected as it was held to be essential that only *asl* or true Rajputs had a claim to be designated as such in this Agency. The criterion in other claims was two-fold. Firstly public opinion had to be in favour of the new designation, or secondly it had to be such that the old designation was so readily recognisable as to admit of the figures being comparable with those obtained at previous Censuses. For these reasons the claims of the Nais and Khanzadas were rejected as the former are not recognised by other Brahmans and the latter have for some years been freely enlisted in the Army as Khanzadas. The applications of the remainder were admitted but no entries were recorded of Kurmi Kshatriya or Rohela Tank Kshatriya. Some of the applications suggested that the Abstraction Offices should summarily alter the return of all persons shown under the better known name of the caste, to the new designation, but this was definitely refused.

Caste to which usually recognised as belonging.	New nomenclature requested by some of the community concerned.
1. Daroga ...	Rawana Rajput.
2. Nai ...	Kuleen-Brahman or Nai-Brahman.
3. Khanzada ...	Muslim Rajput Jadon.
4. Sevag, Rankawat and Bhojak ...	Brahman.
5. Khati or Sutar ...	Jangida Brahman.
6. Mali ...	Sainik Kshatriya.
7. Kurmi or Kunbi ...	Kurmi Kshatriya.
8. Darzi, Chhipa, etc.	Rohela Tank Kshatriya.

Accuracy.

7. In rural areas and in smaller towns every man is usually well known to his neighbour so that the staff had, as a rule, no difficulty in making an accurate return of caste for the hundred or so persons that each enumerator was responsible for. In larger towns and among the travelling public, such accurate knowledge was not always forthcoming. Considering however, as seen in paragraph 2 *supra*, that vague or inaccurate returns were really only possible among under 5 per mille of the whole population, the record of race and caste may be considered reasonably accurate.

* Sidney Low, A Vision of India.

The principal Castes.

8. The diagram prefacing this Chapter shows that 28 large and well defined castes comprise 768 per mille of the population, the nine largest castes, each numbering over 300,000 persons, forming more than half the population of the Agency. In amplification of the summary in paragraph 2 *supra*, the marginal statement shows details of the 42 large castes each numbering over 50,000 persons. In addition to the 9 already referred to, there are 13 which have from 100 to 300,000 persons each while 20 number from 50 to 100,000. In this detail 84 per cent. of the population are accounted for.

STATEMENT OF CASTES NUMBERING OVER 50,000 PERSONS EACH.

Category or Caste, etc.	Total persons.	Per mille of total population.
Over 300,000	**5,814,611**	**517·9**
1. Jat	1,042,153	92·8
2 Brahman	854,634	76·1
3. Chamar	767,263	68·3
4. Bhil	655,647	58·4
5. Rajput	633,830	56·5
6 Mina	607,369	54·1
7. Gujar	526,731	46·9
8. Mali	369,173	32 9
9. Kumhar	357,751	31·9
100,000 to 300,000	**2,262,064**	**201·5**
1. Balai	218,927	19·5
2. Sheikh	210,499	18·8
3. Khati	209,937	18·7
4. Oswal	197,460	17·6
5. Agarwal	183,754	16·3
6. Ahir	182,165	16·2
7. Daroga	177,104	15·8
8. Meo	167,530	14·9
9. Nai	166,096	14·8
10. Bambhi	162,865	14·5
11. Rebari	135,820	12·1
12. Raigar	130,104	11·6
13. Pathan	119,803	10·7
50,000 to 100,000	**1,400,641**	**124·8**
1. Bhangi	99,083	8·8
2. Dhakar	96,158	8·6
3. Koli	90,910	8·1
4. Mahesri	81,819	7·3
5. Lohar	81,070	7·2
6. Teli	80,015	7·1
7. Gadaria	77,370	6·9
8. Jogi	76,204	6·8
9. Sunar	73,455	6·5
10. Bishnoi	69,873	6·2
11. Sadhu	66,597	5·9
12. Naik	62,329	5·6
13. Kachhi	60,510	5·4
14. Khatik	59,527	5·3
15. Kunbi	57,815	5·2
16. Patel	55,867	5·0
17. Fakir	54,859	4 9
18. Sirvi	53,611	4·8
19. Rath	52,671	4·7
20 Dangi	50,898	4·5

The smaller castes.

9. There are 54 castes each with 10 to 50,000 persons which amount in the aggregate to 1,411,775 persons. These are shown in the margin and they represent 125·8 persons per mille of the whole population. By adding these to the 42 large castes already shown in detail we are able to ascertain that out of 393 castes tabulated, not more than 96 are represented in 97 per cent. of the whole population. If our knowledge of the minor ramifications of caste was wider and extended to the entire non-indigenous population, it would probably be possible to connect most of these remaining 297 castes with one or other of the larger ones.

Caste.	Persons.	Caste.	Persons.
Bagri ...	11,165	Kir ...	23,980
Banjara ...	28,409	Kirar ...	15,697
Bauria ...	37,605	Koria ...	11,304
Bhat ...	39,882	Lakhera ...	12,985
Bhishti ...	23,949	Lodha ...	48,503
Bhoi ...	10,340	Meghwal ...	23,273
Bohra ...	15,302	Mirasi ...	17,051
Charan ...	35,548	Mochi ...	13,246
Chhipa ...	33,225	Moghal ...	11,650
Dakot ...	27,353	Pinara ...	26,388
Darzi ...	47,398	Porwal ...	29,359
Dhanak ...	30,735	Purohit ...	45,308
Dhed ...	19,907	Rana ...	10,035
Dhobi ...	43,832	Ranghar ...	24,091
Dholi ...	35,576	Rangrez ...	16,128
Gachha ...	14,525	Rao ...	14,219
Gosain ...	29,648	Rawat ...	27,804
Grassia ...	29,231	Sad ...	29,041
Humar ...	10,541	Sahar ...	19,696
Julaha ...	17,087	Saiyed ...	33,409
Kahar ...	15,143	Saraogi ...	32,648
Kaimkhani ...	85,686	Sargara ...	31,800
Kalal ...	42,876	Silawat ...	13,776
Kasai ...	24,847	Sindhi ...	43,588
Kayastha ...	23,165	Sondhia ...	34,257
Khandelwal ...	48,435	Swami ...	44,937
Khattri ...	14,290	Thori ...	17,899

Different kinds of castes.

10. In the 1901 Census Report for India, it was stated that Hindu castes could be said to be of eight different kinds. Of these the terms *Tribal* and *Functional* apply predominantly to those found in Rajputana wherein we may

describe as Tribal or Racial, the Rajputs, Jats, Gujars, Ahirs, Minas and Bhils. These are well defined rural communities who tend to concentrate in particular localities. To these may be added the Muslim Meos and Raths and such converts to Islam as Ranghars, Kaimkhanis and Khanzadas. *Functional* or *Occupational* castes are not as a rule found concentrated nor are their members exclusively engaged in their traditional occupations. Such castes are Brahmans, Chamars, Malis, Kumhars, Balais, Khatis, Oswals and Agarwals, etc.

The geographical distribution of certain castes.

11. The localities in which the various larger caste communities are to be found are matters of interest.

Bharatpur	... 72,383
Bikaner	... 215,947
Jaipur	... 313,609
Marwar	... 283,933

Jats.—The Jats who number 1,042,153 persons are undoubtedly descendants of early Aryan invaders and they are predominantly found in contiguous parts of Bikaner, Jaipur and Marwar. Their presence in Bharatpur is due to more recent invasions. Figures for these four States are shown in the margin and the figures for Bikaner include 26,537 professing the Sikh religion who have recently immigrated from the Punjab.

Rajputs.—The Rajputs who rule in 18 of the States, etc., are not in consequence as concentrated. Of the total number of 633,830 persons, the bulk is found in the three largest States of Jaipur (113,389), Marwar (187,874) and Mewar (124,174). Their position as Rulers and land owners mitigates against concentration, though large communities exist in northern Jaipur and western Marwar. A note on Rajput clans appears as an Appendix to this Chapter.

Alwar	... 44,007
Bharatpur	... 40,432
Jaipur	... 192,542
Kotah	... 42,357
Mewar	... 84,361

Gujars.—The 526,791 Gujars are chiefly found in the eastern part of the Agency as shown in the marginal distribution. Though herdsmen by tradition, they also extensively engage in agriculture but not, perhaps, with the same degree of skill and patience as Jats and Ahirs.

Ahirs.—The relatively small number of 182,165 Ahirs are almost exclusively found in northern Alwar and the contiguous parts of Jaipur. Most of them belong to the endogamous division of *Jadubansi* but some in parts of Jaipur are of the *Nandbansi* sect.

Bhils.—The 655,647 Bhils are practically all found in Mewar and the Southern States. In spite of a hazy tradition that they originally came from the North, they are really among the earliest inhabitants of this part of the Agency and in the more accessible localities are rapidly becoming Hinduised. A full account of their beliefs and customs can be read in the Mewar Gazetteer from which the following are extracted. The Sun, Moon, Stars and Comets are considered as male gods and of these some think that the Comets have an evil influence. Excepting the Pole star which is the greatest and head of all, the names of other stars are not commonly known. The Earth exists on one of the heads of *Sheshnag* (a snake with a large number of heads) and when the snake turns his back, the Earth is shaken and an earthquake occurs. As regards eclipses they believe that when the Sun or Moon are pressed by their creditors for the payment of their debts, they try to hide and thus cause an eclipse. This belief is however not confined to Bhils alone. The custom of *Ghar Jamai* is common, whereby a youth works for his future father-in-law for a specified number of years before marriage, in lieu of paying *Dapa* or bride money. If intimacy takes place during this period, the couple are allowed to live as man and wife and no marriage ceremony takes place. They still maintain *Bhopas* or witch finders, and formerly, if the witch was found she was subjected to trial by ordeal but this is now prohibited and a fine is inflicted instead. There is said to have existed in former times a proclivity for head-hunting for the heads of their enemies were cut off and hung up in trees. There are very few regular Bhil villages and groups of families occupy rude huts perched on eminences in the immediate vicinity of their fields. At this Census 70 per cent. of all Bhils were returned as Hindus as against 19 per cent. at the last Census.

Minas.—Minas are principally to be found in the east and south east of the Agency in the States of Alwar, Jaipur, Kotah and Mewar. They number in all 607,369 persons and although many are of mixed descent they are among the oldest inhabitants of Rajputana.

Meos.—There is reason to think that the Meos who number 167,530 persons originally sprang from the same stock as the Minas. All are now Muslims and they are found in those parts of Alwar and Bharatpur States known as Mewat.

Other localised castes.—In the east and south east of the Agency other localised castes each numbering over 50,000 are the Dhakars (96,158) and Kachhis (60,510). In the west, the Bishnois (69,873) were formerly a sect but are now regarded as a separate caste. Racially, they are principally Jats and are found almost wholly in Bikaner, Jaisalmer and Marwar. Rebaris who are traditionally camel breeders and graziers now number 135,820 persons of whom the majority are found in contiguous parts of Marwar, Mewar and Sirohi. Those large agricultural communities known variously in other parts of India as Kunbis, Kurmis, Kalbis, Patidars, etc., are represented in the Agency by 57,815 persons of whom the bulk are found in those parts of Marwar and Sirohi which adjoin the Bombay Presidency. The 5,100 Kunbis returned from the scattered parganas of Tonk are probably Kurmis akin to those found in large numbers in the United Provinces and Central India. Among this class of agriculturists, mention should be made of 55,867 Patels, most of whom are found in Banswara and Dungarpur, also of 2,778 Anjnas in tracts adjacent to the Central India Agency. Other particularly localised castes are the Sirvis (53,611) mostly of Marwar, the 52,671 Muslim Raths, all of northern Bikaner and the 50,898 Dangis chiefly of Mewar.

The Functional castes.

12. This term is applied to those castes, etc., whose traditional occupations are usually non-agricultural and who are for this reason found in dispersed communities in varying numbers throughout the Agency. In this category therefore fall the Brahmans, the large numbers who are collectively styled Mahajans, the various artisan castes such as the Kumhars, Khatis, Lohars, and Sunars, etc., and lastly the leather workers and scavengers.

Brahmans.—The Brahmans collectively are, after the Jats, the most numerous community in the Agency. Their total of 854,634 persons is made up of the sub-divisions shown in the margin in order of numerical superiority, and they form over ten per cent. of the population in Dholpur and Jaipur.

SUB-DIVISION.	NUMBER.	SUB-DIVISION.	NUMBER.
Gaur and Adi Gaur ...	231,236	Palliwal ...	24,172
Sanadhya ...	119,727	Bagara ...	16,917
Gujar Gaur ...	61,756	Srimali ...	15,921
Parikh ...	45,536	Saraswat ...	14,963
Khandelwal ...	41,964	Audich ...	14,459
Hariyana ...	33,406	Sikhwal ...	13,124
Daima ...	33,132	Mewaria ...	10,804
Pushkarna ...	31,787	Others ...	152,730

Mahajans.—Of the 638,820 persons who are collectively styled Mahajans no less than 72 per cent. belong to the 3 large castes of Oswal, Agarwal and Mahesri and 47 per cent. are Jains by religion. They are found scattered all over the Agency and many who have their homes here, conduct their business or trade in every part of India only visiting their homes occasionally.

Other functional castes.—Nearly every village of any size has its attendant communities of Kumhars, Khatis, Nais, Lohars and leather workers who are principally Chamars. Among the Hindu Lohars there is a sub-division known as *Gadiya* Lohars from the peculiar shape of their carts in which they travel about the country. A tradition concerning them is that they were placed under a curse by the Brahmans of Chitor and were expelled from that ancient Capital of Mewar. Except when actually slept on, their bedsteads are always placed feet uppermost and they say that until they are restored to Chitor they will always place them so. Recorded caste names that are particularly functional and can hardly perhaps represent true castes, are Chabaksawar (rough rider), Golandaz (artilleryman), Pahalwan (wrestler), Salotri (farrier), and Sipahi (soldier).

Depressed castes.

13. An enquiry into the subject of depressed or untouchable Hindu castes was not devoid of difficulty. At the outset each State Superintendent was asked to supply a list of those considered as being of this description. The replies received were by no means uniform and regarding some there was a considerable divergence of opinion. For instance, a Koli was not considered as depressed in Alwar but was so in Mewar and some other States. For this

reason it was decided to include only those castes concerning which there was unanimity and whose untouchability and lowly position in the social structure was not open to question among other Hindus. The list in the margin shows the depressed castes and the number of persons belonging to each in order of numerical superiority. The Social map in the cover of this volume, its Legend which forms an Appendix to Chapter XI and Provincial Table II show full details concerning the distribution of the depressed castes treated as a whole. They number 1,565,409 persons or 14 per cent. of the whole population but this proportion varies from 1·9 per cent. in Kushalgarh to 20·3 per cent. in Bharatpur. In 1921 no regular enquiry into this subject was made but the India Report of that year shows an estimate of some 2,267,000 persons as belonging to depressed classes in Rajputana. Now this figure could not possibly have been arrived at without including the Bhils who are not considered as untouchable in the sense that the Chamars and allied castes are. I am not at all confident that this enquiry met with much enthusiasm in the States and there were perhaps suspicions that a social uplift campaign was to be inaugurated. In a conservative and aristocratic Hindu society where each caste has a definite position in the scheme of things, such a rumour would undoubtedly be regarded with disfavour.

DEPRESSED CASTES.					
Chamar	...	766,643	Ghancha	...	4,772
Balai	...	218,857	Kalbelia	...	3,740
Bambhi	...	162,863	Kanjar	...	3,553
Raigar	...	130,108	Khangar	...	2,925
Bhangi	...	92,747	Bargi	...	1,598
Sargara	...	31,800	Aheri	...	1,204
Dhanak	...	30,733	Satia	...	1,113
Meghwal	...	23,278	Bansphod	...	926
Dhed	...	19,907	Tirgar	...	708
Thori	...	17,397	Rawal	...	677
Koria	...	11,808	Dabgar	...	652
Bagri	...	10,397	Bazigar	...	372
Garoda	...	8,699	Kuchband	...	326
Sansi	...	6,719	Bidakia	...	63
Nat	...	6,416	Pasi	...	48
Mahar	...	5,362	Sarbhangi	...	23

14. Subsidiary Table 1 shows the variations in numbers recorded in certain castes at each Census since 1901. There appears to be a certain amount of interchange between those recorded as Bambhi, Balai and Raigar which is due more than anything else to the vagaries of enumeration. Pathans and Sheikhs show an increase of 25·0 and 44·9 per cent. respectively since 1921, owing to the absorption of minor Muslim occupational castes. Rajputs have increased by only 7·6 per cent. during the decade but at every Census there is a difficulty of excluding those who more properly belong to the caste of Daroga. Variations shown by other castes do not call for any particular comment except that the increase of 17·9 per cent. in Jats is due to recent Sikh immigration to the northern parts of Bikaner. *Variation in numbers since 1901.*

15. Imperial Table XVIII shows the variation in the population of Bhils, Grassias, Merats, Minas and Rawats at each Census since 1891, and in each instance is an increase recorded during the past 40 years. It is curious to note that while among the Bhils and Minas there is a tendency to be returned in increasing numbers as Hindus rather than as Animists, the reverse is the case with the Grassias who are higher in the social scale than Bhils and most Minas and who on this occasion include 8,258 Animists as against 11 in 1921. The only possible explanation for this phenomenon is that instructions for the guidance of the enumerating staff included one to the effect that, as a general rule, in cases of doubt, those primitive tribes who lived in contact with Hindus were ordinarily to be returned as such, while those whose habitations were in the more inaccessible parts of the country, such as are occupied by Grassias, should be regarded as belonging to Tribal religions. *Variations among semi-primitive tribes.*

16. Subsidiary Table 2 appended to this Chapter shows the principal castes returned by Indian Christians, Muslims, Sikhs, persons of Tribal religions and by persons collectively termed Mahajans. *Castes returned by Christians, Muslims, Sikhs, Tribals, and by Mahajans.*

17. In Bharatpur there is a community of 557 persons who were returned as being of a caste known as Chaube. They are not Brahmans but it is possible that they were formerly Banjaras and have now settled down to agricultural pursuits. At previous Censuses they have been erroneously classified as Brahmans. In the same State 524 persons in Kumher Tehsil were entered as Rajputs with the addition of no clan name. Enquiry showed that their first ancestor who was a Brahman, had forcibly carried off a married Rajput girl and married her, and the descendants are known as Tarkars and not Thakurs (Rajput) as alleged by them. The caste therefore appears as Tarkar *New castes recorded.*

in the record. Certain followers of the *Radhaswami* faith in Marwar belonging to the Pancholi section of Kayasthas recorded themselves as *Satsangis*, an entry which was accepted by the State authorities. They number 381 and may be regarded as a new sectarian caste.

Europeans and Anglo-Indians.

18. Imperial Table XIX shows that there are 932 Europeans and persons of allied races in the Agency of whom 656 were returned from the States of Jaipur, Marwar and Sirohi. The majority of these are connected with the Railway at the large centres of Bandikui, Phulera, Gangapur, Jodhpur and Abu Road. The same may be said of the 828 Anglo-Indians of whom 718 were returned from those same three States. The marginal statement shows the distribution in detail. One would expect to find some connection between the total number of Europeans and Anglo-Indians and the total number of those whose mother tongue is some European or similar language, but it is curious to note that the former number is 1,760 whereas the latter is 1,909. A possible explanation is that some Indian Christians including Goanese have returned English or Portuguese as their mother tongue.

State.		Europeans and Allied races	Anglo-Indians.	Total.
Rajputana	...	*932*	*828*	*1,760*
Abu	...	62	18	80
Alwar	...	20	4	24
Banswara	...	3	...	3
Bharatpur	...	28	6	34
Bikaner	...	33	12	45
Bundi	...	17	...	17
Dholpur	...	9	5	14
Jaipur	...	427	436	863
Jhalawar	...	3	...	3
Kishangarh	...	...	8	8
Kotah	...	20	24	44
Marwar	...	103	80	183
Mewar	...	66	8	74
Partabgarh	...	1	...	1
Shahpura	...	1	...	1
Sirohi	...	126	202	328
Tonk	...	13	25	38

PART II.—BY STATES, ETC.

Reference to statistics.

19. Imperial Table XVII Part II shows the more numerically important castes in each State. The percentage of the population so shown varies from 92 in Jaipur to 60 in Abu and Lawa as will be seen by the marginal statement. In only seven of the States, etc., does the population shown by caste represent less than 80 per cent. of the total population. In former Reports it was the practice to select for this Table a number of castes that formed a certain percentage of the total population of the Agency and to exhibit in tabular form their distribution in each State. The disadvantage of this method is that certain castes that are found exclusively perhaps in only one State are not of sufficient numerical importance in relation to the population of the whole Agency to be exhibited except as 'others' or 'minor castes'. An instance of this is the caste of 'Dhed' who number 19,907 of whom 19,681 are found in Sirohi where they are more numerous than any other caste. For this reason Part II of the Caste Table has been compiled in its present and perhaps more interesting form. In deference to a suggestion made prior to the Census that the Table should exhibit a distribution by castes in units smaller than States such as Tehsils, etc., Provincial Table III has been prepared. For this Table 50 castes of general or local interest numbering in the aggregate 886 per mille of the total population have been selected and from it can be traced the detailed distribution of each of them.

Percentage of total population shown by Castes in Imperial Table XVII Part II.

State		Percentage	State		Percentage
Abu	...	60	Karauli	...	91
Alwar	...	89	Kishangarh	...	67
Banswara	...	88	Kotah	...	88
Bharatpur	...	84	Kushalgarh	...	89
Bikaner	...	85	Lawa	...	60
Bundi	...	80	Marwar	...	90
Dholpur	...	86	Mewar	...	87
Dungarpur	...	89	Partabgarh	...	71
Jaipur	...	92	Shahpura	...	66
Jaisalmer	...	84	Sirohi	...	88
Jhalawar	...	69	Tonk	...	79

20. The statement in the margin shows the most numerous caste in each State except Abu and Lawa, together with its proportion to the whole State population. These proportions vary from 84 per cent. in the case of the Bhils in Kushalgarh to 9 per cent. for the Dheds of Sirohi. It will be seen that Bhils are the most numerous community in Banswara, Dungarpur, Kushalgarh, Mewar and Partabgarh though in Mewar they only form 14 per cent. of the population. Jats are the most numerous in Bikaner, Jaipur, Kishangarh and Marwar though in no State do they exceed 23 per cent. of the population. The mixed nature of the population in Bharatpur, Dholpur, Kotah and Tonk is shown by the fact that in each of these States the depressed Chamars exceed in numbers any other caste, though their proportions to the entire population of each State is only 16, 17, 12 and 13 per cent. respectively. The depressed castes in each State are shown in Subsidiary Table 3 at the end of this Chapter. Numerous Castes.

THE MOST NUMEROUS CASTE IN EACH STATE.

State.	Caste.	Persons.	Percentage of State population.
Alwar ...	Meo ...	117,381	16
Banswara ...	Bhil ...	144,925	64
Bharatpur ...	Chamar ...	79,181	16
Bikaner ...	Jat ...	215,947	23
Bundi ...	Mina ...	33,910	16
Dholpur ...	Chamar ...	42,405	17
Dungarpur ...	Bhil ...	123,350	54
Jaipur ...	Jat ...	313,609	12
Jaisalmer ...	Rajput ...	20,068	26
Jhalawar ...	Sondhia ...	27,179	25
Karauli ...	Mina ...	32,022	23
Kishangarh ...	Jat ...	15,529	18
Kotah ...	Chamar ...	83,022	12
Kushalgarh ...	Bhil ...	29,985	84
Marwar ...	Jat ...	283,933	13
Mewar ...	Bhil ...	216,283	14
Partabgarh ...	Bhil ...	29,445	38
Shahpura ...	Gujar ...	5,179	10
Sirohi ...	Dhed ...	19,681	9
Tonk ...	Chamar ...	40,123	13

21. Provincial Table III shows the distribution of certain castes in each tehsil, pargana, etc., of every State and we are able therefrom to determine the presence or absence of them in any particular locality. From this Table in which Mahajans are treated as one caste, the following statement has been prepared which shows for each rural administrative unit except in Abu, Jaisalmer and Lawa, the largest community found therein. Abu and Lawa consist of one unit each and the castes found therein are shown in Imperial Table XVII Part II. As regards Jaisalmer the 50 selected castes only amount in the aggregate in some of the units to a very small proportion of the sparse population, but on the whole, Hindu Rajputs appear generally to be in the majority in most parts of the State:— Castes in Tehsils, etc.

STATEMENT SHOWING THE CASTES WHICH FORM THE LARGEST COMMUNITY IN EACH ADMINISTRATIVE UNIT.

Caste, etc.	State.	Tehsils, etc.	Caste, etc.	State.	Tehsils, etc.
Jat ...	Bharatpur ...	Bharatpur, Dig, Kumher, Nadbai.	Chamar.—*Concld.*	Kotah ...	Baran, Barod, Chechat, Digod, Kanwas, Kishanganj, Ladpura, Sangod, Shahabad.
	Bikaner ...	Every Tehsil.			
	Jaipur ...	Malpura, Sambhar, Shekhawati, Torawati, Khetri, Sikar.		Tonk ...	Nimbahera, Sironj, Tonk.
	Kishangarh.	Arain, Kishangarh, Rupnagar, Sarwar.	Bhil ...	Banswara ...	Every Tehsil.
	Marwar ...	Bilara, Didwana, Jodhpur, Malani, Merta, Nagaur, Parbatsar, Sambhar-Marwar.		Dungarpur...	Every Tehsil.
				Jhalawar ...	Patan.
				Kotah ...	Asnawar.
				Kushalgarh.	Every Tehsil.
				Mewar ...	Chitorgarh, Kherwara, Magra, Udaipur.
	Mewar ...	Bhilwara, Kapasin, Rashmi.		Partabgarh.	Every Tehsil.
Brahman.	Alwar ...	Thana Ghazi.		Sirohi ...	Madar, Rohera.
	Jaipur ...	Amber, Sawai Jaipur.	Mahajan.	Marwar ...	Bali, Jalore, Pachbhadra, Siwana.
	Dholpur ...	Rajakhera.			
Chamar.	Alwar ...	Katumbar.		Sirohi ...	Posaliya.
	Bharatpur ...	Rupbas, Uchain, Weir.	Rajput ...	Marwar ...	Phalodi, Shergarh, Sheo.
	Dholpur ...	Bari, Gird, Baseri.		Mewar ...	Khamnor, Kumalgarh, Rajnagar.

STATEMENT SHOWING THE CASTES WHICH FORM THE LARGEST COMMUNITY IN EACH ADMINISTRATIVE UNIT.—*Concluded.*

Caste, etc.	State.	Tehsils, etc.
Mina	Alwar	Partabgarh, Rajgarh, Reni.
	Bundi	Dei, Gaindoli, Patan.
	Dholpur	Sir Muthra.
	Jaipur	Dausa, Gangapur, Hindaun, Sawai Madhopur, Uniara.
	Karauli	Hazur, Mandrail, Sapotra, Utgir.
	Kotah	Aklerah, Chhippa-barod, Itawa, Kunjer, Mangrol.
	Mewar	Chhoti Sadri, Girwa, Jahazpur.
	Tonk	Aligarh, Chhabra.
Gujar	Alwar	Bansur, Narayanpur.
	Bharatpur	Bayana.
	Bundi	Baroondhan, Hindoli.
	Karauli	Machilpur.
	Mewar	Asind, Hurra, Mandalgarh, Saharan.
Mali	Kotah	Antah.
Rebari	Sirohi	Pamera.
Meo	Alwar	Alwar, Govindgarh, Khairthal, Kishangarh, Lachmangarh, Malakhera, Ramgarh, Tijara, Tapukrah.
Meo.-*Cld.*	Bharatpur	Kaman, Nagar, Pahari.
Ahir	Alwar	Ajeraka, Bahror, Mandhan, Mandawar, Nimrana.
	Jaipur	Kotkasim.
Kachhi	Dholpur	Kolari.
Sondhia.	Jhalawar	Awar, Dag, Gangdhar, Pachpahar.
	Tonk	Pirawa.
Lodha	Kotah	Bakani, Manohar Thana.
Dhed	Sirohi	Barlut, Magra, Sirohi.
Dhakar.	Kotah	Khanpur.
Grassia	Sirohi	Bhakar, Pindwara, Santhpur.
Sirvi	Marwar	Desuri, Sojat.
Kumhar	Marwar	Jaitaran.
Kunbi	Marwar	Jaswantpura.
Rebari	Marwar	Pali.
Bishnoi	Marwar	Sanchore.

It is curious to note that Mahajans are the majority community in five contiguous units in Marwar and Sirohi.

1.—VARIATION IN CASTE, TRIBE, ETC., SINCE 1901.

CASTE, TRIBE OR RACE.	PERSONS.				PERCENTAGE OF VARIATION.			PROPORTION, PER MILLE, TO TOTAL POPULATION,* 1931.	REASONS FOR MARKED VARIATION.
	1931.	1921.	1911.	1901.	1921-31.	1911-21.	1901-11.		
1	2	3	4	5	6	7	8	9	10
1. Agarwal ...	183,754	168,156	199,629	223,209	+ 9·3	− 15·8	− 10·6	16·3	
2. Ahir ...	182,165	163,311	169,129	159,434	+ 11·5	− 3·4	+ 6·1	16·2	
3. Balai ...	218,927	203,091	197,511	313,174	+ 7·8	+ 2·8	− 36·9	19·5	See Note against Raigar. Bambhi returned as Balai in 1901.
4. Bambhi ...	162,865	159,276	133,826	1,133	+ 2·3	+ 19·0	+ 11,711·7	14·5	
5. Bhil ...	655,647	549,531	448,910	339,786	+ 19·3	+ 22·4	+ 32·1	58·4	
6. Brahman ...	854,634	772,156	922,810	1,012,396	+ 10·7	− 16·3	− 8·8	76·1	
7. Chamar ...	767,263	696,904	734,110	688,023	+ 10·1	− 5·1	+ 6·7	68·3	
8. Daroga ...	177,104	160,735	177,520	155,908	+ 10·2	− 9·5	+ 13·9	15·8	Includes Chakar in 1921, 1911 and 1901.
9. Gujar ...	526,791	484,130	500,046	462,739	+ 8·8	− 3·2	+ 8·1	46·9	
10. Jat ...	1,042,153	883,716	928,486	845,909	+ 17·9	− 4·8	+ 9·8	92·8	
11. Khati ...	209,937	142,804	134,992	152,037	+ 47·0	+ 5·8	− 11·2	18·7	Includes Sutar in 1931.
12. Kumhar ...	357,751	299,055	309,234	264,521	+ 19·6	− 3·3	+ 16·9	31·9	
13. Mali ...	369,178	316,632	336,876	313,285	+ 16·6	− 6·0	+ 7·5	32·9	
14. Meo ...	167,530	152,550	165,690	168,596	+ 9·8	− 7·9	− 1·7	14·9	
15. Mina ...	607,369	515,241	558,689	477,129	+ 17·9	− 7·8	+ 17·1	54·1	
16. Nai ...	166,096	148,627	162,463	154,763	+ 11·8	− 8·5	+ 5·0	14·8	
17. Oswal ...	197,460	180,954	209,965	209,188	+ 9·1	− 13·8	+ ·4	17·6	
18. Pathan ...	119,803	95,867	108,291	105,890	+ 25·0	− 11·5	+ 2·3	10·7	Probably includes many minor castes differently returned at previous Censuses
19. Raigar ...	130,104	76,841	81,568	84,296	+ 69·3	− 5·8	− 3·2	11·6	Partially returned as Balai and Bambhi in 1921.
20. Rajput (Hindu and Jain) ...	633,830	588,885	632,907	585,784	+ 7·6	− 7·0	+ 8·0	56·5	
(More important clans.)									
(a) Chauhan ...	*88,694*	*91,760*	*106,510*	*86,460*	− *3·3*	− *13·8*	+ *23·2*	*139·9*	Classification at previous Censuses not in all cases accurate.
(b) Jadon, including Bhatti ...	*61,849*	*60,201*	*71,957*	*74,666*	+ *2·7*	− *16·3*	− *3 6*	*97 6*	
(c) Kachwaha ...	*96,429*	*83,216*	*98,030*	*100,208*	+ *15·9*	− *15·1*	− *2·2*	*152·1*	
(d) Jhala ...	*5,068*	*4,143*	*4,105*	*5,446*	+ *22 3*	+ *·9*	− *24 6*	*8 0*	
(e) Ponwar ...	*36,088*	*33,792*	*45,430*	*43,435*	+ *6·8*	− *25·6*	+ *4 6*	*57 0*	
(f) Rathor ...	*163,288*	*154,358*	*176,757*	*123,734*	+ *5·8*	− *12·7*	+ *42 9*	*257 6*	
(g) Sisodia, including Gahlot ...	*54,738*	*71,388*	*61,543*	*51,366*	− *23·3*	+ *16·0*	+ *19·8*	*86 4*	
(h) Tonwar ...	*20,868*	*18,012*	*21,527*	*19,723*	+ *15 9*	− *16·3*	+ *9·1*	*32·9*	
(i) Parihar ...	*22,453*	*14,350*	*16,367*	*9,448*	+ *56·5*	− *12 3*	+ *73·2*	*35·4*	
21. Rebari ...	135,820	123,653	129,918	99,099	+ 9·8	− 4·8	+ 31·1	12·1	
22. Sheikh ...	210,499	145,226	182,019	242,046	+ 44·9	− 20·2	− 24·8	18 8	Probably includes many minor castes differently returned at previous Censuses
23. Europeans and Allied Races. ...	932	840	1,179	969	+ 11·0	− 28·8	+ 21·7	·08	
British subjects ...	*856*	*804*	*1,127*	*885*	+ *6·5*	− *28 7*	+ *27·3*	*·07*	
24. Anglo-Indians ...	828	641	529	503	+ 29·2	+ 21·2	+ 5 2	07	

* Figures for Rajput clans represent proportion per mille to total population of Rajputs only.

2(a).—CASTES, ETC., RETURNED BY INDIAN CHRISTIANS.

Agarwal	5	Bhil	183	Kunbi	4	As Indian Christian.	3,573
Ahir	1	Brahman	4	Paraiyan	1		
Balai	44	Chamar	40	Marehta	3	Total	4,021
Bhangi	212	Kumhar	1				

(b).—CASTES, ETC., RETURNED BY MUSLIMS.

Bhat	1,620	Jat	1,257	Makrani	1,320	Ranghar	24,079
Bhatiara	1,415	Jogi	2,094	Mali	2,692	Rangrez	15,826
Bhishti	23,863	Julaha	16,655	Manihar	6,716	Rath	52,671
Bisati	3,384	Kaimkhani	35,685	Meo	167,514	Saiyed	33,409
Bohra	15,302	Kalal	3,082	Merat	3,084	Sheikh	210,499
Chhipa	7,553	Kasai	24,826	Mirasi	15,483	Silawat	9,582
Deswali	5,854	Khanzada	8,616	Mochi	1,420	Sindhi	48,587
Dhobi	5,049	Khati	1,863	Moghal	11,650	Sipahi	1,425
Dholi	4,710	Khoja	1,071	Mulla	1,780	Teli	30,495
Fakir	54,777	Kumhar	6,919	Nai	8,894	Minor Castes	20,982
Gaddi	5,326	Kunjra	4,427	Niaria	2,447	Unspecified	2,663
Ghancha	1,657	Labhana	5,742	Pathan	119,799		
Ghosi	1,611	Lakhera	2,019	Pinara	18,489		
Hammal	1,383	Lohar	13,659	Rana	1,500	Total	1,069,325

(c).—CASTES, ETC., RETURNED BY SIKHS.

Agarwal	12	Darzi	10	Khattri	571	Rangrez	2
Ahir	13	Gujar	2	Kumhar	1,221	Sadhu	20
Bauria	1,274	Jat	26,942	Lodha	2	Sikligar	12
Bazigar	88	Jhinwar	38	Lohar	20	Sunar	55
Bhangi	5,680	Julaha	6	Mali	142	Swami	4
Bhat	2	Kabirpanthi	1	Manihar	1	Unspecified	1,194
Brahman	17	Kahar	94	Mochi	10		
Chamar	566	Kalal	9	Nai	208		
Charan	2	Kambo	726	Naik	1		
Chhipa	174	Khati	2,455	Nanakpanthi	31	Total	41,605

(d).—CASTES, ETC., RETURNED BY THOSE OF TRIBAL RELIGIONS.

Bagri	755	Chamar	1	Kathiara	39	Sadhu	1
Balai	6	Dangi	9	Kharol	6	Sahar	170
Bambhi	2	Dholi	4	Mina	20,336	Sansi	428
Banjara	149	Grassia	8,258	Moghia	134	Unspecified	6
Bauria	350	Jogi	1	Naik	1		
Bavaria	126	Kalbelia	25	Nat	91		
Bhil	198,005	Kanjár	182	Patel	7	Total	229,092

(e).—MAHAJAN CASTES.

Agarwal	183,754	Jaiswal	2,494	Narsinghpura	8,515	Saraogi	82,648
Bagerwal	3,418	Khandelwal	48,485	Nima	1,381	Minor Castes	4,970
Bijabargi	7,477	Mahesri	81,819	Oswal	197,460	Caste unspecified	7,214
Chitora	2,109	Mawar	8,884	Palliwal	4,362		
Humar	10,541	Nagda	4,030	Porwal	29,359	Total	638,820

Of 300,748 Jains all save 1,256 belong to the above castes.

3.—Distribution of Depressed Castes.

CASTE.	Rajputana.	ABU	ALWAR.	BANSWARA.	BHARATPUR.	BIKANER.	BUNDI.	DHOLPUR.	DUNGARPUR.	JAIPUR.	JAISALMER.	JHALAWAR.	KARAULI.	KISHANGARH.	KOTAH.	KUSHALGARH.	LAWA.	MARWAR.	MEWAR.	PARTABGARH.	SHAHPURA.	SIROHI.	TONK.
Total ...	***1,565,409***	***487***	***101,079***	***11,365***	***98,972***	***125,284***	***32,238***	***45,309***	***11,165***	***396,791***	***8,836***	***18,778***	***22,481***	***14,255***	***102,849***	***676***	***492***	***301,887***	***169,271***	***5,350***	***9,088***	***32,578***	***56,178***
Aheri ...	**1,204**	...	27	...	78	92	...	...	...	...	...	...	...	...	853	...	...	...	159	...	...	...	...
Bagri ...	**10,397**	11	1	...	...	...	188	...	...	727	...	1,646	18	444	254	...	24	1,759	1,545	...	148	1,050	2,582
Balai ...	**218,857**	31	5,099	8,183	1,011	2,667	8,875	...	3,241	68,886	...	5,803	5	4,964	4,951	12	30	42,703	66,613	1,120	1,591	368	3,709
Bambhi ...	**162,863**	1	...	12	...	561	1	...	8	16	...	21	...	...	250	7	7	158,008	3,498	108	...	22	348
Bansphod.	**926**	...	34	...	...	...	...	...	122	...	...	...	...	...	...	...	...	...	...	70	...	416	284
Bargi ...	**1,593**	..	...	...	333	...	...	...	...	416	...	...	...	...	...	...	...	844	...	...	...	...	...
Bazigar ...	**372**	...	...	...	...	238	...	...	30	9	...	...	...	48	...	3	...	33	...	...	...	11	...
Bhangi ..	**92,747**	208	10,494	527	6,177	9,816	1,967	2,269	666	23,470	45	847	1,805	861	6,978	...	48	15,059	6,109	414	511	1,290	4,186
Bidakia ...	**63**	...	...	...	63	...	...	...	...	...	...	...	...	...	...	...	...	...	...	...	...	...	...
Chamar ...	**766,643**	89	79,546	6,161	79,181	75,005	18,654	42,405	6,545	234,442	1,035	10,582	21,083	8,443	83,022	359	286	6,224	49,434	3,526	4,917	681	40,123
Dabgar ...	**652**	...	...	28	...	31	...	...	189	1	...	...	...	10	38	1	...	337	...	15	...	52	...
Dhanak ...	**30,733**	...	3,399	...	10	8,601	...	274	...	14,411	...	41	35	27	...	...	...	514	3,167	...	45	64	145
Dhed ...	**19,907**	9	...	...	...	...	...	...	...	2	...	...	...	...	...	...	...	...	215	...	...	19,681	...
Garoda ...	**8,699**	...	...	...	...	494	...	...	...	...	421	...	...	...	...	8	...	6,755	158	...	...	868	...
Ghancha ...	**4,772**	5	...	478	...	6	...	...	...	...	...	...	...	11	...	246	...	2,964	745	...	...	314	8
Kalbelia ...	**3,740**	...	...	...	82	70	408	106	95	92	...	121	...	...	138	...	...	275	2,284	60	9	...	...
Kanjar ...	**3,553**	4	309	...	173	204	409	...	43	407	...	2	1	3	37	...	...	...	1,619	...	...	...	342
Khangar ...	**2,926**	...	8	...	...	...	79	...	...	750	...	6	6	5	1,086	...	...	...	...	...	...	...	985
Koria ...	**11,303**	...	...	...	11,301	...	...	...	...	...	...	...	...	...	...	...	...	...	...	...	...	2	...
Kuchband.	**326**	...	101	...	...	40	...	...	...	74	...	22	...	...	...	...	...	...	34	21	...	34	...
Mahar ...	**5,362**	...	61	...	...	5	709	...	...	1,059	...	...	...	...	3,528	...	...	...	...	...	...	...	...
Meghwal ...	**23,273**	21	...	...	...	10,524	28	...	...	...	7,385	...	...	...	622	...	...	...	4,205	...	...	538	...
Nat ...	**6,416**	...	266	11	566	89	115	255	79	2,078	...	193	26	140	254	...	...	1,405	821	5	24	59	30
Pasi ..	**43**	...	...	...	2	...	...	...	...	24	...	...	...	...	3	...	...	...	...	...	...	10	4
Raigar ...	**130,103**	3	1,734	...	...	5,013	805	...	...	54,648	...	...	...	4,254	44	...	97	32,284	25,977	...	1,881	149	3,264
Rawal ...	**677**	...	...	...	...	24	...	...	5	105	...	15	...	17	27	...	...	...	474	10	...	...	...
Sansi ...	**6,719**	...	...	1	...	2,568	...	...	...	674	...	1	...	...	673	12	...	2,270	417	...	...	6	97
Sarbhangi.	**23**	...	...	...	...	...	...	...	...	...	...	...	2	...	...	...	...	...	21	...	...	...	...
Sargara ...	**31,300**	105	...	795	...	1	...	...	176	...	...	...	...	28	...	...	...	21,598	1,786	...	12	6,778	71
Satia ...	**1,113**	...	...	...	...	39	...	...	...	...	...	28	...	...	81	...	...	965	...	...	...	...	...
Thori	**17,397**	...	...	174	...	9,696	...	...	16	...	...	...	...	...	10	28	...	7,431	39	1	...	2	...
Tirgar	**708**	...	...	...	...	...	...	...	...	...	...	...	...	...	...	...	...	459	11	...	...	238	...

APPENDIX.

The Rajput Clans of Rajputana.

History.

1. The various authorities on the ancient History of India hold divided opinions as to the origin of the Rajputs. Most are agreed that they came from beyond the northern confines of India. Colonel Tod, a Political Officer in Rajputana more than a hundred years ago, and author of that classic work "The Annals and Antiquities of Rajasthan", ascribes to them a Scythic origin. Another authority maintains that the origin of many clans dates from the Saka or the Kushan invasion which began about the middle of the second century B.C. Yet another historian claims for them descent from the White Huns who destroyed the Gupta Empire in A.D. 480. The bards (Charans) give various clans mythical descent from Sun, Moon and Fire. The tribes of the Solar line being the Sesodias of Mewar, Banswara, Dungarpur, Partabgarh and Shahpura, the Kachwahas (or more correctly Kushwahas), of Jaipur and Alwar, the Rathors of Marwar, Bikaner and Kishangarh and the Bargujars of no particular State. Of the Lunar line there are the Jadons of Jaisalmer and Karauli and the Tonwars who now rule in no State in Rajputana. The clans which claim descent from Agni, the element of fire, are the Ponwars, Chauhans of Bundi, Kotah and Sirohi, the Parihars and Solankis, although recent research scholars maintain that the Chauhans and Parihars belong to the Solar and the Solankis to the Lunar line.

There were supposed to be thirty six Royal Races of Rajputs, many of whom are not found in Rajputana at the present day. Among them is the Huna or Hun and inscriptions have been found recording the fact of ancestors of Sesodia and other Rajput kings having Hun wives.

Although there were doubtless those whom we now know as Rajputs in Rajputana before the seventh century, many of the dynasties now ruling were established between the seventh and the beginning of the eleventh century A.D. The Sesodia branch of the Gahlots migrated from Gujarat and occupied what is now the south-western portion of Mewar, their earliest inscription being dated 646 A.D. Next came the Parihars who began to rule at Mandore, the ancient capital of Marwar, a few years later, and they were followed in the eighth century by the Chauhans and Jadons who settled down at Sambhar and in Jaisalmer respectively. Lastly, in the tenth century the Ponwars and Solankis began to be powerful in the south-west.

It is interesting to note that, of these Rajput clans, only three are now represented by the Ruling Princes of Rajputana, namely, the Sesodias, Jadons and Chauhans; and of these three, only two are still to be found in their original settlements, the Chauhans having moved gradually south-west and south-east to Sirohi, Bundi and Kotah. Later on the Jadons obtained a footing in Karauli about the middle of the eleventh century, though they had lived in the vicinity for a very long time; the Kachwahas came from Gwalior to Jaipur about 1128; the Rathors settled in Marwar in the beginning of the thirteenth century; and the Jhala State of Jhalawar did not come into existence till 1838.

The Principal Clans.

2. Of all the Hindu Rajputs found at the present time in Rajputana, 91 per cent. belong to one or other of the well defined exogamous clans known as Bargujar, Chauhan, Gahlot, Gaur, Jadon, Jhala, Kachwaha, Parihar, Ponwar, Rathor, Solanki and Tonwar. Within some of these there are important sub-divisions which in some cases have outnumberd the parent clan and except for the tie of exogamy, have almost, a separate existence. For instance, the clan of Chauhan includes the Haras of Bundi and Kotah and the Deoras of Sirohi; Gahlot includes the far more numerous and important sub-division of Sesodia who rule in Mewar, Banswara, Dungarpur, Partabgarh and Shahpura; Jadon includes the far famed Bhattis of Jaisalmer while the numerous clan of Kachwaha includes the Narukas of Alwar. The clans which are represented by the Ruling Princes can therefore be summarised as in the marginal statement. The remaining six clans of Bargujar, Gaur, Parihar, Ponwar, Solanki and Tonwar which, in the aggregate, only comprise 17 per cent. of all Rajputs do not now rule in any State in Rajputana.

Clan.		States.
Chauhan	...	Bundi Kotah, Sirohi.
Gahlot	...	Mewar. Banswara, Dungarpur, Partabgarh, Shahpura.
Jadon	...	Karauli, Jaisalmer.
Jhala	...	Jhalawar.
Kachwaha	...	Jaipur, Alwar.
Rathor	...	Marwar, Bikaner, Kishangarh.

The structure of the clans.

3. The Rajput States have a constitution which differs from that of any other group of States in India. An ordinary person would not perhaps suspect a radical difference between say, Gwalior and Marwar. He might indeed assume that Gwalior was a State in which a Mahratta Prince ruled over Mahrattas and that the Prince of Marwar ruled over Rajputs and would probably be surprised to learn that there are

very few Mahrattas in Gwalior and that there are more Rajputs there than there are in Marwar. The marginal statement shows the percentage of Rajputs in the population of each Rajput State. The real difference is that the Gwalior Prince represents a single family of a successful Captain of armies who annexed, in the 18th. century, all the territory he could lay hands on, while the Marwar and other Rajput Princes of Rajputana are the heads of clans which have for several centuries been lords of the soil which now make up the territory of the Rajput States. Such a State, where its peculiar structure has been least modified means the territory over which a particular clan or division of a clan, claims dominion for its Chief and political predominance for itself by right of occupation or conquest. The Ruler therefore instead of being an absolute despot exercises a jurisdiction more or less limited over an aristocracy consisting principally of his kinsmen and connections. He is the hereditary Chief of the dominant clan and the nearest legitimate descendant of the former founder. But even primogeniture has been required to qualify up to a low standard of competency and when direct heirs fail there is the right of adoption from one or other branch of the stock group, and there are not wanting instances of internal strife when the nobles have not unanimously approved of the choice.

Alwar	... 8	Karauli	...4
Banswara	... 2	Kishangarh	...5
Bikaner	... 6	Kotah	...2
Bundi	... 2	Marwar	...9
Dungarpur	... 4	Mewar	...8
Jaipur	... 4	Partabgarh	...4
Jaisalmer	...26	Shahpura	...3
Jhalawar	... 3	Sirohi	...7

In all these States there are various signs of feudalism, such as quotas for service, fees on succession and aids on special occasions, but before the constitution can be termed feudal in its entirety, it is as well to examine what is meant by feudalism according to Western standards. The origin of the system was the necessity for protection against a common enemy. An individual could ask for protection in return for service befitting a free man, or a poor land owner could place his land under a powerful one for protection. A King would view this with displeasure as it tended to weaken his authority; so, in course of time came about a system whereby rich land owners became vassals of the King under obligation of finding so many horses, men, etc., for the service of the State. There was not necessarily any community of kinship. In the Rajput States we have therefore some of the features of feudalism, but the essential difference is the system by which the land is held by the branch families and this is the basis of the constitution and forms a characteristic distinction. This is not accurately feudal, as the nobles really claim to be coparceners with the rulers in their right to dominion over the soil and to the fruits of it. In most of the States the Ruler and his nobles really constitute a *fr'erage* though this is not so apparent in Mewar where nearly half of the great nobles belong to other clans. In this State it is said that formerly the estate holders used to move round every three years. The system was a check to the imbibing of local attachment, and the prohibition against erecting forts for refuge or defiance prevented its growth if acquired. It produced the object intended, obedience to the Chief and unity against the restless Moghul.

The vassals of Marwar where the *fr'erage* is perhaps strongest are of two kinds. Some are deemed to have obtained their lands by conquest and their holdings are irrevocable and must be perpetuated by adoption on the failure of lineal issue. The others may, on lapses, be resumed and added to the fisc. Some years ago when there was a dispute between a Prince and some of his nobles the representation from the latter to the British Government contained the expression, "When our services are acceptable, then he is our lord; when not, we are again his brothers and kin, claimants and laying claim to the land." This may be described as the essence of the constitution of the clans that has survived through many centuries of disruption. Though feudalism is apparent in quotas for service, reliefs on succession, and aids on special occasions, many States have substituted cash payments for quotas for service but the move is not popular with the great nobles as it tends to increase the Prince's power and to lessen their own. There have in the past been many serious disputes between the Princes and their nobles; the Princes striving always to depress and break down the power of their great nobles and the latter determined to restrict the strength of their rulers. British paramountcy is favourable to the Princes on such occasions, as the inclination is to support a strong central administration. There is no doubt that but for British intervention many of the States would have broken up under the flood of the Mahratta armies and the status of the clans dissolved. Their survival gives us the best specimens of early institutions within the purview of comparatively settled civilisation. But peace and prosperity are not favourable to early institutions any more than are war and rapine. The more efficient, according to modern standards, does the administration of a State become, the more these old institutions tend to disappear and in many States their only relics are seen in the outward ceremonies and rituals of Durbars, etc., though the clansmen have always a restless, though sometimes a resigned eye looking for movements that clash with their ideas or rights and privileges.

Instructions for the Census.

4. At each Census during the past thirty years, an attempt has been made to obtain an accurate record of the strength of the various clans. It cannot be said that the results have been satisfactory nor, in spite of careful instructions, can perfection be claimed for the figures now published in this Appendix. Adequate instructions for the guidance of Enumerators were by no means easy to draw up. In the first place it was necessary that all save pure Rajputs should be excluded; secondly, Enumerators could not be expected to be familiar with a long string of clan names and, thirdly, the Jaipur, Marwar and Bikaner Darbars desired that figures for the more important sub-divisions of the Kachwahas and Rathors should be obtained. With all these difficulties to contend with it was finally decided to issue to Enumerators the comparatively short list shown in the margin with additional instructions that for a person giving his or her clan as Rathor or Kachwaha, a further entry of the name of the sub-clan was to be made. In accordance with the wishes of the three Darbars referred to, figures for the important sub-divisions shown in the margin were separately tabulated. The difference between the Kachwaha and Rathor lists is that the former provides for every sub-division of the clan known in Rajputana however small or obscure, whereas the latter only contains 17 sub-clan names, all the remaining being amalgamated under 'other Rathors.' In spite of the comprehensive nature of the Kachwaha list 20 per cent. of the clan were returned as 'unspecified' and the result is that as many of them probably belong to one or other of the 24 sub-clans, the return is to some extent deficient. Especially is this the case in the parent State of Jaipur, where out of 59,095 members of the clan, no fewer than 11,797 are shown as 'unspecified' Kachwahas. The detailed list of 117 sub-divisions of this clan is shown as Annexure I.

Clan	
1. Bargujar.	
2. Chauhan.	*Hara* *Deora* *Nirbhan*
3. Gahlot.	*Sesodia*
4. Gaur.	
5. Jadon.	*Bhatti*
6. Jhala.	
7. Parihar.	
8. Ponwar	
9. Solanki.	
10. Tonwar.	
11. Kachwaha.	
12. Rathor.	

SUB-DIVISIONS OF THE KACHWAHA AND RATHOR CLANS.

Kachwaha.	Rathor.
1. Askarnot.	1. Chandel.*
2. Balbhadrot.	2. Jaitawat.
3. Balapota.	3. Deorajot.
4. Banbirpota.	4 Kumpawat.
5. Bankawat.	5. Kandhlot.
6 Bikalpota.	6. Champawat.
7. Chatturbhujot.	7. Mandlawat.
8. Hamirde.	8. Bala.
9. Khangarot.	9. Karamsot.
10. Kilanot.	10 Jodha.
11. Kumbhani.	11. Bika.
12. Kumbhawat.	12. Mertia.
13. Madhani.	13. Udawat.
14. Naruka.	14. Narawat.
15. Nathawat.	15 Bidawat
16. Pichanot.	16. Gaharwal.*
17. Pratapota.	17. Pattawat.
18. Puranmalot.	18. Others.
19. Rajawat Mansinghot, etc.	
20. Ramsinghot.	
21. Shekhawat.	
22. Saindasot.	
23. Sheobrahmpota.	
24. Surtanot.	
25. Unspecified Kachwahas.	

* These are not, accurately speaking, Rathor Sub-clans.

As regards the Rathors, the 17 sub-clans exhibited were selected for their importance or numerical superiority leaving 147 others to be amalgamated as 'other Rathors'. There is therefore some scope perhaps for finding a considerable number under this collective designation but not, it is thought, as many as 47 per cent. as the return shows. In the three States of Jaipur, Jaisalmer and Mewar out of 40,407 Rathors no fewer than 29,081 have been shown as 'others', many of whom, we have no reason to doubt, belong to one or other of the named clans.

A detailed examination of the figures received from all States shows that 27 per cent. of all Rathors showed no additional sub-division and therefore had perforce to be classified as 'other Rathors'. The return is therefore rather more defective than that for the Kachwaha clan, but both are a very great improvement on the results obtained at previous Censuses. A detailed list of the Rathor sub-divisions is shown as Annexure II.

Results obtained.

5. With this brief review of what is involved by an enumeration of the clans, we may proceed to consider the results obtained. The statement in the margin shows in order of numerical superiority the strength of each of the 12 important exogamous clans. As previously stated these figures represent 91 per cent. of all Hindu Rajputs in Rajputana, the remaining 9 per cent. being 29,928 persons of minor and in some cases obscure, clans chiefly returned from localities bordering on the United Provinces and Gwalior State, and 26,881 persons whose claim to be considered as Rajputs is doubtful. Among these latter are 20,660 persons in Mewar who permit widow re-marriage and are definitely considered to be *kam asl.* The Table opposite shows the detailed distribution of these 12 clans in the various States, etc., of the Agency.

Clan.	Persons.	Males.	Females.
Rathor ...	163,288	90,745	72,543
Kachwaha ...	96,429	60,880	35,549
Chauhan ...	88,694	46,699	41,995
Jadon ...	61,849	33,285	28,564
Gahlot ...	54,738	30,142	24,596
Ponwar ...	36,088	21,111	14,977
Parihar ...	22,453	11,406	11,047
Tonwar ...	20,868	11,200	9,668
Solanki ...	19,089	10,232	8,857
Gaur ...	5,307	3,061	2,246
Jhala ...	5,068	2,753	2,315
Bargujar ...	3,147	1,711	1,436
Total.	577,018	323,225	253,793

DETAILED DISTRIBUTION OF THE MAIN EXOGAMOUS CLANS.

STATE OR DISTRICT.	BARGUJAR.			CHAUHAN.			GAHLOT.			GAUR.			JADON.			JHALA.		
	Persons.	Males.	Females.	Persons.	Males.	Females.	Persons.	Males.	Females.	Persons.	Males.	Females.	Persons.	Males.	Females.	Persons.	Males.	Females.
1	2	3	4	5	6	7	8	9	10	11	12	13	14	15	16	17	18	19
Abu ...	...	...	...	**9**	8	1	...	...	...	...	...	...	...	...	...	...	...	...
Alwar ...	**1,290**	704	586	**8,698**	4,971	3,727	**103**	50	53	**316**	184	132	**1,026**	418	608	...	...	...
Banswara ...	...	...	...	**1,554**	856	698	**902**	467	435	**4**	3	1	**30**	16	14	**161**	98	63
Bharatpur ...	**200**	81	119	**1,400**	768	632	**448**	209	239	**365**	125	240	**2,382**	1,307	1,075	...	...	...
Bikaner ...	**228**	126	102	**3,845**	1,974	1,871	**1,202**	629	573	**358**	178	180	**9,846**	5,052	4,794	**4**	1	3
Bundi ...	...	...	...	**2,256**	1,365	891	**216**	75	141	**136**	77	59	**85**	29	56	**63**	21	42
Dholpur ...	**42**	23	19	**1,880**	745	1,135	**114**	46	68	**4**	1	3	**1,245**	818	427	...	...	...
Dungarpur ...	...	...	...	**3,399**	1,772	1,627	**1,567**	763	804	...	...	...	**28**	15	13	**30**	15	15
Jaipur ...	**963**	485	478	**13,033**	5,856	7,177	**1,253**	704	549	**1,177**	603	574	**3,704**	996	2,708	**39**	16	23
Jaisalmer ...	**4**	1	3	**729**	407	322	**435**	224	211	**2**	1	1	**9,829**	6,783	3,046	**137**	24	113
Jhalawar ...	**14**	10	4	**504**	244	260	**166**	88	78	**34**	19	15	**90**	42	48	**1,165**	706	459
Karauli ...	**172**	126	46	**639**	166	473	**25**	16	9	**22**	6	16	**3,603**	2,619	984	**5**	...	5
Kishangarh ...	**12**	5	7	**242**	144	98	**163**	25	138	**56**	22	34	**154**	86	68	...	...	...
Kotah ...	**59**	36	23	**4,939**	2,782	2,157	**1,364**	738	626	**665**	342	323	**588**	325	263	**468**	234	234
Kushalgarh (Chiefship) ...	**15**	7	8	**62**	31	31	**28**	14	14	**16**	5	11	**8**	2	6	**14**	7	7
Lawa (Estate) ...	...	...	...	**4**	1	3	**1**	1	...	...	...	...	...	...	...	...	...	...
Marwar ...	**133**	104	29	**22,206**	11,334	10,872	**8,110**	4,022	4,088	**658**	507	151	**24,743**	12,410	12,333	**54**	33	21
Mewar ...	...	...	...	**14,323**	7,485	6,838	**35,486**	20,232	15,254	**739**	442	297	**3,325**	1,815	1,510	**2,444**	1,513	931
Partabgarh ...	**11**	3	8	**531**	235	296	**1,495**	937	558	**15**	4	11	**202**	95	107	**64**	24	40
Shahpura ...	...	...	...	**85**	43	42	**523**	316	207	**65**	36	29	**99**	46	53	**1**	1	...
Sirohi ...	**4**	...	4	**5,732**	3,613	2,119	**750**	373	377	**8**	5	3	**429**	217	212	**45**	32	13
Tonk ...	...	...	...	**2,624**	1,399	1,225	**387**	213	174	**667**	501	166	**433**	199	234	**374**	28	346
Total Rajputana ...	**3,147**	**1,711**	**1,436**	**88,694**	**46,699**	**41,995**	**54,738**	**30,142**	**24,596**	**5,307**	**3,061**	**2,246**	**61,849**	**33,285**	**28,564**	**5,068**	**2,753**	**2,315**

DETAILED DISTRIBUTION OF THE MAIN EXOGAMOUS CLANS.—*Concluded.*

STATE OR DISTRICT.	KACHWAHA.			PARIHAR.			PONWAR.			RATHOR.			SOLANKI.			TONWAR.		
	Persons.	Males.	Females.	Persons.	Males.	Females.	Persons.	Males.	Females.	Persons	Males	Females	Persons.	Males	Females.	Persons.	Males	Females.
1	20	21	22	23	24	25	26	27	28	29	30	31	32	33	34	35	36	37
Abu ...	...	...	...	4	4	...	2	1	1	12	8	4	1	1	...	...	...	...
Alwar ...	8,892	5,466	3,426	21	10	11	431	110	321	1,036	529	507	30	12	18	905	354	551
Banswara ...	44	27	17	24	18	11	51	22	29	642	294	348	247	128	119	38	23	15
Bharatpur ...	1,667	940	727	37	14	23	1,604	826	778	246	155	91	54	31	23	210	78	132
Bikaner ...	7,370	3,588	3,782	1,769	897	872	2,743	1,427	1,316	23,985	16,286	7,699	320	167	153	2,003	943	1,060
Bundi ...	482	207	275	9	3	6	36	14	22	225	116	109	805	452	353	18	8	10
Dholpur ...	247	107	140	385	198	187	9,557	6,618	2,939	114	45	69	164	108	61	3,006	1,178	1,828
Dungarpur ...	130	61	69	36	18	18	1,192	782	410	2,396	1,159	1,237	523	279	244	53	28	25
Jaipur ...	59,095	43,132	15,963	63	13	50	1,200	496	704	16,370	3,922	12,448	915	488	427	10,680	6,518	4,162
Jaisalmer ...	2	1	1	288	113	175	1,948	1,148	800	3,687	1,344	2,343	2,232	1,176	1,056	733	371	362
Jhalawar ...	3	2	1	53	25	28	110	51	59	15	9	6	2	2	...	78	46	32
Karauli ...	575	151	424	...	...	...	321	75	246	38	16	22	21	11	10	173	57	116
Kishangarh ...	1,091	370	721	19	7	12	128	75	53	1,979	1,288	691	30	14	16	13	10	3
Kotah ...	1,623	857	766	95	50	45	534	273	261	1,474	827	647	984	545	439	533	298	235
Kushalgarh (Chiefship) ...	...	...	...	...	...	...	36	19	17	119	59	60	8	3	5	...	...	...
Lawa (Estate) ...	45	29	16	...	...	...	...	...	...	22	10	12	2	1	1	...	...	...
Marwar ...	11,918	4,183	7,735	11,084	5,824	5,260	14,008	8,153	5,855	85,812	52,477	33,335	4,245	2,232	2,013	1,164	595	569
Mewar ...	2,328	1,307	1,021	8,276	4,068	4,208	...	...	...	20,350	10,110	10,240	5,894	3,269	2,625	852	418	434
Partabgarh ...	49	20	29	53	29	24	171	79	92	407	148	259	166	61	105	20	3	17
Shahpura ...	157	69	88	7	2	5	45	25	20	307	134	173	61	28	33	1	1	...
Sirohi ...	36	28	8	230	118	112	1,875	917	958	2,923	1,176	1,747	1,277	681	596	41	32	9
Tonk ...	675	335	340	...	...	...	96	...	96	1,129	633	496	1,108	548	560	347	239	108
Total Rajputana ...	**96,429**	**60,880**	**35,549**	**22,453**	**11,406**	**11,047**	**36,088**	**21,111**	**14,977**	**163,288**	**90,745**	**72,543**	**19,089**	**10,232**	**8,857**	**20,868**	**11,200**	**9,668**

6. Where a particular clan dominates all others in a State, as is the case with the Rathors in Bikaner and Marwar, and the Kachwahas in Jaipur, the law of exogamy has the effect of showing a comparative deficiency in females in the parent State and an excess in the neighbouring one. For instance, in Jaipur there are only 15,963 females of the Kachwaha clan to 43,132 males, whereas in the neighbouring State of Marwar there are 4,183 males and 7,735 females of this clan. For similar reasons, out of 16,370 Rathors in Jaipur, 12,448 are females. **The effect of exogamy.**

7. The proportions between the sexes in each clan have already been referred to in Chapter V but it would not be out of place here to emphasise the fact that the low ratio of females among Rajputs taken as a whole, to which attention is invariably drawn in every Census Report, would be for the remaining eleven clans, as high as 832 females per 1,000 males if the Kachwaha figures were omitted. This ratio compares very favourably with those shown by the racially allied Ahirs, Gujars and Jats which are 851, 841 and 845 respectively. The Kachwaha ratio is as low as 584 and the reasons for this very marked deficiency of females have been discussed in Chapter V of this Report. **Sex proportions.**

We may now proceed to consider the figures for each clan separately.

8. The following statement shows the strength of each of the important sub-clans as recorded at this Census together with figures for males in the States of Marwar, Bikaner, Kishangarh and Mewar. The relative numbers of males and females in some of the sub-clans point to faulty classification and erroneous inclusion among 'others' vide figures for Karamsot, Jodha, Bika, Mertia and Bidawat. **Rathor.**

SUB-CLAN.	TOTAL RAJPUTANA.			MARWAR.	BIKANER.	KISHANGARH.	MEWAR.
	Persons	Males.	Females.	Males.	Males.	Males	Males
1	2	3	4	5	6	7	8
Chandel ...	154	92	62	...	47	1	...
Jaitawat ...	923	547	376	448	...	...	...
Deorajot ...	2,741	1,301	1,440	1,301	...	...	...
Kumpawat ...	4,195	2,625	1,570	2,547	1	...	...
Kandhlot ...	2,466	1,807	659	...	1,807	...	...
Champawat ...	5,869	3,295	2,574	1,995	3	189	640
Mandlawat ...	479	345	134	32	304	...	...
Bala ...	3,248	1,688	1,560	595	5	...	1,031
Karamsot ...	3,426	2,284	1,142	1,724	229	327	...
Jodha ...	13,563	7,708	5,855	6,575	151	189	...
Bika ...	10,023	6,520	3,503	3	6,188	184	...
Mertia ...	24,445	14,768	9,677	13,787	105	52	...
Udawat ...	3,665	2,217	1,448	1,842	308	3	...
Narawat ...	172	87	85	86	...	...	...
Bidawat ...	8,554	5,077	3,477	169	4,621	...	...
Pattawat ...	2,587	1,361	1,226	1,289	60	...	...
Other Rathors ...	76,778	39,028	37,750	20,184	2,462	393	8,439
Total ...	163,288	90,745	72,543	52,477	16,286	1,288	10,110

9. The statement overleaf shows the numbers in each of the sub-clans together with the number of males in the States of Jaipur, Alwar, Bikaner and Marwar. Here again, the large numbers shown as 'unspecified' suggest an omission to record the correct sub-clan especially in Jaipur State where 'unspecified' number 11,797 out of 18,836 recorded in the whole Agency. The figures for the Naruka and Shekhawat sub-clans may however be taken as approximately correct, since persons of these two sub-clans seldom use any other name when asked to state their clan. The twelve important families in Jaipur known as the *Bara Kothris* are represented by serial numbers 1, 6, 8, 9, 14, 15 and 19, no figures having been recorded for the remaining five, viz., Askarnot, Ramsinghot, Pratapota, Saindasot and Puranmalot. **Kachwaha.**

SUB-CLAN	TOTAL RAJPUTANA.			JAIPUR.	ALWAR.	BIKANER.	MARWAR.
	Persons.	Males.	Females.	Males.	Males	Males.	Males.
1. Balbhadrot	71	47	24	47	...	...	...
2. Balapota	693	379	314	315	...	63	...
3. Banbirpota	34	15	19	15	...	...	...
4. Bankawat	406	156	250	118	80	...	...
5. Bikalputa, etc.	691	438	253	276	162	...	...
6. Chattarbhujot	149	102	47	102	...	...	...
7. Hamirde *	2,183	1,872	311	435	109	1	...
8. Khangarot	1,936	1,235	701	1,120	...	...	86
9. Kilanot	2,207	1,324	883	1,187	132	...	...
10. Kumbhani	59	28	31	28	...	...	...
11. Kumbhawat	450	266	184	219	45	1	...
12. Madhani	18	1	17	...	...	...	...
13. Naruka	9,377	4,960	4,417	1,665	2,297	72	458
14. Nathawat	2,212	1,301	911	1,045	29	12	59
15. Pichanot	740	373	367	256	94	...	...
16. Rajawat Mansinghot, etc. ...	5,838	3,161	2,677	2,061	228	34	197
17. Shekhawat	50,004	32,672	17,332	24,567	2,046	2,612	2,964
18. Sheobrahmpota	49	39	10	39	...	...	...
19. Surtanot	476	305	171	300	...	...	...
20. Unspecified Kachwahas ...	18,836	12,706	6,130	9,337	294	793	469
Total ...	**96,429**	**60,880**	**35,549**	**43,132**	**5,466**	**3,588**	**4,183**

* 802 Males returned in Mewar.

Chauhan.

10. The list of clans issued to Enumerators shows, in addition to the parent clan of Chauhan, the sub-clans of Hara, Deora, and Nirbhan. The general distribution statement shows that the clan is found in varying numbers in every State in the Agency. The statement below however shows the localities in which the specified sub-clans are chiefly found. Other sub-clans are Bhadauriya, Khinchi, Mohil, Sanchorra and Songirra but the numbers in each were not recorded, though several entries of them were observed, and were classified under the parent clan.

State.	Chauhan.		Hara.		Deora.		Nirbhan.	
	Males.	Females.	Males.	Females.	Males.	Females.	Males.	Females.
Kotah ..	987	904	1,758	1,214	35	39	2	..
Bundi ..	158	82	1,207	809	..	..	..	..
Sirohi ..	801	846	14	10	2,795	1,261	3	2
Mewar ..	4,613	3,970	196	425	2,676	2,443	..	..
Jaipur ..	3,911	5,493	151	296	29	12	1,765	1,376
Other States.	20,738	19,216	1,147	345	3,293	2,927	420	325
Total ..	**31,208**	**30,511**	**4,473**	**3,099**	**8,828**	**6,682**	**2,190**	**1,703**

Jadon.

11. The 61,849 persons belonging to this clan include 48,080 of the Bhatti sub-clan which is found almost exclusively in the States of Jaisalmer, Bikaner and Marwar. The clan as a whole was recorded in every State except in the Lawa Estate. Of the 13,769 persons returned as Jadons, only 3,596 are of the parent State of Karauli. A few were returned as Jarechas which is a sub-clan commonly found in Kathiawar. The 48,080 Bhattis are distributed as shown in the margin, the principal sub-divisions of them being known as Jessa, Kelan, Khianh, Maldot, Pugaliya and Rawalot.

Jaisalmer ...	9,829
Bikaner ...	9,817
Marwar ...	24,739
Elsewhere ...	3,695
Total ...	48,080

Gahlot.

12. The powerful sub-clan of Sesodia is ten times as numerous as the parent clan from which it is an offshoot. The figures in the margin show the numbers recorded at this Census. Of the Gahlots pure and simple, more than half are found in Marwar and the remainder are scattered in small numbers throughout most of the other States. The Sesodia States of Mewar, Banswara, Dungarpur, Partabgarh and Shahpura contain 80 per cent. of all male Sesodias and if Marwar be added 88 per cent. of all females. The principal sub-divisions are Asaich, Aharya, Mangaliya, Pipara

Clan.	Persons.	Males.	Females.
Gahlot.	4,974	2,476	2,498
Sesodia	49,764	27,666	22,098

Chondawat, Kishnawat, Mainawat, Ranawat, Saktawat, Sangawat, Sarangdeot, Kanawat Kumbhawat and Lunawat. In Mewar there are 50,659 male Rajputs who belong to one or other of the twelve main exogamous clans. Of these only 19,790 are Sesodias and an explanation of their comparative paucity probably lies in the fact that only ten of the nineteen great Nobles of the State are Sesodias. The marginal statement shows the Estates in order of precedence and the clan of each Noble. This peculiar condition of Mewar society is without parallel elsewhere in Rajputana and most of the Estates held by those who are not the Ruler's clansmen date back to the days when Mewar was harassed by the Delhi Emperors and the Ranas of Chitor were in sore need of all the assistance they could get from their fellow Rajputs who made common cause with them against the invaders.

Estate.		Clan.
Bari Sadri	...	Jhala
Bedla	...	Chauhan
Kotharia	...	Chauhan
Salumbar	...	Sesodia (Chondawat)
Bijolian	...	Ponwar
Deogarh	...	Sesodia (Chondawat)
Begun	...	Sesodia (Chondawat)
Delwara	...	Jhala
Meja	...	Sesodia (Chondawat)
Amet	...	Sesodia (Chondawat)
Gogunda	...	Jhala
Kanor	...	Sesodia (Sarangdeot)
Bhindar	...	Sesodia (Saktawat)
Badnor	...	Rathor
Bansi	...	Sesodia (Saktawat)
Bhainsrorgarh	...	Sesodia (Chondawat)
Parsoli	...	Chauhan
Kurabar	...	Sesodia (Chondawat)
Sardargarh	...	Dodia

13. In spite of the comparatively simple instructions issued to Enumerators several entries were made of sub-clans which, on further examination, had to be tabulated as shown in the margin. Among the 29,928 persons classified as belonging to either minor or unspecified clans, mention should be made of such clans as Sikarwal, Bais, Surajbansi, etc., which though numerous in the United Provinces are of little importance in Rajputana. **Other Clans.**

Parihar	Solanki
Chanderiya	*Baghela*
Sindhu	*Khairara*
Inda	*Dayaldas*
Ponwar	Jhala
Sankla	*Makwana*
Dabi	Tonwar
Salawat	*Borahna*
Bhail	*Jatu*
Kabbha	
Soda	
Hunnar	

ANNEXURE 1.

CLASSIFIED LIST OF KACHWAHA SUB-DIVISIONS.

Sub-division.	Classified under—	Sub-division.	Classified under—
1. Akherajot	Naruka	60. Kiratsinghot	Rajawat Mansinghot, etc.
2. Akhnawat	Balapota	61. Kitawat	Hamirde
3. Alkanji	Naruka	62. Kumbhani	Kumbhani
4. Amarsinghot	Shekhawat	63. Kumbhawat	Kumbhawat
5. Askarnot	Askarnot	64. Ladkhani	Shekhawat
6. Balapota	Balapota	65. Lalawat	Naruka
7. Balbhadrot	Balbhadrot	66. Madhani Rajawat	Madhani
8. Banbirpota	Banbirpota	67. Mangalpota	Banbirpota
9. Bankawat	Bankawat	68. Manohardasot	Nathawat
10. Banmalidasot	Madhani	69. Mansinghot-Rajawat	Rajawat Mansinghot, etc.
11. Barepota	Banbirpota	70. Melag	Bikalpota
12. Bhaironji	Shekhawat	71. Mer ka Kachwaha	Bikalpota
13. Bhankrot	Hamirde	72. Milkhpuriya	Shekhawat
14. Bhojpota	Bikalpota	73. Mohandasot	Bikalpota
15. Bhojraji	Shekhawat	74. Mokawat	Balapota
16. Biharidasji	Naruka	75. Mukandasji	Naruka
17. Bijawat	Balapota	76. Napawat	Hamirde
18. Bikalpota	Bikalpota	77. Naruka	Naruka
19. Bikawat	Bikalpota	78. Nata-Jaita	Naruka
20. Biranpota	Banbirpota	79. Nathawat	Nathawat
21. Bithaldasot	Bikalpota	80. Parasramji	Shekhawat
22. Bithalpota	Balapota	81. Partabsinghot	Shekhawat
23. Chattarbhujot	Chattarbhujot	82. Patilpota	Balapota
24. Chattarsinghot	Sheobrahmpota	83. Pichanot	Pichanot
25. Chitarji	Naruka	84. Pratapota	Pratapota
26. Chitori ka Kachwaha	Bikalpota	85. Purana Kachwaha	Bikalpota
27. Dasawat	Naruka	86. Puranmalot	Puranmalot
28. Dasrathpota	Bikalpota	87. Radharka	Bikalpota
29. Dausa ka Kachwaha	Bikalpota	88. Rajawat	Rajawat Mansinghot, etc.
30. Delhnot	Bikalpota	89. Ralhanot	Bikalpota
31. Deosinghot	Sheobrahmpota	90. Ramsahaiji	Nathawat
32. Dhirawat	Bikalpota	91. Ramsinghot	Ramsinghot
33. Dogia	Hamirde	92. Ranchordasji	Naruka
34. Durjansinghot	Rajawat Mansinghot, etc.	93. Raojika	Shekhawat
35. Dwarkadasji	Naruka	94. Ratanji	Naruka
36. Gadh ka Kachwaha	Bikalpota	95. Ratanawat	Shekhawat
37. Girdharji	Shekhawat	96. Rawat ka Kachwaha	Bikalpota
38. Gogawat	Hamirde	97. Sagatsinghot	Rajawat Mansinghot, etc.
39. Gopalji	Shekhawat	98. Sainsmalji	Naruka
40. Hamirde	Hamirde	99. Saindasot	Saindasot
41. Himmatsinghot	Rajawat Mansinghot, etc.	100. Sanwaldasji	Naruka
42. Isrisinghot	Naruka	101. Sanwatpota	Bikalpota
43. Jagmalot	Bikalpota	102. Shamsinghji	Naruka
44. Jagannathot	Bankawat	103. Shekhawat	Shekhawat
45. Jaitalpota	Bikalpota	104. Sheobrahmpota	Sheobrahmpota
46. Jasrapota	Bikalpota	105. Singaji	Naruka
47. Jaswant ka Kachwaha	Bikalpota	106. Singawat	Bikalpota
48. Jhamawat	Bikalpota	107. Somant ka Kachwaha	Balapota
49. Jhunjhar Singhot	Rajawat Mansinghot, etc.	108. Somesarpota or Ranawat	Bikalpota
50. Jodhsinghot	Naruka	109. Soora ka Kachwaha	Bikalpota
51. Jogi Kachwaha	Hamirde	110. Soordasot	Bikalpota
52. Kaphurji	Bikalpota	111. Soorsinghot	Madhani
53. Karnaji	Naruka	112. Sundardasot	Bankawat
54. Karnawat	Balapota	113. Surtanot	Surtanot
55. Khangarot	Khangarot	114. Tajkhani	Shekhawat
56. Khehnawat	Bikalpota	115. Tejawat	Naruka
57. Khinchawat	Bikalpota	116. Ugrawat	Balapota
58. Kilanot	Kilanot	117. Ugrsenji	Shekhawat
59. Kilansinghot	Rajawat Mansinghot, etc.		

ANNEXURE II.

CLASSIFIED LIST OF RATHOR SUB-DIVISIONS.

Sub-division.	Classified under—	Sub-division.	Classified under—
1. Akherajot	Rathor	83. Kesodasot	Bidawat and Mertia
2. Amarsinghot	Bika	84. Khangarot	Bidawat
3. Amrawat	Bika	85. Khetsinghot	Rathor
4. Anopsinghot	Mertia	86. Khipsa	Rathor
5. Arjanot	Rathor	87. Kiratsinghot	Bika
6. Arkmalot	Rathor	88. Kishansinghot	Bika
7. Armalot	Rathor	89. Kitpalot	Rathor
8. Ashal	Rathor	90. Kokar	Rathor
9. Badhawat	Rathor	91. Koticha	Rathor
10. Bhagawat	Bika	92. Kumpawat	Kumpawat
11. Bairawat	Rathor	93. Lakhawat	Rathor
12. Bairsalot	Bidawat	94. Lumbawat	Rathor
13. Bala	Bala	95. Madhawat	Bidawat
14. Ballot	Champawat	96. Madhodasot	Mertia
15. Balmera	Rathor	97. Mahecha	Rathor
16. Bandar	Rathor	98. Mallinath	Rathor
17. Banbhirot	Rathor	99. Mandlawat	Mandlawat
18. Banirot	Kandhlot	100. Mandhanot	Rathor
19. Barmalot	Rathor	101. Manohardasot	Bidawat
20. Barsinghot	Rathor	102. Mepa	Rathor
21. Behar	Rathor	103. Mertia	Mertia
22. Bhataru	Rathor	104. Mohania	Rathor
23. Bhimot	Rathor	105. Mohania Raipalot	Rathor
24. Bhimrajot	Bika and Bidawat	106. Mulu	Rathor
25. Bhojrajot	Bidawat	107. Napawat	Udawat
26. Bhopalot	Champawat	108. Narawat	Narawat
27. Bidawat	Bidawat	109. Narnot	Bika
28. Bijawat	Rathor	110. Nathot	Rathor
29. Bika	Bika	111. Nimawat	Bika
30. Bisawat	Bika	112. Pattawat	Rathor
31. Bitaldasot	Champawat	113. Partabsinghot	Bika
32. Bitwassia Udawat	Rathor	114. Phalsundia	Rathor
33. Chachak	Rathor	115. Phittak	Rathor
34. Chajjar	Rathor	116. Pirthirajot	Bika and Bidawat
35. Champawat	Champawat	117. Pithar	Rathor
36. Chandawat	Rathor	118. Pohar	Rathor
37. Chandel	Chandel	119. Polia	Rathor
38. Chappunnia	Rathor	120. Pokharna	Rathor
39. Chundawat	Rathor	121. Pryagdasot	Udawat
40. Dandul	Rathor	122. Punawat	Rathor
41. Danga	Rathor	123. Raghodasot	Kandhlot
42. Davecha	Rathor	124. Raghunathsinghot	Mertia
43. Dayaldasot	Bidawat	125. Raipalot	Rathor
44. Debidasot	Udawat	126. Rajak	Rathor
45. Deorajot	Deorajot	127. Rajvi	Bika
46. Dharniya	Rathor	128. Ramawat	Bika
47. Dhenawat	Bidawat	129. Ramdasot	Bidawat
48 Duhuria	Rathor	130. Ranawat	Rathor
49. Domgrsiot	Bidawat	131. Randha	Rathor
50. Dimgrot	Rathor	132. Randhirot	Rathor
51. Edanot	Champawat	133. Rardhana	Bidawat
52. Gaharwal	Gaharwal	134. Rashawat	Rathor
53. Gaindasot	Mertia	135. Ratansinghot	Bika
54. Garsiot	Bika	136. Rawattot	Kandhlot
55. Gonecha	Rathor	137. Rirmalot	Rathor
56. Gopaldasot	Kandhlot	138. Rupawat	Rathor
57. Gopinathot	Mertia	139 Sainsmalot	Rathor
58. Gugadeot	Rathor	140. Sandawat	Rathor
59. Hairawat	Bidawat	141. Sangawat	Udawat
60. Harchandot	Rathor	142. Sanhidasot	Kandhlot
61. Harkawat	Rathor	143. Sanwaldasot	Bidawat
62. Hathundiya	Rathor	144. Sarangot	Bika
63. Iduria	Rathor	145. Shattawat	Rathor
64. Jagmalot	Rathor	146. Sheobar	Rathor
65. Jaisinghot	Rathor	147. Shihawat	Bidawat
66. Jaitawat	Jaitawat	148. Shindal	Rathor
67. Jaitmalot	Rathor	149. Shinrajot	Rathor
68. Jhujharria	Rathor	150. Shikhawat	Udawat
69. Jodha	Jodha	151. Simalot	Rathor
70. Jogaiyat	Rathor	152. Soonda	Rathor
71. Jolu	Rathor	153. Sultanot	Mertia
72. Joraiyat	Rathor	154. Surajmalot	Bika
73. Kabbha	Rathor	155. Tejsinghot	Bika and Bidawat
74. Kairecha	Rathor	156 Thatti	Rathor
75. Kallawat	Rathor	157. Tiloksiot	Udawat
76. Kalliandasot	Mertia	158. Tumaliya	Rathor
77. Kanawat	Rathor	159. Udaikarnot	Bidawat
78. Kandhlot	Kandhlot	160. Udawat	Udawat
79. Kanhasaraya	Rathor	161. Uga	Rathor
80. Karbarria	Rathor	162. Uhar	Rathor
81. Karamsot	Karamsot	163. Undar	Rathor
82. Karnot	Rathor	164. Zalimsinghot	Mertia

GENERAL SUMMARY

OF

MAIN STATISTICS.

GENERAL SUMMARY OF MAIN STATISTICS IN EACH STATE, ETC.

Agency, State or District.	Population.	Mean Density of population per Square Mile	Percentage of population living in Towns.	Percentage of Variation in Population.		Number in every 10,000 of the population who were born—		Number in 10,000 of the population who belong to each of the Main Religions.						Number of Females to 1,000 Males.	Number of Literate Males per 1,000 of the Male population. (All ages 5 and over).
				1921—31.	1911—21.	Within the Agency, State, etc.	Elsewhere.	Hindu.	Muslim.	Jain.	Tribal.	Sikh.	Christian.		
1	2	3	4	5	6	7	8	9	10	11	12	13	14	15	16
Rajputana ...	**11,225,712**	**87**	**13·9**	**+ 14·2**	**− 6·5**	**9,705**	**295**	**8,522**	**953**	**268**	**204**	**37**	**5**	**908**	**76**
1. Abu District ...	4,532	756	91·9	+ 25·7	− 16·0	3,244	6,756	7,718	1,765	46	...	119	309	646	267
2. Alwar ...	749,751	238	10·0	+ 6·9	− 11·4	9,223	777	7,322	2,620	51	...	...	1	892	74
3. Banswara ...	225,106	141	4·6	+ 18·3	+ 15·0	9,628	372	5,351	289	204	4,146	...	9	1,010	50
4. Bharatpur ...	486,954	247	14·7	− 1·9	− 11·2	8,617	1,383	7,967	1,931	49	...	3	13	849	91
5. Bikaner ...	936,218	41	24·1	+ 41·9	− 5·9	8,277	1,723	7,711	1,512	307	...	432	3	868	85
6. Bundi ...	216,722	98	14·8	+ 15·9	− 14·5	9,354	646	9,336	475	185	...	2	1	916	52
7. Dholpur ...	254,986	209	14·1	+ 10·8	− 12·7	8,899	1,101	9,248	661	71	4	10	2	815	69
8. Dungarpur ...	227,544	158	7·7	+ 20·2	+ 18·9	9,578	422	9,407	338	255	...	...	...	988	59
9. Jaipur ...	2,631,775	169	17·0	+ 12·5	− 11·8	9,741	259	9,052	815	112	10	1	6	897	74
10. Jaisalmer ...	76,255	5	9·3	+ 12·7	− 23·4	9,311	689	6,789	2,900	120	189	1	...	801	53
11. Jhalawar ...	107,890	134	15·5	+ 12·2	− 0·1	7,676	2,324	8,944	793	244	...	2	5	909	128
12. Karauli ...	140,525	114	17·2	+ 5·1	− 8·8	8,722	1,278	9,447	520	32	...	...	1	831	77
13. Kishangarh ...	85,744	100	21·5	+ 10·3	− 10·8	8,109	1,891	8,887	769	260	74	...	2	927	120
14. Kotah ...	685,804	121	8·6	+ 8·8	− 1·4	9,123	877	9,166	686	76	43	4	13	932	91
15. Kushalgarh (Chiefship) ...	35,564	105	8·6	+ 22·0	+ 32·5	8,906	1,094	9,596	240	164	...	...	...	1,008	48
16. Lawa (Estate) ...	2,790	147	...	+ 23·3	− 11·8	6,631	3,369	9,108	391	484	...	...	...	981	65
17. Marwar ...	2,125,982	61	13·3	+ 15·4	− 10·5	9,877	123	8,604	832	535	15	...	3	915	80
18. Mewar ...	1,566,910	124	7·5	+ 14·6	+ 6·7	9,844	156	8,628	344	421	608	...	3	941	65
19. Partabgarh ...	76,539	87	14·1	+ 14·1	+ 7·0	8,235	1,765	5,402	511	581	3,495	1	9	963	124
20. Shahpura ...	54,233	134	17·1	+ 12·7	+ 1·5	8,184	1,816	8,952	469	261	...	...	...	943	104
21. Sirohi ...	216,528	111	10·7	+ 16·0	+ 1·0	9,071	929	8,949	302	716	...	...	23	989	95
22. Tonk ...	317,360	125	20·1	+ 10·2	− 5·0	8,714	1,286	8,277	1,394	216	111	...	1	930	39

GENERAL SUMMARY OF MAIN STATISTICS IN EACH STATE, ETC.—*Concluded.*

Agency, State or District.	Number of Males literate in English per 10,000 of the Male Population. (All ages 5 and over).	Number in 10,000 of the Population who speak each of the Principal Languages.							Number in 100,000 Persons who are—				Percentage of Population supported by—				
		Rajasthani.	Western Hindi.	Bhili.	Sindhi.	Panjabi.	Gujarati.	Others.	Insane.	Deaf-mutes.	Blind.	Lepers.	Agricultural Occupations.	Industrial Occupations	Commercial Occupations.	Professional Occupations.	Other Occupations.
1	17	18	19	20	21	22	23	24	25	26	27	28	29	30	31	32	33
Rajputana ...	**56**	**7,667**	**1,533**	**641**	**11**	**111**	**18**	**19**	**23**	**28**	**282**	**5**	**72**	**12**	**5**	**5**	**6**
1. Abu District ...	917	2,438	4,396	1,999	...	...	...	1,167	22	110	154	...	11	31	8	9	41
2. Alwar ...	54	5,654	4,340	...	...	...	...	6	25	74	413	6	78	12	5	4	6
3. Banswara ...	14	120	28	9,810	...	...	...	36	41	72	165	8	87	6	3	2	2
4. Bharatpur ...	54	1,337	8,650	...	...	...	...	13	19	23	562	5	71	14	6	4	5
5. Bikaner ...	93	8,415	152	...	94	1,288	3	48	26	10	309	4	79	8	4	3	6
6. Bundi ...	25	9,889	63	7	...	...	...	91	39	44	288	7	71	13	4	5	7
7. Dholpur ...	49	28	9,864	...	...	...	...	108	17	76	425	6	80	10	4	4	2
8. Dungarpur ...	16	143	111	9,644	...	1	96	5	27	11	159	2	87	6	3	2	2
9. Jaipur ...	57	8,533	1,447	...	...	...	...	20	21	8	256	2	64	15	5	6	10
10. Jaisalmer ...	20	9,475	1	1	495	3	9	16	9	35	135	3	68	22	5	6	4
11. Jhalawar ...	87	5,388	4,505	21	...	...	...	186	48	109	252	16	69	12	6	6	7
12. Karauli ...	21	49	9,941	...	...	...	...	10	26	95	369	4	74	13	4	5	4
13. Kishangarh ...	78	9,968	20	...	...	...	...	17	44	16	478	...	71	12	5	6	6
14. Kotah ...	59	8,886	1,057	1	...	...	...	56	34	41	333	12	75	13	4	4	4
15. Kushalgarh (Chiefship).	56	700	236	8,740	...	...	...	324	53	93	135	14	92	3	2	2	1
16. Lawa (Estate) ...	33	9,982	14	...	...	...	...	4	...	143	430	...	55	26	5	7	7
17. Marwar ...	75	9,888	29	80	...	...	...	8	18	31	303	6	71	14	5	5	5
18. Mewar ...	23	8,779	51	1,103	...	4	43	20	15	9	83	1	74	11	8	5	2
19. Partabgarh ...	73	5,992	176	3,504	...	...	116	212	41	51	201	48	80	8	4	5	3
20. Shahpura ...	95	9,982	13	...	...	...	...	5	28	18	315	...	75	11	4	4	6
21. Sirohi ...	85	8,208	207	1,404	1	4	147	29	36	23	545	7	71	11	7	8	8
22. Tonk ...	16	8,750	1,246	2	...	...	...	2	35	49	291	10	68	11	4	4	13

TABLE I.

Area, Houses and Population.

EXPLANATORY NOTE.

The States in Rajputana are arranged in this Table alphabetically.

The apparent increase in the area of 72 square miles, as compared with the figure quoted in 1921, is due to a portion of the Agency having been re-surveyed and former figures adjusted and to the addition of 2 uninhabited square miles to Bikaner from the Punjab.

The area and population of the places under British Administration in Rajputana are as follows:—

Unit.	State.	Area.	Population.		
			Total.	Males.	Females.
Abu District.	Sirohi.	6 Sq. miles.	4,532	2,753	1,779
Kherwara.	Mewar.	1 Sq. mile.	1,899	1,266	633
Kotra.	Mewar.	1 " "	929	534	395
Erinpura.	Sirohi.	1 " "	1,645	914	731
Deoli Agency.	Mewar.	Not available.	1,052	530	522

They have been included in the Tables in the figures of the States in which they are situated, but Abu District is shown as a separate unit, while the Deoli Agency leased area figures are included in those of Ajmer-Merwara.

Column 3 of the Table shows ½ a town each against Jaipur and Marwar. This is due to the jointly owned Town and Shamlat area of Sambhar, detailed figures for which appear in Imperial Table V and Provincial Tables.

TABLE I —AREA, HOUSES AND POPULATION

AGENCY AND STATE OR DISTRICT.	Area in square miles.	Inhabited Towns.	Inhabited Villages.	OCCUPIED HOUSES.			POPULATION.								
							PERSONS.			MALES.			FEMALES.		
				Total.	In Towns.	In Villages.	Total.	Urban.	Rural.	Total.	Urban.	Rural.	Total.	Urban.	Rural.
1	2	3	4	5	6	7	8	9	10	11	12	13	14	15	16
RAJPUTANA.	*129,059*	*145*	*33,688*	*2,392,110*	*306,271*	*2,083,839*	*11,225,712*	*1,556,305*	*9,669,407*	*5,885,028*	*813,605*	*5,071,423*	*5,340,684*	*742,700*	*4,597,984*
Abu District	6	1	4	**1,186**	1,095	91	**4,532**	4,165	367	**2,753**	2,539	214	**1,779**	1,626	153
Alwar	3,158	7	1,758	**154,310**	14,733	139,577	**749,751**	75,591	674,160	**396,261**	39,921	356,340	**353,490**	35,670	317,820
Banswara	1,606	1	1,096	**45,179**	2,165	43,014	**225,106**	10,444	214,662	**111,983**	5,141	106,842	**113,123**	5,303	107,820
Bharatpur	1,978	7	1,816	**104,246**	12,696	91,550	**486,954**	71,474	415,480	**263,325**	38,568	224,757	**223,629**	32,906	190,723
Bikaner	23,317	15	2,742	**185,418**	42,532	142,886	**936,218**	225,148	711,070	**501,153**	117,338	383,815	**435,065**	107,810	327,255
Bundi	2,220	4	809	**48,335**	7,061	41,274	**216,722**	32,058	184,664	**113,101**	16,505	96,596	**103,621**	15,553	88,068
Dholpur	1,221	3	525	**54,905**	8,047	46,858	**254,986**	36,084	218,902	**140,497**	19,233	121,264	**114,489**	16,851	97,638
Dungarpur...	1,447	3	749	**46,822**	4,070	42,752	**227,544**	17,601	209,943	**114,480**	8,701	105,779	**113,064**	8,900	104,164
Jaipur	15,579	38½	5,873	**566,662**	86,068	480,594	**2,631,775**	446,677	2,185,098	**1,387,067**	233,943	1,153,124	**1,244,708**	212,734	1,031,974
Jaisalmer	16,062	1	496	**18,337**	1,779	16,558	**76,255**	7,120	69,135	**42,342**	3,706	38,636	**33,913**	3,414	30,499
Jhalawar	810	2	432	**23,580**	3,566	20,014	**107,890**	16,758	91,132	**56,518**	8,506	48,012	**51,372**	8,252	43,120
Karauli.	1,242	3	374	**30,938**	4,263	26,675	**140,525**	24,162	116,363	**76,729**	13,146	63,583	**63,796**	11,016	52,780
Kishangarh	858	3	229	**18,352**	3,812	14,540	**85,744**	18,381	67,363	**44,494**	9,761	34,733	**41,250**	8,620	32,630
Kotah	5,684	4	2,525	**153,688**	11,363	142,325	**685,804**	59,046	626,758	**355,056**	31,175	323,881	**330,748**	27,871	302,877
Kushalgarh (Chiefship)	340	1	282	**6,420**	804	5,616	**35,564**	3,069	32,495	**17,754**	1,551	16,203	**17,810**	1,518	16,292
Lawa (Estate)	19	...	11	**608**	...	608	**2,790**	...	2,790	**1,445**	...	1,445	**1,345**	...	1,345
Marwar	35,016	25½	4,126	**449,459**	57,597	391,862	**2,125,982**	283,463	1,842,519	**1,109,912**	146,842	963,070	**1,016,070**	136,621	879,449
Mewar	12,694	15	8,070	**334,790**	21,359	313,431	**1,566,910**	117,938	1,448,972	**807,184**	61,953	745,231	**759,726**	55,985	703,741
Partabgarh...	886	1	470	**16,279**	1,910	14,369	**76,539**	10,845	65,694	**38,991**	5,601	33,390	**37,548**	5,244	32,304
Shahpura	405	1	116	**11,658**	2,181	9,477	**54,233**	9,298	44,935	**27,907**	4,689	23,218	**26,326**	4,609	21,717
Sirohi...	1,958	4	409	**49,450**	5,837	43,613	**216,528**	23,063	193,465	**111,675**	12,203	99,472	**104,853**	10,860	93,993
Tonk	2,553	5	1,276	**71,488**	15,333	56,155	**317,360**	58,920	258,440	**164,401**	32,583	131,818	**152,959**	31,337	121,622

TABLE II.

Variation in Population Since 1881.

EXPLANATORY NOTE.

The figures for Rajputana for 1881 do not agree with the corresponding figures in the Volume of India Tables, as the former include 167, 850 persons of the 3 Parganas of the Tonk State, Chhabra, Pirawa and Sironj, which were situated in 1881 in the Central India Agency, but were omitted in the India Tables from the totals for that Agency, figures being given for Central India States only.

The States in Rajputana are arranged in this Table alphabetically.

The figures for Abu District relating to 1881 (columns 7, 19 and 25) are included in the Sirohi figures.

The figures for Dholpur State include, throughout, the population of Nimrol village, the figures for which were hitherto excluded from the State totals in Imperial Tables and included in Provincial Tables.

The figures for the Mewar State exclude, throughout, the population of Nandwai Pargana of Indore and Gangapur Pargana of Gwalior, which have hitherto been included in the State totals in Imperial Tables.

TABLE II.

Variation in Population Since 1881.

TABLE II.—VARIATION IN

AGENCY AND STATE OR DISTRICT.	PERSONS.						VARIATION—INCREASE(+), DECREASE(—).				
	1931.	1921.	1911.	1901.	1891.	1881.	1921 to 1931	1911 to 1921	1901 to 1911	1891 to 1901	1881 to 1891
1	2	3	4	5	6	7	8	9	10	11	12
RAJPUTANA.	*11,225,712*	*9,831,755*	*10,518,345*	*9,842,482*	*12,153,631*	*10,102,105*	*+1,393,957*	*−686,590*	*+675,863*	*−2,311,149*	*+2,051,526*
Abu District ...	4,532	3,606	4,292	4,068	3,076	Not available	+ 926	− 686	+ 224	+ 992	...
Alwar	749,751	701,154	791,688	828,487	767,786	682,926	+ 48,597	− 90,534	− 36,799	+ 60,701	+ 84,860
Banswara ...	225,106	190,362	165,463	149,128	180,268	104,000	+ 34,744	+ 24,899	+ 16,335	− 31,140	+ 76,268
Bharatpur ...	486,954	496,437	588,785	626,665	640,303	645,540	− 9,483	− 62,348	− 67,880	− 13,638	− 5,237
Bikaner ...	936,218	659,685	700,983	584,755	832,065	509,077	+ 276,533	− 41,298	+ 116,228	− 247,310	+ 322,988
Bundi ...	216,722	187,068	218,730	171,227	295,675	254,701	+ 29,654	− 31,662	+ 47,503	− 124,448	+ 40,974
Dholpur ...	254,986	230,188	263,593	271,496	279,890	249,657	+ 24,798	− 33,405	− 7,903	− 8,394	+ 30,233
Dungarpur ...	227,544	189,272	159,192	100,103	98,448	86,429	+ 38,272	+ 30,080	+ 59,089	+ 1,655	+ 12,019
Jaipur	2,631,775	2,338,802	2,636,647	2,658,666	2,823,966	2,527,142	+ 292,973	− 297,845	− 22,019	− 165,300	+ 296,824
Jaisalmer ...	76,255	67,652	88,311	73,370	115,701	108,143	+ 8,603	− 20,659	+ 14,941	− 42,331	+ 7,558
Jhalawar ...	107,890	96,182	96,271	90,175	151,097	150,361	+ 11,708	− 89	+ 6,096	− 60,922	+ 736
Karauli ...	140,525	133,730	146,587	156,786	156,587	148,670	+ 6,795	− 12,857	− 10,199	+ 199	+ 7,917
Kishangarh ...	85,744	77,734	87,191	90,970	125,516	112,633	+ 8,010	− 9,457	− 3,779	− 34,546	+ 12,883
Kotah	685,804	630,060	639,089	544,879	718,771	707,402	+ 55,744	− 9,029	+ 94,210	− 173,892	+ 11,369
Kushalgarh (Chiefship)	35,564	29,162	22,005	16,222	5,775	Not available	+ 6,402	+ 7,157	+ 5,783	+ 10,447	...
Lawa (Estate) ...	2,780	2,262	2,564	2,671	3,360	2,682	+ 528	− 302	− 107	− 689	+ 678
Marwar... ...	2,125,982	1,841,642	2,057,553	1,935,565	2,528,178	1,757,618	+ 284,340	− 215,911	+ 121,988	− 592,613	+ 770,560
Mewar ...	1,566,910	1,366,980	1,281,284	1,018,805	1,710,579	1,443,144	+ 199,930	+ 85,696	+ 262,479	− 691,774	+ 267,435
Partabgarh ...	76,539	67,110	62,704	52,025	87,975	79,298	+ 9,429	+ 4,406	+ 10,679	− 35,950	+ 8,677
Shahpura ...	54,233	48,130	47,397	42,676	63,646	51,750	+ 6,103	+ 733	+ 4,721	− 20,970	+ 11,896
Sirohi	216,528	186,639	184,835	150,476	184,900	142,903	+ 29,889	+ 1,804	+ 34,359	− 34,424	+ 41,997
Tonk	317,360	287,898	303,181	273,267	380,069	338,029	+ 29,462	− 15,283	+ 29,914	− 106,802	+ 42,040

Net variation in period 1881-1931. Increase(+) Decrease(−)	MALES.						FEMALES.					
	1931.	1921.	1911.	1901.	1891.	1881.	1931.	1921.	1911.	1901.	1891.	1881.
13	14	15	16	17	18	19	20	21	22	23	24	25
+1,123,607	*5,885,028*	*5,178,428*	*5,509,023*	*5,165,931*	*6,427,145*	*5,461,527*	*5,340,684*	*4,653,327*	*5,069,322*	*4,676,551*	*5,726,486*	*4,640,578*
...	2,758	2,147	2,628	2,381	1,209	Not available	1,779	1,459	1,669	1,687	1,167	Not available
+ 66,825	396,261	371,975	418,659	481,085	408,898	360,884	358,490	329,179	878,029	397,452	368,888	322,542
+ 121,106	111,988	94,562	81,620	78,553	92,540	58,498	118,128	95,800	88,848	75,575	87,728	50,602
− 158,586	268,325	272,345	302,254	335,156	347,830	350,475	228,629	224,092	256,531	291,509	292,473	295,065
+ 427,141	501,153	347,690	371,489	306,462	440,114	298,684	435,065	311,995	329,494	278,298	391,951	215,393
− 37,979	113,101	97,635	118,211	88,731	156,033	138,103	108,621	89,433	105,519	82,496	139,642	121,598
+ 5,329	140,497	127,078	144,455	147,880	157,123	188,342	114,489	103,110	119,138	123,616	122,767	111,315
+ 141,115	114,480	95,233	79,105	50,050	49,444	44,568	118,064	94,089	80,087	50,053	49,004	41,861
+ 104,633	1,387,067	1,242,742	1,385,750	1,405,458	1,505,765	1,365,194	1,244,708	1,096,[illegible]	1,250,897	1,258,208	1,318,201	1,161,948
− 31,888	42,342	37,882	48,500	39,389	62,699	61,127	38,918	29,770	39,811	33,981	53,002	47,016
− 42,471	56,518	50,318	50,084	46,737	80,389	81,708	51,372	45,864	46,237	43,488	70,708	68,058
− 8,145	76,729	73,647	80,081	85,356	84,555	80,645	63,796	60,083	66,606	71,430	72,022	68,025
− 26,889	44,494	40,859	45,718	47,475	65,038	59,098	41,250	36,875	41,473	43,495	60,478	53,535
− 21,598	355,056	327,015	380,324	280,912	375,210	371,255	330,748	303,045	308,765	268,967	343,561	336,147
...	17,754	14,575	10,956	8,229	2,920	Not available	17,810	14,587	11,049	7,998	2,855	Not available
+ 108	1,445	1,199	1,302	1,326	1,728	1,360	1,345	1,068	1,262	1,345	1,632	1,322
+ 368,364	1,109,912	971,115	1,075,269	1,015,531	1,329,478	978,065	1,016,070	870,527	982,284	920,034	1,198,700	784,553
+ 128,766	807,184	705,396	664,287	532,046	894,577	772,685	759,726	661,584	616,997	486,759	816,002	670,459
− 2,759	38,991	34,090	31,735	26,036	45,842	41,118	37,548	33,020	30,969	25,989	42,133	38,180
+ 2,488	27,907	24,819	24,595	22,221	33,248	27,217	26,326	23,811	29,802	20,455	30,408	[illegible]
+ 73,625	111,675	96,938	95,666	79,089	96,713	76,132	104,853	89,701	89,169	71,437	88,187	66,771
− 20,669	164,401	149,168	156,390	140,928	200,097	176,869	152,959	138,730	146,791	182,339	179,972	161,160

TABLE III.

Towns and Villages Classified by Population.

EXPLANATORY NOTE.

As in Tables I and II, the States in Rajputana are arranged in this Table alphabetically.

TABLE III.—Towns and Villages Classified by Population.

Agency and State or District.	Total Number of Inhabited Towns and Villages.	Population.	Under 500. Number.	Under 500. Population.	500–1,000. Number.	500–1,000. Population.	1,000–2,000. Number.	1,000–2,000. Population.	2,000–5,000. Number.	2,000–5,000. Population.	5,000–10,000 Number.	5,000–10,000 Population.	10,000–20,000. Number.	10,000–20,000. Population.	20,000–50,000. Number.	20,000–50,000. Population.	50,000–100,000 Number.	50,000–100,000 Population	100,000 and over. Number.	100,000 and over. Population.	Encampments, Boat and Railway Population un-classed.
1	2	3	4	5	6	7	8	9	10	11	12	13	14	15	16	17	18	19	20	21	22
RAJPUTANA.	*33,833*	*11,225,712*	*28,688*	*4,771,209*	*3,511*	*2,415,979*	*1,180*	*1,606,227*	*348*	*1,008,165*	*70*	*489,940*	*26*	*359,836*	*7*	*243,726*	*2*	*180,601*	*1*	*144,179*	*5,850*
Abu District	5	4,532	4	367	...	...	...	...	1	4,165	...	...	...	...	...	...	...	...	...	...	...
Alwar	1,765	749,751	1,369	303,219	271	184,421	99	133,048	22	60,576	3	19,295	...	...	1	47,582	...	...	...	...	1,610
Banswara	1,097	225,106	1,019	146,779	59	39,671	14	19,254	4	8,749	...	...	1	10,444	...	...	...	...	...	...	209
Bharatpur	1,323	486,954	1,075	207,836	186	124,344	49	66,959	8	25,343	3	20,880	1	11,166	1	30,173	...	...	...	...	253
Bikaner	2,757	936,218	2,389	403,292	269	180,696	73	97,455	14	40,471	7	53,345	3	52,895	1	21,965	1	85,927	...	...	172
Bundi	813	216,722	734	117,269	55	37,617	17	23,040	5	14,275	1	6,486	1	17,991	...	...	...	...	...	...	44
Dholpur	528	254,986	380	84,692	108	75,198	32	44,320	5	14,692	1	6,449	2	29,635	...	...	...	...	...	...	...
Dungarpur	752	227,544	637	114,238	84	57,464	27	36,190	2	5,529	2	14,123	...	...	...	...	...	...	...	...	...
Jaipur	5,911½	2,631,775	4,693½	930,598	784½	555,197	291	406,107	106	318,495	28½	163,127	6	87,416	1	26,297	...	...	1	144,179	359
Jaisalmer	497	76,255	471	51,014	20	12,487	5	5,634	...	...	1	7,120	...	...	...	...	...	...	...	...	...
Jhalawar	434	107,890	408	63,383	24	15,861	1	1,136	4	10,752	1	6,316	1	10,442	...	...	...	...	...	...	...
Karauli	877	140,525	805	55,062	49	33,575	19	25,378	3	6,839	...	...	1	19,671	...	...	...	...	...	...	...
Kishangarh	232	85,744	197	38,944	23	16,399	8	9,926	3	8,546	...	...	1	11,929	...	...	...	...	...	...	...
Kotah	2,529	685,804	2,290	379,381	155	103,838	62	87,189	20	65,368	...	...	1	11,471	1	37,876	...	...	...	...	681
Kushalgarh (Chiefship)	283	35,564	279	30,611	3	1,884	...	...	1	3,069	...	...	...	...	...	...	...	...	...	...	...
Lawa (Estate)... ...	11	2,790	10	620	...	...	...	...	1	2,170	...	...	...	...	...	...	...	...	...	...	...
Marwar...	4,151½	2,125,982	2,951½	653,929	802½	555,883	277	372,547	99	273,788	15½	111,443	5	63,315	...	...	1	94,674	...	...	403
Mewar	8,085	1,566,910	7,488	895,154	412	278,840	140	191,508	86	102,880	7	43,494	1	10,402	1	44,035	...	...	...	...	597
Partabgarh	471	76,539	448	48,347	18	12,435	4	4,621	...	...	...	...	1	10,784	...	...	...	...	...	...	352
Shahpura	117	54,233	86	17,467	21	14,111	8	10,879	1	2,478	1	9,298	...	...	...	...	...	...	...	...	...
Sirohi	418	216,528	282	58,402	81	58,638	38	50,808	10	30,360	2	17,188	...	...	...	...	...	...	...	...	1,132
Tonk	1,281	317,360	1,172	170,605	86	57,420	16	20,228	3	9,620	2	11,376	1	12,275	1	35,798	...	...	...	...	38

TABLE IV.

Towns Classified by Population with Variation Since 1881.

EXPLANATORY NOTE.

A Town, as defined in the Census Code, includes every Municipality and every other continuous collection of houses inhabited by not less than 5,000 persons and having urban characteristics. Discretion is, however, granted to the Local Administration to treat, as Towns, places with less than 5,000 inhabitants, provided they possess urban characteristics.

Sri Ganganagar and Hanumangarh in Bikaner State and Kapasin in Mewar State have been treated as Towns, for the first time at this Census, on account of the expansion of trade and, in Bikaner, the opening of canals and new Railways.

The Capitals of the larger States have, in accordance with previous custom, been treated as Cities though, properly speaking, Jaipur is the only Town that has the requisite qualification of not less than 100,000 inhabitants.

TABLE IV.—Towns Classified by Population

AGENCY AND TOWN.	STATE OR DISTRICT.	Description of Town (Municipality, Suburbs, Cantonments, etc.)	POPULATION. 1931.	1921.	1911.	1901.	1891.	1881.	VARIATION. 1921-31.
1	2	3	4	5	6	7	8	9	10
RAJPUTANA.	**Urban Population.**	...	***1,556,305***	***1,321,171***	***1,379,262***	***1,459,106***	***1,581,304***	***1,361,430***	***+ 235,134***
CITIES.	**10 Cities** ..	Total ...	***558,201***	***470,533***	***487,269***	***549,738***	***579,516***	***510,878***	***+ 87,668***
1. Alwar	Alwar	M.	47,900	44,760	41,305	56,771	51,427	49,867	+ 3,140
2. Bharatpur ...	Bharatpur	M.	30,173	33,495	33,918	43,601	67,555	66,163	− 3,322
3. Bikaner... ...	Bikaner	M.	85,927	69,410	55,326	53,075	50,513	33,154	+ 16,517
4 Bundi	Bundi	...	17,991	16,105	19,598	19,318	22,544	20,744	+ 1,886
5. Dholpur ...	Dholpur	M.	19,586	16,206	19,922	19,310	17,028	15,833	+ 3,380
6. Jaipur	Jaipur	M.	144,179	120,207	137,098	160,167	158,787	142,578	+ 23,972
7. Jodhpur ...	Marwar	M.	94,736	73,480	79,756	79,109	80,405	63,329	+ 21,256
8. Kotah	Kotah	M.	37,876	31,707	32,753	33,657	38,620	40,270	+ 6,169
9. Tonk	Tonk	...	35,798	30,374	33,864	38,759	45,044	40,726	+ 5,424
10. Udaipur ...	Mewar	...	44,035	34,789	38,229	45,976	46,693	38,214	+ 9,246
TOWNS.	**135 Towns** ...	Total ...	***998,104***	***850,638***	***891,993***	***909,368***	***1,001,788***	***850,552***	***+147,466***
Class III.	***20,000 to 50,000***	Total ...	***48,262***	***38,012***	***38,355***	***37,180***	***33,911***	***28,405***	***+ 10,250***
11. Churu	Bikaner	M.	21,965	16,932	16,038	15,657	14,014	10,666	+ 5,033
12. Sikar	Jaipur	...	26,297	21,080	22,317	21,523	19,897	17,739	+ 5,217
Class IV.	***10,000 to 20,000***	...	***334,935***	***284,925***	***297,613***	***298,326***	***324,449***	***287,311***	***+ 50,010***
13. Banswara ...	Banswara	M.	10,444	8,588	7,665	7,038	8,234	7,908	+ 1,856
14. Baran	Kotah	M.	11,471	10,157	9,507	7,892	7,067	7,714	+ 1,314
15. Bari	Dholpur	Town Council	10,049	9,565	11,401	11,603	12,092	11,547	+ 484
16 Bhilwara ...	Mewar	...	10,402	9,100	8,763	10,346	10,843	8,175	+ 1,302
17. Dig	Bharatpur	M.	11,166	11,798	13,147	15,409	15,166	15,828	− 632
18. Fatehpur ...	Jaipur	...	19,505	17,315	17,294	16,393	16,580	14,781	+ 2,190
19 Hindaun ...	—do.—	...	10,825	8,687	10,640	11,938	12,996	12,761	+ 2,138
20. Jhalrapatan Chhaoni ...	Jhalawar	M.	10,442	9,985	11,474	14,315	23,363	20,308	+ 457
21. Jhunjhunu ...	Jaipur	...	14,272	11,950	13,266	12,279	12,267	9,588	+ 2,322
22. Karauli... ...	Karauli	M.	19,671	19,579	19,803	23,482	23,124	25,607	+ 92
23. Kishangarh ...	Kishangarh	M.	11,929	9,452	10,418	12,668	15,457	14,824	+ 2,477
24. Kuchaman ...	Marwar	...	10,262	8,104	9,605	10,749	12,816	13,052	+ 2,158
25. Lachmangarh ...	Jaipur	...	12,839	10,353	10,828	10,176	9,507	8,718	+ 2,486
26. Ladnun	Marwar	...	13,275	10,181	9,685	8,064	7,404	5,188	+ 3,094
27. Nagaur	—do.—	M.	13,837	10,227	12,960	13,377	17,191	14,067	+ 3,610
28. Nawalgarh ...	Jaipur	...	16,902	12,570	14,059	12,315	12,567	10,032	+ 4,332
29. Pali	Marwar	M.	10,974	10,129	12,939	12,673	17,150	13,345	+ 845
30. Partabgarh ...	Partabgarh	M.	10,845	9,182	8,329	9,819	14,819	12,430	+ 1,663
31. Phalodi ...	Marwar	M.	14,982	12,801	13,825	13,924	10,497	9,448	+ 2,181
32. Ramgarh ...	Jaipur	...	13,073	11,479	11,556	11,023	12,197	11,313	+ 1,594
33. Ratangarh ...	Bikaner	M.	16,338	13,468	12,808	11,744	10,536	7,580	+ 2,870
34. Sambhar ...	½ Jaipur	... }	6,296	5,814	5,548	5,437	6,181	5,397	+ 482
	½ Marwar	M. }	6,297	5,813	5,546	5,436	6,181	5,397	+ 484
	Total ...	... }	12,593	11,627	11,094	10,873	12,362	10,794	+ 966
35. Sardarshahr ...	Bikaner	M.	19,407	14,348	12,375	10,052	9,196	5,824	+ 5,059
36. Sironj	Tonk	...	12,275	11,760	12,091	10,417	11,737	11,356	+ 515
37. Sujangarh ...	Bikaner	M.	17,157	12,520	12,086	9,762	9,781	5,238	+ 4,637
Class V.	***5,000 to 10,000***	...	***445,910***	***374,171***	***386,136***	***402,797***	***439,876***	***362,874***	***+ 71,739***
38. Bali	Marwar	M.	5,779	4,882	5,593	5,186	5,354	4,438	+ 897
39. Balotra	—do.—	M.	5,601	5,142	5,408	5,118	5,435	...	+ 459
40. Barmer	—do.—	...	9,240	7,184	6,380	6,064	5,610	...	+ 2,056
41. Bayana	Bharatpur	...	7,252	6,954	7,029	6,867	8,085	8,758	+ 298
42. Bhindar ...	Mewar	...	5,651	5,069	4,630	5,172	6,700	6,522	+ 582
43. Bhinmal	Marwar	M.	6,082	5,032	5,214	4,545	5,736	5,224	+ 1,050
44 Bhusawar ...	Bharatpur	...	5,768	5,295	4,309	6,690	7,419	6,480	+ 473
45. Bidasar ...	Bikaner	...	5,812	5,165	4,791	4,087	4,392	3,627	+ 647
46. Bilara ...	Marwar	...	7,451	6,364	8,606	8,695	11,384	7,699	+ 1,087
47. Bissau	Jaipur	...	7,735	6,941	6,388	7,726	8,041	6,546	+ 794
48. Chaumu ...	—do.—	...	7,807	6,712	6,497	9,300	8,570	3,928	+ 1,095
49. Chhabra ...	Tonk	...	5,462	5,251	6,164	6,724	7,426	8,040	+ 211
50. Chhoti Sadri ...	Mewar	...	5,615	4,757	4,576	5,050	5,368	4,521	+ 858
51. Chitorgarh ...	—do.—	...	8,041	8,015	7,332	7,593	9,354	6,931	+ 26
52. Chirawa ...	Jaipur	...	9,566	7,992	7,979	7,065	6,701	5,489	+ 1,574
53 Dausa	—do—	...	7,691	6,637	5,191	7,540	8,416	7,384	+ 1,054
54. Deogarh ...	Mewar	...	5,082	4,885	5,461	5,884	7,400	6,846	+ 197
55 Didwana ...	Marwar	M.	8,448	6,760	10,122	9,410	11,376	6,617	+ 1,688
56. Dungarpur ...	Dungarpur	M.	8,560	7,327	6,470	6,094	6,431	6,449	+ 1,233
57. Gangapur ...	Jaipur	...	8,943	6,587	5,780	5,155	5,880	5,880	+ 2,356

WITH VARIATION SINCE 1881.

TABLE IV.

Towns Classified by Population.

TION—INCREASE (+), DECREASE (−).				Variation in period 1881 to 1931—Increase (+) Decrease (−)	MALES.			FEMALES.			Serial Number.
1911-21.	1901-11	1891-01.	1881-91.		1931.	1921.	1911.	1931.	1921	1911.	
11	12	13	14	15	16	17	18	19	20	21	
− ***58,091***	− ***79,844***	− ***122,198***	+ ***219,874***	+ ***194,875***	***813,605***	***687,602***	***707,606***	***742,700***	***633,569***	***671,656***	
− ***16,736***	− ***62,469***	− ***29,778***	+ ***68,638***	+ ***47,323***	***300,199***	***250,442***	***253,850***	***258,002***	***220,091***	***233,419***	
+ 8,455	− 15,466	+ 5,344	+ 1,560	− 1,967	25,584	23,433	22,254	22,816	21,327	19,051	1
− 423	− 9,688	− 23,954	+ 1,892	− 35,000	16,786	19,268	18,803	13,437	14,227	15,115	2
+ 13,584	+ 2,751	+ 2,562	+ 17,859	+ 52,773	45,832	36,712	28,275	40,095	32,698	27,551	3
− 3,498	+ 285	− 3,231	+ 1,800	− 2,753	9,179	8,179	9,805	8,812	7,926	9,793	4
− 3,716	+ 612	+ 2,282	+ 1,195	+ 3,753	10,535	8,519	10,783	9,051	7,687	9,139	5
− 16,891	− 23,069	+ 1,880	+ 16,209	+ 1,601	77,933	64,382	70,846	66,246	55,825	66,252	6
− 6,276	+ 647	− 1,296	+ 17,076	+ 31,407	52,165	39,747	41,838	42,571	33,733	37,918	7
− 1,046	− 904	− 4,963	− 1,650	− 2,394	20,259	10,790	16,949	17,617	14,917	15,804	8
− 3,490	− 4,895	− 7,185	+ 5,218	− 4,928	18,201	15,097	16,887	17,597	15,277	17,027	9
+ 1,560	− 12,747	− 717	+ 8,479	+ 5,821	23,775	18,315	17,460	20,260	16,474	15,769	10
− ***41,355***	− ***17,375***	− ***92,420***	+ ***151,236***	+ ***147,552***	***513,406***	***437,160***	***453,756***	***484,698***	***413,478***	***438,237***	
− ***343***	+ ***1,175***	+ ***3,269***	+ ***5,506***	+ ***19,857***	***24,470***	***19,199***	***19,297***	***23,792***	***18,813***	***19,058***	
+ 894	+ 381	+ 1,643	+ 3,348	+ 11,299	11,107	8,462	7,793	10,858	8,470	8,245	11
− 1,237	+ 794	+ 1,626	+ 2,158	+ 8,558	13,363	10,787	11,504	12,934	10,848	10,813	12
− ***12,688***	− ***713***	− ***26,123***	+ ***37,138***	+ ***47,624***	***170,826***	***145,208***	***148,901***	***164,109***	***139,717***	***148,712***	
+ 923	+ 627	− 1,196	+ 326	+ 2,536	5,141	4,202	3,720	5,303	4,386	3,936	13
+ 650	+ 1,615	+ 825	− 647	+ 3,757	5,999	5,382	4,973	5,472	4,775	4,534	14
− 1,836	− 202	− 489	+ 545	− 1,498	5,250	5,034	5,755	4,799	4,531	5,646	15
+ 337	− 1,583	+ 3	+ 2,168	+ 2,227	5,452	4,689	4,613	4,950	4,411	4,150	16
− 1,349	− 2,262	+ 243	− 662	− 4,662	5,934	6,330	7,076	5,232	5,468	6,071	17
+ 21	+ 901	− 187	+ 1,849	+ 4,774	9,481	8,617	8,280	10,024	8,698	9,014	18
− 1,953	− 1,298	− 1,058	+ 235	− 1,936	5,867	4,683	5,787	4,958	4,004	4,903	19
− 1,489	− 2,841	− 9,048	+ 3,060	− 9,861	5,258	4,993	5,597	5,184	4,992	5,877	20
− 1,316	+ 987	+ 12	+ 2,729	+ 4,734	7,563	6,174	6,575	6,709	5,776	6,691	21
− 224	− 3,679	+ 358	− 2,483	− 5,986	10,885	11,164	10,548	8,836	8,415	9,255	22
− 966	− 2,245	− 2,794	+ 633	− 2,895	6,894	5,097	5,448	5 535	4,855	4,975	23
− 1,501	− 1,144	− 2,067	− 236	− 2,790	5,161	3,999	4,754	5,101	4,105	4,851	24
− 475	+ 652	+ 669	+ 794	+ 4,126	6,324	4,960	5,024	6,515	5,393	5,804	25
+ 496	+ 1,621	+ 660	+ 2,221	+ 3,092	6,418	4,774	4,574	6,857	5,407	5,111	26
− 2,733	− 417	− 3,814	+ 3,124	− 230	6,924	4,977	6,442	6,913	5,250	6,518	27
− 1,489	+ 1,744	− 252	+ 2,535	+ 6,870	8,547	6,304	6,874	8,355	6,266	7,185	28
− 2,810	+ 266	− 4,477	+ 3,805	− 2,371	5,600	5,227	6,580	5,374	4,902	6,359	29
+ 853	− 1,490	− 5,000	+ 2,389	− 1,585	5,601	4,666	4,186	5,244	4,516	4,143	30
− 1,024	− 99	+ 3,427	+ 1,049	+ 5,534	7,091	6,175	6,375	7,891	6,626	7,450	31
− 77	+ 533	− 1,174	+ 884	+ 1,760	6,553	5,645	5,657	6,520	5,834	5,890	32
+ 665	+ 1,059	+ 1,208	+ 2,956	+ 8,758	8,197	6,506	6,078	8,141	6,872	6,725	33
+ 266	+ 111	− 744	+ 784	+ 899	3,369	3,174	2,997	2,927	2,640	2,551	34
+ 267	+ 110	− 745	+ 784	+ 900	3,370	3,175	2,995	2,927	2,638	2,551	
+ 533	+ 221	− 1,489	+ 1,568	+ 1,799	6,739	6,349	5,992	5,854	5,278	5,102	
+ 1,973	+ 2,323	+ 856	+ 3,372	+ 13,583	9,714	7,006	6,008	9,693	7,342	6,867	35
− 881	+ 1,674	− 1,320	+ 881	+ 919	6,264	5,995	6,088	6,011	5,765	6,008	36
+ 434	+ 2,324	− 19	+ 4,543	+ 11,919	8,519	6,170	5,948	8,638	6,350	6,138	37
− ***11.965***	− ***16,661***	− ***37,079***	+ ***77,002***	+ ***83,036***	***229,962***	***192,572***	***197.348***	***215,948***	***181,599***	***188,788***	
− 711	+ 407	− 168	+ 916	+ 1,341	2,853	2,440	2,732	2,926	2,442	2,961	38
− 266	+ 200	− 317	...	...	2,864	2,791	2,802	2,737	2,351	2,606	39
+ 804	+ 816	+ 454	...	...	4,825	3,725	3,285	4,415	3,159	3,095	40
− 75	+ 162	− 1,218	− 673	− 1,506	3,351	3,753	3,714	3,401	3,201	3,315	41
+ 439	− 542	− 1,618	+ 268	− 871	2,810	2,511	2,345	2,841	2,558	2,285	42
− 182	+ 660	− 1,191	+ 512	+ 858	3,134	2,449	2,598	2,948	2,583	2,616	43
+ 986	− 2,331	− 729	+ 930	− 712	2,980	2,735	2,252	2,788	2,560	2,057	44
+ 374	+ 754	− 355	+ 765	+ 2,185	2,848	2,592	2,350	2,964	2,643	2,441	45
− 2,242	− 89	− 2,689	+ 3,685	− 248	3,800	3,308	4,453	3,651	3,056	4,153	46
+ 103	− 888	− 315	+ 1,495	+ 1,189	3,855	3,401	3,208	3,880	3,540	3,635	47
+ 215	− 2,303	+ 730	+ 4,612	+ 3,879	4,071	3,427	3,225	3,736	3,285	3,472	48
− 913	− 560	− 702	− 614	− 2,578	2,762	2,614	3,108	2,700	2,637	3,056	49
+ 181	− 474	− 318	+ 847	+ 1,094	2,982	2,487	2,344	2,633	2,270	2,282	50
+ 683	− 261	− 1,761	+ 2,433	+ 1,110	4,280	4,267	3,939	3,761	3,748	3,393	51
+ 13	+ 914	+ 364	+ 1,212	+ 4,077	4,816	3,860	3,891	4,750	4,132	4,063	52
+ 1,446	− 2,349	− 876	+ 1,032	+ 307	3,980	3,457	2,672	3,711	3,180	2,519	53
− 576	+ 77	− 2,016	+ 554	− 1,764	2,510	2,506	2,638	2,572	2,379	2,423	54
− 3,362	+ 712	− 1,966	+ 4,759	+ 1,826	4,421	3,597	5,438	4,022	3,163	4,684	55
+ 857	+ 376	− 337	− 18	+ 2,111	4,418	3,703	3,116	4,142	3,624	3,354	56
+ 807	+ 625	− 725	...	+ 3,063	4,846	3,645	3,199	4,097	2,942	2,581	57

TABLE IV.—TOWNS CLASSIFIED BY POPULATION

AGENCY AND TOWN.	STATE OR DISTRICT.	Description of Town (Municipality, Suburbs, Cantonments, etc.)	POPULATION. 1931.	1921.	1911.	1901.	1891	1881.	VARIATION 1921-31.
1	2	3	4	5	6	7	8	9	10
Class V—*Contd.*									
58. Jaisalmer ...	Jaisalmer ...	...	7,120	4,835	7,420	7,187	10,509	10,965	+ 2,285
59. Jalore... ...	Marwar ...	...	7,114	6,270	7,624	7,443	9,656	6,394	+ 844
60. Kaman ...	Bharatpur ...	...	7,860	7,873	8,912	12,083	11,417	13,199	− 13
61. Kapasin ...	Mewar	...	5,400	...	...	...	...	...	...
62. Khandela ...	Jaipur	...	9,101	6,990	8,206	9,156	10,067	7,949	+ 2,111
63. Kharari (Abu Road) ...	Sirohi	M.	9,725	8,199	7,180	6,661	4,438	...	+ 1,526
64. Khetri ...	Jaipur	...	7,878	6,039	7,125	8,587	8,418	5,288	+ 1,339
65. Kotputli ...	—do.—	...	8,739	7,157	6,879	8,439	7,589	8,084	+ 1,582
66. Lakheri ...	Bundi	...	6,530	4,176	1,824	1,703	2,323	1,889	+ 2,354
67. Lalsote ...	Jaipur	...	5,921	5,501	6,697	8,181	8,168	8,743	+ 420
68. Lohawat ...	Marwar	...	5,011	4,663	4,814	5,322	5,866	2,479	+ 348
69. Makrana ...	—do.—	...	8,713	7,727	6,545	5,157	3,865	...	+ 986
70. Malpura ...	Jaipur	...	5,996	5,373	6,140	6,502	8,345	8,212	+ 623
71. Mandawa ...	—do.—	...	6,956	5,630	5,536	5,165	4,942	4,409	+ 1,326
72. Mundwa ...	Marwar	...	5,234	4,254	5,027	5,121	5,213	4,265	+ 980
73. Nathdwara ...	Mewar	...	8,506	8,524	5,424	8,591	9,331	8,458	− 18
74. Nawan ...	Marwar	...	5,997	4,824	5,657	5,640	5,126	4,142	+ 1,173
75. Nimaj ...	—do.—	...	5,021	4,441	5,015	4,104	5,744	4,371	+ 580
76. Nimbahera ...	Tonk	...	5,946	5,141	4,278	5,446	5,482	6,289	+ 805
77. Nim-ka-Thana ..	Jaipur	...	6,150	5,547	5,946	6,741	5,733	2,711	+ 603
78. Nohar ...	Bikaner	M.	6,089	5,187	5,133	4,698	5,655	3,784	+ 952
79 Patan ...	Jhalawar	M.	6,316	6,083	7,190	7,955	10,783	11,469	+ 233
80. Pipar ...	Marwar	...	7,961	6,494	7,556	6,785	8,153	6,608	+ 1,467
81. Rajakhera ...	Dholpur	Town Council	6,449	5,639	6,890	6,600	6,786	6,274	+ 810
82. Rajaldesar ...	Bikaner	M.	7,204	6,573	5,459	4,366	4,397	3,635	+ 631
83. Rajgarh ...	Alwar	M.	7,683	7,469	9,865	11,008	10,302	9,749	+ 214
84. Rajgarh ...	Bikaner	M.	9,828	5,621	4,526	4,186	4,677	3,726	+ 4,207
85. Reni ...	—do.—	M.	6,335	5,785	5,904	5,745	6,553	5,198	+ 550
86. Sadri ...	Marwar	...	7,684	6,035	4,742	6,621	7,596	3,640	+ 1,649
87. Sagwara ...	Dungarpur ...	M.	5,563	5,539	4,499	4,034	4,085	3,665	+ 24
88. Sawai Madhopur	Jaipur	...	8,216	7,450	11,166	10,828	13,972	14,075	+ 766
89 Shahpura ...	Shahpura	...	9,298	8,296	7,929	8,974	11,718	10,647	+ 1,002
90. Shahpura ...	Jaipur	...	5,041	4,500	3,683	5,245	4,590	3,758	+ 541
91. Sri Madhopur	—do.—	...	6,995	6,699	6,738	6,892	6,130	6,847	+ 296
92. Singhana ...	—do.—	...	5,020	4,674	5,268	5,176	5,901	5,259	+ 346
93. Sirohi ...	Sirohi	M.	7,463	6,197	6,615	5,651	6,207	5,699	+ 1,266
94. Sojat ...	Marwar	M.	9,894	8,797	10,049	11,107	12,624	10,394	+ 1,097
95. Sri Dungargarh	Bikaner	M.	8,212	6,382	8,973	2,679	2,469	...	+ 1,830
96. Sri Ganganagar	—do.—	M.	9,943	1,741	1,700	...	377	...	+ 8,202
97. Surajgarh ...	Jaipur	...	6,082	5,349	5,992	5,248	5,561	5,250	+ 733
98. Tijara ...	Alwar	M.	6,272	6,264	6,561	7,784	7,049	7,728	+ 8
99. Toda Bhim ...	Jaipur	...	5,219	4,891	6,886	6,629	7,053	7,142	+ 328
100. Udaipur ...	—do.—	...	7,144	6,441	7,743	8,638	10,848	9,161	+ 703
Class VI.	**Under** ***5,000***	...	***168,997***	***153,530***	***169,889***	***171,065***	***203,552***	***171,962***	***+15,467***
101. Amber ...	Jaipur	...	4,576	3,689	...	...	...	...	+ 887
102. Bahadurpur ...	Alwar	M.	3,586	3,459	4,236	4,087	4,254	4,171	+ 127
103. Bahror ...	—do.—	M.	4,132	4,108	5,253	5,540	5,719	5,583	+ 24
104. Bairat ...	Jaipur	...	4,973	4,470	5,273	5,687	5,748	5,649	+ 503
105. Bamanwas ...	—do.—	...	3,731	3,505	4,292	5,204	5,806	6,125	+ 226
106. Banera ...	Mewar	...	4,519	4,126	4,335	4,261	5,760	4,718	+ 393
107. Baswa ...	Jaipur	...	4,471	4,289	5,532	5,908	6,117	5,791	+ 182
108. Begun ...	Mewar	...	4,364	3,837	4,385	3,625	5,882	5,641	+ 527
109. Bhadra ...	Bikaner	M.	3,783	3,058	2,835	...	3,256	...	+ 725
110. Chatsu ...	Jaipur	...	4,131	3,375	3,949	4,902	7,870	6,219	+ 756
111. Erinpura ...	Sirohi	...	1,645	2,617	3,033	3,206	3,466	...	− 972
112. Galiakot ...	Dungarpur ...	M.	3,478	4,268	3,014	1,989	1,479	1,504	− 790
113. Govindgarh ...	Alwar	M.	2,848	3,038	3,879	4,932	5,243	4,989	− 190
114. Hanumangarh	Bikaner	M.	3,468	1,788	1,467	...	1,367	...	+ 1,680
115. Jahazpur ...	Mewar	...	3,856	3,633	3,986	3,309	5,106	4,676	+ 223
116. Jaitaran ...	Marwar	...	3,521	3,204	4,371	4,038	4,891	...	+ 317
117. Keshoraipatan	Bundi	...	2,811	2,004	3,429	3,687	4,258	3,987	+ 807
118. Kherwara ...	Mewar	...	1,899	1,599	2,016	2,289	648	...	+ 300
119. Kotra ...	—do.—	...	929	857	746	903	150	...	+ 72
120. Kumher ...	Bharatpur... ...	...	4,653	4,774	5,075	6,240	6,661	7,806	− 121
121. Kushalgarh ...	Kushalgarh (Chiefship) ...	M.	3,069	2,731	2,594	2,838	2,819	2,990	+ 338
122. Mandrail ...	Karauli	...	2,701	2,314	2,514	...	...	...	+ 387
123. Mangrol ...	Kotah	M.	4,855	4,205	4,789	5,156	5,714	5,906	+ 650

TION—INCREASE (+), DECREASE (−).				Variation in period 1881 to 1931 — Increase (+) Decrease (−)	MALES.			FEMALES.			Serial Number.
1911-21.	1901-11.	1891-01.	1881-91.		1931.	1921.	1911.	1931.	1921.	1911.	
11	12	13	14	15	16	17	18	19	20	21	
− 2,585	+ 288	− 3,372	− 456	− 3,845	3,706	2,433	3,667	3,414	2,402	3,753	58
− 1,354	+ 181	− 2,213	+ 3,262	+ 720	3,665	3,082	3,791	3,449	3,188	3,833	59
− 1,089	− 3,171	+ 666	− 1,782	− 5,339	4,204	4,253	4,867	3,656	3,620	4,045	60
...	...	...	...	...	2,786	...	...	2,614	...	...	61
− 1,216	− 950	− 911	+ 2,118	+ 1,152	4,517	3,420	3,995	4,584	3,570	4,211	62
+ 1,019	+ 519	+ 2,223	...	...	5,420	4,789	4,007	4,305	3,410	3,173	63
− 1,086	− 1,412	+ 119	+ 3,135	+ 2,095	3,936	3,157	3,718	3,442	2,882	3,407	64
+ 278	− 1,560	+ 850	− 495	+ 655	4,511	3,542	3,443	4,228	3,615	3,436	65
+ 2,352	+ 121	− 620	+ 484	+ 4,691	3,495	2,320	931	3,035	1,856	893	66
− 1,196	− 1,434	− 82	− 580	− 2,822	3,062	2,852	3,300	2,859	2,649	3,397	67
− 151	− 508	− 44	+ 2,867	+ 2,582	2,497	2,408	2,472	2,514	2,260	2,342	68
+ 1,182	+ 1,388	+ 1,292	...	...	4,412	4,090	3,581	4,301	3,637	2,964	69
− 767	− 362	− 1,843	+ 138	− 2,216	3,204	2,844	3,230	2,792	2,529	2,910	70
+ 94	+ 371	+ 223	+ 533	+ 2,547	3,488	2,850	2,754	3,468	2,780	2,782	71
− 773	− 94	− 92	+ 948	+ 969	2,555	2,155	2,478	2,679	2,099	2,554	72
+ 3,100	− 3,167	− 740	+ 873	+ 48	4,496	4,553	2,906	4,010	3,971	2,518	73
− 833	+ 17	+ 514	+ 984	+ 1,855	3,123	2,576	2,963	2,874	2,248	2,694	74
− 574	+ 911	− 1,640	+ 1,373	+ 650	2,533	2,252	2,520	2,488	2,189	2,495	75
+ 863	− 1,168	− 36	− 807	− 343	3,076	2,759	2,260	2,570	2,382	2,018	76
− 899	− 795	+ 1,008	+ 3,022	+ 3,439	3,329	3,022	3,291	2,821	2,525	2,655	77
+ 4	+ 435	− 957	+ 1,871	+ 2,305	3,075	2,571	2,518	3,014	2,566	2,615	78
− 1,107	− 765	− 2,828	− 686	− 5,153	3,248	3,046	3,547	3,068	3,037	3,643	79
− 1,062	+ 771	− 1,368	+ 1,545	+ 1,353	3,913	3,241	3,796	4,048	3,253	3,760	80
− 751	− 219	− 177	+ 512	+ 175	3,448	3,042	3,527	3,001	2,597	2,863	81
+ 1,114	+ 1,093	− 81	+ 762	+ 3,569	3,465	3,122	2,669	3,739	3,451	2,790	82
− 2,396	− 1,143	+ 706	+ 558	− 2,066	4,025	3,828	4,954	3,658	3,641	4,911	83
+ 1,095	+ 890	− 541	+ 951	+ 6,102	5,134	2,957	2,262	4,694	2,664	2,264	84
− 119	+ 159	− 808	+ 1,355	+ 1,137	3,103	2,805	2,873	3,232	2,980	3,031	85
+ 1,293	− 1,879	− 975	+ 3,956	+ 4,044	3,707	3,006	2,889	3,977	3,029	2,353	86
+ 1,040	+ 465	− 51	+ 420	+ 1,898	2,557	2,772	2,109	3,006	2,767	2,390	87
− 3,716	+ 838	− 3,644	− 103	− 5,859	4,293	3,820	5,900	3,923	3,630	5,266	88
+ 367	− 1,045	− 2,744	+ 1,071	− 1,349	4,689	4,223	4,074	4,609	4,073	3,855	89
+ 867	− 1,612	+ 655	+ 832	+ 1,283	2,562	2,280	1,904	2,479	2,220	1,729	90
− 89	− 154	+ 762	− 717	+ 148	3,555	3,506	3,367	3,440	3,193	3,371	91
− 594	+ 92	− 725	+ 642	− 239	2,379	2,174	2,422	2,641	2,500	2,846	92
− 418	+ 964	− 556	+ 508	+ 1,764	3,820	3,221	3,272	3,643	2,976	3,343	93
− 1,252	− 1,058	− 1,517	+ 2,230	− 500	4,838	4,451	4,971	5,056	4,846	5,078	94
+ 2,409	+ 1,294	+ 210	...	...	4,028	3,177	2,089	4,184	3,205	1,884	95
+ 41	...	...	...	...	6,255	931	951	3,688	810	749	96
− 643	+ 749	− 313	+ 311	+ 882	3,019	2,569	2,962	3,063	2,780	3,080	97
− 297	− 1,223	+ 735	− 674	− 1,451	3,182	3,161	3,341	3,090	3,108	3,220	98
− 1,995	+ 257	− 424	− 89	− 1,923	2,735	2,555	3,519	2,484	2,336	3,367	99
− 1,302	− 895	− 1,705	+ 1,182	− 2,017	4,011	3,564	4,450	3,133	2,877	3,284	100
− 16,359	*− 1,176*	*− 32,487*	*+ 31,590*	*− 2,965*	*88,148*	*80,181*	*88,210*	*80,849*	*73,349*	*81,679*	
...	...	...	...	...	2,627	2,088	...	1,949	1,601	...	101
− 777	+ 149	− 167	+ 83	− 585	1,848	1,780	2,098	1,738	1,720	2,133	102
− 1,145	− 287	− 179	+ 186	− 1,401	2,136	2,111	2,685	1,996	1,997	2,568	103
− 803	− 364	− 111	+ 99	− 676	2,406	2,180	2,549	2,567	2,290	2,724	104
− 787	− 1,002	− 512	− 319	− 2,394	1,943	1,855	2,229	1,788	1,650	2,063	105
− 209	+ 74	− 1,409	+ 1,042	− 199	2,247	2,058	2,144	2,272	2,068	2,191	106
− 1,243	− 876	− 209	+ 326	− 1,320	2,356	2,234	2,820	2,115	2,055	2,712	107
− 548	+ 760	− 2,257	+ 241	− 1,277	2,148	1,908	2,204	2,216	1,984	2,181	108
+ 223	...	...	...	...	1,977	1,576	1,442	1,806	1,482	1,393	109
− 574	− 953	− 2,938	+ 1,651	− 2,088	2,195	1,783	2,099	1,936	1,592	1,850	110
− 416	− 173	− 260	...	...	914	1,798	1,856	731	819	1,177	111
+ 354	+ 1,925	+ 510	− 25	+ 1,974	1,726	2,263	1,965	1,752	2,005	1,949	112
− 846	− 1,053	− 311	+ 254	− 2,146	1,483	1,582	1,993	1,360	1,451	1,886	113
+ 321	...	...	...	...	2,012	966	828	1,456	822	639	114
− 353	+ 587	− 1,707	+ 430	− 820	1,968	1,876	2,105	1,888	1,757	1,881	115
− 1,167	+ 338	− 858	...	...	1,733	1,584	2,108	1,788	1,620	2,263	116
− 1,425	− 258	− 571	+ 321	− 1,126	1,487	1,042	1,715	1,324	962	1,714	117
− 417	− 273	+ 1,641	...	...	1,266	1,029	1,205	633	570	721	118
+ 111	− 157	+ 753	...	...	534	485	461	395	372	265	119
− 801	− 1,165	− 421	− 645	− 2,653	2,442	2,574	2,679	2,211	2,200	2,396	120
+ 187	− 244	+ 19	− 171	+ 79	1,551	1,387	1,276	1,518	1,394	1,318	121
− 200	...	...	...	...	1,366	1,132	1,279	1,335	1,182	1,235	122
− 581	− 367	− 558	− 192	− 1,051	2,515	2,117	2,429	2,340	2,088	2,360	123

TABLE IV.—Towns Classified by Population

Agency and Town.	State or District.	Description of Town (Municipality, Suburb, Cantonment, etc.)	Population. 1931.	1921.	1911.	1901.	1891.	1881.	Varia- 1921-31.
1	2	3	4	5	6	7	8	9	10
Class VI—*Contd.*									
124. Manoharpur ...	Jaipur	...	3,908	3,672	2,094	5,032	4,644	3,570	+ 236
125. Merta ...	Marwar	M.	4,424	3,579	4,397	4,361	7,135	6,682	+ 845
126. Mt. Abu ...	Abu District ...	M.	4,165	2,804	3,286	3,488	2,585	...	+ 1,361
127. Nainwa ...	Bundi	...	4,726	3,996	4,960	4,501	6,093	5,254	+ 730
128. Naraina ...	Jaipur	...	4,703	3,758	5,190	5,266	5,071	4,974	+ 945
129. Nawai ...	—do.—	...	4,834	4,042	4,730	4,432	5,832	4,501	+ 792
130. Pachbhadra ...	Marwar	...	1,414	1,636	2,158	3,194	5,125	4,271	− 222
131. Pirawa ...	Tonk	...	4,439	4,378	4,562	4,771	5,627	5,681	+ 61
132. Pokaran ...	Marwar	...	4,516	4,433	5,314	7,125	7,895	6,467	+ 83
133. Pur ...	Mewar	...	4,948	4,555	4,423	4,498	6,800	5,757	+ 393
134. Ramgarh ...	Alwar	M.	3,175	2,834	3,505	5,179	5,099	5,101	+ 341
135. Rupnagar ...	Kishangarh ...	M.	2,452	2,186	2,988	3,676	5,011	5,665	+ 266
136. Salumbar ...	Mewar	...	4,691	4,399	4,506	4,692	6,020	5,574	+ 292
137. Samod ...	Jaipur	...	2,353	2,120	2,306	3,257	6,582	3,676	+ 233
138. Sangod ...	Kotah	M.	4,844	4,778	5,543	4,369	5,046	5,006	+ 66
139. Sapotra ...	Karauli	...	1,790	1,594	1,630	...	...	...	+ 196
140. Sarwar ...	Kishangarh ...	M.	4,000	3,790	4,418	4,520	5,904	5,361	+ 210
141 Sheoganj ...	Sirohi	M.	4,230	3,599	4,010	4,361	...	...	+ 631
142. Suratgarh ...	Bikaner	M.	3,680	3,592	2,791	2,308	2,650	1,331	+ 88
143. Toda Raisingh	Jaipur	...	4,798	4,192	4,432	3,847	5,649	5,546	+ 606
144. Uniara ...	—do.—	...	4,311	4,102	4,613	4,461	5,728	4,680	+ 209
145. Weir ...	Bharatpur... ...	...	4,602	4,548	5,130	5,711	6,324	7,210	+ 54

Statement showing the variation between the Urban Population as now shown and that shown in 1921.

	1921.	1911.	1891.	Remarks.
Rajputana Agency 1931	1,321,171	1,379,262	1,581,304	
Rajputana Agency 1921	1,317,642	1,373,260	1,571,413	
Variation	+ 3,529	+ 6,002	+ 9,891	
(Previous known population shown for comparison).				
New Towns in 1931	+ 3,529	+ 3,167	+ 1,744	Sri Ganganagar and Hanumangarh.
New Town in 1921	...	+ 2,835	+ 3,256	Bhadra
New Town in 1901	...	...	+ 4,891	Jaitaran.

Towns Classified by Population.

TION—INCREASE (+), DECREASE (–).				Variation in period 1881 to 1931— Increase (+) Decrease (–).	MALES.			FEMALES.			Serial Number.
1911-21.	1901-11.	1891-01.	1881-91.		1931.	1921.	1911.	1931.	1921.	1911.	
11	12	13	14	15	16	17	18	19	20	21	
+ 1,578	– 2,938	+ 888	+ 1,074	+ 888	1,939	1,875	1,084	1,969	1,797	1,010	124
– 818	+ 86	– 2,774	+ 453	– 2,258	2,299	1,851	2,288	2,125	1,728	2,114	125
– 482	– 202	+ 903	...	...	2,539	1,668	2,083	1,626	1,136	1,203	126
– 964	+ 459	– 1,592	+ 839	– 528	2,344	2,015	2,509	2,382	1,981	2,451	127
– 1,432	– 76	+ 195	+ 97	– 271	2,729	2,077	3,255	1,974	1,681	1,935	128
– 688	+ 298	– 1,400	+ 1,331	+ 333	2,682	2,192	2,851	2,202	1,850	1,879	129
– 522	– 1,036	– 1,931	+ 854	– 2,857	712	888	1,098	702	748	1,060	130
– 184	– 209	– 856	– 54	– 1,242	2,280	2,194	2,262	2,159	2,184	2,300	131
– 1,381	– 1,311	– 770	+ 1,428	– 1,951	2,229	2,197	2,863	2,287	2,236	2,951	132
+ 132	– 75	– 2,302	+ 1,043	– 809	2,503	2,373	2,209	2,445	2,182	2,214	133
– 671	– 1,674	+ 80	– 2	– 1,926	1,663	1,549	1,860	1,512	1,285	1,645	134
– 802	– 688	– 1,335	– 654	– 3,213	1,281	1,113	1,519	1,171	1,073	1,469	135
– 107	– 186	– 1,337	+ 455	– 883	2,196	2,088	2,144	2,495	2,311	2,362	136
– 686	– 451	– 3,325	+ 2,906	– 1,323	1,245	1,082	1,381	1,108	1,038	1,425	137
– 765	+ 1,174	– 677	+ 40	– 162	2,402	2,472	2,767	2,442	2,306	2,776	138
– 86	...	...	...	...	945	789	835	845	805	795	139
– 628	– 102	– 1,384	+ 543	– 1,361	2,086	1,986	2,218	1,914	1,804	2,200	140
– 411	– 351	...	...	...	2,049	1,743	1,888	2,181	1,856	2,122	141
+ 801	+ 393	– 261	+ 828	+ 1,849	2,072	1,942	1,490	1,608	1,650	1,301	142
– 240	+ 585	– 1,802	+ 103	– 748	2,481	2,143	2,321	2,817	2,049	2,111	143
– 511	+ 152	– 1,267	+ 1,048	– 369	2,221	2,129	2,353	2,090	1,973	2,260	144
– 582	– 581	– 1,113	– 386	– 2,608	2,421	2,503	2,678	2,181	2,045	2,452	145

TABLE V.

Towns arranged territorially with population by Religion.

EXPLANATORY NOTE.

In this Table Towns are arranged territorially. The Capital town of the State is placed at the top of each group and the remaining towns are arranged in alphabetical order.

The figures for Hindus include those for Aryas, Brahmos and Deo Samajists.

The column for "Others" includes the following :—

State.	Towns etc.	Religion.	Persons.	Males.	Females.
Dholpur.	Dholpur City.	Buddhist.	1	1	...
Sirohi.	Kharari (Abu Road).	Jew.	38	18	20

TABLE V.—Towns Arranged Territorially

Agency, State or District and Town.	Municipality, Cantonment, etc.	Urban Population.			Hindu.			Muslim.		
		Persons.	Males.	Females.	Persons.	Males.	Females.	Persons.	Males.	Females.
1	2	3	4	5	6	7	8	9	10	11
RAJPUTANA.	...	***1,556,305***	***813,605***	***742,700***	***1,074,055***	***566,726***	***507,329***	***383,045***	***198,701***	***184,344***
Abu District.	...	***4,165***	***2,539***	***1,626***	***3,171***	***1,914***	***1,257***	***774***	***492***	***282***
1. Mount. Abu	M.	4,165	2,539	1,626	3,171	1,914	1,257	774	492	282
Alwar.	...	***75,591***	***39,921***	***35,670***	***52,042***	***27,607***	***24,435***	***21,796***	***11,406***	***10,390***
2. Alwar City.	M.	47,900	25,584	22,316	32,568	17,392	15,176	14,278	7,637	6,641
3. Bahadurpur.	M.	3,586	1,848	1,738	2,064	1,089	975	1,487	743	744
4. Behror.	M.	4,132	2,136	1,996	3,338	1,749	1,589	741	361	380
5. Govindgarh.	M.	2,843	1,483	1,360	1,816	968	848	962	477	485
6. Rajgarh.	M.	7,683	4,025	3,658	6,629	3,478	3,151	1,007	521	486
7. Ramgarh.	M.	3,175	1,663	1,512	2,169	1,125	1,044	794	434	360
8. Tijara.	M.	6,272	3,182	3,090	3,458	1,806	1,652	2,527	1,233	1,294
Banswara.	...	***10,444***	***5.141***	***5,303***	***6,970***	***3,467***	***3,503***	***2,957***	***1,382***	***1,575***
9. Banswara.	M.	10,444	5,141	5,303	6,970	3,467	3,503	2,957	1,382	1,575
Bharatpur.	...	***71,474***	***38,568***	***32,906***	***51,488***	***27,742***	***23,746***	***18,130***	***9,813***	***8,317***
10. Bharatpur City. ...	M.	30,173	16,736	13,437	20,216	11,214	9,002	9,117	5,055	4,062
11. Bhusawar.	...	5,768	2,980	2,788	4,147	2,140	2,007	1,612	835	777
12. Bayana.	...	7,252	3,851	3,401	5,257	2,767	2,490	1,838	989	849
13. Dig.	M.	11,166	5,934	5,232	8,543	4,572	3,971	2,339	1,203	1,136
14. Kaman	...	7,860	4,204	3,656	6,350	3,409	2,941	1,189	642	547
15. Kumher.	...	4,653	2,442	2,211	3,434	1,799	1,635	1,040	543	497
16. Weir.	...	4,602	2,421	2,181	3,541	1,841	1,700	995	546	449
Bikaner.	...	***225,148***	***117,338***	***107,810***	***156,279***	***82,767***	***73,512***	***46.296***	***24,545***	***21,751***
17. Bikaner City.	M.	85,927	45,832	40,095	61,697	33,448	28,249	16,858	9,048	7,810
18. Bhadra.	M.	3,783	1,977	1,806	2,492	1,301	1,191	1,200	642	558
19. Bidasar.	...	5,812	2,848	2,964	3,336	1,705	1,631	928	467	436
20. Churu.	M.	21,965	11,107	10,858	13,644	6,914	6,730	6,671	3,423	3,248
21. Dungargarh.	M.	8,212	4,028	4,184	5,889	2,923	2,966	909	502	407
22. Hanumangarh.	M.	3,468	2,012	1,456	2,343	1,380	963	926	512	414
23. Nohar.	M.	6,089	3,075	3,014	4,258	2,157	2,101	1,590	809	781
24. Rajaldesar.	M.	7,204	3,465	3,739	5,089	2.537	2,552	748	388	360
25. Rajgarh.	M.	9,828	5,134	4,694	6,000	3,230	2,770	2,885	1,502	1,383
26. Ratangarh.	M.	16,338	8,197	8,141	12,247	6,139	6,108	3,411	1,761	1,650
27. Reni.	M.	6,335	3,103	3,232	4,737	2,355	2,382	1,096	521	575
28. Sardarshahr.	M.	19,407	9,714	9,693	11,930	6,104	5,826	3,512	1,903	1,609
29. Sri Ganganagar. ...	M.	9,943	6,255	3,688	8,174	5,136	3,038	1,325	820	505
30. Sujangarh.	M.	17,157	8,519	8,638	11,625	5,881	5,744	3,554	1,808	1,746
31. Suratgarh.	M.	3,680	2,072	1,608	2,818	1,557	1,261	688	419	269
Bundi.	...	***32,058***	***16,505***	***15,553***	***24,416***	***12,564***	***11,852***	***6,231***	***3,200***	***3,031***
32. Bundi City.	...	17,991	9,179	8,812	13,341	6,775	6,566	3,901	1,999	1,902
33. Keshoraipatan.	...	2,811	1,487	1,324	2,028	1,084	944	767	396	371
34. Lakheri.	...	6,530	3,495	3,035	5,840	3,106	2,734	589	327	262
35. Nainwa.	...	4,726	2,344	2,382	3,207	1,599	1,608	974	478	496
Dholpur.	...	***36,084***	***19,233***	***16,851***	***26,025***	***14,038***	***11,987***	***9,416***	***4,848***	***4,568***
36. Dholpur City.	M.	19,586	10,535	9,051	13,520	7,388	6,132	5,881	3,044	2,837
37. Bari.	...	10,049	5,250	4,799	7,127	3,777	3,350	2,891	1,457	1,434
38. Rajakhera.	...	6,449	3,448	3,001	5,378	2,873	2,505	644	347	297
Dungarpur.	...	***17,601***	***8,701***	***8,900***	***10,373***	***5,289***	***5,084***	***5.844***	***2,731***	***3,113***
39. Dungarpur.	M.	8,560	4,418	4,142	5,260	2,808	2,452	2,525	1,217	1,308
40. Galiakot.	M.	5,563	2,557	3,006	3,576	1,707	1,869	1,617	673	944
41. Sagwara.	M.	3,478	1,726	1,752	1,537	774	763	1,702	841	861
Jaipur.	...	***446,677***	***233,943***	***212,734***	***316,491***	***166,544***	***149,947***	***117,057***	***60,635***	***56,422***
42. Jaipur City.	M.	144,179	77,933	66,246	92,364	50,076	42,288	44,072	23,780	20,292
43 Amber	...	4,576	2,627	1,949	3,824	2,185	1,639	728	431	297
44. Bairat.	...	4,973	2,406	2,567	3,739	1,833	1,906	949	451	498
45. Bamanwas.	...	3,731	1,943	1,788	3,483	1,801	1,682	167	101	66
46. Baswa.	...	4,471	2,356	2,115	4,031	2,142	1,889	350	175	175
47. Bissau.	...	7,735	3,855	3,880	5,283	2,673	2,610	2,425	1,168	1,257
48. Chaksu.	...	4,131	2,195	1,936	3,157	1,684	1,473	856	448	408
49. Chaumu.	...	7,807	4,071	3,736	5,981	3,109	2,872	1,709	897	812
50. Chirawa.	...	9,566	4,816	4,750	8,231	4,149	4,082	1,312	654	658
51. Dausa	...	7,691	3,980	3,711	6,227	3,248	2,979	1,374	691	683

JAIN.			CHRISTIAN.			TRIBAL.			ZOROASTRIAN.			SIKH.			OTHERS.			Serial Number.
Persons.	Males.	Females	Persons.	Males.	Females.	Persons.	Males.	Females	Persons	Males	Females.	Persons.	Males.	Females.	Persons.	Males	Females.	
12	13	14	15	16	17	18	19	20	21	22	23	24	25	26	27	28	29	
92,565	***44,176***	***48,389***	***3,307***	***1,794***	***1,513***	***1,574***	***1,076***	***498***	***289***	***156***	***133***	***1,431***	***957***	***474***	***39***	***19***	***20***	
21	***10***	***11***	***140***	***84***	***56***	...	...	...	***19***	***11***	***8***	***40***	***28***	***12***	...	...	...	
21	10	11	140	84	56	...	...	...	19	11	8	40	28	12	...	...	...	1
1,653	***850***	***803***	***64***	***38***	***26***	...	...	...	...	...	...	***36***	***20***	***16***	...	...	...	
961	500	461	57	35	22	...	...	...	...	...	...	36	20	16	...	...	...	2
35	16	19	...	...	...	...	...	...	...	...	...	...	...	...	...	...	...	3
58	26	27	...	...	...	...	...	...	...	...	...	...	...	...	...	...	...	4
65	38	27	...	...	...	...	...	...	...	...	...	...	...	...	...	...	...	5
40	23	17	7	3	4	...	...	...	...	...	...	...	...	...	...	...	...	6
212	104	108	...	...	...	...	...	...	...	...	...	...	...	...	...	...	...	7
287	143	144	...	...	...	...	...	...	...	...	...	...	...	...	...	...	...	8
370	***192***	***178***	***83***	***39***	***44***	***58***	***56***	***2***	***1***	***1***	...	***5***	***4***	***1***	...	...	...	
370	192	178	83	39	44	58	56	2	1	1	...	5	4	1	...	...	...	9
1,199	***643***	***556***	***601***	***332***	***269***	...	...	...	***5***	***3***	***2***	***51***	***35***	***16***	...	...	...	
435	233	202	363	206	157	...	...	...	2	1	1	40	27	13	...	...	...	10
9	5	4	...	...	...	...	...	...	...	...	...	...	...	...	...	...	...	11
152	91	61	2	2	...	...	...	...	3	2	1	...	...	...	...	...	...	12
204	116	88	79	42	37	...	...	...	...	...	...	1	1	...	...	...	...	13
242	116	126	79	37	42	...	...	...	...	...	...	...	...	...	...	...	...	14
91	43	48	78	45	33	...	...	...	...	...	...	10	7	3	...	...	...	15
66	34	32	...	...	...	...	...	...	...	...	...	...	...	...	...	...	...	16
21,504	***9,299***	***12,205***	***178***	***104***	***74***	...	...	...	***16***	***9***	***7***	***875***	***614***	***261***	...	...	...	
6,957	3,059	3,898	139	86	53	...	...	...	15	8	7	261	183	78	...	...	...	17
91	34	57	...	...	...	...	...	...	...	...	...	...	...	...	...	...	...	18
1,552	655	897	...	...	...	...	...	...	...	...	...	1	1	...	...	...	...	19
1,633	761	872	14	7	7	...	...	...	...	...	...	3	2	1	...	...	...	20
1,411	600	811	...	...	...	...	...	...	...	...	...	3	3	...	...	...	...	21
79	37	42	...	...	...	...	...	...	...	...	...	120	83	37	...	...	...	22
228	97	131	...	...	...	...	...	...	...	...	...	13	12	1	...	...	...	23
1,367	540	827	...	...	...	...	...	...	...	...	...	...	...	...	...	...	...	24
940	399	541	...	...	...	...	...	...	...	...	...	3	3	...	...	...	...	25
669	289	380	6	5	1	...	...	...	...	...	...	5	3	2	...	...	...	26
502	227	275	...	...	...	...	...	...	...	...	...	...	...	...	...	...	...	27
3,964	1,706	2,258	...	...	...	...	...	...	...	...	...	1	1	...	...	...	...	28
20	11	9	...	...	...	...	...	...	...	...	...	424	288	136	...	...	...	29
1,972	828	1,144	5	1	4	...	...	...	...	...	...	1	1	...	...	...	...	30
119	56	63	14	5	9	...	...	...	1	1	...	40	34	6	...	...	...	31
1,367	***710***	***657***	***29***	***21***	***8***	***5***	***3***	***2***	***3***	***3***	...	***7***	***4***	***3***	...	...	...	
739	398	341	...	...	...	5	3	2	3	3	...	2	1	1	...	...	...	32
16	7	9	...	...	...	...	...	...	...	...	...	...	...	...	...	...	...	33
72	41	31	29	21	8	...	...	...	...	...	...	...	...	...	...	...	...	34
540	264	276	...	...	...	...	...	...	...	...	...	5	3	2	...	...	...	35
480	***268***	***212***	***63***	***21***	***42***	...	...	...	...	...	...	***99***	***57***	***42***	***1***	***1***	...	
41	34	7	63	21	42	...	...	...	...	...	...	80	47	33	1	1	...	36
12	6	6	...	...	...	...	...	...	...	...	...	19	10	9	...	...	...	37
427	228	199	...	...	...	...	...	...	...	...	...	...	...	...	...	...	...	38
1,369	***673***	***696***	***7***	***4***	***3***	...	...	...	...	...	...	***8***	***4***	***4***	...	...	...	
763	387	376	4	2	2	...	...	...	...	...	...	8	4	4	...	...	...	39
370	177	193	...	...	...	...	...	...	...	...	...	...	...	...	...	...	...	40
236	109	127	3	2	1	...	...	...	...	...	...	...	...	...	...	...	...	41
12,238	***6,302***	***5,936***	***658***	***319***	***339***	***14***	***8***	***6***	***40***	***22***	***18***	***179***	***113***	***66***	...	...	...	
7,242	3,828	3,414	329	143	186	8	4	4	17	8	9	147	91	58	...	...	...	42
24	11	13	...	...	...	...	...	...	...	...	...	...	...	...	...	...	...	43
285	122	163	...	...	...	...	...	...	...	...	...	...	...	...	...	...	...	44
81	41	40	...	...	...	...	...	...	...	...	...	...	...	...	...	...	...	45
90	39	51	...	...	...	...	...	...	...	...	...	...	...	...	...	...	...	46
27	14	13	...	...	...	...	...	...	...	...	...	...	...	...	...	...	...	47
118	63	55	...	...	...	...	...	...	...	...	...	...	...	...	...	...	...	48
117	65	52	...	...	...	...	...	...	...	...	...	...	...	...	...	...	...	49
22	12	10	...	...	...	...	...	...	...	...	...	1	1	...	...	...	...	50
90	41	49	...	...	...	...	...	...	...	...	...	...	...	...	...	...	...	51

TABLE V.—TOWNS ARRANGED TERRITORIALLY

AGENCY, STATE OR DISTRICT AND TOWN.	MUNICIPALITY, CANTONMENT, etc.	URBAN POPULATION.			HINDU.			MUSLIM.		
		Persons.	Males.	Females.	Persons.	Males.	Females.	Persons.	Males.	Females.
1	2	3	4	5	6	7	8	9	10	11
Jaipur—*Contd.*										
52. Fatehpur.	...	19,505	9,481	10,024	12,991	6,461	6,530	5,974	2,764	3,210
53. Gangapur.	...	8,943	4,846	4,097	6,475	3,485	2,990	2,076	1,155	921
54. Hindaun.	...	10,825	5,867	4,958	8,586	4,707	3,879	2,143	1,099	1,044
55. Jhunjhunu.	...	14,272	7,563	6,709	8,199	4,407	3,792	5,888	3,059	2,829
56. Khandela.	...	9,101	4,517	4,584	5,886	2,897	2,989	3,095	1,561	1,534
57. Khetri.	...	7,378	3,936	3,442	5,293	2,855	2,438	2,051	1,069	982
58. Kotputli.	...	8,739	4,511	4,228	6,866	3,520	3,346	1,873	991	882
59. Lachmangarh	...	12,839	6,324	6,515	10,531	5,133	5,398	2,269	1,175	1,094
60. Lalsot.	...	5,921	3,062	2,859	5,385	2,806	2,579	439	205	234
61. Malpura.	...	5,996	3,204	2,792	3,912	2,097	1,815	1,739	929	810
62. Mandawa	...	6,956	3,488	3,468	5,752	2,854	2,898	1,204	634	570
63. Manoharpur.	...	3,908	1,939	1,969	2,995	1,513	1,482	913	426	487
64. Naraina.	...	4,703	2,729	1,974	3,577	2,149	1,428	984	508	476
65. Nawai.	...	4,834	2,632	2,202	3,950	2,167	1,783	548	301	247
66. Nawalgarh.	...	16,902	8,547	8,355	13,447	6,838	6,609	3,444	1,702	1,742
67. Nim-ka-Thana	...	6,150	3,329	2,821	5,378	2,899	2,474	772	428	344
68. Ramgarh.	...	13,073	6,553	6,520	9,527	4,792	4,735	3,401	1,697	1,704
69. ¼ Sambhar	...	6,296	3,369	2,927	3,994	2,125	1,869	2,207	1,188	1,019
70. Samod.	...	2,353	1,245	1,108	2,112	1,119	993	239	126	113
71. Sawai Madhopur. ...	...	8,216	4,293	3,923	5,750	3,009	2,741	2,046	1,069	977
72. Shahpura.	...	5,041	2,562	2,479	4,138	2,105	2,028	908	457	451
73. Sikar.	...	26,297	13,363	12,934	14,217	7,384	6,833	11,321	5,624	5,697
74. Singhana.	...	5,020	2,379	2,641	2,570	1,261	1,309	2,438	1,111	1,327
75. Sri Madhopur	...	6,995	3,555	3,440	6,222	3,177	3,045	725	355	370
76. Surajgarh	...	6,082	3,019	3,063	4,641	2,341	2,300	1,435	676	759
77. Toda Bhim	...	5,219	2,735	2,484	4,264	2,235	2,029	939	490	449
78. Toda Raisingh ...	...	4,798	2,481	2,317	3,774	1,947	1,827	616	318	298
79. Udaipur	...	7,144	4,011	3,133	6,299	3,586	2,713	835	419	416
80. Uniara	...	4,311	2,221	2,090	3,450	1,775	1,675	593	303	290
Jaisalmer.	...	***7,120***	***3,706***	***3,414***	***5,942***	***3,073***	***2,869***	***926***	***518***	***408***
81. Jaisalmer	...	7,120	3,706	3,414	5,942	3,073	2,869	926	518	408
Jhalawar.	...	***16,758***	***8,506***	***8,252***	***11,218***	***5,785***	***5,433***	***4,812***	***2,354***	***2,458***
82. Jhalrapatan (Chhaoni) ...	...	10,442	5,258	5,184	7,102	3,628	3,474	3,170	1,539	1,631
83. Patan	...	6,316	3,248	3,068	4,116	2,157	1,959	1,642	815	827
Karauli.	...	***24,162***	***13,146***	***11,016***	***19,321***	***10,615***	***8,706***	***4,459***	***2,344***	***2,115***
84. Karauli	M.	19,671	10,835	8,836	15,090	8,428	6,662	4,213	2,228	1,985
85. Mandrail	...	2,701	1,366	1,335	2,541	1,299	1,242	160	67	93
86. Sapotra	...	1,790	945	845	1,690	888	802	86	49	37
Kishangarh.	...	***18,381***	***9,761***	***8,620***	***13,200***	***7,054***	***6,146***	***4,013***	***2,099***	***1,914***
87. Kishangarh	M.	11,929	6,394	5,535	8,406	4,530	3,876	2,777	1,477	1,300
88. Rupnagar	M.	2,452	1,281	1,171	1,934	1,019	915	386	191	195
89. Sarwar	M.	4,000	2,086	1,914	2,860	1,505	1,355	850	431	419
Kotah	...	***59,046***	***31,175***	***27,871***	***41,233***	***22,053***	***19,180***	***15,952***	***8,127***	***7,825***
90. Kotah City	M.	37,876	20,259	17,617	25,614	13,995	11,619	11,018	5,599	5,419
91. Baran	M.	11,471	5,999	5,472	8,729	4,598	4,131	2,410	1,229	1,181
92. Mangrol	M.	4,855	2,515	2,340	3,191	1,669	1,522	1,486	750	736
93. Sangod.	M.	4,844	2,402	2,442	3,699	1,791	1,908	1,038	549	489
Kushalgarh (Chiefship)	...	***3,069***	***1,551***	***1,518***	***2,054***	***1,033***	***1,021***	***446***	***232***	***214***
94. Kushalgarh	M.	3,069	1,551	1,518	2,054	1,033	1,021	446	232	214
Marwar.	...	***283,463***	***146,842***	***136,621***	***191,190***	***100,561***	***90,629***	***63,532***	***32,960***	***30,572***
95. Jodhpur City	M.	94,736	52,165	42,571	66,199	36,899	29,300	23,239	12,495	10,744
96. Bali	M.	5,779	2,853	2,926	3,918	2,017	1,901	502	242	260
97. Balotra	M.	5,601	2,864	2,737	3,809	1,962	1,847	922	462	460
98. Barmer	...	9,240	4,825	4,415	6,515	3,447	3,068	1,082	584	498
99. Bhinmal	...	6,082	3,134	2,948	4,293	2,308	1,985	346	193	153
100. Bilara	...	7,451	3,800	3,651	6,411	3,289	3,122	623	317	306
101. Didwana	M.	8,443	4,421	4,022	5,584	2,992	2,592	2,670	1,345	1,325
102. Jaitaran	...	3,521	1,733	1,788	2,398	1,199	1,190	697	330	367
103. Jalore.	M.	7,114	3,665	3,449	5,185	2,767	2,418	685	334	351
104. Kuchaman.	...	10,262	5,161	5,101	7,052	3,522	3,530	2,726	1,389	1,337
105. Ladnun	...	13,275	6,418	6,857	6,286	3,109	3,177	4,056	2,053	2,003
106. Lohawat	...	5,011	2,497	2,514	4,064	2,103	1,961	134	80	54

JAIN.			CHRISTIAN.			TRIBAL.			ZOROASTRIAN.			SIKH.			OTHERS.			Serial Number.
Persons.	Males.	Females.	Persons.	Males.	Females.	Persons.	Males.	Females.	Persons.	Males.	Females.	Persons.	Males.	Females.	Persons.	Males.	Females	
12	13	14	15	16	17	18	19	20	21	22	23	24	25	26	27	28	29	
540	256	284	...	...	...	...	...	...	...	...	...	...	...	...	...	...	...	52
93	45	48	266	142	124	...	...	...	19	11	8	14	8	6	...	...	...	53
87	58	29	9	3	6	...	...	...	...	...	...	...	...	...	...	...	...	54
183	95	88	2	2	...	...	...	...	...	...	...	...	...	...	...	...	...	55
120	59	61	...	...	...	...	...	...	...	...	...	...	...	...	...	...	...	56
16	5	11	9	2	7	...	...	...	...	...	...	9	5	4	...	...	...	57
...	...	...	...	...	...	...	...	...	...	...	...	...	...	...	...	...	...	58
39	16	23	...	...	...	...	...	...	...	...	...	...	...	...	...	...	...	59
97	51	46	...	...	...	...	...	...	...	...	...	...	...	...	...	...	...	60
342	175	167	...	...	...	...	...	...	...	...	...	3	3	...	...	...	...	61
...	...	...	...	...	...	...	...	...	...	...	...	...	...	...	...	...	...	62
...	...	...	...	...	...	...	...	...	...	...	...	...	...	...	...	...	...	63
138	69	69	4	3	1	...	...	...	...	...	...	...	...	...	...	...	...	64
336	164	172	...	...	...	...	...	...	...	...	...	...	...	...	...	...	...	65
10	6	4	1	1	...	...	...	...	...	...	...	...	...	...	...	...	...	66
5	2	3	...	...	...	...	...	...	...	...	...	...	...	...	...	...	...	67
140	62	78	...	...	...	...	...	...	...	...	...	5	2	3	...	...	...	68
75	43	32	13	8	5	6	4	2	1	1	...	...	...	...	...	...	...	69
2	...	2	...	...	...	...	...	...	...	...	...	...	...	...	...	...	...	70
420	215	205	...	...	...	...	...	...	...	...	...	...	...	...	...	...	...	71
...	...	...	...	...	...	...	...	...	...	...	...	...	...	...	...	...	...	72
748	349	399	8	4	4	...	...	...	3	2	1	...	...	...	...	...	...	73
12	7	5	...	...	...	...	...	...	...	...	...	...	...	...	...	...	...	74
31	12	19	17	11	6	...	...	...	...	...	...	...	...	...	...	...	...	75
6	2	4	...	...	...	...	...	...	...	...	...	...	...	...	...	...	...	76
16	10	6	...	...	...	...	...	...	...	...	...	...	...	...	...	...	...	77
408	216	192	...	...	...	...	...	...	...	...	...	...	...	...	...	...	...	78
10	6	4	...	...	...	...	...	...	...	...	...	...	...	...	...	...	...	79
268	143	125	...	...	...	...	...	...	...	...	...	...	...	...	...	...	...	80
164	***65***	***99***	...	...	...	***86***	***48***	***38***	...	...	...	***2***	***2***	...	...	...	...	
164	65	99	...	...	...	86	48	38	...	...	...	2	2	...	...	...	...	81
718	***361***	***357***	***5***	***4***	***1***	...	...	...	...	...	...	***5***	***2***	***3***	...	...	...	
160	85	75	5	4	1	...	...	...	...	...	...	5	2	3	...	...	...	82
558	276	282	...	...	...	...	...	...	...	...	...	...	...	...	...	...	...	83
366	***180***	***186***	***16***	***7***	***9***	...	...	...	...	...	...	...	...	...	...	...	...	
352	172	180	16	7	9	...	...	...	...	...	...	...	...	...	...	...	...	84
...	...	...	...	...	...	...	...	...	...	...	...	...	...	...	...	...	...	85
14	8	6	...	...	...	...	...	...	...	...	...	...	...	...	...	...	...	86
1,050	***552***	***498***	***15***	***8***	***7***	***101***	***46***	***55***	...	...	...	***2***	***2***	...	...	...	...	
732	379	353	12	6	6	...	...	...	...	...	...	2	2	...	...	...	...	87
129	69	60	3	2	1	...	...	...	...	...	...	...	...	...	...	...	...	88
189	104	85	...	...	...	101	46	55	...	...	...	...	...	...	...	...	...	89
1,548	***811***	***737***	***112***	***62***	***50***	***123***	***78***	***45***	***4***	***2***	***2***	***74***	***42***	***32***	...	...	...	
1,034	537	497	108	58	50	39	34	5	...	...	...	63	36	27	...	...	...	90
313	160	153	4	4	...	...	...	...	4	2	2	11	6	5	...	...	...	91
94	52	42	...	...	...	84	44	40	...	...	...	...	...	...	...	...	...	92
107	62	45	...	...	...	...	...	...	...	...	...	...	...	...	...	...	...	93
569	***286***	***283***	...	...	...	...	...	...	...	...	...	...	...	...	...	...	...	
569	286	283	...	...	...	...	...	...	...	...	...	...	...	...	...	...	...	94
27,940	***12,866***	***15,074***	***623***	***344***	***279***	***115***	***80***	***35***	***43***	***21***	***22***	***20***	***10***	***10***	...	...	...	
4,773	2,465	2,308	441	251	190	30	29	...	43	21	22	12	5	7	...	...	...	95
1,359	594	765	...	...	...	...	...	...	...	...	...	...	...	...	...	...	...	96
870	440	430	...	...	...	...	...	...	...	...	...	...	...	...	...	...	...	97
1,639	790	849	4	4	...	...	...	...	...	...	...	...	...	...	...	...	...	98
1,441	631	810	2	2	...	...	...	...	...	...	...	...	...	...	...	...	...	99
417	194	223	...	...	...	...	...	...	...	...	...	...	...	...	...	...	...	100
189	84	105	...	...	...	...	...	...	...	...	...	...	...	...	...	...	...	101
426	204	222	...	...	...	...	...	...	...	...	...	...	...	...	...	...	...	102
1,244	564	680	...	...	...	...	...	...	...	...	...	...	...	...	...	...	...	103
484	250	234	...	...	...	...	...	...	...	...	...	...	...	...	...	...	...	104
2,933	1,256	1,677	...	...	...	...	...	...	...	...	...	...	...	...	...	...	...	105
805	309	496	...	...	...	8	5	3	...	...	...	...	...	...	...	...	...	106

TABLE V.—Towns Arranged Territorially

Agency, State or District and Town.	Municipality, Cantonment, etc.	Urban Population.			Hindu.			Muslim.		
		Persons.	Males.	Females.	Persons.	Males.	Females.	Persons.	Males.	Females.
1	2	3	4	5	6	7	8	9	10	11
Marwar—*Contd.*										
107. Makrana	...	8,713	4,412	4,301	3,507	1,861	1,646	5,188	2,541	2,647
108. Merta	M.	4,424	2,299	2,125	2,977	1,588	1,389	1,173	580	593
109. Mundwa	...	5,234	2,555	2,679	4,320	2,100	2,220	853	421	432
110. Nagaur	M.	13,837	6,924	6,913	7,394	3,694	3,700	4,576	2,364	2,212
111. Nawan	...	5,997	3,123	2,874	4,727	2,461	2,266	983	516	467
112. Nimaj	...	5,021	2,533	2,488	4,311	2,194	2,117	448	225	223
113. Pachbhadra	...	1,414	712	702	932	483	449	27	15	12
114. Pali	M.	10,974	5,600	5,374	5,599	2,833	2,766	3,747	1,946	1,801
115. Phalodi	M.	14,982	7,091	7,891	10,597	5,064	5,533	1,876	965	911
116. Pipar	...	7,961	3,913	4,048	4,985	2,471	2,514	2,191	1,099	1,092
117. Pokaran	...	4,516	2,229	2,287	3,707	1,819	1,888	796	400	396
118. Sadri	...	7,684	3,707	3,977	5,460	2,806	2,654	172	88	84
½ Sambhar	M.	6,297	3,370	2,927	3,999	2,128	1,871	2,204	1,188	1,016
119. Sojat	M.	9,894	4,838	5,056	6,961	3,445	3,516	1,616	788	828
Mewar.	...	***117,938***	***61,953***	***55,985***	***81,516***	***42,905***	***38,611***	***23,760***	***12,294***	***11,466***
120. Udaipur City	...	44,035	23,775	20,260	26,973	14,614	12,359	10,988	5,772	5,216
121. Banera	...	4,519	2,247	2,272	3,498	1,711	1,787	831	434	397
122. Begun	...	4,364	2,148	2,216	3,005	1,495	1,510	945	457	488
123. Bhilwara	...	10,402	5,452	4,950	7,289	3,815	3,474	2,372	1,244	1,128
124. Bhindar	...	5,651	2,810	2,841	3,795	1,901	1,894	946	459	487
125. Chhoti Sadri	...	5,615	2,982	2,633	4,203	2,235	1,968	787	415	372
126. Chitorgarh	...	8,041	4,280	3,761	5,839	3,115	2,724	1,609	854	755
127. Deogarh	...	5,082	2,510	2,572	3,812	1,909	1,903	457	204	253
128. Jahazpur	...	3,856	1,968	1,888	2,555	1,303	1,252	1,222	617	605
129. Kapasin	...	5,400	2,786	2,614	4,013	2,051	1,962	842	437	405
130. Kherwara	...	1,899	1,266	633	1,455	987	468	364	222	142
131. Kotra	...	929	534	395	652	389	263	256	135	121
132. Nathdwara	...	8,506	4,496	4,010	7,263	3,840	3,423	827	430	397
133. Pur	...	4,948	2,503	2,445	3,860	1,957	1,903	540	272	268
134. Salumbar	...	4,691	2,196	2,495	3,304	1,583	1,721	774	342	432
Partabgarh.	...	***10,845***	***5,601***	***5,244***	***6,051***	***3,176***	***2,875***	***2,076***	***1,055***	***1,021***
135. Partabgarh	M.	10,845	5,601	5,244	6,051	3,176	2,875	2,076	1,055	1,021
Shahpura.	...	***9,298***	***4,689***	***4,609***	***7,194***	***3,640***	***3,554***	***1,604***	***799***	***805***
136. Shahpura	...	9,298	4,689	4,609	7,194	3,640	3,554	1,604	799	805
Sirohi.	...	***23,063***	***12,203***	***10,860***	***16,090***	***8,665***	***7,425***	***3,543***	***1,927***	***1,616***
137. Sirohi	M.	7,463	3,820	3,643	5,703	2,975	2,728	611	320	291
138. Erinpura	...	1,645	914	731	1,470	823	647	168	87	81
139. Kharari (Abu Road) ...	M.	9,725	5,420	4,305	6,593	3,689	2,904	2,274	1,264	1,010
140. Sheoganj	M.	4,230	2,049	2,181	2,324	1,178	1,146	490	256	234
Tonk.	...	***63,920***	***32,583***	***31,337***	***31,791***	***16,234***	***15,557***	***29,421***	***14,940***	***14,481***
141. Tonk City	...	35,798	18,201	17,597	15,657	7,974	7,683	19,329	9,789	9,540
142. Chhabra	...	5,462	2,762	2,700	3,582	1,801	1,781	1,742	893	849
143. Nimbahera	...	5,946	3,076	2,870	3,422	1,744	1,678	1,864	976	888
144. Pirawa	...	4,439	2,280	2,159	2,160	1,119	1,041	1,557	794	763
145. Sironj	...	12,275	6,264	6,011	6,970	3,596	3,374	4,929	2,488	2,441

JAIN.			CHRISTIAN.			TRIBAL.			ZOROASTRIAN.			SIKH.			OTHERS.			Serial Number.
Persons.	Males.	Females.	Persons.	Males.	Fe-males.	Persons.	Males.	Fe-males.	Persons.	Males	Fe-males.	Persons.	Males	Fe-males	Persons.	Males.	Fe-males	
12	13	14	15	16	17	18	19	20	21	22	23	24	25	26	27	28	29	
17	9	8	...	...	...	...	...	...	...	...	...	1	1	...	...	...	...	107
274	131	143	...	...	...	...	...	...	...	...	...	...	...	...	...	...	...	108
37	21	16	24	13	11	...	...	...	...	...	...	...	...	...	...	...	...	109
1,783	803	980	133	62	71	...	...	...	...	...	...	1	1	...	...	...	...	110
275	139	136	6	4	2	...	...	...	...	...	...	6	3	3	...	...	...	111
262	114	148	...	...	...	...	...	...	...	...	...	...	...	...	...	...	...	112
455	214	241	...	...	...	...	...	...	...	...	...	...	...	...	...	...	...	113
1,555	778	777	...	...	...	73	43	30	...	...	...	...	...	...	...	...	...	114
2,509	1,062	1,447	...	...	...	...	...	...	...	...	...	...	...	...	...	...	...	115
785	343	442	...	...	...	...	...	...	...	...	...	...	...	...	...	...	...	116
13	10	3	...	...	...	...	...	...	...	...	...	...	...	...	...	...	...	117
2,052	813	1,239	...	...	...	...	...	...	...	...	...	...	...	...	...	...	...	118
76	43	33	13	8	5	5	3	2	...	...	...	...	...	...	...	...	...	
1,317	605	712	...	...	...	...	...	...	...	...	...	...	...	...	...	...	...	119
11,572	***6,003***	***5,569***	***161***	***102***	***59***	***921***	***644***	***277***	...	...	...	***8***	***5***	***3***	...	...	...	
5,076	2,706	2,370	94	53	41	896	625	271	...	...	...	8	5	3	...	...	...	120
190	102	88	...	...	...	...	...	...	...	...	...	...	...	...	...	...	...	121
414	196	218	...	...	...	...	...	...	...	...	...	...	...	...	...	...	...	122
740	392	348	...	...	...	1	1	...	...	...	...	...	...	...	...	...	...	123
910	450	460	...	...	...	...	...	...	...	...	...	...	...	...	...	...	...	124
621	330	291	4	2	2	...	...	...	...	...	...	...	...	...	...	...	...	125
590	309	281	2	1	1	1	1	...	...	...	...	...	...	...	...	...	...	126
805	389	416	1	1	...	7	7	...	...	...	...	...	...	...	...	...	...	127
79	48	31	...	...	...	...	...	...	...	...	...	...	...	...	...	...	...	128
545	298	247	...	...	...	...	...	...	...	...	...	...	...	...	...	...	...	129
12	5	7	60	45	15	8	7	1	...	...	...	...	...	...	...	...	...	130
13	7	6	...	...	...	8	3	5	...	...	...	...	...	...	...	...	...	131
416	226	190	...	...	...	...	...	...	...	...	...	...	...	...	...	...	...	132
548	274	274	...	...	...	...	...	...	...	...	...	...	...	...	...	...	...	133
613	271	342	...	...	...	...	...	...	...	...	...	...	...	...	...	...	...	134
2,597	***1,270***	***1,327***	***22***	***12***	***10***	***82***	***75***	***7***	***13***	***9***	***4***	***4***	***4***	...	...	...	...	
2,597	1,270	1,327	22	12	10	82	75	7	13	9	4	4	4	...	...	...	...	135
499	***250***	***249***	***1***	...	***1***	...	...	...	...	...	...	...	...	...	...	...	...	
499	250	249	1	...	1	...	...	...	...	...	...	...	...	...	...	...	...	136
2,748	***1,245***	***1,503***	***490***	***266***	***224***	...	...	...	***145***	***75***	***70***	***9***	***7***	***2***	***38***	***18***	***20***	
1,137	516	621	6	4	2	...	...	...	...	...	...	6	5	1	...	...	...	137
5	2	3	2	2	...	...	...	...	...	...	...	...	...	...	...	...	...	138
190	112	78	482	260	222	...	...	...	145	75	70	3	2	1	38	18	20	139
1,416	615	801	...	...	...	...	...	...	...	...	...	...	...	...	...	...	...	140
2,593	***1,340***	***1,253***	***39***	***27***	***12***	***69***	***38***	***31***	...	...	...	***7***	***4***	***3***	...	...	...	
762	406	356	37	25	12	9	5	4	...	...	...	4	2	2	...	...	...	141
137	67	70	...	...	...	...	...	...	...	...	...	1	1	...	...	...	...	142
599	322	277	2	2	...	59	32	27	...	...	...	...	...	...	...	...	...	143
720	366	354	...	...	...	...	...	...	...	...	...	2	1	1	...	...	...	144
375	179	196	...	...	...	1	1	...	...	...	...	...	...	...	...	...	...	145

TABLE VI.

Birth-Place.

EXPLANATORY NOTE.

This Table shows the birth-places of persons enumerated in Rajputana and is divided into two parts:—

Part I.—For States and Districts as a whole.

Part II.—For Cities only.

The figures for Provinces and States which are adjacent to Rajputana are given in detail.

District, State, Province, or Country where born.	Population of Agency.			District or State					
				Abu District.			Alwar.		
	Persons.	Males.	Females.	Persons.	Males.	Females.	Persons.	Males.	Females.
1	2	3	4	5	6	7	8	9	10
Total Population ...	11,225,712	5,885,028	5,340,684	4,532	2,753	1,779	749,751	396,261	353,490
A. Born in India ...	11,224,686	5,884,346	5,340,340	4,484	2,724	1,760	749,727	396,246	353,481
I. Born within the Agency of Enumeration ...	10,894,773	5,747,387	5,147,386	3,030	1,837	1,193	725,708	392,300	333,408
(i) Within the State ...	10,543,213	5,627,226	4,915,987	1,470	829	641	691,479	385,076	306,403
(ii) In other Rajputana States	351,560	120,161	231,399	1,560	1,008	552	34,229	7,224	27,005
II. (a) Born in Provinces, Districts or States in India adjacent to Rajputana ...	322,270	133,324	188,946	1,327	800	527	23,400	3,783	19,617
(*i*) *British Territory* ...	214,848	94,723	120,125	994	600	394	16,066	2,956	13,110
Ajmer-Merwara ...	21,522	7,875	13,647	410	233	177	212	111	101
Bombay	9,970	4,671	5,299	92	49	43	18	13	5
Delhi	1,962	1,053	909	22	9	13	333	118	215
Punjab	113,855	57,502	56,353	180	109	71	13,808	2,243	11,565
United Provinces of Agra and Oudh ...	67,539	23,622	43,917	290	200	90	1,695	471	1,224
(*ii*) *Indian States* ...	107,422	38,601	68,821	333	200	133	7,334	827	6,507
Bombay States ...	4,362	1,642	2,720	21	10	11	...	...	...
Central India Agency ...	26,335	9,629	16,706	48	23	25	43	21	22
Gwalior State ...	46,601	14,940	31,661	...	...	...	121	35	86
Punjab States Agency ...	26,527	10,845	15,682	99	68	31	7,152	761	6,391
Western India Agency ...	3,597	1,545	2,052	165	99	66	18	10	8
(b) Born in other Provinces and States in India...	6,597	3,255	3,342	98	65	33	139	69	70
(*i*) *British Territory* ...	5,087	2,395	2,692	45	31	14	90	54	36
Bengal	1,003	553	450	12	9	3	26	21	5
Central Provinces and Berar	2,914	1,108	1,806	12	6	6	18	9	9
Other Provinces ...	1,170	734	436	21	16	5	46	24	22
(*ii*) *Other Indian States* ...	1,510	860	650	53	34	19	49	15	34
(c) French and Portuguese Settlements ...	163	122	41	16	14	2	1	1	...
(d) India Unspecified ...	883	258	625	13	8	5	479	93	386
B. Born in other Asiatic Countries ...	521	390	131	4	3	1	10	8	2
(*i*) *Within British Dominions.*	3	2	1	...	...	...	1	...	1
Ceylon	3	2	1	...	...	...	1	...	1
(*ii*) *Outside British Dominions.*	518	388	130	4	3	1	9	8	1
Afghanistan	260	233	27	2	2	...	3	2	1
China	2	1	1	...	...	...	...	...	...
Nepal	230	139	91	...	...	...	6	6	...
Elsewhere	26	15	11	2	1	1	...	...	...
C. Born in Europe. ...	440	276	164	40	24	16	11	7	4
(i) United Kingdom and Ireland	405	257	148	37	23	14	10	6	4
(ii) British Possessions in Europe.	1	...	1	1	...	1	...	...	...
(iii) Continental Europe ...	34	19	15	2	1	1	1	1	...
D. Born in Africa. ...	28	8	20	...	...	...	...	...	...
(*i*) *Within British Dominions.*	6	1	5	...	...	...	...	...	...
Kenya (British East Africa)	6	1	5	...	...	...	...	...	...
(*ii*) *Africa Unspecified* ...	22	7	15	...	...	...	...	...	...
E. Born in America ...	23	5	18	2	1	1	1	...	1
(*i*) *Within British Dominions.*	7	1	6	...	...	...	...	...	...
Canada	7	1	6	...	...	...	...	...	...
(*ii*) *Outside British Dominions.*	6	2	4	...	...	...	...	...	...
United States ...	6	2	4	...	...	...	...	...	...
(*iii*) *America Unspecified* ...	10	2	8	2	1	1	1	...	1
F. Born in Australasia ...	14	3	11	2	1	1	2	...	2
(*i*) *Within British Dominions.*	11	2	9	2	1	1	2	...	2
Australia	6	2	4	2	1	1	...	...	...
Fiji Islands	5	...	5	...	...	...	2	...	2
(*ii*) *Australasia Unspecified* ...	3	1	2	...	...	...	...	...	...

Part I.—Districts and States.

where Enumerated.

Banswara.			Bharatpur.			Bikaner.			Bundi.		
Persons.	Males.	Females.	Persons.	Males.	Females.	Persons.	Males.	Females.	Persons.	Males.	Females.
11	12	13	14	15	16	17	18	19	20	21	22
225,106	***111,983***	***113,123***	***486,954***	***263,325***	***223,629***	***936,218***	***501,153***	***435,065***	***216,722***	***113,101***	***103,621***
225,098	***111,978***	***113,120***	***486,918***	***263,311***	***223,607***	***936,149***	***501,094***	***435,055***	***216,710***	***113,094***	***103,616***
221,724	***110,702***	***111,022***	***448,772***	***253,537***	***195,235***	***832,330***	***440,198***	***392,132***	***214,429***	***111,856***	***102,573***
216,732	109.268	107,464	**419,628**	245,232	174,396	**774,915**	412,608	362,307	**202,719**	106,910	95,809
4,992	1,434	3,558	**29,144**	8,305	20,839	**57,415**	27,590	29,825	**11,710**	4,946	6,764
3,292	***1,229***	***2,063***	***37,857***	***9,612***	***28,245***	***103,159***	***60,521***	***42,638***	***2,213***	***1,194***	***1,019***
1,102	***383***	***719***	***37,363***	***9,404***	***27,959***	***86,470***	***51,183***	***35,287***	***1,095***	***694***	***401***
10	6	4	**169**	68	101	**652**	440	212	**282**	138	144
946	280	666	**145**	80	65	**209**	114	95	**83**	49	34
...	...	...	**205**	93	112	**268**	190	78	**20**	17	8
26	23	3	**8,588**	2,355	6,233	**81,899**	48,207	33,692	**292**	230	62
120	74	46	**28, 256**	6,808	21,448	**3,442**	2,232	1,210	**418**	260	153
2,190	***846***	***1,344***	***494***	***208***	***286***	***16,689***	***9,338***	***7,351***	***1,118***	***500***	***618***
1,072	428	644	**3**	2	1	...	...	...	...	...	...
981	360	621	**86**	47	39	**87**	52	35	**609**	255	354
121	48	73	**294**	94	200	**133**	42	91	**509**	245	264
...	...	...	**105**	59	46	**16,390**	9,193	7,197	...	...	...
16	10	6	**6**	6	...	**79**	51	28	...	...	...
78	***44***	***34***	***208***	***131***	***77***	***610***	***336***	***274***	***48***	***27***	***21***
55	***26***	***29***	***121***	***84***	***37***	***487***	***269***	***218***	***38***	***21***	***17***
13	6	7	**41**	31	10	**240**	124	116	**17**	11	6
15	2	13	**25**	14	11	**82**	51	31	**7**	3	4
27	18	9	**55**	39	16	**165**	94	71	**14**	7	7
23	***18***	***5***	***87***	***47***	***40***	***123***	***67***	***56***	***10***	***6***	***4***
4	***3***	***1***	***4***	***4***	...	***35***	***29***	***6***	***20***	***17***	***3***
...	...	...	***77***	***27***	***50***	***15***	***10***	***5***	...	...	...
5	***5***	...	***5***	***3***	***2***	***49***	***48***	***1***	***2***	***2***	...
...	...	...	***1***	***1***	...	...	...	...	...	...	...
...	...	...	**1**	1	...	...	...	...	...	...	...
5	***5***	...	***4***	***2***	***2***	***49***	***48***	***1***	***2***	***2***	...
4	4	...	**2**	1	1	**49**	48	1	**2**	2	...
...	...	...	...	...	...	...	...	...	...	...	...
1	1	...	...	...	...	...	...	...	...	...	...
...	...	...	**2**	1	1	...	...	...	...	...	...
...	...	...	***19***	***8***	***11***	***16***	***10***	***6***	***10***	***5***	***5***
...	...	...	**18**	8	10	**15**	10	5	**5**	4	1
...	...	...	...	...	...	...	...	...	...	...	...
...	...	...	**1**	...	1	**1**	...	1	**5**	1	4
...	...	...	***8***	***3***	***5***	***2***	***1***	***1***	...	...	...
...	...	...	...	...	...	...	...	...	...	...	...
...	...	...	...	...	...	...	...	...	...	...	...
...	...	...	***8***	***3***	***5***	***2***	***1***	***1***	...	...	...
3	...	***3***	***1***	...	***1***	***1***	...	***1***	...	...	...
3	...	**3**	...	...	...	...	...	...	...	...	...
3	...	3	...	...	...	...	...	...	...	...	...
...	...	...	...	...	...	...	...	...	...	...	...
...	...	...	...	...	...	...	...	...	...	...	...
...	...	...	***1***	...	***1***	***1***	...	***1***	...	...	...
...	...	...	***3***	...	***3***	***1***	...	***1***	...	...	...
...	...	...	***3***	...	***3***	...	...	...	...	...	...
...	...	...	...	...	...	...	...	...	...	...	...
...	...	...	**3**	...	3	...	...	...	...	...	...
...	...	...	...	...	...	***1***	...	***1***	...	...	...

District, State, Province, or Country where born.	District or State									
	Dholpur.			Dungarpur.			Jaipur.			Jaisal-
	Persons	Males.	Females.	Persons.	Males.	Females.	Persons.	Males.	Females.	Persons.
1	23	24	25	26	27	28	29	30	31	32
Total Population ...	254,986	140,497	114,489	227,544	114,480	113,064	2,631,775	1,387,067	1,244,708	76,255
A. Born in India ...	254,969	140,489	114,480	227,477	114,437	113,040	2,631,535	1,386,922	1,244,613	76,252
I. Born within the Agency of Enumeration ...	230,783	134,529	96,254	224,079	113,293	110,786	2,610,011	1,378,104	1,231,907	75,473
(i) Within the State ...	226,923	132,202	93,721	217,938	111,598	106,340	2,563,584	1,366,514	1,197,070	70,998
(ii) In other Rajputana States...	3,860	1,327	2,533	6,141	1,695	4,446	46,427	11,590	34,837	4,475
II. (a) Born in Provinces, Districts, or States in India adjacent to Rajputana ...	24,068	5,906	18,162	3,329	1,107	2,222	20,276	8,189	12,087	710
(i) *British Territory* ...	17,260	4,505	12,755	1,858	647	1,211	17,096	7,364	9,732	628
Ajmer-Merwara ...	47	27	20	11	6	5	3,991	1,170	2,821	1
Bombay	5	4	1	1,705	558	1,147	794	444	350	575
Delhi	55	22	33	...	...	...	608	334	274	4
Punjab	287	177	110	29	16	13	5,949	2,239	3,710	27
United Provinces of Agra and Oudh ...	16,866	4,275	12,591	113	67	46	5,754	3,177	2,577	21
(ii) *Indian States* ...	6,808	1,401	5,407	1,471	460	1,011	3,180	825	2,355	82
Bombay States ...	...	...	...	1,183	341	842	9	5	4	6
Central India Agency ...	156	51	105	167	72	95	453	205	248	34
Gwalior State ...	6,596	1,319	5,277	56	30	26	442	145	297	6
Punjab States Agency ...	54	29	25	...	...	...	2,276	470	1,806	34
Western India Agency ...	2	2	...	65	17	48	...	...	...	2
(b) Born in other Provinces and States in India...	118	54	64	68	36	32	1,007	536	471	61
(i) *British Territory* ...	97	46	51	32	28	4	828	435	393	58
Bengal ...	29	14	15	...	...	...	360	186	174	1
Central Provinces and Berar	42	19	23	...	...	...	159	80	79	56
Other Provinces ...	26	13	13	32	28	4	309	169	140	1
(ii) *Other Indian States* ...	21	8	13	36	8	28	179	101	78	3
(c) French and Portuguese Settlements ...	...	...	...	1	1	...	13	9	4	...
(d) India Unspecified ...	...	...	...	...	...	...	228	84	144	8
B. Born in Other Asiatic Countries ...	7	5	2	67	43	24	63	47	16	3
(i) *Within British Dominions.*	...	...	...	...	...	...	...	...	...	...
Ceylon ...	...	...	...	...	...	...	...	...	...	...
(ii) *Outside British Dominions.*	7	5	2	67	43	24	63	47	16	3
Afghanistan	3	3	...	...	...	...	25	24	1	3
China	...	...	...	...	...	...	2	1	1	...
Nepal	2	2	...	66	42	24	31	17	14	...
Elsewhere	2	...	2	1	1	...	5	5	...	...
C. Born in Europe ...	10	3	7	...	...	...	161	92	69	...
(i) United Kingdom and Ireland	9	2	7	...	...	...	150	83	67	...
(ii) British Possessions in Europe.	...	...	...	...	...	...	...	...	...	...
(iii) Continental Europe ...	1	1	...	...	...	...	11	9	2	...
D. Born in Africa ...	...	...	...	...	...	...	8	3	5	...
(i) *Within British Dominions.*	...	...	...	...	...	...	...	...	...	...
Kenya (British East Africa.)	...	...	...	...	...	...	...	...	...	...
(ii) *Africa Unspecified* ...	...	...	...	...	...	...	8	3	5	...
E. Born in America ...	...	...	...	...	...	...	6	2	4	...
(i) *Within British Dominions.*	...	...	...	...	...	...	...	...	...	...
Canada	...	...	...	...	...	...	...	...	...	...
(ii) *Outside British Dominions*	...	...	...	...	...	...	6	2	4	...
United States ...	...	...	...	...	...	...	6	2	4	...
(iii) *America Unspecified* ...	...	...	...	...	...	...	...	...	...	...
F. Born in Australasia ...	...	...	...	...	...	...	2	1	1	...
(i) *Within British Dominions*	...	...	...	...	...	...	2	1	1	...
Australia	...	...	...	...	...	...	2	1	1	...
Fiji Islands	...	...	...	...	...	...	...	...	...	...
(ii) *Australasia Unspecified* ...	...	...	...	...	...	...	...	...	...	...

where Enumerated.

...mer.		Jhalawar.			Karauli.			Kishangarh.			Kotah.		
Males.	Females.	Persons.	Males.	Females.	Persons.	Males.	Females	Persons.	Males.	Females.	Persons.	Males.	Females.
33	34	35	36	37	38	39	40	41	42	43	44	45	46
42,342	33,913	107,890	56,518	51,372	140,525	76,729	63,796	85,744	44,494	41,250	685,804	355,056	330,748
42,342	33,910	107,875	56,505	51,370	140,516	76,723	63,793	85,743	44,493	41,250	685,694	354,974	330,720
41,977	33,496	92,983	51,519	41,464	136,908	75,816	61,092	79,596	42,721	36,875	660,645	343,737	316,908
40,948	30,050	82,818	47,271	35,547	122,571	71,610	50,961	69,527	39,995	29,532	625,660	326,639	299,021
1,029	3,446	10,165	4,248	5,917	14,337	4,206	10,131	10,069	2,726	7,343	34,985	17,098	17,887
333	377	14,731	4,879	9,852	3,508	880	2,628	6,126	1,761	4,365	22,578	10,285	12,293
287	341	614	396	218	1,170	357	813	5,958	1,684	4,274	5,599	3,471	2,128
...	1	108	68	40	20	10	10	5,640	1,457	4,183	657	349	308
252	323	75	51	24	36	6	30	79	49	30	775	481	294
2	2	12	7	5	14	6	8	37	26	11	53	24	29
16	11	74	49	25	40	22	18	15	14	1	783	541	242
17	4	345	221	124	1,060	313	747	187	138	49	3,331	2,076	1,255
46	36	14,117	4,483	9,634	2,338	523	1,815	168	77	91	16,979	6,814	10,165
6	...	2	2	...	10	7	3	58	35	23	...	...	...
18	16	8,026	2,570	5,456	34	14	20	39	14	25	5,510	2,222	3,288
5	1	6,036	1,872	4,164	2,220	463	1,757	70	27	43	11,469	4,592	6,877
17	17	11	7	4	18	11	7	1	1	...	...	...	...
...	2	42	32	10	56	28	28	...	...	...	...	...	...
32	29	129	93	36	99	26	73	21	11	10	2,451	939	1,512
30	28	35	24	11	91	24	67	16	10	6	2,326	846	1,480
1	...	6	3	3	28	10	18	1	1	...	17	10	7
29	27	8	4	4	2	1	1	13	7	6	2,258	796	1,462
...	1	21	17	4	61	13	48	2	2	...	51	40	11
2	1	94	69	25	8	2	6	5	1	4	125	93	32
...	...	2	2	...	...	...	...	...	...	...	5	3	2
...	8	30	12	18	1	1	...	...	...	...	15	10	5
...	3	13	11	2	8	6	2	1	1	...	91	74	17
...	...	...	...	...	...	...	...	...	...	...	1	1	...
...	...	...	...	...	...	...	...	...	...	...	1	1	...
...	3	13	11	2	8	6	2	1	1	...	90	73	17
...	3	5	5	...	3	3	...	1	1	...	72	64	8
...	...	...	...	...	...	...	...	...	...	...	...	...	...
...	...	8	6	2	5	3	2	...	...	...	14	8	6
...	...	...	...	...	...	...	...	...	...	...	4	1	3
...	...	2	2	...	...	...	...	...	...	...	17	8	9
...	...	2	2	...	...	...	...	...	...	...	8	4	4
...	...	...	...	...	...	...	...	...	...	...	...	...	...
...	...	...	...	...	...	...	...	...	...	...	9	4	5
...	...	...	...	...	1	...	1	...	...	...	2	...	2
...	...	...	...	...	...	...	...	...	...	...	...	...	...
...	...	...	...	...	...	...	...	...	...	...	...	...	...
...	...	...	...	...	1	...	1	...	...	...	2	...	2
...	...	...	...	...	...	...	...	...	...	...	...	...	...
...	...	...	...	...	...	...	...	...	...	...	...	...	...
...	...	...	...	...	...	...	...	...	...	...	...	...	...
...	...	...	...	...	...	...	...	...	...	...	...	...	...
...	...	...	...	...	...	...	...	...	...	...	...	...	...
...	...	...	...	...	...	...	...	...	...	...	...	...	...
...	...	...	...	...	...	...	...	...	...	...	...	...	...
...	...	...	...	...	...	...	...	...	...	...	...	...	...
...	...	...	...	...	...	...	...	...	...	...	...	...	...
...	...	...	...	...	...	...	...	...	...	...	...	...	...
...	...	...	...	...	...	...	...	...	...	...	...	...	...

District. State, Province or Country where born.	District or State									
	Kushalgarh (Chiefship.)			Lawa (Estate.)			Marwar.			Me-
	Persons.	Males.	Females.	Persons.	Males.	Females.	Persons.	Males.	Females.	Persons.
1	47	48	49	50	51	52	53	54	55	56
Total Population ...	35,564	17,754	17,810	2,790	1,445	1,345	2,125,982	1,109,912	1,016,070	1,566,910
A. Born in India ...	35,559	17,749	17,810	2,790	1,445	1,345	2,125,902	1,109,860	1,016,042	1,566,736
I. Born within the Agency of Enumeration ...	33,032	16,723	16,309	2,760	1,438	1,322	2,117,208	1,104,995	1,012,213	1,553,394
(i) Within the State ...	31,673	16,234	15,439	1,850	1,257	593	2,099,877	1,100,699	999,178	1,542,467
(ii) In other Rajputana States.	1,359	489	870	910	181	729	17,331	4,296	18,085	10,927
II. (a) Born in Provinces, Districts or States in India adjacent to Rajputana.	2,490	1,001	1,489	30	7	23	8,095	4,500	3,595	13,160
(i) *British Territory* ...	880	355	525	30	7	23	6,984	3,951	3,033	6,309
Ajmer-Merwara ...	3	1	2	25	8	22	1,418	673	745	3,495
Bombay	855	337	518	...	...	...	1,200	666	534	1,490
Delhi	...	...	...	...	...	...	138	72	66	43
Punjab	...	...	...	1	...	1	1,207	808	399	306
United Provinces of Agra and Oudh ...	22	17	5	4	4	...	3,021	1,732	1,289	975
(ii) *Indian States* ...	1,610	646	964	...	...	...	1,111	549	562	6,851
Bombay States ...	81	35	46	...	...	...	56	37	19	1,319
Central India Agency ...	1,450	571	879	...	...	...	241	153	88	1,705
Gwalior State ...	75	38	37	...	...	...	154	60	94	3,534
Punjab States Agency ...	1	1	...	...	...	...	87	53	34	185
Western India Agency ...	3	1	2	...	...	...	573	246	327	108
(b) Born in other Provinces and States in India ...	37	25	12	...	...	...	558	343	215	171
(i) *British Territory* ...	6	5	1	...	...	...	324	201	123	107
Bengal	1	...	1	...	...	...	128	65	63	44
Central Provinces and Berar	...	...	...	...	...	...	52	32	20	29
Other Provinces ...	5	5	...	...	...	...	144	104	40	34
(ii) *Other Indian States* ...	31	20	11	...	...	...	234	142	92	64
(c) French and Portuguese Settlements ...	...	...	...	...	...	...	41	22	19	5
(d) India Unspecified ...	...	...	...	...	...	...	...	...	...	6
B. Born in other Asiatic Countries.	5	5	...	...	...	...	20	17	3	117
(i) *Within British Dominions.*	...	...	...	...	...	...	...	...	...	...
Ceylon	...	...	...	...	...	...	...	...	...	...
(ii) *Outside British Dominions.*	5	5	...	...	...	...	20	17	3	117
Afghanistan	2	2	...	...	...	...	12	12	...	40
China	...	...	...	...	...	...	...	...	...	...
Nepal	3	3	...	...	...	...	3	2	1	77
Elsewhere	...	...	...	...	...	...	5	3	2	...
C. Born in Europe ...	...	...	...	...	...	...	51	34	17	54
(i) United Kingdom and Ireland.	...	...	...	...	...	...	51	34	17	52
(ii) British Possessions in Europe.	...	...	...	...	...	...	...	...	...	...
(iii) Continental Europe. ...	...	...	...	...	...	...	...	...	...	2
D. Born in Africa ...	...	...	...	...	...	...	6	1	5	...
(i) *Within British Dominions.*	...	...	...	...	...	...	6	1	5	...
Kenya (British East Africa)	...	...	...	...	...	...	6	1	5	...
(ii) *Africa Unspecified* ...	...	...	...	...	...	...	...	...	...	...
E. Born in America ...	...	...	...	...	...	...	1	...	1	3
(i) *Within British Dominions.*	...	...	...	...	...	...	1	...	1	3
Canada	...	...	...	...	...	...	1	...	1	3
(ii) *Outside British Dominions.*	...	...	...	...	...	...	...	...	...	...
United States ...	...	...	...	...	...	...	...	...	...	...
(iii) *America Unspecified* ...	...	...	...	...	...	...	...	...	...	...
F. Born in Australasia ...	...	...	...	...	...	...	2	...	2	...
(i) *Within British Dominions.*	...	...	...	...	...	...	2	...	2	...
Australia	...	...	...	...	...	...	2	...	2	...
Fiji Islands	...	...	...	...	...	...	...	...	...	...
(ii) *Australasia Unspecified* ...	...	...	...	...	...	...	...	...	...	...

Part I.—Districts and States.

where Enumerated.

war.		Partabgarh.			Shahpura.			Sirohi.			Tonk.		
Males.	Females.	Persons.	Males.	Females.	Persons.	Males.	Females.	Persons.	Males.	Females.	Persons.	Males.	Females.
57	58	59	60	61	62	63	64	65	66	67	68	69	70
807,184	***759,726***	***76,539***	***38,991***	***37,548***	***54,233***	***27,907***	***26,326***	***216,528***	***111,675***	***104,853***	***317,360***	***164,401***	***152,959***
807,064	***759,672***	***76,517***	***38,974***	***37,543***	***54,222***	***27,897***	***26,325***	***216,473***	***111,640***	***104,833***	***317,340***	***164,385***	***152,955***
801,214	***752,180***	***69,067***	***36,398***	***32,669***	***50,929***	***26,990***	***23,939***	***210,096***	***108,598***	***101,498***	***301,816***	***158,905***	***142,911***
796,675	745,792	**63,032**	33,768	29,264	**44,386**	25,392	18,994	**196,410**	103,362	93,048	**276,556**	152,139	124,417
4,539	6,388	**6,035**	2,630	3,405	**6,543**	1,598	4,945	**13,686**	5,236	8,450	**25,260**	6,766	18,494
5,723	***7,437***	***7,349***	***2,502***	***4,847***	***3,284***	***902***	***2,382***	***5,960***	***2,822***	***3,138***	***15,328***	***5,388***	***9,940***
3,322	***2,987***	***215***	***142***	***73***	***3,224***	***878***	***2,346***	***2,737***	***1,496***	***1,241***	***1,196***	***641***	***555***
1,661	1,834	**78**	46	32	**3,166**	844	2,322	**638**	318	320	**439**	246	243
818	672	**31**	14	17	...	...	...	**816**	330	486	**41**	26	15
81	12	**8**	8	...	**2**	2	...	**88**	59	29	**52**	33	19
222	84	**7**	5	2	**11**	7	4	**267**	176	91	**59**	43	16
590	385	**91**	69	22	**45**	25	20	**928**	563	365	**555**	293	262
2,401	***4,450***	***7,134***	***2,360***	***4,774***	***60***	***24***	***36***	***3,223***	***1,326***	***1,897***	***14,132***	***4,747***	***9,385***
476	843	**11**	4	7	**6**	1	5	**522**	250	272	**3**	3	...
729	976	**3,260**	1,124	2,136	**37**	16	21	**156**	76	80	**3,213**	1,036	2,177
1,003	2,581	**3,804**	1,197	2,607	**16**	6	10	**43**	24	19	**10,902**	3,695	7,207
117	68	**1**	...	1	...	...	...	**106**	51	55	**7**	7	...
76	82	**58**	35	23	**1**	1	...	**2,396**	925	1,471	**7**	6	1
118	***53***	***97***	***73***	***24***	***9***	***5***	***4***	***400***	***203***	***197***	***190***	***89***	***101***
74	***33***	***60***	***44***	***16***	***3***	***3***	...	***120***	***83***	***37***	***148***	***57***	***91***
31	13	**3**	3	...	...	...	...	**15**	10	5	**21**	17	4
18	11	**16**	8	8	...	...	...	**21**	9	12	**99**	20	79
25	9	**41**	33	8	**3**	3	...	**84**	64	20	**28**	20	8
44	***20***	***37***	***29***	***8***	***6***	***2***	***4***	***280***	***120***	***160***	***42***	***32***	***10***
4	***1***	***4***	***1***	***3***	...	...	...	***12***	***12***	...	...	...	...
5	***1***	...	...	...	...	...	...	***5***	***5***	...	***6***	***3***	***3***
70	***47***	***21***	***16***	***5***	***10***	***10***	...	***3***	***2***	***1***	***17***	***14***	***3***
...	...	...	...	...	...	...	...	...	...	...	...	...	...
...	...	...	...	...	...	...	...	...	...	...	...	...	...
70	***47***	***21***	***16***	***5***	***10***	***10***	...	***3***	***2***	***1***	***17***	***14***	***3***
33	7	**7**	5	2	**10**	10	...	...	...	...	**15**	12	3
...	...	...	...	...	...	...	...	...	...	...	...	...	...
37	40	**13**	11	2	...	...	...	**1**	1	...	...	...	...
...	...	**1**	...	1	...	...	...	**2**	1	1	**2**	2	...
49	***5***	***1***	***1***	...	***1***	...	***1***	***44***	***31***	***13***	***3***	***2***	***1***
48	4	**1**	1	...	**1**	...	1	**43**	30	13	**3**	2	1
...	...	...	...	...	...	...	...	...	...	...	...	...	...
1	1	...	...	...	...	...	...	**1**	1	...	...	...	...
...	...	...	...	...	...	...	...	***1***	...	***1***	...	...	...
...	...	...	...	...	...	...	...	...	...	...	...	...	...
...	...	...	...	...	...	...	...	...	...	...	...	...	...
...	...	...	...	...	...	...	...	***1***	...	***1***	...	...	...
1	***2***	...	...	...	...	...	...	***5***	***1***	***4***	...	...	...
1	***2***	...	...	...	...	...	...	...	...	...	...	...	...
1	2	...	...	...	...	...	...	...	...	...	...	...	...
...	...	...	...	...	...	...	...	...	...	...	...	...	...
...	...	...	...	...	...	...	...	...	...	...	...	...	...
...	...	...	...	...	...	...	...	***5***	***1***	***4***	...	...	...
...	...	...	...	...	...	...	...	***2***	***1***	***1***	...	...	...
...	...	...	...	...	...	...	...	...	...	...	...	...	...
...	...	...	...	...	...	...	...	...	...	...	...	...	...
...	...	...	...	...	...	...	...	...	...	...	...	...	...
...	...	...	...	...	...	...	...	***2***	***1***	***1***	...	...	...

TABLE VI.—BIRTH-PLACE.

State, Province or Country where born.	Population of Cities.			City where					
				Alwar.			Bharatpur.		
	Persons.	Males.	Females.	Persons.	Males.	Females.	Persons.	Males.	Females.
1	2	3	4	5	6	7	8	9	10
Total Population ...	*558,201*	*300,199*	*258,002*	*47,900*	*25,584*	*22,316*	*30,173*	*16,736*	*13,437*
A. Born in India ...	*557,853*	*299,999*	*257,854*	*47,888*	*25,576*	*22,312*	*30,152*	*16,727*	*13,425*
I. Born within the Agency of Enumeration ...	*530,072*	*285,279*	*244,793*	*46,292*	*24,882*	*21,410*	*26,244*	*15,141*	*11,103*
(i) Within the State ...	**506,845**	273,579	233,266	**44,845**	24,335	20,510	**25,319**	14,754	10,565
(ii) In other Rajputana States	**23,227**	11,700	11,527	**1,447**	547	900	**925**	387	538
II. (a) Born in Provinces, Districts or States in India adjacent to Rajputana ...	*26,153*	*13,705*	*12,448*	*1,505*	640	865	*3,819*	*1,527*	*2,292*
(i) *British Territory* ...	*21,550*	*11,421*	*10,129*	*1,350*	*578*	*772*	*3,692*	*1,467*	*2,225*
Ajmer-Merwara ...	**2,055**	1,081	974	**110**	70	40	**83**	33	50
Bombay	**1,260**	686	574	**6**	5	1	**53**	23	30
Delhi	**927**	480	447	**171**	68	103	**106**	48	58
Punjab	**4,201**	2,623	1,578	**605**	270	335	**210**	132	78
United Provinces of Agra and Oudh ...	**13,107**	6,551	6,556	**458**	165	293	**3,240**	1,231	2,009
(ii) *Indian States* ...	*4,603*	*2,284*	*2,319*	*155*	*62*	*93*	*127*	*60*	*67*
Bombay States ...	**88**	55	33	...	...	...	...	...	...
Central India Agency ...	**1,103**	539	564	**17**	8	9	**31**	20	11
Gwalior State ...	**2,402**	1,036	1,366	**34**	11	23	**69**	25	44
Punjab States Agency ...	**815**	523	292	**99**	40	59	**27**	15	12
Western India Agency ...	**195**	131	64	**5**	3	2	...	...	...
(b) Born in other Provinces and States in India ...	*1,486*	*918*	*568*	*87*	*52*	*35*	*71*	*47*	*24*
(i) *British Territory* ...	*1,088*	*701*	*387*	*55*	*42*	*13*	*50*	*34*	*16*
Bengal	**533**	306	227	**23**	20	3	**10**	7	3
Central Provinces and Berar.	**244**	176	68	**8**	7	1	**17**	11	6
Other Provinces ...	**311**	219	92	**24**	15	9	**23**	16	7
(ii) *Other Indian States* ...	*398*	*217*	*181*	*32*	*10*	*22*	*21*	*13*	*8*
(c) French and Portuguese Settlements ...	*100*	*73*	*27*	*1*	*1*	...	*5*	*5*	...
(d) India Unspecified ...	*42*	*24*	*18*	*3*	*1*	*2*	*13*	*7*	*6*
B. Born in other Asiatic Countries ...	*183*	*117*	*66*	*3*	*2*	*1*	*4*	*2*	*2*
(i) *Within British Dominions.*	*1*	*1*	...	...	...	...	*1*	*1*	...
Ceylon	**1**	1	...	...	...	...	**1**	1	...
(ii) *Outside British Dominions.*	*182*	*116*	*66*	*3*	*2*	*1*	*3*	*1*	*2*
Afghanistan	**81**	67	14	**3**	2	1	**2**	1	1
Nepal	**91**	44	47	...	...	...	...	...	...
Elsewhere	**10**	5	5	...	...	...	**1**	...	1
C. Born in Europe ...	*148*	*79*	*69*	*9*	*6*	*3*	*15*	*6*	*9*
(i) United Kingdom and Scotland ...	**142**	75	67	**8**	5	3	**14**	6	8
(ii) Continental Europe ...	**6**	4	2	**1**	1	...	**1**	...	1
D. Born in Africa ...	*11*	*4*	*7*	...	...	...	*2*	*1*	*1*
(i) *Within British Dominions.*	*6*	*1*	*5*	...	...	...	...	...	...
Kenya (British East Africa)	**6**	1	5	...	...	...	...	...	...
(ii) *Africa Unspecified* ...	*5*	*3*	*2*	...	...	...	*2*	*1*	*1*
E. Born in America ...	*3*	...	*3*	...	...	...	...	...	...
(i) *Within British Dominions.*	*3*	...	*3*	...	...	...	...	...	...
Canada	**3**	...	3	...	...	...	...	...	...
F. Born in Australasia ...	*3*	...	*3*	...	...	...	...	...	...
(i) *Within British Dominions.*	*2*	...	*2*	...	...	...	...	...	...
Australia	**2**	...	2	...	...	...	...	...	...
(ii) *Australasia Unspecified* ...	*1*	...	*1*	...	...	...	...	...	...

PART II.—CITIES.

Enumerated.

Bikaner.			Bundi.			Dholpur.			Jaipur.			Jodhpur.		
Persons.	Males.	Females.	Persons.	Males.	Females	Persons.	Males.	Females.	Persons.	Males.	Females.	Persons.	Males.	Females.
11	12	13	14	15	16	17	18	19	20	21	22	23	24	25
85,927	45,832	40,095	17,991	9,179	8,812	19,586	10,535	9,051	144,179	77,933	66,246	94,736	52,165	42,571
85,906	45,819	40,087	17,989	9,177	8,812	19,570	10,528	9,042	144,119	77,900	66,219	94,670	52,126	42,544
81,304	42,873	38,431	17,604	8,992	8,612	16,143	9,257	6,886	139,825	75,422	64,403	90,061	49,415	40,646
75,999	39,704	36,205	16,559	8,509	8,050	15,940	9,170	6,770	137,700	74,381	63,869	88,657	48,611	40,046
5,305	3,169	2,136	1,045	483	562	203	87	116	2,125	1,091	1,034	1,404	804	600
4,295	2,757	1,538	373	178	195	3,333	1,224	2,109	3,870	2,242	1,628	4,244	2,478	1,766
3,616	2,279	1,337	271	147	124	2,135	828	1,307	3,728	2,165	1,563	3,770	2,192	1,578
366	223	143	103	41	62	9	2	7	444	193	251	415	254	161
161	77	84	28	17	11	3	2	1	227	126	101	405	205	200
152	108	44	7	6	1	41	16	25	296	157	139	69	37	32
1,238	786	452	32	16	16	96	55	41	857	554	303	708	485	223
1,699	1,085	614	101	67	34	1,986	753	1,233	1,904	1,135	769	2,173	1,211	962
679	478	201	102	31	71	1,198	396	802	142	77	65	474	286	188
...	...	...	...	...	...	...	...	...	...	...	...	56	37	19
65	41	24	75	23	52	122	45	77	77	38	39	181	117	64
54	39	15	27	8	19	1,027	323	704	65	39	26	75	23	52
500	358	142	...	...	...	47	26	21	...	...	...	34	23	11
60	40	20	...	...	...	2	2	...	...	...	...	128	86	42
259	152	107	11	6	5	94	47	47	411	224	187	324	211	113
206	123	83	11	6	5	76	40	36	344	190	154	181	124	57
106	60	46	9	6	3	26	13	13	222	115	107	90	48	42
38	17	21	...	...	...	35	17	18	32	19	13	16	13	3
62	46	16	2	...	2	15	10	5	90	56	34	75	63	12
53	29	24	...	...	...	18	7	11	67	34	33	143	87	56
35	29	6	1	1	...	...	...	...	8	8	...	41	22	19
13	8	5	...	...	...	...	...	...	5	4	1	...	...	...
3	3	...	2	2	...	6	4	2	21	17	4	8	6	2
...	...	...	...	...	...	...	...	...	...	...	...	...	...	...
...	...	...	...	...	...	...	...	...	...	...	...	...	...	...
3	3	...	2	2	...	6	4	2	21	17	4	8	6	2
3	3	...	2	2	...	3	3	...	11	11	...	5	5	...
...	...	...	...	...	...	1	1	...	7	3	4	2	1	1
...	...	...	...	...	...	2	...	2	3	3	...	1	...	1
15	9	6	...	...	...	10	3	7	38	15	23	49	32	17
14	9	5	...	...	...	9	2	7	36	13	23	49	32	17
1	...	1	...	...	...	1	1	...	2	2	...	...	...	...
2	1	1	...	...	...	...	...	...	1	1	...	6	1	5
...	...	...	...	...	...	...	...	...	...	...	...	6	1	5
...	...	...	...	...	...	...	...	...	...	...	...	6	1	5
2	1	1	...	...	...	...	...	...	1	1	...	...	...	...
...	...	...	...	...	...	...	...	...	...	...	...	1	...	1
...	...	...	...	...	...	...	...	...	...	...	...	1	...	1
...	...	...	...	...	...	...	...	...	...	...	...	1	...	1
1	...	1	...	...	...	...	...	...	...	...	...	2	...	2
...	...	...	...	...	...	...	...	...	...	...	...	2	...	2
...	...	...	...	...	...	...	...	...	...	...	...	2	...	2
1	...	1	...	...	...	...	...	...	...	...	...	...	...	...

TABLE VI.—Birth-Place.—Part II.—Cities.—*Concluded.*

State, Province or Country where born.	City where Enumerated.								
	Kotah.			Tonk.			Udaipur.		
	Persons.	Males.	Females.	Persons.	Males.	Females.	Persons.	Males.	Females.
1	26	27	28	29	30	31	32	33	34
Total Population ...	37,876	20,259	17,617	35,798	18,201	17,597	44,035	23,775	20,260
A. Born in India ...	37,833	20,228	17,605	35,785	18,189	17,596	43,941	23,729	20,212
I. Born within the Agency of Enumeration ...	34,668	18,390	16,278	35,183	17,873	17,310	42,748	23,034	19,714
(i) Within the State ...	27,166	14,449	12,717	32,495	17,025	15,470	42,165	22,691	19,474
(ii) In other Rajputana States.	7,502	3,941	3,561	2,688	848	1,840	583	343	240
II. (a) Born in Provinces, Districts or States in India adjacent to Rajputana ...	3,033	1,736	1,297	547	273	274	1,134	650	484
(*i*) *British Territory* ...	1,932	1,170	762	410	207	203	646	388	258
Ajmer-Merwara ...	236	118	118	141	62	79	148	85	63
Bombay	253	165	88	18	10	8	106	56	50
Delhi	25	...	25	41	25	16	19	15	4
Punjab	318	234	84	28	18	10	109	73	36
United Provinces of Agra and Oudh ...	1,100	653	447	182	92	90	264	159	105
(*ii*) *Indian States* ...	1,101	566	535	137	66	71	488	262	226
Bombay States ...	...	...	...	...	...	...	32	18	14
Central India Agency ...	393	185	208	61	27	34	81	35	46
Gwalior State ...	708	381	327	73	36	37	270	151	119
Punjab States Agency ...	...	...	...	3	3	...	105	58	47
Western India Agency ...	...	...	...	...	...	...	...	...	...
(b) Born in other Provinces and States in India ...	128	99	29	49	40	9	52	40	12
(*i*) *British Territory* ...	105	94	11	28	23	5	32	25	7
Bengal	9	6	3	15	13	2	23	18	5
Central Provinces and Berar.	90	85	5	2	2	...	6	5	1
Other Provinces ...	6	3	3	11	8	3	3	2	1
(*ii*) *Other Indian States* ...	23	5	18	21	17	4	20	15	5
(c) French and Portuguese Settlements ...	4	3	1	...	...	...	5	4	1
(d) India Unspecified ...	...	...	...	6	3	3	2	1	1
B. Born in other Asiatic Countries ...	40	30	10	10	10	...	86	41	45
(*i*) *Within British Dominions.*	...	...	...	...	...	...	...	...	...
Ceylon	...	...	...	...	...	...	...	...	...
(*ii*) *Outside British Dominions.*	40	30	10	10	10	...	86	41	45
Afghanistan	29	23	6	8	8	...	15	9	6
Nepal	10	7	3	...	...	...	71	32	39
Elsewhere	1	...	1	2	2	...	...	...	...
C. Born in Europe ...	3	1	2	3	2	1	6	5	1
(i) United Kingdom and Scotland ...	3	1	2	3	2	1	6	5	1
(ii) Continental Europe ...	...	...	...	...	...	...	...	...	...
D. Born in Africa ...	...	...	...	...	...	...	...	...	...
(*i*) *Within British Dominions.*	...	...	...	...	...	...	...	...	...
Kenya (British East Africa).	...	...	...	...	...	...	...	...	...
(*ii*) *Africa Unspecified* ...	...	...	...	...	...	...	...	...	...
E. Born in America ...	...	...	...	...	...	...	2	...	2
(*i*) *Within British Dominions.*	...	...	...	...	...	...	2	...	2
Canada	...	...	...	...	...	...	2	...	2
F. Born in Australasia ...	...	...	...	...	...	...	...	...	...
(*i*) *Within British Dominions.*	...	...	...	...	...	...	...	...	...
Australia	...	...	...	...	...	...	...	...	...
(*ii*) *Australasia Unspecified* ...	...	...	...	...	...	...	...	...	...

TABLE VII.

Age, Sex and Civil Condition.

EXPLANATORY NOTE.

This Table is divided into three parts, each showing the distribution of population by age, sex and civil condition.

PART A.—Shows, for the Agency, the distribution of the total population (All Religions) and of each religion.

PART B.—Shows, for each State and Abu District, the distribution of the population (All Religions) and of each numerous religion.

PART C.—Shows, for each City, the distribution of the total population (All Religions).

In Part B the age periods are given in less detail than in Part A.

The term "Hindu" includes "Arya", "Brahmo" & "Deo Samaj".

TABLE VII.—Age, Sex and Civil Condition.—Part A.—Agency Summary.

Age and Religion.	Population.			Unmarried.			Married.			Widowed.		
	Persons.	Males.	Females.	Persons.	Males.	Females.	Persons.	Males.	Females.	Persons.	Males.	Females.
1	2	3	4	5	6	7	8	9	10	11	12	13
All Religions	***11,225,712***	***5,885,028***	***5,340,684***	***4,746,017***	***2,888,862***	***1,857,155***	***5,227,694***	***2,579,453***	***2,648,241***	***1,252,001***	***416,713***	***835,288***
0—1 ...	**346,766**	172,374	174,392	**345,183**	171,708	173,475	**1,465**	621	844	**118**	45	73
1—2 ...	**343,154**	169,005	174,149	**341,088**	168,193	172,895	**2,013**	794	1,219	**53**	18	35
2—3 ...	**359,065**	175,296	183,769	**355,639**	174,073	181,566	**3,313**	1,194	2,119	**113**	29	84
3—4 ...	**349,990**	174,235	175,755	**343,111**	172,032	171,079	**6,654**	2,144	4,510	**225**	59	166
4—5 ...	**336,364**	172,187	164,177	**325,747**	168,642	157,105	**10,053**	3,351	6,702	**564**	194	370
Total 0—5	***1,735,339***	***863,097***	***872,242***	***1,710,768***	***854,648***	***856,120***	***23,498***	***8,104***	***15,394***	***1,073***	***345***	***728***
5—10 ...	**1,472,995**	783,824	689,171	**1,303,089**	735,178	567,911	**166,344**	47,248	119,096	**3,562**	1,398	2,164
10—15 ...	**1,364,988**	745,362	619,626	**1,001,876**	635,214	366,662	**355,369**	107,061	248,308	**7,743**	3,087	4,656
15—20 ...	**1,064,302**	563,456	500,846	**330,176**	287,343	42,833	**711,977**	267,361	444,616	**22,149**	8,752	13,397
20—25 ...	**1,049,804**	544,510	505,294	**182,392**	170,269	12,123	**831,882**	360,223	471,659	**35,530**	14,018	21,512
25—30 ...	**881,282**	460,573	420,709	**68,445**	64,893	3,552	**749,965**	373,215	376,750	**62,872**	22,465	40,407
30—35 ...	**768,253**	403,402	364,851	**44,877**	42,366	2,511	**643,324**	333,343	309,981	**80,052**	27,693	52,359
35—40 ...	**691,035**	362,456	328,579	**31,025**	29,239	1,786	**525,958**	291,025	234,933	**134,052**	42,192	91,860
40—45 ...	**606,013**	321,423	284,590	**24,784**	23,485	1,299	**431,955**	249,988	181,967	**149,274**	47,950	101,324
45—50 ...	**494,616**	269,231	225,385	**17,304**	16,531	773	**299,168**	193,794	105,374	**178,144**	58,906	119,238
50—55 ...	**395,814**	214,115	181,699	**12,759**	12,204	555	**220,289**	147,487	72,802	**162,766**	54,424	108,342
55—60 ...	**272,038**	139,756	132,282	**7,531**	7,156	375	**118,357**	85,688	32,669	**146,150**	46,912	99,238
60—65 ...	**226,578**	112,872	113,706	**5,853**	5,519	334	**88,604**	66,373	22,231	**132,121**	40,980	91,141
65—70 ...	**89,276**	45,521	43,755	**2,207**	2.093	114	**29,750**	23,374	6,376	**57,319**	20.054	37,265
70 & over...	**113,379**	55,430	57,949	**2,931**	2,724	207	**31,254**	25,169	6,085	**79,194**	27,537	51,657
Buddhist ...	***1***	***1***	...	...	...	...	***1***	***1***	...	...	...	...
0—1 ...	...	...	...	...	...	...	...	...	...	...	...	...
1—2 ...	...	...	...	...	...	...	...	...	...	...	...	...
2—3 ...	...	...	...	...	...	...	...	...	...	...	...	...
3—4 ...	...	...	...	...	...	...	...	...	...	...	...	...
4—5 ...	...	...	...	...	...	...	...	...	...	...	...	...
Total 0—5	...	...	...	...	...	...	...	...	...	...	...	...
5—10 ...	...	...	...	...	...	...	...	...	...	...	...	...
10—15 ...	...	...	...	...	...	...	...	...	...	...	...	...
15—20 ...	...	...	...	...	...	...	...	...	...	...	...	...
20—25 ...	...	...	...	...	...	...	...	...	...	...	...	...
25—30 ...	1	1	...	...	...	...	1	1	...	...	...	...
30—35 ...	...	...	...	...	...	...	...	...	...	...	...	...
35—40 ...	...	...	...	...	...	...	...	...	...	...	...	...
40—45 ...	...	...	...	...	...	...	...	...	...	...	...	...
45—50 ...	...	...	...	...	...	...	...	...	...	...	...	...
50—55 ...	...	...	...	...	...	...	...	...	...	...	...	...
55—60 ...	...	...	...	...	...	...	...	...	...	...	...	...
60—65 ...	...	...	...	...	...	...	...	...	...	...	...	...
65—70 ...	...	...	...	...	...	...	...	...	...	...	...	...
70 & over...	...	...	...	...	...	...	...	...	...	...	...	...
Christian...	***5,778***	***3,107***	***2,671***	***3,025***	***1,674***	***1,351***	***2,409***	***1,283***	***1,126***	***344***	***150***	***194***
0—1 ...	**192**	97	95	**192**	97	95	...	...	...	...	...	...
1—2 ...	**155**	80	75	**154**	79	75	**1**	1	...	...	...	...
2—3 ...	**163**	72	91	**162**	72	90	**1**	...	1	...	...	...
3—4 ...	**174**	84	90	**172**	84	88	**2**	...	2	...	...	...
4—5 ...	**219**	112	107	**214**	110	104	**5**	2	3	...	...	...
Total 0—5	***903***	***445***	***458***	***894***	***442***	***452***	***9***	***3***	***6***	...	...	...
5—10 ...	**764**	409	355	**729**	393	336	**34**	16	18	**1**	...	1
10—15 ...	**697**	388	309	**613**	349	264	**74**	35	39	**10**	4	6
15—20 ...	**575**	301	274	**348**	209	139	**216**	88	128	**11**	4	7
20—25 ...	**529**	272	257	**234**	151	83	**281**	115	166	**14**	6	8
25—30 ...	**437**	219	218	**76**	53	23	**339**	154	185	**22**	12	10
30—35 ...	**432**	221	211	**45**	25	20	**358**	178	180	**29**	18	11
35—40 ...	**448**	247	201	**24**	15	9	**379**	207	172	**45**	25	20
40—45 ...	**374**	229	145	**21**	17	4	**314**	192	122	**39**	20	19
45—50 ...	**248**	155	93	**23**	14	9	**181**	125	56	**44**	16	28
50—55 ...	**163**	99	64	**13**	5	8	**110**	80	30	**40**	14	26
55—60 ...	**96**	54	42	**3**	1	2	**52**	38	14	**41**	15	26
60—65 ...	**65**	36	29	**2**	...	2	**37**	29	8	**26**	7	19
65—70 ...	**22**	16	6	...	...	...	**12**	12	...	**10**	4	6
70 & over...	**25**	16	9	...	...	...	**13**	11	2	**12**	5	7

TABLE VII.—AGE, SEX AND CIVIL CONDITION.—PART A.—AGENCY SUMMARY.—*Continued.*

Age and Religion.	Population.			Unmarried.			Married.			Widowed.		
	Persons.	Males.	Females.	Persons.	Males.	Females.	Persons.	Males.	Females.	Persons.	Males.	Females.
1	2	3	4	5	6	7	8	9	10	11	12	13
Hindu ...	***9,578,805***	***5,029,620***	***4,549,185***	***4,003,601***	***2,452,204***	***1,551,397***	***4,493,259***	***2,218,088***	***2,275,171***	***1,081,945***	***359,328***	***722,617***
0—1 ...	**292,761**	145,462	147,299	**291,562**	144,958	146,609	**1,143**	491	652	**56**	18	**38**
1—2 ...	**291,270**	143,288	147,982	**289,504**	142,592	146,912	**1,736**	683	1,053	**30**	13	**17**
2—3 ...	**305,304**	149,074	156,230	**302,373**	148,024	154,349	**2,842**	1,024	1,818	**89**	26	**63**
3—4 ...	**297,246**	148,191	149,055	**291,284**	146,300	144,984	**5,766**	1,836	3,930	**196**	55	**141**
4—5 ...	**285,308**	146,279	139,029	**276,303**	143,339	132,964	**8,544**	2,779	5,765	**461**	161	**300**
Total 0—5	***1,471,889***	***732,294***	***739,595***	***1,451,026***	***725,208***	***725,818***	***20,031***	***6,813***	***13,218***	***832***	***273***	***559***
5—10 ...	**1,251,331**	667,306	584,025	**1,099,440**	624,593	474,847	**148,869**	41,528	107,341	**3,022**	1,185	1,837
10—15 ...	**1,165,093**	638,395	526,698	**841,153**	539,911	301,242	**317,230**	95,786	221,444	**6,710**	2,698	4,012
15—20 ...	**909,809**	483,441	426,368	**273,549**	241,968	31,581	**617,281**	234,007	383,274	**18,979**	7,466	11,513
20—25 ...	**894,041**	464,883	429,158	**150,312**	141,524	8,788	**713,552**	311,570	401,982	**30,177**	11,789	18,388
25—30 ...	**752,208**	394,121	358,087	**57,609**	54,810	2,799	**640,795**	320,254	320,541	**53,804**	19,057	34,747
30—35 ...	**655,590**	344,637	310,953	**38,293**	36,325	1,968	**548,561**	284,687	263,874	**68,736**	23,625	45,111
35—40 ...	**593,383**	311,519	281,864	**27,206**	25,761	1,445	**449,954**	249,299	200,655	**116,223**	36,459	79,764
40—45 ...	**521,082**	276,660	244,422	**21,879**	20,818	1,061	**369,545**	214,157	155,388	**129,658**	41,685	87,973
45—50 ...	**424,930**	231,515	193,415	**15,305**	14,691	614	**254,958**	165,431	89,527	**154,667**	51,393	103,274
50—55 ...	**339,565**	183,797	155,768	**11,292**	10,864	428	**187,184**	125,558	61,626	**141,089**	47,375	93,714
55—60 ...	**233,029**	119,437	113,592	**6,702**	6,407	295	**99,881**	72,496	27,885	**126,446**	40,534	85,912
60—65 ...	**194,619**	96,613	98,006	**5,233**	4,976	257	**74,956**	56,292	18,664	**114,430**	35,345	79,085
65—70 ...	**76,210**	38,547	37,663	**1,994**	1,903	91	**24,760**	19,476	5,284	**49,456**	17,168	32,288
70 & over...	**96,026**	46,455	49,571	**2,608**	2,445	163	**25,702**	20,734	4,968	**67,716**	23,276	44,440
Jain ...	***300,748***	***146,004***	***154,744***	***125,152***	***75,521***	***49,631***	***123,732***	***56,889***	***66,843***	***51,864***	***13,594***	***38,270***
0—1 ...	**9,464**	4,818	4,646	**9,357**	4,775	4,582	**87**	35	52	**20**	8	12
1—2 ...	**8,563**	4,269	4,294	**8,497**	4,243	4,254	**63**	24	39	**3**	2	1
2—3 ...	**8,365**	4,111	4,254	**8,292**	4,087	4,205	**71**	24	47	**2**	...	2
3—4 ...	**7,810**	3,877	3,933	**7,700**	3,837	3,863	**107**	40	67	**3**	...	3
4—5 ...	**7,824**	3,944	3,880	**7,538**	3,818	3,720	**256**	116	140	**30**	10	20
Total 0—5	***42,026***	***21,019***	***21,007***	***41,384***	***20,760***	***20,624***	***584***	***239***	***345***	***58***	***20***	***38***
5—10 ...	**35,634**	18,234	17,400	**33,589**	17,618	15,971	**1,952**	598	1,359	**93**	23	70
10—15 ...	**32,455**	16,684	15,771	**26,900**	15,496	11,404	**5,319**	1,142	4,177	**236**	46	190
15—20 ...	**27,053**	13,036	14,017	**8,592**	7,496	1,096	**17,515**	5,346	12,169	**946**	194	752
20—25 ...	**28,427**	13,341	15,086	**5,361**	5,127	234	**21,390**	7,882	13,508	**1,676**	332	1,344
25—30 ...	**23,220**	10,912	12,308	**2,414**	2,331	83	**17,828**	8,030	9,798	**2,978**	551	2,427
30—35 ...	**21,254**	10,059	11,195	**1,828**	1,757	71	**15,553**	7,505	8,048	**3,873**	797	3,076
35—40 ...	**20,124**	9,400	10,724	**1,420**	1,369	51	**12,635**	6,638	5,997	**6,069**	1,393	4,676
40—45 ...	**18,817**	8,925	9,892	**1,248**	1,212	36	**10,773**	6,012	4,761	**6,796**	1,701	5,095
45—50 ...	**16,381**	7,954	8,427	**937**	916	21	**7,844**	4,892	2,952	**7,600**	2,146	5,454
50—55 ...	**13,266**	6,442	6,824	**668**	656	12	**5,797**	3,759	2,038	**6,801**	2,027	4,774
55—60 ...	**8,910**	4,141	4,769	**371**	365	6	**3,030**	2,147	883	**5,509**	1,629	3,880
60—65 ...	**7,034**	3,108	3,926	**247**	241	6	**2,086**	1,533	553	**4,701**	1,334	3,367
65—70 ...	**2,944**	1,344	1,600	**90**	86	4	**748**	596	152	**2,106**	662	1,444
70 & over...	**3,203**	1,405	1,798	**103**	91	12	**678**	575	103	**2,422**	739	1,683
Jew ...	***38***	***18***	***20***	***23***	***9***	***14***	***12***	***7***	***5***	***3***	***2***	***1***
0—1 ...	**1**	1	...	**1**	1	...	...	...	...	...	...	...
1—2 ...	**1**	...	1	**1**	...	1	...	...	...	...	...	...
2—3 ...	**1**	...	1	**1**	...	1	...	...	...	...	...	...
3—4 ...	**1**	1	...	**1**	1	...	...	...	...	...	...	...
4—5 ...	**4**	2	2	**4**	2	2	...	...	...	...	...	...
Total 0—5	***8***	***4***	***4***	***8***	***4***	***4***	...	...	...	...	...	...
5—10 ...	**9**	3	6	**9**	3	6	...	...	...	...	...	...
10—15 ...	**5**	1	4	**5**	1	4	...	...	...	...	...	...
15—20 ...	**2**	1	1	**1**	1	...	**1**	...	1	...	...	...
20—25 ...	...	...	...	...	...	...	...	...	...	...	...	...
25—30 ...	**1**	1	...	...	...	...	...	...	...	**1**	1	...
30—35 ...	**2**	1	1	...	...	...	**1**	...	1	**1**	1	...
35—40 ...	**3**	1	2	...	...	...	**3**	1	2	...	...	...
40—45 ...	**4**	3	1	...	...	...	**4**	3	1	...	...	...
45—50 ...	**2**	1	1	...	...	...	**1**	1	...	**1**	...	1
50—55 ...	...	...	...	...	...	...	...	...	...	...	...	...
55—60 ...	**1**	1	...	...	...	...	**1**	1	...	...	...	...
60—65 ...	**1**	1	...	...	...	...	**1**	1	...	...	...	...
65—70 ...	...	...	...	...	...	...	...	...	...	...	...	...
70 & over...	...	...	...	...	...	...	...	...	...	...	...	...

TABLE VII.—Age, Sex and Civil Condition.—Part A.—Agency Summary.—*Continued.*

Age and Religion	Population			Unmarried.			Married.			Widowed.		
	Persons	Males	Females.	Persons.	Males.	Females	Persons.	Males.	Females.	Persons.	Males.	Females.
1	2	3	4	5	6	7	8	9	10	11	12	13
Muslim ...	***1,069,325***	***565,962***	***503,363***	***472,880***	***280,897***	***191,983***	***494,707***	***246,759***	***247,948***	***101,738***	***38,306***	***63,432***
0—1 ...	**35,003**	17,473	17,530	**34,741**	17,367	17,374	**222**	88	134	**40**	18	22
1—2 ...	**33,725**	16,862	16,863	**33,506**	16,777	16,729	**199**	82	117	**20**	3	17
2—3 ...	**34,536**	16,932	17,604	**34,153**	16,795	17,358	**361**	134	227	**22**	3	19
3—4 ...	**33,967**	16,825	17,142	**33,226**	16,580	16,646	**715**	241	474	**26**	4	22
4—5 ...	**32,777**	16,735	16,042	**31,574**	16,310	15,264	**1,139**	406	733	**64**	19	45
Total 0—5	***170,008***	***84,827***	***85,181***	***167,200***	***83,829***	***83,371***	***2,636***	***951***	***1,685***	***172***	***47***	***125***
5—10 ...	**142,809**	75,807	67,002	**128,788**	71,141	57,647	**13,623**	4,494	9,129	**398**	172	226
10—15 ...	**129,681**	70,234	59,447	**101,649**	61,589	40,060	**27,356**	8,858	18,498	**676**	287	389
15—20 ...	**101,322**	53,427	47,895	**37,275**	30,152	7,123	**62,122**	22,361	39,761	**1,925**	914	1,011
20—25 ...	**102,819**	53,423	49,396	**21,356**	19,180	2,176	**78,225**	32,618	45,607	**3,238**	1,625	1,613
25—30 ...	**86,261**	45,159	41,102	**6,852**	6,360	492	**74,075**	36,326	37,749	**5,334**	2,473	2,861
30—35 ...	**74,645**	39,927	34,718	**3,806**	3,469	337	**64,352**	33,613	30,739	**6,487**	2,845	3,642
35—40 ...	**62,984**	33,955	29,029	**1,970**	1,735	235	**50,889**	28,460	22,429	**10,125**	3,760	6,365
40—45 ...	**53,502**	29,186	24,316	**1,404**	1,237	167	**41,102**	23,991	17,111	**10,996**	3,958	7,038
45—50 ...	**43,256**	24,301	18,955	**892**	776	116	**28,880**	18,843	10,037	**13,484**	4,682	8,802
50—55 ...	**35,117**	19,643	15,474	**675**	580	95	**21,771**	14,652	7,119	**12,671**	4,411	8,260
55—60 ...	**25,007**	13,500	11,507	**385**	326	59	**12,520**	9,001	3,519	**12,102**	4,173	7,929
60—65 ...	**20,835**	11,056	9,779	**319**	260	59	**9,445**	7,011	2,434	**11,071**	3,785	7,286
65—70 ...	**8,870**	4,949	3,921	**111**	94	17	**3,624**	2,830	794	**5,135**	2,025	3,110
70 & over...	**12,209**	6,568	5,641	**198**	169	29	**4,087**	3,250	837	**7,924**	3,149	4,775
Sikh ...	***41,605***	***24,725***	***16,880***	***21,518***	***13,744***	***7,774***	***17,513***	***9,492***	***8,021***	***2,574***	***1,489***	***1,085***
0—1 ...	**1,364**	689	675	**1,360**	685	675	**4**	4	...	...	...	...
1—2 ...	**1,283**	653	630	**1,283**	653	630	...	...	...	...	...	...
2—3 ...	**1,320**	679	641	**1,319**	678	641	**1**	1	...	...	...	...
3—4 ...	**1,312**	685	627	**1,307**	682	625	**5**	3	2	...	...	...
4—5 ...	**1,231**	644	587	**1,218**	637	581	**12**	7	5	**1**	...	1
Total 0—5	***6,510***	***3,350***	***3,160***	***6,487***	***3,335***	***3,152***	***22***	***15***	***7***	***1***	...	***1***
5—10 ...	**5,359**	2,953	2,406	**5,152**	2,872	2,280	**193**	77	116	**14**	4	10
10—15 ...	**4,960**	2,895	2,065	**4,424**	2,706	1,718	**519**	182	337	**17**	7	10
15—20 ...	**4,275**	2,671	1,604	**2,309**	1,856	453	**1,928**	790	1,138	**38**	25	13
20—25 ...	**4,318**	2,651	1,667	**1,547**	1,388	159	**2,700**	1,211	1,489	**71**	52	19
25—30 ...	**3,595**	2,162	1,433	**639**	631	8	**2,824**	1,440	1,384	**132**	91	41
30—35 ...	**3,062**	1,882	1,180	**415**	411	4	**2,495**	1,368	1,127	**152**	103	49
35—40 ...	**2,298**	1,434	864	**183**	183	...	**1,896**	1,111	785	**219**	140	79
40—45 ...	**1,968**	1,235	733	**126**	126	...	**1,576**	944	632	**266**	165	101
45—50 ...	**1,622**	1,063	559	**85**	85	...	**1,197**	788	409	**340**	190	150
50—55 ...	**1,256**	834	422	**59**	59	...	**895**	608	287	**302**	167	135
55—60 ...	**891**	599	292	**40**	40	...	**544**	392	152	**307**	167	140
60—65 ...	**712**	484	228	**31**	31	...	**407**	308	99	**274**	145	129
65—70 ...	**309**	207	102	**9**	9	...	**149**	117	32	**151**	81	70
70 & over...	**470**	305	165	**12**	12	...	**168**	141	27	**290**	152	138
Tribal ...	***229,092***	***115,420***	***113,672***	***119,665***	***64,729***	***54,936***	***95,916***	***46,858***	***49,058***	***13,511***	***3,833***	***9,678***
0—1 ...	**7,971**	3,828	4,143	**7,960**	3,824	4,136	**9**	3	6	**2**	1	1
1—2 ...	**8,153**	3,853	4,300	**8,139**	3,849	4,290	**14**	4	10	...	...	...
2—3 ...	**9,371**	4,427	4,944	**9,334**	4,416	4,918	**37**	11	26	...	...	...
3—4 ...	**9,478**	4,571	4,907	**9,419**	4,547	4,872	**59**	24	35	...	...	...
4—5 ...	**8,986**	4,462	4,524	**8,882**	4,417	4,465	**96**	41	55	**8**	4	4
Total 0—5	***43,959***	***21,141***	***22,818***	***43,734***	***21,053***	***22,681***	***215***	***83***	***132***	***10***	***5***	***5***
5—10 ...	**37,063**	19,099	17,964	**35,357**	18,545	16,812	**1,672**	540	1,132	**34**	14	20
10—15 ...	**32,076**	16,756	15,320	**27,112**	15,153	11,959	**4,870**	1,558	3,312	**94**	45	49
15—20 ...	**21,234**	10,563	10,671	**8,074**	5,647	2,427	**12,910**	4,767	8,143	**250**	149	101
20—25 ...	**19,635**	9,920	9,715	**3,557**	2,884	673	**15,724**	6,822	8,902	**354**	214	140
25—30 ...	**15,531**	7,983	7,548	**845**	701	144	**14,085**	7,002	7,083	**601**	280	321
30—35 ...	**13,242**	6,602	6,640	**486**	376	110	**11,982**	5,982	6,000	**774**	304	470
35—40 ...	**11,767**	5,885	5,882	**220**	174	46	**10,180**	5,298	4,882	**1,367**	413	954
40—45 ...	**10,243**	5,170	5,073	**104**	73	31	**8,621**	4,676	3,945	**1,518**	421	1,097
45—50 ...	**8,160**	4,230	3,930	**61**	48	13	**6,091**	3,708	2,383	**2,008**	479	1,529
50—55 ...	**6,433**	3,294	3,139	**52**	40	12	**4,521**	2,825	1,696	**1,860**	429	1,431
55—60 ...	**4,092**	2,019	2,073	**30**	17	13	**2,321**	1,608	713	**1,741**	394	1,347
60—65 ...	**3,301**	1,568	1,733	**21**	11	10	**1,663**	1,194	469	**1,617**	363	1,254
65—70 ...	**917**	454	463	**3**	1	2	**456**	342	114	**453**	111	347
70 & over...	**1,439**	676	763	**9**	6	3	**605**	458	147	**825**	212	613

TABLE VII.—Age, Sex and Civil Condition.—Part A.—Agency Summary.—*Concluded.*

Age and Religion.	Population.			Unmarried.			Married.			Widowed		
	Persons.	Males.	Females.	Persons	Males	Females.	Persons.	Males.	Females.	Persons.	Males.	Females.
1	2	3	4	5	6	7	8	9	10	11	12	13
Zoroastrian.	*319*	*170*	*149*	*153*	*84*	69	*144*	75	69	*22*	*11*	*11*
0—1 ...	10	6	4	10	6	4	...	...	...	...	...	...
1—2 ...	4	...	4	4	...	4	...	...	...	...	...	...
2—3 ...	5	1	4	5	1	4	...	...	...	...	...	...
3—4 ...	2	1	1	2	1	1	...	...	...	...	...	...
4—5 ...	15	9	6	14	9	5	1	...	1	...	...	...
Total 0—5	*36*	*17*	*19*	*35*	*17*	*18*	*1*	...	*1*	...	...	...
5—10 ...	26	13	13	25	13	12	1	...	1	...	...	...
10—15 ...	21	9	12	20	9	11	1	...	1	...	...	...
15—20 ...	32	16	16	28	14	14	4	2	2	...	...	...
20—25 ...	35	20	15	25	15	10	10	5	5	...	...	...
25—30 ...	27	14	13	10	7	3	17	7	10	...	...	...
30—35 ...	26	13	13	4	3	1	22	10	12	...	...	...
35—40 ...	27	15	12	2	2	...	22	11	11	3	2	1
40—45 ...	23	15	8	2	2	...	20	13	7	1	...	1
45—50 ...	17	12	5	1	1	...	16	11	5	...	...	...
50—55 ...	14	6	8	...	...	...	11	5	6	3	1	2
55—60 ...	12	5	7	...	...	...	8	5	3	4	...	4
60—65 ...	11	6	5	...	...	...	9	5	4	2	1	1
65—70 ...	5	4	1	...	...	...	1	1	...	4	3	1
70 & over...	7	5	2	1	1	...	1	...	1	5	4	1
Religion not returned...	*1*	*1*	...	...	...	...	*1*	*1*	...	...	...	...
0—1 ...	...	...	...	...	...	...	...	...	...	...	...	...
1—2 ...	...	...	...	...	...	...	...	...	...	...	...	...
2—3 ...	...	...	...	...	...	...	...	...	...	...	...	...
3—4 ...	...	...	...	...	...	...	...	...	...	...	...	...
4—5 ...	...	...	...	...	...	...	...	...	...	...	...	...
Total 0—5	...	...	...	...	...	...	...	...	...	...	...	...
5—10 ...	...	...	...	...	...	...	...	...	...	...	...	...
10—15 ...	...	...	...	...	...	...	...	...	...	...	...	...
15—20 ...	...	...	...	...	...	...	...	...	...	...	...	...
20—25 ...	...	...	...	...	...	...	...	...	...	...	...	...
25—30 ...	1	1	...	...	...	...	1	1	...	...	...	...
30—35 ...	...	...	...	...	...	...	...	...	...	...	...	...
35—40 ...	...	...	...	...	...	...	...	...	...	...	...	...
40—45 ...	...	...	...	...	...	...	...	...	...	...	...	...
45—50 ...	...	...	...	...	...	...	...	...	...	...	...	...
50—55 ...	...	...	...	...	...	...	...	...	...	...	...	...
55—60 ...	...	...	...	...	...	...	...	...	...	...	...	...
60—65 ...	...	...	...	...	...	...	...	...	...	...	...	...
65—70 ...	...	...	...	...	...	...	...	...	...	...	...	...
70 & over...	...	...	...	...	...	...	...	...	...	...	...	...

TABLE VII.—Age, Sex and Civil Condition.—Part B.—By States or Districts.

State or District and Religion and Age	Population.			Unmarried.			Married.			Widowed.		
	Persons	Males.	Females.	Persons	Males.	Females	Persons.	Males.	Females.	Persons.	Males.	Females.
1	2	3	4	5	6	7	8	9	10	11	12	13
ABU DISTRICT												
All Religions.	*4,532*	*2,753*	*1,779*	*1,813*	*1,169*	*644*	*2,352*	*1,428*	*924*	*367*	*156*	*211*
0— 1 ...	125	58	67	124	58	66	1	...	1	...	...	...
1— 5 ...	459	231	228	441	225	216	17	6	11	1	...	1
5—10 ...	485	264	221	427	240	187	56	28	38	2	1	1
10—15 ...	505	301	204	375	246	129	125	51	74	5	4	1
15—20 ...	548	332	216	191	166	25	344	157	187	13	9	4
20—30 ...	1,084	686	398	180	165	15	848	489	359	56	32	24
30—40 ...	684	466	218	41	38	3	565	394	171	78	34	44
40—50 ...	380	255	125	17	17	...	266	201	65	97	37	60
50—60 ...	181	112	69	12	10	2	101	81	20	68	21	47
60 and Over.	81	48	33	5	4	1	29	26	3	47	18	29
Christian ...	*140*	*84*	*56*	*79*	*52*	*27*	*56*	*31*	*25*	*5*	*1*	*4*
0— 1 ...	5	3	2	5	3	2	...	...	...	...	...	...
1— 5 ...	17	7	10	17	7	10	...	...	...	...	...	...
5—10 ...	19	9	10	17	9	8	2	...	2	...	...	...
10—15 ...	11	10	1	11	10	1	...	...	...	...	...	...
15—20 ...	13	10	3	10	8	2	3	2	1	...	...	...
20—30 ...	22	11	11	10	8	2	11	3	8	1	...	1
30—40 ...	22	13	9	5	4	1	17	9	8	...	...	...
40—50 ...	16	12	4	3	3	...	12	9	3	1	...	1
50—60 ...	13	8	5	1	...	1	9	7	2	3	1	2
60 and Over.	2	1	1	...	...	...	2	1	1	...	...	...
Hindu ...	*3,498*	*2,099*	*1,399*	*1,365*	*873*	*492*	*1,839*	*1,111*	*728*	*294*	*115*	*179*
0— 1 ...	94	47	47	93	47	46	1	...	1	...	...	...
1— 5 ...	343	168	175	325	162	163	17	6	11	1	...	1
5—10 ...	381	208	173	334	188	146	45	19	26	2	1	1
10—15 ...	404	235	169	295	190	105	104	41	63	5	4	1
15—20 ...	426	256	170	138	121	17	277	126	151	11	9	2
20—30 ...	857	538	319	129	117	12	684	397	287	44	24	20
30—40 ...	531	359	172	29	27	2	435	304	181	67	28	39
40—50 ...	285	187	98	12	12	...	196	149	47	77	26	51
50—60 ...	122	70	52	7	6	1	61	51	10	54	13	41
60 and Over.	55	31	24	3	3	...	19	18	1	33	10	23
Muslim ...	*800*	*512*	*288*	*328*	*218*	*110*	*409*	*257*	*152*	*63*	*37*	*26*
0— 1 ...	23	7	16	23	7	16	...	...	...	...	...	...
1— 5 ...	83	44	39	83	44	39	...	...	...	...	...	...
5—10 ...	79	45	34	70	41	29	9	4	5	...	...	...
10—15 ...	85	55	30	65	45	20	20	10	10	...	...	...
15—20 ...	90	59	31	36	32	4	53	27	26	1	...	1
20—30 ...	182	119	63	37	36	1	134	75	59	11	8	3
30—40 ...	121	87	34	7	7	...	103	74	29	11	6	5
40—50 ...	73	50	23	1	1	...	54	39	15	18	10	8
50—60 ...	43	32	11	4	4	...	29	22	7	10	6	4
60 and Over.	21	14	7	2	1	1	7	6	1	12	7	5
ALWAR.												
All Religions.	*749,751*	*396,261*	*353,490*	*348,111*	*206,395*	*141,716*	*317,738*	*154,926*	*162,812*	*83,902*	*34,940*	*48,962*
0— 1 ...	22,185	10,940	11,245	22,173	10,930	11,243	10	8	2	2	2	...
1— 5 ...	86,996	43,368	43,628	86,824	43,266	43,558	155	95	60	17	7	10
5—10 ...	93,879	50,115	43,764	91,889	49,483	42,406	1,914	600	1,314	76	32	44
10—15 ...	87,711	47,964	39,747	79,659	46,420	33,239	7,859	1,467	6,392	193	77	116
15—20 ...	71,852	37,816	34,036	33,089	25,438	7,651	37,586	11,838	25,748	1,177	540	637
20—30 ...	140,081	71,647	68,434	24,613	21,631	2,982	108,515	46,795	61,720	6,953	3,221	3,732
30—40 ...	102,513	55,193	47,320	5,327	4,978	349	82,752	44,212	38,540	14,434	6,003	8,431
40—50 ...	67,939	37,137	30,802	2,468	2,328	140	45,404	26,828	18,576	20,067	7,981	12,086
50—60 ...	44,202	24,135	20,067	1,266	1,194	72	22,172	14,551	7,621	20,764	8,390	12,374
60 and Over.	32,393	17,946	14,447	803	727	76	11,371	8,532	2,839	20,219	8,687	11,532

TABLE VII.—AGE, SEX AND CIVIL CONDITION —PART B.—BY STATES OR DISTRICTS.—*Continued.*

State or District and Religion and Age.	Population.			Unmarried.			Married.			Widowed.		
	Persons.	Males.	Females.	Persons.	Males.	Females.	Persons.	Males.	Females.	Persons.	Males.	Females.
1	2	3	4	5	6	7	8	9	10	11	12	13
ALWAR— *Concluded.*												
Hindu ...	*549,366*	*290,088*	*259,278*	*253,891*	*151,362*	*102,529*	*230,851*	*112,484*	*118,367*	*64,624*	*26,242*	*38,382*
0— 1 ...	**15,862**	7,802	8,060	**15,850**	7,792	8,058	**10**	8	2	**2**	2	...
1— 5 ...	**62,473**	31,169	31,304	**62,378**	31,106	31,272	**86**	58	28	**9**	5	4
5—10 ...	**68,012**	36,256	31,756	**66,706**	35,868	30,838	**1,257**	368	889	**49**	20	29
10—15 ...	**63,980**	34,902	29,078	**58,137**	33,886	24,251	**5,705**	967	4,738	**138**	49	89
15—20 ...	**52,222**	27,478	24,744	**24,041**	18,576	5,465	**27,313**	8,544	18,769	**868**	358	510
20—30 ...	**102,497**	52,485	50,012	**18,498**	16,266	2,232	**78,714**	33,993	44,721	**5,285**	2,226	3,059
30—40 ...	**75,618**	40,678	34,940	**4,312**	4,097	215	**60,160**	32,196	27,964	**11,146**	4,385	6,761
40—50 ...	**51,084**	27,857	23,227	**2,158**	2,064	94	**33,192**	19,600	13,592	**15,734**	6,193	9,541
50—60 ...	**33,354**	18,170	15,184	**1,102**	1,052	50	**16,228**	10,632	5,596	**16,024**	6,486	9,538
60 and Over.	**24,264**	13,291	10,973	**709**	655	54	**8,186**	6,118	2,068	**15,369**	6,518	8,851
Jain ...	*3,809*	*1,994*	*1,815*	*1,708*	*1,012*	*696*	*1,569*	*764*	*805*	*532*	*218*	*314*
0— 1 ...	**132**	73	59	**132**	73	59	...	...	...	...	...	...
1— 5 ...	**429**	204	225	**426**	203	223	**2**	1	1	**1**	...	1
5—10 ...	**449**	215	234	**439**	210	229	**8**	4	4	**2**	1	1
10—15 ...	**402**	207	195	**360**	199	161	**41**	7	34	**1**	1	...
15—20 ...	**348**	185	163	**143**	123	20	**201**	61	140	**4**	1	3
20—30 ...	**674**	335	339	**106**	102	4	**526**	220	306	**42**	13	29
30—40 ...	**519**	281	238	**39**	39	...	**374**	205	169	**106**	37	69
40—50 ...	**395**	221	174	**27**	27	...	**247**	147	100	**121**	47	74
50—60 ...	**286**	166	120	**26**	26	...	**113**	77	36	**147**	63	84
60 and Over.	**175**	107	68	**10**	10	...	**57**	42	15	**108**	55	53
Muslim ...	*196,460*	*104,110*	*92,350*	*92,454*	*53,982*	*38,472*	*85,270*	*41,651*	*43,619*	*18,736*	*8,477*	*10,259*
0— 1 ...	**6,185**	3,062	3,123	**6,185**	3,062	3,123	...	...	...	...	...	...
1— 5 ...	**24,074**	11,981	12,093	**24,000**	11,943	12,057	**67**	36	31	**7**	2	5
5—10 ...	**25,406**	13,636	11,770	**24,732**	13,397	11,335	**649**	228	421	**25**	11	14
10—15 ...	**23,321**	12,850	10,471	**21,154**	12,330	8,824	**2,113**	493	1,620	**54**	27	27
15—20 ...	**19,272**	10,147	9,125	**8,900**	6,735	2,165	**10,067**	3,231	6,836	**305**	181	124
20—30 ...	**36,885**	18,815	18,070	**6,003**	5,258	745	**29,258**	12,575	16,683	**1,624**	982	642
30—40 ...	**26,357**	14,223	12,134	**975**	842	133	**22,201**	11,800	10,401	**3,181**	1,581	1,600
40—50 ...	**16,451**	9,053	7,398	**283**	237	46	**11,957**	7,075	4,882	**4,211**	1,741	2,470
50—60 ...	**10,557**	5,796	4,761	**138**	116	22	**5,830**	3,841	1,989	**4,589**	1,839	2,750
60 and Over.	**7,952**	4,547	3,405	**84**	62	22	**3,128**	2,372	756	**4,740**	2,113	2,627
BANSWARA.												
All Religions.	*225,106*	*111,983*	*113,123*	*114,687*	*62,844*	*51,843*	*91,969*	*44,861*	*47,108*	*18,450*	*4,278*	*14,172*
0— 1 ...	**8,776**	4,301	4,475	**8,776**	4,301	4,475	...	...	...	...	...	...
1— 5 ...	**32,173**	15,864	16,309	**32,164**	15,864	16,300	**8**	...	8	**1**	...	1
5—10 ...	**34,542**	17,536	17,006	**33,049**	17,164	15,885	**1,458**	366	1,092	**35**	6	29
10—15 ...	**31,203**	15,987	15,216	**26,466**	14,691	11,775	**4,605**	1,267	3,338	**132**	29	103
15—20 ...	**21,339**	10,451	10,888	**8,115**	5,858	2,257	**12,848**	4,476	8,372	**376**	117	259
20—30 ...	**35,171**	17,295	17,876	**4,597**	3,803	794	**29,053**	13,079	15,974	**1,521**	413	1,108
30—40 ...	**25,032**	12,507	12,525	**915**	715	200	**21,099**	11,097	10,002	**3,018**	695	2,323
40—50 ...	**19,059**	9,623	9,436	**344**	269	75	**13,820**	8,230	5,590	**4,895**	1,124	3,771
50—60 ...	**11,296**	5,508	5,788	**169**	121	48	**6,419**	4,333	2,086	**4,708**	1,054	3,654
60 and Over.	**6,515**	2,911	3,604	**92**	58	34	**2,659**	2,013	646	**3,764**	840	2,924
Hindu ...	*120,458*	*59,925*	*60,533*	*56,838*	*31,923*	*24,915*	*51,793*	*25,247*	*26,546*	*11,827*	*2,755*	*9,072*
0— 1 ...	**4,764**	2,337	2,427	**4,764**	2,337	2,427	...	...	...	...	...	...
1— 5 ...	**16,171**	8,092	8,079	**16,163**	8,092	8,071	**7**	...	7	**1**	...	1
5—10 ...	**17,415**	8,894	8,521	**16,330**	8,649	7,681	**1,063**	240	823	**22**	5	17
10—15 ...	**16,160**	8,326	7,834	**12,987**	7,493	5,494	**3,097**	814	2,283	**76**	19	57
15—20 ...	**11,805**	5,735	6,070	**3,775**	2,963	812	**7,806**	2,701	5,105	**224**	71	153
20—30 ...	**19,336**	9,442	9,894	**2,026**	1,786	240	**16,385**	7,429	8,956	**925**	227	698
30—40 ...	**14,002**	6,972	7,030	**402**	318	84	**11,516**	6,207	5,309	**2,084**	447	1,637
40—50 ...	**10,823**	5,441	5,382	**215**	167	48	**7,336**	4,522	2,814	**3,272**	752	2,520
50—60 ...	**6,456**	3,132	3,324	**112**	79	33	**3,329**	2,338	991	**3,015**	715	2,300
60 and Over.	**3,526**	1,554	1,972	**64**	39	25	**1,254**	996	258	**2,208**	519	1,689

TABLE VII.—AGE, SEX AND CIVIL CONDITION.—PART B.—BY STATES OR DISTRICTS.—*Continued.*

State or District and Religion and Age.	Population			Unmarried.			Married.			Widowed		
	Persons.	Males.	Females.	Persons.	Males.	Females.	Persons.	Males.	Females.	Persons.	Males	Females.
1	2	3	4	5	6	7	8	9	10	11	12	13
BANSWARA— *Concluded.*												
Tribal ...	*93,330*	*46,313*	*47,017*	*52,735*	*27,941*	*24,794*	*35,676*	*17,181*	*18,495*	*4,919*	*1,191*	*3,728*
0—1 ...	**3,611**	1,761	1,850	**3,611**	1,761	1,850	...	...	...	...	...	...
1—5 ...	**14,701**	7,141	7,560	**14,701**	7,141	7,560	...	...	...	...	...	...
5—10 ...	**15,618**	7,865	7,753	**15,282**	7,757	7,525	**331**	107	224	**5**	1	4
10—15 ...	**13,657**	6,947	6,710	**12,310**	6,526	5,784	**1,322**	411	911	**25**	10	15
15—20 ...	**8,479**	4,178	4,301	**3,962**	2,580	1,382	**4,447**	1,557	2,890	**70**	41	29
20—30 ...	**13,903**	6,924	6,979	**2,303**	1,768	535	**11,303**	4,995	6,308	**297**	161	136
30—40 ...	**9,567**	4,777	4,790	**440**	330	110	**8,510**	4,254	4,256	**617**	193	424
40—50 ...	**7,060**	3,558	3,502	**76**	51	25	**5,765**	3,228	2,537	**1,219**	279	940
50—60 ...	**4,149**	2,007	2,142	**36**	21	15	**2,749**	1,738	1,011	**1,364**	248	1,116
60 and Over.	**2,585**	1,155	1,430	**14**	6	8	**1,249**	891	358	**1,322**	258	1,064
BHARATPUR.												
All Religions.	*486,954*	*263,325*	*223,629*	*208,152*	*128,639*	*79,513*	*218,114*	*107,534*	*110,580*	*60,688*	*27,152*	*33,536*
0—1 ...	**17,744**	8,768	8,976	**17,728**	8,756	8,972	**16**	12	4	...	...	...
1—5 ...	**56,881**	28,784	28,097	**56,554**	28,629	27,925	**298**	143	155	**29**	12	17
5—10 ...	**61,637**	34,032	27,605	**56,612**	32,480	24,132	**4,897**	1,487	3,410	**128**	65	63
10—15 ...	**57,625**	32,596	25,029	**44,397**	28,328	16,069	**12,835**	4,033	8,802	**393**	235	158
15—20 ...	**45,205**	24,202	21,003	**14,215**	12,334	1,881	**29,803**	11,209	18,594	**1,187**	659	528
20—30 ...	**89,793**	46,900	42,893	**11,541**	11,118	423	**72,268**	32,703	39,565	**5,984**	3,079	2,905
30—40 ...	**69,415**	38,227	31,188	**4,037**	3,969	68	**53,396**	28,860	24,536	**11,982**	5,398	6,584
40—50 ...	**44,576**	25,114	19,462	**1,778**	1,753	25	**27,385**	16,834	10,551	**15,413**	6,527	8,886
50—60 ...	**26,710**	14,974	11,736	**847**	836	11	**11,914**	8,195	3,719	**13,949**	5,943	8,006
60 and Over.	**17,368**	9,728	7,640	**443**	436	7	**5,302**	4,058	1,244	**11,623**	5,234	6,389
Hindu ...	*389,723*	*211,278*	*178,445*	*164,205*	*102,173*	*62,032*	*174,909*	*86,477*	*88,432*	*50,609*	*22,628*	*27,981*
0—1 ...	**14,037**	6,892	7,145	**14,024**	6,881	7,143	**13**	11	2	...	...	...
1—5 ...	**45,116**	22,736	22,380	**44,866**	22,619	22,247	**230**	108	122	**20**	9	11
5—10 ...	**48,777**	26,972	21,805	**44,463**	25,639	18,824	**4,210**	1,279	2,931	**104**	54	50
10—15 ...	**45,699**	25,942	19,757	**34,507**	22,254	12,253	**10,864**	3,494	7,370	**328**	194	134
15—20 ...	**36,099**	19,401	16,698	**10,837**	9,574	1,263	**24,276**	9,299	14,977	**986**	528	458
20—30 ...	**71,863**	37,756	34,107	**9,178**	8,931	247	**57,678**	26,835	31,843	**5,007**	2,490	2,517
30—40 ...	**55,983**	30,961	25,022	**3,534**	3,495	39	**42,380**	22,900	19,480	**10,069**	4,476	5,593
40—50 ...	**36,260**	20,502	15,758	**1,617**	1,606	11	**21,745**	13,381	8,364	**12,898**	5,515	7,383
50—60 ...	**21,785**	12,261	9,524	**772**	769	3	**9,405**	6,467	2,938	**11,608**	5,025	6,583
60 and Over.	**14,104**	7,855	6,249	**407**	405	2	**4,108**	3,113	995	**9,589**	4,337	5,252
Jain ...	*2,390*	*1,288*	*1,102*	*1,058*	*652*	*406*	*915*	*435*	*480*	*417*	*201*	*216*
0—1 ...	**97**	53	44	**97**	53	44	...	...	...	...	...	...
1—5 ...	**235**	108	127	**232**	106	126	**3**	2	1	...	...	...
5—10 ...	**276**	140	136	**266**	137	129	**10**	3	7	...	...	...
10—15 ...	**266**	141	125	**225**	130	95	**39**	10	29	**2**	1	1
15—20 ...	**234**	121	113	**79**	69	10	**147**	49	98	**8**	3	5
20—30 ...	**453**	234	219	**76**	75	1	**331**	142	189	**46**	17	29
30—40 ...	**355**	196	159	**41**	41	...	**220**	119	101	**94**	36	58
40—50 ...	**242**	158	89	**28**	28	...	**99**	61	38	**115**	64	51
50—60 ...	**157**	94	63	**11**	10	1	**52**	37	15	**94**	47	47
60 and Over.	**75**	48	27	**3**	3	...	**14**	12	2	**58**	33	25
Muslim ...	*94,054*	*50,308*	*43,746*	*42,536*	*25,593*	*16,943*	*41,927*	*20,432*	*21,495*	*9,591*	*4,283*	*5,308*
0—1 ...	**3,573**	1,803	1,770	**3,571**	1,803	1,768	**2**	...	2	...	...	...
1—5 ...	**11,429**	5,885	5,544	**11,358**	5,850	5,508	**62**	32	30	**9**	3	6
5—10 ...	**12,482**	6,859	5,623	**11,787**	6,644	5,143	**671**	204	467	**24**	11	13
10—15 ...	**11,576**	6,459	5,117	**9,597**	5,897	3,700	**1,919**	524	1,395	**60**	38	22
15—20 ...	**8,794**	4,686	4,158	**3,273**	2,670	603	**5,332**	1,841	3,491	**189**	125	64
20—30 ...	**17,329**	8,836	8,493	**2,267**	2,096	171	**14,142**	6,177	7,965	**920**	563	357
30—40 ...	**12,961**	7,001	5,960	**457**	431	26	**10,694**	5,691	5,003	**1,810**	879	931
40—50 ...	**8,002**	4,415	3,587	**132**	118	14	**5,489**	3,357	2,132	**2,381**	940	1,441
50—60 ...	**4,733**	2,599	2,134	**61**	56	5	**2,441**	1,678	763	**2,231**	865	1,366
60 and Over.	**3,175**	1,815	1,360	**33**	28	5	**1,175**	928	247	**1,967**	859	1,108

TABLE VII.—Age, Sex and Civil Condition.—Part B.—By States or Districts.—*Continued.*

State or District and Religion and Age.	Population.			Unmarried.			Married.			Widowed.		
	Persons.	Males.	Females.	Persons.	Males.	Females.	Persons.	Males.	Females.	Persons.	Males.	Females.
1	2	3	4	5	6	7	8	9	10	11	12	13
BIKANER.												
All Religions.	*936,218*	*501,153*	*435,065*	*418,731*	*259,383*	*159,348*	*415,522*	*207,512*	*208,010*	*101,965*	*34,258*	*67,707*
0— 1 ...	**29,741**	15,240	14,501	**29,732**	15,233	14,499	**9**	7	2	...	...	...
1— 5 ...	**116,383**	58,854	57,529	**115,859**	58,623	57,236	**500**	224	276	**24**	7	17
5—10 ...	**120,447**	63,832	56,615	**110,166**	61,139	49,027	**10,025**	2,612	7,413	**256**	81	175
10—15 ...	**114,482**	62,147	52,335	**87,446**	54,579	32,867	**26,373**	7,371	19,002	**663**	197	466
15—20 ...	**96,574**	52,312	44,262	**32,979**	28,812	4,167	**61,301**	22,834	38,467	**2,294**	666	1,628
20—30 ...	**162,131**	87,028	75,103	**26,567**	25,280	1,287	**127,115**	59,239	67,876	**8,449**	2,509	5,940
30—40 ...	**112,661**	62,196	50,465	**8,051**	7,901	150	**89,275**	49,541	39,734	**15,335**	4,754	10,581
40—50 ...	**85,551**	47,544	38,007	**4,324**	4,265	59	**57,440**	35,111	22,329	**23,787**	8,168	15,619
50—60 ...	**56,018**	30,527	25,491	**2,307**	2,276	31	**28,877**	19,441	9,436	**24,834**	8,810	16,024
60 and Over.	**42,230**	21,473	20,757	**1,300**	1,275	25	**14,607**	11,132	3,475	**26,323**	9,066	17,257
Hindu ...	*725,084*	*388,017*	*337,067*	*317,390*	*198,640*	*118,750*	*323,615*	*161,258*	*162,357*	*84,079*	*28,119*	*55,960*
0— 1 ...	**22,506**	11,531	10,975	**22,500**	11,527	10,973	**6**	4	2	...	...	...
1— 5 ...	**88,686**	44,874	43,812	**88,396**	44,751	43,645	**269**	116	153	**21**	7	14
5—10 ...	**91,544**	48,515	43,029	**83,591**	46,671	36,920	**7,756**	1,784	5,972	**197**	60	137
10—15 ...	**87,958**	47,769	40,189	**66,002**	41,876	24,126	**21,402**	5,735	15,667	**554**	158	396
15—20 ...	**75,431**	40,820	34,611	**24,253**	21,944	2,309	**49,310**	18,349	30,961	**1,868**	527	1,341
20—30 ...	**124,909**	67,051	57,858	**19,408**	18,810	598	**98,754**	46,320	52,434	**6,747**	1,921	4,826
30—40 ...	**87,041**	48,262	38,779	**6,425**	6,318	107	**68,178**	38,133	30,045	**12,438**	3,811	8,627
40—50 ...	**67,906**	37,862	30,044	**3,695**	3,664	31	**44,531**	27,379	17,152	**19,680**	6,819	12,861
50—60 ...	**44,968**	24,337	20,631	**2,015**	1,991	24	**22,198**	14,933	7,265	**20,755**	7,413	13,342
60 and Over.	**34,135**	16,996	17,139	**1,105**	1,088	17	**11,211**	8,505	2,706	**21,819**	7,403	14,416
Jain ...	*28,773*	*12,479*	*16,294*	*12,057*	*6,952*	*5,105*	*12,197*	*4,788*	*7,409*	*4,519*	*739*	*3,780*
0— 1 ...	**1,011**	531	480	**1,011**	531	480	...	...	...	...	...	...
1— 5 ...	**3,549**	1,756	1,793	**3,503**	1,718	1,785	**46**	38	8	...	...	...
5—10 ...	**3,780**	1,935	1,845	**3,505**	1,842	1,663	**270**	91	179	**5**	2	3
10—15 ...	**3,363**	1,670	1,693	**2,601**	1,526	1,075	**735**	138	597	**27**	6	21
15—20 ...	**2,672**	1,084	1,588	**566**	526	40	**1,952**	539	1,413	**154**	19	135
20—30 ...	**4,802**	1,799	3,003	**475**	445	30	**3,784**	1,298	2,486	**543**	56	487
30—40 ...	**3,606**	1,349	2,257	**185**	170	15	**2,573**	1,082	1,491	**848**	97	751
40—50 ...	**2,712**	1,039	1,673	**118**	104	14	**1,543**	767	776	**1,051**	168	883
50—60 ...	**1,851**	752	1,099	**61**	60	1	**865**	513	352	**925**	179	746
60 and Over.	**1,427**	564	863	**32**	30	2	**429**	322	107	**966**	212	754
Muslim ...	*141,578*	*76,471*	*65,107*	*68,101*	*40,299*	*27,802*	*62,610*	*32,218*	*30,392*	*10,867*	*3,954*	*6,913*
0— 1 ...	**4,897**	2,510	2,387	**4,896**	2,509	2,387	**1**	1	...	...	...	...
1— 5 ...	**19,110**	9,634	9,476	**18,940**	9,575	9,365	**168**	59	109	**2**	...	2
5—10 ...	**19,834**	10,465	9,369	**17,977**	9,787	8,190	**1,817**	663	1,154	**40**	15	25
10—15 ...	**18,271**	9,858	8,413	**14,467**	8,506	5,961	**3,739**	1,826	2,113	**65**	26	39
15—20 ...	**14,301**	7,800	6,501	**5,881**	4,519	1,362	**8,181**	3,183	4,998	**239**	98	141
20—30 ...	**24,710**	13,501	11,209	**4,535**	4,048	487	**19,208**	9,056	10,152	**967**	397	570
30—40 ...	**16,786**	9,370	7,416	**860**	836	24	**14,237**	7,926	6,311	**1,689**	608	1,081
40—50 ...	**11,391**	6,379	5,012	**300**	286	14	**8,622**	5,254	3,368	**2,469**	839	1,630
50—60 ...	**7,081**	4,024	3,057	**133**	127	6	**4,389**	3,006	1,383	**2,559**	891	1,668
60 and Over.	**5,197**	2,930	2,267	**112**	106	6	**2,248**	1,744	504	**2,837**	1,080	1,757
Sikh ...	*40,469*	*24,017*	*16,452*	*21,042*	*13,422*	*7,620*	*16,950*	*9,159*	*7,791*	*2,477*	*1,436*	*1,041*
0— 1 ...	**1,319**	668	651	**1,317**	666	651	**2**	2	...	...	...	...
1— 5 ...	**4,998**	2,573	2,425	**4,980**	2,562	2,418	**17**	11	6	**1**	...	1
5—10 ...	**5,250**	2,895	2,355	**5,055**	2,817	2,238	**181**	74	107	**14**	4	10
10—15 ...	**4,859**	2,834	2,025	**4,348**	2,655	1,693	**494**	172	322	**17**	7	10
15—20 ...	**4,145**	2,599	1,546	**2,266**	1,817	449	**1,846**	760	1,086	**33**	22	11
20—30 ...	**7,655**	4,647	3,008	**2,137**	1,970	167	**5,327**	2,543	2,784	**191**	134	57
30—40 ...	**5,183**	3,187	1,996	**580**	576	4	**4,247**	2,377	1,870	**356**	234	122
40—50 ...	**3,502**	2,236	1,266	**210**	210	...	**2,711**	1,686	1,025	**581**	340	241
50—60 ...	**2,096**	1,402	694	**98**	98	...	**1,411**	978	433	**587**	326	261
60 and Over.	**1,462**	976	486	**51**	51	...	**714**	556	158	**697**	369	328

TABLE VII.—Age, Sex and Civil Condition.—Part B.—By States or Districts.—*Continued.*

State or District and Religion and Age.	Population.			Unmarried.			Married.			Widowed.		
	Persons.	Males.	Females.	Persons.	Males.	Females.	Persons.	Males.	Females.	Persons.	Males.	Females.
1	2	3	4	5	6	7	8	9	10	11	12	13
BUNDI.												
All Religions.	*216,722*	*113,101*	*103,621*	*89,390*	*53,549*	*35,841*	*104,105*	*52,211*	*51,894*	*23,227*	*7,341*	*15,886*
0— 1 ...	**6,469**	3,116	3,353	**6,469**	3,116	3,353	...	...	...	...	...	...
1— 5 ...	**26,093**	12,571	13,522	**25,986**	12,527	13,459	**101**	42	59	**6**	2	4
5—10 ...	**27,798**	14,567	13,231	**24,853**	13,763	11,000	**2,874**	778	2,096	**71**	26	45
10—15 ...	**25,355**	13,773	11,582	**18,666**	11,842	6,824	**6,538**	1,873	4,665	**151**	58	93
15—20 ...	**19,949**	10,425	9,524	**5,844**	5,243	601	**13,688**	5,012	8,676	**417**	170	247
20—30 ...	**38,595**	20,552	18,043	**4,739**	4,484	255	**31,984**	15,350	16,634	**1,872**	718	1,154
30—40 ...	**29,717**	15,301	14,416	**1,382**	1,246	136	**24,078**	12,721	11,357	**4,257**	1,334	2,923
40—50 ...	**22,976**	12,426	10,550	**871**	791	80	**15,512**	9,587	5,925	**6,593**	2,048	4,545
50—60 ...	**12,942**	7,007	5,935	**405**	376	29	**6,766**	4,870	1,896	**5,771**	1,761	4,010
60 and Over.	**6,828**	3,363	3,465	**175**	161	14	**2,564**	1,978	586	**4,089**	1,224	2,865
Hindu ...	*202,329*	*105,482*	*96,847*	*83,713*	*50,069*	*33,644*	*97,174*	*48,693*	*48,481*	*21,442*	*6,720*	*14,722*
0— 1 ...	**6,031**	2,898	3,133	**6,031**	2,898	3,133	...	...	...	...	...	...
1— 5 ...	**24,546**	11,800	12,746	**24,467**	11,777	12,690	**74**	22	52	**5**	1	4
5—10 ...	**26,134**	13,708	12,426	**23,382**	12,965	10,417	**2,689**	718	1,971	**63**	25	38
10—15 ...	**23,752**	12,931	10,821	**17,491**	11,118	6,373	**6,124**	1,759	4,365	**137**	54	83
15—20 ...	**18,585**	9,679	8,906	**5,400**	4,836	564	**12,814**	4,693	8,121	**371**	150	221
20—30 ...	**35,923**	19,097	16,826	**4,321**	4,086	235	**29,908**	14,360	15,548	**1,694**	651	1,043
30—40 ...	**27,665**	14,230	13,435	**1,274**	1,150	124	**22,479**	11,871	10,608	**3,912**	1,209	2,703
40—50 ...	**21,377**	11,569	9,808	**805**	734	71	**14,459**	8,946	5,513	**6,113**	1,889	4,224
50—60 ...	**11,978**	6,469	5,509	**374**	349	25	**6,253**	4,499	1,754	**5,351**	1,621	3,730
60 and Over.	**6,338**	3,101	3,237	**168**	156	12	**2,374**	1,825	549	**3,796**	1,120	2,676
Jain ...	*4,019*	*2,166*	*1,853*	*1,560*	*1,041*	*519*	*1,724*	*877*	*847*	*735*	*248*	*487*
0— 1 ...	**124**	60	64	**124**	60	64	...	...	...	...	...	...
1— 5 ...	**353**	168	185	**349**	168	181	**4**	...	4	...	...	...
5—10 ...	**388**	203	185	**350**	197	153	**34**	5	29	**4**	1	3
10—15 ...	**410**	219	191	**294**	190	104	**109**	28	81	**7**	1	6
15—20 ...	**391**	227	164	**139**	132	7	**230**	87	143	**22**	8	14
20—30 ...	**768**	429	339	**171**	161	10	**512**	245	267	**85**	23	62
30—40 ...	**630**	333	297	**66**	66	...	**402**	214	188	**162**	53	109
40—50 ...	**529**	287	242	**45**	45	...	**270**	164	106	**214**	78	136
50—60 ...	**302**	174	128	**19**	19	...	**123**	99	24	**160**	56	104
60 and Over	**124**	66	58	**3**	3	...	**40**	35	5	**81**	28	53
Muslim ...	*10,292*	*5,398*	*4,894*	*4,082*	*2,416*	*1,666*	*5,164*	*2,612*	*2,552*	*1,046*	*370*	*676*
0— 1 ...	**312**	157	155	**312**	157	155	...	...	...	...	...	...
1— 5 ...	**1,184**	598	586	**1,160**	577	583	**23**	20	3	**1**	1	...
5—10 ...	**1,268**	652	616	**1,113**	597	516	**151**	55	96	**4**	...	4
10—15 ...	**1,185**	617	568	**875**	530	345	**303**	84	219	**7**	3	4
15—20 ...	**965**	514	451	**302**	272	30	**639**	230	409	**24**	12	12
20—30 ...	**1,885**	1,016	869	**243**	233	10	**1,549**	739	810	**93**	44	49
30—40 ...	**1,405**	723	682	**40**	28	12	**1,184**	625	559	**181**	70	111
40—50 ...	**1,064**	565	499	**21**	12	9	**778**	472	306	**265**	81	184
50—60 ...	**660**	362	298	**12**	8	4	**388**	270	118	**260**	84	176
60 and Over.	**364**	194	170	**4**	2	2	**149**	117	32	**211**	75	136
DHOLPUR.												
All Religions.	*254,986*	*140,497*	*114,489*	*108,909*	*70,212*	*38,697*	*113,172*	*55,776*	*57,396*	*32,905*	*14,509*	*18,396*
0— 1 ...	**9,209**	4,697	4,512	**9,209**	4,697	4,512	...	...	...	...	...	...
1— 5 ...	**30,069**	15,426	14,643	**30,064**	15,422	14,642	**5**	4	1	...	...	...
5—10 ...	**31,369**	17,087	14,282	**28,092**	16,242	11,850	**3,202**	807	2,395	**75**	38	37
10—15 ...	**29,937**	17,179	12,758	**21,586**	14,630	6,956	**8,141**	2,438	5,703	**210**	111	99
15—20 ...	**24,398**	13,578	10,820	**7,468**	7,023	445	**16,234**	6,190	10,044	**696**	365	331
20—30 ...	**47,079**	25,713	21,366	**7,162**	7,016	146	**36,618**	17,093	19,525	**3,299**	1,604	1,695
30—40 ...	**35,535**	20,127	15,408	**2,907**	2,848	59	**26,284**	14,390	11,894	**6,344**	2,889	3,455
40—50 ...	**23,878**	13,684	10,194	**1,394**	1,359	35	**14,096**	8,628	5,468	**8,388**	3,697	4,691
50—60 ...	**14,248**	8,055	6,193	**694**	668	26	**5,993**	4,164	1,829	**7,561**	3,223	4,338
60 and Over.	**9,264**	4,951	4,313	**333**	307	26	**2,599**	2,062	537	**6,332**	2,582	3,750

TABLE VII.—Age, Sex and Civil Condition.—Part B.—By States or Districts.—*Continued.*

State or District and Religion and Age.	Population.			Unmarried.			Married.			Widowed.		
	Persons.	Males.	Females.	Persons.	Males.	Females.	Persons.	Males.	Females.	Persons.	Males.	Females.
1	2	3	4	5	6	7	8	9	10	11	12	13
DHOLPUR— *Concluded.*												
Hindu ...	*235,929*	*130,354*	*105,575*	*100,749*	*65,274*	*35,475*	*104,627*	*51,580*	*53,047*	*30,553*	*13,500*	*17,053*
0—1 ...	8,469	4,315	4,154	8,469	4,315	4,154	...	...	...	...	...	...
1—5 ...	27,878	14,359	13,519	27,873	14,355	13,518	5	4	1	...	...	...
5—10 ...	29,027	15,849	13,178	25,943	15,040	10,903	3,013	772	2,241	71	37	34
10—15 ...	27,811	16,008	11,803	19,944	13,585	6,359	7,668	2,819	5,849	199	104	95
15—20 ...	22,621	12,625	9,996	6,886	6,512	374	15,089	5,779	9,310	646	334	312
20—30 ...	43,584	23,882	19,702	6,620	6,524	96	33,884	15,864	18,020	3,080	1,494	1,586
30—40 ...	33,001	18,749	14,252	2,736	2,709	27	24,302	13,329	10,973	5,963	2,711	3,252
40—50 ...	22,026	12,639	9,387	1,313	1,297	16	12,899	7,894	5,005	7,814	3,448	4,366
50—60 ...	13,080	7,409	5,671	657	642	15	5,453	3,783	1,670	6,970	2,984	3,986
60 and Over.	8,432	4,519	3,913	308	295	13	2,314	1,836	478	5,810	2,388	3,422
Muslim ...	*16,842*	*8,903*	*7,939*	*7,196*	*4,327*	*2,869*	*7,674*	*3,753*	*3,921*	*1,972*	*823*	*1,149*
0—1 ...	642	328	314	642	328	314	...	...	...	...	...	...
1—5 ...	1,953	941	1,012	1,953	941	1,012	...	...	...	...	...	...
5—10 ...	2,106	1,119	987	1,925	1,084	841	177	34	143	4	1	3
10—15 ...	1,897	1,049	848	1,467	938	529	421	105	316	9	6	3
15—20 ...	1,558	833	725	516	454	62	1,003	352	651	39	27	12
20—30 ...	3,064	1,601	1,463	463	421	42	2,432	1,088	1,344	169	92	77
30—40 ...	2,213	1,184	1,029	127	98	29	1,779	945	834	307	141	166
40—50 ...	1,625	906	719	60	42	18	1,091	666	425	474	198	276
50—60 ...	1,029	559	470	25	15	10	501	350	151	503	194	309
60 and Over.	755	383	372	18	6	12	270	213	57	467	164	303
DUNGARPUR.												
All Religions.	*227,544*	*114,480*	*113,064*	*105,697*	*59,069*	*46,628*	*102,883*	*50,552*	*52,331*	*18,964*	*4,859*	*14,105*
0—1 ...	7 814	3,835	3,979	7,813	3,835	3,978	1	...	1	...	...	...
1—5 ...	32,040	15,706	16,334	31,984	15,692	16,292	52	12	40	4	2	2
5—10 ...	34,563	17,895	16,668	31,543	16,999	14,544	2,930	885	2,095	40	11	29
10—15 ...	31,728	16,550	15,178	23,823	14,048	9,775	7,800	2,469	5,331	105	33	72
15—20 ...	21,557	10,714	10,843	5,819	4,669	1,150	15,406	5,921	9,485	332	124	208
20—30 ...	35,218	17,670	17,548	3,096	2,716	380	30,761	14,520	16,241	1,361	434	927
30—40 ...	26,147	12,738	13,409	775	554	221	22,082	11,412	10,670	3,290	772	2,518
40—50 ...	20,429	10,420	10,009	483	333	150	14,604	8,701	5,818	5,342	1,296	4,046
50—60 ...	11,639	5,950	5,689	231	150	81	6,586	4,559	2,027	4,822	1,241	3,581
60 and Over.	6,409	3,002	3,407	130	73	57	2,611	1,983	628	3,668	946	2,722
Hindu ...	*214,045*	*107,797*	*106,248*	*100,007*	*55,743*	*44,264*	*96,748*	*47,591*	*49,157*	*17,290*	*4,463*	*12,827*
0—1 ...	7,404	3,642	3,762	7,404	3,642	3,762	...	...	...	...	...	...
1—5 ...	30,592	15,021	15,571	30,555	15,012	15,543	35	8	27	2	1	1
5—10 ...	32,831	17,013	15,818	29,969	16,169	13,800	2,824	834	1,990	38	10	28
10—15 ...	30,059	15,693	14,366	22,503	13,282	9,221	7,456	2,380	5,076	100	31	69
15—20 ...	20,225	10,062	10,163	5,377	4,297	1,080	14,538	5,647	8,891	310	118	192
20—30 ...	32,941	16,561	16,380	2,766	2,405	361	28,929	13,756	15,173	1,246	400	846
30—40 ...	24,364	11,865	12,499	685	472	213	20,691	10,684	10,007	2,988	709	2,279
40—50 ...	18,911	9,633	9,278	421	274	147	13,655	8,184	5,471	4,835	1,175	3,660
50—60 ...	10,771	5,517	5,254	207	127	80	6,169	4,252	1,917	4,395	1,138	3,257
60 and Over.	5,947	2,790	3,157	120	63	57	2,451	1,846	605	3,376	881	2,495
Jain ...	*5,801*	*2,836*	*2,965*	*2,380*	*1,437*	*943*	*2,334*	*1,149*	*1,185*	*1,087*	*250*	*837*
0—1 ...	161	78	83	161	78	83	...	...	...	...	...	...
1—5 ...	531	247	284	528	246	282	2	1	1	1	...	1
5—10 ...	640	324	316	613	312	301	27	12	15	...	...	...
10—15 ...	636	331	305	540	306	234	94	24	70	2	1	1
15—20 ...	573	289	284	206	176	30	355	111	244	12	2	10
20—30 ...	960	486	474	176	170	6	716	302	414	68	14	54
30—40 ...	820	391	429	72	68	4	544	286	258	204	37	167
40—50 ...	773	383	390	54	52	2	378	247	131	341	84	257
50—60 ...	480	221	259	22	21	1	174	127	47	284	78	211
60 and Over.	227	86	141	8	8	...	44	39	5	175	39	136

TABLE VII.—AGE, SEX AND CIVIL CONDITION.—PART B.—BY STATES OR DISTRICTS.—*Continued.*

State or District and Religion and Age.	Population.			Unmarried.			Married.			Widowed.		
	Persons.	Males.	Females.	Persons.	Males.	Females.	Persons.	Males.	Females.	Persons.	Males.	Females.
1	2	3	4	5	6	7	8	9	10	11	12	13
DUNGARPUR. *Concluded.*												
Muslim ...	*7,682*	*3,838*	*3,844*	*3,300*	*1,884*	*1,416*	*3,797*	*1,810*	*1,987*	*585*	*144*	*441*
0— 1 ...	249	115	134	248	115	133	1	...	1	...	...	...
1— 5 ...	913	438	475	897	434	463	15	3	12	1	1	...
5—10 ...	1,091	557	534	960	517	443	129	39	90	2	1	1
10—15 ...	1,033	526	507	780	460	320	250	65	185	3	1	2
15—20 ...	756	361	395	233	194	39	513	163	350	10	4	6
20—30 ...	1,313	620	693	152	139	13	1,115	462	653	46	19	27
30—40 ...	961	481	480	18	14	4	846	442	404	97	25	72
40—50 ...	743	402	341	8	7	1	569	358	211	166	37	129
50—60 ...	388	212	176	2	2	...	243	180	63	143	30	113
60 and Over.	235	126	109	2	2	...	116	98	18	117	26	91
JAIPUR.												
All Religions.	*2,631,775*	*1,387,067*	*1,244,708*	*1,055,776*	*661,170*	*394,606*	*1,274,171*	*620,997*	*653,174*	*301,828*	*104,900*	*196,928*
0— 1 ...	74,320	37,057	37,263	74,118	36,960	37,158	169	81	88	33	16	17
1— 5 ...	319,737	159,541	160,196	315,810	158,255	157,555	3,752	1,227	2,525	175	59	116
5—10 ...	339,744	183,105	156,639	292,668	171,237	121,431	46,244	11,560	34,684	832	308	524
10—15 ...	313,610	173,663	139,947	215,984	145,163	70,821	95,861	27,835	68,026	1,765	665	1,100
15—20 ...	236,137	125,534	110,603	63,851	59,521	4,330	167,552	64,268	103,284	4,734	1,745	2,989
20—30 ...	450,823	232,235	218,588	51,587	49,652	1,935	376,286	174,331	201,955	22,950	8,252	14,698
30—40 ...	353,998	186,640	167,358	20,259	19,550	709	283,438	149,894	133,544	50,301	17,196	33,105
40—50 ...	262,743	142,314	120,429	11,702	11,354	348	175,257	104,407	70,850	75,784	26,553	49,231
50—60 ...	166,521	88,860	77,661	6,165	5,983	182	84,742	56,794	27,948	75,614	26,083	49,531
60 and Over.	114,142	58,118	56,024	3,632	3,495	137	40,870	30,600	10,270	69,640	24,023	45,617
Hindu ...	*2,383,304*	*1,256,918*	*1,126,386*	*957,049*	*601,617*	*355,432*	*1,150,464*	*559,831*	*590,633*	*275,791*	*95,470*	*180,321*
0— 1 ...	66,776	33,254	33,522	66,659	33,196	33,463	105	54	51	12	4	8
1— 5 ...	289,119	144,469	144,650	286,129	143,480	142,649	2,834	936	1,898	156	53	103
5—10 ...	307,385	166,049	141,336	265,613	155,893	109,720	41,046	9,901	31,145	726	255	471
10—15 ...	284,394	157,981	126,413	196,097	132,518	63,579	86,731	24,891	61,840	1,566	572	994
15—20 ...	213,283	113,782	99,501	57,583	54,102	3,481	151,443	58,147	93,296	4,257	1,533	2,724
20—30 ...	407,814	210,057	197,757	46,417	44,922	1,495	340,476	157,744	182,732	20,921	7,391	13,530
30—40 ...	322,086	169,677	152,409	18,793	18,226	567	256,995	135,706	121,289	46,298	15,745	30,553
40—50 ...	238,584	129,002	109,582	10,758	10,496	262	158,299	94,216	64,083	69,527	24,290	45,237
50—60 ...	150,847	80,310	70,537	5,647	5,530	117	76,061	50,953	25,108	69,139	23,827	45,312
60 and Over.	103,016	52,337	50,679	3,353	3,254	99	36,474	27,283	9,191	63,189	21,300	41,889
Jain ...	*29,492*	*15,518*	*13,974*	*11,339*	*7,475*	*3,864*	*12,838*	*6,270*	*6,568*	*5,315*	*1,773*	*3,542*
0— 1 ...	821	418	403	806	412	394	8	3	5	7	3	4
1— 5 ...	2,792	1,373	1,419	2,758	1,357	1,401	31	15	16	3	1	2
5—10 ...	3,068	1,626	1,442	2,795	1,557	1,238	263	67	196	10	2	8
10—15 ...	2,871	1,551	1,320	2,171	1,395	776	676	150	526	24	6	18
15—20 ...	2,586	1,321	1,265	729	702	27	1,774	602	1,172	83	17	66
20—30 ...	5,245	2,675	2,570	872	853	19	3,897	1,719	2,178	476	103	373
30—40 ...	4,228	2,237	1,991	465	460	5	2,814	1,497	1,317	949	280	669
40—50 ...	3,751	2,079	1,672	402	399	3	1,937	1,200	737	1,412	480	932
50—60 ...	2,527	1,397	1,130	242	242	...	984	678	316	1,291	477	814
60 and Over	1,603	841	762	99	98	1	444	339	105	1,060	404	656
Muslim ...	*214,581*	*112,338*	*102,243*	*85,297*	*50,906*	*34,391*	*108,829*	*53,864*	*54,965*	*20,455*	*7,568*	*12,887*
0— 1 ...	6,532	3,290	3,242	6,466	3,259	3,207	54	23	31	12	8	4
1— 5 ...	27,201	13,369	13,832	26,307	13,091	13,216	878	273	605	16	5	11
5—10 ...	28,684	15,114	13,570	23,739	13,501	10,238	4,852	1,563	3,289	93	50	43
10—15 ...	25,804	13,851	11,953	17,335	11,033	6,302	8,302	2,736	5,566	167	82	85
15—20 ...	19,840	10,228	9,612	5,381	4,620	761	14,075	5,421	8,654	384	187	197
20—30 ...	37,035	19,138	17,897	4,141	3,777	364	31,356	14,610	16,746	1,538	751	787
30—40 ...	27,122	14,435	12,687	964	838	126	23,150	12,440	10,710	3,008	1,157	1,851
40—50 ...	19,984	10,993	8,991	516	438	78	14,698	8,790	5,908	4,770	1,765	3,005
50—60 ...	12,959	7,043	5,916	269	207	62	7,564	5,074	2,490	5,126	1,762	3,364
60 and Over.	9,420	4,877	4,543	179	142	37	3,900	2,934	966	5,341	1,801	3,540

TABLE VII.—AGE, SEX AND CIVIL CONDITION.—PART B —BY STATES OR DISTRICTS —*Continued.*

State or District and Religion and Age.	Population.			Unmarried.			Married.			Widowed.		
	Persons	Males.	Females.	Persons.	Males.	Females.	Persons.	Males.	Females.	Persons.	Males.	Females.
1	2	3	4	5	6	7	8	9	10	11	12	13
JAISALMER.												
All Religions.	*76,255*	*42,342*	*33,913*	*37,266*	*24,926*	*12,340*	*28,496*	*14,187*	*14,309*	*10,493*	*3,229*	*7,264*
0 – 1 ...	1,982	988	994	1,982	988	994	...	...	...	...	...	...
1 – 5 ...	9,174	4,670	4,504	9,155	4,666	4,489	16	3	13	3	1	2
5 – 10 ...	10,090	5,676	4,414	9,458	5,555	3,903	614	115	499	18	6	12
10 – 15 ...	9,367	5,549	3,818	7,676	5,194	2,482	1,640	346	1,294	51	9	42
15 – 20 ...	7,432	4,267	3,165	3,466	3,141	325	3,744	1,092	2,652	222	34	188
20 – 30 ...	13,393	7,362	6,031	3,541	3,432	109	8,840	3,732	5,108	1,012	198	814
30 – 40 ...	10,402	5,786	4,616	1,222	1,198	24	7,032	4,047	2,985	2,148	541	1,607
40 – 50 ...	7,791	4,444	3,347	495	484	11	4,284	2,984	1,300	3,012	976	2,036
50 – 60 ...	4,266	2,380	1,886	192	190	2	1,703	838	865	2,371	852	1,519
60 and Over.	2,358	1,220	1,138	79	78	1	623	530	93	1,656	612	1,044
Hindu ...	*51,769*	*28,551*	*23,218*	*24,828*	*16,829*	*7,999*	*19,293*	*9,540*	*9,753*	*7,648*	*2,182*	*5,466*
0 – 1 ...	1,299	673	626	1,299	673	626	...	...	...	...	...	...
1 – 5 ...	6,186	3,171	3,015	6,168	3,168	3,000	15	2	13	3	1	2
5 – 10 ...	6,771	3,808	2,963	6,312	3,734	2,578	449	72	377	10	2	8
10 – 15 ...	6,365	3,774	2,591	5,134	3,526	1,608	1,193	243	950	38	5	33
15 – 20 ...	5,087	2,917	2,170	2,280	2,130	150	2,628	766	1,862	179	21	158
20 – 30 ...	9,100	4,958	4,142	2,277	2,245	32	6,052	2,588	3,464	771	125	646
30 – 40 ...	7,131	3,925	3,206	806	802	4	4,731	2,749	1,982	1,594	374	1,220
40 – 50 ...	5,416	3,034	2,382	355	354	1	2,830	1,980	850	2,231	700	1,531
50 – 60 ...	2,863	1,559	1,304	144	144	...	1,041	834	207	1,678	581	1,097
60 and Over.	1,551	732	819	53	53	...	354	306	48	1,144	373	771
Muslim ...	*22,116*	*12,502*	*9,614*	*11,251*	*7,334*	*3,917*	*8,319*	*4,206*	*4,113*	*2,546*	*962*	*1,584*
0 – 1 ...	609	274	335	609	274	335	...	...	...	...	...	...
1 – 5 ...	2,723	1,362	1,361	2,722	1,361	1,361	1	1	...	...	...	...
5 – 10 ...	2,996	1,689	1,307	2,844	1,647	1,197	145	39	106	7	3	4
10 – 15 ...	2,689	1,600	1,089	2,275	1,501	774	402	95	307	12	4	8
15 – 20 ...	2,094	1,211	883	1,064	910	154	991	283	708	39	13	26
20 – 30 ...	3,884	2,170	1,714	1,154	1,084	70	2,511	1,018	1,493	219	68	151
30 – 40 ...	2,955	1,691	1,264	386	370	16	2,079	1,168	911	490	153	337
40 – 50 ...	2,151	1,292	859	127	120	7	1,331	922	409	693	250	443
50 – 60 ...	1,272	758	514	45	43	2	613	469	144	614	246	368
60 and Over.	743	455	288	25	24	1	246	206	40	472	225	247
Tribal ...	*1,444*	*815*	*629*	*752*	*491*	*261*	*541*	*267*	*274*	*151*	*57*	*94*
0 – 1 ...	44	25	19	44	25	19	...	...	...	...	...	...
1 – 5 ...	181	100	81	181	100	81	...	...	...	...	...	...
5 – 10 ...	213	124	89	201	121	80	11	2	9	1	1	...
10 – 15 ...	206	118	88	176	113	63	29	5	24	1	...	1
15 – 20 ...	154	84	70	78	62	16	73	22	51	3	...	3
20 – 30 ...	244	143	101	61	59	2	173	80	93	10	4	6
30 – 40 ...	170	96	74	8	8	...	140	79	61	22	9	13
40 – 50 ...	111	60	51	2	2	...	70	44	26	39	14	25
50 – 60 ...	82	42	40	1	1	...	32	24	8	49	17	32
60 and Over.	39	23	16	...	...	...	13	11	2	26	12	14
JHALAWAR.												
All Religions.	*107,890*	*56,518*	*51,372*	*39,604*	*24,986*	*14,618*	*54,415*	*27,202*	*27,213*	*13,871*	*4,330*	*9,541*
0 – 1 ...	3,159	1,582	1,577	3,158	1,582	1,576	1	...	1	...	...	...
1 – 5 ...	11,505	5,745	5,760	11,324	5,709	5,615	169	35	134	12	1	11
5 – 10 ...	12,861	6,694	6,167	10,654	6,228	4,426	2,168	457	1,711	39	9	30
10 – 15 ...	12,420	6,481	5,939	8,017	5,336	2,681	4,305	1,116	3,189	98	29	69
15 – 20 ...	10,799	5,527	5,272	2,660	2,454	206	7,844	2,992	4,852	295	81	214
20 – 30 ...	19,003	9,907	9,096	2,109	2,034	75	15,741	7,549	8,192	1,153	324	829
30 – 40 ...	15,091	7,854	7,237	781	757	24	11,666	6,361	5,305	2,644	736	1,908
40 – 50 ...	11,622	6,242	5,380	544	535	9	7,309	4,574	2,735	3,769	1,133	2,636
50 – 60 ...	6,783	3,863	2,920	225	220	5	3,462	2,618	844	3,096	1,025	2,071
60 and Over.	4,647	2,623	2,024	132	131	1	1,750	1,500	250	2,765	992	1,773

TABLE VII.—Age, Sex and Civil Condition.—Part B.—By States or Districts.—*Continued.*

State or District and Religion and Age.	Population.			Unmarried.			Married.			Widowed.		
	Persons.	Males.	Females.	Persons.	Males.	Females.	Persons.	Males.	Females.	Persons.	Males.	Females.
1	2	3	4	5	6	7	8	9	10	11	12	13
JHALAWAR—*Concluded.*												
Hindu ...	*96,634*	*50,705*	*45,929*	*34,991*	*22,189*	*12,802*	*49,122*	*24,592*	*24,530*	*12,521*	*3,924*	*8,597*
0—1 ...	**2,844**	1,429	1,415	**2.844**	1,429	1,415	...	...	...	...	...	...
1—5 ...	**10,339**	5,175	5,164	**10,165**	5,142	5,023	**163**	32	131	**11**	1	10
5—10 ...	**11,523**	6,016	5,507	**9,409**	5,562	3,847	**2,077**	446	1,631	**37**	8	29
10—15 ...	**11,162**	5,829	5,333	**7,001**	4,725	2,276	**4.068**	1,076	2,992	**93**	28	65
15—20 ...	**9,708**	4,965	4,743	**2,281**	2,123	158	**7,150**	2,767	4,383	**277**	75	202
20—30 ...	**17,037**	8,890	8,147	**1,801**	1,744	57	**14,175**	6,855	7,320	**1,061**	291	770
30—40 ...	**13,505**	7,040	6,465	**683**	666	17	**10,406**	5,703	4,703	**2,416**	671	1,745
40—50 ...	**10,369**	5,570	4,799	**487**	481	6	**6.481**	4,061	2,420	**3,401**	1,028	2,373
50—60 ...	**6,045**	3,442	2,603	**202**	199	3	**3,054**	2,318	736	**2,789**	925	1,864
60 and Over.	**4,102**	2,349	1,753	**118**	118	...	**1,548**	1,334	214	**2,436**	897	1,539
Jain ...	*2,630*	*1,390*	*1,240*	*1,033*	*685*	*348*	*1,188*	*576*	*612*	*409*	*129*	*280*
0—1 ...	**59**	30	29	**59**	30	29	...	...	...	...	...	...
1—5 ...	**226**	118	108	**225**	117	108	**1**	1	...	...	...	...
5—10 ...	**279**	141	138	**260**	139	121	**19**	2	17	...	...	...
10—15 ...	**280**	144	136	**220**	134	86	**59**	10	49	**1**	...	1
15—20 ...	**244**	134	110	**79**	76	3	**158**	57	101	**7**	1	6
20—30 ...	**465**	244	221	**87**	87	...	**336**	147	189	**42**	10	32
30—40 ...	**416**	210	206	**43**	43	...	**296**	148	148	**77**	19	58
40—50 ...	**339**	191	148	**33**	33	...	**197**	121	76	**109**	37	72
50—60 ...	**190**	110	80	**16**	16	...	**86**	60	26	**88**	34	54
60 and Over.	**132**	68	64	**11**	10	1	**36**	30	6	**85**	28	57
Muslim ...	*8,558*	*4,377*	*4,181*	*3,555*	*2,094*	*1,461*	*4,070*	*2,011*	*2,059*	*933*	*272*	*661*
0—1 ...	**256**	123	133	**255**	123	132	**1**	...	1	...	...	...
1—5 ...	**933**	449	484	**927**	447	480	**5**	2	3	**1**	...	1
5—10 ...	**1,052**	532	520	**978**	522	456	**72**	9	63	**2**	1	1
10—15 ...	**972**	504	468	**791**	473	318	**177**	30	147	**4**	1	3
15—20 ...	**842**	424	418	**298**	253	45	**533**	166	367	**11**	5	6
20—30 ...	**1,488**	764	724	**218**	200	18	**1,221**	542	679	**49**	22	27
30—40 ...	**1,154**	594	560	**54**	47	7	**953**	504	449	**147**	43	104
40—50 ...	**906**	475	431	**24**	21	3	**625**	387	238	**257**	67	190
50—60 ...	**544**	308	236	**7**	5	2	**319**	237	82	**218**	66	152
60 and Over.	**411**	204	207	**3**	3	...	**164**	134	30	**244**	67	177
KARAULI.												
All Religions.	*140,525*	*76,729*	*63,796*	*59,688*	*38,279*	*21,409*	*63,318*	*31,073*	*32,245*	*17,519*	*7,377*	*10,142*
0—1 ...	**4,869**	2,482	2,387	**4,869**	2,482	2,387	...	...	...	...	...	...
1—5 ...	**16,013**	8,094	7,919	**15,955**	8,078	7,877	**48**	12	36	**10**	4	6
5—10 ...	**18,467**	10,116	8,351	**16,184**	9,548	6,636	**2,244**	546	1,698	**39**	22	17
10—15 ...	**17,631**	9,921	7,710	**12,525**	8,404	4,121	**4,990**	1,458	3,532	**116**	59	57
15—20 ...	**13,056**	7,157	5,899	**3,791**	3,556	235	**8,926**	3,437	5,489	**339**	164	175
20—30 ...	**25,092**	13,617	11,475	**3,639**	3,560	79	**19,825**	9,262	10,563	**1,628**	795	833
30—40 ...	**18,856**	10,486	8,370	**1,431**	1,400	31	**14,205**	7,674	6,531	**3,220**	1,412	1,808
40—50 ...	**13,212**	7,450	5,762	**738**	713	25	**7,902**	4,837	3,065	**4,572**	1,900	2,672
50—60 ...	**8,079**	4,509	3,570	**370**	357	13	**3,574**	2,589	1,085	**4,135**	1,613	2,522
60 and Over.	**5,250**	2,897	2,358	**186**	181	5	**1,604**	1,308	296	**3,460**	1,408	2,052
Hindu ...	*132,759*	*72,578*	*60,181*	*56,459*	*36,282*	*20,177*	*59,698*	*29,281*	*30,417*	*16,602*	*7,015*	*9,587*
0—1 ...	**4,579**	2,345	2,234	**4,579**	2,345	2,234	...	...	...	...	...	...
1—5 ...	**15,151**	7,676	7,475	**15,100**	7,662	7,438	**42**	10	32	**9**	4	5
5—10 ...	**17,515**	9,599	7,916	**15,344**	9,056	6,288	**2,136**	524	1,612	**35**	19	16
10—15 ...	**16,720**	9,412	7,308	**11,857**	7,960	3,897	**4,754**	1,396	3,358	**109**	56	53
15—20 ...	**12,302**	6,764	5,538	**3,541**	3,335	206	**8,439**	3,272	5,167	**322**	157	165
20—30 ...	**23,671**	12,873	10,798	**3,424**	3,360	64	**18,693**	8,749	9,944	**1,554**	764	790
30—40 ...	**17,856**	9,941	7,915	**1,371**	1,353	18	**13,401**	7,231	6,170	**3,084**	1,357	1,727
40—50 ...	**12,472**	7,016	5,456	**706**	688	18	**7,413**	4,524	2,889	**4,353**	1,804	2,549
50—60 ...	**7,591**	4,233	3,358	**357**	347	10	**3,328**	2,360	968	**3,906**	1,526	2,380
60 and Over.	**4,902**	2,719	2,183	**180**	176	4	**1,492**	1,215	277	**3,230**	1,328	1,902

TABLE VII.—Age, Sex and Civil Condition.—Part B.—By States or Districts.—*Continued.*

State or District and Religion and Age	Population.			Unmarried.			Married.			Widowed		
	Persons.	Males.	Females.	Persons.	Males.	Females.	Persons.	Males.	Females.	Persons.	Males	Females.
1	2	3	4	5	6	7	8	9	10	11	12	13
KARAULI.—*Concluded.*												
Muslim ...	*7,301*	*3,914*	*3,387*	*3,025*	*1,879*	*1,146*	*3,435*	*1,705*	*1,730*	*841*	*330*	*511*
0— 1 ...	277	132	145	277	132	145	...	...	...	...	...	...
1— 5 ...	810	390	420	803	388	415	6	2	4	1	...	1
5—10 ...	891	490	401	784	466	318	103	21	82	4	3	1
10—15 ...	853	480	373	623	419	204	223	58	165	7	3	4
15—20 ...	707	370	337	235	209	26	456	154	302	16	7	9
20—30 ...	1,349	713	636	204	190	14	1,081	494	587	64	29	35
30—40 ...	939	512	427	55	42	13	763	420	343	121	50	71
40—50 ...	687	401	286	27	20	7	457	293	164	203	88	115
50—60 ...	458	257	201	11	8	3	236	171	65	211	78	133
60 and Over.	330	169	161	6	5	1	110	92	18	214	72	142
KISHANGARH												
All Religions.	*85,744*	*44,494*	*41,250*	*30,142*	*18,732*	*11,410*	*45,117*	*22,343*	*22,774*	*10,485*	*3,419*	*7,066*
0— 1 ...	2,341	1,180	1,161	2,283	1,157	1,126	58	23	35	...	...	...
1— 5 ...	10,779	5,317	5,462	9,983	5,067	4,916	773	236	537	23	14	9
5—10 ...	11,173	5,887	5,286	8,255	4,889	3,366	2,853	962	1,891	65	36	29
10—15 ...	10,147	5,393	4,754	5,570	3,753	1,817	4,476	1,586	2,890	101	54	47
15—20 ...	7,984	4,109	3,875	1,521	1,432	89	6,273	2,583	3,690	190	94	96
20—30 ...	14,700	7,699	7,001	1,319	1,276	43	12,601	6,120	6,481	780	303	477
30—40 ...	11,520	5,901	5,619	562	533	29	9,106	4,838	4,268	1,852	530	1,323
40—50 ...	9,306	5,046	4,260	400	385	15	5,877	3,670	2,207	3.029	991	2,038
50—60 ...	5,088	2,695	2,393	169	162	7	2,300	1,695	605	2,619	838	1,781
60 and Over.	2,706	1,267	1,439	80	78	2	800	630	170	1,826	559	1,267
Hindu ...	*76,263*	*39,506*	*36,757*	*26,514*	*16,464*	*10,050*	*40,473*	*20,009*	*20,464*	*9,276*	*3,033*	*6,243*
0— 1 ...	2,085	1,055	1,030	2,035	1,034	1,001	50	21	29	...	...	...
1— 5 ...	9,633	4,772	4,861	8,915	4,534	4,381	698	225	473	20	13	7
5—10 ...	9,970	5,260	4,710	7,268	4,322	2,946	2,641	908	1,738	61	35	26
10—15 ...	9,053	4,824	4,229	4.847	3,284	1,563	4,114	1,491	2,623	92	49	43
15—20 ...	7,113	3,660	3,453	1,284	1,211	73	5,666	2,367	3,299	163	82	81
20—30 ...	13,080	6,825	6,255	1,113	1,076	37	11,305	5,490	5,815	662	259	403
30—40 ...	10,246	5,229	5,017	484	459	25	8,128	4,297	3,831	1.634	473	1,161
40—50 ...	8,236	4,455	3,781	349	334	15	5,190	3,226	1,964	2.697	895	1,802
50—60 ...	4,463	2,342	2,121	148	141	7	1,999	1,460	539	2,316	741	1,575
60 and Over.	2,384	1,084	1,300	71	69	2	682	529	153	1,631	486	1,145
Jain ...	*2,231*	*1,187*	*1,044*	*907*	*600*	*307*	*892*	*453*	*439*	*432*	*134*	*298*
0— 1 ...	55	27	28	55	27	28	...	...	...	...	...	...
1— 5 ...	216	108	108	216	108	108	...	...	...	...	...	...
5—10 ...	234	128	106	219	123	96	13	5	8	2	...	2
10—15 ...	222	121	101	179	111	68	41	9	32	2	1	1
15—20 ...	188	95	93	60	55	5	119	37	82	9	3	6
20—30 ...	391	208	183	74	72	2	280	126	154	37	10	27
30—40 ...	353	196	157	46	46	...	226	126	100	81	24	57
40—50 ...	313	176	137	36	36	...	153	100	53	124	40	84
50—60 ...	183	98	85	16	16	...	51	42	9	116	40	76
60 and Over	76	30	46	6	6	...	9	8	1	61	16	45
Muslim ...	*6,597*	*3,467*	*3,130*	*2,463*	*1,509*	*954*	*3,395*	*1,715*	*1,680*	*739*	*243*	*496*
0— 1 ...	187	92	95	179	90	89	8	2	6	...	...	...
1— 5 ...	839	395	444	765	385	380	71	9	62	3	1	2
5—10 ...	865	441	424	689	396	293	174	44	130	2	1	1
10—15 ...	783	397	386	494	320	174	283	73	210	6	4	2
15—20 ...	620	325	295	162	151	11	442	166	276	16	8	8
20—30 ...	1,112	607	505	122	118	4	915	457	458	75	32	43
30—40 ...	846	441	405	30	27	3	684	382	302	132	32	100
40—50 ...	697	382	315	14	14	...	483	314	169	200	54	146
50—60 ...	410	240	170	5	5	...	233	180	53	172	55	117
60 and Over.	238	147	91	3	3	...	102	88	14	133	56	77

TABLE VII.—AGE, SEX AND CIVIL CONDITION.—PART B.—BY STATES OR DISTRICTS.—*Continued.*

State or District and Religion and Age.	Population.			Unmarried.			Married.			Widowed.		
	Persons.	Males.	Females.	Persons.	Males.	Females	Persons.	Males.	Females.	Persons.	Males.	Females.
1	2	3	4	5	6	7	8	9	10	11	12	13
KOTAH.												
All Religions.	*685,804*	*355,056*	*330,748*	*284,591*	*168,842*	*115,749*	*324,416*	*160,913*	*163,503*	*76,797*	*25,301*	*51,496*
0— 1 ...	**22,278**	10,896	11,382	**22,230**	10,866	11,364	**42**	29	13	**6**	1	5
1— 5 ...	**77,116**	37,926	39,190	**76,690**	37,727	38,963	**379**	182	197	**47**	17	30
5—10 ...	**84,486**	43,743	40,743	**79,274**	42,573	36,701	**5,085**	1,129	3,956	**127**	41	86
10—15 ...	**80,063**	41,885	38,178	**63,532**	38,228	25,304	**16,190**	3,543	12,647	**341**	114	227
15—20 ...	**66,627**	33,936	32,691	**20,832**	18,425	2,407	**44,496**	14,980	29,516	**1,299**	531	768
20—30 ...	**125,555**	65,340	60,215	**15,216**	14,599	617	**104,075**	48,165	55,910	**6,264**	2,576	3,688
30—40 ...	**95,163**	49,482	45,681	**3,471**	3,281	190	**77,285**	41,312	35,973	**14,407**	4,889	9,518
40—50 ...	**71,871**	38,538	33,333	**2,061**	1,948	113	**47,786**	29,749	18,037	**22,024**	6,841	15,183
50—60 ...	**39,963**	21,396	18,567	**899**	838	61	**20,599**	14,848	5,751	**18,465**	5,710	12,755
60 and Over.	**22,682**	11,914	10,768	**386**	357	29	**8,479**	6,976	1,503	**13,817**	4,581	9,236
Hindu ...	*629,416*	*325,624*	*303,792*	*260,810*	*154,753*	*106,057*	*297,945*	*147,575*	*150,370*	*70,661*	*23,296*	*47,365*
0— 1 ...	**20,349**	9,922	10,427	**20,308**	9,898	10,410	**35**	23	12	**6**	1	5
1— 5 ...	**70,790**	34,779	36,011	**70,406**	34,602	35,804	**341**	162	179	**43**	15	28
5—10 ...	**77,613**	40,217	37,396	**72,779**	39,140	33,639	**4,723**	1,402	3,321	**111**	35	76
10—15 ...	**73,675**	38,570	35,105	**58,316**	35,147	23,169	**15,055**	3,320	11,735	**304**	103	201
15—20 ...	**61,197**	31,167	30,030	**18,967**	16,816	2,151	**41,052**	13,867	27,185	**1,178**	484	694
20—30 ...	**115,275**	59,962	55,313	**13,737**	13,200	537	**95,804**	44,395	51,409	**5,734**	2,367	3,367
30—40 ...	**87,374**	45,394	41,980	**3,200**	3,025	175	**70,871**	37,868	33,003	**13,303**	4,501	8,802
40—50 ...	**65,935**	35,212	30,723	**1,903**	1,804	99	**43,677**	27,108	16,569	**20,355**	6,300	14,055
50—60 ...	**36,542**	19,540	17,002	**838**	787	51	**18,730**	13,493	5,237	**16,974**	5,260	11,714
60 and Over.	**20,666**	10,861	9,805	**356**	334	22	**7,657**	6,297	1,360	**12,653**	4,230	8,423
Jain ...	*5,194*	*2,759*	*2,435*	*2,145*	*1,385*	*760*	*2,192*	*1,106*	*1,086*	*857*	*268*	*589*
0— 1 ...	**161**	85	76	**161**	85	76	...	...	...	...	...	...
1— 5 ...	**479**	233	246	**476**	233	243	**3**	...	3	...	...	...
5—10 ...	**551**	272	279	**524**	264	260	**26**	7	19	**1**	1	...
10—15 ...	**537**	276	261	**433**	258	175	**98**	18	80	**6**	...	6
15—20 ...	**507**	282	225	**175**	173	2	**317**	105	212	**15**	4	11
20—30 ...	**986**	539	447	**184**	184	...	**710**	332	378	**92**	23	69
30—40 ...	**751**	401	350	**87**	87	...	**496**	272	224	**168**	42	126
40—50 ...	**647**	367	280	**63**	63	...	**330**	219	111	**254**	85	169
50—60 ...	**389**	210	179	**24**	23	1	**159**	111	48	**206**	76	130
60 and Over.	**186**	94	92	**18**	15	3	**53**	42	11	**115**	37	78
Muslim ...	*47,068*	*24,531*	*22,537*	*19,732*	*11,636*	*8,096*	*22,345*	*11,261*	*11,084*	*4,991*	*1,634*	*3,357*
0— 1 ...	**1,634**	821	813	**1,627**	815	812	**7**	6	1	...	...	...
1— 5 ...	**5,323**	2,647	2,676	**5,293**	2,629	2,664	**26**	16	10	**4**	2	2
5—10 ...	**5,736**	2,951	2,785	**5,419**	2,874	2,545	**302**	72	230	**15**	5	10
10—15 ...	**5,305**	2,753	2,552	**4,333**	2,563	1,770	**942**	179	763	**30**	11	19
15—20 ...	**4,510**	2,297	2,213	**1,543**	1,334	209	**2,869**	924	1,945	**98**	39	59
20—30 ...	**8,567**	4,468	4,099	**1,208**	1,147	61	**6 953**	3,151	3,802	**406**	170	236
30—40 ...	**6,456**	3,389	3,067	**176**	163	13	**5,409**	2,908	2,501	**871**	318	553
40—50 ...	**4,894**	2,715	2,179	**87**	76	11	**3,480**	2,215	1,265	**1,327**	424	903
50—60 ...	**2,879**	1,564	1,315	**34**	27	7	**1,622**	1,180	442	**1,223**	357	866
60 and Over.	**1,764**	926	838	**12**	8	4	**735**	610	125	**1,017**	308	709
Tribal ...	*2,923*	*1,515*	*1,408*	*1,258*	*737*	*521*	*1,442*	*707*	*735*	*223*	*71*	*152*
0— 1 ...	**99**	50	49	**99**	50	49	...	...	...	...	...	...
1— 5 ...	**397**	209	188	**391**	207	184	**6**	2	4	...	...	...
5—10 ...	**402**	212	190	**377**	208	169	**25**	4	21	...	...	...
10—15 ...	**362**	193	169	**281**	172	109	**80**	21	59	**1**	...	1
15—20 ...	**286**	124	162	**64**	55	9	**215**	66	149	**7**	3	4
20—30 ...	**561**	281	280	**37**	36	1	**499**	232	267	**25**	13	12
30—40 ...	**400**	214	186	**5**	5	...	**348**	190	158	**47**	19	28
40—50 ...	**254**	149	105	**3**	3	...	**178**	124	54	**73**	22	51
50—60 ...	**114**	59	55	**1**	1	...	**63**	46	17	**50**	12	38
60 and Over.	**48**	24	24	...	...	...	**28**	22	6	**20**	2	18

TABLE VII.—AGE, SEX AND CIVIL CONDITION.—PART B.—BY STATES OR DISTRICTS.—*Continued.*

State or District and Religion and Age.	Population.			Unmarried.			Married.			Widowed.		
	Persons.	Males.	Females.	Persons.	Males.	Females.	Persons.	Males.	Females.	Persons.	Males.	Females.
1	2	3	4	5	6	7	8	9	10	11	12	13
KUSHALGARH (Chiefship)												
All Religions.	*35,564*	*17,754*	*17,810*	*19,285*	*10,395*	*8,890*	*14,026*	*6,810*	*7,216*	*2,253*	*549*	*1,704*
0—1 ...	1,166	582	584	1,166	582	584	...	...	...	...	...	...
1—5 ...	5,889	2,804	3,085	5,886	2,803	3,083	3	1	2	...	...	...
5—10 ...	5,627	2,864	2,763	5,494	2,831	2,663	133	33	100	...	...	...
10—15 ...	4,733	2,467	2,266	4,248	2,325	1,923	482	141	341	3	1	2
15—20 ...	2,950	1,502	1,448	1,384	951	433	1,537	585	1,002	29	16	13
20—30 ...	5,640	2,814	2,826	872	722	150	4,602	2,022	2,580	166	70	96
30—40 ...	4,071	2,043	2,028	136	114	22	3,589	1,830	1,759	346	99	247
40—50 ...	2,758	1,392	1,366	52	36	16	2,138	1,218	920	568	138	430
50—60 ...	1,613	772	841	30	19	11	1,022	643	379	561	110	451
60 and Over.	1,117	514	603	17	12	5	520	387	133	580	115	465
Hindu ...	*34,127*	*17,004*	*17,123*	*18,611*	*10,000*	*8,611*	*13,406*	*6,503*	*6,903*	*2,110*	*501*	*1,609*
0—1 ...	1,126	563	563	1,126	563	563	...	...	...	...	...	...
1—5 ...	5,741	2,737	3,004	5,739	2,736	3,003	2	1	1	...	...	...
5—10 ...	5,417	2,754	2,663	5,293	2,722	2,571	124	32	92	...	...	...
10—15 ...	4,544	2,364	2,180	4,081	2,225	1,856	460	138	322	3	1	2
15—20 ...	2,808	1,422	1,386	1,325	901	424	1,455	505	950	28	16	12
20—30 ...	5,384	2,680	2,704	827	682	145	4,410	1,935	2,475	147	63	84
30—40 ...	3,871	1,951	1,920	125	106	19	3,433	1,755	1,678	313	90	223
40—50 ...	2,601	1,304	1,297	48	34	14	2,029	1,147	882	524	123	401
50—60 ...	1,545	733	812	30	19	11	984	613	371	531	101	430
60 and Over.	1,090	496	594	17	12	5	509	377	132	564	107	457
LAWA (Estate)												
All Religions.	*2,790*	*1,445*	*1,345*	*1,054*	*663*	*391*	*1,433*	*693*	*740*	*303*	*89*	*214*
0—1 ...	105	50	55	105	50	55	...	...	...	...	...	...
1—5 ...	338	168	170	335	167	168	3	1	2	...	...	...
5—10 ...	350	189	161	284	173	111	64	15	49	2	1	1
10—15 ...	343	189	154	206	149	57	134	38	96	3	2	1
15—20 ...	279	147	132	58	58	...	217	87	130	4	2	2
20—30 ...	495	244	251	43	43	...	427	195	232	25	6	19
30—40 ...	366	188	178	10	10	...	312	166	146	44	12	32
40—50 ...	262	141	121	8	8	...	174	110	64	80	23	57
50—60 ...	158	82	76	3	3	...	77	59	18	78	20	58
60 and Over.	94	47	47	2	2	...	25	22	3	67	23	44
Hindu ...	*2,546*	*1,314*	*1,232*	*963*	*598*	*365*	*1,320*	*640*	*680*	*263*	*76*	*187*
0—1 ...	91	41	50	91	41	50	...	...	...	...	...	...
1—5 ...	314	155	159	311	154	157	3	1	2	...	...	...
5—10 ...	325	173	152	263	158	105	60	14	46	2	1	1
10—15 ...	315	171	144	188	135	53	124	34	90	3	2	1
15—20 ...	255	136	119	54	54	...	199	81	118	2	1	1
20—30 ...	446	222	224	38	38	...	388	179	209	20	5	15
30—40 ...	339	172	167	9	9	...	291	153	138	39	10	29
40—50 ...	236	131	105	6	6	...	166	107	59	64	18	46
50—60 ...	139	72	67	2	2	...	69	53	16	68	17	51
60 and Over.	86	41	45	1	1	...	20	18	2	65	22	43
MARWAR.												
All Religions.	*2,125,982*	*1,109,912*	*1,016,070*	*926,394*	*564,450*	*361,944*	*956,738*	*473,719*	*483,019*	*242,850*	*71,743*	*171,107*
0—1 ...	63,457	31,425	32,032	62,616	31,099	31,517	808	320	488	33	6	27
1—5 ...	279,735	139,967	139,768	269,908	136,544	133,364	9.501	3,345	6,156	326	78	248
5—10 ...	288,147	153,528	134,619	250,955	140,951	110,004	36,328	12,198	24,130	864	379	485
10—15 ...	258,933	142,520	116,413	191,741	119,782	71,959	65,543	22,101	43,442	1,649	637	1,012
15—20 ...	199,963	107,769	92,194	68,079	58,920	9,159	127,706	47,510	80,196	4,178	1,339	2,839
20—30 ...	349,339	180,813	168,526	53,035	49,360	3,675	279,118	126,549	152,569	17,186	4,904	12,282
30—40 ...	267,606	137,834	129,772	15,517	14,138	1,379	211,660	112,985	98,675	40,429	10,711	29,718
40—50 ...	210,187	112,255	97,932	8,619	8,087	532	137,282	85,095	52,187	64,286	19,123	45,163
50—60 ...	125,950	65,320	60,630	3,828	3,649	179	62,182	43,215	18,967	59,940	18,456	41,484
60 and Over.	82,665	38,481	44,184	2,096	1,970	126	26,610	20,401	6,209	53,959	16,110	37,849

TABLE VII.—AGE, SEX AND CIVIL CONDITION.—PART B.—BY STATES OR DISTRICTS.—*Continued.*

State or District and Religion and Age.	Population			Unmarried.			Married			Widowed.		
	Persons.	Males.	Females.	Persons.	Males.	Females.	Persons	Males.	Females.	Persons.	Males.	Females.
1	2	3	4	5	6	7	8	9	10	11	12	13
MARWAR.—*Concluded.*												
Hindu ...	*1,831,441*	*962,012*	*869,429*	*795,648*	*487,232*	*308,416*	*830,857*	*413,477*	*417,380*	*204,936*	*61,303*	*143,633*
0— 1 ...	**53,979**	26,686	27,293	**53,299**	26,412	26,887	**663**	271	392	**17**	8	14
1— 5 ...	**241,709**	120,918	120,791	**232,979**	117,880	115,099	**8,490**	2,971	5,519	**240**	67	173
5—10 ...	**248,526**	132,884	115,602	**214,955**	121,562	93,393	**32,865**	10,951	21,914	**706**	321	385
10—15 ...	**224,048**	124,104	99,944	**163,878**	103,476	60,402	**58,773**	20,065	38,708	**1,397**	563	834
15—20 ...	**173,837**	94,540	79,297	**58,876**	51,351	7,525	**111,435**	42,028	69,407	**3,526**	1,161	2,365
20—30 ...	**300,216**	156,692	143,524	**45,487**	42,405	3,082	**240,734**	110,188	130,546	**13,995**	4,099	9,896
30—40 ...	**229,937**	119,320	110,617	**13,371**	12,142	1,229	**183,005**	98,151	84,854	**33,561**	9,027	24,534
40—50 ...	**180,775**	97,492	83,283	**7,574**	7,043	531	**118,932**	74,037	44,895	**54,269**	16,412	37,857
50—60 ...	**107,747**	56,886	51,361	**3,364**	3,208	156	**53,493**	37,338	16,155	**50,890**	15,840	35,050
60 and Over.	**70,667**	33,040	37,627	**1,865**	1,753	112	**22,467**	17,477	4,990	**46,335**	13,810	32,525
Jain ...	*113,669*	*52,587*	*61,082*	*48,183*	*28,278*	*19,905*	*44,601*	*19,521*	*25,080*	*20,885*	*4,788*	*16,097*
0— 1 ...	**3,572**	1,839	1,733	**3,527**	1,823	1,704	**45**	16	29	...	...	...
1— 5 ...	**13,124**	6,606	6,518	**12,863**	6,516	6,347	**247**	86	161	**14**	4	10
5—10 ...	**14,080**	7,176	6,904	**13,326**	6,943	6,383	**715**	224	491	**39**	9	30
10—15 ...	**12,305**	6,213	6,092	**10,556**	5,843	4,713	**1,659**	354	1,305	**90**	16	74
15—20 ...	**9,583**	4,359	5,224	**3,158**	2,614	544	**6,066**	1,688	4,398	**339**	57	282
20—30 ...	**18,942**	8,289	10,653	**2,768**	2,629	139	**14,305**	5,365	8,940	**1,869**	295	1,574
30—40 ...	**15,491**	6,703	8,788	**1,015**	968	47	**10,367**	4,989	5,378	**4,109**	746	3,363
40—50 ...	**13,117**	5,738	7,379	**590**	576	14	**6,721**	3,794	2,927	**5,806**	1,368	4,438
50—60 ...	**8,251**	3,526	4,725	**251**	243	8	**3,084**	1,975	1,109	**4,916**	1,308	3,608
60 and Over.	**5,204**	2,138	3,066	**129**	123	6	**1,372**	1,030	342	**3,703**	985	2,718
Muslim ...	*176,863*	*93,234*	*83,629*	*80,470*	*47,792*	*32,678*	*79,593*	*39,864*	*39,729*	*16,800*	*5,578*	*11,222*
0— 1 ...	**5,730**	2,809	2,921	**5,618**	2,774	2,844	**96**	32	64	**16**	3	13
1— 5 ...	**24,288**	12,161	12,127	**23,467**	11,866	11,601	**749**	288	461	**72**	7	65
5—10 ...	**24,921**	13,190	11,731	**22,090**	12,131	9,959	**2,713**	1,010	1,703	**118**	49	69
10—15 ...	**22,059**	11,909	10,150	**16,859**	10,199	6,660	**5,043**	1,652	3,391	**157**	58	99
15—20 ...	**16,169**	8,687	7,482	**5,882**	4,850	1,032	**9,981**	3,717	6,264	**306**	120	186
20—30 ...	**29,502**	15,497	14,005	**4,677**	4,251	426	**23,535**	10,753	12,782	**1,290**	493	797
30—40 ...	**21,690**	11,538	10,152	**1,111**	1,014	97	**17,866**	9,607	8,259	**2,713**	917	1,796
40—50 ...	**15,996**	8,863	7,133	**452**	416	36	**11,387**	7,118	4,269	**4,157**	1,329	2,828
50—60 ...	**9,801**	5,323	4,478	**212**	197	15	**5,503**	3,831	1,672	**4,086**	1,295	2,791
60 and Over.	**6,707**	3,257	3,450	**102**	94	8	**2,720**	1,356	864	**3,885**	1,307	2,578
Tribal ...	*3,241*	*1,653*	*1,588*	*1,738*	*939*	*799*	*1,331*	*663*	*668*	*172*	*51*	*121*
0— 1 ...	**156**	79	77	**153**	79	74	**3**	...	3	...	...	...
1— 5 ...	**518**	241	277	**507**	241	266	**11**	...	11	...	...	...
5—10 ...	**517**	274	243	**495**	267	228	**22**	7	15	...	...	...
10—15 ...	**439**	243	196	**387**	225	162	**50**	18	32	**2**	...	2
15—20 ...	**300**	139	161	**127**	79	48	**171**	60	111	**2**	...	2
20—30 ...	**531**	257	274	**56**	39	17	**452**	204	248	**23**	14	9
30—40 ...	**367**	202	165	**10**	7	3	**325**	183	142	**32**	12	20
40—50 ...	**229**	120	109	**2**	1	1	**131**	108	73	**46**	11	35
50—60 ...	**112**	64	48	**1**	1	...	**76**	55	21	**35**	8	27
60 and Over.	**72**	34	38	...	...	...	**40**	28	12	**32**	6	26
MEWAR.												
All Religions.	*1,566,910*	*807,184*	*759,726*	*623,252*	*372,378*	*250,874*	*777,709*	*386,559*	*391,150*	*165,949*	*48,247*	*117,702*
0— 1 ...	**50,359**	24,973	25,386	**50,263**	24,938	25,325	**96**	35	61	...	...	...
1— 5 ...	**193,223**	93,992	99,231	**188,873**	92,713	96,160	**4,180**	1,224	2,956	**170**	55	115
5—10 ...	**209,541**	110,377	99,164	**176,781**	100,655	76,126	**32,118**	9,479	22,639	**642**	243	399
10—15 ...	**198,691**	107,522	91,169	**132,084**	85,690	46,394	**65,264**	21,241	44,023	**1,343**	591	752
15—20 ...	**154,862**	81,333	73,529	**38,390**	33,723	4,667	**113,327**	46,046	67,281	**3,145**	1,564	1,581
20—30 ...	**264,564**	139,518	125,046	**24,211**	22,722	1,489	**227,851**	111,744	116,107	**12,502**	5,052	7,450
30—40 ...	**194,265**	98,948	95,322	**6,097**	5,735	362	**160,160**	84,797	75,363	**28,008**	8,411	19,597
40—50 ...	**159,168**	81,385	77,808	**4,064**	3,857	207	**108,274**	64,320	43,954	**46,850**	18,208	38,642
50—60 ...	**93,065**	47,131	45,934	**1,742**	1,658	84	**48,844**	33,984	14,860	**42,479**	11,489	30,990
60 and Over.	**49,152**	22,010	27,142	**747**	687	60	**17,595**	18,689	3,906	**30,810**	7,634	23,176

TABLE VII —Age, Sex and Civil Condition.—Part B.—By States or Districts.—*Continued.*

State or District and Religion and Age.	Population.			Unmarried.			Married.			Widowed.		
	Persons.	Males.	Females.	Persons.	Males.	Females.	Persons	Males.	Females.	Persons.	Males.	Females.
1	2	3	4	5	6	7	8	9	10	11	12	13
MEWAR.— *Concluded.*												
Hindu ...	*1,352,029*	*696,380*	*655,649*	*527,863*	*317,352*	*210,511*	*678,924*	*337,448*	*341,476*	*145,242*	*41,580*	*103,662*
0— 1 ...	**43,417**	21,582	21,835	**43,338**	21,553	21,785	**79**	29	50	**...**	...	...
1— 5 ...	**164,893**	80,308	84,585	**161,032**	79,209	81,823	**3,707**	1,050	2,657	**154**	49	105
5—10 ...	**179,940**	94,957	84,983	**149,595**	86,014	63,581	**29,767**	8,723	21,044	**578**	220	358
10—15 ...	**172,409**	93,518	78,891	**111,454**	73,419	38,035	**59,747**	19,558	40,189	**1,208**	541	667
15—20 ...	**134,764**	70,999	63,765	**32,070**	23,547	8,523	**99,939**	41,060	58,879	**2,755**	1,892	863
20—30 ...	**228,826**	120,844	107,982	**20,035**	18,844	1,191	**197,882**	97,584	100,298	**10,909**	4,416	6,493
30—40 ...	**167,265**	85,007	82,258	**4,951**	4,656	295	**137,913**	73,119	64,794	**24,401**	7,232	17,169
40—50 ...	**137,472**	70,001	67,471	**3,329**	3,165	164	**93,117**	55,387	37,730	**41,026**	11,449	29,577
50—60 ...	**80,264**	40,403	39,861	**1,421**	1,353	68	**41,707**	29,194	12,513	**37,136**	9,856	27,280
60 and Over.	**42,779**	18,761	24,018	**638**	592	46	**15,066**	11,744	3,322	**27,075**	6,425	20,650
Jain ...	*66,001*	*34,086*	*31,915*	*27,732*	*17,049*	*10,683*	*28,118*	*13,860*	*14,258*	*10,151*	*3,177*	*6,974*
0— 1 ...	**2,103**	1,040	1,063	**2,097**	1,037	1,060	**6**	3	3	**...**	...	...
1— 5 ...	**6,836**	3,397	3,439	**6,704**	3,344	3,360	**125**	51	74	**7**	2	5
5—10 ...	**7,648**	3,911	3,737	**7,236**	3,783	3,453	**391**	123	268	**21**	5	16
10—15 ...	**7,244**	3,828	3,416	**6,012**	3,552	2,460	**1,179**	265	914	**53**	11	42
15—20 ...	**6,279**	3,282	2,997	**2,143**	1,910	233	**3,954**	1,322	2,632	**182**	50	132
20—30 ...	**11,538**	6,012	5,526	**1,834**	1,766	68	**8,923**	4,035	4,888	**781**	211	570
30—40 ...	**9,147**	4,785	4,362	**810**	788	22	**6,446**	3,459	2,987	**1,891**	538	1,353
40—50 ...	**8,034**	4,201	3,833	**574**	556	18	**4,440**	2,700	1,740	**3,020**	945	2,075
50—60 ...	**4,804**	2,502	2,302	**246**	242	4	**2,033**	1,407	626	**2,525**	853	1,672
60 and Over.	**2,368**	1,128	1,240	**76**	71	5	**621**	495	126	**1,671**	562	1,109
Muslim ...	*53,833*	*28,346*	*25,487*	*20,852*	*12,458*	*8,394*	*28,088*	*14,204*	*13,884*	*4,893*	*1,684*	*3,209*
0— 1 ...	**1,834**	948	886	**1,827**	947	880	**7**	1	6	**...**	...	...
1— 5 ...	**6,377**	3,161	3,216	**6,169**	3,097	3,072	**204**	63	141	**4**	1	3
5—10 ...	**6,893**	3,612	3,281	**5,815**	3,275	2,540	**1,050**	326	724	**28**	11	17
10—15 ...	**6,310**	3,347	2,963	**4,366**	2,732	1,634	**1,901**	598	1,303	**43**	17	26
15—20 ...	**5,074**	2,620	2,454	**1,370**	1,176	194	**3,601**	1,390	2,211	**103**	54	49
20—30 ...	**9,488**	5,010	4,478	**973**	929	44	**8,105**	3,866	4,239	**410**	215	195
30—40 ...	**7,197**	3,816	3,381	**173**	160	13	**6,257**	3,361	2,896	**767**	295	472
40—50 ...	**5,599**	3,063	2,536	**100**	90	10	**4,204**	2,582	1,622	**1,295**	391	904
50—60 ...	**3,283**	1,780	1,503	**41**	37	4	**1,960**	1,372	588	**1,282**	371	911
60 and Over.	**1,778**	989	789	**18**	15	3	**799**	645	154	**961**	329	632
Tribal ...	*94,544*	*48,061*	*46,483*	*46,535*	*25,337*	*21,198*	*42,374*	*20,932*	*21,442*	*5,635*	*1,792*	*3,843*
0— 1 ...	**2,990**	1,392	1,598	**2,986**	1,390	1,596	**4**	2	2	**...**	...	...
1— 5 ...	**15,055**	7,096	7,959	**14,906**	7,033	7,873	**144**	60	84	**5**	3	2
5—10 ...	**15,001**	7,864	7,137	**14,076**	7,550	6,526	**910**	307	603	**15**	7	8
10—15 ...	**12,657**	6,786	5,871	**10,190**	5,947	4,243	**2,428**	817	1,611	**39**	22	17
15—20 ...	**8,683**	4,390	4,293	**2,771**	2,058	713	**5,807**	2,264	3,543	**105**	68	37
20—30 ...	**14,620**	7,590	7,030	**1,339**	1,153	186	**12,881**	6,229	6,652	**400**	208	192
30—40 ...	**10,584**	5,292	5,292	**158**	126	32	**9,485**	4,824	4,661	**941**	342	599
40—50 ...	**8,045**	4,091	3,954	**60**	45	15	**6,481**	3,627	2,854	**1,504**	419	1,085
50—60 ...	**4,691**	2,433	2,258	**34**	26	8	**3,129**	2,000	1,129	**1,528**	407	1,121
60 and Over.	**2,218**	1,127	1,091	**15**	9	6	**1,105**	802	303	**1,098**	316	782
PARTABGARH												
All Religions.	*76,539*	*38,991*	*37,548*	*33,174*	*19,421*	*13,753*	*34,722*	*17,150*	*17,572*	*8,643*	*2,420*	*6,223*
0— 1 ...	**2,244**	1,077	1,167	**2,243**	1,077	1,166	**1**	...	1	**...**	...	...
1— 5 ...	**9,770**	4,798	4,972	**9,651**	4,765	4,886	**113**	31	82	**6**	2	4
5—10 ...	**10,646**	5,547	5,099	**9,508**	5,259	4,249	**1,110**	275	835	**28**	13	15
10—15 ...	**9,927**	5,195	4,732	**7,386**	4,484	2,902	**2,432**	634	1,798	**59**	27	32
15—20 ...	**7,910**	4,024	3,886	**2,249**	1,883	366	**5,473**	2,064	3,409	**188**	77	111
20—30 ...	**12,715**	6,569	6,146	**1,444**	1,334	110	**10,578**	4,995	5,583	**693**	240	453
30—40 ...	**9,928**	4,989	4,939	**381**	331	50	**7,808**	4,169	3,639	**1,739**	489	1,250
40—50 ...	**7,299**	3,797	3,502	**192**	182	10	**4,638**	2,956	1,682	**2,469**	659	1,810
50—60 ...	**3,968**	2,008	1,960	**81**	74	7	**1,853**	1,405	448	**2,029**	524	1,505
60 and Over.	**2,137**	992	1,145	**39**	32	7	**666**	571	95	**1,432**	389	1,043

TABLE VII.

Age, Sex and Civil Condition.
Part B.—By States or Districts.

TABLE VII.—Age, Sex and Civil Condition.—Part B.—By States or Districts.—*Continued.*

State or District and Religion and Age.	Population.			Unmarried.			Married.			Widowed.		
	Persons.	Males.	Females.	Persons.	Males.	Females.	Persons.	Males.	Females.	Persons.	Males.	Females.
1	2	3	4	5	6	7	8	9	10	11	12	13
PARTABGARH *Concluded.*												
Hindu ...	*41,347*	*21,124*	*20,223*	*15,767*	*9,595*	*6,172*	*20,074*	*10,007*	*10,067*	*5,506*	*1,522*	*3,984*
0— 1 ...	1,195	583	612	1,194	583	611	1	...	1	...	...	...
1— 5 ...	4,752	2,338	2,414	4,653	2,312	2,341	95	25	70	4	1	3
5—10 ...	5,250	2,755	2,495	4,389	2,539	1,850	841	206	635	20	10	10
10—15 ...	5,080	2,675	2,405	3,354	2,179	1,175	1,688	479	1,209	38	17	21
15—20 ...	4,494	2,311	2,188	1,034	986	98	3,345	1,333	2,012	115	42	73
20—30 ...	7,172	3,745	3,427	699	657	42	6,036	2,958	3,078	437	130	307
30—40 ...	5,549	2,796	2,753	235	197	38	4,215	2,298	1,917	1,099	301	798
40—50 ...	4,249	2,188	2,061	134	127	7	2,498	1,621	877	1,617	440	1,177
50—60 ...	2,309	1,138	1,171	47	41	6	992	768	224	1,270	329	941
60 and Over.	1,297	595	702	28	24	4	363	319	44	906	252	654
Jain ...	*4,445*	*2,240*	*2,205*	*1,927*	*1,207*	*720*	*1,779*	*836*	*943*	*739*	*197*	*542*
0— 1 ...	129	57	72	129	57	72	...	...	...	...	...	...
1— 5 ...	451	224	227	451	224	227	...	...	...	...	...	...
5—10 ...	547	286	261	527	284	243	20	2	18	...	...	...
10—15 ...	498	264	234	423	255	168	74	9	65	1	...	1
15—20 ...	408	202	206	138	132	6	256	66	190	14	4	10
20—30 ...	738	367	371	132	132	...	554	227	327	52	8	44
30—40 ...	633	302	331	57	56	1	425	215	210	151	31	120
40—50 ...	539	286	253	38	37	1	299	199	100	202	50	152
50—60 ...	337	172	165	24	24	...	120	92	28	193	56	137
60 and Over.	165	80	85	8	6	2	31	26	5	126	48	78
Muslim ...	*3,914*	*2,045*	*1,869*	*1,655*	*974*	*681*	*1,823*	*916*	*907*	*436*	*155*	*281*
0— 1 ...	114	52	62	114	52	62	...	...	...	...	...	...
1— 5 ...	441	213	228	438	212	226	3	1	2	...	...	...
5—10 ...	518	269	249	479	262	217	36	7	29	3	...	3
10—15 ...	466	242	224	376	225	151	86	16	70	4	1	3
15—20 ...	376	195	181	130	112	18	237	79	158	9	4	5
20—30 ...	668	347	321	95	90	5	534	237	297	39	20	19
30—40 ...	559	289	270	17	15	2	465	246	219	77	28	49
40—50 ...	437	237	200	3	3	...	299	193	106	135	41	94
50—60 ...	227	141	86	3	3	...	124	103	21	100	35	65
60 and Over.	108	60	48	...	...	...	39	34	5	69	26	43
Tribal ...	*26,747*	*13,534*	*13,213*	*13,789*	*7,627*	*6,162*	*11,005*	*5,365*	*5,640*	*1,953*	*542*	*1,411*
0— 1 ...	804	385	419	804	385	419	...	...	...	...	...	...
1— 5 ...	4,116	2,017	2,099	4,099	2,011	2,088	15	5	10	2	1	1
5—10 ...	4,322	2,234	2,088	4,104	2,171	1,933	213	60	153	5	3	2
10—15 ...	3,875	2,011	1,864	3,225	1,622	1,403	634	180	454	16	9	7
15—20 ...	2,624	1,312	1,312	943	700	243	1,632	585	1,047	49	27	22
20—30 ...	4,125	2,103	2,022	517	454	63	3,444	1,567	1,877	164	82	82
30—40 ...	3,167	1,589	1,578	72	63	9	2,686	1,400	1,286	409	126	283
40—50 ...	2,066	1,079	987	15	13	2	1,537	939	598	514	127	387
50—60 ...	1,086	550	536	7	6	1	615	440	175	464	104	360
60 and Over.	562	254	308	3	2	1	229	189	40	330	63	267
SHAHPURA.												
All Religions.	*54,233*	*27,907*	*26,326*	*19,375*	*12,033*	*7,342*	*28,736*	*14,077*	*14,659*	*6,122*	*1,797*	*4,325*
0— 1 ...	1,708	846	862	1,697	842	855	11	4	7	...	...	...
1— 5 ...	6,588	3,280	3,308	6,322	3,207	3,115	241	60	181	25	13	12
5—10 ...	6,811	3,584	3,227	5,203	3,079	2,124	1,572	488	1,084	36	17	19
10—15 ...	6,472	3,483	2,989	3,671	2,506	1,165	2,751	950	1,801	50	27	23
15—20 ...	5,226	2,702	2,524	1,087	1,040	47	4,041	1,610	2,431	98	52	46
20—30 ...	9,347	4,865	4,482	804	784	20	8,130	3,913	4,217	413	168	245
30—40 ...	7,184	3,648	3,536	283	275	8	5,873	3,064	2,809	1,028	309	719
40—50 ...	6,008	3,138	2,870	208	203	5	3,951	2,394	1,557	1,849	541	1,308
50—60 ...	3,358	1,706	1,652	81	78	3	1,687	1,207	480	1,590	421	1,169
60 and Over.	1,531	655	876	19	19	...	479	387	92	1,033	249	784

TABLE VII.—Age, Sex and Civil Condition.—Part B.—By States or Districts.—*Continued.*

State or District and Religion and Age.	Population.			Unmarried.			Married.			Widowed.		
	Persons.	Males.	Females.	Persons.	Males.	Females.	Persons.	Males.	Females.	Persons.	Males.	Females.
1	2	3	4	5	6	7	8	9	10	11	12	13
SHAHPURA.— *Concluded.*												
Hindu ...	*50,273*	*25,845*	*24,428*	*17,898*	*11,098*	*6,800*	*26,786*	*13,120*	*13,666*	*5,589*	*1,627*	*3,962*
0— 1 ...	1,586	794	792	1,575	790	785	11	4	7	...	...	...
1— 5 ...	6,143	3,053	3,090	5,905	2,995	2,910	222	50	172	16	8	8
5—10 ...	6,360	3,344	3,016	4,831	2,863	1,968	1,498	468	1,030	31	13	18
10—15 ...	6,038	3,243	2,795	3,379	2,311	1,068	2,614	909	1,705	45	23	22
15—20 ...	4,849	2,502	2,347	980	941	39	3,776	1,512	2,264	93	49	44
20—30 ...	8,637	4,503	4,134	723	705	18	7,541	3,638	3,903	373	160	213
30—40 ...	6,639	3,374	3,265	235	229	6	5,480	2,863	2,617	924	282	642
40—50 ...	5,532	2,894	2,638	180	177	3	3,659	2,222	1,437	1,693	495	1,198
50—60 ...	3,080	1,549	1,531	73	70	3	1,553	1,104	449	1,454	375	1,079
60 and Over.	1,409	589	820	17	17	...	432	350	82	960	222	738
Jain ...	*1,418*	*757*	*661*	*561*	*373*	*188*	*606*	*301*	*305*	*251*	*83*	*168*
0— 1 ...	42	20	22	42	20	22	...	...	...	...	...	...
1— 5 ...	148	72	76	138	66	72	3	2	1	7	4	3
5—10 ...	137	76	61	128	73	55	9	3	6	...	...	...
10—15 ...	134	80	54	107	73	34	27	7	20	...	...	...
15—20 ...	137	70	67	43	39	4	93	31	62	1	...	1
20—30 ...	252	128	124	40	39	1	192	89	103	20	...	20
30—40 ...	221	121	100	34	34	...	134	73	61	53	14	39
40—50 ...	196	105	91	21	21	...	94	53	41	81	31	50
50—60 ...	114	67	47	6	6	...	47	37	10	61	24	37
60 and Over.	37	18	19	2	2	...	7	6	1	28	10	18
Muslim ...	*2,541*	*1,305*	*1,236*	*915*	*562*	*353*	*1,344*	*656*	*688*	*282*	*87*	*195*
0— 1 ...	80	32	48	80	32	48	...	...	...	...	...	...
1— 5 ...	297	155	142	279	146	133	16	8	8	2	1	1
5—10 ...	314	164	150	244	143	101	65	17	48	5	4	1
10—15 ...	300	160	140	185	122	63	110	34	76	5	4	1
15—20 ...	240	130	110	64	60	4	172	67	105	4	3	1
20—30 ...	458	234	224	41	40	1	397	186	211	20	8	12
30—40 ...	324	153	171	14	12	2	259	128	131	51	13	38
40—50 ...	279	139	140	6	5	1	198	119	79	75	15	60
50—60 ...	164	90	74	2	2	...	87	66	21	75	22	53
60 and Over.	85	48	37	...	...	...	40	31	9	45	17	28
SIROHI.												
All Religions.	*216,528*	*111,675*	*104,853*	*95,215*	*56,554*	*38,661*	*100,804*	*50,081*	*50,723*	*20,509*	*5,040*	*15,469*
0— 1 ...	6,580	3,245	3,335	6,364	3,156	3,208	174	70	104	42	19	23
1— 5 ...	29,394	14,733	14,661	28,665	14,519	14,146	721	214	507	8	...	8
5—10 ...	29,166	15,654	13,512	26,577	14,851	11,726	2,556	791	1,765	33	12	21
10—15 ...	26,353	14,573	11,780	20,876	12,894	7,982	5,397	1,644	3,753	80	35	45
15—20 ...	19,967	10,469	9,498	6,962	5,908	1,054	12,719	4,451	8,268	286	110	176
20—30 ...	35.505	17,854	17,651	4,477	4,138	339	29,639	13,289	16,350	1,389	427	962
30—40 ...	26,995	13,332	13,663	714	603	111	23,007	12,008	10,999	3,274	721	2,553
40—50 ...	21,352	10,980	10,372	330	269	61	15,686	9,573	6,113	5,336	1,138	4,198
50—60 ...	13,118	6,959	6,159	166	142	24	7.675	5,489	2,186	5,277	1,328	3,949
60 and Over	8,098	3,876	4,222	84	74	10	3,230	2,552	678	4,784	1,250	3,534
Hindu ...	*193,785*	*101,044*	*92,741*	*85,697*	*51,144*	*34,553*	*91,121*	*45,621*	*45,500*	*16,967*	*4,279*	*12,688*
0 – 1 ...	5,821	2,862	2,959	5,674	2,804	2,870	129	51	78	18	7	11
1— 5 ...	26,745	13,406	13,339	26,051	13,202	12,849	687	204	483	7	...	7
5—10 ...	26,441	14,251	12,190	23,962	13,495	10,467	2,449	744	1,705	30	12	18
10—15 ...	23,871	13,317	10,554	18,718	11,721	6,997	5,082	1,561	3,521	71	35	36
15—20 ...	17,862	9,496	8,366	6,231	5,346	885	11,399	4,054	7,345	232	96	136
20—30 ...	31,558	16,091	15,467	3,958	3,662	296	26.533	12,075	14,458	1,067	354	713
30—40 ...	24,058	12,030	12,028	602	504	98	20,828	10,931	9,897	2,628	595	2,033
40 50 ...	18,853	9,918	8,935	289	231	58	14,183	8,715	5,468	4,381	972	3,409
50—60 ...	11,480	6,228	5,252	141	118	23	6.903	4,965	1,938	4,436	1,145	3,291
60 and Over	7,096	3,445	3,651	71	61	10	2,928	2,321	607	4,097	1,063	3,034

TABLE VII.—Age, Sex and Civil Condition.—Part B.—By States or Districts.—*Continued.*

State or District and Religion and Age.	Population.			Unmarried.			Married.			Widowed.		
	Persons.	Males.	Females.	Persons.	Males.	Females.	Persons.	Males.	Females.	Persons.	Males.	Females.
1	2	3	4	5	6	7	8	9	10	11	12	13
SIROHI.—*Concluded.*												
Jain ...	*15,508*	*6,696*	*8,812*	*6,251*	*3,475*	*2,776*	*6,291*	*2,685*	*3,606*	*2,966*	*536*	*2,430*
0— 1 ...	**516**	258	258	**479**	243	236	**25**	10	15	**12**	5	**7**
1— 5 ...	**1,717**	874	843	**1,698**	870	828	**18**	4	14	**1**	...	**1**
5—10 ...	**1,789**	902	887	**1,750**	883	867	**37**	19	18	**2**	...	**2**
10—15 ...	**1,601**	769	832	**1,430**	734	696	**166**	35	131	**5**	...	**5**
15—20 ...	**1,394**	584	810	**443**	328	115	**908**	246	662	**43**	10	**33**
20—30 ...	**2,639**	1,057	1,582	**309**	287	22	**2,064**	727	1,337	**266**	43	**223**
30—40 ...	**2,024**	786	1,238	**77**	67	10	**1,388**	634	754	**559**	85	**474**
40—50 ...	**1,822**	680	1,142	**32**	30	2	**973**	526	447	**817**	124	**693**
50—60 ...	**1,232**	499	733	**21**	21	...	**512**	339	173	**699**	139	**560**
60 and Over.	**774**	287	487	**12**	12	...	**200**	145	55	**562**	130	**432**
Muslim ...	*6,538*	*3,561*	*2,977*	*2,902*	*1,732*	*1,170*	*3,097*	*1,617*	*1,480*	*539*	*212*	*327*
0— 1 ...	**226**	116	110	**194**	100	94	**20**	9	11	**12**	7	**5**
1— 5 ...	**845**	413	432	**830**	407	423	**15**	6	9	...	...	...
5—10 ...	**855**	458	397	**785**	431	354	**69**	27	42	**1**	...	**1**
10—15 ...	**808**	448	360	**661**	405	256	**143**	43	100	**4**	...	**4**
15—20 ...	**632**	347	285	**238**	204	34	**384**	139	245	**10**	4	**6**
20—30 ...	**1,170**	625	545	**162**	153	9	**955**	443	512	**53**	29	**24**
30—40 ...	**816**	464	352	**24**	24	...	**711**	402	309	**81**	38	**43**
40—50 ...	**600**	338	262	**6**	6	...	**466**	293	173	**128**	39	**89**
50—60 ...	**375**	218	157	**2**	2	...	**239**	172	67	**134**	44	**90**
60 and Over.	**211**	134	77	...	...	...	**95**	83	12	**116**	51	**65**
TONK.												
All Religions.	*317,360*	*164,401*	*152,959*	*125,711*	*74,773*	*50,938*	*157,738*	*78,849*	*78,889*	*33,911*	*10,779*	*23,132*
0— 1 ...	**10,135**	5,036	5,099	**10,065**	5,003	5,062	**68**	32	36	**2**	1	**1**
1— 5 ...	**38,218**	18,884	19,334	**37,152**	18,472	18,680	**998**	386	612	**68**	26	**42**
5—10 ...	**41,166**	21,532	19,634	**35,163**	19,839	15,324	**5,849**	1,642	4,207	**154**	51	**103**
10—15 ...	**37,752**	20,024	17,728	**25,942**	16,522	9,420	**11,578**	3,409	8,169	**232**	93	**139**
15—20 ...	**29,688**	15,150	14,538	**8,126**	6,788	1,338	**20,912**	8,069	12,843	**650**	293	**357**
20—30 ...	**55,763**	28,755	27,008	**6,045**	5,293	752	**46,972**	22,304	24,668	**2,746**	1,158	**1,588**
30—40 ...	**42,139**	21,977	20,162	**1,603**	1,431	172	**34,610**	18,596	16,014	**5,926**	1,950	**3,976**
40—50 ...	**32,242**	17,329	14,913	**996**	890	106	**22,038**	13,685	8,353	**9,208**	2,754	**6,454**
50—60 ...	**18,691**	9,927	8,764	**408**	356	52	**10,098**	7,147	2,951	**8,185**	2,424	**5,761**
60 and Over.	**11,566**	5,787	5,779	**211**	179	32	**4,615**	3,579	1,036	**6,740**	2,029	**4,711**
Hindu ...	*262,680*	*135,975*	*126,705*	*102,345*	*60,994*	*41,351*	*132,220*	*66,003*	*66,217*	*28,115*	*8,978*	*19,137*
0— 1 ...	**8,447**	4,209	4,238	**8,406**	4,193	4,213	**40**	15	25	**1**	1	...
1— 5 ...	**31,808**	15,656	16,152	**30,888**	15,305	15,583	**866**	331	535	**54**	20	**34**
5—10 ...	**34,174**	17,874	16,300	**28,709**	16,344	12,365	**5,336**	1,488	3,848	**129**	42	**87**
10—15 ...	**31,596**	16,807	14,789	**20,983**	13,601	7,382	**10,407**	3,116	7,291	**206**	90	**116**
15—20 ...	**24,836**	12,724	12,112	**6,336**	5,352	984	**17,932**	7,110	10,822	**568**	262	**306**
20—30 ...	**46,123**	23,850	22,273	**4,439**	3,869	570	**39,382**	18,992	20,390	**2,302**	989	**1,313**
30—40 ...	**34,912**	18,224	16,688	**1,237**	1,126	111	**28,677**	15,448	13,229	**4,998**	1,650	**3,348**
40—50 ...	**26,610**	14,268	12,342	**830**	751	79	**18,016**	11,182	6,834	**7,764**	2,335	**5,429**
50—60 ...	**15,165**	7,934	7,231	**334**	297	37	**8,055**	5,646	2,409	**6,776**	1,991	**4,785**
60 and Over	**9,009**	4,429	4,580	**183**	156	27	**3,509**	2,675	834	**5,317**	1,598	**3,719**
Jain ...	*6,868*	*3,608*	*3,260*	*2,655*	*1,658*	*997*	*3,064*	*1,556*	*1,508*	*1,149*	*394*	*755*
0— 1 ...	**201**	95	106	**197**	92	105	**3**	3	...	**1**	...	**1**
1— 5 ...	**675**	323	352	**660**	319	341	**11**	3	8	**4**	1	**3**
5—10 ...	**752**	389	363	**680**	372	308	**65**	15	50	**7**	2	**5**
10—15 ...	**699**	368	331	**527**	323	204	**161**	44	117	**11**	1	**10**
15—20 ...	**645**	350	295	**198**	182	16	**421**	159	262	**26**	9	**17**
20—30 ...	**1,285**	679	606	**222**	215	7	**971**	440	531	**92**	24	**68**
30—40 ...	**998**	531	467	**99**	87	12	**686**	374	312	**213**	70	**143**
40—50 ...	**812**	443	369	**44**	44	...	**444**	284	160	**324**	115	**209**
50—60 ...	**504**	282	222	**21**	19	2	**215**	158	57	**268**	105	**163**
60 and Over.	**297**	148	149	**7**	5	2	**87**	76	11	**203**	67	**136**

TABLE VII.—Age, Sex and Civil Condition.—Part B.—By States or Districts.—*Concluded.*

State or District and Religion and Age.	Population.			Unmarried.			Married.			Widowed.		
	Persons.	Males.	Females	Persons.	Males.	Females	Persons	Males.	Females.	Persons.	Males.	Females.
1	2	3	4	5	6	7	8	9	10	11	12	13
TONK.—*Concluded.*												
Muslim ...	***44,234***	***22,993***	***21,241***	***19,273***	***11,301***	***7,972***	***20,550***	***10,353***	***10,197***	***4,411***	***1,339***	***3,072***
0— 1 ...	**1,355**	665	690	**1,330**	651	679	**25**	14	11	...	...	...
1— 5 ...	**5,215**	2,652	2,563	**5,102**	2,608	2,499	**104**	44	60	**9**	5	4
5—10 ...	**5,759**	3,014	2,745	**5,362**	2,890	2,472	**384**	118	266	**13**	6	7
10—15 ...	**5,018**	2,626	2,392	**4,158**	2,422	1,736	**850**	203	647	**10**	1	9
15—20 ...	**3,819**	1,897	1,922	**1,525**	1,196	329	**2,242**	681	1,561	**52**	20	32
20—30 ...	**7,721**	3,901	3,820	**1,344**	1,176	168	**6,044**	2,587	3,457	**333**	138	195
30—40 ...	**5,832**	3,020	2,812	**264**	216	48	**4,888**	2,582	2,306	**680**	222	458
40—50 ...	**4,465**	2,428	2,037	**117**	91	26	**3,292**	2,047	1,245	**1,056**	290	766
50—60 ...	**2,863**	1,622	1,241	**51**	39	12	**1,731**	1,274	457	**1,081**	309	772
60 and Over.	**2,187**	1,168	1,019	**20**	17	3	**990**	803	187	**1,177**	348	829

TABLE VII.—Age, Sex and Civil Condition.—Part C.—By Cities (All Religions).

Age and City.	Population.			Unmarried.			Married.			Widowed.		
	Persons.	Males.	Females.	Persons.	Males.	Females.	Persons.	Males.	Females.	Persons.	Males.	Females.
1	2	3	4	5	6	7	8	9	10	11	12	13
Alwar ...	*47,900*	*25,584*	*22,316*	*19,118*	*11,365*	*7,753*	*22,661*	*11,839*	*10,822*	*6,121*	*2,380*	*3,741*
0— 1 ...	**1,487**	739	748	**1,487**	739	748	...	...	...	...	...	...
1— 5 ...	**4,885**	2,452	2,433	**4,879**	2,451	2,428	**4**	1	3	**2**	...	2
5—10 ...	**5,046**	2,581	2,465	**4,951**	2,560	2,391	**88**	20	68	**7**	1	6
10—15 ...	**4,754**	2,482	2,272	**4,232**	2,420	1,812	**513**	61	452	**9**	1	8
15—20 ...	**4,759**	2,481	2,278	**1,726**	1,449	277	**2,938**	990	1,948	**95**	42	58
20—30 ...	**9,611**	5,198	4,413	**1,338**	1,271	67	**7,753**	3,678	4,075	**520**	249	271
30—40 ...	**6,723**	3,819	2,904	**277**	267	10	**5,433**	3,135	2,298	**1,013**	417	596
40—50 ...	**4,756**	2,632	2,124	**119**	112	7	**3,259**	2,040	1,219	**1,378**	480	898
50—60 ...	**3,327**	1,809	1,518	**67**	62	5	**1,732**	1,195	537	**1,528**	552	976
60 and Over.	**2,552**	1,391	1,161	**42**	34	8	**941**	719	222	**1,569**	688	981
Bharatpur ...	*30,173*	*16,736*	*13,437*	*12,133*	*7,619*	*4,514*	*13,879*	*7,371*	*6,508*	*4,161*	*1,746*	*2,415*
0— 1 ...	**1,005**	495	510	**1,001**	495	506	**4**	...	4	...	...	...
1— 5 ...	**3,120**	1,589	1,531	**3,092**	1,580	1,512	**24**	7	17	**4**	2	2
5—10 ...	**3,334**	1,834	1,500	**3,120**	1,780	1,340	**207**	50	157	**7**	4	3
10—15 ...	**3,269**	1,842	1,427	**2,597**	1,657	940	**646**	172	474	**26**	13	13
15—20 ...	**3,116**	1,743	1,378	**1,039**	901	138	**1,987**	797	1,190	**90**	45	45
20—30 ...	**6,020**	3,345	2,675	**847**	797	50	**4,744**	2,339	2,405	**429**	209	220
30—40 ...	**4,405**	2,552	1,853	**246**	232	14	**3,377**	1,986	1,391	**782**	334	448
40—50 ...	**2,989**	1,722	1,267	**112**	105	7	**1,788**	1,188	600	**1,089**	429	660
50—60 ...	**1,737**	969	768	**49**	45	4	**744**	545	199	**944**	379	565
60 and Over.	**1,178**	645	533	**30**	27	3	**358**	287	71	**790**	331	459
Bikaner ...	*85,927*	*45,832*	*40,095*	*32,860*	*21,061*	*11,799*	*41,927*	*22,048*	*19,879*	*11,140*	*2,723*	*8,417*
0— 1 ...	**2,319**	1,168	1,151	**2,319**	1,168	1,151	...	...	...	...	...	...
1— 5 ...	**9,304**	4,680	4,624	**9,280**	4,672	4,608	**24**	8	16	...	...	...
5—10 ...	**9,420**	5,119	4,301	**8,283**	4,866	3,417	**1,120**	245	875	**17**	8	9
10—15 ...	**9,304**	5,108	4,196	**6,558**	4,396	2,162	**2,688**	695	1,993	**58**	17	41
15—20 ...	**9,163**	4,982	4,181	**2,681**	2,441	240	**6,206**	2,461	3,745	**276**	80	196
20—30 ...	**17,162**	9,715	7,447	**2,500**	2,359	141	**13,507**	7,018	6,489	**1,155**	338	817
30—40 ...	**11,842**	6,529	5,313	**646**	608	38	**9,178**	5,444	3,734	**2,018**	477	1,541
40—50 ...	**8,589**	4,489	4,100	**343**	319	24	**5,547**	3,544	2,003	**2,699**	626	2,073
50—60 ...	**5,317**	2,553	2,764	**148**	140	8	**2,575**	1,792	783	**2,594**	621	1,973
60 and Over.	**3,507**	1,489	2,018	**102**	92	10	**1,082**	841	241	**2,323**	556	1,767
Bundi ...	*17,991*	*9,179*	*8,812*	*6,113*	*3,756*	*2,357*	*9,067*	*4,590*	*4,477*	*2,811*	*833*	*1,978*
0— 1 ...	**470**	235	235	**470**	235	235	...	...	...	...	...	...
1— 5 ...	**1,607**	764	843	**1,598**	755	843	**9**	9	...	...	...	...
5—10 ...	**1,740**	937	803	**1,587**	897	690	**146**	40	106	**7**	...	7
10—15 ...	**1,646**	869	777	**1,224**	779	445	**410**	89	321	**12**	1	11
15—20 ...	**1,649**	783	866	**428**	387	41	**1,167**	385	782	**54**	11	43
20—30 ...	**3,478**	1,782	1,696	**461**	421	40	**2,751**	1,285	1,466	**266**	76	190
30—40 ...	**2,831**	1,438	1,393	**154**	125	29	**2,133**	1,155	978	**544**	158	386
40—50 ...	**2,336**	1,213	1,123	**93**	75	18	**1,474**	914	560	**769**	224	545
50—60 ...	**1,417**	740	677	**64**	52	12	**683**	480	203	**670**	208	462
60 and Over.	**817**	418	399	**34**	30	4	**294**	233	61	**489**	155	334
Dholpur ...	*19,586*	*10,535*	*9,051*	*7,775*	*4,745*	*3,030*	*9,159*	*4,761*	*4,398*	*2,652*	*1,029*	*1,623*
0— 1 ...	**722**	369	353	**722**	369	353	...	...	...	...	...	...
1— 5 ...	**2,060**	1,033	1,027	**2,060**	1,033	1,027	...	...	...	...	...	...
5—10 ...	**2,218**	1,175	1,043	**2,052**	1,128	924	**164**	47	117	**2**	...	2
10—15 ...	**2,052**	1,128	924	**1,590**	998	592	**456**	127	329	**6**	3	3
15—20 ...	**1,854**	982	872	**557**	499	58	**1,251**	458	793	**46**	25	21
20—30 ...	**3,722**	2,008	1,714	**509**	475	34	**2,981**	1,423	1,558	**232**	110	122
30—40 ...	**2,719**	1,556	1,163	**159**	143	16	**2,129**	1,225	904	**431**	188	243
40—50 ...	**1,961**	1,083	878	**70**	60	10	**1,228**	773	455	**663**	250	413
50—60 ...	**1,321**	697	624	**31**	24	7	**621**	439	182	**669**	234	435
60 and Over.	**957**	504	453	**25**	16	9	**329**	269	60	**603**	219	384

TABLE VII.—Age, Sex and Civil Condition.—Part C.—By Cities (All Religions).—*Concld.*

Age and City.	Population.			Unmarried.			Married.			Widowed.		
	Persons.	Males.	Females.	Persons.	Males.	Females.	Persons.	Males.	Females.	Persons.	Males.	Females.
1	2	3	4	5	6	7	8	9	10	11	12	13
Jaipur ...	*144,179*	*77,933*	*66,246*	*47,995*	*30,387*	*17,608*	*76,576*	*40,658*	*35,918*	*19,608*	*6,888*	*12,720*
0— 1 ...	3,821	1,929	1,892	3,809	1,922	1,887	9	6	3	3	1	2
1— 5 ...	13,432	6,769	6,663	13,142	6,688	6,454	277	77	200	13	4	9
5—10 ...	14,663	7,889	6,774	12,380	7,255	5,125	2,232	615	1,617	51	19	32
10—15 ...	14,256	7,711	6,545	9,569	6,291	3,278	4,584	1,379	3,205	103	41	62
15—20 ...	14,136	7,543	6,593	3,640	3,200	440	10,141	4,167	5,974	355	176	179
20—30 ...	28,120	15,426	12,694	3,235	3,019	216	23,124	11,637	11,487	1,761	770	991
30—40 ...	21,619	12,016	9,603	1,055	956	99	17,188	9,852	7,336	3,376	1,208	2,168
40—50 ...	16,380	9,075	7,305	609	558	51	10,914	6,899	4,015	4,857	1,618	3,239
50—60 ...	10,590	5,735	4,855	346	314	32	5,403	3,859	1,544	4,841	1,562	3,279
60 and Over.	7,162	3,840	3,322	210	184	26	2,704	2,167	537	4,248	1,489	2,759
Jodhpur ...	*94,736*	*52,165*	*42,571*	*39,043*	*24,904*	*14,139*	*44,534*	*24,029*	*20,505*	*11,159*	*3,232*	*7,927*
0— 1 ...	2,736	1,447	1,289	2,731	1,447	1,284	5	...	5	...	...	...
1— 5 ...	11,237	5,688	5,549	11,072	5,643	5,429	158	42	116	7	3	4
5—10 ...	11,057	6,069	4,988	9,672	5,585	4,087	1,342	411	931	43	23	20
10—15 ...	10,527	6,042	4,485	7,754	5,192	2,562	2,685	804	1,881	88	46	42
15—20 ...	9,908	5,632	4,276	3,336	3,005	331	6,331	2,520	3,811	241	107	134
20—30 ...	18,720	10,831	7,889	2,896	2,689	207	14,769	7,760	7,009	1,055	382	673
30—40 ...	13,097	7,561	5,536	878	736	142	10,107	6,184	3,923	2,112	641	1,471
40—50 ...	9,220	5,024	4,196	442	346	96	5,795	3,840	1,955	2,983	838	2,145
50—60 ...	5,159	2,524	2,635	158	132	26	2,392	1,732	660	2,609	660	1,949
60 and Over.	3,075	1,347	1,728	104	79	25	950	736	214	2,021	532	1,489
Kotah ...	*37,876*	*20,259*	*17,617*	*14,021*	*8,994*	*5,027*	*18,108*	*9,506*	*8,602*	*5,747*	*1,759*	*3,988*
0— 1 ...	1,178	571	607	1,178	571	607	...	...	...	...	...	...
1— 5 ...	3,304	1,678	1,626	3,301	1,676	1,625	1	1	...	2	1	1
5—10 ...	3,663	1,970	1,693	3,455	1,931	1,524	202	37	165	6	2	4
10—15 ...	3,736	2,011	1,725	2,956	1,883	1,073	761	124	637	19	4	15
15—20 ...	4,135	2,248	1,887	1,379	1,274	105	2,653	945	1,708	103	29	74
20—30 ...	7,919	4,421	3,498	1,229	1,184	45	6,126	3,031	3,095	564	206	358
30—40 ...	5,747	3,108	2,639	288	265	23	4,272	2,471	1,801	1,187	372	815
40—50 ...	4,506	2,383	2,123	154	140	14	2,610	1,729	881	1,742	514	1,228
50—60 ...	2,428	1,255	1,173	55	47	8	1,084	830	254	1,289	378	911
60 and Over.	1,260	614	646	26	23	3	399	338	61	835	253	582
Tonk ...	*35,798*	*18,201*	*17,597*	*13,645*	*7,947*	*5,698*	*18,003*	*9,106*	*8,897*	*4,150*	*1,148*	*3,002*
0— 1 ...	995	505	490	995	505	490	...	...	...	...	...	...
1— 5 ...	3,860	1,957	1,903	3,803	1,929	1,874	54	26	28	3	2	1
5—10 ...	4,322	2,231	2,091	3,898	2,105	1,793	418	124	294	6	2	4
10—15 ...	3,825	1,959	1,866	2,929	1,705	1,224	887	252	635	9	2	7
15—20 ...	3,001	1,431	1,570	897	714	183	2,058	698	1,360	46	19	27
20—30 ...	6,337	3,179	3,158	800	725	75	5,260	2,354	2,906	277	100	177
30—40 ...	4,932	2,506	2,426	181	152	29	4,153	2,173	1,980	598	181	417
40—50 ...	3,956	2,057	1,899	98	76	22	2,854	1,725	1,129	1,004	256	748
50—60 ...	2,599	1,399	1,200	32	26	6	1,508	1,099	409	1,059	274	785
60 and Over.	1,971	977	994	12	10	2	811	655	156	1,148	312	836
Udaipur ...	*44,035*	*23,775*	*20,260*	*16,128*	*10,206*	*5,922*	*22,736*	*11,901*	*10,835*	*5,171*	*1,668*	*3,503*
0— 1 ...	1,180	619	561	1,180	619	561	...	...	...	...	...	...
1— 5 ...	4,080	2,104	1,976	4,061	2,102	1,959	18	2	16	1	...	1
5—10 ...	4,877	2,694	2,183	4,451	2,578	1,873	418	114	304	8	2	6
10—15 ...	4,749	2,699	2,050	3,692	2,384	1,308	1,037	307	730	20	8	12
15—20 ...	4,391	2,432	1,959	1,331	1,186	145	2,969	1,203	1,766	91	43	48
20—30 ...	8,992	4,839	4,153	1,027	979	48	7,543	3,687	3,856	422	173	249
30—40 ...	6,511	3,522	2,989	212	199	13	5,372	3,011	2,361	927	312	615
40—50 ...	4,908	2,630	2,278	102	94	8	3,367	2,104	1,263	1,439	432	1,007
50—60 ...	2,875	1,483	1,392	46	42	4	1,483	1,052	431	1,346	389	957
60 and Over.	1,472	753	719	26	23	3	529	421	108	917	309	608

TABLE VIII.

Civil condition by age for selected castes.

EXPLANATORY NOTE.

The castes shown in this and Table XIV comprise 35·9 per cent. of the total population of the selected localities. They are representative of every grade of society and are well defined communities in the localities concerned.

TABLE VIII.

Civil Condition by Age for Selected Castes.

TABLE VIII.—CIVIL CONDITION

CASTE, TRIBE OR RACE.	LOCALITY.	SEX.	POPULATION DEALT WITH.	Unmarried.						
				Total.	0—6.	7—13.	14—16.	17—23.	24—43.	44 & over.
1	2	3	4	5	6	7	8	9	10	11
1. Agarwal ...	Jaipur ...	Males.	45,623	22,764	8,194	7,392	2,091	1,753	2,236	1,098
		Females.	45,651	14,670	8,461	5,780	216	107	62	44
2. Ahir ...	Alwar ...	Males.	38,820	20,628	6,427	6,600	2,655	8,061	1,636	249
		Females.	32,460	13,748	6,570	5,493	1,270	333	65	12
3. Bhangi ...	Jaipur ...	Males.	12,043	5,596	2,565	1,987	508	298	196	42
		Females.	11,474	3,947	2,482	1,328	83	24	28	2
	Marwar ...	Males.	7,902	3,760	1,644	1,237	344	281	178	76
		Females.	7,157	2,801	1,697	891	123	44	88	13
4. Bhil ...	Banswara ...	Males.	72,238	42,269	17,881	15,433	4,319	3,377	1,200	59
		Females.	72,687	36,873	18,585	14,290	2,667	988	309	34
	Dungarpur ...	Males.	62,892	34,183	15,441	12,966	3,226	1,833	539	178
		Females.	60,458	28,953	16,115	11,023	1,297	291	149	78
5. Brahman ...	Marwar ...	Males.	56,150	27,926	9,663	8,710	2,935	3,076	2,609	933
		Females.	54,020	17,381	8,736	6,248	1,065	866	160	306
	Mewar ...	Males.	56,046	24,908	9,141	8,409	2,510	2,161	1,958	729
		Females.	53,562	16,304	9,714	5,843	899	117	166	65
6. Chamar ...	Bharatpur ...	Males.	40,984	17,152	8,285	6,420	1,347	696	354	50
		Females.	38,197	12,776	8,310	4,135	256	51	23	1
	Jaipur ...	Males.	120,697	54,528	24,825	20,535	5,058	2,634	1,181	295
		Females.	113,745	38,582	25,406	12,251	578	225	108	14
	Kotah ...	Males.	41,903	19,277	8,218	7,186	2,185	1,226	374	88
		Females.	41,119	15,007	8,631	5,750	451	107	53	15
7. Grassia ...	Sirohi ...	Males.	8,249	4,604	2,127	1,622	440	296	101	18
		Females.	7,755	3,664	1,972	1,334	255	80	20	3
8. Gujar ...	Bharatpur ...	Males.	22,753	11,760	3,963	4,103	1,311	1,164	987	232
		Females.	17,679	5,980	3,503	2,192	230	42	12	1
	Jaipur ...	Males.	104,216	49,309	19,471	17,161	5,217	3,960	2,891	609
		Females.	88,326	27,492	17,711	9,127	340	165	123	26
9. Jat ...	Bikaner ...	Males.	119,683	61,697	21,617	18,732	6,977	7,554	5,335	1,482
		Females.	96,264	35,526	20,058	13,491	1,586	345	42	4
	Jaipur ...	Males.	170,306	80,669	31,052	27,619	8,797	6,502	5,350	1,849
		Females.	143,303	46,075	29,967	15,039	677	257	103	32
	Marwar ...	Males.	151,744	70,028	28,579	21,874	7,807	6,331	4,067	1,370
		Females.	132,189	45,903	27,524	14,248	2,019	915	917	280
10. Khati ...	Jaipur ...	Males.	27,091	13,058	5,313	4,514	1,283	928	775	245
		Females.	25,684	8,099	5,251	2,711	78	28	24	7
	Mewar ...	Males.	13,889	5,942	2,407	2,150	631	426	259	69
		Females.	13,263	3,953	2,432	1,220	125	89	58	29
11. Khanzada ...	Alwar ...	Males.	3,724	1,983	626	654	245	317	124	17
		Females.	3,668	1,420	688	568	116	36	9	3
12. Kumhar ...	Jaipur ...	Males.	47,571	21,138	9,401	7,661	1,906	1,236	752	182
		Females.	44,842	14,055	9,549	4,264	155	89	41	7
13. Meo ...	Alwar ...	Males.	63,127	33,174	11,774	11,040	4,228	4,302	1,681	149
		Females.	54,254	23,416	11,708	8,652	2,082	780	161	33
	Bharatpur ...	Males.	24,752	12,953	4,780	4,693	1,500	1,044	881	55
		Females.	21,723	8,665	4,591	3,398	544	108	24	5
14. Mina ...	Alwar ...	Males.	27,155	14,212	4,958	4,977	1,845	1,625	669	143
		Females.	24,704	9,872	4,889	3,941	772	206	53	11
	Jaipur ...	Males.	137,471	66,658	25,885	24,028	7,080	5,290	3,629	796
		Females.	123,099	42,254	25,445	15,571	864	172	170	32
	Kotah ...	Males.	33,861	16,508	6,114	5,516	1,969	1,797	910	202
		Females.	30,819	11,529	6,131	4,735	529	70	45	19
15. Oswal ...	Marwar ...	Males.	45,435	24,001	9,038	7,930	2,023	2,386	2,013	611
		Females.	51,361	16,795	8,705	6,945	859	169	81	86
	Mewar ...	Males.	25,218	12,420	4,035	3,748	1,453	1,453	1,228	503
		Females.	23,097	7,669	3,891	3,259	244	181	69	25
16. Rajput ...	Jaipur ...	Males.	65,816	35,325	10,086	10,247	4,154	4,599	4,895	1,894
		Females.	47,573	11,494	6,562	4,278	425	121	77	81
	Marwar ...	Males.	104,518	58,143	15,637	15,778	7,397	8,511	7,718	3,102
		Females.	83,356	29,066	13,635	11,982	1,909	657	511	372
	Mewar ...	Males.	66,345	35,348	11,439	11,835	4,275	4,274	2,631	894
		Females.	57,829	19,894	10,789	7,608	749	244	338	166
17. Rebari ...	Marwar ...	Males.	47,013	22,224	8,782	7,505	2,662	2,095	988	197
		Females.	44,530	15,221	8,697	5,218	798	296	174	38
	Sirohi ...	Males.	10,009	4,632	1,724	1,683	682	378	147	18
		Females.	8,802	2,886	1,780	992	97	84	20	13
18. Sondhia ...	Jhalawar ...	Males.	14,520	6,469	2,203	1,967	646	617	729	307
		Females.	12,659	3,076	1,971	1,049	42	7	7	...

Married.							Widowed.							Serial Number.
Total.	0—6.	7—13.	14—16.	17—23.	24—43.	44 & over.	Total.	0—6.	7—13.	14—16.	17—23.	24—43.	44 & over.	
12	13	14	15	16	17	18	19	20	21	22	23	24	25	
18,409	38	376	950	3,583	8,768	4,699	4,450	1	10	20	96	1,260	3,063	1
21,417	64	1,127	2,388	5,332	9,603	2,908	9,564	7	23	53	334	3,461	5,686	
14,175	22	74	194	1,740	8,446	3,699	4,017	...	3	2	47	1,294	2,671	2
14,819	20	142	735	3,555	8,121	2,246	3,893	2	2	8	60	1,003	2,818	
5,762	30	345	394	955	2,892	1,146	685	1	14	11	42	212	405	3
6,243	56	655	789	1,322	2,811	610	1,284	5	5	8	82	408	826	
3,465	57	207	281	609	1,640	671	677	4	8	26	104	206	329	
3,520	63	264	428	985	1,478	357	836	...	7	14	84	279	502	
27,790	...	382	1,071	4,360	14,716	7,261	2,179	...	3	23	108	737	1,908	4
29,599	4	945	2,594	7,460	14,505	4,091	5,215	...	11	26	90	1,465	4,623	
26,563	5	720	1,774	4,546	13,341	6,177	2,146	...	9	16	124	696	1,301	
27,150	17	1,420	3,336	6,414	12,594	3,369	4,355	...	13	27	62	1,125	3,218	
22,700	182	566	1,102	3,484	10,769	6,597	5,524	14	14	110	369	1,510	3,507	5
24,220	211	1,608	2,390	6,390	10,172	3,449	12,419	12	74	204	644	4,498	6,987	
25,422	129	868	1,414	4,081	12,336	6,644	5,716	5	47	160	296	1,556	3,652	
25,090	227	2,310	2,849	5,999	10,526	3,179	12,168	17	93	143	547	4,328	7,045	
20,518	47	1,213	1,764	3,540	10,532	3,422	3,314	...	36	70	209	1,172	1,827	6
20,957	102	2,396	2,497	4,547	9,888	1,577	4,464	1	32	62	97	1,656	2,616	
58,987	138	2,594	4,173	9,208	30,595	12,279	7,182	12	50	74	190	2,076	4,780	
61,017	326	6,876	7,137	12,044	28,372	6,262	14,146	9	71	95	250	4,368	9,358	
20,432	43	298	847	3,385	11,260	4,599	2,194	...	7	30	97	748	1,312	
20,885	75	1,117	2,679	5,184	9,530	2,300	5,227	6	26	45	113	1,810	3,227	
3,426	25	51	131	428	1,768	1,028	219	...	8	8	10	69	184	7
3,682	30	126	282	810	1,845	589	409	4	1	3	9	55	337	
8,943	14	246	390	1,271	4,844	2,178	2,050	...	7	21	90	796	1,186	8
9,215	24	612	868	1,961	4,778	972	2,484	...	28	19	49	747	1,641	
47,180	157	1,947	2,812	6,652	24,854	10,758	7,727	3	45	69	220	2,467	4,923	
48,486	334	5,799	5,290	9,813	22,705	5,045	12,348	6	71	81	204	3,456	8,580	
48,412	71	1,077	2,444	8,618	24,145	12,062	9,574	...	35	48	229	2,337	6,925	9
47,126	116	3,574	5,431	11,599	20,444	5,962	13,612	3	58	120	408	3,603	9,420	
76,910	215	2,977	4,835	11,946	38,119	18,818	12,727	4	61	110	332	3,812	8,408	
79,707	524	9,646	8,886	15,401	35,094	10,156	17,521	15	83	85	220	4,114	13,004	
67,466	1,468	4,748	5,464	12,761	29,077	13,948	14,250	14	85	363	1,226	3,449	9,113	
66,980	1,955	7,769	7,797	16,158	25,089	8,262	19,306	38	166	331	985	5,841	11,945	
12,005	36	386	640	1,769	6,030	3,144	2,028	...	6	13	52	609	1,348	10
13,840	98	1,457	1,505	2,842	6,201	1,737	3,745	4	18	24	59	1,057	2,588	
6,967	75	332	463	1,309	3,235	1,553	980	...	19	41	94	325	501	
7,024	105	806	861	1,584	2,856	812	2,286	3	28	38	167	619	0,481	
1,425	1	6	15	175	796	432	316	...	...	1	7	89	219	11
1,582	3	26	109	419	882	193	666	...	2	2	16	224	422	
23,387	62	899	1,647	3,929	11,691	5,159	3,046	1	23	24	79	829	2,090	12
24,711	135	3,067	2,933	4,957	11,058	2,566	6,076	7	25	32	96	1,712	4,204	
24,951	23	210	802	3,393	15,169	5,854	5,002	...	7	24	191	1,814	2,966	13
25,371	34	320	1,154	6,437	14,350	3,076	5,467	3	3	20	95	1,504	3,342	
9,847	17	145	335	1,301	5,919	2,130	1,952	...	4	28	86	817	1,017	
10,445	...	330	922	2,387	5,865	941	2,613	...	2	12	39	864	1,696	
11,017	13	77	121	1,498	6,774	2,534	1,926	1	6	8	42	523	1,346	14
11,398	5	109	695	2,829	6,491	1,269	3,434	...	5	6	71	1,314	2,218	
61,132	141	1,633	3,196	8,539	32,939	14,684	9,681	7	44	48	215	3,059	6,308	
63,234	229	4,843	6,516	13,188	31,334	7,124	17,611	19	66	86	309	5,564	11,567	
14,964	44	134	379	2,269	8,327	8,811	2,389	2	8	7	58	878	1,441	
15,179	62	523	1,364	3,935	7,589	1,706	4,111	1	7	20	62	1,263	2,758	
16,989	79	378	541	2,865	8,757	4,369	4,445	4	13	34	220	1,300	2,874	15
21,502	107	795	1,939	5,900	9,964	2,797	13,064	4	19	85	541	5,134	7,281	
10,194	45	146	281	1,790	5,257	2,675	2,604	6	9	49	78	782	1,680	
10,414	50	489	1,081	2,880	4,592	1,322	5,014	4	20	36	210	1,770	2,974	
25,155	34	322	519	3,053	13,456	7,771	5,336	2	6	23	102	1,428	3,775	16
24,269	74	1,068	2,919	5,582	12,122	3,224	11,810	4	31	95	376	3,886	7,418	
37,815	552	684	1,221	4,525	19,397	11,436	3,560	4	31	100	523	2,051	5,851	
35,253	210	1,377	3,288	8,942	15,998	5,448	19,037	11	54	329	928	6,629	11,086	
26,860	101	578	1,028	3,946	14,317	6,890	4,137	1	14	49	196	1,354	2,528	
25,708	446	1,639	2,893	6,120	11,882	2,728	12,227	104	58	79	346	3,979	7,666	
21,213	289	1,180	1,434	3,343	10,203	4,764	3,576	7	35	71	185	1,004	2,274	17
21,665	550	2,226	2,261	4,992	8,880	2,756	7,644	12	28	74	265	2,561	4,704	
4,915	28	247	321	737	2,209	1,292	462	1	3	9	8	114	327	
4,588	111	484	455	972	2,016	550	1,328	...	4	3	17	318	986	
6,860	5	253	425	1,188	3,396	1,598	1,191	...	...	9	37	269	876	18
6,665	86	909	762	1,695	2,607	606	2,918	11	16	70	136	1,189	1,496	

TABLE IX.

INFIRMITIES.

EXPLANATORY NOTE.

The infirmities recorded at the Census were insanity, deaf-mutism, total blindness, and corrosive leprosy.

The Table is divided into two parts:—

Part I.—Shows the distribution of the afflicted persons according to age, and

Part II.—Shows the distribution according to locality.

2. No instances of dual-infirmity were returned.

TABLE IX.—INFIRMITIES.—PART I.—DISTRIBUTION BY AGE.

AGE.	POPULATION AFFLICTED.			INSANE.			DEAF-MUTES.			BLIND.			LEPERS.		
	Persons.	Males.	Females.	Persons.	Males.	Females.	Persons.	Males.	Females.	Persons.	Males.	Females.	Persons.	Males.	Females.
1	2	3	4	5	6	7	8	9	10	11	12	13	14	15	16
Total ...	**37,886**	**17,787**	**20,099**	**2,590**	**1,727**	**863**	**3,126**	**1,896**	**1,230**	**31,627**	**13,782**	**17,845**	**543**	**382**	**161**
0—1 ...	**49**	31	18	**2**	...	2	**4**	4	...	**40**	25	15	**3**	2	1
1—2 ...	**77**	41	36	**2**	1	1	**11**	3	8	**63**	36	27	**1**	1	...
2—3 ...	**128**	61	67	**9**	3	6	**17**	6	11	**102**	52	50	...	...	...
3—4 ...	**164**	87	77	**9**	4	5	**29**	19	10	**124**	63	61	**2**	1	1
4—5 ...	**273**	146	127	**42**	26	16	**65**	35	30	**163**	84	79	**3**	1	2
Total 0—5 ...	**691**	**366**	**325**	**64**	**34**	**30**	**126**	**67**	**59**	**492**	**260**	**232**	**9**	**5**	**4**
5—10 ...	**1,362**	824	538	**195**	125	70	**312**	194	118	**845**	499	346	**10**	6	4
10—15 ...	**1,463**	914	549	**219**	147	72	**332**	209	123	**898**	549	349	**14**	9	5
15—20 ...	**1,433**	896	587	**281**	189	92	**284**	196	88	**841**	497	344	**27**	14	13
20—25 ...	**1,531**	939	592	**290**	203	87	**282**	190	92	**932**	531	401	**27**	15	12
25—30 ...	**1,642**	932	710	**288**	201	87	**254**	162	92	**1,057**	538	519	**43**	31	12
30—35 ...	**1,623**	872	751	**248**	181	67	**224**	143	81	**1,107**	517	590	**44**	31	13
35—40 ...	**2,141**	1,010	1,131	**249**	166	83	**229**	143	86	**1,588**	653	935	**75**	48	27
40—45 ...	**2,258**	1,013	1,245	**204**	182	72	**198**	118	80	**1,790**	718	1,072	**66**	45	21
45—50 ...	**2,937**	1,306	1,631	**180**	109	71	**193**	114	79	**2,484**	1,021	1,463	**80**	62	18
50—55 ...	**2,990**	1,341	1,649	**128**	82	46	**159**	93	66	**2,645**	1,116	1,529	**58**	50	8
55—60 ...	**4,245**	1,735	2,510	**92**	59	33	**136**	77	59	**3,976**	1,567	2,409	**41**	32	
60—65 ...	**4,461**	1,777	2,684	**76**	51	25	**128**	65	63	**4,229**	1,642	2,587	**28**	19	9
65—70 ...	**3,114**	1,338	1,776	**25**	14	11	**81**	40	41	**2,998**	1,276	1,722	**10**	8	2
70 and over. ...	**5,995**	2,524	3,471	**51**	34	17	**188**	85	103	**5,745**	2,398	3,347	**11**	7	4

TABLE IX.—Infirmities.—Part II.—By States or Districts.

Agency, and State or District.	Population Afflicted.			Insane.			Deaf-Mutes.			Blind.			Lepers.		
	Persons.	Males.	Females.	Persons.	Males.	Females.	Persons.	Males.	Females.	Persons.	Males.	Females.	Persons.	Males.	Females.
1	2	3	4	5	6	7	8	9	10	11	12	13	14	15	16
RAJPUTANA.	**37,886**	**17,787**	**20,099**	**2,590**	**1,727**	**863**	**3,126**	**1,896**	**1,230**	**31,627**	**13,782**	**17,845**	**543**	**382**	**161**
Abu District ...	13	7	6	1	1	...	5	2	3	7	4	3	...	...	...
Alwar ...	3,883	1,376	2,007	185	119	66	558	342	216	3,095	1,376	1,719	45	39	6
Banswara ...	647	291	356	93	56	37	163	81	82	372	188	184	19	16	3
Bharatpur ...	2,966	1,331	1,635	93	63	30	110	80	30	2,739	1,168	1,571	24	20	4
Bikaner ...	3,258	1,543	1,715	240	167	73	91	65	26	2,892	1,287	1,605	35	24	11
Bundi ...	710	364	346	85	57	28	95	54	41	515	243	272	15	10	5
Dholpur ...	1,334	582	752	44	27	17	192	120	72	1,083	423	660	15	12	3
Dungarpur ...	454	211	243	62	42	20	26	14	12	361	152	209	5	3	2
Jaipur ...	7,576	3,702	3,874	561	412	149	215	157	58	6,739	3,091	3,648	61	42	19
Jaisalmer ...	139	80	59	7	6	1	27	16	11	103	57	46	2	1	1
Jhalawar ...	459	210	249	52	16	36	118	49	69	272	141	131	17	4	13
Karauli ...	695	329	366	37	24	13	134	85	49	519	217	302	5	3	2
Kishangarh ...	462	197	265	38	25	13	14	8	6	410	164	246	...	...	...
Kotah ...	2,679	1,350	1,329	233	147	86	281	165	116	2,284	977	1,307	81	61	20
Kushalgarh (Chiefship)...	105	57	48	19	12	7	33	17	16	48	23	25	5	5	...
Lawa (Estate) ...	16	7	9	...	...	...	4	2	2	12	5	7	...	...	...
Marwar ...	7,589	3,355	4,234	378	258	120	652	380	272	6,440	2,634	3,806	119	83	36
Mewar ...	1,702	868	834	229	146	83	154	96	58	1,308	620	688	11	6	5
Partabgarh ...	261	134	127	31	25	6	39	28	11	154	65	89	37	16	21
Shahpura ...	196	78	118	15	7	8	10	3	7	171	68	103	...	...	...
Sirohi ...	1,322	589	733	77	46	31	50	26	24	1,180	505	675	15	12	3
Tonk ...	1,220	626	594	110	70	39	155	106	49	923	424	499	32	25	7

TABLE X.

Occupation or Means of Livelihood.

EXPLANATORY NOTE.

This Table corresponds to Imperial Table XVII-A of 1921 and is divided into two parts:—

Part I.—Is an Agency Summary.

Part II.—Shows by States, etc. and Cities the total numbers in each class, sub-class, order and sub-order and also in the agricultural groups 1 to 7 of sub-order 1 (a). In order to economise space, the Government of India approved that figures for the remaining groups should be omitted.

The separate figures for Cities given in Part II are included in the State and District figures as well.

The following Groups are blank for the whole Agency and have therefore been omitted in Part I:—

(8) Cultivators of jhum, taungya and shifting areas. (9) Cinchona. (10) Cocoanut. (11) Coffee. (12) Ganja. (14) Rubber. (15) Tea. (25) Silk-worms. (26) Lac cultivation. (29) Gold. (30) Iron. (31) Lead, silver and zinc. (32) Manganese. (33) Tin and wolfram. (34) Other metallic minerals. (39) Precious and semi-precious stones. (76) Toddy drawers. (104) Labourers employed on harbours, docks, rivers and canals.

TABLE X.—PART I.—OCCUPATION OR MEANS OF LIVELIHOOD.—AGENCY SUMMARY.

Total Earners ...	4,204,710
Total Working Dependents ...	1,720,553
Total Non-working Dependents	5,300,449
Total Population...	11,225,712

Group Numbers.	Occupation.	Total following occupation.	As principal occupation.		As working dependents.		As Subsidiary to other occupation.	
			Males.	Females.	Males.	Females.	Males.	Females.
1	2	3	4	5	6	7	8	9
	Classes A. B. C. & D. ...	***6,366,828***	***3,457,237***	***747,473***	***396,874***	***1,323,679***	***385,396***	***56,169***
	Class A.—Production of Raw Materials ...	***4,534,710***	***2,259,669***	***406,300***	***367,559***	***1,232,253***	***229,112***	***39,817***
	Sub-Class I.—Exploitation of Animals and Vegetation ...	***4,526,020***	***2,253,724***	***404,418***	***367,550***	***1,232,109***	***228,430***	***39,789***
	Order 1.—Pasture and Agriculture.	***4,525,729***	***2,253,483***	***404,411***	***367,545***	***1,232,107***	***228,395***	***39,788***
	(a) Cultivation	***4,268,728***	***2,122,624***	***385,358***	***324,364***	***1,209,695***	***190,700***	***35,987***
1	Non-cultivating proprietors taking rent in money or kind	72,073	58,144	4,588	...	...	9,118	238
2	Estate Agents and Managers of owners.	19,601	17,117	1,468	...	...	987	29
3	Estate Agents and Managers of Government (State Court of Wards) ...	300	268	25	...	...	7	...
4	Rent collectors, clerks, etc. ...	2,076	696	15	...	...	1,819	46
5	Cultivating owners	288,057	258,107	10,833	...	...	14,101	516
6	Tenant cultivators	1,895,944	1,616,712	121,742	...	...	139,959	17,581
7	Agricultural labourers and helpers in agriculture	1,995,677	171,580	247,192	324,364	1,209,695	25,214	17,682
	(b) Cultivation of special crops, fruit, etc. (Planters, managers, clerks and labourers)	***4,625***	***2,888***	***1,218***	***19***	***188***	***283***	***29***
13	Pan-Vine	629	512	96	6	9	6	...
16	Market gardeners, flower and fruit growers	3,996	2,376	1,122	13	179	277	29
	(c) Forestry	***16,716***	***6,060***	***5,095***	***327***	***1,185***	***2,372***	***1,677***
17	Forest officers, rangers, guards, etc. ...	1,172	1,105	1	10	...	55	1
18	Wood-cutters and charcoal burners ...	7,108	1,964	2,538	123	297	1,874	812
19	Collectors of forest produce ...	8,428	2,984	2,555	194	888	948	864
20	Collectors of lac	8	7	1	...	...	...	...
	(d) Stock raising ...	***235,659***	***121,910***	***12,740***	***42,835***	***21,039***	***35,040***	***2,095***
21	Cattle and Buffalo Breeders and keepers.	74,671	42,157	2,458	9,011	4,100	15,495	1,455
22	Breeders of transport animals ...	4,331	3,100	64	575	83	502	7
23	Herdsmen, shepherds and breeders of other animals	156,657	76,653	10,223	33,249	16,856	19,043	633
	(e) Raising of small animals and insects	***1***	***1***	...	...	...	...	...
24	Birds, bees, etc.	1	1	...	...	...	...	...
	Order 2.—Fishing and hunting ...	***291***	***241***	***7***	***5***	***2***	***35***	***1***
27	Fishing and Pearling	209	173	2	5	2	27	...
28	Hunting	82	68	5	...	...	8	1
	Sub-Class II.—Exploitation of Minerals	***8,690***	***5,945***	***1,882***	***9***	***144***	***682***	***28***
	Order 4.—Non-Metallic Minerals.	***8,690***	***5,945***	***1,882***	***9***	***144***	***682***	***28***
35	Coal	16	12	4	...	...	...	...
36	Petroleum	2	2	...	...	...	...	...
37	Building materials (including stone, materials for cement-manufacture and clays)	4,107	2,199	1,294	8	70	510	26
38	Mica	18	16	...	...	...	2	...
40	Salt, saltpetre and other saline substances	4,509	3,693	584	1	74	155	2
41	Other non-metallic minerals ...	38	23	...	...	...	15	...

TABLE X.—PART I.—OCCUPATION OR MEANS OF LIVELIHOOD.—AGENCY SUMMARY.—*Continued.*

Group Numbers.	Occupation.	Total following occupation.	As principal occupation.		As working dependents.		As Subsidiary to other occupation.	
			Males.	Females.	Males.	Females.	Males.	Females.
1	2	3	4	5	6	7	8	9
	Class B.—Preparation and Supply of Material Substances ...	*1,146,769*	*748,004*	*198,327*	*16,989*	*66,767*	*105,793*	*10,889*
	Sub-Class III.—Industry ...	*751,272*	*476,276*	*135,760*	*12,073*	*57,089*	*64,161*	*5,913*
	Order 5.—Textiles	*177,529*	*82,398*	*47,151*	*3,640*	*30,254*	*12,158*	*1,928*
42	Cotton ginning, cleaning and pressing ...	16,322	9,552	3,984	184	1,181	1,282	180
43	Cotton spinning, sizing and weaving ...	132,614	57,854	34,211	2,687	26,795	9,478	1,585
44	Jute pressing, spinning and weaving ...	200	137	34	4	...	25	...
45	Rope, twine, string and other fibres ...	4,020	1,718	1,161	99	281	759	52
46	Wool carding, spinning and weaving ...	2,698	1,236	905	41	286	202	28
47	Silk spinning and weaving ...	2	1	1	...	...	...	...
48	Hair (Horse-hair), etc.	461	197	130	5	11	113	5
49	Dyeing, bleaching, printing, preparation and sponging of textiles ...	19,969	11,089	6,413	558	1,566	275	68
50	Lace, crepe, embroideries, fringes, etc., and insufficiently described textile industries	1,243	614	358	62	184	24	1
	Order 6.—Hides, skins and hard materials from the animal kingdom	*46,299*	*32,922*	*3,827*	*608*	*2,061*	*6,709*	*172*
51	Working in Leather	45,463	32,312	3,733	583	1,984	6,679	172
52	Furriers and persons occupied with feathers, and bristles; brush makers ...	9	9	...	...	...	...	...
53	Bone, ivory, horn, shell, etc. workers (except buttons)	827	601	94	25	77	30	...
	Order 7.—Wood	*69,442*	*49,452*	*5,696*	*1,223*	*2,077*	*10,068*	*926*
54	Sawyers	1,346	1,122	121	32	4	66	1
55	Carpenters, turners and joiners, etc. ...	51,541	42,104	557	897	488	7,418	82
56	Basket makers and other industries of woody materials, including leaves and thatchers and builders working with bamboo, reeds or similar materials ...	16,555	6,226	5,018	294	1,585	2,580	848
	Order 8.—Metals	*25,730*	*21,006*	*1,279*	*428*	*693*	*2,169*	*155*
57	Smelting, forging and rolling of iron and other metals	218	175	1	9	6	27	...
58	Makers of arms, guns, etc.	868	738	64	3	13	42	3
59	Blacksmiths, other workers in iron, makers of implements	21,671	17,665	1,095	273	468	2,018	152
60	Workers in brass, copper and bell metal.	2,543	2,042	88	140	206	67	...
61	Workers in other metals (except precious metals)	335	299	19	3	...	14	...
62	Workers in mints, die-sinkers, etc. ...	100	87	12	...	...	1	...
	Order 9.—Ceramics	*71,375*	*46,482*	*12,842*	*1,243*	*5,226*	*5,137*	*445*
63	Potters and makers of earthen-ware ...	69,825	45,301	12,599	1,228	5,187	5,068	442
64	Brick and tile makers	1,479	1,135	224	13	35	69	3
65	Other workers in ceramics... ...	71	46	19	2	4	...	...
	Order 10.—Chemical products properly so-called and analogous	*20,281*	*14,033*	*2,586*	*281*	*840*	*2,416*	*125*
66	Manufacture of matches, fire-works and other explosives	565	428	34	12	19	72	...
67	Manufacture of aerated and mineral waters and ice	117	111	2	1	...	3	...
68	Manufacture and refining of vegetable oils	19,327	13,254	2,530	268	820	2,330	125
69	Manufacture and refining of mineral oils.	7	3	4	...	...	...	...
70	Others	265	237	16	...	1	11	...
	Order 11.—Food Industries ...	*22,798*	*13,175*	*6,929*	*561*	*783*	*1,012*	*338*
71	Rice pounders and huskers and flour grinders	7,203	754	5,685	29	389	94	302

TABLE X.—PART I.—OCCUPATION OR MEANS OF LIVELIHOOD.—AGENCY SUMMARY.—*Continued.*

Group Numbers.	Occupation.	Total following occupation.	As principal occupation.		As working dependents.		As Subsidiary to other occupation.	
			Males.	Females.	Males.	Females.	Males.	Females.
1	2	3	4	5	6	7	8	9
	Order 11.—Food Industries. *Concluded.*							
72	Grain parchers, etc.	1,677	1,053	314	16	189	92	13
73	Butchers	6,166	5,028	537	88	104	400	14
74	Makers of sugar, molasses and gur ...	90	78	...	...	...	12	...
75	Sweetmeat and condiment makers ...	5,305	4,766	140	105	11	279	4
77	Brewers and distillers	1,416	912	80	317	71	35	1
78	Manufacturers of Tobacco	634	427	139	11	19	35	3
79	Manufacturers of Opium	8	8	...	...	...	...	...
80	Manufacturers of Ganja	16	6	8	...	...	2	...
81	Others	283	143	76	...	...	63	1
	Order 12.—Industries of dress and the toilet	***178,135***	***123,134***	***24,976***	***2,248***	***8,909***	***18,064***	***804***
82	Boot, shoe, sandal and clog makers ...	66,981	48,126	5,612	976	3,252	8,788	227
83	Tailors, milliners, dress-makers and darners	34,294	21,549	8,097	336	1,930	2,146	236
84	Embroiderers, hat-makers and makers of other articles of wear	1,618	135	982	25	486	28	12
85	Washing and cleaning	15,574	7,860	4,960	246	1,418	968	122
86	Barbers, hair-dressers and wig-makers ...	48,579	38,854	2,246	520	1,178	5,734	47
87	Other industries connected with the toilet.	11,089	6,610	3,079	145	700	405	150
	Order 13.—Furniture Industries.	***1,246***	***1,130***	***59***	...	***11***	***40***	6
88	Cabinet-makers, carriage painters, etc. ...	1,201	1,101	55	...	11	30	4
89	Upholsterers, tent-makers, etc. ...	45	29	4	...	...	10	2
	Order 14.—Building Industries ...	***57,846***	***39,832***	***11,571***	***370***	***1,367***	***4,069***	***587***
90	Lime burners, cement workers; Excavators and well-sinkers; Stone-cutters and dressers; Brick-layers and masons; Builders (other than buildings made of bamboo or similar materials), painters, decorators of houses, tilers, plumbers, etc.	57,846	39,882	11,571	370	1,367	4,069	587
	Order 15.—Construction of means of transport.	***228***	***176***	***20***	...	***3***	***28***	**1**
91	Persons engaged in making, assembling or repairing motor vehicles or cycles	98	92	3	...	1	1	1
92	Carriage, cart, palki, etc. makers and wheel-wrights	102	70	5	...	...	27	...
93	Ship, boat, aeroplane builders ...	28	14	12	...	2	...	...
	Order 16.—Production and transmission of physical force. ...	***1,203***	***1,159***	***5***	***17***	...	***21***	***1***
94	Heat, light, electricity, motive power, etc., gas works and electric light and power	1,203	1,159	5	17	...	21	1
	Order 17.—Miscellaneous and undefined Industries. ...	***79,160***	***51,327***	***18,819***	***1,454***	***4,865***	***2,270***	***425***
95	Printers, engravers, book-binders, etc. ...	409	342	46	6	...	15	...
96	Makers of musical instruments ...	32	26	3	...	...	3	...
97	Makers of clocks and surgical or scientific instruments, etc.	227	207	2	4	...	14	...
98	Makers of jewellery and ornaments ...	28,245	25,049	1,160	506	421	1,086	23
99	Other miscellaneous and undefined industries (toy-making, taxidermy, etc.) ...	5,025	3,359	1,035	106	360	156	9
100	Scavenging	45,222	22,344	16,578	832	4,084	996	388
	Sub-Class IV.—Transport ...	***57,953***	***47,127***	***3,061***	***441***	***475***	***6,712***	***137***
	Order 18.—Transport by air ...	***17***	***16***	...	...	...	***1***	...
101	Persons concerned with aerodromes and aeroplanes	17	16	...	...	...	1	...

TABLE X.—PART I.—OCCUPATION OR MEANS OF LIVELIHOOD.—AGENCY SUMMARY.—*Continued.*

Group Numbers.	Occupation.	Total following occupation.	As principal occupation.		As working dependents.		As subsidiary to other occupation.	
			Males.	Females.	Males.	Females.	Males.	Females.
1	2	3	4	5	6	7	8	9
	Order 19.—Transport by water ...	***611***	***501***	...	***1***	...	***109***	...
102	Ship-owners, boat-owners and their employees, officers, mariners, etc. Ship-brokers boatmen and tow men ...	295	213	...	...	...	82	...
103	Persons (other than labourers) employed in harbours, docks, rivers, and canals, including pilots	316	288	...	1	...	27	...
	Order 20.—Transport by road ...	***33,284***	***23,969***	***2,429***	***399***	***421***	***5,932***	***134***
105	Persons (other than labourers) employed on the construction and maintenance of roads and bridges ...	259	169	73	...	3	12	2
106	Labourers employed on roads and bridges.	4,698	3,114	1,221	36	102	208	17
107	Owners, managers and employees (excluding personal servants) connected with mechanically driven vehicles (including trams)	260	237	7	...	...	16	...
108	Owners, managers and employees (excluding personal servants) connected with other vehicles	6,458	5,139	50	41	9	1,203	16
109	Palki, etc., bearers and owners ...	117	95	1	10	...	11	...
110	Pack elephant, camel, mule, ass and bullock, owners and drivers ...	15,584	10,181	653	291	209	4,153	97
111	Porters and messengers	5,958	5,084	424	21	98	329	2
	Order 21.—Transport by rail ...	***22,039***	***20,700***	***610***	***40***	***54***	***632***	***3***
112	Railway employees of all kinds other than coolies	17,355	16,593	158	20	51	523	1
113	Labourers employed on railway construction and maintenance and coolies and porters employed on railway premises.	4,684	4,107	452	11	3	109	2
	Order 22.—Post Office, Telegraph and Telephone services ...	***2,002***	***1,941***	***22***	***1***	...	***38***	...
114	Post Office, Telegraph and Telephone Services	2,002	1,941	22	1	...	38	...
	Sub-Class V.—Trade ...	***337,544***	***224,601***	***59,506***	***4,475***	***9,203***	***34,920***	***4,839***
	Order 23.—Banks, establishments of credit, exchange and insurance	***43,956***	***32,218***	***2,100***	***551***	***460***	***8,488***	***139***
115	Bank managers, money lenders, exchange and insurance agents, money changers and brokers and their employees ...	43,956	32,218	2,100	551	460	8,488	139
	Order 24.—Brokerage commission and export	***3,285***	***2,939***	***26***	***48***	***2***	***270***	...
116	Brokers, Commission agents, commercial travellers, warehouse owners and employees	3,285	2,939	26	48	2	270	...
	Order 25.—Trade in textiles ...	***17,083***	***15,411***	***445***	***250***	***219***	***709***	***49***
117	Trade in piece-goods, wool, cotton, silk, hair and other textiles	17,083	15,411	445	250	219	709	49
	Order 26.—Trade in skins, leather and furs	***3,407***	***2,933***	***93***	***22***	***106***	***252***	***1***
118	Trade in skins, leather, furs, feathers, horn, etc. and the articles made from these	3,407	2,933	93	22	106	252	1
	Order 27.—Trade in wood ...	***2,064***	***874***	***650***	***10***	***70***	***408***	***52***
119	Trade in wood (not fire-wood) ...	492	186	15	...	8	283	...
120	Trade in barks	141	31	102	...	...	6	2

TABLE X.—PART I.—OCCUPATION OR MEANS OF LIVELIHOOD —AGENCY SUMMARY.—*Continued.*

Group Numbers.	Occupation.	Total following occupation.	As principal occupation.		As working dependents.		As subsidiary to other occupation.	
			Males.	Females.	Males.	Females.	Males.	Females.
1	2	3	4	5	6	7	8	9
	Order 27.—Trade in wood.—*Concld.*							
121	Trade in bamboos and canes ...	1,137	603	421	3	18	90	3
122	Trade in thatches and other forest produce	294	54	112	7	44	29	48
	Order 28.—Trade in metals ...	***777***	***680***	***18***	***7***	***3***	***67***	***2***
123	Trade in metals, machinery, knives, tools, etc.	777	680	18	7	3	67	2
	Order 29.—Trade in pottery, bricks and tiles	***314***	***184***	***100***	***11***	***12***	***6***	***1***
124	Trade in pottery, bricks and tiles ...	314	184	100	11	12	6	1
	Order 30.—Trade in chemical products	***1,282***	***756***	***255***	***5***	***11***	***239***	***16***
125	Drugs, dyes, paints, petroleum, explosives, etc.	1,282	756	255	5	11	239	16
	Order 31.—Hotels, cafes, restaurants, etc.	***7,653***	***6,029***	***586***	***86***	***422***	***502***	***28***
126	Vendors of wine, liquors, aerated waters and ice	5,744	4,467	479	50	328	399	21
127	Owners and Managers of hotels, cookshops, sarais, etc (and employees)	685	380	87	6	93	63	6
128	Hawkers of drink and food stuffs ...	1,274	1,182	20	30	1	40	1
	Order 32.—Other trade in food stuffs...	***163,214***	***101,612***	***37,915***	***2,255***	***5,111***	***13,898***	***2,423***
129	Grain and pulse dealers	21,565	19,357	516	366	61	1,255	10
130	Dealers in sweetmeats, sugar and spices.	6,431	4,908	938	25	155	801	104
131	Dealers in dairy product, eggs and poultry.	7,867	3,061	2,928	43	537	669	109
132	Dealers in animals for food ...	1,697	1,315	189	5	7	178	3
133	Dealers in fodder for animals ...	31,678	5,752	17,083	42	1,185	6,455	1,161
134	Dealers in other food stuffs ...	91,863	65,069	16,011	1,765	3,127	4,857	1,085
135	Dealers in tobacco	1,582	1,253	209	5	31	83	1
136	Dealers in opium	931	810	84	4	4	79	...
137	Dealers in ganja	100	88	7	...	4	1	...
	Order 33.—Trade in clothing and toilet articles	***11,368***	***9,860***	***386***	***218***	***327***	***572***	***5***
138	Trade in ready-made clothing and other articles of dress and the toilet (hats, umbrellas, socks, ready-made shoes, perfumes, etc)	11,368	9,860	386	218	327	572	5
	Order 34.—Trade in furniture ...	***1,309***	***907***	***248***	***9***	***15***	***122***	***8***
139	Trade in furniture, carpets, curtains and bedding	224	107	72	1	2	40	2
140	Trade in Hardware, cooking utensils, porcelain, crockery, glassware, bottles, articles for gardening, etc ...	1,085	800	170	8	13	82	6
	Order 35.—Trade in building materials.	***824***	***465***	***257***	***7***	***43***	***34***	***18***
141	Trade in building materials (other than bricks, tiles and woody materials) ...	824	465	257	7	43	34	18
	Order 36.—Trade in means of transport	***7,737***	***6,166***	***208***	***84***	***7***	***1,271***	***1***
142	Dealers and hirers, in mechanical transport, motors, cycles, etc ...	256	200	14	...	...	42	...
143	Dealers and hirers in other carriages, carts, boats, etc.	4,363	3,305	112	62	5	879	...

TABLE X.—Part I.—Occupation or Means of Livelihood.—Agency Summary.—*Continued.*

Group Numbers	Occupation.	Total following occupation	As principal occupation.		As working dependents.		As subsidiary to other occupation.	
			Males.	Females.	Males.	Females.	Males.	Females.
1	2	3	4	5	6	7	8	9
	Order 36.—Trade in means of transport.—*Concluded.*							
144	Dealers and hirers of elephants, camels, horses, cattle, asses, mules, etc. ...	3,118	2,661	82	22	2	350	1
	Order 37.—Trade in fuel ...	***31,973***	***8,038***	***13,843***	***149***	***1,880***	***6,011***	***2,052***
145	Dealers in firewood, charcoal, coal, cow-dung, etc.	31,973	8,038	13,843	149	1,880	6,011	2,052
	Order 38.—Trade in articles of luxury and those pertaining to letters and the arts and sciences	***9,167***	***7,470***	***1,074***	***51***	***225***	***331***	***16***
146	Dealers in precious stones, jewellery (real and imitation), clocks, optical instruments, etc.	2,532	2,346	22	20	24	119	1
147	Dealers in common bangles, bead necklaces, fans, small articles, toys, hunting and fishing tackles, flowers, etc. ...	6,445	4,949	1,049	27	200	205	15
148	Publishers, book-sellers, stationers, dealers in music, pictures, musical instruments and curiosities ...	190	175	8	4	1	7	...
	Order 39.—Trade of other sorts...	***32,131***	***28,059***	***1,302***	***712***	***290***	***1,740***	***28***
149	Dealers in rags, stable refuse, etc. ...	58	50	...	...	...	7	1
150	General store-keepers and shop-keepers otherwise unspecified	29,222	25,516	1,166	622	276	1,615	27
151	Itinerant traders, pedlars and hawkers (of other than food, etc.) ...	1,872	1,627	115	79	6	45	...
152	Other trades (including farmers of pounds, tools and markets)	979	866	21	11	8	73	...
	Class C.—Public administration and liberal arts	***301,671***	***232,450***	***35,425***	***2,632***	***5,314***	***24,584***	***1,266***
	Sub-Class VI.—Public force ...	***59,289***	***55,376***	***106***	***301***	***262***	***3,236***	***8***
	Order 40.—Army	***29,046***	***28,351***	***23***	***63***	***...***	***608***	***1***
153	Army (Imperial)	1,412	1,362	3	3	...	44	...
154	Army (Indian States)	27,631	26,989	20	60	...	564	1
	Order 41.—Navy	***2***	***2***	...	...	...	...	...
155	Navy	2	2	...	...	...	...	...
	Order 42.—Air Force ...	***1***	***1***	...	...	...	...	...
156	Air Force	1	1	...	...	...	...	...
	Order 43.—Police	***30,240***	***27,022***	***83***	***238***	***262***	***2,628***	***7***
157	Police	16,927	16,352	11	35	16	513	...
158	Village watchmen	13,313	10,670	72	203	246	2,115	7
	Sub-Class VII.—Public Administration	***71,581***	***62,088***	***2,644***	***209***	***226***	***6,313***	***101***
	Order 44.—Public Administration.	***71,581***	***62,088***	***2,644***	***209***	***226***	***6,313***	***101***
159	Service of the State	601	511	30	3	2	54	1
160	Service of Indian and Foreign States ...	56,04[illegible]	51,684	1,929	114	76	2,312	39
160 (a)	Ruling Princes and Chiefs of Indian States	12	12	...	...	...	...	...
161	Municipal and other local (not village) service	3,257	2,436	644	1	10	120	37
162	Village officials and servants other than watchmen	11,660	7,412	147	91	138	3,818	24

TABLE X.—PART I.—OCCUPATION OR MEANS OF LIVELIHOOD.—AGENCY SUMMARY.—*Continued.*

Group Number.	Occupation.	Total following occupation.	As principal occupation. Males.	As principal occupation. Females.	As working dependents. Males.	As working dependents. Females.	As subsidiary to other occupation. Males.	As subsidiary to other occupation. Females.
1	2	3	4	5	6	7	8	9
	Sub-Class VIII.—Professions and Liberal Arts	***170,801***	***114,986***	***32,675***	***2,122***	***4,826***	***15,035***	***1,157***
	Order 45.—Religion ...	***119,201***	***83,600***	***18,347***	***1,630***	***2,720***	***12,308***	***596***
163	Priests, ministers, etc.	32,433	23,522	2,752	600	695	4,771	93
164	Monks, nuns, religious mendicants ...	71,356	48,850	14,667	891	1,673	4,942	333
165	Other religious workers ...	4,653	2,847	521	95	310	741	139
166	Servants in religious edifices, burial and burning grounds, pilgrim conductors, circumcisers, etc.	10,759	8,381	407	44	42	1,854	31
	Order 46.—Law	***2,221***	***2,127***	***7***	***6***	...	***81***	...
167	Lawyers of all kinds, including Qazis, Law Agents and Mukhtiars ...	1,433	1,879	7	...	...	47	...
168	Lawyers' clerks, petition writers, etc. ...	788	748	...	6	...	34	...
	Order 47.—Medicine ...	***8,732***	***3,055***	***4,779***	***15***	***484***	***219***	***180***
169	Registered medical practitioners including occulists	543	436	82	...	8	19	3
170	Other persons practising the healing arts without being registered. ...	1,456	1,265	18	11	11	150	1
171	Dentists	34	30	1	...	...	3	...
172	Midwives, vaccinators, compounders, nurses, masseurs, etc.	6,663	1,292	4,677	4	470	46	174
173	Veterinary Surgeons	36	32	1	...	...	1	2
	Order 48.—Instruction ...	***6,618***	***5,776***	***437***	***90***	***15***	***295***	***5***
174	Professors and teachers of all kinds ...	5,889	5,180	368	90	15	281	5
175	Clerks and servants connected with education	729	646	69	...	...	14	...
	Order 49.—Letters, arts and Sciences, (other than 44) ...	***34,029***	***20,428***	***9,105***	***381***	***1,607***	***2,132***	***376***
176	Public scribes, stenographers, etc. ...	55	53	...	...	...	2	...
177	Architects, surveyors, engineers, and their employees (not being State servants).	145	126	3	...	...	16	...
178	Authors, editors, journalists and photographers	302	282	2	1	...	17	...
179	Artists, sculptors and image-makers.	1,224	856	257	25	38	48	...
180	Scientists (Astronomers, botanists, etc).	75	69	...	1	...	5	...
181	Horoscope casters, astrologers, fortune-tellers, wizards, witches and mediums.	1,086	920	39	5	1	121	...
182	Musicians (composers and performers other than military), actors, dancers, etc.	29,453	16,726	8,670	307	1,557	1,822	871
183	Managers and employees of places of public entertainments, race courses, societies, clubs	385	301	30	18	8	28	...
184	Conjurers, acrobats, recitors, exhibitors of curiosities and wild animals, etc. ...	1,304	1,095	104	24	3	73	5
	Class D.—Miscellaneous ...	***383,678***	***217,114***	***107,421***	***9,694***	***19,345***	***25,907***	***4,197***
	Sub-Class IX.—Persons living on their income	***6,883***	***3,888***	***1,474***	***124***	***285***	***1,034***	***78***
	Order 50.—Persons living principally on their income.	***6,883***	***3,888***	***1,474***	***124***	***285***	***1,034***	***78***
185	Proprietors (other than of agricultural land), fund and scholarship holders and pensioners	6,883	3,888	1,474	124	285	1,034	78
	Sub-Class X.—Domestic Service.	***91,876***	***61,061***	***19,544***	***889***	***5,292***	***4,274***	***816***
	Order 51.—Domestic Service ...	***91,876***	***61,061***	***19,544***	***889***	***5,292***	***4,274***	***816***
186	Private motor-drivers and cleaners ...	1,461	1,430	3	4	...	24	...
187	Other domestic service	90,415	59,631	19,541	885	5,292	4,250	816

TABLE X.—PART I.—OCCUPATION OR MEANS OF LIVELIHOOD.—AGENCY SUMMARY.—*Concluded.*

Group Number.	Occupation.	Total following occupation.	As principal occupation.		As working dependents.		As subsidiary to other occupation.	
			Males.	Females.	Males.	Females.	Males.	Females.
1	2	3	4	5	6	7	8	9
	Sub-Class XI.—Insufficiently described occupations ...	***198,762***	***97,535***	***73,536***	***2,552***	***11,015***	***11,754***	***2,370***
	Order 52.—General terms which do not indicate a definite occupation	***198,762***	***97,535***	***73,536***	***2,552***	***11,015***	***11,754***	***2,370***
188	Manufacturers, business men and contractors otherwise unspecified ...	1,994	1,700	87	82	11	163	1
189	Cashiers, accountants, book-keepers, clerks and other employees in unspecified offices and warehouses and shops ...	9,779	8,849	493	129	26	221	61
190	Mechanics otherwise unspecified ...	273	218	48	...	...	7	...
191	Labourers and workmen otherwise unspecified	186,716	86,768	72,958	2,341	10,978	11,363	2,308
	Sub-Class XII.—Unproductive ...	***86,157***	***54,630***	***12,867***	***6,129***	***2,753***	***8,845***	***933***
	Order 53.—Inmates of jails, asylums and alms houses ...	***4,973***	***8***	...	***4,740***	***198***	***27***	...
192	Inmates of jails, asylums and alms houses	4,973	8	...	4,740	198	27	...
	Order 54.—Beggars, vagrants, prostitutes.	***80,108***	***53,780***	***12,732***	***1,376***	***2,555***	***8,737***	***928***
193	Beggars and vagrants	79,868	53,770	12,545	1,376	2,553	8,733	891
194	Procurers and prostitutes	240	10	187	...	2	4	37
	Order 55.—Other unclassified non-productive industries ...	***1,076***	***842***	***135***	***13***	...	***81***	***5***
195	Other unclassified non-productive industries	1,076	842	135	13	...	81	5

TABLE X.—Occupation or Means of Livelihood.—Part II.—By State or District and City.

Serial Number	Agency, State or District and City.	Total Population.	Total of all Classes. Total Population. Total Earners (Principal Occupations). Males.	Total Earners (Principal Occupations). Females.	Total Working Dependants. Males.	Total Working Dependants. Females.	Total Non-working Dependant Population. Males.	Total Non-working Dependant Population. Females.	Total Earners with Subsidiary Occupation. Males.	Total Earners with Subsidiary Occupation. Females.	Class A.—Production of Raw Materials. Total of Class A. Total Earners (Principal Occupations). Males.	Total Earners (Principal Occupations). Females.	Total Working Dependants. Males.	Total Working Dependants. Females.	Total following occupation as Subsidiary to other. Males.	Total following occupation as Subsidiary to other. Females.
1	2	3	4	5	6	7	8	9	10	11	12	13	14	15	16	17
	Rajputana ...	***11,225,712***	***3,457,237***	***747,473***	***396,874***	***1,323,679***	***2,030,917***	***3,269,532***	***385,396***	***56,169***	***2,259,669***	***406,300***	***367,559***	***1,232,253***	***229,112***	***39,817***
1	Abu District ...	4,532	1,900	350	...	5	858	1,424	174	17	198	40	...	...	79	10
2	Alwar ...	749,751	247,086	81,747	15,162	91,990	134,013	229,758	29,728	2,694	166,388	17,251	13,691	83,820	17,981	1,749
3	Banswara ...	225,106	45,342	10,048	24,002	51,605	42,639	51,470	7,085	1,435	85,420	5,826	23,766	51,523	4,786	1,273
4	Bharatpur ...	486,954	152,011	24,486	17,110	26,636	94,204	172,507	28,953	2,182	104,196	10,771	16,462	25,414	18,872	1,294
5	Bikaner ...	936,218	239,435	25,280	86,846	127,001	174,872	282,094	22,062	1,526	160,835	8,090	85,669	125,274	8,010	698
6	Bundi ...	216,722	68,664	23,850	6,142	17,708	38,295	62,563	4,764	630	46,035	13,903	5,740	16,529	2,137	323
7	Dholpur ...	254,986	93,146	9,756	2,190	20,916	45,161	83,817	14,405	371	73,923	6,706	1,914	18,909	10,209	238
8	Dungarpur ...	227,544	48,345	3,425	21,226	43,442	44,909	66,197	6,357	227	37,252	1,895	20,214	41,942	8,621	172
9	Jaipur ...	2,631,775	763,582	139,311	135,922	315,245	487,563	790,152	50,671	4,483	430,595	45,873	119,852	272,151	26,435	2,366
10	Jaisalmer ...	76,255	27,998	3,277	469	2,243	13,875	28,393	13,060	967	19,271	875	369	967	11,932	640
11	Jhalawar ...	107,890	37,648	9,658	1,258	5,618	17,612	36,096	4,198	399	24,806	6,060	1,126	5,403	1,753	165
12	Karauli ...	140,525	46,835	4,718	4,977	23,934	24,917	35,144	14,522	776	31,068	2,028	4,584	21,647	9,859	574
13	Kishangarh ...	85,744	23,306	6,232	5,740	8,929	15,858	26,089	3,204	139	13,437	4,356	5,279	8,359	1,778	93
14	Kotah ...	685,804	230,386	96,588	12,015	52,580	112,655	181,580	19,162	2,612	161,669	71,944	11,074	50,296	9,908	1,556
15	Kushalgarh (Chiefship)	35,564	9,278	477	1,027	8,072	7,449	9,261	198	19	8,142	126	999	8,015	53	3
16	Lawa (Estate) ...	2,790	811	166	18	119	616	1,060	19	...	469	60	12	74	4	...
17	Marwar ...	2,125,982	699,185	202,176	11,588	205,080	399,139	608,814	83,768	18,732	456,229	135,205	9,315	195,507	55,926	15,075
18	Mewar ...	1,566,910	522,820	106,922	20,412	239,284	263,952	413,520	65,538	15,541	366,225	52,240	18,406	226,549	35,590	10,911
19	Partabgarh ...	76,539	19,390	5,813	6,074	12,968	18,527	18,767	4,347	2,186	12,979	3,635	5,991	12,953	2,780	2,036
20	Shahpura ...	54,233	18,315	2,947	5,434	10,866	9,158	12,513	3,669	606	7,767	723	5,350	10,563	2,234	425
21	Sirohi ...	216,528	66,672	12,257	12,203	25,046	32,800	67,550	2,646	253	40,952	5,708	11,762	23,377	1,899	44
22	Tonk ...	317,360	99,992	28,489	7,059	34,802	57,350	90,168	6,871	374	63,813	12,985	5,984	32,981	8,821	237
	Cities ...	***558,201***	***190,265***	***45,906***	***5,306***	***5,134***	***104,628***	***206,962***	***7,462***	***728***	***14,845***	***2,609***	***241***	***1,044***	***2,998***	***121***
1	Alwar ...	47,900	15,190	3,146	571	678	9,828	18,492	247	105	1,417	569	27	114	48	45
2	Bharatpur ...	30,173	10,271	1,731	239	107	6,226	11,599	471	53	558	29	7	4	36	...
3	Bikaner ...	85,927	28,772	5,900	241	24	16,819	34,171	2,038	98	2,104	99	1	14	1,438	27
4	Bundi ...	17,991	6,350	2,704	103	30	2,726	6,078	533	24	783	401	7	4	176	7
5	Dholpur ...	19,586	6,460	1,079	265	223	3,810	7,749	999	36	782	103	55	172	561	8
6	Jaipur ...	144,179	47,523	9,381	1,778	2,558	28,632	54,307	1,680	142	4,194	448	91	384	310	22
7	Jodhpur ...	94,736	36,760	9,917	1,075	666	14,330	31,988	301	19	1,852	309	...	1	32	1
8	Kotah ...	37,876	13,233	4,464	320	161	6,706	12,992	467	65	563	105	...	6	152	4
9	Tonk ...	35,798	10,609	3,182	158	303	7,434	14,162	214	31	1,369	385	50	238	57	2
10	Udaipur ...	44,035	15,097	4,452	556	384	8,122	15,424	562	158	1,278	161	3	107	188	5

TABLE X.—Occupation or Means of Livelihood.—Part II.—By State or District and City.—*Continued.*

CLASS A.—PRODUCTION OF RAW MATERIALS.—*Continued.*
SUB-CLASS I.—EXPLOITATION OF ANIMALS AND VEGETATION.

SERIAL NUMBER.	AGENCY, STATE OR DISTRICT AND CITY.	TOTAL OF SUB-CLASS I. Total Earners (Principal Occupations). Males.	Females.	Total Working Dependants. Males.	Females.	Total following occupation as Subsidiary to other. Males.	Females.	TOTAL ORDER 1.—PASTURE AND AGRICULTURE. Total Earners (Principal Occupations). Males.	Females.	Total Working Dependants. Males.	Females.	Total following occupation as Subsidiary to other. Males.	Females.
1	2	18	19	20	21	22	23	24	25	26	27	28	29
	Rajputana ...	***2,253,724***	***404,418***	***367,550***	***1,232,109***	***228,430***	***39,789***	***2,253,483***	***404,411***	***367,545***	***1,232,107***	***228,395***	***39,788***
1	Abu District ...	197	39	...	...	79	10	197	39	...	...	79	10
2	Alwar ...	166,264	17,240	13,690	88,819	17,958	1,748	166,257	17,240	18,690	88,819	17,951	1,748
3	Banswara ...	33,419	5,826	28,766	51,523	4,727	1,273	33,417	5,826	28,766	51,523	4,710	1,278
4	Bharatpur ...	103,958	10,758	16,460	25,414	18,796	1,234	103,953	10,758	16,460	25,414	18,796	1,234
5	Bikaner ...	160,614	8,047	85,668	125,260	7,964	692	160,614	8,047	85,668	125,269	7,964	692
6	Bundi ...	45,972	13,847	5,740	16,529	2,124	323	45,072	13,847	5,740	16,529	2,124	323
7	Dholpur ...	73,884	6,634	1,918	18,895	10,036	221	73,383	6,634	1,918	18,895	10,036	221
8	Dungarpur ...	37,252	1,895	20,214	41,942	8,621	172	37,252	1,895	20,214	41,942	8,621	172
9	Jaipur ...	480,115	45,806	119,849	272,138	26,352	2,365	480,035	45,801	119,849	272,138	26,347	2,364
10	Jaisalmer ...	19,267	875	369	967	11,932	640	19,267	875	369	967	11,932	640
11	Jhalawar ...	24,756	6,038	1,126	5,898	1,746	165	24,756	6,038	1,126	5,398	1,745	165
12	Karauli ...	31,068	2,028	4,584	21,647	9,859	574	31,060	2,028	4,583	21,647	9,859	574
13	Kishangarh ...	13,420	4,356	5,279	8,359	1,778	98	13,420	4,356	5,279	8,359	1,778	98
14	Kotah ...	161,591	70,947	11,074	50,278	9,900	1,550	161,556	70,947	11,074	50,278	9,892	1,550
15	Kushalgarh (Chiefship).	8,142	126	999	8,015	58	8	8,142	126	999	8,015	58	8
16	Lawa (Estate) ...	469	60	12	74	4	...	469	60	12	74	4	...
17	Marwar ...	452,813	184,701	9,315	195,440	55,805	15,073	452,813	184,701	9,315	195,440	55,805	15,078
18	Mewar ...	365,858	52,234	18,406	226,540	35,535	10,911	365,846	52,234	18,406	226,540	35,533	10,911
19	Partabgarh ...	12,970	3,632	5,991	12,946	2,780	2,036	12,969	3,632	5,991	12,946	2,780	2,036
20	Shahpura ...	7,760	728	5,350	10,563	2,232	425	7,760	728	5,350	10,563	2,232	425
21	Sirohi ...	40,884	5,697	11,762	23,877	1,395	44	40,878	5,697	11,762	23,877	1,395	44
22	Tonk ...	68,556	12,914	5,983	82,981	3,759	237	68,467	12,912	5,979	82,979	8,759	237
	Cities ...	***14,682***	***2,500***	***241***	***1,043***	***2,997***	***121***	***14,640***	***2,500***	***241***	***1,043***	***2,997***	***121***
1	Alwar ...	1,412	561	27	114	48	45	1,412	561	27	114	48	45
2	Bharatpur ...	558	29	7	4	35	...	554	29	7	4	35	...
3	Bikaner ...	2,064	99	1	14	1,438	27	2,064	99	1	14	1,438	27
4	Bundi ...	721	350	7	4	176	7	721	350	7	4	176	7
5	Dholpur ...	782	108	55	172	561	8	782	108	55	172	561	8
6	Jaipur ...	4,192	429	91	383	310	22	4,168	429	91	383	310	22
7	Jodhpur ...	1,810	309	...	1	82	1	1,810	309	...	1	82	1
8	Kotah ...	562	105	...	6	152	4	557	105	...	6	152	4
9	Tonk ...	1,369	355	50	238	57	2	1,369	355	50	238	57	2
10	Udaipur ...	1,212	160	8	107	188	5	1,208	160	8	107	188	5

TABLE X.—Occupation or Means of Livelihood.—Part II.—By State or District and City.—*Continued.*

CLASS A.—PRODUCTION OF RAW MATERIALS.—*Continued*
SUB-CLASS I.—EXPLOITATION OF ANIMALS AND VEGETATION.—*Continued.*
ORDER I.—PASTURE AND AGRICULTURE.—*Continued.*

SUB-ORDER I (A).—CULTIVATION.

SERIAL NUMBER.	AGENCY, STATE OR DISTRICT AND CITY.	TOTAL SUB-ORDER I (A).—GROUPS 1-7						GROUP 1.—NON-CULTIVATING PROPRIETORS TAKING RENT IN MONEY OR KIND.					
		Total Earners (Principal Occupations).		Total Working Dependants.		Total following occupation as Subsidiary to other.		Total Earners (Principal Occupations).		Total Working Dependants		Total following occupation as Subsidiary to other.	
		Males.	Females.	Males.	Females	Males.	Females.	Males.	Females.	Males.	Females.	Males	Females.
1	2	30	31	32	33	34	35	36	37	38	39	40	41
	Rajputana ...	**2,122,624**	**385,358**	**324,364**	**1,209,695**	**190,700**	**35,987**	**58,144**	**4,583**	...	...	**9,113**	**233**
1	Abu District ...	140	37	...	...	79	10	2	...	...	...	...	...
2	Alwar ...	158,307	16,383	6,588	80,961	17,167	1,672	6,335	294	...	...	2,217	55
3	Banswara ...	32,635	5,644	23,645	51,409	4,591	1,266	168	21	...	...	36	2
4	Bharatpur ...	98,181	10,574	11,719	25,032	18,124	1,228	3,806	848	...	...	2,116	61
5	Bikaner ...	157,112	7,907	84,131	125,006	5,579	679	2,618	590	...	...	417	1
6	Bundi ...	40,772	18,474	5,446	16,379	1,860	306	195	47	...	...	79	4
7	Dholpur ...	71,214	6,550	1,354	18,758	9,528	217	846	106	...	...	287	2
8	Dungarpur ...	36,686	1,040	13,001	39,925	3,190	122	384	146	...	...	77	...
9	Jaipur ...	412,499	43,236	103,008	262,728	26,195	2,258	16,675	755	...	...	917	17
10	Jaisalmer ...	8,877	235	41	189	4,698	31	312	22	...	...	220	...
11	Jhalawar ...	23,247	5,956	796	5,894	1,628	168	130	22	...	...	69	1
12	Karauli ...	29,140	1,887	3,148	21,135	5,952	498	1,192	111	...	...	358	11
13	Kishangarh ...	12,800	4,292	4,740	8,202	1,679	73	1,021	70	...	...	133	1
14	Kotah ...	145,602	68,566	10,515	50,118	8,709	1,206	4,648	286	...	...	423	13
15	Kushalgarh (Chiefship).	8,122	123	822	7,939	49	3	8	1	...	...	8	...
16	Lawa (Estate) ...	457	60	11	74	4	...	10	5	...	...	1	...
17	Marwar ..	421,434	130,095	8,497	194,488	42,774	14,122	13,120	1,090	...	...	1,118	35
18	Mewar ...	353,448	48,384	15,211	232,783	31,685	10,505	5,590	498	...	...	467	14
19	Partabgarh ...	11,932	2,423	5,303	12,495	1,366	930	278	54	...	...	64	4
20	Shahpura ...	7,172	651	5,276	10,555	2,129	424	160	26	...	...	104	9
21	Sirohi ...	34,171	5,476	11,655	23,325	1,257	42	397	5	...	...	3	...
22	Tonk ...	59,176	12,365	4,462	32,800	3,457	237	299	91	...	...	4	3
	Cities ...	**12,282**	**1,897**	**221**	**988**	**2,903**	**73**	**2,188**	**226**	...	...	**628**	**4**
1	Alwar ...	1,247	521	21	108	31	5	98	8	...	...	10	1
2	Bharatpur ...	408	29	3	3	32	...	124	13	...	...	6	...
3	Bikaner ...	1,752	88	1	14	1,418	27	141	5	...	...	291	...
4	Bundi ...	568	319	7	4	178	6	73	21	...	...	24	...
5	Dholpur ...	629	100	55	172	546	7	90	11	...	...	71	...
6	Jaipur ...	3,737	361	81	336	286	21	558	37	...	...	52	1
7	Jodhpur ...	1,368	57	...	1	30	...	578	24	...	...	8	...
8	Kotah ...	483	70	...	5	151	...	87	32	...	...	53	...
9	Tonk ...	1,107	242	50	238	50	2	106	38	...	...	...	2
10	Udaipur ...	1,083	110	3	107	186	5	333	37	...	...	118	...

TABLE X.—Occupation or Means of Livelihood.—Part II.—By State or District and City.—*Continued.*

CLASS A.—PRODUCTION OF RAW MATERIALS.—*Continued.*
SUB-CLASS I.—EXPLOITATION OF ANIMALS AND VEGETATION.—*Continued.*
ORDER I.—PASTURE AND AGRICULTURE.—*Continued.*

SUB-ORDER I (A).—CULTIVATION.—*Continued.*

Serial Number.	Agency, State or District and City.	Group 2.—Estate Agents and Managers of Owners. Total Earners (Principal Occupations). Males.	Females.	Total Working Dependants. Males.	Females.	Total following occupation as Subsidiary to other. Males.	Females.	Group 3.—Estate Agents and Managers of Government (State Court of Wards). Total Earners (Principal Occupations). Males.	Females.	Total Working Dependants. Males.	Females.	Total following occupation as Subsidiary to other. Males.	Females.
1	2	42	43	44	45	46	47	48	49	50	51	52	53
	Rajputana ...	***17,117***	***1,468***	...	...	***987***	***29***	***268***	***25***	...	...	***7***	...
1	Abu District ...	...	...	...	...	...	...	...	...	...	...	...	...
2	Alwar ...	72	7	...	...	2	...	...	...	...	...	...	...
3	Banswara ...	665	12	...	...	82	...	16	...	...	...	...	...
4	Bharatpur ...	...	...	...	...	...	...	...	...	...	...	...	...
5	Bikaner ...	74	9	...	...	5	...	20	...	...	...	3	...
6	Bundi ...	5	1	...	...	...	...	...	21	...	...	...	...
7	Dholpur ...	...	...	...	...	...	...	...	...	...	...	...	...
8	Dungarpur ...	163	32	...	...	72	...	4	...	...	...	...	...
9	Jaipur ...	10,785	974	...	...	494	6	175	4	...	...	4	...
10	Jaisalmer ...	...	...	...	...	...	...	...	...	...	...	...	...
11	Jhalawar ...	58	15	...	...	7	...	4	...	...	...	...	...
12	Karauli ...	63	...	...	...	12	...	...	...	...	...	...	...
13	Kishangarh ...	...	...	...	...	...	...	...	...	...	...	...	...
14	Kotah ...	1,539	104	...	...	125	...	34	...	...	...	...	...
15	Kushalgarh (Chiefship).	...	...	...	...	...	...	...	...	...	...	...	...
16	Lawa (Estate) ...	...	...	...	...	...	...	...	...	...	...	...	...
17	Marwar ...	890	...	...	...	...	...	4	...	...	...	...	...
18	Mewar ...	2,660	313	...	...	178	23	...	...	...	...	...	...
19	Partabgarh ...	43	...	...	...	9	...	5	...	...	...	...	...
20	Shahpura ...	8	...	...	...	1	...	5	...	...	...	...	...
21	Sirohi ...	...	...	...	...	...	...	...	...	...	...	...	...
22	Tonk ...	92	1	...	...	...	...	1	...	...	...	...	...
	Cities ...	***1,874***	***142***	...	...	***19***	...	***20***	***4***	...	...	...	...
1	Alwar ...	10	...	...	...	...	...	...	...	...	...	...	...
2	Bharatpur ...	...	...	...	...	...	...	...	...	...	...	...	...
3	Bikaner ...	16	...	...	...	...	...	4	...	...	...	...	...
4	Bundi ...	...	...	...	...	...	...	...	...	...	...	...	...
5	Dholpur ...	...	...	...	...	...	...	...	...	...	...	...	...
6	Jaipur ...	1,700	142	...	...	18	...	14	4	...	...	...	...
7	Jodhpur ...	19	...	...	...	...	...	...	...	...	...	...	...
8	Kotah ...	...	...	...	...	...	...	2	...	...	...	...	...
9	Tonk ...	34	...	...	...	...	...	...	...	...	...	...	...
10	Udaipur ...	95	...	...	...	1	...	...	...	...	...	...	...

TABLE X.—Occupation or Means of Livelihood.—Part II.—By State or District and City.—*Continued.*

CLASS A.—PRODUCTION OF RAW MATERIALS.—*Continued.*
SUB-CLASS I.—EXPLOITATION OF ANIMALS AND VEGETATION.—*Continued.*
ORDER I.—PASTURE AND AGRICULTURE.—*Continued.*

Sub-Order I (A). Cultivation.—*Continued.*

Serial Number.	Agency, State or District and City.	Group 4.—Rent Collectors, Clerks, Etc.						Group 5.—Cultivating Owners.					
		Total Earners (Principal Occupations).		Total Working Dependants.		Total following occupation as Subsidiary to other.		Total Earners (Principal Occupations).		Total Working Dependants.		Total following occupation as Subsidiary to other.	
		Males.	Females.	Males.	Females.	Males.	Females.	Males.	Females.	Males.	Females.	Males.	Females.
1	2	54	55	56	57	58	59	60	61	62	63	64	65
	Rajputana ...	**696**	**15**	...	...	**1,319**	**46**	**258,107**	**10,333**	...	...	**14,101**	**516**
1	Abu District ...	...	...	...	...	...	...	42	8	...	...	1	...
2	Alwar ...	...	...	...	...	...	...	34,012	920	...	...	1,305	19
3	Banswara ...	...	...	...	...	...	...	105	58	...	...	77	4
4	Bharatpur ...	...	...	...	...	...	...	34,857	899	...	...	1,147	38
5	Bikaner ...	...	...	...	...	...	...	8,912	272	...	...	278	25
6	Bundi ...	...	...	...	...	...	...	22	5	...	...	7	...
7	Dholpur ...	...	...	...	...	...	...	8,078	155	...	...	1,092	3
8	Dungarpur ...	20	...	...	...	...	...	18,062	5	...	...	1,560	35
9	Jaipur ...	647	15	...	...	1,819	46	11,074	189	...	...	877	28
10	Jaisalmer ...	...	...	...	...	...	...	2,454	24	...	...	684	4
11	Jhalawar ...	...	...	...	...	...	...	295	10	...	...	88	...
12	Karauli ...	...	...	...	...	...	...	876	129	...	...	550	24
13	Kishangarh ...	...	...	...	...	...	...	...	...	...	...	...	...
14	Kotah ...	...	...	...	...	...	...	76,851	5,877	...	...	3,927	260
15	Kushalgarh (Chiefship).	10	...	...	...	...	...	6	...	...	...	1	1
16	Lawa (Estate) ...	...	...	...	...	...	...	...	...	...	...	...	...
17	Marwar ...	...	...	...	...	...	...	44,444	1,188	...	...	1,074	12
18	Mewar ...	19	...	...	...	...	...	17,849	1,125	...	...	1,770	66
19	Partabgarh ...	...	...	...	...	...	...	812	11	...	...	167	2
20	Shahpura ...	...	...	...	...	...	...	46	8	...	...	88	...
21	Sirohi ...	...	...	...	...	...	...	288	8	...	...	15	...
22	Tonk ...	...	...	...	...	...	...	27	7	...	...	3	...
	Cities ...	**6**	...	...	...	...	...	**364**	**19**	...	...	**80**	**8**
1	Alwar ...	...	...	...	...	...	...	36	...	...	...	...	...
2	Bharatpur ...	...	...	...	...	...	...	7	1	...	...	1	...
3	Bikaner ...	...	...	...	...	...	...	6	...	...	...	...	...
4	Bundi ...	...	...	...	...	...	...	...	...	...	...	...	...
5	Dholpur ...	...	...	...	...	...	...	2	4	...	...	54	...
6	Jaipur ...	6	...	...	...	...	...	124	7	...	...	1	8
7	Jodhpur ...	...	...	...	...	...	...	91	...	...	...	13	...
8	Kotah ...	...	...	...	...	...	...	48	...	...	...	8	...
9	Tonk ...	...	...	...	...	...	...	15	5	...	...	...	...
10	Udaipur ...	...	...	...	...	...	...	40	2	...	...	8	...

TABLE X.—OCCUPATION OR MEANS OF LIVELIHOOD.—PART II.—BY STATE OR DISTRICT AND CITY.—*Continued.*

CLASS A.—PRODUCTION OF RAW MATERIALS.—*Continued.*
SUB-CLASS I.—EXPLOITATION OF ANIMALS AND VEGETATION.—*Continued.*
ORDER I.—PASTURE AND AGRICULTURE.—*Continued.*

SUB-ORDER I.—(A) CULTIVATION.—*Continued.*

SERIAL NUMBER.	AGENCY, STATE OR DISTRICT AND CITY.	GROUP 6.—TENANT CULTIVATORS.						GROUP 7.—AGRICULTURAL LABOURERS & HELPERS IN AGRICULTURE.					
		Total Earners (Principal Occupations).		Total Working Dependants.		Total following occupation as subsidiary to other.		Total Earners (Principal Occupations).		Total Working Dependants.		Total following occupation as Subsidiary to other.	
		Males.	Females.	Males.	Females.	Males.	Females.	Males.	Females.	Males.	Females.	Males.	Females.
1	2	66	67	68	69	70	71	72	73	74	75	76	77
	Rajputana ...	***1,616,712***	***121,742***	...	...	***139,959***	***17,531***	***171,580***	***247,192***	***324,364***	***1,209,695***	***25,214***	***17,632***
1	Abu District ...	96	34	...	...	78	10	...	...	...	...	...	...
2	Alwar ...	85,701	5,841	...	...	9,909	228	32,187	9,821	6,588	80,961	4,441	1,875
3	Banswara ...	80,157	1,054	...	...	4,218	720	1,524	4,504	23,645	51,400	178	681
4	Bharatpur ...	46,040	1,457	...	...	10,819	161	18,478	7,875	11,719	25,032	4,542	978
5	Bikaner ...	140,233	6,151	...	...	4,476	214	5,255	885	84,131	125,006	405	439
6	Bundi ...	84,871	2,613	...	...	1,468	44	5,679	10,787	5,446	16,379	306	258
7	Dholpur ...	59,205	4,771	...	...	6,605	72	3,085	1,518	1,354	18,758	1,544	140
8	Dungarpur ...	17,460	...	...	...	1,806	...	643	857	18,001	39,925	175	87
9	Jaipur ...	357,559	15,166	...	...	20,558	876	15,684	26,133	103,003	262,728	1,536	1,290
10	Jaisalmer ...	5,823	108	...	...	3,758	24	288	81	41	189	86	8
11	Jhalawar ...	19,548	435	...	...	948	14	8,212	5,474	796	5,894	516	148
12	Karauli ...	26,695	955	...	...	4,896	802	814	692	3,148	21,135	636	161
13	Kishangarh ...	9,188	2,860	...	...	1,171	5	2,091	1,862	4,740	8,202	375	67
14	Kotah ...	21,417	3,141	...	...	2,059	92	41,118	59,658	10,515	50,118	2,175	841
15	Kushalgarh (Chiefship).	8,084	89	...	...	30	...	64	33	822	7,939	1	2
16	Lawa (Estate) ...	320	4	...	...	8	...	127	51	11	74	...	...
17	Marwar ...	343,749	63,403	...	...	38,596	13,116	20,227	64,404	8,497	194,488	1,991	959
18	Mewar ...	314,197	10,768	...	...	25,127	1,325	13,133	35,680	15,211	222,783	4,143	9,077
19	Partabgarh ...	10,020	311	...	...	566	7	1,274	2,047	5,308	12,495	560	917
20	Shahpura ...	6,684	380	...	...	1,294	141	269	287	5,276	10,555	697	274
21	Sirohi ...	29,181	110	...	...	882	2	4,810	5,358	11,655	23,925	357	40
22	Tonk ...	51,534	3,081	...	...	2,890	184	7,223	9,185	4,462	32,800	560	50
	Cities ...	***6,982***	***931***	...	...	***2,077***	***26***	***848***	***575***	***221***	***988***	***99***	***35***
1	Alwar ...	1,004	440	...	...	20	4	99	64	21	108	1	...
2	Bharatpur ...	281	10	...	...	24	...	46	5	3	3	1	...
3	Bikaner ...	1,406	81	...	...	1,082	5	179	2	1	14	45	22
4	Bundi ...	263	28	...	...	115	...	232	270	7	4	34	6
5	Dholpur ...	526	81	...	...	417	6	11	4	55	172	4	1
6	Jaipur ...	1,226	88	...	...	212	11	109	83	81	336	3	1
7	Jodhpur ...	651	29	...	...	9	...	39	4	...	1	5	...
8	Kotah ...	258	34	...	...	90	...	43	4	...	5	...	...
9	Tonk ...	886	84	...	...	45	...	66	115	50	238	5	...
10	Udaipur ...	531	47	...	...	63	...	31	24	3	107	1	5

TABLE X.—OCCUPATION OR MEANS OF LIVELIHOOD.—PART II.—BY STATE OR DISTRICT AND CITY.—*Continued.*

CLASS A.—PRODUCTION OF RAW MATERIALS—*Continued.*
SUB-CLASS I.—EXPLOITATION OF ANIMALS AND VEGETATION—*Continued.*
ORDER I.—PASTURE AND AGRICULTURE.—*Continued.*

SERIAL NUMBER.	AGENCY, STATE OR DISTRICT AND CITY.	SUB-ORDER 1 (B).—CULTIVATION OF SPECIAL CROPS, FRUIT, ETC. (PLANTERS, MANAGERS, CLERKS AND LABOURERS). Total Earners (Principal Occupations). Males.	Total Earners (Principal Occupations). Females.	Total Working Dependants. Males.	Total Working Dependants. Females.	Total following occupation as Subsidiary to other. Males.	Total following occupation as Subsidiary to other. Females.	SUB-ORDER 1 (C).—FORESTRY. Total Earners (Principal Occupations). Males.	Total Earners (Principal Occupations). Females.	Total Working Dependants. Males.	Total Working Dependants. Females.	Total following occupation as Subsidiary to other. Males.	Total following occupation as Subsidiary to other. Females.
1	2	78	79	80	81	82	83	84	85	86	87	88	89
	Rajputana ...	***2,888***	***1,218***	***19***	***188***	***283***	***29***	***6,060***	***5,095***	***327***	***1,185***	***2,372***	***1,677***
1	Abu District ...	35	...	...	...	...	...	15	1	...	...	...	...
2	Alwar ...	105	17	1	2	14	...	391	141	80	28	55	10
3	Banswara ...	61	24	4	9	...	...	57	...	...	...	...	...
4	Bharatpur ...	345	3	...	...	27	...	57	48	...	...	12	...
5	Bikaner ...	154	16	...	...	21	...	169	5	...	...	15	...
6	Bundi ...	82	33	...	...	5	1	215	43	39	107	11	1
7	Dholpur ...	63	5	...	1	3	...	128	16	...	3	18	...
8	Dungarpur ...	117	...	1	...	22	...	141	738	21	104	274	45
9	Jaipur ...	405	177	7	102	40	...	382	347	26	371	29	19
10	Jaisalmer ...	...	...	...	...	...	...	148	23	7	1	129	1
11	Jhalawar ...	27	59	...	...	...	...	15	1	...	...	1	...
12	Karauli ...	140	21	2	56	124	2	11	...	...	...	3	...
13	Kishangarh ...	9	10	2	...	9	...	50	...	8	...	5	...
14	Kotah ...	19	9	...	4	...	...	1,976	1,896	28	76	231	815
15	Kushalgarh (Chiefship).	3	...	1	...	...	...	8	...	...	...	2	...
16	Lawa (Estate) ...	...	...	...	...	...	...	...	...	...	...	...	...
17	Marwar ...	891	652	...	...	1	6	278	124	2	3	2	...
18	Mewar ...	214	83	...	15	11	20	906	445	52	372	285	190
19	Partabgarh ...	...	...	...	...	...	...	715	1,154	54	27	1,289	1,095
20	Shahpura ...	...	...	1	...	...	...	24	21	...	...	4	1
21	Sirohi ...	34	4	...	...	2	...	158	...	1	3	57	...
22	Tonk ...	184	105	...	...	4	...	141	92	9	...	...	...
	Cities ...	***930***	***443***	***5***	***7***	***24***	***1***	***526***	***57***	***1***	***25***	***28***	***4***
1	Alwar ...	3	1	...	1	...	...	52	15	...	...	...	...
2	Bharatpur ...	...	...	...	...	...	...	16	...	...	...	2	...
3	Bikaner ...	118	6	...	...	9	...	156	5	...	...	10	...
4	Bundi ...	52	29	...	...	...	1	22	...	...	...	...	...
5	Dholpur ...	86	...	...	...	1	...	66	...	...	...	3	...
6	Jaipur ...	242	42	5	6	12	...	45	3	1	24	10	...
7	Jodhpur ...	260	220	...	...	...	...	62	...	...	...	2	...
8	Kotah ...	8	...	...	...	...	...	60	34	...	1	1	4
9	Tonk ...	109	99	...	...	2	...	16	...	...	...	...	...
10	Udaipur ...	102	46	...	...	...	...	31	...	...	...	...	...

TABLE X.—OCCUPATION OR MEANS OF LIVELIHOOD.—PART II.—BY STATE OR DISTRICT AND CITY.—*Continued.*

CLASS A.—PRODUCTION OF RAW MATERIALS.—*Continued.*
SUB-CLASS I.—EXPLOITATION OF ANIMALS AND VEGETATION.—*Continued.*
ORDER I.—PASTURE AND AGRICULTURE.—*Concluded.*

SERIAL NUMBER.	AGENCY, STATE OR DISTRICT AND CITY.	SUB-ORDER I (D).—STOCK-RAISING.						SUB-ORDER I (E).—RAISING OF SMALL ANIMALS AND INSECTS.					
		Total Earners (Principal Occupations).		Total Working Dependants.		Total following occupation as Subsidiary to other.		Total Earners (Principal Occupations).		Total Working Dependants.		Total following occupation as Subsidiary to other.	
		Males.	Females.	Males.	Females.	Males.	Females.	Males.	Females.	Males.	Females.	Males.	Females.
1	2	90	91	92	93	94	95	96	97	98	99	100	101
	Rajputana ...	***121,910***	***12,740***	***42,835***	***21,039***	***35,040***	***2,095***	***1***	...	...	...	...	...
1	Abu District ...	7	1	...	...	...	...	...	...	...	...	...	...
2	Alwar ...	7,454	699	7,091	2,828	715	66	...	...	...	...	...	...
3	Banswara ...	664	158	117	105	119	7	...	...	...	...	...	...
4	Bharatpur ...	5,370	128	4,741	382	633	11	...	...	...	...	...	...
5	Bikaner ...	3,179	119	1,587	268	2,849	13	...	...	...	...	...	...
6	Bundi ...	4,903	297	255	43	248	15	...	...	...	...	...	...
7	Dholpur ...	1,988	63	559	183	487	4	...	...	...	...	...	...
8	Dungarpur ...	308	117	2,191	1,628	185	5	...	...	...	...	...	...
9	Jaipur ...	16,749	2,041	16,813	8,937	1,088	87	...	...	...	...	...	...
10	Jaisalmer ...	10,242	617	821	777	7,105	608	...	...	...	...	...	...
11	Jhalawar ...	1,466	22	880	4	116	2	...	...	...	...	...	...
12	Karauli ...	1,769	120	1,483	457	8,780	74	1	...	...	...	...	...
13	Kishangarh ...	1,061	54	529	157	85	20	...	...	...	...	...	...
14	Kotah ...	13,959	476	531	75	952	29	...	...	...	...	...	...
15	Kushalgarh (Chiefship).	9	8	176	76	2	...	...	...	...	...	...	...
16	Lawa (Estate) ...	12	...	1	...	...	...	...	...	...	...	...	...
17	Marwar ...	30,215	3,830	816	949	13,028	945	...	...	...	...	...	...
18	Mewar ...	11,188	3,322	3,143	3,370	8,602	196	...	...	...	...	...	...
19	Partabgarh ...	892	55	634	424	125	11	...	...	...	...	...	...
20	Shahpura ...	564	51	73	8	99	...	...	...	...	...	...	...
21	Sirohi ...	6,520	217	106	49	79	2	...	...	...	...	...	...
22	Tonk ...	3,966	850	1,508	179	298	...	...	...	...	...	...	...
	Cities ...	***902***	***103***	***14***	***23***	***42***	***43***	...	...	...	...	...	...
1	Alwar ...	110	24	6	5	17	40	...	...	...	...	...	...
2	Bharatpur ...	130	...	4	1	1	...	...	...	...	...	...	...
3	Bikaner ...	38	...	...	...	1	...	...	...	...	...	...	...
4	Bundi ...	79	2	...	...	3	...	...	...	...	...	...	...
5	Dholpur ...	51	3	...	...	11	1	...	...	...	...	...	...
6	Jaipur ...	139	23	4	17	2	1	...	...	...	...	...	...
7	Jodhpur ...	120	32	...	...	...	1	...	...	...	...	...	...
8	Kotah ...	56	1	...	...	...	...	...	...	...	...	...	...
9	Tonk ...	187	14	...	...	5	...	...	...	...	...	...	...
10	Udaipur ...	42	4	...	...	2	...	...	...	...	...	...	...

TABLE X.—Occupation or Means of Livelihood.—Part II.—By State or District and City.—*Continued.*

Serial Number.	Agency, State or District and City.	CLASS A.—PRODUCTION OF RAW MATERIALS.—*Continued.*											
		SUB-CLASS I.—EXPLOITATION OF ANIMALS AND VEGETATION.—*Concluded.*						SUB-CLASS II.—EXPLOITATION OF MINERALS.					
		ORDER 2.—FISHING AND HUNTING.						TOTAL OF SUB-CLASS II.					
		Total Earners (Principal Occupations).		Total Working Dependants.		Total following occupation as Subsidiary to other.		Total Earners (Principal Occupations).		Total Working Dependants.		Total following occupation as Subsidiary to other.	
		Males.	Females.	Males.	Females.	Males.	Females.	Males.	Females.	Males.	Females.	Males.	Females.
1	2	102	103	104	105	106	107	108	109	110	111	112	113
	Rajputana ...	**241**	**7**	**5**	**2**	**35**	**1**	**5,945**	**1,882**	**9**	**144**	**682**	**28**
1	Abu District ...	...	...	...	...	...	...	1	1	...	...	...	...
2	Alwar ...	7	...	...	...	2	...	124	11	1	1	28	1
3	Banswara ...	2	...	...	...	17	...	1	...	...	...	9	...
4	Bharatpur ...	5	...	...	...	...	...	238	18	2	...	76	...
5	Bikaner ...	...	...	...	...	...	...	221	43	1	5	46	1
6	Bundi ...	...	...	...	...	...	...	68	56	...	...	13	...
7	Dholpur ...	1	...	...	...	...	...	539	72	1	14	173	17
8	Dungarpur ...	...	...	...	...	...	...	...	...	...	...	...	...
9	Jaipur ...	80	5	...	...	5	1	480	67	3	13	83	1
10	Jaisalmer ...	...	...	...	...	...	...	4	...	...	...	...	...
11	Jhalawar ...	...	...	...	...	1	...	50	23	...	5	7	...
12	Karauli ...	8	...	1	...	...	...	...	...	...	...	...	...
13	Kishangarh ...	...	...	...	...	...	...	17	...	...	...	...	...
14	Kotah ...	35	...	...	...	8	...	78	997	...	23	3	6
15	Kushalgarh (Chiefship).	...	...	...	...	...	...	...	...	...	...	...	...
16	Lawa (Estate)	...	...	...	...	...	...	...	...	...	...	...	...
17	Marwar ...	...	...	...	...	...	...	3,416	504	...	67	121	2
18	Mewar ...	7	...	...	...	2	...	372	6	...	9	55	...
19	Partabgarh ...	1	...	...	...	...	...	9	3	...	7	...	...
20	Shahpura ...	...	...	...	...	...	...	7	...	...	...	2	...
21	Sirohi ...	6	...	...	...	...	...	68	11	...	...	4	...
22	Tonk ...	89	2	4	2	...	...	257	71	1	...	62	...
	Cities ...	**42**	...	...	...	...	...	**163**	**109**	...	**1**	**1**	...
1	Alwar ...	...	...	...	...	...	...	5	8	...	...	...	...
2	Bharatpur ...	4	...	...	...	...	...	...	...	...	...	1	...
3	Bikaner ...	...	...	...	...	...	...	40	...	...	...	...	...
4	Bundi ...	...	...	...	...	...	...	12	51	...	...	...	...
5	Dholpur ...	...	...	...	...	...	...	...	...	...	...	...	...
6	Jaipur ...	29	...	...	...	...	...	2	19	...	1	...	...
7	Jodhpur ...	...	...	...	...	...	...	42	...	...	...	...	...
8	Kotah ...	5	...	...	...	...	...	1	...	...	...	...	...
9	Tonk ...	...	...	...	...	...	...	...	30	...	...	...	...
10	Udaipur ...	4	...	...	...	...	...	61	1	...	...	...	...

TABLE X.—Occupation or Means of Livelihood.—Part II.—By State or District and City.—*Continued.*

Serial Number.	Agency, State or District and City.	CLASS A.—PRODUCTION OF RAW MATERIALS.—*Concluded.* SUB-CLASS II.—EXPLOITATION OF MINERALS.—*Concluded.* ORDER 4.—NON-METALLIC MINERALS. Total Earners (Principal Occupations). Males.	Total Earners (Principal Occupations). Females.	Total Working Dependants. Males.	Total Working Dependants. Females.	Total following occupation as Subsidiary to other. Males.	Total following occupation as Subsidiary to other. Females.	CLASS B.—PREPARATION AND SUPPLY OF MATERIAL SUBSTANCES. SUB-CLASS III.—INDUSTRY. TOTAL OF CLASS B. Total Earners (Principal Occupations). Males.	Total Earners (Principal Occupations). Females.	Total Working Dependants. Males.	Total Working Dependants. Females.	Total following occupation as Subsidiary to other. Males.	Total following occupation as Subsidiary to other. Females.
1	2	114	115	116	117	118	119	120	121	122	123	124	125
	Rajputana ...	***5,945***	***1,882***	***9***	***144***	***682***	***28***	***748,004***	***198,327***	***16,989***	***66,767***	***105,793***	***10,889***
1	Abu District ...	1	1	...	...	...	...	724	165	...	1	24	2
2	Alwar ...	124	11	1	1	28	1	49,885	9,743	555	5,603	5,906	521
3	Banswara ...	1	...	...	...	9	...	8,435	2,817	171	67	1,282	101
4	Bharatpur ...	238	18	2	...	76	...	32,332	11,588	378	1,068	7,532	769
5	Bikaner ...	221	43	1	5	46	1	44,794	9,069	615	1,311	9,562	256
6	Bundi ...	63	56	...	...	13	...	13,924	5,162	228	828	1,712	204
7	Dholpur ...	539	72	1	14	178	17	12,729	2,277	86	1,920	8,238	107
8	Dungarpur ...	...	...	...	...	...	...	7,839	1,190	768	1,014	1,670	45
9	Jaipur ...	480	67	3	13	83	1	184,778	41,864	10,428	80,594	12,762	1,055
10	Jaisalmer ...	4	...	...	...	...	...	6,140	1,706	80	1,098	796	259
11	Jhalawar ...	50	22	...	5	7	...	7,466	2,026	89	154	1,384	158
12	Karauli ...	...	...	...	...	...	...	9,698	1,714	261	2,005	3,395	159
13	Kishangarh ...	17	...	...	...	...	...	5,752	983	376	431	1,070	12
14	Kotah ...	78	997	...	23	8	6	44,140	18,249	492	1,904	6,302	838
15	Kushalgarh (Chiefship).	...	...	...	...	...	...	664	278	19	41	106	16
16	Lawa (Estate) ...	...	...	...	...	...	...	223	75	6	40	13	...
17	Marwar ..	3,416	504	...	67	121	2	162,852	35,480	921	5,743	20,710	1,950
18	Mewar ...	372	6	...	9	55	...	118,468	48,092	918	10,973	24,287	4,006
19	Partabgarh ...	9	8	...	7	...	...	4,118	1,227	8	14	991	99
20	Shahpura ...	7	...	...	...	2	...	3,397	1,240	25	261	910	94
21	Sirohi ...	68	11	...	...	4	...	16,756	3,827	103	976	809	168
22	Tonk ...	257	71	1	...	62	...	17,900	5,560	562	731	1,847	75
	Cities ...	***163***	***109***	...	***1***	***1***	...	***90,091***	***25,151***	***856***	***3,151***	***2,583***	***286***
1	Alwar ...	5	8	...	...	...	...	6,196	1,950	37	484	135	57
2	Bharatpur ...	...	...	...	...	1	...	4,608	1,088	26	88	241	6
3	Bikaner ...	40	...	...	...	...	...	14,249	3,434	...	2	309	17
4	Bundi ...	12	51	...	...	...	...	2,495	1,526	...	14	183	16
5	Dholpur ...	...	...	...	...	...	...	2,759	590	36	45	273	26
6	Jaipur ...	2	19	...	1	...	...	21,225	4,352	510	1,533	692	67
7	Jodhpur ...	42	...	...	...	...	...	21,194	5,443	245	610	185	2
8	Kotah ...	1	...	...	...	...	...	5,986	2,870	...	91	257	87
9	Tonk ...	...	30	...	...	...	...	3,770	1,380	...	62	183	19
10	Udaipur ...	61	1	...	...	...	...	7,609	3,018	2	222	175	39

TABLE X.—Occupation or Means of Livelihood.—Part II.—By State or District and City.—*Continued.*

CLASS B.—PREPARATION AND SUPPLY OF MATERIAL SUBSTANCES.—*Continued.*
SUB-CLASS III.—INDUSTRY.—*Continued.*

Serial Number.	Agency, State or District and City.	Total Sub-Class III. Total Earners (Principal Occupations). Males.	Females.	Total Working Dependants. Males.	Females.	Total following occupation as Subsidiary to other. Males.	Females	Order 5.—Textiles. Total Earners (Principal Occupations). Males.	Females.	Total Working Dependants. Males.	Females.	Total following occupation as Subsidiary to other. Males.	Females.
1	2	126	127	128	129	130	131	132	133	134	135	136	137
	Rajputana ...	***476,276***	***135,760***	***12,073***	***57,089***	***64,161***	***5,913***	***82,398***	***47,151***	***3,640***	***30,254***	***12,158***	***1,928***
1	Abu District ...	411	59	...	...	13	...	...	...	...	...	...	...
2	Alwar ...	32,222	7,228	454	4,842	3,006	271	6,265	2,285	110	1,588	812	89
3	Banswara ...	5,421	1,554	33	46	475	54	730	57	...	4	98	12
4	Bharatpur ...	20,264	6,676	212	804	2,853	312	4,281	1,680	58	509	585	184
5	Bikaner ...	24,486	7,101	374	1,259	7,742	241	1,050	1,682	16	861	1,016	130
6	Bundi ...	9,566	3,778	167	598	1,160	114	1,278	1,864	24	327	127	45
7	Dholpur ...	7,724	1,602	58	1,591	1,686	85	1,336	260	9	879	279	13
8	Dungarpur ...	4,984	858	528	932	1,267	41	691	52	133	211	191	3
9	Jaipur ...	122,095	32,589	7,305	27,794	6,668	714	24,755	14,592	2,234	17,411	1,206	336
10	Jaisalmer ...	4,646	1,624	22	1,006	302	234	1,360	1,405	4	937	155	231
11	Jhalawar ...	4,570	1,186	27	109	945	101	419	126	...	6	87	15
12	Karauli ...	6,139	1,371	170	1,697	2,100	97	1,560	654	75	1,080	197	56
13	Kishangarh ...	3,845	676	263	402	857	2	1,020	325	94	174	162	1
14	Kotah ...	29,060	12,494	361	1,497	3,988	452	4,258	3,669	108	622	302	100
15	Kushalgarh (Chiefship).	334	199	19	35	53	6	9	...	1	...	1	...
16	Lawa (Estate) ...	169	75	6	40	7	...	55	34	3	9	...	...
17	Marwar ...	108,676	29,692	840	4,829	16,858	1,408	18,008	8,989	582	1,174	4,392	332
18	Mewar ...	65,402	19,594	699	8,294	11,608	1,571	11,730	7,617	125	4,999	2,257	308
19	Partabgarh ...	2,271	962	7	14	562	65	151	67	...	1	23	2
20	Shahpura ...	2,260	982	18	258	718	81	339	334	1	224	147	16
21	Sirohi ...	9,738	1,135	15	403	479	50	1,028	175	1	73	82	2
22	Tonk ...	11,903	4,435	500	579	884	69	2,075	1,275	67	265	89	13
	Cities ...	***53,644***	***19,094***	**677**	**2,876**	***1,447***	***190***	***7,561***	**6,302**	***318***	***1,461***	***225***	***78***
1	Alwar ...	3,753	1,344	28	422	74	22	1,010	451	16	320	21	8
2	Bharatpur ...	2,674	749	18	84	142	3	405	150	...	33	19	...
3	Bikaner ...	7,696	2,436	...	2	115	16	227	286	...	...	7	1
4	Bundi ...	1,582	1,189	...	13	119	15	250	619	...	9	64	15
5	Dholpur ...	1,355	428	19	43	96	10	114	40	2	3	10	...
6	Jaipur ...	13,487	3,580	367	1,374	502	43	2,561	1,856	65	686	33	16
7	Jodhpur ...	13,301	4,589	245	609	114	1	1,611	1,486	235	204	7	...
8	Kotah ...	8,332	1,717	...	84	164	34	410	558	...	49	28	25
9	Tonk ...	2,449	1,249	...	62	81	19	650	656	...	61	7	12
10	Udaipur ...	4,115	1,868	...	183	90	27	323	200	...	96	29	1

TABLE X.

Occupation or Means of Livelihood. Part II.— By State or District and City.

TABLE X.—Occupation or Means of Livelihood.—Part II.—By State or District and City.—*Continued.*

CLASS B.—PREPARATION AND SUPPLY OF MATERIAL SUBSTANCES.—*Continued.*
SUB-CLASS III.—INDUSTRY.—*Continued.*

Serial Number.	Agency, State or District and City.	Order 6.—Hides, Skins and Hard Materials from the Animal Kingdom. Total Earners (Principal Occupations). Males.	Females.	Total Working Dependants. Males.	Females.	Total following occupation as Subsidiary to other. Males.	Females.	Order 7.—Wood. Total Earners (Principal Occupations). Males.	Females.	Total Working Dependants. Males.	Females.	Total following occupation as Subsidiary to other. Males.	Females.
1	2	138	139	140	141	142	143	144	145	146	147	148	149
	Rajputana ...	***32,922***	***3,827***	***608***	***2,061***	***6,709***	***172***	***49,452***	***5,696***	***1,223***	***2,077***	***10,068***	***926***
1	Abu District ...	...	...	...	...	...	...	25	1	...	...	...	...
2	Alwar ...	1,902	84	16	201	199	12	8,394	258	101	121	430	35
3	Banswara ...	1,282	9	...	...	7	...	564	183	1	1	63	9
4	Bharatpur ...	470	32	1	40	252	12	1,956	207	10	20	414	10
5	Bikaner ...	670	68	1	6	123	8	2,554	89	48	22	1,767	9
6	Bundi ...	802	84	20	31	82	6	763	170	15	25	127	28
7	Dholpur ...	62	...	1	...	50	...	784	64	3	70	254	5
8	Dungarpur ...	365	6	26	25	120	...	477	30	40	38	118	4
9	Jaipur ...	6,154	725	439	666	363	4	13,360	1,440	804	973	1,036	96
10	Jaisalmer ...	255	5	...	4	...	...	665	7	5	3	72	...
11	Jhalawar ...	151	35	...	...	33	...	485	141	3	88	151	35
12	Karauli ...	789	12	8	31	1,096	13	493	43	7	48	206	10
13	Kishangarh ...	315	...	21	5	201	...	311	36	30	3	104	...
14	Kotah ...	1,819	272	25	115	231	5	2,686	1,287	26	122	618	114
15	Kushalgarh (Chiefship)	...	...	...	...	...	...	63	26	...	6	5	...
16	Lawa (Estate) ...	...	...	...	...	...	...	6	...	...	...	6	...
17	Marwar ...	11,229	2,089	16	687	1,881	102	11,759	332	21	82	2,683	164
18	Mewar ...	5,181	160	10	177	1,729	8	6,468	829	35	478	1,621	363
19	Partabgarh ...	195	40	1	...	197	2	273	87	...	3	96	26
20	Shahpura ...	88	1	...	...	25	...	170	38	1	2	108	10
21	Sirohi ...	596	113	1	33	58	...	1,073	84	2	...	30	...
22	Tonk ...	1,062	92	22	40	69	...	1,188	388	71	82	164	8
	Cities ...	***1,554***	***502***	***1***	***4***	***8***	***1***	***3,551***	***676***	***20***	***74***	***105***	***11***
1	Alwar ...	75	16	...	...	...	1	276	92	...	4	5	1
2	Bharatpur ...	65	1	...	...	...	...	148	59	2	4	17	1
3	Bikaner ...	79	...	...	...	...	...	709	56	...	...	5	1
4	Bundi ...	25	4	...	...	1	...	83	29	...	...	4	...
5	Dholpur ...	3	...	...	...	1	...	78	8	...	...	11	5
6	Jaipur ...	78	7	1	3	4	...	811	87	18	52	30	...
7	Jodhpur ...	926	481	...	...	...	...	819	77	...	...	3	...
8	Kotah ...	108	2	...	...	...	...	217	66	...	11	4	2
9	Tonk ...	145	32	...	...	...	...	124	62	...	...	5	...
10	Udaipur ...	55	9	...	1	2	...	286	140	...	3	21	1

TABLE X.—Occupation or Means of Livelihood.—Part II.—By State or District and City.—*Continued.*

CLASS A.—PREPARATION AND SUPPLY OF MATERIAL SUBSTANCES—*Continued.*
SUB-CLASS III.—INDUSTRY.—*Continued.*

Serial Number.	Agency, State or District and City.	Order 8.—Metals. Total Earners (Principal Occupations). Males.	Females.	Total Working Dependants. Males.	Females.	Total following occupation as Subsidiary to other. Males.	Females.	Order 9.—Ceramics. Total Earners (Principal Occupations). Males.	Females.	Total Working Dependants. Males.	Females.	Total following occupation as Subsidiary to other. Males.	Females.
1	2	150	151	152	153	154	155	156	157	158	159	160	161
	Rajputana ...	***21,006***	***1,279***	***428***	***693***	***2,169***	***155***	***46,482***	***12,842***	***1,243***	***5,226***	***5,137***	***445***
1	Abu District ...	10	...	...	...	...	...	8	2	...	...	...	...
2	Alwar ...	918	17	3	8	43	...	8,480	581	38	589	165	13
3	Banswara ...	768	75	3	6	55	1	442	822	4	17	3	...
4	Bharatpur ...	782	17	15	...	60	...	2,815	1,029	24	40	117	7
5	Bikaner ...	950	86	45	94	144	9	1,854	877	20	130	682	6
6	Bundi ...	422	47	...	5	26	2	721	201	21	75	37	12
7	Dholpur ...	252	...	...	...	9	...	629	116	8	142	87	1
8	Dungarpur ...	495	9	56	41	114	1	500	77	92	272	117	8
9	Jaipur ...	3,053	282	165	161	73	...	10,972	2,466	784	2,027	616	44
10	Jaisalmer ...	56	...	...	...	1	...	313	85	...	14	5	2
11	Jhalawar ...	388	4	3	...	61	...	441	180	5	14	62	7
12	Karauli ...	165	1	2	3	26	...	380	90	15	158	59	3
13	Kishangarh ...	193	...	17	23	46	...	281	10	38	77	83	...
14	Kotah ...	1,168	75	8	53	144	1	2,351	1,276	44	176	307	75
15	Kushalgarh (Chiefship)	71	2	...	1	12	...	34	15	...	1	4	...
16	Lawa (Estate) ...	1	...	...	...	...	...	8	...	...	...	...	...
17	Marwar ...	5,090	532	73	202	630	135	12,366	8,487	42	674	1,788	147
18	Mewar ...	4,862	106	21	92	647	4	6,626	1,540	35	740	858	85
19	Partabgarh ...	158	10	4	4	33	2	196	168	1	2	34	7
20	Shahpura ...	90	...	...	...	23	...	202	93	2	4	74	2
21	Sirohi ...	758	8	...	...	9	...	1,290	203	3	45	28	1
22	Tonk ...	416	8	13	...	13	...	1,128	624	72	79	66	25
	Cities ...	***2,296***	***229***	***11***	***82***	***18***	...	***2,452***	***633***	***13***	***32***	***51***	...
1	Alwar ...	86	8	...	...	...	...	95	24	...	1	...	...
2	Bharatpur ...	81	1	...	...	1	...	117	71	...	...	...	...
3	Bikaner ...	242	35	...	...	1	...	489	156	...	...	35	...
4	Bundi ...	82	9	...	...	3	...	46	41	...	...	...	...
5	Dholpur ...	44	...	...	...	1	...	36	81	4	7	...	...
6	Jaipur ...	843	95	11	18	9	...	176	49	9	12	3	...
7	Jodhpur ...	401	78	...	60	...	...	1,287	210	...	...	...	...
8	Kotah ...	97	...	...	...	...	...	66	25	...	...	13	...
9	Tonk ...	104	...	...	...	...	...	65	12	...	...	...	...
10	Udaipur ...	316	3	...	4	3	...	75	14	...	12	...	...

TABLE X.—Occupation or Means of Livelihood.—Part II.—By State or District and City.—*Continued.*

SERIAL NUMBER.	AGENCY, STATE OR DISTRICT AND CITY.	CLASS B.—PREPARATION AND SUPPLY OF MATERIAL SUBSTANCES.—*Continued.* SUB-CLASS III.—INDUSTRY.—*Continued.* ORDER 10.—CHEMICAL PRODUCTS PROPERLY SO-CALLED AND ANALOGOUS. Total Earners (Principal Occupations).		Total Working Dependants.		Total following occupation as Subsidiary to other.		ORDER 11.—FOOD INDUSTRY. Total Earners (Principal Occupations).		Total Working Dependants.		Total following occupation as Subsidiary to other.	
		Males.	Females.	Males.	Females.	Males.	Females.	Males.	Females.	Males.	Females.	Males.	Females.
1	2	162	163	164	165	166	167	168	169	170	171	172	173
	Rajputana ...	***14,033***	***2,586***	***281***	***840***	***2,416***	***125***	***13,175***	***6,929***	***561***	***783***	***1,012***	***338***
1	Abu District ...	1	...	...	...	1	...	22	...	...	...	2	...
2	Alwar ...	736	63	1	30	56	...	743	370	1	127	58	42
3	Banswara ...	222	85	16	2	11	...	34	133	1	3	56	11
4	Bharatpur ...	669	208	5	20	45	1	940	936	15	29	185	73
5	Bikaner ...	730	77	8	19	151	...	920	558	4	24	80	23
6	Bundi ...	302	39	5	4	58	...	257	102	4	9	23	1
7	Dholpur ...	555	16	6	30	168	...	175	375	5	47	32	10
8	Dungarpur ...	175	42	34	101	72	3	106	188	...	10	4	8
9	Jaipur ...	2,184	263	114	230	124	2	4,220	858	182	308	188	39
10	Jaisalmer ...	24	1	...	...	...	...	69	4	3	1	8	...
11	Jhalawar ...	186	25	2	...	43	1	62	97	1	7	21	8
12	Karauli ...	278	15	7	60	125	3	281	109	5	13	7	10
13	Kishangarh ...	97	13	1	1	14	1	101	18	3	8	10	...
14	Kotah ...	1,576	479	29	72	245	27	588	489	5	32	42	31
15	Kushalgarh (Chiefship).	15	4	...	...	...	...	15	84	13	2	...	...
16	Lawa (Estate) ...	1	1	...	...	1	...	1	1	...	...	...	...
17	Marwar ...	2,734	379	11	49	588	34	1,921	1,568	19	34	74	5
18	Mewar ...	2,661	514	10	177	555	39	1,847	842	296	109	198	56
19	Partabgarh ...	129	68	...	1	27	...	115	100	...	1	6	6
20	Shahpura ...	85	28	1	1	31	...	30	8	...	1	6	1
21	Sirohi ...	244	53	1	18	33	6	198	66	...	16	3	5
22	Tonk ...	479	213	31	30	68	3	585	178	4	7	14	9
	Cities ...	***978***	***198***	***8***	***3***	***18***	***2***	***3,596***	***1,518***	***40***	***51***	***103***	***42***
1	Alwar ...	27	31	...	1	...	...	285	88	...	5	1	8
2	Bharatpur ...	86	25	...	...	...	...	344	161	11	8	18	...
3	Bikaner ...	139	19	...	...	1	...	348	188	...	...	6	...
4	Bundi ...	59	7	...	...	3	...	82	47	...	...	8	...
5	Dholpur ...	55	...	...	...	2	...	81	67	4	3	3	4
6	Jaipur ...	144	5	8	1	2	2	865	141	15	32	48	...
7	Jodhpur ...	197	24	...	...	3	...	1,008	559	10	...	3	...
8	Kotah ...	124	88	...	1	7	...	147	122	...	8	15	1
9	Tonk ...	115	26	...	...	...	...	215	65	...	...	...	5
10	Udaipur ...	39	23	...	...	...	...	226	130	...	...	6	24

TABLE X.—Occupation or Means of Livelihood.—Part II.—By State or District and City.—*Continued.*

CLASS B.—PREPARATION AND SUPPLY OF MATERIAL SUBSTANCES.—*Continued.*
SUB-CLASS III.—INDUSTRY.—*Continued.*

Serial Number.	Agency, State or District and City.	Order 12.—Industries of Dress and Toilet. Total Earners (Principal Occupations). Males.	Females.	Total Working Dependants. Males	Females	Total following occupation as Subsidiary to other. Males.	Females	Order 13.—Furniture Industries. Total Earners (Principal Occupations). Males.	Females.	Total Working Dependants. Males.	Females.	Total following occupation as Subsidiary to other. Males.	Females.
1	2	174	175	176	177	178	179	180	181	182	183	184	185
	Rajputana ...	***123,134***	***24,976***	***2,248***	***8,909***	***18,064***	***804***	***1,130***	***59***	...	***11***	***40***	***6***
1	Abu District ...	73	12	...	...	3	...	...	...	...	...	...	...
2	Alwar ...	9,479	1,588	75	1,077	1,028	74	26	18	...	6	3	...
3	Banswara ...	821	388	...	1	21	...	4	...	...	...	2	...
4	Bharatpur ...	4,725	787	46	76	696	22	91	5	...	3	3	...
5	Bikaner ...	6,510	2,092	130	354	2,552	20	138	5	...	...	...	...
6	Bundi ...	2,841	340	19	53	558	8	5	...	...	...	...	3
7	Dholpur ...	2,410	407	19	678	659	5	2	...	...	...	1	...
8	Dungarpur ...	1,478	239	125	209	891	2	7	...	...	...	...	...
9	Jaipur ...	33,681	5,186	1,417	8,666	2,181	110	66	2	...	1	1	...
10	Jaisalmer ...	1,611	86	10	46	56	1	...	...	...	...	...	...
11	Jhalawar ...	1,698	809	13	39	415	7	1	...	...	...	2	...
12	Karauli ...	1,059	212	18	182	276	2	...	...	...	...	...	...
13	Kishangarh ...	862	115	37	38	188	...	3	...	...	...	...	...
14	Kotah ...	7,722	1,706	55	209	1,771	55	14	19	...	...	1	3
15	Kushalgarh (Chiefship).	79	17	...	7	22	2	...	...	...	...	...	...
16	Lawa (Estate) ...	18	6	...	...	...	...	...	...	...	...	...	...
17	Marwar ...	26,288	7,600	50	1,856	3,833	346	764	3	...	..	25	...
18	Mewar ...	14,453	2,258	79	740	2,551	186	...	5	...	1	...	...
19	Partabgarh ...	542	181	...	...	107	4	...	...	...	...	...	...
20	Shahpura ...	806	215	4	16	280	5	...	...	...	...	2	...
21	Sirohi ...	3,029	460	6	79	195	2	...	...	...	...	...	...
22	Tonk ...	3,460	863	155	83	286	3	14	2	...	...	...	...
	Cities ...	***11,525***	***3,919***	***71***	***863***	***343***	***15***	***607***	***25***	...	6	6	...
1	Alwar ...	953	256	6	59	17	4	19	18	...	6	1	...
2	Bharatpur ...	572	89	8	8	29	...	88	...	...	...	3	...
3	Bikaner ...	1,614	954	...	2	17	2	128	5	...	...	...	...
4	Bundi ...	590	117	...	4	40	...	...	...	...	...	...	...
5	Dholpur ...	417	94	9	30	34	...	2	...	...	...	1	...
6	Jaipur ...	2,692	618	53	341	86	1	52	...	...	...	1	...
7	Jodhpur ...	2,910	1,157	...	345	7	...	802	...	...	...	...	...
8	Kotah ...	685	197	...	12	85	6	2	...	...	...	...	...
9	Tonk ...	596	194	...	1	11	2	14	2	...	...	...	...
10	Udaipur ...	597	248	...	61	17	...	...	...	...	...	...	...

TABLE X.—Occupation or Means of Livelihood.—Part II.—By State or District and City.—*Continued.*

CLASS B.—PREPARATION AND SUPPLY OF MATERIAL SUBSTANCES.—*Continued.*
SUB-CLASS III.—INDUSTRY.—*Continued.*

Serial Number.	Agency, State or District and City.	Order 14.—Building Industries. Total Earners (Principal Occupations). Males.	Females	Total Working Dependants. Males.	Females.	Total following occupation as Subsidiary to other. Males.	Females.	Order 15.—Construction of Means of Transport. Total Earners (Principal Occupations). Males.	Females.	Total Working Dependants. Males.	Females.	Total following occupation as Subsidiary to other. Males.	Females.
1	2	186	187	188	189	190	191	192	193	194	195	196	197
	Rajputana ...	***39,882***	***11,571***	***370***	***1,367***	***4,069***	***587***	***176***	***20***	...	***3***	***28***	***1***
1	Abu District ...	175	...	...	...	6	...	1	...	...	...	1	...
2	Alwar ...	1,218	276	5	105	139	5	14	...	...	...	1	...
3	Banswara ...	197	188	...	1	121	2	...	...	...	...	...	...
4	Bharatpur ...	1,465	273	8	6	386	30	...	...	...	...	...	...
5	Bikaner ...	5,376	1,091	54	69	384	28	9	...	...	...	...	...
6	Bundi ...	1,777	354	35	15	88	5	3	17	...	2	...	...
7	Dholpur ...	667	72	...	10	95	1	...	...	...	...	...	...
8	Dungarpur ...	276	129	5	...	86	8	...	...	...	...	...	...
9	Jaipur ...	8,790	2,049	180	484	405	28	38	1	...	1	26	...
10	Jaisalmer ...	118	15	...	1	...	...	...	...	...	...	...	...
11	Jhalawar ...	282	48	...	8	79	9	2	...	...	...	...	...
12	Karauli ...	457	2	4	...	91	...	...	...	...	...	...	...
13	Kishangarh ...	341	37	7	24	25	...	...	...	...	...	...	...
14	Kotah ...	4,115	1,273	30	10	258	2	15	...	...	...	...	...
15	Kushalgarh (Chiefship).	47	101	5	18	9	4	...	...	...	...	...	...
16	Lawa (Estate) ...	64	21	3	31	...	...	...	...	...	...	...	...
17	Marwar ...	7,651	1,849	8	219	550	56	91	...	...	...	...	...
18	Mewar ...	5,595	3,515	23	354	821	358	8	2	...	...	...	1
19	Partabgarh ...	222	123	1	2	21	15	...	...	...	...	...	...
20	Shahpura ...	183	105	1	3	7	46	...	...	...	...	...	...
21	Sirohi ...	541	11	1	...	32	...	...	...	...	...	...	...
22	Tonk ...	325	89	...	12	21	...	...	...	...	...	...	...
	Cities ...	***10,068***	***2,351***	***25***	***36***	***130***	***16***	***82***	...	...	...	...	...
1	Alwar ...	536	78	1	8	2	...	7	...	...	...	...	...
2	Bharatpur ...	355	40	2	...	11	...	...	...	...	...	...	...
3	Bikaner ...	2,092	382	...	...	37	12	5	...	...	...	...	...
4	Bundi ...	84	9	...	...	1	...	...	...	...	...	...	...
5	Dholpur ...	844	70	...	...	27	1	...	...	...	...	...	...
6	Jaipur ...	1,518	112	22	24	19	1	5	...	...	...	...	...
7	Jodhpur ...	2,372	232	...	...	17	1	62	...	...	...	...	...
8	Kotah ...	1,018	539	...	...	7	...	...	...	...	...	...	...
9	Tonk ...	181	27	...	...	1	...	...	...	...	...	...	...
10	Udaipur ...	1,568	862	...	4	8	1	8	...	...	...	...	...

TABLE X.—Occupation or Means of Livelihood.—Part II.—By State or District and City.—*Continued.*

CLASS B.—PREPARATION AND SUPPLY OF MATERIAL SUBSTANCES.—*Continued.*
SUB CLASS III.—INDUSTRY.—*Concluded.*

Serial Number.	Agency, State or District and City.	Order 16.—Production and Transmission of Physical Force. Total Earners (Principal Occupations). Males.	Total Earners (Principal Occupations). Females.	Total Working Dependants. Males.	Total Working Dependants. Females.	Total following occupation as Subsidiary to other. Males.	Total following occupation as Subsidiary to other. Females.	Order 17.—Miscellaneous and Undefined Industries. Total Earners (Principal Occupations). Males.	Total Earners (Principal Occupations). Females.	Total Working Dependants. Males.	Total Working Dependants. Females.	Total following occupation as Subsidiary to other. Males.	Total following occupation as Subsidiary to other. Females.
1	2	198	199	200	201	202	203	204	205	206	207	208	209
	Rajputana ...	***1,159***	***5***	***17***	...	***21***	***1***	***51,327***	***18,819***	***1,454***	***4,865***	***2,270***	***425***
1	Abu District ...	2	...	...	...	...	...	100	44	...	...	...	...
2	Alwar ...	29	...	...	...	...	...	4,078	1,788	104	1,090	72	1
3	Banswara ...	18	...	...	...	...	...	354	164	8	11	88	19
4	Bharatpur ...	25	...	...	...	1	...	2,545	1,502	85	121	109	23
5	Bikaner ...	249	1	...	...	2	...	3,481	975	58	180	391	13
6	Bundi ...	110	...	...	...	...	...	695	555	24	52	39	4
7	Dholpur ...	58	...	...	...	1	...	794	288	8	235	51	...
8	Dungarpur ...	14	...	...	...	...	...	400	186	17	25	54	4
9	Jaipur ...	147	2	17	...	14	1	14,725	4,767	969	1,866	430	54
10	Jaisalmer ...	...	...	...	...	...	...	175	16	...	...	5	...
11	Jhalawar ...	9	...	...	...	...	...	556	221	...	7	41	19
12	Karauli ...	...	...	...	...	...	...	727	233	20	172	17	...
13	Kishangarh ...	4	...	...	...	...	...	317	122	20	54	24	...
14	Kotah ...	156	2	...	...	...	...	3,097	1,997	31	86	74	39
15	Kushalgarh (Chiefship).	...	...	...	...	...	...	1	...	...	...	...	...
16	Lawa (Estate) ...	...	...	...	...	...	...	15	12	...	...	...	...
17	Marwar ...	230	...	...	...	...	...	10,545	2,814	18	352	464	82
18	Mewar ...	108	...	...	...	3	...	5,873	2,206	65	432	880	123
19	Partabgarh ...	...	...	...	...	...	...	290	118	...	...	18	1
20	Shahpura ...	...	...	...	...	...	...	272	160	3	7	10	1
21	Sirohi ...	...	...	...	...	...	...	981	3	...	144	9	34
22	Tonk ...	...	...	...	...	...	...	1,811	708	65	31	44	8
	Cities ...	**954**	**3**	**17**	...	**9**	...	**8,420**	**2,738**	**153**	**264**	**431**	**25**
1	Alwar ...	8	...	...	...	...	...	376	282	5	18	27	...
2	Bharatpur ...	22	...	...	...	...	...	391	152	...	36	44	2
3	Bikaner ...	237	1	...	...	2	...	1,894	404	...	...	4	...
4	Bundi ...	96	...	...	...	...	...	126	257	...	...	...	...
5	Dholpur ...	52	...	...	...	1	...	129	113	...	...	5	...
6	Jaipur ...	117	2	17	...	4	...	3,575	608	148	205	263	23
7	Jodhpur ...	192	...	...	...	...	...	1,219	340	...	...	74	...
8	Kotah ...	147	...	...	...	...	...	366	170	...	3	5	...
9	Tonk ...	...	...	...	...	...	...	306	178	...	...	7	...
10	Udaipur ...	83	...	...	...	2	...	544	239	...	2	2	...

TABLE X.—Occupation or Means of Livelihood.—Part II.—By State or District and City.—*Continued.*

CLASS B.—PREPARATION AND SUPPLY OF MATERIAL SUBSTANCES.—*Continued.*
SUB-CLASS IV.—TRANSPORT.

SERIAL NUMBER.	AGENCY, STATE OR DISTRICT AND CITY.	TOTAL OF SUB-CLASS IV.						ORDER 18.—TRANSPORT BY AIR.					
		Total Earners (Principal Occupations).		Total Working Dependants.		Total following occupation as Subsidiary to other.		Total Earners (Principal Occupations).		Total Working Dependants.		Total following occupation as Subsidiary to other.	
		Males.	Females	Males.	Females.	Males.	Females.	Males.	Females.	Males.	Females.	Males.	Females.
1	2	210	211	212	213	214	215	216	217	218	219	220	221
	Rajputana ...	**47,127**	**3,061**	**441**	**475**	**6,712**	**137**	**16**	...	...	...	**1**	...
1	Abu District ...	166	60	...	1	2	...	...	...	...	...	...	...
2	Alwar ...	2,623	45	17	12	528	7	...	...	...	...	...	...
3	Banswara ...	155	26	...	...	204	...	...	...	...	...	...	...
4	Bharatpur ...	2,779	163	15	9	1,158	67	...	...	...	...	...	...
5	Bikaner ...	5,338	138	2	2	570	...	...	...	...	...	...	...
6	Bundi ...	747	108	5	11	84	11	6	...	...	...	1	...
7	Dholpur ...	1,085	18	1	1	309	...	...	...	...	...	...	...
8	Dungarpur ...	107	...	2	3	68	...	...	...	...	...	...	...
9	Jaipur ...	11,972	549	306	182	1,505	9	...	...	...	...	...	...
10	Jaisalmer ...	7	...	...	...	8	...	...	...	...	...	...	...
11	Jhalawar ...	430	27	4	...	49	2	...	...	...	...	...	...
12	Karauli ...	725	51	18	16	354	8	...	...	...	...	...	...
13	Kishangarh ...	288	5	13	...	12	...	...	...	...	...	...	...
14	Kotah ...	5,085	779	14	18	466	12	...	...	...	...	...	...
15	Kushalgarh (Chiefship).	13	...	...	...	18	...	...	...	...	...	...	...
16	Lawa (Estate) ...	3	...	...	...	...	...	...	...	...	...	...	...
17	Marwar ...	8,654	234	10	74	578	...	10	...	...	...	...	...
18	Mewar ...	4,833	771	17	146	628	18	...	...	...	...	...	...
19	Partabgarh ...	194	5	1	...	51	1	...	...	...	...	...	...
20	Shahpura ...	64	1	5	...	19	...	...	...	...	...	...	...
21	Sirohi ...	1,346	99	10	...	45	1	...	...	...	...	...	...
22	Tonk ...	513	1	1	...	71	1	...	...	...	...	...	...
	Cities ...	**11,181**	**344**	**9**	**24**	**283**	**2**	**9**	...	...	...	...	...
1	Alwar ...	531	12	...	...	14	...	...	...	...	...	...	...
2	Bharatpur ...	663	...	...	...	20	...	...	...	...	...	...	...
3	Bikaner ...	2,347	38	...	...	72	...	...	...	...	...	...	...
4	Bundi ...	100	11	...	...	4	...	...	...	...	...	...	...
5	Dholpur ...	536	1	...	...	44	...	...	...	...	...	...	...
6	Jaipur ...	1,464	37	8	22	50	...	...	...	...	...	...	...
7	Jodhpur ...	3,446	5	...	1	17	...	9	...	...	...	...	...
8	Kotah ...	1,124	30	...	...	9	...	...	...	...	...	...	...
9	Tonk ...	221	...	...	...	2	...	...	...	...	...	...	...
10	Udaipur ...	749	201	1	1	51	2	...	...	...	...	...	...

TABLE X.—Occupation or Means of Livelihood.—Part II.—By State or District and City.—*Continued.*

CLASS B.—PREPARATION AND SUPPLY OF MATERIAL SUBSTANCES—*Continued.*
SUB-CLASS IV.—TRANSPORT.—*Continued.*

Serial Number.	Agency, State or District and City.	Order 19.—Transport by Water. Total Earners (Principal Occupations). Males.	Females.	Total Working Dependants. Males.	Females.	Total following occupation as Subsidiary to other. Males.	Females.	Order 20.—Transport by Road. Total Earners (Principal Occupations). Males.	Females.	Total Working Dependants. Males.	Females.	Total following occupation as Subsidiary to other. Males.	Females.
1	2	222	223	224	225	226	227	228	229	230	231	232	233
	Rajputana ...	*501*	...	*1*	...	*109*	...	*23,969*	*2,429*	*399*	*421*	*5,932*	*134*
1	Abu District ...	...	...	...	...	...	...	129	60	...	1	2	...
2	Alwar ...	8	...	...	...	1	...	1,966	41	17	12	507	6
3	Banswara ...	...	...	...	...	6	...	137	26	...	...	195	...
4	Bharatpur ...	2	...	...	...	...	...	1,586	160	14	9	1,133	67
5	Bikaner ...	132	...	1	...	4	...	2,028	41	1	...	490	...
6	Bundi ...	101	...	...	...	23	...	378	95	5	10	56	11
7	Dholpur ...	47	...	...	...	16	...	535	18	1	1	256	...
8	Dungarpur ...	...	...	...	...	...	...	96	...	2	3	68	...
9	Jaipur ...	18	...	...	...	7	...	6,886	500	287	182	1,393	9
10	Jaisalmer ...	...	...	...	...	...	...	1	...	...	...	7	...
11	Jhalawar ...	...	...	...	...	1	...	257	25	4	...	47	2
12	Karauli ...	1	...	...	...	18	...	672	51	18	16	331	8
13	Kishangarh ...	...	...	...	...	...	...	202	5	13	...	9	...
14	Kotah ...	128	...	...	...	19	...	8,556	725	13	11	416	12
15	Kushalgarh (Chiefship).	...	...	...	...	...	...	10	...	...	...	16	...
16	Lawa (Estate) ...	...	...	...	...	...	...	3	...	...	...	...	...
17	Marwar ...	...	...	...	...	...	...	2,001	203	...	30	320	...
18	Mewar ...	58	...	...	...	12	...	2,786	469	17	146	537	16
19	Partabgarh ...	...	...	...	...	...	...	184	5	1	...	51	1
20	Shahpura ...	...	...	...	...	2	...	59	1	5	...	17	...
21	Sirohi ...	...	...	...	...	...	...	79	3	...	...	10	1
22	Tonk ...	6	...	...	...	...	...	418	1	1	...	71	1
	Cities ...	*91*	...	...	...	...	...	*5,569*	*327*	*8*	*23*	*250*	*2*
1	Alwar ...	3	...	...	...	...	...	423	12	...	...	14	...
2	Bharatpur ...	...	...	...	...	...	...	362	...	...	...	19	...
3	Bikaner ...	1	...	...	...	...	...	987	24	...	...	67	...
4	Bundi ...	...	...	...	...	...	...	59	11	...	...	4	...
5	Dholpur ...	10	...	...	...	...	...	227	1	...	...	41	...
6	Jaipur ...	...	...	...	...	...	...	1,236	36	7	22	47	...
7	Jodhpur ...	...	...	...	...	...	...	624	3	...	...	...	...
8	Kotah ...	35	...	...	...	...	...	980	39	...	...	9	...
9	Tonk ...	...	...	...	...	...	...	213	...	...	...	2	...
10	Udaipur ...	42	...	...	...	...	...	558	201	1	1	47	2

TABLE X.—Occupation or Means of Livelihood.—Part II.—By State or District and City.—*Continued.*

CLASS B.—PREPARATION AND SUPPLY OF MATERIAL SUBSTANCES.—*Continued.*
SUB-CLASS IV.—TRANSPORT.—*Concluded.*

Serial Number.	Agency, State or District and City.	Order 21.—Transport by Rail. Total Earners (Principal Occupations). Males.	Order 21. Total Earners. Females.	Order 21. Total Working Dependants. Males.	Order 21. Total Working Dependants. Females.	Order 21. Total following occupation as Subsidiary to other. Males.	Order 21. Total following occupation as Subsidiary to other. Females.	Order 22.—Post Office, Telegraph and Telephone Services. Total Earners (Principal Occupations). Males.	Order 22. Total Earners. Females.	Order 22. Total Working Dependants. Males.	Order 22. Total Working Dependants. Females.	Order 22. Total following occupation as Subsidiary to other. Males.	Order 22. Total following occupation as Subsidiary to other. Females.
1	2	234	235	236	237	238	239	240	241	242	243	244	245
	Rajputana ...	***20,700***	***610***	***40***	***54***	***632***	***3***	***1,941***	***22***	***1***	...	***38***	...
1	Abu District ...	27	...	...	...	...	...	10	...	...	...	...	...
2	Alwar ...	529	3	...	...	9	1	120	1	...	...	6	...
3	Banswara ...	...	...	...	...	...	...	18	...	...	...	3	...
4	Bharatpur ...	1,117	3	1	...	19	...	74	...	...	...	1	...
5	Bikaner ...	3,049	72	...	2	75	...	129	20	...	...	1	...
6	Bundi ...	227	8	...	1	4	...	35	...	...	...	...	...
7	Dholpur ...	472	...	...	...	28	...	31	...	...	...	9	...
8	Dungarpur ...	...	...	...	...	...	...	11	...	...	...	...	...
9	Jaipur ...	4,786	48	18	...	101	...	282	1	1	...	4	...
10	Jaisalmer ...	1	...	...	...	...	...	5	...	...	...	1	...
11	Jhalawar ...	129	2	...	...	...	...	44	...	...	...	1	...
12	Karauli ...	40	...	...	...	3	...	12	...	...	...	2	...
13	Kishangarh ...	63	...	...	...	...	...	23	...	...	...	3	...
14	Kotah ...	1,244	54	1	7	31	...	157	...	...	...	...	...
15	Kushalgarh (Chiefship).	...	...	...	...	...	...	3	...	...	...	2	...
16	Lawa (Estate) ...	...	...	...	...	...	...	...	...	...	...	...	...
17	Marwar ...	5,907	31	10	44	253	...	736	...	...	...	...	...
18	Mewar ...	1,816	302	...	...	74	2	173	...	...	...	5	...
19	Partabgarh ...	1	...	...	...	...	...	9	...	...	...	...	...
20	Shahpura ...	1	...	...	...	...	...	4	...	...	...	...	...
21	Sirohi ...	1,222	87	10	...	35	...	45	...	...	...	...	...
22	Tonk ...	69	...	...	...	...	...	20	...	...	...	...	...
	Cities ...	***5,049***	***17***	...	***1***	***32***	...	***463***	...	***1***	...	***1***	...
1	Alwar ...	69	...	...	...	...	...	36	...	...	...	...	...
2	Bharatpur ...	259	...	...	...	1	...	42	...	...	...	...	...
3	Bikaner ...	1,284	14	...	...	5	...	75	...	...	...	...	...
4	Bundi ...	24	...	...	...	...	...	17	...	...	...	...	...
5	Dholpur ...	279	...	...	...	3	...	20	...	...	...	...	...
6	Jaipur ...	130	1	...	...	3	...	98	...	1	...	...	...
7	Jodhpur ...	2,818	2	...	1	17	...	95	...	...	...	...	...
8	Kotah ...	66	...	...	...	...	...	43	...	...	...	...	...
9	Tonk ...	...	...	...	...	...	...	8	...	...	...	...	...
10	Udaipur ...	120	...	...	...	3	...	29	...	...	...	1	...

TABLE X.—Occupation or Means of Livelihood.—Part II.—By State or District and City.—*Continued.*

CLASS B.—PREPARATION AND SUPPLY OF MATERIAL SUBSTANCES.—*Continued.*
SUB-CLASS V.—TRADE.

SERIAL NUMBER.	AGENCY, STATE OR DISTRICT AND CITY.	TOTAL OF SUB-CLASS V.						ORDER 23.—BANKS, ESTABLISHMENTS OF CREDIT, EXCHANGE AND INSURANCE.					
		Total Earners (Principal Occupations).		Total Working Dependants.		Total following occupation as Subsidiary to other.		Total Earners (Principal Occupations).		Total Working Dependants.		Total following occupation as Subsidiary to other.	
		Males.	Females.	Males.	Females.	Males.	Females.	Males.	Females.	Males.	Females.	Males.	Females.
1	2	246	247	248	249	250	251	252	253	254	255	256	257
	Rajputana ...	**224,601**	**59,506**	**4,475**	**9,203**	**34,920**	**4,839**	**32,218**	**2,100**	**551**	**460**	**8,488**	**139**
1	Abu District ...	147	46	...	...	9	2	1	1	...	...	2	...
2	Alwar ...	15,040	2,475	84	749	2,467	243	2,758	77	11	88	1,311	20
3	Banswara ...	2,859	1,237	138	21	553	47	416	15	...	...	34	...
4	Bharatpur ...	9,289	4,744	151	190	3,526	390	914	45	5	...	1,526	25
5	Bikaner ...	14,970	1,835	289	50	1,250	15	748	264	...	11	59	...
6	Bundi ...	3,611	1,286	56	214	468	79	215	12	...	...	96	5
7	Dholpur ...	3,920	657	27	328	1,288	72	559	20	1	...	601	2
8	Dungarpur ...	2,748	832	238	70	835	4	301	84	40	8	10	...
9	Jaipur ...	50,706	8,276	2,817	2,618	4,594	832	7,090	328	372	158	2,482	26
10	Jaisalmer ...	1,487	82	8	92	486	25	495	30	6	33	218	...
11	Jhalawar ...	2,466	863	8	45	390	55	256	14	1	...	84	2
12	Karauli ...	2,834	202	73	292	941	54	518	42	9	4	342	11
13	Kishangarh ...	1,619	302	100	29	201	10	376	26	22	...	73	...
14	Kotah ...	9,095	4,976	117	389	1,853	374	44	1	...	...	...	...
15	Kushalgarh (Chiefship).	317	79	...	6	35	10	1	...	...	...	...	...
16	Lawa (Estate) ...	51	...	...	...	6	...	2	...	...	...	6	...
17	Marwar ...	45,522	5,554	71	840	3,284	547	10,557	939	30	191	1,054	39
18	Mewar ...	43,233	22,727	202	2,538	12,001	2,417	4,837	151	37	18	293	6
19	Partabgarh ...	1,648	260	...	...	378	33	393	29	...	...	120	3
20	Shahpura ...	1,073	257	7	8	178	13	99	4	...	...	49	...
21	Sirohi ...	5,672	2,102	78	578	285	112	1,237	2	16	...	52	...
22	Tonk ...	5,394	1,124	61	152	442	5	406	16	1	4	76	...
	Cities ...	**25,266**	**5,713**	**170**	**251**	**853**	**94**	**1,955**	**293**	**3**	**21**	**163**	**6**
1	Alwar ...	1,912	594	9	62	47	35	106	14	...	4	17	1
2	Bharatpur ...	1,271	389	8	4	79	3	76	4	...	...	15	...
3	Bikaner ...	4,206	960	...	...	122	1	269	77	...	...	8	...
4	Bundi ...	863	376	...	1	60	1	69	6	...	...	12	...
5	Dholpur ...	868	166	17	2	133	16	75	4	...	...	48	3
6	Jaipur ...	6,324	735	135	137	140	24	533	51	3	2	33	1
7	Jodhpur ...	4,447	849	...	...	54	1	554	120	...	...	20	1
8	Kotah ...	1,530	614	...	7	84	3	36	...	...	...	4	...
9	Tonk ...	1,100	181	...	...	100	...	88	...	...	...	...	...
10	Udaipur ...	2,745	949	1	88	84	10	149	17	...	15	6	...

TABLE X.—OCCUPATION OR MEANS OF LIVELIHOOD.—PART II.—BY STATE OR DISTRICT AND CITY.—*Continued.*

CLASS B.—PREPARATION AND SUPPLY OF MATERIAL SUBSTANCES.—*Continued.*
SUB-CLASS V.—TRADE.—*Continued.*

SERIAL NUMBER.	AGENCY, STATE OR DISTRICT AND CITY.	ORDER 24.—BROKERAGE, COMMISSION AND EXPORT. Total Earners (Principal Occupations). Males.	Females.	Total Working Dependants. Males.	Females.	Total following occupation as Subsidiary to other. Males.	Females.	ORDER 25.—TRADE IN TEXTILES. Total Earners (Principal Occupations). Males.	Females.	Total Working Dependants. Males.	Females.	Total following occupation as Subsidiary to other. Males.	Females.
1	2	258	259	260	261	262	263	264	265	266	267	268	269
	Rajputana ...	**2,939**	**26**	**48**	**2**	**270**	...	**15,411**	**445**	**250**	**219**	**709**	**49**
1	Abu District ...	...	...	...	...	...	...	...	...	...	...	...	...
2	Alwar ...	107	...	...	...	5	...	584	7	...	32	18	5
3	Banswara ...	10	...	...	...	6	...	8	...	...	...	1	...
4	Bharatpur ...	66	...	...	...	66	...	63	7	3	...	18	...
5	Bikaner ...	526	9	11	...	54	...	4,098	22	99	...	161	...
6	Bundi ...	55	...	...	...	1	...	62	...	...	...	26	1
7	Dholpur ...	12	...	...	...	4	...	30	...	...	...	5	...
8	Dungarpur ...	10	...	...	...	2	...	353	4	17	4	15	...
9	Jaipur ...	1,090	10	17	2	36	...	1,514	65	116	95	67	1
10	Jaisalmer ...	2	...	...	...	...	...	60	...	...	...	12	...
11	Jhalawar ...	112	2	...	...	16	...	30	2	...	...	4	...
12	Karauli ...	1	...	...	...	...	...	235	...	1	...	85	...
13	Kishangarh ...	15	...	...	...	...	...	48	17	...	...	...	...
14	Kotah ...	162	2	...	...	31	...	942	77	5	13	124	1
15	Kushalgarh (Chiefship).	1	...	...	...	1	...	24	...	...	...	...	...
16	Lawa (Estate) ...	...	...	...	...	...	...	...	...	...	...	...	...
17	Marwar ...	328	...	...	...	...	...	2,996	6	3	1	29	...
18	Mewar ...	141	2	...	...	3	...	8,518	108	6	74	151	40
19	Partabgarh ...	71	1	...	...	31	...	14	9	...	...	7	1
20	Shahpura ...	4	...	...	...	3	...	93	2	...	...	6	...
21	Sirohi ...	140	...	20	...	...	...	491	...	...	...	1	...
22	Tonk ...	71	...	...	...	11	...	308	119	...	...	29	...
	Cities ...	**631**	**2**	**5**	...	**15**	...	**2,976**	**71**	**18**	**7**	**60**	**2**
1	Alwar ...	56	...	...	...	...	...	172	2	...	...	...	...
2	Bharatpur ...	8	...	...	...	...	...	22	...	...	...	8	...
3	Bikaner ...	21	...	...	...	...	...	942	4	...	...	17	...
4	Bundi ...	48	...	...	...	...	...	42	...	...	...	15	1
5	Dholpur ...	8	...	...	...	1	...	5	...	...	...	1	...
6	Jaipur ...	814	2	5	...	2	...	408	8	18	...	5	...
7	Jodhpur ...	25	...	...	...	...	...	800	...	...	...	...	...
8	Kotah ...	78	...	...	...	1	...	152	29	...	...	10	...
9	Tonk ...	49	...	...	...	11	...	115	16	...	...	3	...
10	Udaipur ...	29	...	...	...	...	...	818	12	...	7	1	1

TABLE X.—OCCUPATION OR MEANS OF LIVELIHOOD.—PART II.—BY STATE OR DISTRICT AND CITY.—*Continued.*

CLASS B.—PREPARATION AND SUPPLY OF MATERIAL SUBSTANCES.—*Continued.*
SUB-CLASS V.—TRADE.—*Continued.*

SERIAL NUMBER.	AGENCY, STATE OR DISTRICT AND CITY.	ORDER 26.—TRADE IN SKINS, LEATHER AND FURS.						ORDER 27.—TRADE IN WOOD.					
		Total Earners (Principal Occupations).		Total Working Dependants.		Total following occupation as Subsidiary to other.		Total Earners (Principal Occupations).		Total Working Dependants.		Total following occupation as Subsidiary to other	
		Males.	Females.	Males.	Females.	Males.	Females.	Males.	Females.	Males.	Females	Males.	Females.
1	2	270	271	272	273	274	275	276	277	278	279	280	281
	Rajputana ...	***2,933***	***93***	***22***	***106***	***252***	***1***	***874***	***650***	***10***	***70***	***408***	***52***
1	Abu District ...	...	...	...	...	...	...	...	...	...	...	...	...
2	Alwar ...	891	1	...	2	21	...	59	24	1	12	7	3
3	Banswara ...	81	3	...	...	2	...	...	...	...	...	...	...
4	Bharatpur ...	28	...	...	...	16	...	27	1	...	...	2	...
5	Bikaner ...	44	...	1	...	36	...	7	6	...	3	8	...
6	Bundi ...	14	...	...	...	...	...	...	14	...	...	...	...
7	Dholpur ...	58	1	...	...	21	...	1	...	...	...	1	...
8	Dungarpur ...	13	6	...	...	3	...	2	...	3	...	...	...
9	Jaipur ...	505	35	21	85	24	...	151	35	3	19	8	1
10	Jaisalmer ...	...	...	...	...	...	...	...	...	...	...	...	...
11	Jhalawar ...	8	6	...	...	1	...	17	...	...	...	...	...
12	Karauli ...	18	...	...	...	1	...	2	...	...	...	1	...
13	Kishangarh ...	22	1	...	5	...	...	36	...	...	...	...	...
14	Kotah ...	85	1	...	...	15	...	55	1	...	...	12	...
15	Kushalgarh (Chiefship).	1	...	...	...	...	...	...	...	...	...	...	...
16	Lawa (Estate) ...	7	...	...	...	...	...	...	...	...	...	...	...
17	Marwar ...	683	18	...	...	52	...	85	63	...	16	7	2
18	Mewar ...	450	18	...	14	53	1	343	472	3	20	308	44
19	Partabgarh ...	10	...	...	...	7	...	46	9	...	...	42	2
20	Shahpura ...	...	...	...	...	...	...	1	...	...	...	8	...
21	Sirohi ...	118	2	...	...	...	...	39	2	...	...	4	...
22	Tonk ...	12	1	...	...	...	...	3	24	...	...	10	...
	Cities ...	***270***	***19***	***5***	...	***5***	...	***101***	***22***	...	***2***	***1***	***1***
1	Alwar ...	6	...	...	...	...	...	22	3	...	2	...	...
2	Bharatpur ...	13	...	...	...	4	...	9	...	...	...	...	...
3	Bikaner ...	6	...	...	...	...	...	3	1	...	...	...	...
4	Bundi ...	...	...	...	...	...	...	...	7	...	...	...	...
5	Dholpur ...	4	...	...	...	...	...	1	...	...	...	1	...
6	Jaipur ...	218	5	5	...	1	...	38	6	...	...	...	1
7	Jodhpur ...	3	13	...	...	...	...	23	5	...	...	...	...
8	Kotah ...	13	...	...	...	...	...	...	...	...	...	...	...
9	Tonk ...	3	...	...	...	...	...	...	...	...	...	...	...
10	Udaipur ...	4	1	...	...	...	...	5	...	...	...	...	...

TABLE X.—Occupation or Means of Livelihood.—Part II.—By State or District and City.—*Continued.*

Serial Number.	Agency, State or District and City.	Class B.—Preparation and Supply of Material Substances.—*Continued.* Sub-Class V.—Trade.—*Continued.* Order 28.—Trade in Metal. Total Earners (Principal Occupations). Males	Females.	Total Working Dependants. Males	Females.	Total following occupation as Subsidiary to other. Males.	Females.	Order 29.—Trade in Pottery, Bricks and Tiles. Total Earners (Principal Occupations). Males.	Females.	Total Working Dependants. Males.	Females.	Total following occupation as Subsidiary to other. Males.	Females.
1	2	282	283	284	285	286	287	288	289	290	291	292	293
	Rajputana ...	**680**	**18**	**7**	**3**	**67**	**2**	**184**	**100**	**11**	**12**	**6**	**1**
1	Abu District ...	...	...	...	...	...	...	...	...	...	...	...	...
2	Alwar ...	47	2	...	...	1	...	21	2	1	...	3	...
3	Banswara ...	...	...	...	...	1	...	...	...	...	...	...	...
4	Bharatpur ...	26	3	...	...	...	2	...	...	...	...	...	...
5	Bikaner ...	19	...	...	...	...	...	1	12	...	...	...	1
6	Bundi ...	...	...	...	...	...	...	...	...	...	...	...	...
7	Dholpur ...	...	...	...	...	...	...	...	...	...	...	...	...
8	Dungarpur ...	28	1	...	...	9	...	...	...	...	...	...	...
9	Jaipur ...	164	1	5	1	1	...	58	27	10	2	3	...
10	Jaisalmer ...	...	...	...	...	...	...	...	...	...	...	...	...
11	Jhalawar ...	...	...	...	...	...	...	...	...	...	...	...	...
12	Karauli ...	46	...	...	...	...	...	...	...	...	...	...	...
13	Kishangarh ...	...	...	...	...	...	...	...	...	...	...	...	...
14	Kotah ...	8	...	1	...	...	...	9	...	...	...	...	...
15	Kushalgarh (Chiefship).	...	...	...	...	...	...	...	...	...	...	...	...
16	Lawa (Estate) ...	...	...	...	...	...	...	...	...	...	...	...	...
17	Marwar ...	90	...	...	...	2	...	...	...	...	...	...	...
18	Mewar ...	73	8	...	2	2	...	96	48	...	...	...	...
19	Partabgarh ...	18	...	...	...	1	...	...	...	...	...	...	...
20	Shahpura ...	1	...	...	...	1	...	...	...	...	...	...	...
21	Sirohi ...	1	...	...	...	...	...	4	11	...	10	...	...
22	Tonk ...	159	3	1	...	49	...	...	...	...	...	...	...
	Cities ...	**155**	**2**	...	...	**19**	...	**11**	**16**	...	**1**	...	...
1	Alwar ...	82	...	...	...	...	...	...	...	...	...	...	...
2	Bharatpur ...	14	2	...	...	...	...	...	...	...	...	...	...
3	Bikaner ...	14	...	...	...	...	...	...	12	...	...	...	...
4	Bundi ...	...	...	...	...	...	...	...	...	...	...	...	...
5	Dholpur ...	...	...	...	...	...	...	...	...	...	...	...	...
6	Jaipur ...	88	...	...	...	1	...	3	4	...	1	...	...
7	Jodhpur ...	...	...	...	...	...	...	...	...	...	...	...	...
8	Kotah ...	2	...	...	...	...	...	8	...	...	...	...	...
9	Tonk ...	36	...	...	...	16	...	...	...	...	...	...	...
10	Udaipur ...	19	...	...	...	2	...	...	...	...	...	...	...

TABLE X.—Occupation or Means of Livelihood.—Part II.—By State or District and City.—*Continued.*

CLASS B.—PREPARATION AND SUPPLY OF MATERIAL SUBSTANCES—*Continued.*
SUB-CLASS V.—TRADE.—*Continued.*

SERIAL NUMBER.	AGENCY, STATE OR DISTRICT AND CITY.	ORDER 30.—TRADE IN CHEMICAL PRODUCTS.						ORDER 31.—HOTELS, CAFES, RESTAURANTS, ETC.					
		Total Earners (Principal Occupations).		Total Working Dependants.		Total following occupation as Subsidiary to other.		Total Earners (Principal Occupations).		Total Working Dependants.		Total following occupation as Subsidiary to other.	
		Males.	Females.	Males.	Females.	Males.	Females.	Males.	Females.	Males.	Females.	Males.	Females.
1	2	294	295	296	297	298	299	300	301	302	303	304	305
	Rajputana ...	*756*	*255*	*5*	*11*	*239*	*16*	*6,029*	*586*	*86*	*422*	*502*	*28*
1	Abu District ...	...	...	...	...	...	...	6	...	...	...	...	...
2	Alwar ...	21	1	...	...	1	...	832	12	6	33	22	...
3	Banswara ...	...	1	...	...	...	...	105	2	...	1	25	...
4	Bharatpur ...	7	1	...	...	...	...	90	9	...	...	11	...
5	Bikaner ...	46	1	...	...	...	...	155	6	...	...	8	...
6	Bundi ...	58	...	...	...	1	1	184	66	...	52	22	2
7	Dholpur ...	54	...	...	...	8	...	70	8	2	8	8	...
8	Dungarpur ...	18	...	...	...	...	...	168	12	1	5	109	...
9	Jaipur ...	259	118	8	5	4	...	1,087	74	52	58	89	4
10	Jaisalmer ...	...	...	...	...	...	...	...	...	...	...	...	...
11	Jhalawar ...	2	16	...	...	10	5	43	9	...	...	16	...
12	Karauli ...	9	...	...	...	...	...	99	...	...	...	17	...
13	Kishangarh ...	12	...	...	...	1	...	62	16	4	8	18	1
14	Kotah ...	26	...	2	...	208	...	198	63	2	2	84	7
15	Kushalgarh (Chiefship).	...	...	...	...	...	...	18	2	...	1	1	...
16	Lawa (Estate) ...	...	...	...	...	...	...	1	...	...	...	...	...
17	Marwar ...	29	...	...	...	1	...	265	1	...	...	5	...
18	Mewar ...	58	48	...	6	6	10	2,982	295	19	268	144	13
19	Partabgarh ...	10	...	...	...	1	...	70	8	...	...	18	1
20	Shahpura ...	...	...	...	...	...	...	12	2	...	...	5	...
21	Sirohi ...	45	...	...	...	8	...	154	2	...	1	5	...
22	Tonk ...	112	69	...	...	...	...	88	4	...	...	...	...
	Cities ...	*159*	*4*	*1*	...	*6*	...	*880*	*78*	*8*	*25*	*30*	*3*
1	Alwar ...	8	...	...	...	...	...	132	2	3	21	...	...
2	Bharatpur ...	7	1	...	...	...	...	29	...	...	...	8	...
3	Bikaner ...	28	1	...	...	...	...	109	6	...	...	...	...
4	Bundi ...	2	...	...	...	1	...	48	22	...	...	9	...
5	Dholpur ...	10	...	...	...	1	...	89	2	2	1	6	...
6	Jaipur ...	66	2	1	...	8	...	285	7	3	...	10	...
7	Jodhpur ...	...	...	...	...	...	...	66	...	...	...	...	...
8	Kotah ...	9	...	...	...	1	...	85	24	...	...	1	8
9	Tonk ...	11	...	...	...	...	...	16	...	...	...	...	...
10	Udaipur ...	18	...	...	...	...	...	126	15	...	8	1	...

TABLE X.—Occupation or Means of Livelihood.—Part II.—By State or District and City.—*Continued.*

CLASS B.—PREPARATION AND SUPPLY OF MATERIAL SUBSTANCES.—*Continued.*
SUB-CLASS V.—TRADE.—*Continued.*

Serial Number.	Agency, State or District and City.	Order 32.—Other Trade in Food Stuffs. Total Earners (Principal Occupations). Males.	Females.	Total Working Dependants. Males.	Females.	Total following occupation as Subsidiary to other. Males.	Females.	Order 33.—Trade in Clothing and Toilet Articles. Total Earners (Principal Occupations). Males.	Females.	Total Working Dependants. Males.	Females.	Total following occupation as Subsidiary to other. Males.	Females.
1	2	306	307	308	309	310	311	312	313	314	315	316	317
	Rajputana ...	*101,612*	*37,915*	*2,255*	*5,111*	*13,898*	*2,423*	*9,860*	*386*	*218*	*327*	*572*	*5*
1	Abu District ...	8	2	...	...	2	2	...	...	...	...	...	...
2	Alwar ...	5,802	1,822	88	517	580	182	130	31	2	9	21	...
3	Banswara ...	1,708	1,159	128	20	314	33	119	1	3	...	23	...
4	Bharatpur ...	5,690	3,176	87	124	868	110	648	4	2	...	85	...
5	Bikaner ...	7,881	1,048	127	27	548	7	187	18	...	3	1	...
6	Bundi ...	1,648	510	45	68	111	40	195	4	1	...	18	...
7	Dholpur ...	2,475	497	28	229	449	64	366	24	...	50	26	1
8	Dungarpur ...	844	193	88	62	142	4	7	...	14	...	...	...
9	Jaipur ...	26,272	5,182	1,448	1,516	1,296	194	3,716	85	181	245	124	1
10	Jaisalmer ...	702	84	1	59	167	25	...	...	...	...	...	...
11	Jhalawar ...	1,272	492	7	86	141	21	212	21	...	...	24	3
12	Karauli ...	1,451	195	87	161	319	38	52	...	...	...	20	...
13	Kishangarh ...	841	163	78	21	103	7	149	2	1	...	5	...
14	Kotah ...	3,874	4,170	89	310	765	350	295	52	...	2	12	...
15	Kushalgarh (Chiefship).	244	68	...	4	33	10	...	...	...	...	...	...
16	Lawa (Estate) ...	5	...	...	...	...	...	...	...	...	...	...	...
17	Marwar ...	16,805	2,680	8	380	964	376	2,796	48	14	...	148	...
18	Mewar ...	18,920	14,251	54	1,089	6,606	923	710	59	...	6	48	...
19	Partabgarh ...	725	186	...	...	120	3	171	7	...	...	17	...
20	Shahpura ...	711	101	5	2	74	7	3	...	...	...	2	...
21	Sirohi ...	1,210	1,390	4	384	95	22	20	12	...	...	...	...
22	Tonk ...	3,520	596	48	102	201	5	140	18	...	12	3	...
	Cities ...	*10,872*	*3,615*	*79*	*164*	*290*	*62*	*1,509*	*76*	*17*	*3*	*14*	...
1	Alwar ...	758	428	5	29	26	33	6	3	...	...	...	...
2	Bharatpur ...	748	271	8	8	32	3	76	...	...	...	...	...
3	Bikaner ...	2,264	536	...	...	23	1	106	10	...	...	1	...
4	Bundi ...	378	47	...	...	10	...	86	...	...	...	1	...
5	Dholpur ...	535	136	14	1	55	15	117	...	...	...	4	...
6	Jaipur ...	2,323	518	52	112	36	3	548	14	17	3	4	...
7	Jodhpur ...	1,600	465	...	...	15	...	326	8	...	...	...	...
8	Kotah ...	798	478	...	6	47	...	100	26	...	...	1	...
9	Tonk ...	570	43	...	...	43	...	41	3	...	...	3	...
10	Udaipur ...	903	698	...	18	3	7	108	17	...	...	...	...

TABLE X.—OCCUPATION OR MEANS OF LIVELIHOOD.—PART II.—BY STATE OR DISTRICT AND CITY.—*Continued.*

CLASS B.—PREPARATION AND SUPPLY OF MATERIAL SUBSTANCES—*Continued.*
SUB-CLASS V.—TRADE.—*Continued.*

SERIAL NUMBER.	AGENCY, STATE OR DISTRICT AND CITY.	ORDER 34.—TRADE IN FURNITURE.						ORDER 35.—TRADE IN BUILDING MATERIALS.					
		Total Earners (Principal Occupations).		Total Working Dependants.		Total following occupation as Subsidiary to other.		Total Earners (Principal Occupations).		Total Working Dependants.		Total following occupation as Subsidiary to other.	
		Males.	Females.	Males.	Females.	Males	Females.	Males.	Females.	Males.	Females	Males.	Females.
1	2	318	319	320	321	322	323	324	325	326	327	328	329
	Rajputana ...	*907*	*248*	*9*	*15*	*122*	*8*	*465*	*257*	*7*	*43*	*34*	*18*
1	Abu District ...	...	...	...	...	...	...	...	...	...	...	...	...
2	Alwar ...	12	9	...	1	...	...	5	31	...	5	1	1
3	Banswara ...	7	...	...	...	14	...	6	2	...	...	11	12
4	Bharatpur ...	...	...	...	...	...	...	5	...	...	...	...	...
5	Bikaner ...	49	11	...	...	17	...	22	9	...	...	1	...
6	Bundi ...	4	50	...	...	1	...	4	16	...	6	1	1
7	Dholpur ...	30	1	1	...	3	...	14	...	...	...	...	...
8	Dungarpur ...	29	...	...	...	1	...	2	...	1	...	1	...
9	Jaipur ...	142	22	6	...	4	...	138	80	6	31	13	3
10	Jaisalmer ...	...	...	...	...	...	...	...	...	...	...	...	...
11	Jhalawar ...	15	1	...	...	2	...	18	17	...	...	3	...
12	Karauli ...	...	...	...	...	...	...	...	...	...	...	...	...
13	Kishangarh ...	...	...	...	...	...	...	...	...	...	...	...	...
14	Kotah ...	54	3	...	...	13	...	39	1	...	...	...	...
15	Kushalgarh (Chiefship).	...	...	...	...	...	...	...	...	...	...	...	...
16	Lawa (Estate) ...	...	...	...	...	...	...	...	...	...	...	...	...
17	Marwar ...	352	15	...	1	6	6	31	...	...	...	...	...
18	Mewar ...	167	129	...	12	60	2	152	87	...	...	3	1
19	Partabgarh ...	...	...	...	...	...	...	...	...	...	...	...	...
20	Shahpura ...	...	...	...	...	...	...	...	...	...	...	...	...
21	Sirohi ...	26	2	...	1	1	...	4	...	...	...	...	...
22	Tonk ...	20	5	2	...	...	...	25	14	...	1	...	...
	Cities ...	*122*	*32*	*3*	...	...	...	*108*	*23*	...	...	*4*	...
1	Alwar ...	...	...	...	...	...	...	8	...	...	...	...	...
2	Bharatpur ...	...	...	...	...	...	...	2	...	...	...	...	...
3	Bikaner ...	21	...	...	...	...	...	22	9	...	...	...	...
4	Bundi ...	...	...	...	...	...	...	...	...	...	...	...	...
5	Dholpur ...	10	1	1	...	...	...	10	...	...	...	...	...
6	Jaipur ...	62	2	2	...	...	...	11	1	...	...	3	...
7	Jodhpur ...	19	2	...	...	...	...	5	...	...	...	...	...
8	Kotah ...	...	...	...	...	...	...	...	...	...	...	...	...
9	Tonk ...	...	...	...	...	...	...	...	...	...	...	...	...
10	Udaipur ...	10	27	...	...	...	...	55	13	...	...	1	...

TABLE X.—Occupation or Means of Livelihood.—Part II.—By State or District and City.—*Continued.*

CLASS B.—PREPARATION AND SUPPLY OF MATERIAL SUBSTANCES.—*Continued.*
SUB-CLASS V.—TRADE.—*Continued.*

Serial Number.	Agency, State or District and City.	Order 36.—Trade in Means of Transport. Total Earners (Principal Occupations). Males.	Females.	Total Working Dependants. Males.	Females.	Total following occupation as Subsidiary to other. Males.	Females.	Order 37.—Trade in Fuel. Total Earners (Principal Occupations). Males.	Females.	Total Working Dependants. Males.	Females.	Total following occupation as Subsidiary to other. Males.	Females.
1	2	330	331	332	333	334	335	336	337	338	339	340	341
	Rajputana ...	*6,166*	*208*	*84*	*7*	*1,271*	*1*	*8,038*	*13,843*	*149*	*1,880*	*6,011*	*2,052*
1	Abu District ...	5	...	...	...	...	...	80	41	...	...	1	...
2	Alwar ...	227	4	...	...	56	1	339	295	2	43	157	27
3	Banswara ...	11	2	...	...	87	...	9	10	...	...	16	...
4	Bharatpur ...	463	1	5	...	186	...	705	1,322	21	63	706	252
5	Bikaner ...	77	10	...	...	78	...	101	846	...	4	233	7
6	Bundi ...	113	1	...	1	54	...	280	580	4	69	41	29
7	Dholpur ...	84	...	...	...	32	...	63	61	...	27	54	4
8	Dungarpur ...	41	2	4	...	12	...	...	...	...	...	...	...
9	Jaipur ...	842	20	28	...	142	...	1,114	1,930	24	259	135	98
10	Jaisalmer ...	...	...	...	...	...	...	...	...	...	...	...	...
11	Jhalawar ...	79	14	...	...	34	...	92	214	...	3	44	24
12	Karauli ...	9	...	...	...	1	...	192	52	25	124	172	5
13	Kishangarh ...	5	...	...	...	...	...	11	75	...	...	...	2
14	Kotah ...	419	22	4	...	143	...	90	76	...	1	10	...
15	Kushalgarh (Chiefship)	15	...	...	...	...	...	...	6	...	1	...	...
16	Lawa (Estate) ...	...	...	...	...	...	...	...	...	...	...	...	...
17	Marwar ...	2,500	13	...	...	277	...	887	1,192	5	186	808	120
18	Mewar ...	410	19	1	2	114	...	8,590	6,719	62	976	4,061	1,870
19	Partabgarh ...	29	...	...	...	6	...	8	8	...	...	5	23
20	Shahpura ...	7	...	...	...	10	...	91	140	2	1	23	6
21	Sirohi ...	782	100	35	4	63	...	860	558	2	173	82	90
22	Tonk ...	98	...	7	...	26	...	131	224	2	...	18	...
	Cities ...	*921*	*5*	...	*1*	*19*	...	*888*	*1,056*	*2*	*10*	*133*	*14*
1	Alwar ...	7	...	...	...	...	...	178	125	...	3	2	1
2	Bharatpur ...	4	...	...	...	...	...	66	40	...	1	18	...
3	Bikaner ...	11	...	...	...	...	...	44	290	...	...	70	...
4	Bundi ...	51	1	...	1	3	...	78	286	...	...	6	...
5	Dholpur ...	24	...	...	...	12	...	10	9	...	...	8	...
6	Jaipur ...	98	1	...	...	2	...	208	64	2	6	23	13
7	Jodhpur ...	579	...	...	...	1	...	172	125	...	...	...	...
8	Kotah ...	81	...	...	...	...	...	33	...	...	...	6	...
9	Tonk ...	4	...	...	...	...	...	11	64	...	...	...	...
10	Udaipur ...	112	3	...	...	1	...	98	53	...	...	10	...

TABLE X.—OCCUPATION OR MEANS OF LIVELIHOOD.—PART II.—BY STATE OR DISTRICT AND CITY—*Continued.*

CLASS B.—PREPARATION AND SUPPLY OF MATERIAL SUBSTANCES.—*Continued.*
SUB-CLASS V.—TRADE.—*Concluded.*

SERIAL NUMBER.	AGENCY, STATE OR DISTRICT AND CITY	ORDER 38.—TRADE IN ARTICLES OF LUXURY AND THOSE PERTAINING TO LETTERS AND THE ARTS AND SCIENCES. Total Earners (Principal Occupations). Males.	Females.	Total Working Dependants. Males.	Females.	Total following occupation as Subsidiary to other. Males.	Females.	ORDER 39.—TRADE OF OTHER SORTS. Total Earners (Principal Occupations). Males.	Females.	Total Working Dependants. Males.	Females.	Total following occupation as Subsidiary to other. Males.	Females.
1	2	342	343	344	345	346	347	348	349	350	351	352	353
	Rajputana ...	***7,470***	***1,074***	***51***	***225***	***331***	***16***	***28,059***	***1,302***	***712***	***290***	***1,740***	***28***
1	Abu District ...	...	...	...	...	...	...	102	2	...	...	4	...
2	Alwar ...	265	98	1	43	24	2	8,495	59	22	14	289	2
3	Banswara ...	46	10	...	...	3	...	889	82	7	...	66	2
4	Bharatpur ...	300	171	5	3	21	...	288	4	23	...	21	...
5	Bikaner ...	757	29	1	2	34	1	807	45	...	...	12	...
6	Bundi ...	128	14	1	1	4	...	706	19	5	17	92	...
7	Dholpur ...	106	50	...	19	25	1	8	...	...	...	6	...
8	Dungarpur ...	66	17	3	8	16	...	876	18	67	2	16	...
9	Jaipur ...	1,128	148	30	69	81	4	5,441	116	500	85	185	5
10	Jaisalmer ...	6	...	...	...	1	...	222	18	1	...	88	...
11	Jhalawar ...	25	34	...	6	8	...	285	21	...	...	8	...
12	Karauli ...	4	...	...	...	...	...	198	8	1	3	33	...
13	Kishangarh ...	13	1	...	...	...	...	29	1	...	...	1	...
14	Kotah ...	319	78	...	1	7	1	8,876	484	64	60	479	15
15	Kushalgarh (Chiefship)	13	4	...	...	...	...	...	...	...	...	...	...
16	Lawa (Estate) ...	...	...	...	...	...	...	86	...	...	...	...	...
17	Marwar ...	1,167	120	...	10	62	1	6,556	459	11	105	874	3
18	Mewar ...	1,737	237	9	42	61	6	6,099	76	11	4	93	1
19	Partabgarh ...	75	8	...	...	7	...	13	...	...	...	1	...
20	Shahpura ...	48	8	...	...	2	...	8	...	...	...	...	...
21	Sirohi ...	1,086	21	1	...	29	...	10	...	...	...	...	...
22	Tonk ...	181	81	...	33	2	...	180	...	...	...	22	...
	Cities ...	***1,338***	***223***	***14***	***14***	***18***	***6***	***2,370***	***176***	***15***	***3***	***76***	...
1	Alwar ...	48	3	...	2	2	...	388	14	1	1	...	...
2	Bharatpur ...	13	18	...	...	...	...	179	3	...	...	4	...
3	Bikaner ...	227	12	...	...	2	...	119	2	...	...	1	...
4	Bundi ...	46	7	...	...	...	...	25	...	...	...	3	...
5	Dholpur ...	19	14	...	...	1	...	1	...	...	...	...	...
6	Jaipur ...	428	44	18	12	1	4	758	11	14	1	16	...
7	Jodhpur ...	210	12	...	...	1	...	565	104	...	...	17	...
8	Kotah ...	79	16	...	...	2	...	161	41	...	1	15	...
9	Tonk ...	16	5	...	...	...	...	140	...	...	...	20	...
10	Udaipur ...	257	99	1	...	9	2	44	1	...	...	...	...

TABLE X.—OCCUPATION OR MEANS OF LIVELIHOOD.—PART II.—BY STATE OR DISTRICT AND CITY.—*Continued.*

CLASS C.—PUBLIC ADMINISTRATION AND LIBERAL ARTS.
SUB-CLASS VI.—PUBLIC FORCE.

SERIAL NUMBER.	AGENCY, STATE OR DISTRICT AND CITY.	TOTAL OF CLASS C.						TOTAL OF SUB-CLASS VI.					
		Total Earners (Principal Occupations).		Total Working Dependants.		Total following occupation as Subsidiary to other.		Total Earners (Principal Occupations).		Total Working Dependants.		Total following occupation as Subsidiary to other.	
		Males.	Females.	Males.	Females.	Males.	Females.	Males.	Females.	Males.	Females.	Males.	Females.
1	2	854	855	856	857	858	859	860	861	862	863	864	865
	Rajputana ...	***232,450***	***35,425***	***2,632***	***5,314***	***24,584***	***1,266***	***55,376***	***106***	***301***	***262***	***3,236***	***8***
1	Abu District ...	195	16	...	...	1	...	85	...	...	...	...	...
2	Alwar ...	18,174	670	108	812	2,408	48	8,458	8	9	...	810	...
3	Banswara ...	1,860	264	8	7	589	18	262	2	...	...	98	...
4	Bharatpur ...	7,281	874	18	26	954	42	2,188	...	2	...	295	...
5	Bikaner ...	12,501	1,247	100	284	1,781	68	8,259	9	6	..	128	...
6	Bundi ...	4,858	721	68	88	482	18	1,191	4	...	...	54	1
7	Dholpur ...	4,468	162	6	2	558	14	1,708	...	...	...	92	...
8	Dungarpur ...	1,780	89	84	9	708	...	516	...	1	...	188	...
9	Jaipur ...	69,289	5,726	1,848	2,802	5,757	165	14,412	78	278	259	1,256	4
10	Jaisalmer ...	1,817	152	19	71	69	10	417	...	...	...	9	...
11	Jhalawar ...	8,025	808	5	4	881	18	884	2	...	...	52	1
12	Karauli ...	8,965	261	21	41	809	14	1,191	1	8	...	108	...
13	Kishangarh ...	2,578	198	15	15	215	2	788	...	2	...	40	...
14	Kotah ...	14,128	1,565	20	55	1,518	65	4,149	5	...	...	197	2
15	Kushalgarh (Chiefship).	898	15	1	...	28	...	116	...	...	...	8	...
16	Lawa (Estate) ...	77	8	...	...	1	...	14	...	...	...	...	...
17	Marwar ...	44,084	15,040	185	1,187	2,810	295	8,258	...	...	1	119	...
18	Mewar ...	84,557	7,502	188	994	4,691	451	8,018	8	...	1	219	...
19	Partabgarh ...	1,657	886	2	...	455	26	404	1	...	...	55	...
20	Shahpura ...	1,127	286	2	8	225	16	211	...	...	...	18	...
21	Sirohi ...	8,824	251	5	86	102	8	692	...	...	...	4	...
22	Tonk ...	6,877	801	4	28	102	8	8,225	8	...	1	51	...
	Cities ...	***52,041***	***4,199***	***126***	***158***	***958***	***159***	***18,316***	***12***	***11***	...	***87***	***1***
1	Alwar ...	5,494	150	16	17	26	...	2,447	...	...	...	...	...
2	Bharatpur ...	8,222	129	2	...	59	20	1,866	...	...	...	...	...
3	Bikaner ...	5,856	429	8	...	58	14	2,280	8	...	...	...	...
4	Bundi ...	2,868	886	...	...	111	1	781	...	...	...	29	1
5	Dholpur ...	2,289	106	1	...	108	...	1,066	...	...	...	20	...
6	Jaipur ...	12,641	855	96	111	824	24	2,888	4	11	...	84	...
7	Jodhpur ...	7,995	857	4	12	56	10	8,125	...	...	...		...
8	Kotah ...	4,288	471	...	4	40	6	1,865	...	...	...	1	...
9	Tonk ...	8,409	99	...	...	4	...	1,862	...	...	...	1	...
10	Udaipur ...	5,079	717	4	14	177	84	1,686	...	...	...	2	...

TABLE X.—Occupation or Means of Livelihood.—Part II.—By State or District and City.—*Continued.*

SERIAL NUMBER.	AGENCY, STATE OR DISTRICT AND CITY.	CLASS C.—PUBLIC ADMINISTRATION AND LIBERAL ARTS.—*Continued.* SUB-CLASS VI.—PUBLIC FORCE.—*Continued.*											
		ORDER 40.—ARMY.						ORDER 41.—NAVY.					
		Total Earners (Principal Occupations).		Total Working Dependants.		Total following occupation as Subsidiary to other.		Total Earners (Principal Occupations).		Total Working Dependants.		Total following occupation as Subsidiary to other	
		Males.	Females.	Males.	Females.	Males.	Females.	Males.	Females.	Males.	Females.	Males.	Females
1	2	366	367	368	369	370	371	372	373	374	375	376	377
	Rajputana ...	***28,351***	***23***	***63***	...	***608***	***1***	***2***	...	...	...	...	...
1	Abu District ...	46	...	...	...	...	...	...	...	...	...	...	...
2	Alwar ...	2,435	...	2	...	31	...	...	...	...	...	...	...
3	Banswara ...	49	...	...	...	...	...	...	...	...	...	...	...
4	Bharatpur ...	1,196	...	...	...	32	...	...	...	...	...	...	...
5	Bikaner ...	1,959	7	3	...	21	...	...	...	...	...	...	...
6	Bundi ...	863	3	...	...	32	1	...	...	...	...	...	...
7	Dholpur ...	1,068	...	...	...	21	...	...	...	...	...	...	...
8	Dungarpur ...	133	...	...	...	26	...	...	...	...	...	...	...
9	Jaipur ...	7,204	6	56	...	144	...	2	...	...	...	...	...
10	Jaisalmer ...	183	...	...	...	9	...	...	...	...	...	...	...
11	Jhalawar ...	387	...	...	...	3	...	...	...	...	...	...	...
12	Karauli ...	998	1	2	...	90	...	...	...	...	...	...	...
13	Kishangarh ...	619	...	...	...	30	...	...	...	...	...	...	...
14	Kotah ...	1,218	3	...	...	...	...	...	...	...	...	...	...
15	Kushalgarh (Chiefship).	...	...	...	...	...	...	...	...	...	...	...	...
16	Lawa (Estate) ...	...	...	...	...	...	...	...	...	...	...	...	...
17	Marwar ...	1,652	...	...	...	1	...	...	...	...	...	...	...
18	Mewar ...	6,092	3	...	...	162	...	...	...	...	...	...	...
19	Partabgarh ...	25	...	...	...	...	...	...	...	...	...	...	...
20	Shahpura ...	80	...	...	...	1	...	...	...	...	...	...	...
21	Sirohi ...	162	...	...	...	...	...	...	...	...	...	...	...
22	Tonk ...	1,982	...	...	...	5	...	...	...	...	...	...	...
	Cities ...	***13,219***	***9***	***2***	...	***52***	***1***	...	...	...	...	...	...
1	Alwar ...	2,075	...	...	...	...	...	...	...	...	...	...	...
2	Bharatpur ...	1,026	...	...	...	...	...	...	...	...	...	...	...
3	Bikaner ...	1,881	7	...	...	...	...	...	...	...	...	...	...
4	Bundi ...	628	...	...	...	23	1	...	...	...	...	...	...
5	Dholpur ...	887	...	...	...	9	...	...	...	...	...	...	...
6	Jaipur ...	1,121	2	2	...	18	...	...	...	...	...	...	...
7	Jodhpur ...	1,595	...	...	...	...	...	...	...	...	...	...	...
8	Kotah ...	1,081	...	...	...	...	...	...	...	...	...	...	...
9	Tonk ...	1,586	...	...	...	1	...	...	...	...	...	...	...
10	Udaipur ...	1,339	...	...	...	1	...	...	...	...	...	...	...

TABLE X.—OCCUPATION OR MEANS OF LIVELIHOOD.—PART II.—BY STATE OR DISTRICT AND CITY.—*Continued.*

CLASS C.—PUBLIC ADMINISTRATION AND LIBERAL ARTS.—*Continued.*
SUB-CLASS VI.—PUBLIC FORCE.—*Concluded.*

SERIAL NUMBER.	AGENCY, STATE OR DISTRICT AND CITY.	ORDER 42.—AIR FORCE.						ORDER 43.—POLICE.					
		Total Earners (Principal Occupations).		Total Working Dependants.		Total following occupation as Subsidiary to other.		Total Earners (Principal Occupations).		Total Working Dependants.		Total following occupation as Subsidiary to other.	
		Males.	Females.	Males.	Females.	Males.	Females.	Males.	Females.	Males.	Females.	Males.	Females.
1	2	378	379	380	381	382	383	384	385	386	387	388	389
	Rajputana ...	**1**	...	...	...	...	...	**27,022**	**83**	**238**	**262**	**2,628**	**7**
1	Abu District ...	1	...	...	...	...	...	33	...	...	...	...	...
2	Alwar ...	...	...	...	...	...	...	1,018	3	7	...	279	...
3	Banswara ...	...	...	...	...	...	...	213	2	...	...	98	...
4	Bharatpur ...	...	...	...	...	...	...	992	...	2	...	263	...
5	Bikaner ...	...	...	...	...	...	...	1,300	2	3	...	107	...
6	Bundi ...	...	...	...	...	...	...	328	1	...	...	22	...
7	Dholpur ...	...	...	...	...	...	...	635	...	...	...	71	...
8	Dungarpur ...	...	...	...	...	...	...	333	...	1	...	107	...
9	Jaipur ...	...	...	...	...	...	...	7,206	67	222	259	1,112	4
10	Jaisalmer ...	...	...	...	...	...	...	234	...	...	...	...	...
11	Jhalawar ...	...	...	...	...	...	...	447	2	...	...	49	1
12	Karauli ...	...	...	...	...	...	...	198	...	1	...	13	...
13	Kishangarh ...	...	...	...	...	...	...	169	...	2	...	10	...
14	Kotah ...	...	...	...	...	...	...	2,931	2	...	...	197	2
15	Kushalgarh (Chiefship).	...	...	...	...	...	...	116	...	...	...	3	...
16	Lawa (Estate) ...	...	...	...	...	...	...	14	...	...	...	...	...
17	Marwar ...	...	...	...	...	...	...	6,601	...	...	1	118	...
18	Mewar ...	...	...	...	...	...	...	1,921	...	...	1	57	...
19	Partabgarh ...	...	...	...	...	...	...	379	1	...	...	55	...
20	Shahpura ...	...	...	...	...	...	...	131	...	...	...	17	...
21	Sirohi ...	...	...	...	...	...	...	580	...	...	...	4	...
22	Tonk ...	...	...	...	...	...	...	1,243	3	...	1	46	...
	Cities ...	...	...	...	...	...	...	**5,097**	**3**	**9**	...	**35**	...
1	Alwar ...	...	...	...	...	...	...	372	...	...	...	...	...
2	Bharatpur ...	...	...	...	...	...	...	340	...	...	...	...	...
3	Bikaner ...	...	...	...	...	...	...	399	1	...	...	...	...
4	Bundi ...	...	...	...	...	...	...	153	...	...	...	6	...
5	Dholpur ...	...	...	...	...	...	...	179	...	...	...	11	...
6	Jaipur ...	...	...	...	...	...	...	1,267	2	9	...	16	...
7	Jodhpur ...	...	...	...	...	...	...	1,530	...	...	...	...	...
8	Kotah ...	...	...	...	...	...	...	284	...	...	...	1	...
9	Tonk ...	...	...	...	...	...	...	276	...	...	...	...	...
10	Udaipur ...	...	...	...	...	...	...	297	...	...	...	1	...

TABLE X.—Occupation or Means of Livelihood.—Part II.—By State or District and City.—*Continued.*

Serial Number.	Agency, State or District and City.	CLASS C.—PUBLIC ADMINISTRATION AND LIBERAL ARTS.—*Continued.*											
		SUB-CLASS VII.—PUBLIC ADMINISTRATION.						SUB-CLASS VIII.—PROFESSIONS AND LIBERAL ARTS.					
		TOTAL OF SUB-CLASS VII, ALSO ORDER 44.—PUBLIC ADMINISTRATION.						TOTAL OF SUB-CLASS VIII.					
		Total Earners (Principal Occupations)		Total Working Dependants.		Total following occupation as Subsidiary to other.		Total Earners (Principal Occupations).		Total Working Dependants.		Total following occupation as Subsidiary to other.	
		Males.	Females.	Males.	Females.	Males.	Females.	Males.	Females.	Males.	Females.	Males.	Females.
1	2	390	391	392	393	394	395	396	397	398	399	400	401
	Rajputana ...	**62,088**	**2,644**	**209**	**226**	**6,313**	**101**	**114,986**	**32,675**	**2,122**	**4,826**	**15,035**	**1,157**
1	Abu District ...	57	6	...	...	...	...	53	10	...	...	1	...
2	Alwar ...	4,829	188	34	80	1,261	6	4,892	484	65	282	842	42
3	Banswara ...	618	58	...	...	278	...	980	209	3	7	213	18
4	Bharatpur ...	3,110	76	...	...	223	25	1,933	298	11	26	436	17
5	Bikaner ...	4,334	96	...	1	780	3	4,908	1,142	94	233	828	60
6	Bundi ...	1,986	313	4	...	106	1	1,676	404	59	33	322	11
7	Dholpur ...	1,597	27	1	...	90	...	1,163	185	5	2	371	14
8	Dungarpur ...	617	34	4	...	411	...	647	48	29	9	164	...
9	Jaipur ...	17,141	495	187	154	1,080	28	37,786	5,158	1,428	1,889	3,471	188
10	Jaisalmer ...	126	24	3	1	...	...	1,274	128	16	70	60	10
11	Jhalawar ...	1,836	57	3	...	87	5	855	249	2	4	242	12
12	Karauli ...	1,536	135	2	10	367	7	1,238	125	16	31	339	7
13	Kishangarh ...	1,109	68	2	...	67	...	681	125	11	15	108	2
14	Kotah ...	5,982	487	3	16	711	16	3,992	1,123	17	39	610	47
15	Kushalgarh (Chiefship).	218	7	1	...	14	...	50	8	...	...	11	...
16	Lawa (Estate) ...	40	2	...	...	...	...	23	1	...	...	1	...
17	Marwar ...	7,545	177	11	...	468	4	28,286	14,863	174	1,136	2,223	291
18	Mewar ...	5,480	324	3	1	223	2	21,064	7,175	180	992	4,249	449
19	Partabgarh ...	467	5	...	...	97	...	786	330	2	...	303	26
20	Shahpura ...	591	78	...	2	81	3	325	158	2	6	126	18
21	Sirohi ...	1,239	25	1	1	18	1	1,393	226	4	35	80	2
22	Tonk ...	2,180	22	...	10	11	...	1,022	276	4	17	40	8
	Cities ...	**22,790**	**1,517**	**32**	**23**	**326**	**40**	**10,935**	**2,670**	**83**	**135**	**545**	**118**
1	Alwar ...	2,354	67	9	3	13	...	698	88	7	14	13	...
2	Bharatpur ...	1,870	19	...	...	28	19	486	110	2	...	31	1
3	Bikaner ...	1,330	76	...	...	6	...	1,746	845	3	...	52	14
4	Bundi ...	1,241	298	...	...	10	...	346	98	...	...	72	...
5	Dholpur ...	862	25	...	...	39	...	311	81	1	...	44	...
6	Jaipur ...	6,309	373	28	20	162	18	3,944	478	62	91	128	6
7	Jodhpur ...	3,684	118	...	...	24	1	1,186	789	4	12	32	9
8	Kotah ...	2,190	229	...	...	13	...	688	242	...	4	26	6
9	Tonk ...	1,148	10	...	...	1	...	404	89	...	...	2	...
10	Udaipur ...	2,807	307	...	...	80	2	1,186	410	4	14	145	82

TABLE X.—OCCUPATION OR MEANS OF LIVELIHOOD.—PART II.—BY STATE OR DISTRICT AND CITY.—*Continued.*

CLASS C.—PUBLIC ADMINISTRATION AND LIBERAL ARTS.—*Continued.*
SUB-CLASS VIII.—PROFESSIONS AND LIBERAL ARTS.—*Continued.*

SERIAL NUMBER.	AGENCY, STATE OR DISTRICT AND CITY.	ORDER 45.—RELIGION.						ORDER 46.—LAW.					
		Total Earners (Principal Occupations).		Total Working Dependants.		Total following occupation as Subsidiary to other.		Total Earners (Principal Occupations).		Total Working Dependants.		Total following occupation as Subsidiary to other	
		Males.	Females.	Males.	Females.	Males.	Females.	Males.	Females.	Males.	Females.	Males.	Females.
1	2	402	403	404	405	406	407	408	409	410	411	412	413
	Rajputana ...	***83,600***	***18,347***	***1,630***	***2,720***	***12,308***	***596***	***2,127***	***7***	***6***	...	***81***	...
1	Abu District ...	9	...	...	...	...	...	2	...	...	...	...	...
2	Alwar ...	8,156	115	46	115	651	16	127	...	4	...	11	...
3	Banswara ...	667	117	3	...	174	11	12	...	...	...	2	...
4	Bharatpur ...	986	38	8	...	807	5	131	...	...	...	8	...
5	Bikaner ...	2,403	344	7	7	533	29	260	...	...	...	3	...
6	Bundi ...	1,068	151	8	8	215	4	2	...	...	...	...	...
7	Dholpur ...	651	21	3	1	264	...	68	...	...	...	3	...
8	Dungarpur ...	479	30	29	6	156	...	13	...	...	...	...	...
9	Jaipur ...	30,799	3,417	1,191	1,437	3,019	115	559	...	1	...	11	...
10	Jaisalmer ...	896	24	12	23	49	...	1	...	...	...	...	...
11	Jhalawar ...	294	19	1	...	144	1	45	...	...	...	8	...
12	Karauli ...	798	31	10	3	292	3	29	...	...	...	4	...
13	Kishangarh ...	236	31	...	...	46	2	18	...	...	...	...	...
14	Kotah ...	1,938	279	7	21	518	24	198	...	...	...	15	...
15	Kushalgarh (Chiefship).	16	3	...	...	2	...	8	...	...	...	2	...
16	Lawa (Estate) ...	22	1	...	...	1	...	...	...	...	...	...	...
17	Marwar ...	21,443	10,680	140	626	1,741	86	370	...	...	...	3	...
18	Mewar ...	16,020	2,968	160	467	3,791	288	164	6	...	...	3	...
19	Partabgarh ...	501	76	2	...	257	12	13	1	...	...	4	...
20	Shahpura ...	171	9	1	...	95	...	11	...	...	...	3	...
21	Sirohi ...	561	9	1	...	84	...	23	...	...	...	...	...
22	Tonk ...	418	34	1	6	19	...	78	...	1	...	1	...
	Cities ...	***5,211***	***789***	***50***	***104***	***383***	***91***	***1,015***	...	***4***	...	***15***	...
1	Alwar ...	283	16	2	3	7	...	60	...	3	...	...	...
2	Bharatpur ...	181	13	2	...	10	...	52	...	...	...	2	...
3	Bikaner ...	1,032	110	3	...	89	1	90	...	...	...	1	...
4	Bundi ...	210	41	...	...	58	...	2	...	...	...	...	...
5	Dholpur ...	117	4	...	...	17	...	46	...	...	...	2	...
6	Jaipur ...	2,011	170	80	80	90	5	347	...	1	...	5	...
7	Jodhpur ...	303	188	...	4	4	9	243	...	...	...	2	...
8	Kotah ...	243	63	...	3	23	6	60	...	...	...	2	...
9	Tonk ...	224	25	...	...	2	...	27	...	...	...	...	...
10	Udaipur ...	607	159	4	14	183	70	88	...	...	...	1	...

TABLE X.—Occupation or Means of Livelihood.—Part II.—By State or District and City.—*Continued.*

CLASS C.—PUBLIC ADMINISTRATION AND LIBERAL ARTS.—*Continued.*
SUB-CLASS VIII.—PROFESSIONS AND LIBERAL ARTS.—*Continued.*

Serial Number.	Agency, State or District and City.	Order 47.—Medicine. Total Earners (Principal Occupations). Males.	Females.	Total Working Dependants. Males.	Females.	Total following occupation as Subsidiary to other. Males.	Females.	Order 48.—Instruction. Total Earners (Principal Occupations). Males.	Females.	Total Working Dependants. Males.	Females.	Total following occupation as Subsidiary to other. Males.	Females.
1	2	414	415	416	417	418	419	420	421	422	423	424	425
	Rajputana ...	***3,055***	***4,779***	***15***	***484***	***219***	***180***	***5,776***	***437***	***90***	***15***	***295***	***5***
1	Abu District ...	10	4	...	...	...	...	24	6	...	...	1	...
2	Alwar ...	182	151	1	82	20	15	344	15	1	...	18	...
3	Banswara ...	29	41	...	...	2	2	84	7	...	...	3	...
4	Bharatpur ...	178	188	...	8	24	12	295	22	1	...	13	...
5	Bikaner ...	302	128	...	1	17	4	507	59	...	...	14	...
6	Bundi ...	190	118	4	18	27	6	138	12	35	...	45	1
7	Dholpur ...	79	30	...	...	15	...	137	13	...	...	10	...
8	Dungarpur ...	27	2	...	...	2	...	81	4	...	...	3	...
9	Jaipur ...	820	386	8	60	39	5	1,458	92	44	10	101	...
10	Jaisalmer ...	6	5	...	...	...	...	11	...	...	...	2	...
11	Jhalawar ...	56	47	...	...	9	3	101	16	...	...	11	...
12	Karauli ...	47	27	1	3	5	3	53	1	...	...	4	...
13	Kishangarh ...	38	20	1	...	...	...	65	5	...	...	3	...
14	Kotah ...	381	381	...	4	7	16	625	73	...	...	10	...
15	Kushalgarh (Chiefship).	6	2	...	...	...	...	20	1	...	...	...	...
16	Lawa (Estate) ...	...	...	...	...	...	...	...	...	...	...	...	...
17	Marwar ...	339	722	...	116	36	21	741	42	...	3	23	4
18	Mewar ...	285	2,197	...	186	12	74	712	32	8	2	21	...
19	Partabgarh ...	28	143	...	...	2	5	68	5	...	...	6	...
20	Shahpura ...	18	106	...	3	1	12	44	5	...	...	1	...
21	Sirohi ...	51	23	...	...	1	2	140	12	1	...	4	...
22	Tonk ...	43	58	...	3	...	...	128	15	...	...	2	...
	Cities ...	***921***	***582***	***4***	***7***	***46***	***16***	***1,525***	***223***	***6***	...	***31***	...
1	Alwar ...	62	40	1	3	1	...	95	6	...	...	2	...
2	Bharatpur ...	102	62	...	...	6	1	82	15	...	...	7	...
3	Bikaner ...	155	42	...	...	7	3	168	39	...	...	1	...
4	Bundi ...	27	17	...	...	6	...	41	4	...	...	5	...
5	Dholpur ...	51	40	...	...	3	...	51	13	...	...	5	...
6	Jaipur ...	215	68	3	4	7	...	421	53	6	...	7	...
7	Jodhpur ...	189	87	...	...	13	...	223	25	...	...	...	...
8	Kotah ...	56	58	...	...	...	...	188	37	...	...	1	...
9	Tonk ...	26	33	...	...	...	...	58	15	...	...	...	...
10	Udaipur ...	38	135	...	...	3	12	198	16	...	...	3	...

TABLE X.—OCCUPATION OR MEANS OF LIVELIHOOD.—PART II.—BY STATE OR DISTRICT AND CITY.—*Continued.*

SERIAL NUMBER.	AGENCY, STATE OR DISTRICT AND CITY.	CLASS C.—PUBLIC ADMINISTRATION AND LIBERAL ARTS.—*Concluded.* SUB-CLASS VIII.—PROFESSIONS AND LIBERAL ARTS.—*Concluded.* ORDER 49.—LETTERS, ARTS AND SCIENCES (OTHER THAN 44). Total Earners (Principal Occupations).		Total Working Dependants.		Total following occupation as Subsidiary to other.		CLASS D.—MISCELLANEOUS. TOTAL OF CLASS D. Total Earners (Principal Occupations).		Total Working Dependants.		Total following occupation as Subsidiary to other.	
		Males.	Females.	Males.	Females.	Males.	Females.	Males.	Females.	Males.	Females.	Males.	Females.
1	2	426	427	428	429	430	431	432	433	434	435	436	437
	Rajputana ...	***20,428***	***9,105***	***381***	***1,607***	***2,132***	***376***	***217,114***	***107,421***	***9,694***	***19,345***	***25,907***	***4,197***
1	Abu District ...	8	...	...	...	...	...	788	129	...	4	70	5
2	Alwar ...	1,088	203	13	85	142	11	17,639	4,088	808	2,255	3,848	376
3	Banswara ...	186	44	...	7	32	...	1,627	1,141	62	8	528	48
4	Bharatpur ...	348	50	2	18	84	...	8,252	1,758	257	133	1,595	187
5	Bikaner ...	1,486	611	87	225	256	27	21,805	6,874	462	272	2,759	514
6	Bundi ...	278	128	12	12	35	...	3,852	3,564	111	323	438	90
7	Dholpur ...	228	71	2	1	79	14	2,031	611	184	85	410	12
8	Dungarpur ...	47	12	...	3	3	...	1,474	258	210	477	358	10
9	Jaipur ...	4,100	1,263	184	382	301	18	78,925	46,348	8,799	10,198	5,717	897
10	Jaisalmer ...	360	99	4	47	9	10	770	544	51	107	268	58
11	Jhalawar ...	350	167	1	4	70	8	2,351	1,264	88	57	680	58
12	Karauli ...	311	66	5	20	34	1	2,104	715	111	241	459	29
13	Kishangarh ...	324	69	10	15	59	...	1,629	700	70	124	141	32
14	Kotah ...	855	390	10	14	60	7	10,454	4,880	429	825	1,439	158
15	Kushalgarh (Chiefship).	9	2	...	...	7	...	79	58	8	16	11	...
16	Lawa (Estate) ...	1	...	...	...	...	...	42	28	...	5	1	...
17	Marwar ...	5,393	3,469	34	391	420	180	36,020	16,451	1,167	2,698	4,322	1,412
18	Mewar ...	3,875	1,972	12	387	422	87	8,570	4,088	905	768	1,020	178
19	Partabgarh ...	176	105	...	...	34	9	641	615	78	1	121	25
20	Shahpura ...	81	38	1	3	26	1	1,024	748	57	84	800	71
21	Sirohi ...	618	177	2	35	41	...	5,640	2,971	383	657	336	43
22	Tonk ...	355	169	2	8	18	8	11,902	9,648	509	562	1,601	54
	Cities ...	***2,263***	***1,076***	***19***	***24***	***70***	***11***	***33,288***	***13,947***	***4,083***	***781***	***923***	***162***
1	Alwar ...	198	21	1	8	3	...	2,088	477	491	68	38	8
2	Bharatpur ...	69	20	...	...	6	...	1,888	485	204	15	135	27
3	Bikaner ...	301	154	...	...	4	10	7,068	1,938	237	8	233	40
4	Bundi ...	66	31	...	...	3	...	754	391	96	12	68	...
5	Dholpur ...	46	24	1	...	17	...	680	280	178	6	62	4
6	Jaipur ...	950	187	13	7	19	1	9,463	8,726	1,081	530	804	29
7	Jodhpur ...	278	439	4	8	13	...	5,719	3,308	826	43	28	6
8	Kotah ...	186	84	...	1	...	...	2,446	1,518	320	60	18	18
9	Tonk ...	69	16	...	...	...	...	2,061	1,268	108	3	20	10
10	Udaipur ...	155	100	...	...	5	...	1,136	556	547	41	22	25

TABLE X.—Occupation or Means of Livelihood.—Part II.—By State or District and City.—*Continued.*

SERIAL NUMBER.	AGENCY, STATE OR DISTRICT AND CITY.	CLASS D.—MISCELLANEOUS.—*Continued.*											
		SUB-CLASS IX.—PERSONS LIVING ON THEIR INCOME.						SUB-CLASS X.—DOMESTIC SERVICE.					
		TOTAL OF SUB-CLASS IX, ALSO ORDER 50.—PERSONS LIVING PRINCIPALLY ON THEIR INCOME.						TOTAL OF SUB-CLASS X, ALSO ORDER 51.—DOMESTIC SERVICE.					
		Total Earners (Principal Occupations).		Total Working Dependants.		Total following occupation as Subsidiary to other.		Total Earners (Principal Occupations).		Total Working Dependants.		Total following occupation as Subsidiary to other.	
		Males.	Females.	Males.	Females.	Males.	Females.	Males.	Females.	Males.	Females.	Males.	Females.
1	2	438	439	440	441	442	443	444	445	446	447	448	449
	Rajputana ...	***3,888***	***1,474***	***124***	***285***	***1,034***	***78***	***61,061***	***19,544***	***889***	***5,292***	***4,274***	***816***
1	Abu District ...	3	...	...	...	...	...	238	45	...	...	10	...
2	Alwar ...	605	50	10	43	296	6	3,118	488	24	187	261	126
3	Banswara ...	89	61	...	2	127	9	596	623	...	1	125	21
4	Bharatpur ...	774	169	...	2	132	7	2,805	643	12	74	460	53
5	Bikaner ...	98	19	8	6	86	...	8,168	2,386	18	20	227	11
6	Bundi ...	62	51	...	1	12	...	755	325	2	48	70	3
7	Dholpur ...	161	86	...	1	26	3	688	194	...	15	62	2
8	Dungarpur ...	...	2	...	...	...	...	413	66	23	124	117	3
9	Jaipur ...	906	177	95	55	202	3	14,081	4,606	628	3,389	900	145
10	Jaisalmer ...	2	2	...	...	...	...	480	42	...	14	26	1
11	Jhalawar ...	190	169	...	...	19	1	691	197	3	11	86	12
12	Karauli ...	58	120	...	4	28	8	505	140	12	36	82	3
13	Kishangarh ...	81	48	1	85	2	...	228	138	1	10	5	29
14	Kotah ...	361	268	1	21	15	11	3,060	968	4	48	125	20
15	Kushalgarh (Chiefship).	2	...	...	...	...	...	38	52	...	8	...	...
16	Lawa (Estate) ...	...	...	...	...	...	...	13	20	...	4	1	...
17	Marwar ...	267	100	9	56	40	23	16,385	4,388	67	635	1,311	240
18	Mewar ...	74	34	...	6	40	5	4,680	2,798	65	448	354	107
19	Partabgarh ...	21	22	...	...	6	2	343	869	...	...	29	19
20	Shahpura ...	6	4	...	8	...	...	188	74	3	18	21	15
21	Sirohi ...	27	1	...	...	3	...	1,588	223	4	29	29	...
22	Tonk ...	201	91	...	...	...	...	2,005	814	23	188	23	6
	Cities ...	***1,871***	***654***	***60***	***40***	***100***	***22***	***14,969***	***5,370***	***94***	***249***	***302***	***57***
1	Alwar ...	277	18	2	5	4	1	675	162	1	15	2	1
2	Bharatpur ...	429	104	...	...	4	2	949	265	7	7	89	24
3	Bikaner ...	40	10	...	...	2	...	3,114	934	...	...	12	...
4	Bundi ...	47	45	...	...	5	...	299	146	...	1	34	...
5	Dholpur ...	115	61	...	...	18	2	415	161	...	6	24	2
6	Jaipur ...	538	105	52	10	58	2	3,318	1,244	86	211	117	3
7	Jodhpur ...	72	84	6	15	...	1	2,863	989	...	...	12	...
8	Kotah ...	141	169	...	9	...	10	1,435	435	...	7	...	1
9	Tonk ...	188	84	...	...	...	...	1,087	545	...	...	4	5
10	Udaipur ...	29	29	...	1	9	4	814	489	...	2	8	21

TABLE X.—Occupation or Means of Livelihood.—Part II.—By State or District and City.—*Continued.*

Serial Number.	Agency, State or District and City.	Class D.—Miscellaneous.—*Continued.*											
		Sub-Class XI.—Insufficiently described occupations.						Sub-Class XII.—Unproductive.					
		Total of Sub-Class XI, also Order 52.—General terms which do not indicate a definite occupation.						Total of Sub-Class XII.					
		Total Earners (Principal Occupations).		Total Working Dependants.		Total following occupation as Subsidiary to other.		Total Earners (Principal Occupations).		Total Working Dependants.		Total following occupation as Subsidiary to other.	
		Males.	Females.	Males.	Females.	Males.	Females.	Males.	Females.	Males.	Females.	Males.	Females.
1	2	450	451	452	453	454	455	456	457	458	459	460	461
	Rajputana ...	***97,535***	***73,536***	***2,552***	***11,015***	***11,754***	***2,370***	***54,630***	***12,867***	***6,129***	***2,753***	***8,845***	***933***
1	Abu District ...	528	81	...	4	55	5	14	8	...	...	5	...
2	Alwar ...	7,540	8,037	156	1,718	1,972	220	6,881	558	618	307	814	24
3	Banswara ...	88	207	...	3	98	14	904	250	62	2	178	4
4	Bharatpur ...	1,241	624	16	85	801	67	3,432	322	229	22	702	10
5	Bikaner ...	8,482	2,758	13	25	1,580	392	4,557	1,711	423	221	866	111
6	Bundi ...	2,074	3,002	8	247	200	81	961	186	101	27	151	6
7	Dholpur ...	167	44	2	11	42	1	1,015	287	182	58	280	6
8	Dungarpur ...	97	67	9	162	2	2	964	123	178	191	239	5
9	Jaipur ...	50,570	39,108	1,771	5,689	3,657	678	13,368	2,462	1,305	1,065	958	71
10	Jaisalmer ...	121	411	5	66	129	48	167	89	46	27	108	9
11	Jhalawar ...	656	705	4	30	221	21	814	108	81	16	404	24
12	Karauli ...	344	326	11	170	118	13	1,197	129	88	31	231	5
13	Kishangarh ...	593	396	4	15	8	1	777	118	64	14	126	2
14	Kotah ...	2,373	2,810	13	178	127	62	4,660	789	411	78	1,172	60
15	Kushalgarh (Chiefship).	...	...	...	...	...	...	39	6	8	13	11	...
16	Lawa (Estate) ...	15	...	...	...	...	...	14	8	...	1	...	...
17	Marwar ...	11,532	7,926	109	1,583	1,468	604	7,836	4,087	989	419	1,503	545
18	Mewar ...	1,915	1,018	19	203	214	48	1,901	238	821	116	412	18
19	Partabgarh ...	87	95	...	...	9	1	190	129	73	1	77	8
20	Shahpura ...	397	625	19	13	118	51	483	45	85	5	161	5
21	Sirohi ...	2,230	2,317	135	553	178	28	1,795	430	194	75	126	15
22	Tonk ...	6,485	7,984	258	810	1,257	88	3,211	754	228	64	321	10
	Cities ...	***13,079***	***6,619***	***46***	***242***	***396***	***34***	***3,369***	***1,304***	***3,883***	***250***	***125***	***49***
1	Alwar ...	871	258	4	15	25	1	260	44	484	28	7	...
2	Bharatpur ...	336	78	...	...	36	...	169	38	197	8	6	1
3	Bikaner ...	3,001	656	...	...	171	...	908	388	287	8	48	40
4	Bundi ...	308	180	...	...	8	...	105	20	96	11	16	...
5	Dholpur ...	85	20	1	...	14	...	65	88	172	...	6	...
6	Jaipur ...	4,637	2,068	41	214	112	28	975	809	902	95	17	1
7	Jodhpur ...	2,329	1,901	...	...	11	5	455	384	820	28	5	...
8	Kotah ...	615	859	...	13	2	5	255	55	320	31	16	2
9	Tonk ...	669	579	...	...	14	...	117	60	108	3	2	5
10	Udaipur ...	233	20	...	...	3	...	60	18	547	38	2	...

TABLE X.—Occupation or Means of Livelihood.—Part II.—By State or District and City.—*Continued.*

CLASS D.—MISCELLANEOUS.—*Continued.*
SUB-CLASS XII.—UNPRODUCTIVE.—*Continued.*

SERIAL NUMBER.	AGENCY, STATE OR DISTRICT AND CITY.	ORDER 53.—INMATES OF JAILS, ASYLUMS AND ALMS HOUSES. Total Earners (Principal Occupations).		Total Working Dependants.		Total following occupation as Subsidiary to other.		ORDER 54.—BEGGARS, VAGRANTS, PROSTITUTES. Total Earners (Principal Occupations).		Total Working Dependants.		Total following occupation as Subsidiary to other.	
		Males.	Females.	Males.	Females.	Males.	Females.	Males.	Females.	Males.	Females.	Males.	Females.
1	2	462	463	464	465	466	467	468	469	470	471	472	473
	Rajputana ...	8	...	***4,740***	***198***	***27***	...	***53,780***	***12,732***	***1,376***	***2,555***	***8,737***	***928***
1	Abu District ...	...	...	...	...	...	...	14	3	...	...	5	...
2	Alwar ...	...	...	458	6	2	...	6,381	558	165	301	812	24
3	Banswara ...	...	...	61	2	...	...	904	250	1	...	178	4
4	Bharatpur ...	...	...	197	9	...	...	3,432	322	32	18	702	10
5	Bikaner ...	...	...	250	8	...	...	4,390	1,711	173	218	863	106
6	Bundi ...	...	...	96	11	...	...	957	186	5	16	151	6
7	Dholpur ...	...	...	172	...	...	...	1,015	287	10	58	280	6
8	Dungarpur ...	...	...	71	...	...	...	964	123	107	191	239	5
9	Jaipur ...	...	...	862	22	...	...	12,798	2,459	440	1,043	895	71
10	Jaisalmer ...	...	...	37	1	...	...	167	89	9	26	108	9
11	Jhalawar ...	...	...	67	4	...	...	814	198	14	12	404	24
12	Karauli ...	...	...	56	1	...	...	1,197	120	32	30	231	5
13	Kishangarh ...	...	...	58	1	...	...	777	118	11	13	126	2
14	Kotah ...	...	...	320	28	...	...	4,635	786	91	50	1,172	60
15	Kushalgarh (Chiefship).	...	...	...	...	...	...	39	6	8	19	11	...
16	Lawa (Estate) ...	...	...	...	...	...	...	14	8	...	1	...	...
17	Marwar ...	...	...	848	27	25	...	7,816	4,037	134	892	1,478	545
18	Mewar ...	...	...	802	70	...	...	1,901	238	19	40	412	18
19	Partabgarh ...	...	...	78	1	...	...	190	129	...	...	77	3
20	Shahpura ...	...	...	29	...	...	...	433	45	6	8	161	5
21	Sirohi ...	...	...	159	4	...	...	1,789	801	85	71	111	15
22	Tonk ...	8	...	144	3	...	...	3,208	754	84	61	321	10
	Cities ...	...	...	***3,802***	***151***	**2**	...	***3,142***	***1,303***	**81**	**99**	**118**	**49**
1	Alwar ...	...	...	458	6	2	...	260	44	81	22	5	...
2	Bharatpur ...	...	...	197	8	...	...	169	38	...	...	6	1
3	Bikaner ...	...	...	287	8	...	...	804	338	...	...	45	40
4	Bundi ...	...	...	96	11	...	...	105	20	...	...	16	...
5	Dholpur ...	...	...	172	...	...	...	65	88	...	...	6	...
6	Jaipur ...	...	...	852	22	...	...	852	308	50	78	15	1
7	Jodhpur ...	...	...	820	27	...	...	455	384	...	1	5	...
8	Kotah ...	...	...	320	28	...	...	255	55	...	8	16	2
9	Tonk ...	...	...	108	8	...	...	117	60	...	...	2	5
10	Udaipur ...	...	...	547	88	...	...	60	18	...	...	2	...

TABLE X.—Occupation or Means of Livelihood.—Part II.—By State or District and City.—*Concluded.*

CLASS D.—MISCELLANEOUS.—*Concluded.*
SUB-CLASS XII.—UNPRODUCTIVE.—*Concluded.*

ORDER 55.—OTHER UNCLASSIFIED NON-PRODUCTIVE INDUSTRIES.

Serial Number.	Agency, State or District and City.	Total Earners (Principal Occupations).		Total Working Dependants.		Total following occupation as Subsidiary to other.	
		Males.	Females.	Males.	Females.	Males.	Females.
1	2	474	475	476	477	478	479
	Rajputana ...	842	135	13	...	81	5
1	Abu District ...	...	...	...	...	...	...
2	Alwar ...	...	...	...	...	...	...
3	Banswara ...	...	...	...	...	...	...
4	Bharatpur ...	...	...	...	...	...	...
5	Bikaner ...	167	...	...	...	...	...
6	Bundi ...	4	...	...	...	8	5
7	Dholpur ...	...	...	...	...	...	...
8	Dungarpur ...	...	...	...	...	...	...
9	Jaipur ...	570	3	13	...	63	...
10	Jaisalmer ...	...	...	...	...	...	...
11	Jhalawar ...	...	...	...	...	...	...
12	Karauli ...	...	...	...	...	...	...
13	Kishangarh ...	...	...	...	...	...	...
14	Kotah ...	25	3	...	...	...	...
15	Kushalgarh (Chiefship) ...	...	...	...	...	...	...
16	Lawa (Estate) ...	...	...	...	...	...	...
17	Marwar ...	20	...	...	...	...	...
18	Mewar ...	...	...	...	...	...	...
19	Partabgarh ...	...	...	...	...	...	...
20	Shahpura ...	...	...	...	...	...	...
21	Sirohi ...	56	129	...	...	15	...
22	Tonk ...	...	...	...	...	...	...
	Cities ...	227	1	...	...	5	...
1	Alwar ...	...	...	...	...	...	...
2	Bharatpur ...	...	...	...	...	...	...
3	Bikaner ...	104	...	...	...	3	...
4	Bundi ...	...	...	...	...	...	...
5	Dholpur ...	...	...	...	...	...	...
6	Jaipur ...	123	1	...	...	2	...
7	Jodhpur ...	...	...	...	...	...	...
8	Kotah ...	...	...	...	...	...	...
9	Tonk ...	...	...	...	...	...	...
10	Udaipur ...	...	...	...	...	...	...

TABLE XI.

Occupation by Caste, Tribe or Race.

EXPLANATORY NOTE.

This Table has only been compiled for Europeans and Anglo-Indians.

TABLE XI.—OCCUPATION BY CASTE, TRIBE OR RACE.

OCCUPATION OF EUROPEANS AND ANGLO-INDIANS.

AGENCY, STATE AND DISTRICT.	TOTAL NUMBER OF Earners and working dependants.		Non-working dependants.	Sub-class I. Exploitation of Animals and Vegetation.		Sub-class II. Exploitatoin of Minerals.		Sub-class III. Industry.		Sub-class IV. Transport.		Sub-class V. Trade.		Sub-class VI. Public Force.		Sub-class VII Public Administration.		Sub-class VIII. Professions and Liberal Arts.		Sub-class IX. Persons living on their income.		Sub-class X. Domestic Service.		Sub-class XI. Insufficiently described Occupations.	
	Males.	Females.	Both sexes.	Males.	Females.	Males.	Females.	Males.	Females.	Males.	Females.	Males.	Females.	Males.	Females.	Males.	Females.	Males.	Females.	Males.	Females.	Males.	Females.	Males.	Females.
1	2	3	4	5	6	7	8	9	10	11	12	13	14	15	16	17	18	19	20	21	22	23	24	25	26
										(a) Europeans.															
Rajputana ...	*346*	*57*	*529*	*1*	...	*5*	...	*13*	*1*	*178*	...	*4*	*1*	66	...	*33*	*3*	*33*	*43*	*8*	...	*2*	*9*	*3*	...
Abu District ...	17	4	41	...	...	...	...	...	...	2	...	...	...	10	...	...	...	3	4	1	...	...	...	1	...
Alwar ...	8	2	10	...	...	...	...	...	...	1	...	...	...	1	...	5	1	1	1	...	...	...	...	...	...
Banswara ...	...	3	...	...	...	...	...	...	...	...	...	...	...	...	...	...	...	...	3	...	...	...	...	...	...
Bharatpur ...	9	4	15	...	...	...	...	1	...	...	...	...	...	3	...	4	...	...	2	...	...	1	2	...	...
Bikaner ...	16	4	13	...	...	...	...	1	...	7	...	2	...	2	...	1	...	2	1	1	...	...	3	...	...
Bundi ...	10	...	7	...	...	...	...	6	...	...	...	...	...	...	...	...	...	2	...	...	...	1	...	1	...
Dholpur ...	2	4	3	...	...	...	...	...	...	1	...	...	...	...	...	1	...	...	4	...	...	...	...	...	...
Jaipur ...	138	21	268	1	...	...	...	5	1	101	...	1	1	5	...	10	1	10	17	4	...	...	1	1	...
Jhalawar ...	2	...	1	...	...	...	...	...	...	...	...	...	...	...	...	...	...	1	...	1	...	...	...	...	...
Kotah ...	10	8	2	...	...	...	...	...	...	4	...	...	...	...	...	...	...	6	8	...	...	...	...	...	...
Marwar ...	40	5	58	...	...	5	...	...	...	24	...	1	...	...	...	7	1	3	2	...	...	...	2	...	...
Mewar ...	47	...	19	...	...	...	...	...	...	2	...	...	...	41	...	3	...	1	...	...	...	...	...	...	...
Partabgarh ...	1	...	...	...	...	...	...	...	...	...	...	...	...	...	...	1	...	...	...	...	...	...	...	...	...
Shahpura ...	...	1	...	...	...	...	...	...	...	...	...	...	...	...	...	...	...	...	1	...	...	...	...	...	...
Sirohi ...	44	...	82	...	...	...	...	...	...	36	...	...	...	2	...	1	...	4	...	1	...	...	...	...	...
Tonk ...	2	1	10	...	...	...	...	...	...	...	...	...	...	2	...	...	...	...	...	...	...	...	1	...	...
										(b) Anglo-Indians.															
Rajputana ...	224	22	582	*1*	*1*	...	...	5	...	178	*1*	2	...	2	...	12	...	13	19	1	...	7	*1*	3	...
Abu District ...	4	2	12	...	...	...	...	...	...	...	...	...	...	...	...	...	...	2	2	...	...	...	...	2	...
Alwar ...	4	...	...	...	...	...	...	...	...	2	...	...	...	...	...	1	...	...	...	...	...	1	...	...	...
Bharatpur ...	1	...	5	...	...	...	...	...	...	1	...	...	...	...	...	...	...	...	...	...	...	...	...	...	...
Bikaner ...	3	1	8	...	...	...	...	1	...	2	...	...	...	...	...	...	...	...	...	...	...	...	1	...	...
Dholpur ...	1	2	2	...	...	...	...	...	...	1	...	...	...	...	...	...	...	...	2	...	...	...	...	...	...
Jaipur ...	113	6	317	...	...	...	...	2	...	102	1	2	...	...	...	1	...	3	5	...	...	2	...	1	...
Kishangarh ...	2	...	6	...	...	...	...	1	...	...	...	...	...	...	...	1	...	...	...	...	...	...	...	...	...
Kotah ...	6	1	17	...	...	...	...	...	...	5	...	...	...	...	...	...	...	1	1	...	...	...	...	...	...
Marwar ...	32	2	46	...	...	...	...	1	...	20	...	...	...	...	...	7	...	4	2	...	...	...	...	...	...
Mewar ...	5	1	2	...	...	...	...	...	...	...	...	...	...	...	...	2	...	2	1	1	...	...	...	...	...
Sirohi ...	42	6	154	...	...	...	...	...	...	41	...	...	...	...	...	...	...	1	6	...	...	...	...	...	...
Tonk ...	11	1	13	1	1	...	...	...	...	4	...	...	...	2	...	...	...	...	...	...	...	4	...	...	...

TABLE XII.

Educated Unemployment.

EXPLANATORY NOTE.

This Table is divided into two parts. Part I shows figures for educated unemployment by Class and Part II by Degrees.

The minimum qualification for being considered as 'Educated' was the passing of the Matriculation or equivalent Examination.

TABLE XII.

Educated Unemployment.
Part I.—By Class.
Part II.—By Degrees.

TABLE XII.—EDUCATED UNEMPLOYMENT.

PART I.—BY CLASS.

Class.	Total Unemployed.	Aged 20—24.		Aged 25—29.		Aged 30—34.		Aged 35—39.	
		Unemployed for less than one year.	Unemployed for one year or more.	Unemployed for less than one year.	Unemployed for one year or more.	Unemployed for less than one year.	Unemployed for one year or more.	Unemployed for less than one year.	Unemployed for one year or more.
1	2	3	4	5	6	7	8	9	10
Brahmans ...	29	12	7	1	7	1	...	...	1
Depressed Hindus.	...	...	...	...	...	...	...	...	...
Other Hindus.									
(a) Kayasthas ...	13	6	2	2	2	...	...	1	...
(b) Mahajans ...	14	7	5	1	...	...	1	...	...
(c) Others ...	20	7	8	2	1	1	1	...	...
Muslims ...	18	3	7	3	4	...	...	...	1
Anglo-Indians ...	...	...	...	...	...	...	...	...	...
All other classes ...	...	...	...	...	...	...	...	...	...
Total ...	94	35	29	9	14	2	2	1	2

Total of English knowing unemployed under 20 years 29
" " " " " over 40 years 5
Total of educated unemployed whose fathers were soldiers 1
" " " " " " " cultivators 14
" " " " " " " artizans ... ... Nil
" " " " " " " menials or servants ... 1
" " " " passed Matric. or S.L.C. who though not totally unemployed failed to obtain employment with which they are satisfied ... 13

PART II.—BY DEGREES.

Degree	Total Unemployed.	Aged 20—24		Aged 25—29.		Aged 30—34.		Aged 35—39.	
		Unemployed for less than one year.	Unemployed for one year or more.	Unemployed for less than one year.	Unemployed for one year or more.	Unemployed for less than one year.	Unemployed for one year or more.	Unemployed for less than one year.	Unemployed for one year or more.
1	2	3	4	5	6	7	8	9	10
British Degrees ...	...	...	...	...	...	...	...	...	...
Continental Degrees.	...	...	...	...	...	...	...	...	...
American Degrees...	...	...	...	...	...	...	...	...	...
Other Foreign Degrees	...	...	...	...	...	...	...	...	...
Indian Degrees:—									
Medical ...	1	...	...	...	...	1	...	...	...
Legal ...	6	...	...	3	3	...	...	...	...
Agricultural ...	...	...	...	...	...	...	...	...	...
Commerce ...	1	1	...	...	...	...	...	...	...
M. A. ...	2	1	...	1	...	...	...	...	...
M. Sc. ...	...	...	...	...	...	...	...	...	...
B. A. ...	10	3	4	1	2	...	...	...	...
B. Sc. ...	1	1	...	...	...	...	...	...	...
B. Eng. or L.C.E.	...	...	...	...	...	...	...	...	...
B.T. or L.T. ...	...	...	...	...	...	...	...	...	...
Sch.L.C. or Matric.	73	29	25	4	9	1	2	1	2
Total ...	94	35	29	9	14	2	2	1	2

TABLE XIII.

Literacy by Religion and Age.

EXPLANATORY NOTE.

This Table deals with the literacy of the population, classified by religion and age-periods, and in general arrangement, closely follows Table VII.

The literates shown in Columns 5-7 include literates in English, appearing in Columns 11-13. The totals in Columns 2-4, therefore, represent the aggregates of columns 5-10 only.

Christians have been sub-divided into (a) Indians, and (b) Others in part A of the Table to illustrate the extent of literacy among Indian Christians.

As in Table VII the term 'Hindu' includes Arya, Brahmo and Deo Samaj.

TABLE XIII.—Literacy by Religion and Age.—Part A.—Agency Summary.

Religion and Age.	Population.									Literate in English.		
	Total.			Literate.			Illiterate.					
	Persons.	Males.	Females.	Persons.	Males.	Females.	Persons.	Males.	Females.	Persons.	Males.	Females.
1	2	3	4	5	6	7	8	9	10	11	12	13
All Religions.	*11,225,712*	*5,885,028*	*5,340,684*	*407,136*	*381,602*	*25,534*	*10,818,576*	*5,503,426*	*5,315,150*	*29,895*	*28,209*	*1,686*
0—5 ...	1,735,339	863,097	872,242	990	714	276	1,734,349	862,888	871,966	99	76	23
5—10 ...	1,472,995	783,824	689,171	20,205	18,073	2,132	1,452,790	765,751	687,039	1,354	1,230	124
10—15 ...	1,364,988	745,362	619,626	35,295	32,077	3,218	1,329,693	713,285	616,408	2,815	2,616	199
15—20 ...	1,064,302	563,456	500,846	52,173	48,270	3,903	1,012,129	515,186	496,943	5,159	4,910	249
20 and over.	5,588,088	2,929,289	2,658,799	298,473	282,468	16,005	5,289,615	2,646,821	2,642,794	20,468	19,877	1,091
Buddhist ...	*1*	*1*	...	...	...	...	*1*	*1*	...	...	...	...
0—5 ...	...	...	...	...	...	...	...	...	...	...	...	...
5—10 ...	...	...	...	...	...	...	...	...	...	...	...	...
10—15 ...	...	...	...	...	...	...	...	...	...	...	...	...
15—20 ...	...	...	...	...	...	...	...	...	...	...	...	...
20 and over.	1	1	...	...	...	...	1	1	...	...	...	...
Christian ...	*5,778*	*3,107*	*2,671*	*3,060*	*1,782*	*1,278*	*2,718*	*1,325*	*1,393*	*2,004*	*1,156*	*848*
(a) Indian.	*4,021*	*2,149*	*1,872*	*1,590*	*959*	*631*	*2,431*	*1,190*	*1,241*	*674*	*422*	*252*
0—5 ...	641	307	334	26	15	11	615	292	323	6	5	1
5—10 ...	591	319	272	182	113	69	409	206	203	48	27	21
10—15 ...	552	314	238	233	145	88	319	169	150	66	42	24
15—20 ...	414	223	191	221	135	86	193	88	105	98	63	35
20 and over.	1,823	986	837	928	551	377	895	435	460	456	285	171
(b) Others.	*1,757*	*958*	*799*	*1,470*	*823*	*647*	*287*	*135*	*152*	*1,330*	*734*	*596*
0—5 ...	262	138	124	61	40	21	201	98	103	36	23	13
5—10 ...	173	90	83	138	76	62	35	14	21	120	68	52
10—15 ...	145	74	71	135	71	64	10	3	7	124	67	57
15—20 ...	161	78	83	146	75	71	15	3	12	133	70	63
20 and over	1,016	578	438	990	561	429	26	17	9	917	506	411
Hindu ...	*9,578,805*	*5,029,620*	*4,549,185*	*284,306*	*267,817*	*16,489*	*9,294,499*	*4,761,803*	*4,532,696*	*21,548*	*20,915*	*633*
0—5 ...	1,471,889	732,294	739,595	557	412	145	1,471,332	731,882	739,450	35	27	8
5—10 ...	1,251,331	667,306	584,025	13,844	12,487	1,357	1,237,487	654,819	582,668	905	864	41
10—15 ...	1,165,093	638,395	526,698	24,702	22,616	2,086	1,140,391	615,779	524,612	2,057	1,965	92
15—20 ...	909,809	483,441	426,368	37,022	34,411	2,611	872,787	449,030	423,757	3,902	3,787	115
20 and over.	4,780,683	2,508,184	2,272,499	208,181	197,891	10,290	4,572,502	2,310,293	2,262,209	14,649	14,272	377
Jain ...	*300,748*	*146,004*	*154,744*	*80,270*	*75,960*	*4,310*	*220,478*	*70,044*	*150,434*	*2,604*	*2,541*	*63*
0—5 ...	42,026	21,019	21,007	188	140	48	41,838	20,879	20,959	11	11	...
5—10 ...	35,634	18,234	17,400	4,153	3,800	353	31,481	14,434	17,047	145	141	4
10—15 ...	32,455	16,684	15,771	7,045	6,526	519	25,410	10,158	15,252	295	291	4
15—20 ...	27,053	13,036	14,017	9,842	9,234	608	17,211	8,802	18,409	483	472	11
20 and over.	163,580	77,031	86,549	59,042	56,260	2,782	104,538	20,771	83,767	1,670	1,626	44
Jew ...	*38*	*18*	*20*	*30*	*16*	*14*	*8*	*2*	*6*	*22*	*14*	*8*
0—5 ...	8	4	4	4	2	2	4	2	2	2	2	...
5—10 ...	9	3	6	7	3	4	2	...	2	3	1	2
10—15 ...	5	1	4	5	1	4	...	...	...	5	1	4
15—20 ...	2	1	1	2	1	1	...	...	...	2	1	1
20 and over.	14	9	5	12	9	3	2	...	2	10	9	1
Muslim ...	*1,069,325*	*565,962*	*503,363*	*37,484*	*34,340*	*3,144*	*1,031,841*	*531,622*	*500,219*	*3,251*	*3,169*	*82*
0—5 ...	170,008	84,827	85,181	143	99	44	169,865	84,728	85,137	6	6	...
5—10 ...	142,809	75,807	67,002	1,807	1,541	266	141,002	74,266	66,736	115	113	2
10—15 ...	129,681	70,234	59,447	3,046	2,625	421	126,635	67,609	59,026	241	227	14
15—20 ...	101,322	53,427	47,895	4,697	4,225	472	96,625	49,202	47,423	482	468	14
20 and over.	525,505	281,667	243,838	27,791	25,850	1,941	497,714	255,817	241,897	2,407	2,355	52

TABLE XIII.—Literacy by Religion and Age.—Part A.—Agency Summary.—*Concluded.*

Religion and Age.	Population.									Literate in English.		
	Total.			Literate.			Illiterate.					
	Persons.	Males.	Females.	Persons.	Males.	Females.	Persons.	Males.	Females.	Persons.	Males.	Females.
1	2	3	4	5	6	7	8	9	10	11	12	13
Sikh ...	*41,605*	*24,725*	*16,880*	*1,699*	*1,503*	*196*	*39,906*	*23,222*	*16,684*	*331*	*321*	*10*
0—5 ...	6,510	3,350	3,160	7	4	3	6,503	3,346	3,157	2	2	...
5—10 ...	5,359	2,953	2,406	58	44	14	5,301	2,909	2,392	12	12	...
10—15 ...	4,960	2,895	2,065	114	83	31	4,846	2,812	2,034	22	21	1
15—20 ...	4,275	2,671	1,604	211	170	41	4,064	2,501	1,563	45	41	4
20 and over.	20,501	12,856	7,645	1,309	1,202	107	19,192	11,654	7,538	250	245	5
Tribal ...	*229,092*	*115,420*	*113,672*	*47*	*45*	*2*	*229,045*	*115,375*	*113,670*	...	...	...
0—5 ...	43,959	21,141	22,818	...	...	...	43,959	21,141	22,818	...	...	...
5—10 ...	37,063	19,099	17,964	2	2	...	37,061	19,097	17,964	...	...	...
10—15 ..	32,076	16,756	15,320	2	2	...	32,074	16,754	15,320	...	...	...
15—20 ...	21,234	10,563	10,671	6	6	...	21,228	10,557	10,671	...	...	...
20 and over.	94,760	47,861	46,899	37	35	2	94,723	47,826	46,897	...	...	...
Zoroastrian.	*319*	*170*	*149*	*240*	*139*	*101*	*79*	*31*	*48*	*135*	*93*	*42*
0—5 ...	36	17	19	4	2	2	32	15	17	1	...	1
5—10 ...	26	13	13	14	7	7	12	6	6	6	4	2
10—15 ...	21	9	12	13	8	5	8	1	7	5	2	3
15—20 ...	32	16	16	26	13	13	6	3	3	14	8	6
20 and over.	204	115	89	183	109	74	21	6	15	109	79	30
Religion Not Returned.	*1*	*1*	...	...	...	...	*1*	*1*	...	...	...	...
0—5 ...	...	...	...	...	...	...	...	...	...	...	...	...
5—10 ...	...	...	...	...	...	...	...	...	...	...	...	...
10—15 ...	...	...	...	...	...	...	...	...	...	...	...	...
15—20 ...	...	...	...	...	...	...	...	...	...	...	...	...
20 and over.	1	1	...	...	...	...	1	1	...	...	...	...

TABLE XIII.—Literacy by Religion and Age.—Part B.—By State or District.

State or District, Age and Religion.	Population.									Literate in English.		
	Total.			Literate.			Illiterate.					
	Persons.	Males.	Females.	Persons.	Males.	Females.	Persons.	Males.	Females.	Persons.	Males.	Females.
1	2	3	4	5	6	7	8	9	10	11	12	13
ABU DISTRICT.												
All Religions.	*4,532*	*2,753*	*1,779*	*829*	*663*	*166*	*3,703*	*2,090*	*1,613*	*281*	*227*	*54*
0—5 ...	**584**	289	295	**7**	4	3	**577**	285	292	**1**	1	...
5—10 ...	**485**	264	221	**61**	38	23	**424**	226	198	**18**	13	5
10—15 ...	**505**	301	204	**85**	63	22	**420**	238	182	**20**	15	5
15—20 ...	**548**	332	216	**109**	88	21	**439**	244	195	**33**	27	6
20 and over.	**2,410**	1,567	843	**567**	470	97	**1,843**	1,097	746	**209**	171	38
Christian ...	*140*	*84*	*56*	*104*	*68*	*36*	*36*	*16*	*20*	*87*	*54*	*33*
(Indian) ...	*60*	*41*	*19*	*37*	*27*	*10*	*23*	*14*	*9*	*25*	*15*	*10*
0—5 ...	**13**	7	6	...	...	...	**13**	7	6	...	...	...
5—10 ...	**3**	2	1	**1**	...	1	**2**	2	...	**1**	...	1
10—15 ...	**3**	3	...	**3**	3	...	...	...	...	**1**	1	...
15—20 ...	**5**	5	...	**3**	3	...	**2**	2	...	**2**	2	...
20 and over.	**36**	24	12	**30**	21	9	**6**	3	3	**21**	12	9
(Others) ...	*80*	*43*	*37*	*67*	*41*	*26*	*13*	*2*	*11*	*62*	*39*	*23*
0—5 ...	**9**	3	6	**3**	2	1	**6**	1	5	**1**	...	1
5—10 ...	**16**	7	9	**10**	6	4	**6**	1	5	**9**	6	3
10—15 ...	**8**	7	1	**8**	7	1	...	...	...	**8**	7	1
15—20 ...	**8**	5	3	**7**	5	2	**1**	...	1	**7**	5	2
20 and over.	**39**	21	18	**39**	21	18	...	...	...	**37**	21	16
Hindu ...	*3,498*	*2,099*	*1,399*	*488*	*391*	*97*	*3,010*	*1,708*	*1,302*	*117*	*105*	*12*
0—5 ...	**437**	215	222	**4**	2	2	**433**	213	220	...	...	...
5—10 ...	**381**	208	173	**34**	20	14	**347**	188	159	**5**	4	1
10—15 ...	**404**	235	169	**51**	34	17	**353**	201	152	**6**	5	1
15—20 ...	**426**	256	170	**68**	53	15	**358**	203	155	**14**	12	2
20 and over.	**1,850**	1,185	665	**331**	282	49	**1,519**	903	616	**92**	84	8
Muslim ...	*890*	*512*	*288*	*185*	*169*	*16*	*615*	*343*	*272*	*49*	*46*	*3*
0—5 ...	**106**	51	55	...	...	...	**106**	51	55	...	...	...
5—10 ...	**79**	45	34	**15**	12	3	**64**	33	31	**3**	3	...
10—15 ...	**85**	55	30	**20**	18	2	**65**	37	28	**3**	3	...
15—20 ...	**90**	59	31	**22**	22	...	**68**	37	31	**5**	5	...
20 and over.	**440**	302	138	**128**	117	11	**312**	185	127	**38**	35	3
ALWAR												
All Religions.	*749,751*	*396,261*	*353,490*	*26,850*	*25,420*	*1,430*	*722,901*	*370,841*	*352,060*	*1,906*	*1,853*	*53*
0—5 ...	**109,181**	54,308	54,873	**48**	35	13	**109,133**	54,273	54,860	...	...	...
5—10 ...	**93,879**	50,115	43,764	**1,197**	1,084	113	**92,682**	49,031	43,651	**69**	67	2
10—15 ...	**87,711**	47,964	39,747	**2,082**	1,915	167	**85,629**	46,049	39,580	**162**	157	5
15—20 ...	**71,852**	37,816	34,036	**3,315**	3,070	245	**68,537**	34,746	33,791	**340**	333	7
20 and over.	**387,128**	206,058	181,070	**20,208**	19,816	392	**366,920**	186,742	180,178	**1,335**	1,296	39
Hindu ...	*549,366*	*290,088*	*259,278*	*23,338*	*22,141*	*1,197*	*526,028*	*267,947*	*258,081*	*1,622*	*1,583*	*39*
0—5 ...	**78,335**	38,971	39,364	**27**	24	3	**78,308**	38,947	39,361	...	...	...
5—10 ...	**68,012**	36,256	31,756	**1,019**	931	88	**66,993**	35,325	31,668	**62**	60	2
10—15 ...	**63,980**	34,902	29,078	**1,809**	1,671	138	**62,171**	33,231	28,940	**144**	140	4
15—20 ...	**52,222**	27,478	24,744	**2,913**	2,702	211	**49,309**	24,776	24,533	**298**	292	6
20 and over	**286,817**	152,481	134,336	**17,570**	16,813	757	**269,247**	135,668	133,579	**1,118**	1,091	27
Jain ...	*3,809*	*1,994*	*1,815*	*1,309*	*1,212*	*97*	*2,500*	*782*	*1,718*	*56*	*56*	...
0—5 ...	**561**	277	284	**10**	5	5	**551**	272	279	...	...	...
5—10 ...	**449**	215	234	**73**	62	11	**376**	153	223	**1**	1	...
10—15 ...	**402**	207	195	**115**	101	14	**287**	106	181	**5**	5	...
15—20 ...	**348**	185	163	**159**	140	19	**189**	45	144	**9**	9	...
20 and over	**2,049**	1,110	939	**952**	904	48	**1,097**	206	891	**41**	41	...

TABLE XIII.—Literacy by Religion and Age.—Part B.—By State or District.—*Continued.*

State or District, Age and Religion.	Population. Total. Persons.	Total. Males.	Total. Females.	Literate. Persons.	Literate. Males.	Literate. Females.	Illiterate. Persons.	Illiterate. Males.	Illiterate. Females.	Literate in English. Persons.	Literate in English. Males.	Literate in English. Females.
1	2	3	4	5	6	7	8	9	10	11	12	13
ALWAR *Concluded.*												
Muslim ...	*196,460*	*104,110*	*92,350*	*2,131*	*2,020*	*111*	*194,329*	*102,090*	*92,239*	*190*	*188*	*2*
0— 5 ...	30,259	15,043	15,216	7	5	2	30,252	15,038	15,214	...	...	...
5—10 ...	25,406	13,636	11,770	98	87	11	25,308	13,549	11,759	4	4	...
10—15 ...	23,321	12,850	10,471	151	138	13	23,170	12,712	10,458	10	10	...
15—20 ...	19,272	10,147	9,125	236	223	13	19,036	9,924	9,112	31	31	...
20 and over.	98,202	52,434	45,768	1,639	1,567	72	96,563	50,867	45,696	145	143	2
BANSWARA.												
All Religions.	*225,106*	*111,983*	*113,123*	*4,896*	*4,588*	*308*	*220,210*	*107,395*	*112,815*	*151*	*133*	*18*
0— 5 ...	40,949	20,165	20,784	3	1	2	40,946	20,164	20,782	...	...	...
5—10 ...	34,542	17,536	17,006	240	216	24	34,302	17,320	16,982	2	2	...
10—15 ...	31,203	15,987	15,216	424	388	36	30,779	15,599	15,180	10	10	...
15—20 ...	21,339	10,451	10,888	634	588	46	20,705	9,863	10,842	30	28	2
20 and over.	97,073	47,844	49,229	3,595	3,395	200	93,478	44,449	49,029	109	93	16
Hindu ...	*120,458*	*59,925*	*60,533*	*2,573*	*2,384*	*189*	*117,885*	*57,541*	*60,344*	*119*	*114*	*5*
0— 5 ...	20,935	10,429	10,506	2	1	1	20,933	10,428	10,505	...	...	...
5—10 ...	17,415	8,894	8,521	142	125	17	17,273	8,769	8,504	2	2	...
10—15 ...	16,160	8,326	7,834	239	216	23	15,921	8,110	7,811	8	8	...
15—20 ...	11,805	5,735	6,070	334	305	29	11,471	5,430	6,041	25	25	...
20 and over.	54,143	26,541	27,602	1,856	1,737	119	52,287	24,804	27,483	84	79	5
Tribal ...	*93,330*	*46,313*	*47,017*	*3*	*3*	...	*93,327*	*46,310*	*47,017*	...	..	...
0— 5 ...	18,312	8,902	9,410	...	...	...	18,312	8,902	9,410	...	...	...
5—10 ...	15,618	7,865	7,753	1	1	...	15,617	7,864	7,753	...	...	...
10—15 ...	13,657	6,947	6,710	1	1	...	13,656	6,946	6,710	...	...	...
15—20 ...	8,479	4,178	4,301	...	...	...	8,479	4,178	4,301	...	...	...
20 and over.	37,264	18,421	18,843	1	1	...	37,263	18,420	18,843	...	...	...
BHARATPUR.												
All Religions.	*486,954*	*263,325*	*223,629*	*21,988*	*20,522*	*1,466*	*464,966*	*242,803*	*222,163*	*1,282*	*1,215*	*67*
0— 5 ...	74,625	37,552	37,073	32	28	4	74,593	37,524	37,069	...	...	...
5—10 ...	61,637	34,032	27,605	1,266	1,131	135	60,371	32,901	27,470	46	42	4
10—15 ...	57,625	32,596	25,029	2,173	1,955	218	55,452	30,641	24,811	122	113	9
15—20 ...	45,205	24,202	21,003	2,829	2,563	266	42,376	21,639	20,737	204	193	11
20 and over.	247,862	134,943	112,919	15,688	14,845	843	232,174	120,098	112,076	910	867	43
Hindu ...	*389,723*	*211,278*	*178,445*	*18,706*	*17,619*	*1,087*	*371,017*	*193,659*	*177,358*	*937*	*905*	*32*
0— 5 ...	59,153	29,628	29,525	28	25	3	59,125	29,603	29,522	...	...	...
5—10 ...	48,777	26,972	21,805	1,072	964	108	47,705	26,008	21,697	28	25	3
10—15 ...	45,699	25,942	19,757	1,855	1,686	169	43,844	24,256	19,588	93	86	7
15—20 ...	36,099	19,401	16,698	2,420	2,227	193	33,679	17,174	16,505	154	148	6
20 and over.	199,995	109,335	90,660	13,331	12,717	614	186,664	96,618	90,046	662	646	16
Jain ...	*2,390*	*1,288*	*1,102*	*916*	*831*	*85*	*1,474*	*457*	*1,017*	*45*	*44*	*1*
0— 5 ...	332	161	171	3	2	1	329	159	170	...	...	...
5—10 ...	276	140	136	60	48	12	216	92	124	2	2	...
10—15 ...	266	141	125	98	79	19	168	62	106	4	4	...
15—20 ...	234	121	113	112	98	14	122	23	99	9	8	1
20 and over.	1,282	725	557	643	604	39	639	121	518	30	30	...
Muslim ...	*94,054*	*50,308*	*43,746*	*2,223*	*1,975*	*248*	*91,831*	*48,333*	*43,498*	*230*	*227*	*3*
0— 5 ...	15,002	7,688	7,314	1	1	...	15,001	7,687	7,314	...	...	...
5—10 ...	12,482	6,859	5,623	125	112	13	12,357	6,747	5,610	12	12	...
10—15 ...	11,576	6,459	5,117	209	181	28	11,367	6,278	5,089	21	20	1
15—20 ...	8,794	4,636	4,158	286	230	56	8,508	4,406	4,102	35	34	1
20 and over.	46,200	24,666	21,534	1,602	1,451	151	44,598	23,215	21,383	162	161	1

TABLE XIII.—Literacy by Religion and Age.—Part B.—By State or District.—*Continued.*

State or District, Age and Religion.	Population.									Literate in English.		
	Total.			Literate.			Illiterate.					
	Persons.	Males.	Females.	Persons.	Males.	Females.	Persons.	Males.	Females	Persons.	Males.	Females.
1	2	3	4	5	6	7	8	9	10	11	12	13
BIKANER.												
All Religions.	*936,218*	*501,153*	*435,065*	*39,408*	*36,299*	*3,109*	*896,810*	*464,854*	*431,956*	*4,135*	*3,988*	*147*
0—5 ...	146,124	74,094	72,080	46	33	13	146,078	74,061	72,017	6	4	2
5—10 ...	120.447	63,882	56,615	1,947	1,718	229	118,500	62,114	56,386	197	188	9
10—15 ...	114,482	62,147	52,335	3,577	3,168	409	110,905	58,979	51,926	420	400	20
15—20 ...	96,574	52,312	44,262	5,558	4,983	575	91,016	47,329	43,687	744	720	24
20 and over.	458,591	248,768	209,823	28,280	26,397	1,883	430,311	222,371	207,940	2,768	2,676	92
Hindu ...	*725,084*	*388,017*	*337,067*	*29,074*	*26,908*	*2,166*	*696,010*	*361,109*	*334,901*	*3,179*	*3,081*	*98*
0—5 ...	111,192	56,405	54.787	30	21	9	111,162	56,384	54,778	5	3	2
5—10 ...	91,544	48,515	43,029	1,455	1,286	169	90,089	47,229	42,860	151	144	7
10—15 ...	87,958	47,769	40,189	2,653	2,375	278	85,305	45,394	39,911	332	315	17
15—20 ...	75,431	40,820	34,611	4,168	3,765	408	71,263	37,055	34,208	599	583	16
20 and over.	358,959	194,508	164,451	20,768	19,461	1,307	338,191	175,047	163,144	2,092	2,036	56
Jain ...	*28,773*	*12,479*	*16,294*	*6,076*	*5,522*	*554*	*22,697*	*6,957*	*15,740*	*308*	*305*	*3*
0—5 ...	4,560	2,287	2,273	8	6	2	4,552	2,281	2,271	...	...	...
5—10 ...	3,780	1,925	1,845	319	283	36	3,461	1,652	1,809	21	20	1
10—15 ...	3,363	1,670	1,693	590	519	71	2,773	1,151	1,622	41	40	1
15—20 ...	2,672	1,084	1,588	823	729	94	1,849	355	1,494	58	58	...
20 and over.	14,398	5,503	8,895	4,336	3,985	351	10,062	1,518	8,544	188	187	1
Muslim ...	*141,578*	*76,471*	*65,107*	*2,862*	*2,645*	*217*	*138,716*	*73,826*	*64,890*	*329*	*328*	*1*
0—5 ...	24,007	12,144	11,863	3	3	...	24,004	12,141	11,863	...	...	...
5—10 ...	19.834	10,465	9,369	132	118	14	19,702	10,347	9,355	12	12	...
10—15 ...	18,271	9,858	8,413	245	212	35	18,026	9,646	8,380	26	26	...
15—20 ...	14,301	7,800	6,501	396	358	38	13,905	7,442	6,463	50	50	...
20 and over.	65,165	36,204	28,961	2,086	1,954	132	63,079	34,250	28,829	241	240	1
Sikh ...	*40,469*	*24,017*	*16,452*	*1,258*	*1,143*	*115*	*39,211*	*22,874*	*16,337*	*216*	*214*	*2*
0—5 ...	6,317	3,241	3,076	3	3	...	6,314	3,238	3,076	1	1	...
5—10 ...	5,250	2,895	2,355	36	27	9	5,214	2,868	2,346	9	9	...
10—15 ...	4,859	2,834	2,025	79	56	23	4,780	2,778	2,002	15	15	...
15—20 ...	4,145	2,599	1,546	157	128	29	3,988	2,471	1,517	29	28	1
20 and over.	19,898	12,448	7,450	983	929	54	18,915	11,519	7,896	162	161	1
BUNDI.												
All Religions.	*216,722*	*113,101*	*103,621*	*5,448*	*5,115*	*333*	*211,274*	*107,986*	*103,288*	*257*	*244*	*13*
0—5 ...	32,562	15,687	16,875	8	3	5	32,554	15,684	16,870	...	...	...
5—10 ...	27,798	14,567	13,231	213	186	27	27,585	14,381	13,204	8	7	1
10—15 ...	25.355	13,773	11,582	366	326	40	24,989	13,447	11,542	17	15	2
15—20 ...	19,949	10,425	9,524	587	545	42	19,362	9,880	9,482	37	36	1
20 and over.	111,058	58,649	52,409	4,274	4,055	219	106,784	54,594	52,190	195	186	9
Hindu ...	*202,329*	*105,482*	*96,847*	*4,200*	*3,934*	*266*	*198,129*	*101,548*	*96,581*	*205*	*197*	*8*
0—5 ...	30,577	14,698	15,879	6	3	3	30,571	14,695	15,876	...	...	...
5—10 ...	26,134	13,708	12,426	152	133	19	25,982	13,575	12,407	6	5	1
10—15 ...	23,752	12,931	10,821	268	239	29	23,484	12,692	10,792	13	12	1
15—20 ...	18,585	9,679	8,906	442	406	36	18,143	9,273	8,870	31	30	1
20 and over	103,281	54,466	48,815	3,332	3,153	179	99,949	51,818	48,636	155	150	5
Jain ...	*4,019*	*2,166*	*1,853*	*949*	*920*	*29*	*3,070*	*1,246*	*1,824*	*9*	*9*	...
0—5 ...	477	228	249	1	...	1	476	228	248	...	...	...
5—10 ...	388	208	185	38	35	3	350	168	182	...	...	...
10—15 ...	410	219	191	63	59	4	347	160	187	...	...	...
15—20 ...	391	227	164	96	92	4	295	135	160	2	2	...
20 and over.	2,353	1,289	1,064	751	734	17	1,602	555	1,047	7	7	...

TABLE XIII.—Literacy by Religion and Age.—Part B.—By State or District.—*Continued.*

State or District, Age and Religion.	Population.									Literate in English.		
	Total.			Literate.			Illiterate.					
	Persons.	Males.	Females.	Persons.	Males.	Females	Persons.	Males.	Females.	Persons.	Males.	Females.
1	2	3	4	5	6	7	8	9	10	11	12	13
BUNDI *Concluded.*												
Muslim ...	*10,292*	*5,398*	*4,894*	*257*	*224*	*33*	*10,035*	*5,174*	*4,861*	*24*	*23*	*1*
0— 5 ...	1,496	755	741	1	...	1	1,495	755	740	...	...	...
5—10 ...	1,268	652	616	21	17	4	1,247	635	612	2	2	...
10—15 ...	1,185	617	568	31	24	7	1,154	593	561	4	3	1
15—20 ...	965	514	451	44	42	2	921	472	449	3	3	...
20 and over.	5,378	2,860	2,518	160	141	19	5,218	2,719	2,499	15	15	...
DHOLPUR.												
All Religions	*254,986*	*140,497*	*114,489*	*8,865*	*8,247*	*618*	*246,121*	*132,250*	*113,871*	*633*	*588*	*45*
0— 5 ...	39,278	20,123	19,155	...	...	...	39,278	20,123	19,155	...	...	...
5—10 ...	31,369	17,087	14,282	361	828	88	31,008	16,764	14,244	14	12	2
10—15 ..	29,937	17,179	12,758	732	670	62	29,205	16,509	12,696	36	34	2
15—20 ...	24,398	13,578	10,820	1,147	1,039	108	23,251	12,539	10,712	97	89	8
20 and over.	130,004	72,530	57,474	6,625	6,215	410	123,379	66,315	57,064	486	453	33
Hindu ...	*235,929*	*130,354*	*105,575*	*7,587*	*7,147*	*440*	*228,342*	*123,207*	*105,135*	*493*	*474*	*19*
0— 5 ...	36,347	18,674	17,673	...	...	...	36,347	18,674	17,673	...	...	...
5—10 ...	29,027	15,849	13,178	308	282	26	28,719	15,567	13,152	11	9	2
10—15 ...	27,811	16,008	11,803	633	589	44	27,178	15,419	11,759	31	29	2
15—20 ...	22,621	12,625	9,996	977	902	75	21,644	11,723	9,921	76	73	3
20 and over.	120,123	67,198	52,925	5,669	5,374	295	114,454	61,824	52,630	375	363	12
Muslim ...	*16,842*	*8,903*	*7,939*	*872*	*764*	*108*	*15,970*	*8,139*	*7,831*	*73*	*73*	...
0— 5 ...	2,595	1,269	1,326	...	...	...	2,595	1,269	1,326	...	...	...
5—10 ...	2,106	1,119	987	34	26	8	2,072	1,093	979	...	1	...
10—15 ...	1,897	1,049	848	65	53	12	1,832	996	836	...	...	...
15—20 ...	1,558	833	725	114	93	21	1,444	740	704	9	9	...
20 and over.	8,686	4,633	4,053	659	592	67	8,027	4,041	3,986	63	63	...
DUNGARPUR.												
All Religions.	*227,544*	*114,480*	*113,064*	*5,863*	*5,564*	*299*	*221,681*	*108,916*	*112,765*	*158*	*149*	*9*
0— 5 ...	39,854	19,541	20,313	2	...	2	39,852	19,541	20,311	...	...	...
5—10 ...	34,563	17,895	16,668	415	384	31	34,148	17,511	16,637	6	6	...
10—15 ...	31,728	16,550	15,178	663	618	45	31,065	15,932	15,133	15	14	1
15—20 ...	21,557	10,714	10,843	815	767	48	20,742	9,947	10,795	32	29	3
20 and over.	99,842	49,780	50,062	3,968	3,795	173	95,874	45,985	49,889	105	100	5
Hindu ...	*214,045*	*107,797*	*106,248*	*2,981*	*2,768*	*213*	*211,064*	*105,029*	*106,035*	*105*	*97*	*8*
0— 5 ...	37,996	18,663	19,333	...	...	...	37,996	18,663	19,333	...	...	...
5—10 ...	32,831	17,018	15,818	240	220	20	32,591	16,793	15,798	6	6	...
10—15 ...	30,059	15,693	14,366	369	342	27	29,690	15,351	14,339	12	11	1
15—20 ...	20,225	10,062	10,163	405	372	33	19,820	9,690	10,130	21	19	2
20 and over.	92,934	46,366	46,568	1,967	1,834	133	90,967	44,532	46,435	66	61	5
Jain ...	*5,801*	*2,836*	*2,965*	*1,744*	*1,684*	*60*	*4,057*	*1,152*	*2,905*	*10*	*10*	...
0— 5 ...	692	325	367	...	...	...	692	325	367	...	...	...
5—10 ...	640	324	316	108	99	9	532	225	307	...	...	...
10—15 ...	636	331	305	178	166	12	458	165	293	1	1	...
15—20 ...	573	289	284	247	238	9	326	51	275	1	1	...
20 and over.	3,260	1,567	1,693	1,211	1,181	30	2,049	386	1,663	8	8	...
Muslim ...	*7,682*	*3,838*	*3,844*	*1,125*	*1,104*	*21*	*6,557*	*2,734*	*3,823*	*38*	*38*	...
0— 5 ...	1,162	553	609	...	...	...	1,162	553	609	...	...	...
5—10 ...	1,091	557	534	67	65	2	1,024	492	532	...	...	...
10—15 ...	1,033	526	507	116	110	6	917	416	501	2	2	...
15—20 ...	756	361	395	160	155	5	596	206	390	9	9	...
20 and over.	3,640	1,841	1,799	782	774	8	2,858	1,067	1,791	27	27	...

TABLE XIII.—LITERACY BY RELIGION AND AGE.—PART B.—BY STATE OR DISTRICT.—*Continued.*

State or District, Age and Religion.	Population									Literate in English.		
	Total.			Literate			Illiterate.					
	Persons.	Males.	Females.	Persons.	Males.	Females.	Persons.	Males.	Females.	Persons.	Males.	Females.
1	2	3	4	5	6	7	8	9	10	11	12	13
JAIPUR.												
All Religions.	*2,631,775*	*1,387,067*	*1,241,708*	*93,339*	*87,834*	*5,505*	*2,538,436*	*1,299,233*	*1,239,203*	*7,458*	*6,821*	*637*
0— 5 ...	394,057	196,598	197,459	255	196	59	393,802	196,402	197,400	39	32	7
5—10 ...	339,744	183,105	156,639	4,179	3,730	449	335,565	179,375	156,190	350	292	58
10—15 ...	313,610	173,663	139,947	7,254	6,644	610	306,356	167,019	139,337	607	531	76
15—20 ...	236,137	125,534	110,603	11,186	10,427	759	224,951	115,107	109,844	1,157	1,076	81
20 and over.	1,348,227	708,167	640,060	70,465	66,837	3,628	1,277,762	641,330	636,432	5,305	4,890	415
Hindu ...	*2,383,304*	*1,256,918*	*1,126,386*	*75,430*	*71,707*	*3,723*	*2,307,874*	*1,185,211*	*1,122,663*	*5,006*	*4,833*	*173*
0— 5 ...	355,895	177,723	178,172	172	148	29	355,723	177,580	178,143	16	15	1
5—10 ...	307,385	166,049	141,336	3,275	2,991	284	304,110	163,058	141,052	187	175	12
10—15 ...	284,394	157,981	126,413	5,895	5,488	407	278.499	152,493	126,006	393	365	28
15—20 ...	213,283	113,782	99,501	9,210	8,696	514	204,073	105,086	98,987	833	803	30
20 and over.	1,222,347	641,383	580,964	56,878	54,389	2,489	1,165,469	586,994	578,475	3,577	3,475	102
Jain ...	*29,492*	*15,518*	*13,974*	*9,075*	*8,536*	*539*	*20,417*	*6,982*	*13,435*	*502*	*495*	*7*
0— 5 ...	3,613	1,791	1,822	17	13	4	3,596	1,778	1,818	1	1	...
5—10 ...	3,068	1,626	1,442	416	373	43	2,652	1,253	1,399	32	32	...
10—15 ...	2,871	1,551	1,320	672	609	63	2,199	942	1,257	51	51	...
15—20 ...	2,586	1,321	1,265	971	888	83	1,615	433	1,182	87	85	2
20 and over.	17,354	9,229	8,125	6,999	6,653	346	10,355	2,576	7,779	331	326	5
Muslim ...	*214,581*	*112,338*	*102,243*	*7,607*	*6,865*	*742*	*206,974*	*105,473*	*101,501*	*938*	*917*	*21*
0— 5 ...	33,733	16,659	17,074	31	16	15	33,702	16,643	17,059	2	2	...
5—10 ...	28,684	15,114	13,570	341	279	62	28,343	14,835	13,508	27	26	1
10—15 ...	25,804	13,851	11,953	547	462	85	25,257	13,389	11,868	56	53	3
15—20 ...	19,840	10,228	9,612	881	774	107	18,959	9,454	9,505	133	131	2
20 and over.	106,520	56,486	50,034	5,807	5,334	473	100,713	51,152	49,561	720	705	15
JAISALMER.												
All Religions.	*76,255*	*42,342*	*33,913*	*2,010*	*1,957*	*53*	*74,245*	*40,385*	*33,860*	*74*	*74*	...
0— 5 ...	11,156	5,658	5,498	...	...	...	11,156	5,658	5,498	...	...	...
5—10 ...	10,090	5,676	4,414	50	48	2	10,040	5,628	4,412	1	1	...
10—15 ...	9,367	5,549	3,818	125	122	3	9,242	5,427	3,815	2	2	...
15—20 .	7,432	4,267	3,165	256	248	8	7,176	4,019	3,157	11	11	...
20 and over.	38,210	21,192	17,018	1,579	1,539	40	36,631	19,653	16,978	60	60	...
Hindu ...	*51,769*	*28,551*	*23,218*	*1,801*	*1,753*	*48*	*49,968*	*26,798*	*23,170*	*73*	*73*	...
0— 5 ...	7,485	3,844	3,641	...	...	...	7,485	3,844	3,641	...	...	...
5—10 ..	6,771	3,808	2,963	45	43	2	6,726	3,765	2,961	1	1	...
10—15 ...	6,365	3,774	2,591	113	110	3	6.252	3,664	2,588	2	2	...
15—20 ...	5,087	2,917	2,170	231	224	7	4,856	2,693	2,163	10	10	...
20 and over.	26,061	14,208	11,853	1,412	1,376	36	24,649	12,832	11,817	60	60	...
Muslim ...	*22,116*	*12,502*	*9,614*	*48*	*43*	*5*	*22,068*	*12,459*	*9,609*	*1*	1	...
0— 5 ...	3,332	1,636	1,696	...	...	...	3,332	1,636	1,696	...	...	...
5—10 ...	2,996	1,689	1,307	...	...	...	2,996	1,689	1,307	...	...	...
10—15 ...	2,689	1,600	1,089	1	1	...	2,688	1,599	1,089	...	...	...
15—20 ...	2,094	1,211	883	6	5	1	2,088	1,206	882	1	1	...
20 and over.	11,005	6,366	4,639	41	87	4	10,964	6,329	4,635	...	...	...
Tribal ...	*1,444*	*815*	*629*	...	...	...	*1,444*	*815*	*629*	...	...	...
0— 5 ...	225	125	100	...	...	...	225	125	100	...	...	...
5—10 ...	213	124	89	...	...	...	213	124	89	...	...	...
10—15 ..	206	118	88	...	...	...	206	118	88	...	...	...
15—20 ...	154	84	70	...	...	...	154	84	70	...	...	...
20 and over.	646	364	282	...	...	...	646	364	282	...	...	...

TABLE XIII.—LITERACY BY RELIGION AND AGE.—PART B.—BY STATE OR DISTRICT.—*Continued.*

State or District, Age and Religion.	Population. Total.			Literate.			Illiterate.			Literate in English.		
	Persons.	Males.	Females.	Persons.	Males.	Females.	Persons.	Males.	Females.	Persons.	Males.	Females.
1	2	3	4	5	6	7	8	9	10	11	12	13
JHALAWAR.												
All Religions.	*107,890*	*56,518*	*51,372*	*7,132*	*6,303*	*829*	*100,758*	*50,215*	*50,543*	*439*	*427*	*12*
0—5 ...	**14,664**	7,327	7,337	**25**	20	5	**14,639**	7,307	7,332	...	...	...
5—10 ...	**12,861**	6,694	6,167	**634**	512	122	**12,227**	6,182	6,045	**10**	10	...
10—15 ...	**12,420**	6,481	5,939	**889**	736	153	**11,531**	5,745	5,786	**33**	32	1
15—20 ...	**10,799**	5,527	5,272	**942**	821	121	**9,857**	4,706	5,151	**83**	81	2
20 and over.	**57,146**	30,489	26,657	**4,642**	4,214	428	**52,504**	26,275	26,229	**313**	304	9
Hindu ...	*96,634*	*50,705*	*45,929*	*4,792*	*4,289*	*503*	*91,842*	*46,416*	*45,426*	*315*	*306*	*9*
0—5 ...	**13,183**	6,604	6,579	**12**	10	2	**13,171**	6,594	6,577	...	...	...
5—10 ...	**11,523**	6,016	5,507	**417**	339	78	**11,106**	5,677	5,429	**8**	8	...
10—15 ...	**11,162**	5,829	5,333	**587**	487	100	**10,575**	5,342	5,233	**23**	22	1
15—20 ...	**9,708**	4,965	4,743	**625**	551	74	**9,083**	4,414	4,669	**56**	55	1
20 and over.	**51,058**	27,291	23,767	**3,151**	2,902	249	**47,907**	24,389	23,518	**228**	221	7
Jain ...	*2,630*	*1,390*	*1,240*	*979*	*840*	*139*	*1,651*	*550*	*1,101*	*48*	*47*	*1*
0—5 ...	**285**	148	137	**5**	5	...	**280**	143	137	...	...	...
5—10 ...	**279**	141	138	**84**	65	19	**195**	76	119	**1**	1	...
10—15 ...	**280**	144	136	**118**	95	23	**162**	49	113	**6**	6	...
15—20 ...	**244**	134	110	**125**	104	21	**119**	30	89	**8**	8	...
20 and over.	**1,542**	823	719	**647**	571	76	**895**	252	643	**33**	32	1
Muslim ...	*8,558*	*4,377*	*4,181*	*1,341*	*1,157*	*184*	*7,217*	*3,220*	*3,997*	*67*	*66*	*1*
0—5 ...	**1,189**	572	617	**8**	5	3	**1,181**	567	614	...	...	...
5—10 ...	**1,052**	532	520	**133**	108	25	**919**	424	495	**1**	1	...
10—15 ...	**972**	504	468	**184**	154	30	**788**	350	438	**4**	4	...
15—20 ...	**842**	424	418	**189**	163	26	**653**	261	392	**18**	17	1
20 and over.	**4,503**	2,345	2,158	**827**	727	100	**3,676**	1,618	2,058	**44**	44	...
KARAULI.												
All Religions.	*140,525*	*76,729*	*63,796*	*5,384*	*5,106*	*278*	*135,141*	*71,623*	*63,518*	*149*	*140*	*9*
0—5 ...	**20,882**	10,576	10,306	**1**	1	...	**20,881**	10,575	10,306	...	...	...
5—10 ...	**18,467**	10,116	8,351	**192**	179	13	**18,275**	9,937	8,338	**2**	1	1
10—15 ...	**17,631**	9,921	7,710	**405**	374	31	**17,226**	9,547	7,679	**10**	8	2
15—20 ...	**13,056**	7,157	5,899	**715**	663	52	**12,341**	6,494	5,847	**22**	20	2
20 and over.	**70,489**	38,959	31,530	**4,071**	3,889	182	**66,418**	35,070	31,348	**115**	111	4
Hindu ...	*132,759*	*72,578*	*60,181*	*4,825*	*4,601*	*224*	*127,934*	*67,977*	*59,957*	*114*	*106*	*8*
0—5 ...	**19,730**	10,021	9,709	**1**	1	...	**19,729**	10,020	9,709	...	...	...
5—10 ...	**17,515**	9,599	7,916	**168**	160	8	**17,347**	9,439	7,908	**2**	1	1
10—15 ...	**16,720**	9,412	7,308	**359**	337	22	**16,361**	9,075	7,286	**9**	7	2
15—20 ...	**12,302**	6,764	5,538	**635**	594	41	**11,667**	6,170	5,497	**16**	14	2
20 and over.	**66,492**	36,782	29,710	**3,662**	3,509	153	**62,830**	33,273	29,557	**87**	84	3
Muslim ...	*7,301*	*3,914*	*3,387*	*375*	*347*	*28*	*6,926*	*3,567*	*3,359*	*13*	*13*	...
0—5 ...	**1,087**	522	565	...	...	...	**1,087**	522	565	...	...	...
5—10 ...	**891**	490	401	**14**	12	2	**877**	478	399	...	...	...
10—15 ...	**853**	480	373	**26**	23	3	**827**	457	370	...	...	...
15—20 ...	**707**	370	337	**52**	47	5	**655**	323	332	**1**	1	...
20 and over.	**3,763**	2,052	1,711	**283**	265	18	**3,480**	1,787	1,693	**12**	12	...
KISHANGARH.												
All Religions	*85,744*	*44,494*	*41,250*	*4,872*	*4,560*	*312*	*80,872*	*39,934*	*40,938*	*302*	*295*	*7*
0—5 ...	**13,120**	6,497	6,623	**5**	4	1	**13,115**	6,493	6,622	...	...	...
5—10 ...	**11,173**	5,887	5,286	**262**	238	24	**10,911**	5,649	5,262	**13**	13	...
10—15 ...	**10,147**	5,393	4,754	**413**	382	31	**9,734**	5,011	4,723	**27**	27	...
15—20 ...	**7,984**	4,109	3,875	**579**	541	38	**7,405**	3,568	3,837	**60**	60	...
20 and over.	**43,320**	22,608	20,712	**3,613**	3,395	218	**39,707**	19,213	20,494	**202**	195	7

TABLE XIII.—Literacy by Religion and Age —Part B.—By State or District.—*Continued.*

State or District, Age and Religion.	Population.									Literate in English.		
	Total			Literate.			Illiterate.					
	Persons.	Males	Females.	Persons.	Males.	Females.	Persons.	Males.	Females.	Persons.	Males.	Females.
1	2	3	4	5	6	7	8	9	10	11	12	13
KISHANGARH *Concluded.*												
Hindu	***76,263***	***39,506***	***36,757***	***3,595***	***3,379***	***216***	***72,668***	***36,127***	***36,541***	***242***	***238***	***4***
0— 5 ...	**11,718**	5,827	5,891	**3**	2	1	**11,715**	5,825	5,890	...	...	...
5—10 ...	**9,970**	5,260	4,710	**189**	173	16	**9,781**	5,087	4,694	**9**	9	...
10—15 ...	**9,053**	4,824	4,229	**309**	288	21	**8,744**	4,536	4,208	**19**	19	...
15—20 ...	**7,113**	3,660	3,453	**442**	412	30	**6,671**	3,248	3,423	**48**	48	...
20 and over.	**38,409**	19,935	18,474	**2,652**	2,504	148	**35,757**	17,431	18,326	**166**	162	4
Jain ...	***2,231***	***1,187***	***1,044***	***870***	***803***	***67***	***1,361***	***384***	***977***	***30***	***29***	***1***
0— 5 ...	**271**	135	136	**2**	2	...	**269**	133	136	...	...	...
5—10 ...	**234**	128	106	**53**	47	6	**181**	81	100	**2**	2	...
10—15 ...	**222**	121	101	**70**	62	8	**152**	59	93	**5**	5	...
15—20 ...	**188**	95	93	**85**	79	6	**103**	16	87	**7**	7	...
20 and over.	**1,316**	708	608	**660**	613	47	**656**	95	561	**16**	15	1
Muslim ...	***6,597***	***3,467***	***3,130***	***392***	***369***	***23***	***6,205***	***3,098***	***3,107***	***20***	***19***	***1***
0— 5 ...	**1,026**	487	539	...	...	...	**1,026**	487	539	...	...	...
5—10 ...	**865**	441	424	**18**	16	2	**847**	425	422	...	...	...
10—15 ...	**783**	397	386	**32**	30	2	**751**	367	384	**1**	1	...
15—20 ...	**620**	325	295	**51**	49	2	**569**	276	293	**4**	4	...
20 and over.	**3,303**	1,817	1,486	**291**	274	17	**3,012**	1,543	1,469	**15**	14	1
KOTAH.												
All Religions.	***685,804***	***355,056***	***330,748***	***30,452***	***27,893***	***2,559***	***655,352***	***327,163***	***328,189***	***1,914***	***1,813***	***101***
0— 5 ...	**99,394**	48,822	50,572	**151**	85	66	**99,243**	48,737	50,506	**6**	4	2
5—10 ...	**84,486**	43,743	40,743	**2,095**	1,832	263	**82,391**	41,911	40,480	**49**	45	4
10—15 ...	**80,063**	41,885	38,178	**3,312**	2,902	410	**76,751**	38,983	37,768	**158**	147	11
15—20 ...	**66,627**	33,936	32,691	**4,217**	3,800	417	**62,410**	30,136	32,274	**375**	357	18
20 and over.	**355,234**	186,670	168,564	**20,677**	19,274	1,403	**334,557**	167,896	167,161	**1,326**	1,260	66
Hindu ...	***629,416***	***325,624***	***303,792***	***24,096***	***22,361***	***1,735***	***605,320***	***303,263***	***302,057***	***1,452***	***1,403***	***49***
0— 5 ...	**91,139**	44,701	46,438	**97**	48	49	**91,042**	44,653	46,389	**4**	2	2
5—10 ...	**77,613**	40,217	37,396	**1,657**	1,482	175	**75,956**	38,735	37,221	**37**	35	2
10—15 ...	**73,675**	38,570	35,105	**2,640**	2,360	280	**71,035**	36,210	34,825	**123**	117	6
15—20 ...	**61,197**	31,167	30,030	**3,320**	3,037	283	**57,877**	28,130	29,747	**286**	275	11
20 and over.	**325,792**	170,969	154,823	**16,382**	15,434	948	**309,410**	155,535	153,875	**1,002**	974	28
Jain ...	***5,194***	***2,759***	***2,435***	***1,868***	***1,664***	***204***	***3,326***	***1,095***	***2,231***	***67***	***65***	***2***
0— 5 ...	**640**	318	322	**13**	10	3	**627**	308	319	**1**	1	...
5—10 ...	**551**	272	279	**114**	91	23	**437**	181	256	**1**	...	1
10—15 ...	**537**	276	261	**181**	151	30	**356**	125	231	**5**	4	1
15—20 ...	**507**	282	225	**258**	220	38	**249**	62	187	**19**	19	...
20 and over	**2,959**	1,611	1,348	**1,302**	1,192	110	**1,657**	419	1,238	**41**	41	...
Muslim ...	***47,068***	***24,531***	***22,537***	***3,814***	***3,487***	***327***	***43,254***	***21,044***	***22,210***	***270***	***267***	***3***
0— 5 ...	**6,957**	3,468	3,489	**32**	22	10	**6,925**	3,446	3,479	...	...	...
5—10 ...	**5,736**	2,951	2,785	**251**	215	36	**5,485**	2,736	2,749	**7**	7	...
10—15 ...	**5,305**	2,753	2,552	**384**	335	49	**4,921**	2,418	2,503	**19**	19	...
15—20 ...	**4,510**	2,297	2,213	**544**	494	50	**3,966**	1,803	2,163	**51**	51	...
20 and over.	**24,560**	13,062	11,498	**2,603**	2,421	182	**21,957**	10,641	11,316	**193**	190	3
Tribal ...	***2,923***	***1,515***	***1,408***	***1***	***1***	...	***2,922***	***1,514***	***1,408***	...	...	...
0— 5 ...	**496**	259	237	...	...	...	**496**	259	237	...	...	...
5—10 ...	**402**	212	190	...	...	...	**402**	212	190	...	...	...
10—15 ...	**362**	193	169	...	...	...	**362**	193	169	...	...	...
15—20 ...	**286**	124	162	...	...	...	**286**	124	162	...	...	...
20 and over.	**1,377**	727	650	**1**	1	...	**1,376**	726	650	...	...	...

TABLE XIII.—LITERACY BY RELIGION AND AGE.—PART B.—BY STATE AND DISTRICT.—*Continued.*

State or District, Age and Religion.	Population.									Literate in English.		
	Total.			Literate.			Illiterate.					
	Persons.	Males.	Females.	Persons.	Males.	Females.	Persons.	Males.	Females.	Persons.	Males.	Females.
1	2	3	4	5	6	7	8	9	10	11	12	13
KUSHALGARH (Chiefship)												
All Religions.	***35,564***	***17,754***	***17,810***	***751***	***696***	***55***	***34,813***	***17,058***	***17,755***	***80***	***80***	...
0—5 ...	**7,055**	3,386	3,669	...	...	...	**7,055**	3,386	3,669	...	...	...
5—10 ...	**5,627**	2,864	2,763	**52**	45	7	**5,575**	2,819	2,756	**2**	2	...
10—15 ...	**4,733**	2,467	2,266	**83**	72	11	**4,650**	2,395	2,255	**10**	10	...
15—20 ...	**2,950**	1,502	1,448	**105**	95	10	**2,845**	1,407	1,438	**21**	21	...
20 and over.	**15,199**	7,535	7,664	**511**	484	27	**14,688**	7,051	7,637	**47**	47	...
Hindu ...	***34,127***	***17,004***	***17,123***	***411***	***378***	***33***	***33,716***	***16,626***	***17,090***	***63***	***63***	...
0—5 ...	**6,867**	3,300	3,567	...	...	...	**6,867**	3,300	3,567	...	...	...
5—10 ...	**5,417**	2,754	2,663	**28**	24	4	**5,389**	2,730	2,659	**1**	1	...
10—15 ...	**4,544**	2,364	2,180	**44**	37	7	**4,500**	2,327	2,173	**6**	6	...
15—20 ...	**2,808**	1,422	1,386	**58**	52	6	**2,750**	1,370	1,380	**16**	16	...
20 and over.	**14,491**	7,164	7,327	**281**	265	16	**14,210**	6,899	7,311	**40**	40	...
LAWA (Estate).												
All Religions.	***2,790***	***1,445***	***1,345***	***92***	***80***	***12***	***2,698***	***1,365***	***1,333***	***4***	***4***	...
0—5 ...	**443**	218	225	...	...	...	**443**	218	225	...	...	...
5—10 ...	**350**	189	161	**2**	2	...	**348**	187	161	...	...	...
10—15 ...	**343**	189	154	**6**	6	...	**337**	183	154	...	...	...
15—20 ...	**279**	147	132	**12**	11	1	**267**	136	131	...	...	...
20 and over.	**1,375**	702	673	**72**	61	11	**1,303**	641	662	**4**	4	...
Hindu ...	***2,546***	***1,314***	***1,232***	***52***	***41***	***11***	***2,494***	***1,273***	***1,221***	***4***	***4***	...
0—5 ...	**405**	196	209	...	...	...	**405**	196	209	...	...	...
5—10 ...	**325**	173	152	**2**	2	...	**323**	171	152	...	...	...
10—15 ...	**315**	171	144	**3**	3	...	**312**	168	144	...	...	...
15—20 ...	**255**	136	119	**8**	7	1	**247**	129	118	...	...	...
20 and over.	**1,246**	638	608	**39**	29	10	**1,207**	609	598	**4**	4	...
MARWAR.												
All Religions.	***2,125,982***	***1,109,912***	***1,016,070***	***79,797***	***74,956***	***4,841***	***2,046,185***	***1,034,956***	***1,011,229***	***7,359***	***7,091***	***268***
0—5 ...	**343,192**	171,392	171,800	**300**	231	69	**342,892**	171,161	171,731	**25**	20	5
5—10 ...	**288,147**	153,528	134,619	**4,021**	3,633	388	**284,126**	149,890	134,236	**448**	434	14
10—15 ...	**258,933**	142,520	116,413	**7,133**	6,569	564	**251,800**	135,951	115,849	**878**	842	36
15—20 ...	**199,963**	107,769	92,194	**10,534**	9,865	669	**189,429**	97,904	91,525	**1,331**	1,276	55
20 and over.	**1,035,747**	534,703	501,044	**57,809**	54,653	3,156	**977,938**	480,050	497,888	**4,677**	4,519	158
Hindu ...	***1,831,441***	***962,012***	***869,429***	***44,058***	***41,439***	***2,619***	***1,787,383***	***920,573***	***866,810***	***5,576***	***5,446***	***130***
0—5 ...	**295,688**	147,604	148,084	**145**	112	33	**295,543**	147,492	148,051	**7**	5	2
5—10 ...	**248,526**	132,834	115,692	**2,097**	1,885	212	**246,429**	130,949	115,480	**325**	319	6
10—15 ...	**224,048**	124,104	99,944	**3,978**	3,658	320	**220,070**	120,446	99,624	**664**	647	17
15—20 ...	**173,837**	94,540	79,297	**6,162**	5,748	414	**167,675**	88,792	78,883	**1,053**	1,020	33
20 and over.	**889,342**	462,930	426,412	**31,676**	30,036	1,640	**857,666**	432,894	424,772	**3,527**	3,455	72
Jain ...	***113,669***	***52,587***	***61,082***	***29,901***	***28,384***	***1,517***	***83,768***	***24,203***	***59,565***	***1,028***	***982***	***46***
0—5 ...	**16,696**	8,445	8,251	**97**	73	24	**16,599**	8,372	8,227	**5**	5	...
5—10 ...	**14,080**	7,176	6,904	**1,616**	1,514	102	**12,464**	5,662	6,802	**68**	66	2
10—15 ...	**12,305**	6,213	6,092	**2,664**	2,536	128	**9,641**	3,677	5,964	**120**	118	2
15—20 ...	**9,583**	4,359	5,224	**3,656**	3,501	155	**5,927**	858	5,069	**168**	160	8
20 and over.	**61,005**	26,394	34,611	**21,868**	20,760	1,108	**39,137**	5,634	33,503	**667**	633	34
Muslim ...	***176,863***	***93,234***	***83,629***	***5,436***	***4,873***	***563***	***171,427***	***88,361***	***83,066***	***567***	***536***	***31***
0—5 ...	**30,018**	14,970	15,048	**40**	33	7	**29,978**	14,937	15,041	**3**	3	...
5—10 ...	**24,921**	13,190	11,731	**262**	212	50	**24,659**	12,978	11,681	**38**	38	...
10—15 ...	**22,059**	11,909	10,150	**447**	351	96	**21,612**	11,558	10,054	**75**	67	8
15—20 ...	**16,169**	8,687	7,482	**660**	576	84	**15,509**	8,111	7,398	**82**	74	8
20 and over.	**83,696**	44,478	39,218	**4,027**	3,701	326	**79,669**	40,777	38,892	**369**	354	15

TABLE XIII.—LITERACY BY RELIGION AND AGE.—PART B.—BY STATE OR DISTRICT.—*Continued.*

State or District, Age and Religion.	Population.									Literate in English.		
	Total.			Literate.			Illiterate.					
	Persons	Males.	Females.	Persons.	Males.	Females.	Persons.	Males.	Females.	Persons.	Males.	Females.
1	2	3	4	5	6	7	8	9	10	11	12	13
MARWAR.— *Concluded.*												
Tribal ...	*3,241*	*1,653*	*1,588*	*29*	*29*	...	*3,212*	*1,624*	*1,588*	...	...	...
0—5 ...	**674**	320	354	...	...	...	**674**	320	354	...	...	...
5—10 ...	**517**	274	243	...	...	...	**517**	274	243	...	...	...
10—15 ...	**439**	243	196	...	...	...	**439**	243	196	...	...	...
15—20 ...	**300**	139	161	**6**	6	...	**294**	133	161	...	...	...
20 and over.	**1,311**	677	634	**23**	23	...	**1,288**	654	634	...	...	...
MEWAR.												
All Religions.	*1,566,910*	*807,184*	*759,726*	*46,491*	*44,759*	*1,732*	*1,520,419*	*762,425*	*757,994*	*1,609*	*1,565*	*44*
0—5 ...	**243,582**	118,965	124,617	**8**	8	...	**243,574**	118,957	124,617	...	...	...
5—10 ...	**209,541**	110,377	99,164	**1,768**	1,661	107	**207,773**	108,716	99,057	**54**	52	2
10—15 ...	**198,691**	107,522	91,169	**3,544**	3,335	209	**195,147**	104,187	90,960	**135**	132	3
15—20 ...	**154,862**	81,333	73,529	**5,834**	5,592	242	**149,028**	75,741	73,287	**311**	309	2
20 and over.	**760,234**	388,987	371,247	**35,337**	34,163	1,174	**724,897**	354,824	370,073	**1,109**	1,072	37
Hindu ...	*1,352,029*	*696,380*	*655,649*	*24,891*	*23,852*	*1,039*	*1,327,138*	*672,528*	*654,610*	*1,114*	*1,098*	*16*
0—5 ...	**208,310**	101,890	106,420	**1**	1	...	**208,309**	101,889	106,420	...	...	...
5—10 ...	**179,940**	94,957	84,983	**907**	856	51	**179,033**	94,101	84,932	**43**	43	...
10—15 ...	**172,409**	93,518	78,891	**1,839**	1,728	111	**170,570**	91,790	78,780	**104**	103	1
15—20 ...	**134,764**	70,999	63,765	**3,114**	2,969	145	**131,650**	68,030	63,620	**222**	222	...
20 and over.	**656,606**	335,016	321,590	**19,030**	18,298	732	**637,576**	316,718	320,858	**745**	730	15
Jain ...	*66,001*	*34,086*	*31,915*	*17,001*	*16,591*	*410*	*49,000*	*17,495*	*31,505*	*234*	*232*	*2*
0—5 ...	**8,939**	4,437	4,502	**4**	4	...	**8,935**	4,433	4,502	...	...	...
5—10 ...	**7,648**	3,911	3,737	**688**	656	32	**6,960**	3,255	3,705	**7**	7	...
10—15 ...	**7,244**	3,828	3,416	**1,343**	1,284	59	**5,901**	2,544	3,357	**22**	22	...
15—20 ...	**6,279**	3,282	2,997	**2,118**	2,057	61	**4,161**	1,225	2,936	**52**	52	...
20 and over.	**35,891**	18,628	17,263	**12,848**	12,590	258	**23,043**	6,038	17,005	**153**	151	2
Muslim ...	*53,833*	*28,346*	*25,487*	*4,394*	*4,146*	*248*	*49,439*	*24,200*	*25,239*	*162*	*155*	*7*
0—5 ...	**8,211**	4,109	4,102	**3**	3	...	**8,208**	4,106	4,102	...	...	...
5—10 ...	**6,893**	3,612	3,281	**161**	141	20	**6,732**	3,471	3,261	**1**	1	...
10—15 ...	**6,310**	3,347	2,963	**333**	300	33	**5,977**	3,047	2,930	**5**	5	...
15—20 ...	**5,074**	2,620	2,454	**564**	531	33	**4,510**	2,089	2,421	**20**	19	1
20 and over.	**27,345**	14,658	12,687	**3,333**	3,171	162	**24,012**	11,487	12,525	**136**	130	6
Tribal ...	*94,544*	*48,061*	*46,483*	*6*	*6*	...	*94,538*	*48,055*	*46,483*	...	...	...
0—5 ...	**18,045**	8,488	9,557	...	...	...	**18,045**	8,488	9,557	...	...	...
5—10 ...	**15,001**	7,864	7,137	**1**	1	...	**15,000**	7,863	7,137	...	...	...
10—15 ...	**12,657**	6,786	5,871	**1**	1	...	**12,656**	6,785	5,871	...	...	...
15—20 ...	**8,683**	4,390	4,293	...	...	...	**8,683**	4,390	4,298	...	...	...
20 and over.	**40,158**	20,533	19,625	**4**	4	...	**40,154**	20,529	19,625	...	...	...
PARTABGARH												
All Religions.	*76,539*	*38,991*	*37,548*	*4,501*	*4,122*	*379*	*72,038*	*34,869*	*37,169*	*250*	*243*	*7*
0—5 ...	**12,014**	5,875	6,139	**1**	1	...	**12,013**	5,874	6,139	...	...	...
5—10 ...	**10,646**	5,547	5,099	**242**	215	27	**10,404**	5,332	5,072	**4**	3	1
10—15 ...	**9,927**	5,195	4,732	**402**	362	40	**9,525**	4,833	4,692	**15**	14	1
15—20 ...	**7,910**	4,024	3,886	**621**	555	66	**7,289**	3,469	3,820	**53**	51	2
20 and over.	**36,042**	18,350	17,692	**3,235**	2,989	246	**32,807**	15,361	17,446	**178**	175	3
Hindu ...	*41,347*	*21,124*	*20,223*	*2,474*	*2,308*	*166*	*38,873*	*18,816*	*20,057*	*141*	*136*	*5*
0—5 ...	**5,947**	2,921	3,026	...	...	...	**5,947**	2,921	3,026	...	...	...
5—10 ...	**5,250**	2,755	2,495	**121**	110	11	**5,129**	2,645	2,484	**1**	...	1
10—15 ...	**5,080**	2,675	2,405	**215**	199	16	**4,865**	2,476	2,389	**6**	5	1
15—20 ...	**4,494**	2,311	2,183	**365**	339	26	**4,129**	1,972	2,157	**29**	28	1
20 and over	**20,576**	10,462	10,114	**1,773**	1,660	113	**18,803**	8,802	10,001	**105**	103	2

TABLE XIII.—Literacy by Religion and Age.—Part B.—By State or District.—*Continued.*

State or District, Age and Religion.	Population.									Literate in English.		
	Total.			Literate.			Illiterate.					
	Persons.	Males.	Females.	Persons.	Males.	Females.	Persons.	Males.	Females.	Persons.	Males.	Females.
1	2	3	4	5	6	7	8	9	10	11	12	13
PARTABGARH *Concluded.*												
Jain ...	*4,445*	*2,240*	*2,205*	*1,641*	*1,449*	*192*	*2,804*	*791*	*2,013*	*87*	*87*	...
0—5 ...	**580**	281	299	...	...	...	**580**	281	299	...	...	...
5—10 ...	**547**	286	261	**104**	89	15	**443**	197	246	**3**	3	...
10—15 ...	**498**	264	234	**161**	139	22	**337**	125	212	**8**	8	...
15—20 ...	**408**	202	206	**210**	173	37	**198**	29	169	**19**	19	...
20 and over.	**2,412**	1,207	1,205	**1,166**	1,048	118	**1,246**	159	1,087	**57**	57	...
Muslim. ...	*3,914*	*2,045*	*1,869*	*356*	*342*	*14*	*3,558*	*1,703*	*1,855*	*12*	*11*	*1*
0—5 ...	**555**	265	290	...	...	...	**555**	265	290	...	...	...
5—10 ...	**518**	269	249	**15**	14	1	**503**	255	248	...	...	...
10—15 ...	**466**	242	224	**25**	23	2	**441**	219	222	...	...	...
15—20 ...	**376**	195	181	**43**	41	2	**333**	154	179	**2**	2	...
20 and over.	**1,999**	1,074	925	**273**	264	9	**1,726**	810	916	**10**	9	1
Tribal ...	*26,747*	*13,534*	*13,213*	*3*	*3*	...	*26,744*	*13,531*	*13,213*	...	...	...
0—5 ...	**4,920**	2,402	2,518	...	...	...	**4,920**	2,402	2,518	...	...	...
5—10 ...	**4,322**	2,234	2,088	...	...	...	**4,322**	2,234	2,088	...	...	...
10—15 ...	**3,875**	2,011	1,864	...	...	...	**3,875**	2,011	1,864	...	...	...
15—20 ...	**2,624**	1,312	1,312	...	...	...	**2,624**	1,312	1,312	...	...	...
20 and over.	**11,006**	5,575	5,431	**3**	3	...	**11,003**	5,572	5,431	...	...	...
SHAHPURA.												
All Religions.	*54,233*	*27,907*	*26,326*	*2,695*	*2,481*	*214*	*51,538*	*25,426*	*26,112*	*235*	*225*	*10*
0—5 ...	**8,296**	4,126	4,170	**1**	...	1	**8,295**	4,126	4,169	...	...	...
5—10 ...	**6,811**	3,584	3,227	**194**	166	28	**6,617**	3,418	3,199	**8**	6	2
10—15 ...	**6,472**	3,483	2,989	**308**	269	39	**6,164**	3,214	2,950	**38**	36	2
15—20 ...	**5,226**	2,702	2,524	**364**	327	37	**4,862**	2,375	2,487	**61**	60	1
20 and over.	**27,428**	14,012	13,416	**1,828**	1,719	109	**25,600**	12,293	13,307	**128**	123	5
Hindu ...	*50,273*	*25,845*	*24,428*	*1,973*	*1,806*	*167*	*48,300*	*24,039*	*24,261*	*196*	*187*	*9*
0—5 ...	**7,729**	3,847	3,882	**1**	...	1	**7,728**	3,847	3,881	...	...	...
5—10 ...	**6,360**	3,344	3,016	**151**	128	23	**6,209**	3,216	2,993	**8**	6	2
10—15 ...	**6,038**	3,243	2,795	**235**	204	31	**5,803**	3,039	2,764	**32**	30	2
15—20 ...	**4,849**	2,502	2,347	**269**	242	27	**4,580**	2,260	2,320	**52**	51	1
20 and over.	**25,297**	12,909	12,388	**1,317**	1,232	85	**23,980**	11,677	12,303	**104**	100	4
Jain ...	*1,418*	*757*	*661*	*540*	*497*	*43*	*878*	*260*	*618*	*33*	*33*	...
0—5 ...	**190**	92	98	...	...	...	**190**	92	98	...	...	...
5—10 ...	**137**	76	61	**34**	29	5	**103**	47	56	...	...	...
10—15 ...	**134**	80	54	**57**	49	8	**77**	31	46	**6**	6	...
15—20 ...	**137**	70	67	**68**	59	9	**69**	11	58	**8**	8	...
20 and over.	**820**	439	381	**381**	360	21	**439**	79	360	**19**	19	...
Muslim ...	*2,541*	*1,305*	*1,236*	*181*	*178*	*3*	*2,360*	*1,127*	*1,233*	*5*	*5*	...
0—5 ...	**377**	187	190	...	...	...	**377**	187	190	...	...	...
5—10 ...	**314**	164	150	**9**	9	...	**305**	155	150	...	...	...
10—15 ...	**300**	160	140	**16**	16	...	**284**	144	140	...	...	...
15—20 ...	**240**	130	110	**27**	26	1	**213**	104	109	**1**	1	...
20 and over.	**1,310**	664	646	**129**	127	2	**1,181**	537	644	**4**	4	...
SIROHI.												
All Religions.	*216,528*	*111,675*	*104,853*	*9,761*	*8,960*	*801*	*206,767*	*102,715*	*104,052*	*986*	*812*	*174*
0—5 ...	**35,974**	17,978	17,996	**94**	61	33	**35,880**	17,917	17,963	**22**	15	7
5—10 ...	**29,166**	15,654	13,512	**682**	597	85	**28,484**	15,057	13,427	**51**	32	19
10—15 ...	**26,353**	14,573	11,780	**1,041**	935	106	**25,312**	13,638	11,674	**96**	73	23
15—20 ...	**19,967**	10,469	9,498	**1,206**	1,102	104	**18,761**	9,367	9,394	**134**	111	23
20 and over.	**105,068**	53,001	52,067	**6,738**	6,265	473	**98,330**	46,736	51,594	**683**	581	102

TABLE XIII.—LITERACY BY RELIGION AND AGE.—PART B.—BY STATE OR DISTRICT.—*Concluded.*

State or District, Age and Religion.	Population.									Literate in English.		
	Total.			Literate.			Illiterate.					
	Persons.	Males.	Females.	Persons.	Males.	Females.	Persons.	Males.	Females.	Persons.	Males.	Females.
1	2	3	4	5	6	7	8	9	10	11	12	13
SIROHI. *Concluded.*												
Hindu ...	*193,785*	*101,044*	*92,741*	*4,528*	*4,228*	*300*	*189,257*	*96,816*	*92,441*	*401*	*392*	*9*
0— 5 ...	**32,566**	16,268	16,298	**28**	19	9	**32,538**	16,249	16,289	**3**	2	1
5—10 ...	**26,441**	14,251	12,190	**307**	276	31	**26,134**	13,975	12,159	**11**	10	1
10—15 ...	**23,871**	13,317	10,554	**476**	437	39	**23,395**	12,880	10,515	**35**	34	1
15—20 ...	**17,862**	9,496	8,366	**575**	534	41	**17,287**	8,962	8,325	**56**	56	...
20 and over.	**93,045**	47,712	45,333	**3,142**	2,962	180	**89,903**	44,750	45,153	**296**	290	6
Jain ...	*15,508*	*6,696*	*8,812*	*3,961*	*3,778*	*183*	*11,547*	*2,918*	*8,629*	*95*	*95*	...
0— 5 ...	**2,233**	1,132	1,101	**25**	17	8	**2,208**	1,115	1,093	**4**	4	...
5—10 ...	**1,789**	902	887	**295**	273	22	**1,494**	629	865	**4**	4	...
10—15 ...	**1,601**	769	832	**454**	424	30	**1,147**	345	802	**12**	12	...
15—20 ...	**1,394**	584	810	**477**	452	25	**917**	132	785	**23**	23	...
20 and over.	**8,491**	3,309	5,182	**2,710**	2,612	98	**5,781**	697	5,084	**52**	52	...
Muslim ...	*6,538*	*3,561*	*2,977*	*783*	*678*	*105*	*5,755*	*2,883*	*2,872*	*112*	*107*	*5*
0— 5 ...	**1,071**	529	542	**17**	11	6	**1,054**	518	536	**1**	1	...
5—10 ...	**855**	458	397	**39**	28	11	**816**	430	386	**6**	5	1
10—15 ...	**808**	448	360	**64**	51	13	**744**	397	347	**10**	9	1
15—20 ...	**632**	347	285	**98**	87	11	**534**	260	274	**11**	10	1
20 and over.	**3,172**	1,779	1,393	**565**	501	64	**2,607**	1,278	1,329	**84**	82	2
TONK.												
All Religions.	*317,360*	*164,401*	*152,959*	*5,712*	*5,477*	*235*	*311,648*	*158,924*	*152,724*	*233*	*222*	*11*
0 – 5 ...	**48,353**	23,920	24,433	**3**	3	...	**48,350**	23,917	24,433	...	...	...
5—10 ...	**41,166**	21,532	19,634	**132**	130	2	**41,034**	21,402	19,632	**2**	2	...
10 – 15 ...	**37,752**	20,024	17,728	**278**	266	12	**37,474**	19,758	17,716	**4**	4	...
15—20 ...	**29,688**	15,150	14,538	**608**	580	28	**29,080**	14,570	14,510	**23**	22	1
20 and over.	**160,401**	83,775	76,626	**4,691**	4,498	193	**155,710**	79,277	76,433	**204**	194	10
Hindu ...	*262,680*	*135,975*	*126,705*	*2,433*	*2,383*	*50*	*260,247*	*133,592*	*126,655*	*74*	*74*	...
0 – 5 ...	**40,255**	19,865	20,390	...	...	...	**40,255**	19,865	20,390	...	...	...
5—10 ...	**34,174**	17,874	16,300	**58**	57	1	**34,116**	17,817	16,299	**1**	1	...
10 15 ...	**31,596**	16,807	14,789	**132**	128	4	**31,464**	16,679	14,785	**2**	2	...
15—20 ...	**24,836**	12,724	12,112	**281**	274	7	**24,555**	12,450	12,105	**7**	7	...
20 and over.	**131,819**	68,705	63,114	**1,962**	1,924	38	**129,857**	66,781	63,076	**64**	64	...
Jain ...	*6,868*	*3,608*	*3,260*	*1,075*	*1,025*	*50*	*5,793*	*2,583*	*3,210*	*5*	*5*	...
0— 5 ...	**876**	418	458	**3**	3	...	**873**	415	458	...	...	...
5—10 ...	**752**	389	363	**32**	32	...	**720**	357	363	...	...	...
10—15 ...	**699**	368	331	**62**	59	3	**637**	309	328	...	...	...
15—20 ...	**645**	350	295	**123**	115	8	**522**	235	287	**1**	1	...
20 and over.	**3,896**	2,083	1,813	**855**	816	39	**3,041**	1,267	1,774	**4**	4	...
Muslim ...	*44,234*	*22,993*	*21,241*	*2,182*	*2,057*	*125*	*42,052*	*20,936*	*21,116*	*135*	*133*	*2*
0— 5 ...	**6,570**	3,317	3,253	...	...	...	**6,570**	3,317	3,253	...	...	...
5—10 ...	**5,759**	3,014	2,745	**42**	41	1	**5,717**	2,973	2,744	**1**	1	...
10 – 15 ...	**5,018**	2,626	2,392	**84**	79	5	**4,934**	2,547	2,387	**2**	2	...
15—20 ...	**3,819**	1,897	1,922	**201**	189	12	**3,618**	1,708	1,910	**12**	12	...
20 and over.	**23,068**	12,139	10,929	**1,855**	1,748	107	**21,213**	10,391	10,822	**120**	118	2

TABLE XIII.—LITERACY BY RELIGION AND AGE.—PART C.—BY CITIES. (ALL RELIGIONS).

City and Age.	Population.									Literate in English		
	Total.			Literate.			Illiterate.					
	Persons.	Males.	Females.	Persons.	Males.	Females.	Persons	Males.	Females.	Persons.	Males.	Females.
1	2	3	4	5	6	7	8	9	10	11	12	13
Alwar ...	*47,900*	*25,584*	*22,316*	*6,524*	*5,893*	*631*	*41,376*	*19,691*	*21,685*	*1,225*	*1,181*	*44*
0—5 ...	**6,372**	3,191	3,181	**8**	3	5	**6,364**	3,188	3,176	...	...	...
5—10 ...	**5,046**	2,581	2,465	**310**	253	57	**4,736**	2,328	2,408	**49**	47	2
10—15 ...	**4,754**	2,482	2,272	**500**	421	79	**4,254**	2,061	2,193	**106**	102	4
15—20 ...	**4,759**	2,481	2,278	**794**	702	92	**3,965**	1,779	2,186	**219**	212	7
20 and over.	**26,969**	14,849	12,120	**4,912**	4,514	398	**22,057**	10,335	11,722	**851**	820	31
Bharatpur.	*30,173*	*16,736*	*13,437*	*4,796*	*4,077*	*719*	*25,377*	*12,659*	*12,718*	*901*	*849*	*52*
0—5 ...	**4,125**	2,084	2,041	**5**	4	1	**4,120**	2,080	2,040	...	...	...
5—10 ...	**3,334**	1,834	1,500	**283**	230	53	**3,051**	1,604	1,447	**38**	35	3
10—15 ...	**3,269**	1,842	1,427	**501**	402	99	**2,768**	1,440	1,328	**94**	88	6
15—20 ...	**3,116**	1,743	1,373	**682**	552	130	**2,434**	1,191	1,243	**162**	154	8
20 and over.	**16,329**	9,233	7,096	**3,325**	2,889	436	**13,004**	6,344	6,660	**607**	572	35
Bikaner ...	*85,927*	*45,832*	*40,095*	*12,419*	*11,159*	*1,260*	*73,508*	*34,673*	*38,835*	*2,014*	*1,901*	*113*
0—5 ...	**11,623**	5,848	5,775	**1**	...	1	**11,622**	5,848	5,774	...	...	...
5—10 ...	**9,420**	5,119	4,301	**559**	471	88	**8,861**	4,648	4,213	**101**	93	8
10—15 ...	**9,304**	5,108	4,196	**1,034**	875	159	**8,270**	4,233	4,037	**201**	185	16
15—20 ...	**9,163**	4,982	4,181	**1,737**	1,504	233	**7,426**	3,478	3,948	**336**	316	20
20 and over.	**46,417**	24,775	21,642	**9,088**	8,309	779	**37,329**	16,466	20,863	**1,376**	1,307	69
Bundi ...	*17,991*	*9,179*	*8,812*	*2,501*	*2,263*	*238*	*15,490*	*6,916*	*8,574*	*190*	*183*	*7*
0—5 ...	**2,077**	999	1,078	**2**	...	2	**2,075**	999	1,076	...	...	...
5—10 ...	**1,740**	937	803	**107**	86	21	**1,633**	851	782	**6**	5	1
10—15 ...	**1,646**	869	777	**191**	157	34	**1,455**	712	743	**17**	15	2
15—20 ...	**1,649**	783	866	**296**	269	27	**1,353**	514	839	**31**	31	...
20 and over.	**10,879**	5,591	5,288	**1,905**	1,751	154	**8,974**	3,840	5,134	**136**	132	4
Dholpur ...	*19,586*	*10,535*	*9,051*	*2,854*	*2,403*	*451*	*16,732*	*8,132*	*8,600*	*536*	*491*	*45*
0—5 ...	**2,782**	1,402	1,380	...	...	...	**2,782**	1,402	1,380	...	...	...
5—10 ...	**2,218**	1,175	1,043	**104**	81	23	**2,114**	1,094	1,020	**13**	11	2
10—15 ...	**2,052**	1,128	924	**218**	175	43	**1,834**	953	881	**35**	33	2
15—20 ...	**1,854**	982	872	**390**	307	83	**1,464**	675	789	**87**	79	8
20 and over.	**10,680**	5,848	4,832	**2,142**	1,840	302	**8,538**	4,008	4,530	**401**	368	33
Jaipur ...	*144,179*	*77,933*	*66,246*	*19,201*	*17,057*	*2,144*	*124,978*	*60,876*	*64,102*	*3,338*	*3,065*	*273*
0—5 ...	**17,253**	8,698	8,555	**33**	33	...	**17,220**	8,665	8,555	**4**	4	...
5—10 ...	**14,663**	7,889	6,774	**917**	728	189	**13,746**	7,161	6,585	**147**	119	28
10—15 ...	**14,256**	7,711	6,545	**1,483**	1,232	251	**12,773**	6,479	6,294	**299**	258	41
15—20 ...	**14,136**	7,543	6,593	**2,351**	2,053	298	**11,785**	5,490	6,295	**589**	546	43
20 and over.	**83,871**	46,092	37,779	**14,417**	13,011	1,406	**69,454**	33,081	36,373	**2,299**	2,138	161
Jodhpur ...	*94,736*	*52,165*	*42,571*	*17,597*	*15,782*	*1,815*	*77,139*	*36,383*	*40,756*	*5,515*	*5,310*	*205*
0—5 ...	**13,973**	7,135	6,838	**118**	95	23	**13,855**	7,040	6,815	**16**	13	3
5—10 ...	**11,057**	6,069	4,988	**1,330**	1,145	185	**9,727**	4,924	4,803	**383**	370	13
10—15 ...	**10,527**	6,042	4,485	**2,336**	2,053	283	**8,191**	3,989	4,202	**770**	735	35
15—20 ...	**9,908**	5,632	4,276	**2,886**	2,583	303	**7,022**	3,049	3,973	**1,069**	1,026	43
20 and over.	**49,271**	27,287	21,984	**10,927**	9,906	1,021	**38,344**	17,381	20,963	**3,277**	3,166	111
Kotah ...	*37,876*	*20,259*	*17,617*	*5,948*	*5,079*	*869*	*31,928*	*15,180*	*16,748*	*995*	*943*	*52*
0—5 ...	**4,482**	2,249	2,233	**23**	12	11	**4,459**	2,237	2,222	**2**	1	1
5—10 ...	**3,663**	1,970	1,693	**391**	306	85	**3,272**	1,664	1,608	**31**	28	3
10—15 ...	**3,736**	2,011	1,725	**640**	512	128	**3,096**	1,499	1,597	**101**	95	6
15—20 ...	**4,135**	2,248	1,887	**884**	754	130	**3,251**	1,494	1,757	**214**	206	8
20 and over.	**21,860**	11,781	10,079	**4,010**	3,495	515	**17,850**	8,286	9,564	**647**	613	34

TABLE XIII.

Literacy by Religion and Age.
Part C. –By Cities. (All Religions).

TABLE XIII.—LITERACY BY RELIGION AND AGE.—PART C.—BY CITIES. (ALL RELIGIONS).—*Concld*

City and Age.	Population.									Literate in English.		
	Total			Literate.			Illiterate.					
	Persons.	Males.	Females	Persons	Males	Females.	Persons.	Males.	Females.	Persons.	Males	Females.
1	2	3	4	5	6	7	8	9	10	11	12	13
Tonk ...	***35,798***	***18,201***	***17,597***	***1,967***	***1,807***	***160***	***33,831***	***16,394***	***17,437***	***165***	***155***	***10***
0 – 5 ...	**4,855**	2,462	2,393	...	...	...	**4,855**	2,462	2,393	...	...	...
5—10 ...	**4,322**	2,231	2,091	**40**	39	1	**4,282**	2,192	2,090	**1**	1	...
10 –15 ...	**3,825**	1,959	1,866	**81**	74	7	**3,744**	1,885	1,859	**3**	3	...
15 –20 ...	**3,001**	1,431	1,570	**188**	172	16	**2,813**	1,259	1,554	**17**	16	1
20 and over.	**19,795**	10,118	9,677	**1,658**	1,522	136	**18,137**	8,596	9,541	**144**	135	9
Udaipur ...	***44,035***	***23,775***	***20,260***	***8,320***	***7,915***	***405***	***35,715***	***15,860***	***19,855***	***777***	***750***	***27***
0— 5 ...	**5,260**	2,723	2,537	...	...	...	**5,260**	2,723	2,537	...	...	...
5—10 ...	**4,877**	2,694	2,183	**312**	284	28	**4.565**	2,410	2,155	**14**	12	2
10 - 15 ...	**4,749**	2,699	2,050	**644**	598	46	**4,105**	2,101	2,004	**49**	47	2
15—20 ...	**4,391**	2,432	1,959	**1,048**	999	49	**3,343**	1,433	1,910	**151**	149	2
20 and over	**24,758**	13,227	11,531	**6,316**	6,034	282	**18,442**	7,193	11,249	**563**	542	21

TABLE XIV.

Literacy by selected Castes, Tribes or Races.

EXPLANATORY NOTE.

The castes shown in this and Table VIII comprise 35·9 per cent. of the total Population of the selected localities. They are representative of every grade of society and are well defined communities in the localities concerned.

TABLE XIV.—LITERACY BY SELECTED CASTES, TRIBES OR RACES.

CASTE, TRIBE OR RACE.	LOCALITY.	POPULATION (7 YEARS AND OVER).											
		TOTAL.			LITERATE.			ILLITERATE.			LITERATE IN ENGLISH (7 YEARS AND OVER).		
		Persons.	Males.	Females.	Persons.	Males.	Females	Persons.	Males.	Females.	Persons.	Males.	Females.
1	2	3	4	5	6	7	8	9	10	11	12	13	14
1 Agarwal ...	Jaipur ...	**74,509**	37,390	37,119	**19,616**	18,914	702	**54,893**	18,476	36,417	**775**	764	11
2. Ahir ...	Alwar ...	**58,239**	32,371	25,868	**468**	456	12	**57,771**	31,915	25,856	**8**	8	...
3. Bhangi ...	Jaipur and Marwar ...	**29,972**	15,644	14,328	**217**	166	51	**29,755**	15,478	14,277	**11**	11	...
4. Bhil ...	Banswara and Dungarpur ...	**200,227**	101,808	98,424	**93**	90	3	**200,134**	101,713	98,421	**3**	2	1
5 Brahman ...	Marwar and Mewar ...	**181,727**	93,062	88,665	**23,289**	22,053	1,236	**158,438**	71,009	87,429	**2,586**	2,550	36
6. Chamar ...	Bharatpur, Jaipur and Kotah ...	**312,211**	162,016	150,195	**741**	708	33	**311,470**	161,318	150,157	**6**	6	...
7. Grassia ...	Sirohi ...	**11,846**	6,097	5,749	**50**	50	...	**11,796**	6,047	5,749	...	...	...
8. Gujar ...	Bharatpur and Jaipur ...	**187,788**	103,361	84,427	**915**	874	41	**186,873**	102,487	84,386	**34**	33	1
9. Jat ...	Bikaner, Jaipur and Marwar ...	**650,269**	358,713	291,556	**4,572**	4,370	202	**645,697**	354,343	291,354	**555**	552	3
10. Khati ...	Jaipur and Mewar ...	**64,203**	33,149	31,054	**1,156**	1,137	19	**63,047**	32,012	31,035	**189**	188	1
11. Khanzada ...	Alwar ...	**6,074**	3,097	2,977	**125**	119	6	**5,949**	2,978	2,971	**12**	12	...
12. Kumhar ...	Jaipur ...	**73,258**	38,107	35,151	**440**	431	9	**72,818**	37,676	35,142	**30**	30	...
13. Meo ...	Alwar and Bharatpur ...	**130,926**	71,285	59,641	**389**	388	1	**130,537**	70,897	59,640	**3**	3	...
14. Mina ...	Alwar, Jaipur and Kotah ...	**303,168**	161,327	141,841	**1,603**	1,553	50	**301,565**	159,774	141,791	**25**	24	1
15. Oswal ...	Marwar and Mewar ...	**119,143**	57,446	61,697	**38,858**	37,264	1,594	**80,285**	20,182	60,103	**1,061**	1,025	36
16 Rajput ...	Jaipur, Marwar and Mewar ...	**355,796**	198,873	156,923	**15,732**	14,001	1,731	**340,064**	184,872	155,192	**1,935**	1,897	38
17 Rebari ...	Marwar and Sirohi ...	**88,423**	46,191	42,232	**278**	258	20	**88,145**	45,933	42,212	**30**	30	...
18. Sondhia ...	Jhalawar ...	**22,903**	12,312	10,591	**142**	141	1	**22,761**	12,171	10,590	...	...	...

TABLE XV.

Language.

EXPLANATORY NOTE.

Languages of numerical insignificance in Part I have been amalgamated under 'Others' in each group. Their details are as follows:—

Languages	Persons.	Males.	Females.
A. Vernaculars of India	**2,654**	**1,725**	**929**
Assamese	3	3	...
Balochi ...	191	111	80
Bengali	818	476	342
Burmese Unspecified ...	5	5	...
Central Pahari ...	51	47	4
Kanarese	6	3	3
Kashmeri	11	7	4
Khandeshi	85	42	43
Konkani	11	5	6
Malayalam	4	1	3
Nimadi	3	3	...
Nepali	245	120	125
Oriya	14	12	2
Pahari Unspecified	383	329	54
Pashto	585	410	175
Sanskrit	1	1	...
Tamil	131	98	33
Telugu	107	52	55
B. Vernaculars of Asiatic and African countries ...	**127**	**86**	**41**
Arabic	16	9	7
Hebrew	1	1	...
Persian	99	71	28
Turkish	7	5	2
Not Returned	1	...	1
African Unspecified	3	...	3
C. European Languages	**87**	**57**	**30**
Danish	6	1	5
Dutch	2	1	1
French	8	4	4
Gaelic (Scotch)	3	3	...
German	9	8	1
Greek	1	1	...
Irish	4	4	...
Italian	3	1	2
Portuguese	50	34	16
Slavonic (Russian)	1	...	1

TABLE XV.—Part I.—Language.

AGENCY, STATE OR DISTRICT.	POPULATION.			A.—VERNACULARS OF INDIA.—(I).—VERNACULARS OF RAJPUTANA.								
				TOTAL VERNACULARS OF INDIA.			TOTAL VERNACULARS OF RAJPUTANA.			MARWARI.		
	Persons.	Males.	Females.	Persons.	Males.	Females.	Persons.	Males.	Females.	Persons.	Males.	Females.
1	2	3	4	5	6	7	8	9	10	11	12	13
RAJPUTANA ...	*11,225,712*	*5,885,028*	*5,340,684*	*11,223,676*	*5,883,892*	*5,339,784*	*11,078,124*	*5,803,751*	*5,274,373*	*5,618,885*	*2,939,125*	*2,679,760*
Abu District ...	**4,532**	2,753	1,779	**4,420**	2,691	1,729	**4,004**	2,420	1,584	**1,064**	664	400
Alwar ...	**749,751**	396,261	353,490	**749,681**	396,222	353,459	**749,324**	396,000	353,324	**814**	360	454
Banswara ...	**225,106**	111,983	113,123	**225,102**	111,983	113,119	**224,518**	111,671	112,847	**1,763**	796	967
Bharatpur ...	**486,954**	263,325	223,629	**486,909**	263,303	223,606	**486,340**	262,954	223,386	**632**	357	275
Bikaner ...	**936,218**	501,153	435,065	**936,146**	501,112	435,034	**824,102**	438,069	386,033	**785,111**	416,461	368,650
Bundi ...	**216,722**	113,101	103,621	**216,694**	113,081	103,613	**215,242**	112,250	102,992	**51,451**	26,720	24,731
Dholpur ...	**254,986**	140,497	114,489	**254,969**	140,493	114,476	**252,221**	139,759	112,462	**413**	204	209
Dungarpur ...	**227,544**	114,480	113,064	**227,544**	114,480	113,064	**225,222**	113,646	111,576	**3,128**	1,401	1,727
Jaipur ...	**2,631,775**	1,387,067	1,244,708	**2,630,782**	1,386,531	1,244,251	**2,626,607**	1,384,109	1,242,498	**931,700**	494,983	436,717
Jaisalmer ...	**76,255**	42,342	33,913	**76,255**	42,342	33,913	**76,037**	42,240	33,797	**72,242**	40,113	32,129
Jhalawar ...	**107,890**	56,518	51,372	**107,884**	56,514	51,370	**106,717**	55,872	50,845	**860**	471	389
Karauli ...	**140,525**	76,729	63,796	**140,521**	76,726	63,795	**140,393**	76,662	63,731	**551**	291	260
Kishangarh ...	**85,744**	44,494	41,250	**85,744**	44,494	41,250	**85,600**	44,393	41,207	**17,899**	9,979	7,920
Kotah ...	**685,804**	355,056	330,748	**685,748**	355,024	330,724	**681,979**	352,825	329,154	**8,804**	4,720	4,084
Kushalgarh (Chiefship) ...	**35,564**	17,754	17,810	**35,564**	17,754	17,810	**35,139**	17,486	17,653	**15**	7	8
Lawa (Estate) ...	**2,790**	1,445	1,345	**2,790**	1,445	1,345	**2,789**	1,445	1,344	**15**	6	9
Marwar ...	**2,125,982**	1,109,912	1,016,070	**2,125,815**	1,109,802	1,016,013	**2,124,477**	1,109,050	1,015,427	**2,092,869**	1,091,919	1,000,950
Mewar ...	**1,566,910**	807,184	759,726	**1,566,829**	807,119	759,710	**1,557,909**	802,414	755,495	**1,369,320**	705,152	664,168
Partabgarh ...	**76,539**	38,991	37,548	**76,538**	38,990	37,548	**75,375**	38,362	37,013	**433**	234	199
Shahpura ...	**54,233**	27,907	26,326	**54,232**	27,907	26,325	**54,207**	27,891	26,316	**50,795**	26,939	23,856
Sirohi ...	**216,528**	111,675	104,853	**216,167**	111,487	104,680	**212,626**	109,866	102,760	**176,518**	90,870	85,648
Tonk ...	**317,360**	164,401	152,959	**317,342**	164,392	152,950	**317,296**	164,367	152,929	**52,488**	26,478	26,010

TABLE XV.—Part I.—Language.—*Continued.*

A.—VERNACULARS OF INDIA —(I).—VERNACULARS OF RAJPUTANA.—*Continued.*

AGENCY, STATE OR DISTRICT.	Central Eastern Rajasthani			North Eastern Rajasthani.			Malvi.			Western Hindi.		
	Persons.	Males.	Females.	Persons.	Males.	Females.	Persons.	Males.	Females.	Persons.	Males.	Females.
1	14	15	16	17	18	19	20	21	22	23	24	25
RAJPUTANA ...	*2,157,974*	*1,122,076*	*1,035,898*	*478,941*	*252,474*	*226,467*	*350,856*	*182,346*	*168,510*	*1,721,186*	*926,351*	*794,835*
Abu District ...	19	12	7	22	15	7	...	...	...	1,992	1,928	764
Alwar ...	29,917	15,097	14,820	393,182	207,854	185,328	...	...	...	325,388	172,676	152,712
Banswara ...	4	1	8	...	...	...	1,070	518	557	636	373	268
Bharatpur ...	204	118	86	64,285	34,211	30,074	...	...	...	421,214	228,266	192,948
Bikaner ...	2,700	1,236	1,464	11	11	...	32	20	12	14,248	8,264	5,984
Bundi ...	161,496	84,347	77,149	23	18	5	255	110	145	1,368	781	587
Dholpur ...	279	140	133	9	8	1	...	...	...	251,520	139,401	112,119
Dungarpur ...	...	...	...	...	...	...	132	56	76	2,518	1,358	1,160
Jaipur ...	1,293,377	677,138	616,239	20,626	9,888	10,738	113	60	53	380,761	202,034	178,727
Jaisalmer ...	...	...	...	...	...	...	7	6	1	4	3	1
Jhalawar ...	106	63	43	...	...	...	56,624	29,918	26,706	48,604	25,139	23,465
Karauli ...	140	67	73	2	1	1	...	...	...	139,700	76,303	63,397
Kishangarh ...	67,441	34,236	33,205	48	39	15	40	14	96	172	131	41
Kotah ...	471,579	242,265	229,314	92	78	14	128,963	67,806	61,657	72,469	38,401	34,068
Kushalgarh (Chiefship) ...	...	...	...	...	...	...	2,474	1,206	1,268	838	444	394
Lawa (Estate) ...	2,770	1,435	1,335	...	...	...	...	...	...	4	4	...
Marwar ...	8,191	4,411	3,780	11	...	11	124	43	81	6,220	3,609	2,611
Mewar ...	2,507	1,329	1,176	282	160	122	3,447	1,673	1,774	8,074	3,916	4,158
Partabgarh ...	2	2	...	15	10	5	45,410	23,117	22,293	1,345	716	629
Shahpura ...	3,250	874	2,376	14	8	6	79	29	50	69	41	28
Sirohi ...	995	536	459	160	89	71	48	24	24	4,486	2,506	1,980
Tonk ...	112,997	58,763	54,234	159	90	69	112,038	58,251	53,787	39,556	20,757	18,799

TABLE XV.—PART I.—LANGUAGE.—*Continued.*

AGENCY, STATE OR DISTRICT.	A.—VERNACULARS OF INDIA.—*Continued.* (1).—VERNACULARS OF RAJPUTANA.—*Concluded.* BHILI. Persons.	BHILI. Males.	BHILI. Females.	SINDHI. Persons.	SINDHI. Males.	SINDHI. Females.	RATHI DIALECT OF PANJABI. Persons.	RATHI DIALECT OF PANJABI. Males.	RATHI DIALECT OF PANJABI. Females.	GIPSY LANGUAGES. Persons	GIPSY LANGUAGES. Males.	GIPSY LANGUAGES. Females.
1	26	27	28	29	30	31	32	33	34	35	36	37
RAJPUTANA ...	719,640	364,830	354,810	12,840	7,165	5,675	9,036	5,014	4,022	8,766	4,370	4,396
Abu District ...	906	500	406	1	1	...	...	...	...	...	...	...
Alwar ...	...	...	...	...	...	...	...	...	...	23	13	10
Banswara ...	220,821	109,888	110,933	1	1	...	...	...	...	223	99	124
Bharatpur ...	...	...	...	5	2	3	...	...	...	...	...	...
Bikaner ...	...	...	...	8,833	4,925	3,908	9,036	5,014	4,022	4,131	2,138	1,993
Bundi ...	161	65	96	...	...	...	...	...	...	488	209	279
Dholpur ...	...	...	...	...	...	...	...	...	...	...	...	...
Dungarpur ...	219,444	110,831	108,613	...	...	...	...	...	...	...	...	...
Jaipur ...	4	1	3	26	5	21	...	...	...	...	...	...
Jaisalmer ...	7	7	...	3,777	2,111	1,666	...	...	...	...	...	...
Jhalawar ...	224	118	106	9	9	...	...	...	...	290	154	136
Karauli ...	...	...	...	...	...	...	...	...	...	...	...	...
Kishangarh ...	...	...	...	...	...	...	...	...	...	...	...	...
Kotah ...	44	27	17	1	1	...	...	...	...	27	27	...
Kushalgarh (Chiefship).	31,085	15,505	15,580	3	1	2	...	...	...	724	323	401
Lawa (Estate) ...	...	...	...	...	...	...	...	...	...	...	...	...
Marwar ...	16,915	8,985	7,930	147	83	64	...	...	...	...	...	...
Mewar ...	172,760	89,481	83,279	14	12	2	...	...	...	1,505	691	814
Partabgarh ...	26,814	13,566	13,248	1	1	...	...	...	...	1,355	716	639
Shahpura ...	...	...	...	...	...	...	...	...	...	...	...	...
Sirohi ...	30,397	15,828	14,569	22	13	9	...	...	...	...	...	...
Tonk ...	58	28	30	...	...	...	...	...	...	...	...	...

TABLE XV.—PART I.—LANGUAGE.—*Continued.*

A.—VERNACULARS OF INDIA.—*Continued.*—(II).—VERNACULARS OF INDIA FOREIGN TO RAJPUTANA.

AGENCY, STATE OR DISTRICT.	TOTAL VERNACULARS OF INDIA FOREIGN TO RAJPUTANA.			MARATHI.			PANJABI (INCLUDES WESTERN PANJABI)			GUJARATI.		
	Persons.	Males.	Females.	Persons.	Males.	Females.	Persons.	Males.	Females.	Persons.	Males.	Females.
1	38	39	40	41	42	43	44	45	46	47	48	49
RAJPUTANA. ...	***145,552***	***80,141***	***65,411***	***2,433***	***880***	***1,553***	***116,261***	***65,731***	***50,530***	***20,064***	***9,971***	***10,093***
Abu District ...	**416**	271	145	**39**	24	15	**129**	86	43	**202**	128	74
Alwar ...	**357**	222	135	**9**	2	7	**148**	93	55	**74**	34	40
Banswara ...	**584**	312	272	**15**	6	9	**10**	9	1	**475**	244	231
Bharatpur ...	**569**	349	220	**48**	26	22	**297**	198	99	**155**	80	75
Bikaner ...	**112,044**	63,043	49,001	**104**	70	34	**111,491**	62,767	48,724	**303**	94	209
Bundi ...	**1,452**	831	621	**33**	19	14	**107**	72	35	**527**	307	220
Dholpur ...	**2,748**	734	2,014	**735**	88	647	**291**	182	109	...	...	...
Dungarpur ...	**2,322**	834	1,488	**19**	8	11	**27**	11	16	**2 185**	763	1,422
Jaipur ...	**4,175**	2,422	1,753	**335**	191	144	**1,688**	1,055	633	**912**	484	428
Jaisalmer ...	**218**	102	116	...	...	...	**25**	15	10	**70**	29	41
Jhalawar ...	**1,167**	642	525	**29**	19	10	**64**	49	15	**954**	490	464
Karauli ...	**128**	64	64	**10**	2	8	**10**	6	4	**20**	9	11
Kishangarh ...	**144**	101	43	**132**	91	41	**9**	7	2	...	...	...
Kotah ...	**3,769**	2,199	1,570	**231**	138	93	**687**	418	269	**2,249**	1,194	1,055
Kushalgarh (Chiefship) ...	**425**	268	157	**7**	2	5	**2**	2	...	**410**	259	151
Lawa (Estate) ...	**1**	...	1	...	...	...	**1**	...	1	...	...	...
Marwar ...	**1,338**	752	586	**77**	41	36	**513**	312	201	**613**	318	295
Mewar ...	**8,920**	4,705	4,215	**433**	53	380	**668**	385	283	**6,818**	3,673	3,145
Partabgarh ...	**1,163**	628	535	**28**	17	11	**1**	...	1	**888**	466	422
Shahpura ...	**25**	16	9	...	...	...	**1**	1	...	**13**	4	9
Sirohi ...	**3,541**	1,621	1,920	**142**	81	61	**86**	59	27	**3,196**	1,395	1,801
Tonk ...	**46**	25	21	**7**	2	5	**6**	4	2	...	...	...

TABLE XV.—Part I.—Language.—*Continued.*

AGENCY, STATE OR DISTRICT.	A.—VERNACULARS OF INDIA.—(II).—VERNACULARS OF INDIA FOREIGN TO RAJPUTANA—*Concluded.* BIHARI.			EASTERN HINDI.			OTHERS.			B.—VERNACULARS OF ASIATIC AND AFRICAN COUNTRIES. TOTAL.		
	Persons.	Males.	Females.	Persons.	Males.	Females.	Persons.	Males.	Females.	Persons	Males.	Females.
1	50	51	52	53	54	55	56	57	58	59	60	61
RAJPUTANA ...	2,425	827	1,598	1,715	1,007	708	2,654	1,725	929	127	86	41
Abu District ...	...	...	...	32	25	7	14	8	6	8	3	5
Alwar ...	83	55	28	...	...	...	43	38	5	51	28	23
Banswara ...	...	...	...	...	...	...	84	53	31	...	...	...
Bharatpur ...	43	25	18	...	...	...	26	20	6	...	...	...
Bikaner ...	13	9	4	...	...	...	133	103	30	16	12	4
Bundi ...	731	385	346	...	...	...	54	48	6	1	1	...
Dholpur ...	1,525	333	1,192	...	...	...	197	131	66	2	...	2
Dungarpur ...	...	...	...	41	17	24	50	35	15	...	...	...
Jaipur ...	...	...	...	651	357	294	589	335	254	34	31	3
Jaisalmer ...	...	...	...	...	...	...	123	58	65	...	...	...
Jhalawar ...	...	...	...	42	27	15	78	57	21	1	...	1
Karauli ...	...	...	...	...	...	...	88	47	41	4	3	1
Kishangarh ...	...	...	...	...	...	...	3	3	...	...	...	...
Kotah ...	...	...	...	221	139	82	381	310	71	...	...	...
Kushalgarh (Chiefship).	...	...	...	...	...	...	6	5	1	...	...	...
Lawa (Estate) ...	...	...	...	...	...	...	...	...	...	...	...	...
Marwar ...	...	...	...	...	...	...	135	81	54	2	2	...
Mewar ...	3	3	...	728	442	286	270	149	121	...	...	...
Partabgarh ...	27	17	10	...	...	...	219	128	91	...	...	...
Shahpura ...	...	...	...	...	...	...	11	11	...	...	...	...
Sirohi ...	...	...	...	...	...	...	117	86	31	8	6	2
Tonk ...	...	...	...	...	...	...	33	19	14	...	...	...

TABLE XV.—PART I—LANGUAGE.—*Concluded.*

AGENCY, STATE OR DISTRICT.	C.—EUROPEAN LANGUAGES.								
	TOTAL.			ENGLISH.			OTHER EUROPEAN LANGUAGES.		
	Persons.	Males.	Females.	Persons.	Males.	Females.	Persons.	Males.	Females.
1	62	63	64	65	66	67	68	69	70
RAJPUTANA ...	1,909	1,050	859	1,822	993	829	87	57	30
Abu District ...	104	59	45	99	55	44	5	4	1
Alwar ...	19	11	8	18	10	8	1	1	...
Banswara ...	4	...	4	4	...	4	...	...	...
Bharatpur ...	45	22	23	45	22	23	...	...	...
Bikaner ...	56	29	27	54	28	26	2	1	1
Bundi ...	27	19	8	6	5	1	21	14	7
Dholpur ...	15	4	11	14	3	11	1	1	...
Dungarpur ...	...	...	...	...	...	...	...	...	...
Jaipur ...	959	505	454	922	480	442	37	25	12
Jaisalmer ...	...	...	...	...	...	...	...	...	...
Jhalawar ...	5	4	1	3	2	1	2	2	...
Karauli ...	...	...	...	...	...	...	...	...	...
Kishangarh ...	...	...	...	...	...	...	...	...	...
Kotah ...	56	32	24	49	29	20	7	3	4
Kushalgarh (Chiefship)	...	...	...	...	...	...	...	...	...
Lawa (Estate) ...	...	...	...	...	...	...	...	...	...
Marwar ...	165	108	57	165	108	57	...	...	...
Mewar ...	81	65	16	79	63	16	2	2	...
Partabgarh ...	1	1	...	1	1	...	...	...	...
Shahpura ...	1	...	1	1	...	1	...	...	...
Sirohi ...	353	182	171	345	178	167	8	4	4
Tonk ...	18	9	9	17	9	8	1	...	1

TABLE XV.—PART II.—BILINGUALISM.

AREA OF BILINGUALISM.	MOTHER TONGUE.—RAJASTHANI.									MOTHER TONGUE.—BHILI.				
	NUMBER OF PERSONS SPEAKING MOTHER TONGUE.	SUBSIDIARY LANGUAGES.								NUMBER OF PERSONS SPEAKING MOTHER TONGUE	SUBSIDIARY LANGUAGES.			
		Gujarati.		Bhili.		Sindhi.		Panjabi.			Rajasthani.		Gujarati.	
		Males.	Females.	Males.	Females.	Males.	Females.	Males.	Females.		Males	Females	Males.	Females.
1	2	3	4	5	6	7	8	9	10	11	12	13	14	15
North-West Bikaner (Ganganagar and Suratgarh Nizamats) ...	111,749	...	...	...	...	...	...	69	56	...	...	...	...	...
West and South-West Marwar (Mallani and Sanchore Parganas) ...	262,412	64	443	...	...	5,119	4,788	...	...	...	...	...	...	...
Sirohi ...	177,721	109	35	45	8	...	...	...	...	30,397	1,112	1,108	164	112
West Jaisalmer (Shahgarh Ghotru Pargana) ...	...	...	...	...	...	...	...	...	...	...	...	...	...	...
South-West Mewar (Kherwara District) ...	10,562	10	...	1,200	1,117	...	...	...	...	61,546	59	225	...	...
Banswara ...	2,837	...	...	14	84	...	...	...	...	220,821	3	2	...	5
Dungarpur ...	...	...	...	...	...	...	...	...	...	219,444	...	...	1,844	1,050
Kushalgarh (Chiefship) ...	2,489	...	1	2	...	...	...	...	...	...	...	...	...	...
Partabgarh ...	45,860	...	...	1	1	...	...	...	...	26,814	65	64	...	...

TABLE XV.—PART II.—BILINGUALISM.—*Concluded.*

AREA OF BILINGUALISM	MOTHER TONGUE.—SINDHI.					MOTHER TONGUE.—PANJABI.					MOTHER TONGUE.—GUJARATI.						
	NUMBER OF PERSONS SPEAKING MOTHER TONGUE.	SUBSIDIARY LANGUAGES.				NUMBER OF PERSONS SPEAKING MOTHER TONGUE.	SUBSIDIARY LANGUAGES.				NUMBER OF PERSONS SPEAKING MOTHER TONGUE.	SUBSIDIARY LANGUAGES.					
		Rajasthani.		Gujarati.			Rajasthani.		Sindhi.			Bhili.		Rajasthani.		Sindhi	
		Males.	Females.	Males.	Females.		Males.	Females.	Males.	Females.		Males.	Females.	Males.	Females.	Males.	Females.
1	16	17	18	19	20	21	22	23	24	25	26	27	28	29	30	31	32
North-West Bikaner (Ganganagar and Suratgarh Nizamats) ...	...	...	...	...	...	**111,491**	146	180	13	...	...	...	...	...	...	...	...
West and South-West Marwar (Mallani and Sanchore Parganas) ...	**147**	42	23	...	...	...	...	...	...	...	**613**	...	...	131	253	6	1
Sirohi ...	...	...	...	...	...	...	...	...	...	...	**3,196**	24	40	373	830	...	...
West Jaisalmer (Shahgarh Ghotru Paragna) ...	**3,091**	17	...	...	...	**25**	6	...	...	...	**70**	...	...	5	4	...	...
South-West Mewar (Kherwara District) ...	...	...	...	...	...	...	...	...	...	...	**354**	4	7	122	132	...	...
Banswara ...	...	...	...	...	...	...	...	...	...	...	**475**	4	97	...	...	...	...
Dungarpur ...	...	...	...	...	...	...	...	...	...	...	...	...	...	...	...	...	...
Kushalgarh (Chiefship) ...	...	...	...	...	...	...	...	...	...	...	**410**	1	...	7	6	...	...
Partabgarh ...	...	...	...	...	...	...	...	...	...	...	...	...	...	...	...	...	...

TABLE XVI.

Religion.

EXPLANATORY NOTE.

The details of Christians are given below:—

Sect.	Persons.	Males.	Females
Anglican Communion	941	484	457
India United Churches.	1,514	797	717
Methodists	893	485	408
Minor and Unspecified Protestants	334	180	154
Roman Catholics.	1,465	823	642
Others.	631	338	293
TOTAL ...	5,778	3,107	2,671

TABLE XVI.—Religion.

AGENCY, STATE OR DISTRICT.	POPULATION.			HINDU.								
				TOTAL.			BRAHMANIC.			ARYA		
	Persons.	Males.	Females.	Persons.	Males.	Females.	Persons	Males.	Females	Persons.	Males.	Females.
1	2	3	4	5	6	7	8	9	10	11	12	13
RAJPUTANA ...	***11,225,712***	***5,885,028***	***5,340,684***	***9,578,805***	***5,029,620***	***4,549,185***	***9,567,234***	***5,023,365***	***4,543,869***	***11,471***	***6,196***	***5,275***
Abu District ...	**4,532**	2,753	1,779	**3,498**	2,099	1,399	**3,498**	2,099	1,399	...	...	...
Alwar ...	**749,751**	396,261	353,490	**549,366**	290,088	259,278	**548,956**	289,879	259,077	**410**	209	201
Banswara ...	**225,106**	111,983	113,123	**120,458**	59,925	60,533	**120,452**	59,921	60,531	**6**	4	2
Bharatpur ...	**486,954**	263,325	223,629	**389,723**	211,278	178,445	**387,969**	210,343	177,626	**1,747**	930	817
Bikaner ...	**936,218**	501,153	435,065	**725,084**	388,017	337,067	**721,926**	386,259	335,667	**3,125**	1,736	1,389
Bundi ...	**216,722**	113,101	103,621	**202,329**	105,482	96,847	**202,324**	105,479	96,845	**5**	3	2
Dholpur ...	**254,986**	140,497	114,489	**235,929**	130,354	105,575	**235,809**	130,297	105,512	**120**	57	63
Dungarpur ...	**227,544**	114,480	113,064	**214,045**	107,797	106,248	**214,042**	107,795	106,247	**3**	2	1
Jaipur ...	**2,631,775**	1,387,067	1,244,708	**2,383,304**	1,256,918	1,126,386	**2,382,219**	1,256,285	1,125,934	**1,085**	633	452
Jaisalmer ...	**76,255**	42,312	33,913	**51,769**	28,551	23,218	**51,769**	28,551	23,218	...	...	...
Jhalawar ...	**107,890**	56,518	51,372	**96,634**	50,705	45,929	**96,501**	50,629	45,872	**133**	76	57
Karauli ...	**140,525**	76,729	63,796	**132,759**	72,578	60,181	**132,759**	72,578	60,181	...	...	...
Kishangarh ...	**85,744**	44,494	41,250	**76,263**	39,506	36,757	**76,197**	39,464	36,733	**66**	42	24
Kotah ...	**685,804**	355,056	330,748	**629,416**	325,624	303,792	**628,626**	325,207	303,419	**742**	395	347
Kushalgarh (Chiefship).	**35,564**	17,754	17,810	**34,127**	17,004	17,123	**34,127**	17,004	17,123	...	...	...
Lawa (Estate) ...	**2,790**	1,445	1,345	**2,546**	1,314	1,232	**2,541**	1,310	1,231	**5**	4	1
Marwar ...	**2,125,982**	1,109,912	1,016,070	**1,831,441**	962,012	869,429	**1,829,298**	960,902	868,396	**2,143**	1,110	1,033
Mewar ...	**1,566,910**	807,184	759,726	**1,352,029**	696,380	655,649	**1,351,873**	696,273	655,600	**144**	97	47
Partabgarh ...	**76,539**	38,991	37,548	**41,347**	21,124	20,223	**41,347**	21,124	20,223	...	...	...
Shahpura ...	**54,233**	27,907	26,326	**50,273**	25,845	24,428	**48,547**	24,953	23,594	**1,726**	892	834
Sirohi ...	**216,528**	111,675	104,853	**193,785**	101,044	92,741	**193,779**	101,040	92,739	**6**	4	2
Tonk ...	**317,360**	164,401	152,959	**262,680**	135,975	126,705	**262,675**	135,973	126,702	**5**	2	3

TABLE XVI.—Religion —*Continued.*

AGENCY, STATE OR DISTRICT.	HINDU.—*Concluded.* BRAHMO.			DRO SAMAJ.			SIKH.			BUDDHIST.		
	Persons.	Males.	Females.	Persons.	Males.	Females.	Persons.	Males.	Females.	Persons	Males	Females
1	14	15	16	17	18	19	20	21	22	23	24	25
RAJPUTANA. ...	44	32	12	56	27	29	41,605	24,725	16,880	1	1	...
Abu District ...	...	...	...	...	...	...	54	37	17	...	...	...
Alwar ...	...	...	...	...	...	...	37	21	16	...	...	...
Banswara ...	...	...	...	...	...	...	5	4	1	...	...	...
Bharatpur ...	7	5	2	...	...	...	157	102	55	...	...	...
Bikaner ...	25	17	8	8	5	3	40,469	24,017	16,452	...	...	...
Bundi ...	...	...	...	...	...	...	45	28	17	...	...	...
Dholpur ...	...	...	...	...	...	...	254	160	94	1	1	...
Dungarpur ...	...	...	...	...	...	...	9	5	4	...	...	...
Jaipur ...	...	...	...	...	...	...	189	120	69	...	...	...
Jaisalmer ...	...	...	...	...	...	...	9	8	1	...	...	...
Jhalawar ...	...	...	...	...	...	...	18	15	3	...	...	...
Karauli ...	...	...	...	...	...	...	1	1	...	...	...	...
Kishangarh ...	...	...	...	...	...	...	2	2	...	...	...	...
Kotah ...	...	...	...	48	22	26	273	151	122	...	...	...
Kushalgarh (Chiefship) ...	...	...	...	...	...	...	...	...	...	...	...	...
Lawa (Estate) ...	...	...	...	...	...	...	...	...	...	...	...	...
Marwar ...	...	...	...	...	...	...	34	17	17	...	...	...
Mewar ...	12	10	2	...	...	...	23	17	6	...	...	...
Partabgarh ...	...	...	...	...	...	...	6	6	...	...	...	...
Shahpura ...	...	...	...	...	...	...	...	...	...	...	...	...
Sirohi ...	...	...	...	...	...	...	10	8	2	...	...	...
Tonk ...	...	...	...	...	...	...	10	6	4	...	...	...

TABLE XVI.—RELIGION.—*Continued.*

AGENCY, STATE OR DISTRICT.	JAIN.											
	TOTAL JAIN.			SWETAMBARI.			DIGAMBARI.			BAISTOLA (DHUNDIA).		
	Persons.	Males.	Females.	Persons.	Males.	Females.	Persons.	Males.	Females.	Persons.	Males.	Females.
1	26	27	28	29	30	31	32	33	34	35	36	37
RAJPUTANA ...	*300,748*	*146,004*	*154,744*	*134,615*	*63,411*	*71,204*	*76,237*	*39,366*	*36,871*	*50,228*	*25,058*	*25,170*
Abu District ...	**21**	10	11	**21**	10	11	...	...	...	...	...	...
Alwar ...	**3,809**	1,994	1,815	**1,169**	606	563	**2,438**	1,286	1,152	**34**	14	20
Banswara ...	**4,597**	2,342	2,255	**404**	214	190	**4,180**	2,119	2,061	**13**	9	4
Bharatpur ...	**2,390**	1,288	1,102	**917**	506	411	**1,462**	775	687	**2**	2	...
Bikaner ...	**28,773**	12,479	16,294	**3,558**	1,722	1,836	**1,001**	451	550	**3,664**	1,629	2,035
Bundi ...	**4,019**	2,166	1,853	**135**	76	59	**3,767**	2,026	1,741	**34**	20	14
Dholpur ...	**1,799**	994	805	**8**	5	3	**1,756**	966	790	**8**	8	...
Dungarpur ...	**5,801**	2,836	2,965	**1,631**	820	811	**4,167**	2,015	2,152	**3**	1	2
Jaipur ...	**29,492**	15,518	13,974	**4,903**	2,535	2,368	**23,236**	12,282	10,954	**593**	295	298
Jaisalmer ...	**917**	466	451	**917**	466	451	...	...	...	...	...	...
Jhalawar ...	**2,630**	1,390	1,240	**1,526**	824	702	**646**	325	321	**438**	229	209
Karauli ...	**448**	229	219	**380**	188	192	**68**	41	27	...	...	...
Kishangarh ...	**2,231**	1,187	1,044	**509**	285	224	**916**	492	424	**770**	392	378
Kotah ...	**5,194**	2,759	2,435	**1,221**	661	560	**3,546**	1,874	1,672	**212**	111	101
Kushalgarh (Chiefship).	**583**	297	286	**219**	116	103	**364**	181	183	...	...	...
Lawa (Estate) ...	**135**	75	60	**4**	3	1	**131**	72	59	...	...	...
Marwar ...	**113,669**	52,587	61,082	**83,522**	38,316	45,206	**5,013**	2,427	2,586	**18,921**	9,035	9,886
Mewar ...	**66,001**	34,086	31,915	**13,576**	7,036	6,540	**16,721**	8,489	8,232	**24,268**	12,654	11,614
Partabgarh ...	**4,445**	2,240	2,205	**1,791**	893	898	**2,339**	1,205	1,134	**315**	142	173
Shahpura ...	**1,418**	757	661	**621**	327	294	**505**	262	243	**292**	168	124
Sirohi ...	**15,508**	6,696	8,812	**15,470**	6,678	8,792	**38**	18	20	...	...	...
Tonk ...	**6,868**	3,608	3,260	**2,113**	1,124	989	**3,943**	2,060	1,883	**661**	349	312

TABLE XVI.—RELIGION.—*Continued.*

AGENCY, STATE OR DISTRICT.	JAIN.—*Concluded.*						MUSLIM.					
	TERAPANTHI.			OTHERS.			TOTAL.			SUNNI.		
	Persons.	Males.	Females.	Persons.	Males.	Females.	Persons.	Males.	Females.	Persons.	Males.	Females.
1	38	39	40	41	42	43	44	45	46	47	48	49
RAJPUTANA ...	*38,563*	*17,568*	*20,995*	*1,105*	*601*	*504*	*1,069,325*	*565,962*	*503,363*	*1,041,361*	*551,416*	*489,945*
Abu District ...	...	...	...	...	...	...	800	512	288	633	400	233
Alwar ...	69	38	31	99	50	49	196,460	104,110	92,350	195,346	103,565	91,781
Banswara ...	...	...	...	...	...	...	6,510	3,300	3,210	4,529	2,312	2,217
Bharatpur ...	8	4	4	1	1	...	94,054	50,308	43,746	92,543	49,515	43,028
Bikaner ...	20,549	8,676	11,873	1	1	...	141,578	76,471	65,107	140,787	76,048	64,739
Bundi ...	49	28	21	34	16	18	10,292	5,398	4,894	9,773	5,126	4,647
Dholpur ...	27	15	12	...	...	...	16,842	8,903	7,939	15,879	8,413	7,466
Dungarpur ...	...	...	...	...	...	...	7,682	3,838	3,844	4,406	2,282	2,124
Jaipur ...	238	118	120	522	288	234	214,581	112,338	102,243	209,770	109,782	99,988
Jaisalmer ...	...	...	...	...	...	...	22,116	12,502	9,614	22,051	12,469	9,582
Jhalawar ...	4	2	2	16	10	6	8,558	4,377	4,181	7,764	3,994	3,770
Karauli ...	...	...	...	...	...	...	7,301	3,914	3,387	7,291	3,908	3,383
Kishangarh ...	36	18	18	...	...	...	6,597	3,467	3,130	6,242	3,282	2,960
Kotah ...	128	64	64	87	49	38	47,068	24,531	22,537	45,817	23,852	21,965
Kushalgarh (Chiefship).	...	...	...	...	...	...	854	453	401	572	297	275
Lawa (Estate) ...	...	...	...	...	...	...	109	56	53	109	56	53
Marwar ...	6,213	2,809	3,404	...	...	...	176,863	93,234	83,629	174,555	91,994	82,561
Mewar ...	11,210	5,782	5,428	226	125	101	53,833	28,346	25,487	47,354	24,877	22,477
Partabgarh ...	...	...	...	...	...	...	3,914	2,045	1,869	3,321	1,728	1,593
Shahpura ...	...	...	...	...	...	...	2,541	1,305	1,236	2,541	1,305	1,236
Sirohi ...	...	...	...	...	...	...	6,538	3,561	2,977	6,299	3,452	2,847
Tonk ...	32	14	18	119	61	58	44,234	22,993	21,241	43,779	22,759	21,020

TABLE XVI.—Religion.—*Continued.*

AGENCY, STATE OR DISTRICT.	MUSLIM.—*Concluded.*									TRIBAL.		
	SHIA.			AHAL-I-HADIS.			UNSPECIFIED					
	Persons.	Males.	Females.	Persons.	Males.	Females.	Persons.	Males.	Females.	Persons.	Males.	Females.
1	50	51	52	53	54	55	56	57	58	59	60	61
RAJPUTANA ...	**21,818**	**11,247**	**10,571**	**2,004**	**1,053**	**951**	**4,142**	**2,246**	**1,896**	**229,092**	**115,420**	**113,672**
Abu District ...	17	14	3	2	2	...	148	96	52	...	...	...
Alwar ...	723	342	381	6	2	4	385	201	184	...	...	...
Banswara ...	1,981	988	993	...	...	...	...	...	...	93,330	46,313	47,017
Bharatpur ...	1,511	793	718	...	...	...	...	...	...	...	...	...
Bikaner ...	775	416	359	12	5	7	4	2	2	...	...	...
Bundi ...	492	257	235	...	...	...	27	15	12	5	3	2
Dholpur ...	629	327	302	324	160	164	10	3	7	98	64	34
Dungarpur ...	3,276	1,556	1,720	...	...	...	...	...	...	...	...	...
Jaipur ...	1,608	837	771	9	9	...	3,194	1,710	1,484	2,599	1,349	1,250
Jaisalmer ...	65	33	32	...	...	...	...	...	...	1,444	815	629
Jhalawar ...	791	381	410	3	2	1	...	...	...	...	...	...
Karauli ...	9	6	3	...	...	...	1	...	1	...	...	...
Kishangarh ...	68	33	35	287	152	135	...	...	...	636	324	312
Kotah ...	878	463	415	53	24	29	320	192	128	2,923	1,515	1,408
Kushalgarh (Chiefship)...	271	149	122	...	...	...	11	7	4	...	...	...
Lawa (Estate) ...	...	...	...	...	...	...	...	...	...	...	...	...
Marwar ...	1,039	560	479	1,269	680	589	...	...	...	3,241	1,653	1,588
Mewar ...	6,437	3,449	2,988	...	...	...	42	20	22	94,544	48,061	46,483
Partabgarh ...	593	317	276	...	...	...	...	...	...	26,747	13,534	13,218
Shahpura ...	...	...	...	...	...	...	...	...	...	...	...	...
Sirohi ...	232	105	127	7	4	3	...	...	...	...	...	...
Tonk ...	423	221	202	32	13	19	...	...	...	3,525	1,789	1,736

TABLE XVI.—Religion.—*Concluded.*

AGENCY, STATE OR DISTRICT.	ZOROASTRIAN.			CHRISTIAN.			JEW.			RELIGION NOT RETURNED.		
	Persons.	Males.	Females.	Persons.	Males.	Females.	Persons.	Males.	Females.	Persons	Males	Females.
1	62	63	64	65	66	67	68	69	70	71	72	73
RAJPUTANA ...	319	170	149	5,778	3,107	2,671	38	18	20	1	1	...
Abu District ...	19	11	8	140	84	56	...	...	...	...	...	...
Alwar ...	...	...	...	79	48	31	...	...	...	...	...	...
Banswara ...	1	1	...	205	98	107	...	...	...	...	...	...
Bharatpur ...	5	3	2	625	346	279	...	...	...	...	...	...
Bikaner ...	16	9	7	298	160	138	...	...	...	...	...	...
Bundi ...	3	3	...	29	21	8	...	...	...	...	...	...
Dholpur ...	...	...	...	63	21	42	...	...	...	...	...	...
Dungarpur ...	...	...	...	7	4	3	...	...	...	...	...	...
Jaipur ...	52	29	23	1,558	795	763	...	...	...	...	...	...
Jaisalmer ...	...	...	...	...	...	...	...	...	...	...	...	...
Jhalawar ...	...	...	...	50	31	19	...	...	...	...	...	...
Karauli ...	...	...	...	16	7	9	...	...	...	...	...	...
Kishangarh ...	...	...	...	15	8	7	...	...	...	...	...	...
Kotah ...	16	6	10	914	470	444	...	...	...	...	...	...
Kushalgarh (Chiefship)	...	...	...	...	...	...	...	...	...	...	...	...
Lawa (Estate) ...	...	...	...	...	...	...	...	...	...	...	...	...
Marwar ...	48	23	25	686	386	300	...	...	...	...	...	...
Mewar ...	...	...	...	479	293	186	...	...	...	1	1	...
Partabgarh ...	13	9	4	67	33	34	...	...	...	...	...	...
Shahpura ...	...	...	...	1	...	1	...	...	...	...	...	...
Sirohi ...	146	76	70	503	272	231	38	18	20	...	...	...
Tonk ...	...	...	...	43	30	13	...	...	...	...	...	...

TABLE XVII.

Race, Tribe or Caste.

EXPLANATORY NOTE.

This Table is divided into two Parts.

Part I shows the castes returned in the Agency as a whole, together with particulars regarding religion.

Part II shows the more numerous castes found in each State, etc.

The following amalgamations have been made:—

Brahman	includes	Sevag.
Chamar	,,	Jatiya.
Dadupanthi	,,	Naga.
Daroga	,,	Chakar, Chela, Golapurab, Hazuri, Pasbania.
Jogi	,,	Nath.
Kalbelia	,,	Sapera.
Kahar	,,	Dhimar.
Khati	,,	Barhai, Karigar, Sutar.
Kunbi	,,	Kurmi.
Merat	,,	Chita, Kathat.
Rawat	,,	Gorat, Mer.
Thathera	,,	Kalaigar.

Bhojak is included in Brahman except for 2,754 persons returned from Mewar. Kharadi is included in Khati except in Shahpura and Partabgarh. Unspecified includes those who genuinely do not believe in the caste system as well as those for whom an entry in column in the schedule was overlooked.

TABLE XVII.—Race, Tribe or Caste.—Part I.—Agency Summary.

(B=Budhist; C=Christian; H=Hdindu; J=Jain; M=Muslim; S=Sikh; T=Tribal, Z=Zoroastrian).

Caste.	Religion.	Population. Persons.	Males.	Females.
1	2	3	4	5
Total Population.		***11,225,712***	***5,885,028***	***5,340,684***
Afghan ...	M	**69**	**40**	**29**
Agarwal ...		**183,754**	**94,376**	**89,378**
	C	5	2	3
	H	173,387	88,869	84,518
	J	10,349	5,496	4,858
	M	1	1	...
	S	12	8	4
Aheri ...	H	**1,204**	**640**	**564**
Ahir ...		**182,165**	**98,431**	**83,734**
	C	1	...	1
	H	182,139	98,426	83,713
	M	12	2	10
	S	13	3	10
Anjna ...	H	**2,778**	**1,440**	**1,338**
Arab ...	M	**12**	**6**	**6**
Arya ...	H	**896**	**497**	**399**
Bachhra ...	H	**129**	**63**	**66**
Badi ...	H	**708**	**330**	**378**
Bagerwal ...		**3,418**	**1,755**	**1,663**
	H	372	183	189
	J	3,046	1,572	1,474
Bagri ...		**11,165**	**5,852**	**5,313**
	H	10,397	5,446	4,951
	M	13	8	5
	T	755	398	357
Bahrupia ...	H	**37**	**16**	**21**
Baid ...	H	**45**	**22**	**23**
Baidnor ...	H	**3**	...	**3**
Balai ...		**218,927**	**113,543**	**105,384**
	C	44	25	19
	H	218,857	113,501	105,356
	M	20	13	7
	T	6	4	2
Baluch ...	M	**628**	**351**	**277**
Bambhi ...		**162,865**	**84,420**	**78,445**
	H	162,863	84,419	78,444
	T	2	1	1
Bandhera ...	H	**1,107**	**525**	**582**
Banjara ...		**23,409**	**12,337**	**11,072**
	H	22,632	11,888	10,744
	M	628	375	253
	T	149	74	75
Banoda ...	H	**5**	**2**	**3**
Banotia ...	M	**1**	**1**	...
Bansphod ...		**927**	**373**	**554**
	H	926	373	553
	M	1	...	1
Bara ...	H	**37**	**21**	**16**
Baraseni ...	H	**5**	**3**	**2**
Bargi ...	H	**1,593**	**703**	**890**
Bargonda ...	H	**300**	**263**	**37**
Bari ...	H	**1,944**	**946**	**998**
Baria ...		**283**	**72**	**211**
	H	274	72	202
	M	9	...	9
Basara ...	H	**791**	**400**	**391**
Basdev ...	H	**1**	**1**	...
Bauria ...		**37,605**	**19,015**	**18,590**
	H	35,965	18,164	17,801
	M	16	4	12
	S	1,274	676	598
	T	350	171	179
Bavaria ...		**1,552**	**841**	**711**
	H	1,426	775	651
	T	126	66	60
Bazigar ...		**467**	**258**	**209**
	H	372	215	157
	M	7	2	5
	S	88	41	47
Bengali ...		**375**	**207**	**168**
	H	309	171	138
	M	66	36	30
Beria ...	H	**700**	**324**	**376**
Bhagat ...		**494**	**212**	**282**
	H	483	209	274
	M	11	3	8
Bhagwal ...	H	**2**	**2**	...
Bhand ...		**1,535**	**807**	**728**
	H	1,315	697	618
	M	220	110	110
Bhandari ...	H	**17**	**13**	**4**
Bhangi ...		**99,083**	**50,906**	**48,177**
	C	212	126	86
	H	92,747	47,346	45,401
	M	444	219	225
	S	5,680	3,215	2,465
Bhangri ...	H	**58**	**24**	**34**
Bharawa ...	H	**498**	**277**	**221**
Bharbunja ...		**3,643**	**1,963**	**1,680**
	H	2,826	1,507	1,319
	M	817	456	361
Bhargava ...	H	**1,359**	**730**	**629**
Bharti ...	H	**81**	**81**	...
Bharwa ...		**14**	**10**	**4**
	H	9	7	2
	M	5	3	2
Bhat ...		**39,882**	**19,995**	**19,887**
	H	38,260	19,301	18,959
	M	1,620	692	928
	S	2	2	...
Bhateora ...		**108**	**58**	**50**
	H	2	2	...
	J	106	56	50
Bhatia ...		**113**	**29**	**84**
	H	107	26	81
	M	6	3	3
Bhatiara ...		**1,452**	**796**	**656**
	H	37	20	17
	M	1,415	776	639
Bhatphor ...	H	**45**	**19**	**26**
Bhatu ...	H	**3**	**2**	**1**
Bhawaiya ...	H	**181**	**116**	**65**
Bhil ...		**655,647**	**332,625**	**323,022**
	C	133	65	68
	H	457,509	233,302	224,207
	T	198,005	99,258	98,747
Bhishti ...		**23,949**	**12,744**	**11,205**
	H	86	39	47
	M	23,863	12,705	11,158
Bhoi ...	H	**10,340**	**5,261**	**5,079**
Bhojak ...		**2,754**	**1,369**	**1,385**
	H	2,712	1,346	1,366
	J	42	23	19
Bhomiya ...	H	**34**	**34**	...
Bhopa ...	H	**1,787**	**897**	**890**
Bhubalia ...	H	**43**	**23**	**20**
Bidakia ...	H	**63**	**44**	**19**
Bijabani ...	H	**16**	**12**	**4**
Bijabargi ...		**7,477**	**3,886**	**3,591**
	H	7,387	3,828	3,559
	J	90	58	32
Bijawat ...	H	**45**	**23**	**22**
Bisa Mahajan ...	H	**1**	**1**	...
Bisati ...	M	**3,384**	**1,768**	**1,616**
Bishnoi ...	H	**69,873**	**37,010**	**32,863**
Bodla ...	M	**308**	**169**	**139**
Bohra ...	M	**15,302**	**7,851**	**7,451**
Brahmachari ...	H	**1**	**1**	...
Brahm Bhatt ...	H	**32**	**7**	**25**
Brahman ...		**854,634**	**442,020**	**412,614**
	C	4	3	1
	H	854,575	441,990	412,585
	J	38	19	19
	S	17	8	9
Audich ...		*14,459*	*6,878*	*7,581*
Bagara ...		*16,917*	*8,582*	*8,335*
Daima ...		*33,132*	*16,596*	*16,536*
Gaur and Adi Gaur		*231,236*	*121,566*	*109,670*
Gujar Gaur ...		*61,756*	*31,906*	*29,850*
Hariyana ...		*33,406*	*16,834*	*16,572*
Khandelwal ...		*41,964*	*21,104*	*20,860*
Mewaria ...		*10,804*	*5,614*	*5,190*
Palliwal ...		*24,172*	*12,324*	*11,848*
Parikh ...		*45,536*	*22,733*	*22,803*
Pushkarna ...		*31,787*	*16,570*	*15,217*
Sanadhya ...		*112,727*	*61,482*	*51,245*
Saraswat ...		*14,963*	*8,154*	*6,809*

TABLE XVII.—Race, Tribe or Caste.—Part I.—Agency Summary.—*Continued.*

Caste.	Religion.	Population. Persons.	Males.	Females.
1	2	3	4	5
Sikhwal ...		*13,124*	*6,645*	*6,479*
Srimali ...		*15,921*	*7,900*	*8,021*
Others ...		*152,730*	*77,132*	*75,598*
Brijbasi ...	H	2	2	...
Chabaksawar ...	M	15	9	6
Chadwa ...	M	732	385	347
Chakra ...		287	136	151
	H	91	2	89
	M	196	134	62
Chamar ...		767,263	394,422	372,841
	C	40	17	23
	H	766,643	394,035	372,608
	M	13	11	2
	S	566	358	208
	T	1	1	...
Chamta ...	H	155	70	85
Charan ...		35,548	19,271	16,277
	H	35,546	19,271	16,275
	S	2	...	2
Charwadar ...		508	245	263
	H	284	129	155
	M	224	116	108
Chaturseni ...	H	36	36	...
Chaube ...	H	557	309	248
Chaurasiya ...	H	14	6	8
Chhipa ...		33,225	17,238	15,987
	H	25,498	13,326	12,272
	M	7,553	3,911	3,642
	S	174	101	73
Chirar ...	H	1,227	534	693
Chitara ...		80	47	33
	H	10	5	5
	M	70	42	28
Chitora ...		2,109	1,132	977
	H	1,079	599	480
	J	1,030	533	497
Chobdar ...		2,479	1,365	1,114
	H	1,784	1,030	754
	M	695	335	360
Chopdia ...	H	1	1	...
Christian ...		5,330	2,865	2,465
(a) Indians ...	C	3,573	1,907	1,666
(b) Others ...	C	1,757	958	799
Chungar ...	M	574	288	286
Dabgar ...		696	222	474
	H	652	199	453
	M	44	23	21
Dadupanthi ...		6,122	5,690	432
	H	6,120	5,688	432
	M	2	2	...
Dai ...	M	1	...	1
Dakot ...		27,353	14,154	13,199
	H	27,322	14,128	13,194
	J	20	19	1
	M	11	7	4
Dangi ...		50,898	25,802	25,096
	H	50,889	25,793	25,096
	T	9	9	...
Daroga ...		177,104	88,658	88,446
	H	177,051	88,633	88,418
	J	19	8	11
	M	34	17	17
Darugar ...		92	39	53
	H	21	9	12
	M	71	30	41
Darzi ...		47,398	24,755	22,643
	H	47,078	24,577	22,501
	J	3	1	2
	M	307	169	138
	S	10	8	2
Deogar ...	M	11	7	4
Desantri ...	H	162	95	67
Deswali ...		5,861	3,054	2,807
	H	7	4	3
	M	5,854	3,050	2,804
Dhakar ...		96,158	50,728	45,430
	H	96,157	50,727	45,430
	J	1	1	...
Dhanak ...		30,735	14,330	16,405
	H	30,733	14,328	16,405
	M	2	2	...
Dhankuta ...	H	469	115	354
Dhargiya ...	H	5	3	2
Dhed ...	H	19,907	10,339	9,568
Dhobi ...		43,832	22,492	21,340
	H	38,783	19,897	18,886
	M	5,049	2,595	2,454
Dholi ...		35,576	18,125	17,451
	H	30,862	15,636	15,226
	M	4,710	2,485	2,225
	T	4	4	...
Dom ...		930	468	462
	H	598	295	303
	M	332	173	159
Fakir ...		54,859	28,857	26,002
	H	82	48	34
	M	54,777	28,809	25,968
Farrash ...		239	119	120
	H	4	2	2
	M	235	117	118
Farrukhi ...	M	16	10	6
Gachha ...	H	14,525	7,183	7,342
Gadaria ...	H	77,370	39,903	37,467
Gaddi ...		5,349	3,082	2,267
	H	23	15	8
	M	5,326	3,067	2,259
Gandharp ...		9	4	5
	H	1	1	...
	J	1	1	...
	M	7	2	5
Gandhi ...		390	233	157
	H	358	214	144
	M	32	19	13
Garoda ...	H	8,699	4,599	4,100
Gatrara ...		122	69	53
	H	35	21	14
	M	87	48	39
Gawaria ...	H	5,354	2,559	2,795
Gayna ...	H	12	2	10
Ghancha ...		6,429	4,133	2,296
	H	4,772	3,270	1,502
	M	1,657	863	794
Ghanchi ...	H	5,371	2,879	2,492
Ghasiara ...		36	14	22
	H	6	1	5
	M	30	13	17
Ghati ...	H	35	34	1
Ghosi ...		1,884	983	901
	H	273	155	118
	M	1,611	828	783
Golandaz ...		19	3	16
	H	2	1	1
	M	17	2	15
Gond ...	H	403	199	204
Gonja ...	H	274	147	127
Gor ...	M	11	7	4
Gosain ...	H	29,648	16,042	13,606
Goswami ...	H	243	145	98
Gowár ...	H	517	233	284
Grassia ...		29,231	15,211	14,020
	H	20,973	10,827	10,146
	T	8,258	4,384	3,874
Gujar ...		526,791	286,171	240,620
	H	526,017	285,731	240,286
	J	1	...	1
	M	771	438	333
	S	2	2	...
Gujrati ...	H	15	4	11
Gurkha ...	H	61	57	4
Guru ...	H	165	94	71
Gurwal ...	H	24	14	10
Habura ...	H	18	8	10
Haji ...	M	1	...	1
Halwai ...		205	106	99
	H	128	63	65
	J	51	25	26
	M	26	18	8
Hammal ...		1,385	687	698
	H	2	1	1
	M	1,383	686	697
Harsola ...	H	31	13	18
Hijra ...		73	73	...
	H	37	37	...
	M	36	36	...
Hiranbaz ...	M	11	7	4
Hoshiyara ...	M	45	27	18

TABLE XVII.—RACE, TRIBE OR CASTE.—PART I.—AGENCY SUMMARY.—*Continued.*

Caste.	Religion.	Population. Persons.	Males.	Females.
1	2	3	4	5
Humar ...		**10,541**	**5,242**	**5,299**
	H	7	5	2
	J	10,534	5,237	5,297
Hurkiya ...		**5**	**5**	...
	H	2	2	...
	M	3	3	...
Illaya ...	M	**79**	**69**	**10**
Jagri ...		**918**	**305**	**613**
	H	906	304	602
	M	12	1	11
Jaiswal ...		**2,494**	**1,437**	**1,057**
	H	81	35	46
	J	2,412	1,401	1,011
	M	1	1	...
Jathi		**36**	**27**	**9**
	H	35	26	9
	M	1	1	...
Janwa ...	H	**3,697**	**2,004**	**1,693**
Jarrah ...	M	**1**	...	**1**
Jasondia ...		**92**	**51**	**41**
	H	88	51	37
	M	4	...	4
Jat ...		**1,042,153**	**564,799**	**477,354**
	H	1,013,945	547,486	466,459
	J	9	5	4
	M	1,257	754	503
	S	26,942	16,554	10,888
Jatav ...	H	**66**	**41**	**25**
Jati ...		**222**	**148**	**74**
	H	55	47	8
	J	167	101	66
Jew ...	Jew	**38**	**18**	**20**
Jhinwar ...		**165**	**94**	**71**
	H	110	70	40
	M	17	...	17
	S	38	24	14
Jingar ...		**176**	**91**	**85**
	H	175	90	85
	M	1	1	...
Jogi ...		**76,204**	**40.319**	**35,885**
	H	74,109	39,242	34,867
	M	2,094	1,076	1,018
	T	1	1	...
Jotgi ...	H	**14**	**9**	**5**
Julaha ...		**17,087**	**8,895**	**8,192**
	H	426	258	168
	M	16,655	8,634	8,021
	S	6	3	3
Kabirpanthi ...		**413**	**266**	**147**
	H	409	263	146
	M	3	2	1
	S	1	1	...
Kachara ...		**651**	**339**	**312**
	H	647	337	310
	M	4	2	2
Kachhi ...		**60,510**	**32,065**	**28,445**
	H	60,409	31,988	28,421
	J	1	...	1
	M	100	77	23
Kagzi ...		**28**	**26**	**2**
	H	27	25	2
	M	1	1	...
Kahar ...		**15,143**	**7,958**	**7,185**
	H	15,034	7,900	7,134
	M	15	3	12
	S	94	55	39
Kaimkhani ...		**35,686**	**18,681**	**17,005**
	H	1	1	...
	M	35,685	18,680	17,005
Kakhera ...	H	**6**	**2**	**4**
Kalal ...		**42,876**	**21,924**	**20,952**
	H	39,735	20,384	19,401
	M	3,082	1,540	1,542
	S	9	...	9
Kalawat ...		**262**	**143**	**119**
	H	89	47	42
	M	173	96	77
Kalbelia ...		**3,765**	**1,961**	**1,804**
	H	3,740	1,945	1,795
	T	25	16	9
Kallandar ...	M	**248**	**144**	**104**
Kamar ...		**614**	**333**	**281**
	H	605	328	277
Kamar (*Ctd.*) ...	M	9	5	4
Kambo ...		**768**	**437**	**331**
	H	3	3	...
	M	39	38	1
	S	726	396	330
Kamlia ...	H	**150**	**76**	**74**
Kamnigar ...		**248**	**134**	**114**
	H	51	34	17
	M	197	100	97
Kanchan ...	M	**2**	**2**	...
Kanjar ...		**3,764**	**1,812**	**1,952**
	H	3,553	1,674	1,879
	M	29	16	13
	T	182	122	60
Kapri ...	H	**586**	**264**	**322**
Karolia ...	M	**1**	**1**	...
Kasai ...		**24,847**	**12,639**	**12,208**
	H	21	9	12
	M	24,826	12,630	12,196
Kathiara ...		**1,086**	**530**	**556**
	H	992	484	508
	M	55	26	29
	T	39	20	19
Katthak ...	H	**54**	**25**	**29**
Katwal ...	H	**108**	**44**	**64**
Kavalia ...	H	**48**	**39**	**9**
Kayastha ...		**23,165**	**12,728**	**10,437**
	H	23,164	12,727	10,437
	J	1	1	...
Kazi ...	M	**925**	**501**	**424**
Khairadi ...		**59**	**21**	**38**
	H	51	18	33
	M	8	3	5
Khandelwal ...		**48,435**	**25,833**	**22,602**
	H	46,355	24,720	21,635
	J	2,077	1,112	965
	M	3	1	2
Khangar ...		**2,969**	**1,488**	**1,481**
	H	2,925	1,455	1,470
	M	44	33	11
Khanzada ...		**8,674**	**4,402**	**4,272**
	H	58	33	25
	M	8,616	4,369	4,247
Kharaeta ...	H	**167**	**80**	**87**
Kharol ...		**7,477**	**3,788**	**3,689**
	H	7,468	3,786	3,682
	M	3	1	2
	T	6	1	5
Kharpalta ...	H	**39**	**18**	**21**
Kharwar ...	H	**5,762**	**2,751**	**3,011**
Khati ...		**209,937**	**109,135**	**100,802**
Jangida Brahman		*1,053*	*479*	*574*
	H	205,618	106,684	98,934
	J	1	...	1
	M	1,863	991	872
	S	2,455	1,460	995
Khatik ...		**59,527**	**30,266**	**29,261**
	H	59,520	30,260	29,260
	M	7	6	1
Khattri ...		**14,290**	**7,712**	**6,578**
	H	13,714	7,371	6,343
	J	1	1	...
	M	4	4	...
	S	571	336	235
Khawaswal ...	H	**1,588**	**836**	**752**
Khedi ...	H	**1**	**1**	...
Kheldar ...	M	**34**	**18**	**16**
Khent ...	H	**709**	**368**	**341**
Kher ...	H	**467**	**277**	**190**
Kherwa ...	H	**413**	**312**	**101**
Khilji ...	M	**1**	...	**1**
Khoja ...	M	**1,071**	**543**	**528**
Khumra ...	M	**161**	**93**	**68**
Kilanot ...	H	**9**	**4**	**5**
Kir ...		**23,980**	**12,387**	**11,593**
	H	23,979	12,386	11,593
	M	1	1	...
Kirar ...	H	**15,697**	**8,028**	**7,669**
Koli ...		**90,910**	**46,735**	**44,175**
	H	90,625	46,593	44,032
	M	285	142	143
Koria ...		**11,304**	**5,991**	**5,313**
	H	11,303	5,990	5,313

TABLE XVII.—Race, Tribe or Caste.—Part I —Agency Summary.—*Continued.*

Caste.	Religion.	Population. Persons.	Males	Females.
1	2	3	4	5
Koria (*Ctd.*) ...	M	1	1	...
Kotwal ...	M	212	115	97
Kuchband ...	H	326	188	138
Kumhar ...		357,751	185,518	172,233
	C	1	...	1
	H	349,605	180,980	168,625
	J	5	2	3
	M	6,919	3,893	3,026
	S	1,221	643	578
Kumrawat ...	H	3,072	1,602	1,470
Kunbi ...		57,815	30,257	27,558
	C	4	3	1
	H	57,811	30,254	27,557
Kundigar ...	H	4	2	2
Kunjra ...		4,440	2,199	2,241
	H	13	9	4
	M	4,427	2,190	2,237
Labhana ...		8,904	4,477	4,427
	H	3,162	1,534	1,628
	M	5,742	2,943	2,799
Lakhera ...		12,985	6,785	6,200
	H	10,966	5,755	5,211
	M	2,019	1,030	989
Langah ...	M	151	91	60
Langhawa ...	M	29	13	16
Loda ...	H	9,057	4,841	4,216
Lodha ...		48,503	25,665	22,838
	H	48,482	25,655	22,827
	M	19	8	11
	S	2	2	...
Lohar ...		81,070	42,013	39,057
	H	67,391	35,063	32,328
	M	13,659	6,939	6,720
	S	20	11	9
Lok ...	H	1,023	510	513
Machhi ...	M	796	392	404
Madari ...		186	121	65
	H	1	1	...
	M	185	120	65
Madrasi Paraiyan ...	C	1	1	...
Maha Brahman ...	H	231	110	121
Mahajan Unspecified.		7,214	3,629	3,585
	H	6,097	3,042	3,055
	J	1,117	587	530
Mahar ...	H	5,362	2,526	2,836
Mahawat ...	M	561	327	234
Mahesri ...		81,819	41,736	40,083
	H	81,522	41,560	39,962
	J	297	176	121
Mahoba ...	M	58	...	58
Majvi ...	M	138	70	68
Makrani ...	M	1,320	659	661
Mali ...		369,173	192,611	176,562
Sainik Kshatriya ...		*57,927*	*30,228*	*27,699*
	H	366,338	191,070	175,268
	J	1	...	1
	M	2,692	1,458	1,234
	S	142	83	59
Malkana ...		39	24	15
	H	24	10	14
	M	15	14	1
Malkhani ...	M	6	6	...
Mallah ...		2,191	1,223	968
	H	2,173	1,216	957
	M	18	7	11
Mallik ...	M	31	24	7
Malzada ...	M	43	19	24
Manga ...	H	3	3	...
Manihar ...		7,082	3,675	3,407
	H	365	203	162
	M	6,716	3,471	3,245
	S	1	1	...
Marehta ...		547	316	231
	C	3	...	3
	H	544	316	228
Marwari ...	H	26	12	14
Mathuria ...	H	996	524	472
Mavan ...	H	1	...	1
Mawar ...		8,884	4,669	4,215
	H	8,880	4,666	4,214
	J	4	3	1
Meghwal ...	H	23,273	12,133	11,140
Mehra ...	H	115	60	55
Memar ...	H	7	7	...
Meo ...		167,530	89,810	77,720
	H	16	12	4
	M	167,514	89,798	77,716
Merat ...	M	3,084	1,671	1,413
Meratwal ...		641	326	315
	H	627	318	309
	J	2	1	1
	M	12	7	5
Metwal ...	H	955	469	486
Mina ...		607,369	321,211	286,158
	H	587,029	310,782	276,247
	M	4	3	1
	T	20,336	10,426	9,910
Mirasi ...		17,051	8,811	8,240
	H	1,568	825	743
	M	15,483	7,986	7,497
Mochi ...		13,246	6,878	6,368
	H	11,816	6,083	5,733
	M	1,420	785	635
	S	10	10	...
Modi ...		37	14	23
	H	31	14	17
	J	6	...	6
Moghal ...	M	11,650	6,079	5,571
Moghia ...		6,079	3,099	2,980
	H	5,945	3,046	2,899
	T	134	53	81
Mohammadi ...	M	8	5	3
Momia ...	M	94	86	8
Mor ...		602	281	321
	H	197	98	99
	M	405	183	222
Motisar ...	H	132	99	33
Mujawar ...	M	779	354	425
Mulla ...	M	1,780	978	802
Multani ...	M	182	82	100
Murid ...	M	223	94	129
Nadwania ...	H	65	38	27
Nagar ...	H	130	60	70
Nagda ...		4,030	2,008	2,022
	H	69	37	32
	J	3,961	1,971	1,990
Nagdara ...	J	647	337	310
Nagori ...	M	941	500	441
Nai ...		166,096	86,581	79,515
	H	156,993	81,759	75,234
	J	1	...	1
	M	8,894	4,691	4,203
	S	208	131	77
Naik ...		62,329	32,201	30,128
	H	62,116	32,094	30,022
	M	211	106	105
	S	1	...	1
	T	1	1	...
Namadgar ...	M	47	27	20
Nanakpanthi ...	S	31	9	22
Nanakshahi ...		559	440	119
	H	557	438	119
	M	2	2	...
Nao-Muslim ...	M	131	68	63
Narsinghpura ...		8,515	4,153	4,362
	H	25	12	13
	J	8,490	4,141	4,349
Nat ...		7,083	3,694	3,389
	H	6,416	3,331	3,085
	M	576	307	269
	T	91	56	35
Nena ...	J	2	2	...
Niaria ...		2,458	1,370	1,088
	H	11	6	5
	M	2,447	1,364	1,083
Nima ...	H	1,331	686	645
Odh ...		7,757	3,905	3,852
	H	7,512	3,774	3,738
	M	245	131	114
Oswal ...		197,460	94,687	102,773
	H	4,360	2,399	1,961
	J	193,100	92,288	100,812
Pahalwan ...	M	7	2	5
Paink ...	M	10	7	3
Pajawgir ...	M	446	230	216
Palliwal ...		4,362	2,198	2,164

TABLE XVII.—Race, Tribe or Caste.—Part I.—Agency Summary.—*Continued.*

Caste.	Religion.	Population. Persons.	Males.	Females.
1	2	3	4	5
Palliwal (*Contd.*) ...	H	1,151	535	616
	J	3,211	1,663	1,548
Pannigar ...	H	45	27	18
Parsi ...	Z	319	170	149
Pasi ...	H	43	28	15
Patel ...		55,867	28,346	27,521
	H	55,860	28,339	27,521
	T	7	7	...
Pathan ...		119,803	63,543	56,260
	H	4	3	1
	M	119,799	63,540	56,259
Pattidar ...	H	65	41	24
Patwa ...		2,850	1,438	1,412
	H	2,724	1,358	1,366
	J	39	28	11
	M	87	52	35
Payak ...	H	204	113	91
Phadali ...	M	427	214	213
Pinara ...		26,388	13,710	12,678
	H	7,949	4,279	3,670
	M	18,439	9,431	9,008
Pir ...	M	3	2	1
Pirzada ...	M	189	108	81
Pokhra ...	H	229	127	102
Porwal ...		29,359	13,274	16,085
	H	3,040	1,635	1,405
	J	26,319	11,639	14,680
Prabhu ...	H	2	2	...
Purabia ...	H	2,290	1,245	1,045
Purbi ...	H	458	242	216
Puria ...	H	47	28	19
Purohit ...	H	45,308	23,179	22,129
Qurreshi ...	M	699	362	337
Raigar ...		130,104	66,591	63,513
	H	130,103	66,591	63,512
	M	1	...	1
Rajakhera Rajput ...	H	4,717	2,765	1,952
Rajput ...		633,830	352,827	281,003
	H	633,827	352,826	281,001
	J	3	1	2
Rana ...		10,035	5,070	4,965
	H	8,535	4,376	4,159
	M	1,500	694	806
Randi ...		293	6	287
	H	125	5	120
	M	168	1	167
Randiwal ...	M	4	4	...
Randizada ...		12	12	...
	H	9	9	...
	M	3	3	...
Rangaswami ...	H	10	7	3
Ranghar ...		24,091	13,209	10,882
	H	12	9	3
	M	24,079	13,200	10,879
Rangrez ...		16,128	8,343	7,785
	H	293	136	157
	J	7	2	5
	M	15,826	8,208	7,623
	S	2	2	...
Rao ...		14,219	7,089	7,130
	H	14,188	7,076	7,112
	M	31	13	18
Rath ...	M	52,671	28,679	23,992
Rathi ...	H	1,472	812	660
Rawal ...	H	677	372	305
Rawala ...	H	5,716	3,818	1,898
Rawat ...	H	27,804	14,352	13,452
Rebari ...		135,820	69,430	66,390
	H	135,649	69,314	66,335
	M	171	116	55
Runiar ...	H	13	5	8
Rustagi ...	H	370	199	171
Sabugar ...		211	92	119
	H	4	3	1
	M	207	89	118
Sad ...		29,044	15,944	13,100
	H	29,039	15,944	13,095
	M	5	...	5
Sadhu ...		66,597	36,063	30,534
	H	65,753	35,661	30,092
	J	823	381	442
	S	20	20	...
	T	1	1	...

Caste.	Religion.	Population. Persons.	Males.	Females.
1	2	3	4	5
Sahar ...		19,696	10,024	9,672
	H	19,526	9,935	9,591
	T	170	89	81
Sailwal ...		285	161	124
	H	64	36	28
	J	221	125	96
Sain ...	M	3	2	1
Sais ...		107	97	10
	H	77	77	...
	M	30	20	10
Saiyed ...	M	33,409	17,787	15,622
Salotri ...	M	1	1	...
Salvi ...	H	262	130	132
Samija ...	M	186	87	99
Sangtarash ...	H	614	321	293
Sansi ...		7,148	3,848	3,300
	H	6,719	3,595	3,124
	M	1	...	1
	T	428	253	175
Saraogi ...		32,648	17,100	15,548
	H	214	134	80
	J	32,434	16,966	15,468
Sarbhangi ...	H	23	8	15
Sargara ...	H	31,300	15,392	15,908
Satia ...	H	1,113	567	546
Satsangi ...	H	381	180	201
Shandhan ...	M	1	...	1
Shehnaichi ...	M	2	2	...
Sheikh ...	M	210,499	111,773	98,726
Shishagar ...	M	34	16	18
Shorgar ...		587	316	271
	H	75	39	36
	M	512	277	235
Sijvi ...	H	2	2	...
Sikligar ...		2,083	1,029	1,054
	H	2,036	994	1,042
	M	35	29	6
	S	12	6	6
Silawat ...		13,776	6,715	7,061
	H	4,244	2,055	2,189
	M	9,532	4,660	4,872
Sindhi ...		43,588	23,164	20,424
	H	1	1	...
	M	43,587	23,163	20,424
Singiwala ...		227	143	84
	H	203	129	74
	M	24	14	10
Sipahi ...		1,431	774	657
	H	6	3	3
	M	1,425	771	654
Sirkiwala ...	M	43	28	15
Sirvi ...	H	53,611	27,749	25,862
Sompara ...	H	300	126	174
Sondhia ...	H	34,257	18,194	16,063
Sowan ...	H	1	1	...
Sufi ...	M	23	10	13
Sunar ...		73,455	38,082	35,373
	H	73,355	38,022	35,333
	J	3	2	1
	M	42	26	16
	S	55	32	23
Surwal ...	H	42	26	16
Swami ...		44,937	25,025	19,912
	H	44,933	25,023	19,910
	S	4	2	2*
Takara ...	H	16	7	9
Tamboli ...		6,104	3,182	2,922
	H	6,087	3,171	2,916
	M	17	11	6
Tank ...	H	9	5	4
Tanchra ...	H	12	5	7
Taragi ...	H	1,871	1,011	860
Tarkar ...	H	524	276	248
Tarkash ...	M	16	6	10
Tavayaf ...		535	106	429
	H	53	...	53
	M	482	106	376
Teli ...		80,015	41,822	38,193
	H	49,500	25,503	23,997
	J	20	2	18
	M	30,495	16,317	14,178
Thathera ...		2,856	1,458	1,398
	H	2,806	1,485	1,371

TABLE XVII.—Race, Tribe or Caste.—Part I.—Agency Summary.—*Concluded.*

Caste.	Religion.	Population.		
		Persons.	Males.	Females
1	2	3	4	5
Thathera (*Ctd.*) ...	M	50	23	27
Thori ...		**17,399**	**9,672**	**7,727**
	H	17,397	9,670	7,727
	M	2	2	...
Tikkiwal ...	H	**27**	**20**	**7**
Tirgar ...		**762**	**486**	**276**
	H	708	454	254
	M	54	32	22
Turk ...	M	**45**	**24**	**21**
Udasi ...	H	**16**	**15**	**1**
Usta ...	M	**374**	**181**	**193**
Vaid ...	H	**3,112**	**1,623**	**1,489**
Unspecified ...		**5,079**	**2,736**	**2,343**
	H	1,179	635	544
	J	35	17	18
	M	2,663	1,556	1,107
	S	1,194	522	672
	T	6	4	2
	B	1	1	...
	Not returned	1	1	...

TABLE XVII.—Race, Tribe or Caste.—Part II.—By States or District.

Locality and Caste.	POPULATION.	
	Males.	Females.
1	2	3
RAJPUTANA.	**5,885,028**	**5,340,684**
Abu ...	**2,753**	**1,779**
Agarwal ...	116	104
Bhangi ...	117	91
Bhil ...	486	414
Brahman ...	151	82
Koli ...	153	180
Lok ...	117	122
Mochi ...	127	81
Sargara ...	67	88
Sheikh ...	200	131
Others ...	1,219	586
Alwar ...	**396,261**	**353,490**
Agarwal ...	6,081	6,287
Ahir ...	88,820	82,460
Balai ...	2,629	2,470
Bhangi ...	5,305	5,189
Bhishti ...	4,171	3,751
Brahman ...	31,297	28,279
Bagara ...	*1,315*	*1,339*
Gaur & Adi Gaur.	*22,632*	*20,381*
Hariyana ...	*2,279*	*2,187*
Others ...	*5,071*	*4,372*
Chamar ...	40,669	38,887
Daroga ...	2,721	2,615
Fakir ...	9,558	8,868
Gujar ...	23,777	20,230
Jat ...	18,161	14,688
Jogi ...	4,089	3,831
Khandelwal ...	5,259	4,794
Khati ...	6,745	6,729
Jangida Brahman	*416*	*506*
Koli ...	5,515	5,291
Kumhar ...	8,668	8,103
Mali ...	15,618	14,068
Saini Kshatriya	*53*	*59*
Mawar ...	4,357	3,897
Meo ...	68,127	54,254
Mina ...	27,155	24,704
Nai ...	6,226	5,547
Pathan ...	2,856	2,567
Rajput ...	13,665	10,851
Sheikh ...	4,985	4,401
Others ...	44,207	40,734
Banswara ...	**111,983**	**113,123**
Balai ...	,1641	1,542
Bhil ...	72,238	72,687
Bhoi ...	1,125	1,158
Brahman ...	4,378	5,159
Audich ...	*1,578*	*1,967*
Bhojak ...	*425*	*450*
Bhatt ...	*503*	*559*
Gaur & Adi Gaur.	*330*	*464*
Trivedi Mewara	*576*	*741*
Others ...	*966*	*978*
Chamar ...	3,156	3,005
Daroga ...	982	1,139
Humar ...	1,667	1,592
Jogi ...	1,191	1,221
Kalal ...	1,255	1,286
Lohar ...	1,080	1,072
Patel ...	7,347	7,550
Rajput ...	1,999	1,819
Others ...	13,914	13,893
Bharatpur ...	**263,325**	**223,629**
Agarwal ...	8,508	7,467
Bhangi ...	3,449	2,949
Bhishti ...	2,366	1,967
Brahman ...	23,602	19,285
Bagara ...	*1,038*	*847*
Bharatpur (*Concld.*)		
Brahman (*Concld.*)		
Gaur & Adi Gaur.	*5,606*	*4,726*
Hawasi ...	*692*	*609*
Sanadhya ...	*14.800*	*11,725*
Others ...	*1,466*	*1,328*
Chamar ...	40,984	38,197
Dhakar ...	2,303	1.996
Fakir ...	5,196	4,527
Gadaria ...	2,528	2,150
Gujar ...	22,753	17,679
Jat ...	40,426	31,957
Kachhi ...	2,875	2,431
Khandelwal ...	2,539	2,145
Khati ...	3,745	3,234
Jangida Brahman	*60*	*64*
Koria ...	5,988	5,313
Kumhar ...	5,035	4,493
Mali ...	9,354	8,035
Meo ...	24,752	21,728
Mina ...	5,845	4,999
Nai ...	4,447	3,807
Rajput ...	5,206	4,329
Others ...	41,124	34,096
Bikaner ...	**501,153**	**435,065**
Agarwal ...	9,930	9,974
Bauria ...	4,905	4,418
Bhangi ...	8,212	6,875
Bishnoi ...	8,894	7,521
Brahman ...	41,683	40,052
Bhojak ...	*1,186*	*1,215*
Daima ...	*1,571*	*1,505*
Gaur & Adi Gaur.	*9,936*	*9,297*
Gujar Gaur ...	*2,676*	*2,806*
Khandelwal ...	*2,916*	*2,826*
Parikh ...	*7,220*	*7,799*
Pushkarna ...	*4,588*	*5,282*
Saraswat ...	*4,235*	*3,812*
Others ...	*7,005*	*6,010*
Chamar ...	40,378	35,196
Daroga ...	7,040	6,689
Dhanak ...	4,649	3,752
Jat ...	119,633	96,264
Kaimkhani ...	5,186	4,240
Khati ...	13,098	10,972
Jangida Brahman	*3*	*4*
Khattri ...	3,674	2,813
Kumhar ...	20,494	17,407
Mahesri ...	7,429	9,372
Mali ...	8,153	7,618
Meghwal ...	5,424	5,100
Nai ...	10,829	9,431
Naik ...	12,402	11,480
Oswal ...	11,957	15,611
Rajput ...	32,365	23,147
Rath ...	28,679	23,992
Sunar ...	6,157	5,563
Swami ...	6,118	6,691
Teli ...	3,802	3,237
Thori ...	5,573	4,125
Others ...	72,294	63,625
Bundi ...	**113,101**	**103,621**
Balai ...	3,549	5,326
Bhangi ...	946	1,110
Bhil ...	2,787	2,708
Brahman ...	8,430	8,234
Gaur & Adi Gaur.	*710*	*725*
Gujar Gaur ...	*2,992*	*2,688*
Sanadhya ...	*1,329*	*1,211*
Sanklwal ...	*456*	*567*
Others ...	*2,943*	*3,043*
Chamar ...	8,453	10,201
Daroga ...	1,498	1,521
Dhakar ...	3,593	3,340
Gujar ...	15,105	12,608
Bundi (*Concld.*)		
Jat ...	1,627	936
Khati ...	1,595	1,489
Kir ...	1,476	1,465
Kumhar ...	2,754	2,520
Mahesri ...	1,282	1,037
Mali ...	8,881	8,513
Mina ...	18,600	15,810
Nai ...	1,870	1,712
Pathan ...	1,818	1,387
Rajput ...	2,699	2,445
Sadhu ...	1,810	853
Teli ...	1,714	1,574
Others ...	23,114	19,387
Dholpur	**140,497**	**114,489**
Agarwal ...	4,454	3,499
Brahman ...	16,059	11,955
Sanadhya ...	*14,880*	*11,093*
Others ...	*1,179*	*862*
Chamar ...	22,597	19,808
Daroga ...	3,364	2,508
Dhobi ...	1,982	1,810
Gadaria ...	3,831	3,407
Gujar ...	12,488	8,269
Kachhi ...	14,210	12,307
Khati ...	2,411	1,874
Koli ...	4,162	3,685
Kumhar ...	1,936	1,653
Lodha ...	5,757	4,918
Mina ...	5,893	5,104
Nai ...	2,369	1,904
Pathan ...	2,442	2,166
Rajakhera Rajput	2,765	1,952
Rajput ...	11,749	9,084
Sheikh ...	3,234	2,867
Others ...	18,849	15,719
Dungarpur.	**114,480**	**113,064**
Balai ...	1,702	1,539
Banjara ...	1,285	1,302
Bhil ...	62,892	60,458
Brahman ...	5,798	7,235
Audich ...	*1,113*	*1,271*
Bhatt ...	*922*	*1,099*
Bhojak ...	*726*	*886*
Chaubisa ...	*504*	*622*
Gaur & Adi Gaur.	*897*	*1,243*
Trivedi Mewara	*969*	*1,388*
Others ...	*667*	*726*
Chamar ...	3,849	3,196
Daroga ...	1,372	1,668
Humar ...	1,842	1,508
Jogi ...	1,152	1,151
Kalal ...	1,259	1,323
Khati ...	1,055	1,007
Kumhar ...	1,187	1,168
Lohar ...	1,454	1,381
Patel ...	12,553	12,578
Rajput ...	5,088	4,836
Others ...	12,992	12,714
Jaipur. ...	**1,387,067**	**1,244,708**
Agarwal ...	45,623	45,651
Ahir ...	40,262	34,114
Balai ...	32,607	30,787
Bhangi ...	12,048	11,474
Brahman ...	142,951	135,007
Bagara ...	*7,076*	*6,695*
Baragaon ...	*2,029*	*1,901*
Gaur & Adi Gaur.	*61,952*	*57,886*
Gujar Gaur ...	*5,539*	*4,900*
Hariyana ...	*13,622*	*13,503*
Khandelwal ...	*12,281*	*12,343*
Parikh ...	*8,548*	*7,966*

TABLE XVII.—RACE, TRIBE OR CASTE.—PART II.—BY STATES OR DISTRICT.—*Continued.*

Locality and Caste.	POPULATION.	
	Males.	Females.
1	2	3
Jaipur (*Concld*).		
Brahman (*Concld.*)		
Sanadhya ...	*15,799*	*14,555*
Others ...	*16,105*	*15,258*
Chamar ...	120,697	113,745
Dadupanthi ...	5,305	116
Daroga ...	16,755	17,484
Dhanak ...	7,242	7,169
Dhobi ...	5,714	5,441
Gujar ...	104,216	88,826
Jat ...	170,306	148,303
Jogi ...	13,036	11,607
Kaimkhani ...	8,487	8,076
Khandelwal ...	15,247	13,113
Khati ...	27,091	25,684
Khatik ...	10,563	10,254
Koli ...	19,449	18,617
Kumhar ...	47,571	44,842
Mali ...	72,045	64,886
Mina ...	137,471	128,099
Nai ...	20,869	19,343
Naik ...	8,580	8,041
Pathan ...	17,466	15,612
Raigar ...	28,099	26,550
Rajput ...	65,816	47,573
Sadhu ...	6,149	4,851
Saiyed ...	5,684	4,828
Saraogi ...	10,451	9,901
Sheikh ...	47,237	48,163
Sunar ...	7,800	7,349
Swami ...	7,782	5,825
Others ...	106,508	99,574
Jaisalmer	**42,342**	**33,913**
Bhil ...	1,116	832
Bishnoi ...	1,946	1,700
Brahman ...	2,040	1,881
Pushkarna ...	*1,383*	*1,321*
Others ...	*657*	*510*
Daroga ...	1,228	1,143
Kumhar ...	770	764
Mahesri ...	1,276	1,121
Meghwal ...	4,036	3,299
Nai ...	582	456
Rajput ...	11,620	8,443
Ranghar ...	6,522	5,046
Sheikh ...	4,755	3,469
Others ...	6,451	5,604
Jhalawar ...	**56,518**	**51,372**
Balai ...	2,725	2,613
Bhil ...	1,650	1,600
Brahman ...	3,143	2,705
Gaur & Adi Gaur.	*1,058*	*537*
Gujar Gaur ...	*423*	*381*
Sanadhya ...	*354*	*273*
Others ...	*1,308*	*1,514*
Chamar ...	5,346	5,190
Dhakar ...	1,068	970
Gujar ...	2,574	2,238
Kumhar ...	1,248	1,099
Mali ...	1,079	1,042
Nai ...	1,049	954
Pathan ...	1,882	1,827
Rajput ...	1,879	1,692
Sondhia ...	14,520	12,659
Teli ...	1,147	1,000
Others ...	17,708	16,198
Karauli ...	**76,729**	**63,796**
Agarwal ...	4,077	3,383
Bhangi ...	692	613
Brahman ...	8,123	6,725
Chaturvedi ...	*678*	*478*

Locality and Caste.	POPULATION.	
	Males.	Females.
1	2	3
Karauli (*Concld.*)		
Brahman (*Concld*)		
Sanadhya ...	*6,659*	*5,401*
Others ...	*886*	*846*
Chamar ...	10,946	10,137
Fakir ...	560	477
Gujar ...	9,032	6,132
Jogi ...	960	781
Kachhi ...	5,396	4,428
Kahar ...	585	455
Khati ...	1,119	972
Koli ...	1,234	1,994
Kumhar ...	2,580	1,341
Mali ...	965	836
Mina ...	17,290	14,732
Nai ...	1,022	871
Pathan ...	987	811
Rajput ...	3,494	2,604
Sheikh ...	750	657
Others ...	6,967	5,847
Kishangarh ...	**44,494**	**41,250**
Balai ...	2,530	2,434
Brahman ...	3,120	2,883
Daima ...	*669*	*603*
Gaur & Adi Gaur.	*257*	*299*
Gujar Gaur ...	*380*	*276*
Khandelwal ...	*569*	*558*
Parikh ...	*366*	*342*
Others ...	*879*	*805*
Chamar ...	1,795	1,648
Daroga ...	1,183	1,164
Gujar ...	3,852	3,417
Jat ...	8,080	7,449
Kumhar ...	1,355	1,274
Mahesri ...	862	760
Mali ...	2,132	2,056
Oswal ...	859	757
Raigar ...	2,211	2,043
Rajput ...	2,059	1,852
Others ...	14,456	13,513
Kotah ...	**355,056**	**330,748**
Agarwal ...	3,348	2,921
Ahir ...	3,965	3,566
Bhangi ...	3,540	3,439
Bhil ...	12,406	11,669
Brahman ...	19,737	16,770
Daima ...	*695*	*662*
Gaur & Adi Gaur	*2,745*	*1,855*
Gujar Gaur ...	*5,088*	*4,369*
Gujrati ...	*697*	*673*
Sanadhya ...	*4,853*	*4,182*
Sankliwal ...	*648*	*560*
Shri Gaur ...	*729*	*739*
Others ...	*4,372*	*3,730*
Chamar ...	41,908	41,119
Dhakar ...	22,710	22,068
Dhobi ...	2,800	2,685
Gujar ...	22,740	19,617
Jat ...	2,941	2,357
Jogi ...	2,677	2,704
Julaha ...	3,349	3,221
Kachhi ...	4,447	4,327
Khati ...	4,454	4,054
Kirar ...	6,020	5,778
Koli ...	5,112	4,868
Kumhar ...	7,506	7,394
Loda ...	4,818	4,139
Lodha ...	13,023	12,059
Lohar ...	3,297	3,091
Mali ...	23,013	22,089
Mina ...	33,861	30,819
Nai ...	5,522	5,218
Pathan ...	7,043	6,442
Rajput ...	7,905	6,652

Locality and Caste.	POPULATION.	
	Males.	Females.
1	2	3
Kotah (*Concld.*)		
Rawat ...	3,337	3,269
Sadhu ...	4,068	3,477
Sahar ...	8,730	8,451
Sheikh ...	4,960	4,379
Teli ...	4,613	4,328
Others ...	60,971	57,828
Kushalgarh ...	**17,754**	**17,810**
Bhil ...	14,072	15,013
Brahman ...	236	229
Audich ...	*63*	*54*
Trivedi Mewara	*95*	*114*
Others ...	*78*	*61*
Labhana ...	285	355
Rajput ...	312	308
Others ...	1,049	1,905
Lawa ...	**1,445**	**1,345**
Brahman ...	47	34
Daima ...	*24*	*10*
Others ...	*23*	*24*
Chamar ...	144	142
Daroga ...	80	90
Gujar ...	144	114
Jat ...	223	216
Koli ...	70	69
Mali ...	104	116
Rajput ...	42	33
Others ...	501	532
Marwar ...	**1,109,912**	**1,016,070**
Balai ...	23,676	19,027
Bambhi ...	81,942	76,006
Bauria ...	12,179	12,337
Bhangi ...	7,952	7,157
Bhat ...	10,134	10,0[illegible]
Bhil ...	28,356	22,[illegible]
Bishnoi ...	25,[illegible]	23,[illegible]
Brahman ...	56,150	54,020
Audich ...	*1,551*	*1,749*
Bhojak ...	*2,802*	*3,[illegible]79*
Daima ...	*4,352*	*4,[illegible]*
Gaur & Adi Gaur.	*10,094*	*8,024*
Gujar Gaur ...	*2,737*	*3,434*
Khandelwal ...	*2,814*	*2,[illegible]72*
Palliwal ...	*1,947*	*1,759*
Parikh ...	*3,095*	*3,[illegible]*
Pushkarna ...	*9,344*	*7,[illegible]*
Sankhwal ...	*1,203*	*1,[illegible]80*
Saraswat ...	*1,478*	*1,013*
Srimali ...	*6,106*	*6,207*
Others ...	*7,757*	*8,429*
Charan ...	7,[illegible]	[illegible]
Daroga ...	2[illegible],[illegible]74	25,922
Darzi ...	[illegible]	7,746
Dholi ...	5,206	4,952
Gachha ...	7,183	7,[illegible]42
Gujar ...	11,845	9,545
Jat ...	151,744	132,1[illegible]
Khati ...	24,385	23,[illegible]05
Kumhar ...	45,871	41,976
Kunbi ...	19,280	17,346
Lohar ...	10,474	9,797
Mahesri ...	12,402	11,253
Mali ...	30,175	27,640
(*Sainik Kshatriya*)		
Mina ...	11,890	10,565
Nai ...	15,786	15,130
Oswal ...	45,435	51,361
Patel ...	7,664	7,351
Pathan ...	7,545	6,347
Porwal ...	5,557	7,710
Purohit ...	22,658	21,664
Raigar ...	16,285	15,999

TABLE XVII.—Race, Tribe or Caste.—Part II.—By States or District.—*Concluded.*

Locality and Caste.	POPULATION.	
	Males.	Females.
1	2	3
Marwar (*Concld.*)		
Rajput ...	104,518	83,356
Rebari ...	47,013	44,530
Sad ...	15,025	12,282
Sargara ...	10,489	11,109
Sheikh ...	23,537	20,844
Sindhi ...	22,370	19,748
Sirvi ...	27,350	25,569
Sunar ...	10,226	9,911
Swami ...	6,951	5,365
Others ...	106,960	97,143
Mewar ...	**807,184**	**759,726**
Balai ...	34,410	32,209
Bhil ...	110,148	106,135
Brahman ...	56,016	53,562
Audich ...	*1,743*	*1,950*
Chaubisa ...	*1,840*	*1,834*
Daima ...	*3,995*	*3,889*
Gaur & Adi Gaur.	*2,271*	*1,832*
Gujar Gaur ...	*9,918*	*9,440*
Khandelwal ...	*1,802*	*1,746*
Mewaria ...	*5,289*	*4,894*
Nagda ...	*3,233*	*3,130*
Palliwal ...	*7,497*	*7,240*
Parikh ...	*1,724*	*1,754*
Sanadhya ...	*1,779*	*1,811*
Sukhwal ...	*6,126*	*5,907*
Others ...	*8,829*	*8,135*
Chamar ...	24,845	24,590
Dangi ...	21,061	21,014
Daroga ...	18,745	19,474
Dhakar ...	14,639	11,111
Dholi ...	5,773	5,567
Gadaria ...	27,388	25,983
Grassia ...	4,324	3,854
Gujar ...	44,186	40,175
Jat ...	41,267	39,106
Jogi ...	6,231	5,621
Kalal ...	7,864	7,164
Khati ...	13,990	13,263
Khatik ...	7,209	7,131
Kumhar ...	25,560	24,365
Lohar ...	10,599	9,728
Mahesri ...	11,846	9,949
Mali ...	11,448	10,698
Mina ...	40,504	42,069
Nai ...	9,464	8,936
Oswal ...	25,218	23,097
Pathan ...	6 637	5,783
Raigar ...	13,521	12,456
Rajput ...	66,345	17,829
Rawat ...	7,411	6,552
Rebari ...	5,611	5,894
Sadhu ...	11,231	10,697
Sheikh ...	5.291	4,734
Mewar (*Concld.*)		
Teli ...	9,866	9,389
Others ...	108,307	101,122
Partabgarh	**38,991**	**37,548**
Anjna ...	506	509
Bhil ...	14,897	14,548
Brahman ...	1,683	1,531
Audich ...	*334*	*327*
Gaur & Adi Gaur.	*158*	*151*
Jodhpura ...	*224*	*194*
Mewaria ...	*325*	*294*
Others ...	*642*	*565*
Chamar ...	1,767	1,795
Daroga ...	959	1,009
Gadaria ...	853	825
Humar ...	992	982
Jogi ...	884	906
Kumhar ...	1,712	1,608
Kunbi ...	836	768
Oswal ...	661	689
Rajput ...	1,698	1,664
Others ...	11,548	10,714
Shahpura ...	**27,907**	**26,326**
Balai ...	815	776
Bhil ...	1,376	1,331
Brahman ...	1,985	1,782
Daima ...	*325*	*309*
Gujar Gaur ...	*574*	*527*
Parikh ...	*233*	*131*
Sanawar ...	*80*	*75*
Sukhwal ...	*253*	*277*
Others ...	*470*	*463*
Chamar ...	2,465	2,452
Daroga ...	756	815
Gadaria ...	768	778
Gujar ...	2,700	2,479
Jat ...	2,161	2,018
Kumhar ...	1,603	1,520
Mali ...	1,432	1,816
Mina ...	575	481
Raigar ...	938	898
Rajput ...	728	674
Others ...	9,655	9,016
Sirohi	**111,675**	**104,853**
Bhat ...	1,079	1,134
Bhil ...	9,994	8,952
Brahman ...	7,667	8,037
Gaurwal ...	*1,219*	*1,624*
Palliwal ...	*2,026*	*2,138*
Others ...	*4,422*	*4,275*
Sirohi (*Concld.*)		
Daroga ...	1,694	1,647
Dhed ...	10,203	9,478
Ghanchi ...	2,879	2,402
Grassia ...	8,249	7,755
Khati ...	1,770	1,542
Koli ...	3,379	3,059
Kumhar ...	6,434	5,967
Kunbi ...	4,556	4,171
Lohar ...	1,423	1,230
Mali ...	3,014	2,859
Mina ...	3,907	3,227
Nai ...	1,237	1,287
Oswal ...	3,533	4,630
Porwal ...	3,085	4,104
Rajput ...	8,150	6,918
Rebari ...	10,009	8,802
Sargara ...	3,491	3,237
Sheikh ...	1,453	1,125
Sunar ...	1,057	1,091
Others ...	13,412	12,059
Tonk ...	**164,401**	**152,959**
Agarwal ...	2,231	1,376
Ahir ...	5,041	4,592
Balai ...	1,919	1,790
Bhangi ...	1,636	2,560
Bhil ...	2,701	2,618
Brahman ...	7,794	7,267
Gaur & Adi Gaur.	*2,167*	*1,754*
Gujar Gaur ...	*1,093*	*1,065*
Sanadhya ...	*1,931*	*1,819*
Others ...	*2,603*	*2,629*
Chamar ...	20,603	19,520
Dangi ...	3,705	3,143
Dhakar ...	3,078	2,875
Gadaria ...	2,002	1,784
Gujar ...	8,926	7,850
Jat ...	5,514	5,024
Kachhi ...	3,755	3,520
Khati ...	2,918	2,478
Koli ...	2,802	2,830
Kumhar ...	3,377	3,309
Kunbi ...	2,702	2,398
Lodha ...	2,037	1,723
Mali ...	4,235	3,944
Mina ...	9,558	8,796
Nai ...	2,671	2,872
Pathan ...	9,257	8,533
Pinara ...	1,596	1,675
Raigar ...	1,660	1,604
Rajput ...	5,278	4,835
Sadhu ...	1,703	1,481
Saiyed ...	1,618	1,441
Sheikh ...	4,568	3,980
Sondhia ...	3,243	3,007
Teli ...	2,977	2,853
Others ...	33,296	31,780

TABLE XVIII.

Variation in Population of Selected Tribes.

EXPLANATORY NOTE.

The Tribes, selected for this Table, are those of a primitive or quasi-primitive origin. The figures for Rawats include those who, at previous Censuses, have been shown as Mers or Merat Gorats.

TABLE XVIII.—VARIATION IN POPULATION OF SELECTED TRIBES.

Tribe.	Persons.					Variation—(Increase+, Decrease−).				Net variation 1891 to 1931. Increase+ Decrease−.	Males.					Females.				
	1931.	1921.	1911.	1901.	1891.	1921 to 1931.	1911 to 1921.	1901 to 1911.	1891 to 1901.		1931.	1921.	1911.	1901.	1891.	1931.	1921.	1911.	1901.	1891.
1	2	3	4	5	6	7	8	9	10	11	12	13	14	15	16	17	18	19	20	21
Bhil ...	655,647	549,531	448,910	339,786	470,332	+106,116	+100,621	+109,124	−130,546	+185,315	332,625	281,066	229,266	175,116	243,081	323,022	268,465	219,644	164,670	227,251
Christian.	133	...	...	...		+ 133	...	...			65	...	...	...		68	...	...	...	
Hindu ...	457,509	103,589	63,004	9,245		+ 353,920	+ 40,585	+ 53,759			233,302	54,529	33,022	4,611		224,207	49,060	29,982	4,634	
Jain ...	...	1	...	...	470,332	− 1	+ 1	...	− 130,546	+185,315	...	1	...	...	243,081	...	...	...	...	227,251
Muslim ...	...	4	3	...		− 4	+ 1	+ 3			...	2	2	...		...	2	1	...	
Tribal ...	198,005	445,937	385,903	330,541		− 247,932	+ 60,084	+ 55,362			99,258	226,534	196,242	170,505		98,747	219,403	189,661	160,096	
Grassia ...	29,231	24,910	17,419	12,297	14,948	+ 4,321	+ 7,491	+ 5,122	− 2,651	+14,283	15,211	12,835	8,918	6,411	7,890	14,020	12,075	8,501	5,886	7,058
Hindu ...	20,973	24,877	16,268	5		− 3,904	+ 8,609	+ 16,263			10,827	12,814	8,331	1		10,146	12,063	7,937	4	
Muslim ...	...	22	...	...	14,948	− 22	+ 22	...	− 2,651	+ 14,283	...	10	...	...	7,890	...	12	...	...	7,058
Tribal ...	8,258	11	1,151	12,292		+ 8,247	− 1,140	− 11,141			4,384	11	587	6,410		3,874	...	564	5,882	
Merat ...	3,084	1,685	2,310	30	553	+ 1,399	− 625	+ 2,280	− 523	+ 2,531	1,671	920	1,296	16	294	1,413	765	1,014	14	259
Muslim ...	3,084	1,685	2,310	30	553	+ 1,399	− 625	+ 2,280	− 523	+ 2,531	1,671	920	1,296	16	294	1,413	765	1,014	14	259
Mina ...	607,369	515,241	558,689	477,129	536,422	+ 92,128	− 43,448	+ 81,560	− 59,293	+ 70,947	321,211	273,736	296,205	251,646	286,593	286,158	241,505	262,484	225,483	249,829
Hindu ...	587,029	483,674	512,506	461,093	536,422	+ 103,355	− 28,832	+ 51,413	− 75,329	+ 50,607	310,782	257,418	279,411	243,102	286,593	276,247	226,261	240,095	217,991	249,829
Muslim ...	4	90	139	1	...	− 86	− 49	+ 138	+ 1	+ 4	3	32	64	1	...	1	58	75	...	...
Tribal ...	20,336	31,477	46,044	16,035	...	− 11,141	− 14,567	+ 30,009	+ 16,035	+ 20,336	10,426	16,291	23,730	8,543	...	9,910	15,186	22,314	7,492	...
Rawat ...	27,804	26,722	27,417	12,544	8,934	+ 1,082	− 695	+ 14,873	+ 3,610	+ 18,870	14,352	14,558	14,708	6,440	4,734	13,452	12,164	12,709	6,104	4,200
Hindu ...	27,804	26,722	27,417	12,544	8,934	+ 1,082	− 695	+ 14,873	+ 3,610	+ 18,870	14,352	14,558	14,708	6,440	4,734	13,452	12,164	12,709	6,104	4,200

TABLE XIX.

European and Allied Races and Anglo-Indians by Race and Age.

EXPLANATORY NOTE.

This Table corresponds with Table XVI of 1921 and is divided into two Parts:—

Part A. Gives Statistics by Age and by State or District for all European and Allied Races.

Part B. Gives similar statistics for Anglo-Indians.

Europeans have been sub-divided into (i) British subjects and (ii) Others. Both the Parts show figures for Cities separately and these are included also in the State figures.

The States or Cities which do not contain any European or Anglo-Indian population have been omitted.

No Armenians were returned.

TABLE XIX.—European and Allied Races and Anglo-Indians by Race and Age.

Part A.—European and Allied Races.

Agency and State, District or City.	Total.			(A).—British Subjects.																		(B).—Others.																	
				All Ages.			0—13.		14—16.		17—23.		24—33.		34—43.		44—53.		54 and over.		All Ages.			0—13.		14—16.		17—23.		24—33.		34—43.		44—53.		54 and over.	
	Persons.	Males.	Females.	Persons.	Males.	Females.	Males.	Females.	Males.	Females.	Males.	Females.	Males.	Females.	Males.	Females.	Males.	Females.	Males.	Females.	Persons.	Males.	Females.	Males.	Females.	Males.	Females.	Males.	Females.	Males.	Females.	Males.	Females.	Males.	Females.	Males.	Females.
1	2	3	4	5	6	7	8	9	10	11	12	13	14	15	16	17	18	19	20	21	22	23	24	25	26	27	28	29	30	31	32	33	34	35	36	37	38
RAJPUTANA ...	*932*	*508*	*424*	*856*	*463*	*393*	*99*	*85*	*15*	*23*	*59*	*50*	*82*	*80*	*74*	*75*	*90*	*49*	*44*	*31*	*76*	*45*	*31*	*10*	*10*	*2*	*3*	*3*	*2*	*6*	*3*	*10*	*4*	*8*	*7*	*6*	*2*
Abu District ...	62	33	29	61	33	28	10	12	3	1	5	2	5	4	3	5	6	2	1	2	1	...	1	...	...	...	...	...	...	...	...	...	...	...	1	...	...
Alwar ...	20	12	8	19	11	8	2	1	...	1	1	...	6	5	...	...	2	1	...	...	1	1	...	...	...	...	...	1	...	...	...	...	...	...	...	...	...
Banswara ...	3	...	3	3	...	3	...	...	...	...	...	...	...	1	...	1	...	...	...	1	...	...	...	...	...	...	...	...	...	...	...	...	...	...	...	...	...
Bharatpur ...	28	12	16	28	12	16	2	4	...	...	2	1	1	3	5	4	2	2	...	2	...	...	...	...	...	...	...	...	...	...	...	...	...	...	...	...	...
Bikaner ...	33	17	16	31	16	15	...	2	1	...	...	1	2	4	3	1	7	5	3	2	2	1	1	...	...	...	...	...	...	...	...	1	1	...	...	...	...
Bundi ...	17	11	6	12	6	6	1	2	...	...	1	1	3	2	1	1	...	...	...	...	5	5	...	...	...	...	...	...	...	2	...	2	...	1	...	...	...
Dholpur ...	9	2	7	9	2	7	...	...	...	...	...	...	1	3	...	3	...	...	1	1	...	...	...	...	...	...	...	...	...	...	...	...	...	...	...	...	...
Jaipur ...	427	225	202	367	190	177	50	37	7	18	16	28	24	29	35	36	37	21	21	18	60	35	25	10	10	2	3	2	2	4	3	6	2	6	3	5	2
Jhalawar ...	3	2	1	3	2	1	...	...	...	...	...	...	...	...	...	...	...	...	2	1	...	...	...	...	...	...	...	...	...	...	...	...	...	...	...	...	...
Kotah ...	20	10	10	13	7	6	...	...	...	...	...	...	3	1	1	1	1	...	2	4	7	3	4	...	...	...	...	...	...	...	...	1	1	1	3	1	...
Marwar ...	103	54	49	103	54	49	11	9	...	3	6	7	11	13	12	9	8	6	6	2	...	...	...	...	...	...	...	...	...	...	...	...	...	...	...	...	...
Mewar ...	66	51	15	66	51	15	1	2	2	...	21	2	17	8	2	2	6	5	2	1	...	...	...	...	...	...	...	...	...	...	...	...	...	...	...	...	...
Partabgarh ...	1	1	...	1	1	...	...	...	...	...	...	...	...	...	...	...	1	...	...	...	...	...	...	...	...	...	...	...	...	...	...	...	...	...	...	...	...
Shahpura ...	1	...	1	1	...	1	...	...	...	...	...	...	...	...	...	...	...	1	...	...	...	...	...	...	...	...	...	...	...	...	...	...	...	...	...	...	...
Sirohi ...	126	72	54	126	72	54	19	14	2	5	7	7	9	10	11	11	19	5	5	2	...	...	...	...	...	...	...	...	...	...	...	...	...	...	...	...	...
Tonk ...	13	6	7	13	6	7	3	2	...	...	...	1	...	2	1	1	1	1	1	...	...	...	...	...	...	...	...	...	...	...	...	...	...	...	...	...	...
CITIES ...	*274*	*129*	*145*	*263*	*120*	*143*	*20*	*20*	*2*	*6*	*10*	*15*	*20*	*39*	*25*	*22*	*21*	*25*	*22*	*16*	*11*	*9*	*2*	*2*	...	...	...	*1*	...	*2*	...	*1*	*1*	...	*1*	*3*	...
Alwar ...	17	10	7	16	9	7	2	1	...	1	1	...	5	4	...	...	1	1	...	...	1	1	...	...	...	...	...	1	...	...	...	...	...	...	...	...	...
Bharatpur ...	23	9	14	23	9	14	2	4	...	...	1	1	1	2	5	3	...	2	...	2	...	...	...	...	...	...	...	...	...	...	...	...	...	...	...	...	...
Bikaner ...	31	16	15	29	15	14	...	2	1	...	...	1	1	3	3	1	7	5	3	2	2	1	1	...	...	...	...	...	...	...	...	1	1	...	...	...	...
Dholpur ...	9	2	7	9	2	7	...	...	...	...	...	...	1	3	...	3	...	...	1	1	...	...	...	...	...	...	...	...	...	...	...	...	...	...	...	...	...
Jaipur ...	75	36	39	67	29	38	3	3	...	2	2	4	4	10	8	6	3	8	9	5	8	7	1	2	...	...	...	...	...	2	...	...	...	...	1	3	...
Jodhpur ...	86	44	42	86	44	42	10	6	...	3	5	6	8	13	8	7	8	5	5	2	...	...	...	...	...	...	...	...	...	...	...	...	...	...	...	...	...
Kotah ...	4	1	3	4	1	3	...	...	...	...	...	...	...	...	...	...	...	...	1	3	...	...	...	...	...	...	...	...	...	...	...	...	...	...	...	...	...
Tonk ...	13	6	7	13	6	7	3	2	...	...	...	1	...	2	1	1	1	1	1	...	...	...	...	...	...	...	...	...	...	...	...	...	...	...	...	...	...
Udaipur ...	16	5	11	16	5	11	...	2	1	...	1	2	...	2	...	1	1	3	2	1	...	...	...	...	...	...	...	...	...	...	...	...	...	...	...	...	...

TABLE XIX.—European and Allied Races and Anglo-Indians by Race and Age.—Part B.—Anglo-Indians.

Agency and State, District or City.	All Ages.			0—3.		4—6.		7—13.		14—16.		17—19.		20—29.		30—39.		40—49.		50—59.		60—69.		70 & Over.	
	Persons.	Males.	Females.	Males.	Females.	Males.	Females.	Males.	Females.	Males.	Females.	Males.	Females.	Males.	Females.	Males.	Females.	Males.	Females.	Males.	Females.	Males.	Females.	Males.	Females.
1	2	3	4	5	6	7	8	9	10	11	12	13	14	15	16	17	18	19	20	21	22	23	24	25	26
RAJPUTANA ...	*828*	*452*	*376*	*53*	*53*	*40*	*32*	*76*	*62*	*20*	*19*	*34*	*36*	*71*	*49*	*75*	*66*	*54*	*32*	*18*	*10*	*9*	*11*	*2*	*6*
Abu District ...	18	10	8	1	1	1	1	1	1	1	...	2	1	1	1	...	1	2	1	1	1	...	...	...	...
Alwar ...	4	4	...	...	...	...	...	...	...	...	...	...	...	...	...	2	...	1	...	1	...	...	...	...	...
Bharatpur ...	6	4	2	2	...	1	...	...	...	...	...	...	1	...	1	1	...	...	...	...	...	...	...	...	...
Bikaner ...	12	4	8	...	1	...	1	1	...	...	1	...	1	1	3	1	1	...	...	1	...	...	...	...	...
Dholpur ...	5	1	4	...	...	...	...	...	1	...	...	...	...	...	...	1	1	...	...	...	1	...	1	...	...
Jaipur ...	436	233	203	29	27	22	16	43	34	9	9	18	23	37	23	37	40	25	19	8	5	4	4	1	8
Kishangarh ...	8	6	2	...	...	1	...	2	...	...	...	1	...	...	...	2	1	...	...	...	...	...	1	...	...
Kotah ...	24	12	12	1	1	1	1	2	2	1	1	...	...	...	...	4	4	2	1	...	...	...	1	1	1
Marwar ...	80	52	28	2	3	1	2	8	6	2	2	5	2	12	3	9	3	7	2	4	3	2	...	...	2
Mewar ...	8	7	1	...	...	1	...	...	...	...	...	1	...	1	...	1	..	1	1	1	...	1	...	...	...
Sirohi ...	202	97	105	16	20	8	11	17	18	6	6	6	8	14	16	16	14	12	8	...	...	2	4	...	...
Tonk ...	25	22	3	2	...	4	...	2	...	1	...	1	...	5	2	1	1	4	...	2	...	...	...	...	...
CITIES ...	*127*	*87*	*40*	*6*	*4*	*6*	*3*	*10*	*4*	*2*	*3*	*7*	*3*	*18*	*7*	*15*	*5*	*11*	*3*	*7*	*4*	*3*	*2*	*2*	*2*
Alwar ...	4	4	...	...	...	...	...	...	...	...	...	...	...	...	...	2	...	1	...	1	...	...	...	...	...
Bharatpur ...	5	3	2	2	...	1	...	...	...	...	...	...	1	...	1	...	...	...	...	...	...	...	...	...	...
Bikaner ...	12	4	8	...	1	...	1	1	...	...	1	...	1	1	3	1	1	...	...	1	...	...	...	...	...
Dholpur ...	5	1	4	...	...	...	...	...	1	...	...	...	...	...	...	1	1	...	...	...	1	...	1	...	...
Jaipur ...	4	4	...	...	...	...	...	...	...	...	...	...	...	1	...	2	...	...	...	...	...	...	...	1	...
Jodhpur ...	67	45	22	2	3	1	2	7	3	2	2	5	1	11	1	7	3	6	2	2	3	2	...	...	2
Kotah ...	3	2	1	...	...	...	...	...	...	...	...	...	...	...	...	1	...	...	...	...	...	...	1	1	...
Tonk ...	19	17	2	2	...	3	...	2	...	...	...	1	...	4	2	...	...	3	...	2	...	...	...	...	...
Udaipur ...	8	7	1	...	...	1	...	...	...	...	...	1	...	1	...	1	...	1	1	1	...	1	...	...	...

PROVINCIAL TABLE I.

Area, Houses and Population of Administrative Units.

EXPLANATORY NOTE.

The Provincial Tables in this volume give statistics for the Administrative Units in the States and the District of Abu, e. g. for Tehsils, Nizamats, Parganas, towns or whatever the local unit may be called.

This Table shows for each unit its area, number of towns, villages and houses, population of 1931, density of population per square mile, population of 1921 and percentage of variations for 1911-21 and 1921-31.

The Capitals of States have been printed first in each case.

Many of the units have been completely changed since 1921 and adjustments have been made where possible in columns 9 to 11.

The difference in the area of Alwar, Bharatpur and Jaipur when compared with Imperial Table I, is due to the fact that the figures shown in this Table are based on the Revenue records of the States and those in Imperial Table I on the Imperial Survey of India.

The figures for Mewar and Marwar do not include the population of 115 inhabited villages which are situated in Ajmer-Merwara and administered by the British Government but which belong to these States. Their details are shown below:—

Serial No	Name of State.	Area in Sq. miles.	No. of inhabited villages.	No. of Occupied houses.	Population.		
					Males.	Females.	Total.
1	2	3	4	5	6	7	8
1	Mewar villages ...	221	93	9,852	23,092	21,371	44,463
2	Marwar villages ...	50	22	1,951	4,598	4,248	8,846
	Total. ...	271	115	11,803	27,690	25,619	53,309

PROVINCIAL TABLE I.—AREA, HOUSES AND POPULATION OF ADMINISTRATIVE UNITS.

State or District and Administrative Unit (Pargana, Tehsil, Town, etc.).	Approximate area in square miles.	Inhabited towns.	Inhabited villages.	Occupied houses.	POPULATION. 1931. Persons.	1931. Males.	1931. Females.	1921. Both Sexes.	PERCENTAGE OF VARIATION. 1921-31.	1911-21.	Number of persons per square mile in 1931.
1	2	3	4	5	6	7	8	9	10	11	12
RAJPUTANA ...	*130,215*	*145*	*33,688*	*2,392,110*	*11,225,712*	*5,885,028*	*5,340,684*	*9,831,755*	+ *14·2*	– *6·5*	*87*
Abu District ...	*6*	*1*	*4*	*1,186*	*4,532*	*2,753*	*1,779*	*3,606*	+ *25·7*	– *16·0*	*756*
Alwar State ...	*3,217*	*7*	*1,758*	*154,310*	*749,751*	*396,261*	*353,490*	*701,154*	+ *6·9*	– *11·4*	*234*
Alwar City ...	4·39	1	...	9,491	**47,900**	25,584	22,316	44,760	+ 7·01	+ 8·4	10,912
Alwar ...	348·11	1	100	9,423	**43,705**	23,020	20,685	40,708	+ 7·8	Figures of 1911 population of the units are not available.	126
Ajeraka ...	104	...	66	6,146	**29,920**	15,745	14,175	29,760	+ ·5		288
Bahror ...	152	1	85	9,352	**47,099**	24,509	22,590	42,804	+ 10·08		310
Bansur ...	209	...	87	8,575	**41,278**	22,069	19,209	38,799	+ 6·3		198
Govindgarh ...	93	1	82	6,240	**28,176**	14,745	13,431	23,708	+ 18·9		303
Katumbar ...	179	...	112	10,114	**49,668**	26,784	22,884	44,018	+ 12·8		278
Khairthal ...	109	...	63	6,618	**31,374**	16,486	14,888	29,330	+ 7·0		288
Kishangarh ...	112	...	95	6,831	**31,083**	16,797	14,286	29,146	+ 6·6		278
Lachmangarh ...	214	...	143	9,714	**49,472**	26,049	23,423	45,898	+ 7·8		232
Malakhera ...	146	...	97	7,234	**35,011**	18,597	16,414	33,346	+ 4·9		240
Mandhan ...	91	...	55	5,348	**26,692**	13,526	13,166	24,146	+ 10·5		294
Mandawar ...	105	...	66	6,320	**31,079**	16,708	14,371	29,456	+ 5·5		296
Narayanpur ...	103	...	51	4,904	**24,485**	12,704	11,781	22,083	+ 10·9		238
Partabgarh ...	205	...	74	4,016	**17,661**	9,190	8,471	19,735	– 10·5		87
Rajgarh ...	149	1	79	7,321	**34,467**	17,774	16,693	32,504	+ 6·04		232
Ramgarh ...	123	1	85	6,881	**33,036**	17,725	15,311	34,519	– 4·3		269
Reni ...	213	...	89	6,843	**33,817**	17,585	16,232	28,564	+ 18·4		159
Thana Ghazi ...	74	...	56	5,077	**23,541**	12,304	11,237	22,069	+ 6·7		319
Tijara ...	149	1	99	7,563	**39,620**	21,112	18,508	37,089	+ 6·9		266
Tapukrah ...	105	...	94	5,142	**27,058**	14,603	12,455	24,328	+ 11·2		258
Circles ...	204·50	...	62	3,515	**15,594**	8,452	7,142	16,059	– 2·9		78
Nimrana Estate ...	25	...	18	1,642	**8,015**	4,193	3,822	8,385	– 4·4	– 4·0	321
Banswara State ...	*1,606*	*1*	*1,096*	*45,179*	*225,106*	*111,983*	*113,123*	*190,362*	+ *18·3*	+ *15·0*	*141*
Banswara Town ...	8	1	...	2,165	**10,444**	5,141	5,303	8,588	+ 21·6	+ 12·04	1,305
Khalsa Villages ...	625	...	350	17,994	**87,607**	43,477	44,130	81,377	+ 7·7	+ 15·4	140
Jagir and Other Villages	973	...	746	25,020	**127,055**	63,365	63,690	100,397	+ 26·5	+ 15·0	131
Bharatpur State ...	*1,972*	*7*	*1,316*	*104,246*	*486,954*	*263,325*	*223,629*	*496,437*	– *1·9*	– *11·2*	*247*
Bharatpur City ...	10	1	...	5,834	**30,173**	16,736	13,437	33,495	– 9·9	– 1·2	3,017
Bharatpur ...	186	...	166	8,190	**36,473**	19,754	16,719	39,547	– 7·8	– 12·0	196
Bayana ...	310	1	156	12,785	**57,714**	31,605	26,109	59,405	– 2·9	– 12·5	187
Dig ...	193	1	103	9,392	**47,658**	25,833	21,825	49,744	– 4·2	– 9·8	247
Kaman ...	137	1	108	7,858	**37,524**	20,076	17,448	37,405	+ ·3	– 6·9	274
Kumher ...	186	1	108	8,315	**40,370**	21,918	18,452	40,758	– 1·1	– 11·3	216
Nadbai ...	173	...	110	9,598	**43,265**	23,154	20,111	43,422	– ·4	– 13·6	250
Nagar ...	181	...	163	9,914	**47,086**	25,108	21,978	43,233	+ 8·9	– 14·1	261
Pahari ...	146	...	124	8,595	**36,355**	19,332	17,023	35,531	+ 2·3	– 15·4	249
Rupbas ...	213	...	93	7,473	**34,089**	18,732	15,357	36,673	– 7·0	– 18·4	224
Uchain ...		...	45	3,231	**14,452**	7,910	6,542	15,622	– 7·5	– 19·8	
Weir ...	237	2	140	13,061	**61,795**	33,167	28,628	61,602	+ ·3	– 7·2	261
Bikaner State ...	*23,317*	*15*	*2,742*	*185,418*	*936,218*	*501,153*	*435,065*	*659,685*	+ *41·9*	– *5·9*	*41*
Bikaner City ...	81	1	...	17,589	**85,927**	45,832	40,095	69,410	+ 28·8	+ 24·3	2,772
Bikaner Nisamat.											
Bikaner ...	4,475	...	198	11,699	**53,807**	28,057	25,750	45,822	+ 17·4	– 13·6	12
Lunkaransar ...	3,115	...	145	6,221	**28,684**	15,282	13,402	26,136	+ 9·7	– 17·2	10
Surpura ...	2,185	...	166	12,227	**56,992**	29,825	27,167	48,881	+ 16·6	– 11·7	26
Ganganagar Nisamat.											
Ganganagar ...	715	1	215	11,664	**62,448**	35,788	26,660	12,359	+ 405·3	Not available.	88
Karanpur ...	817	...	168	6,274	**30,525**	17,367	13,158	3,522	+ 766·7		97
Padampur ...	256	...	150	3,667	**18,832**	10,933	7,899	3,359	+ 460·6		74
Raisingnagar ...	516	...	150	2,961	**14,571**	8,458	6,113	3,613	+ 303·8		29

PROVINCIAL TABLE I.—AREA, HOUSES AND POPULATION OF ADMINISTRATIVE UNITS.—*Contd.*

State or District and Administrative Unit (Pargana, Tehsil, Town, etc.).	Approximate area in square miles.	Inhabited towns	Inhabited villages.	Occupied houses.	POPULATION. 1931. Persons.	1931. Males.	1931. Females	1921. Both Sexes.	PERCENTAGE OF VARIATION. 1921-31.	1911-21.	Number of persons per square mile in 1931.
1	2	3	4	5	6	7	8	9	10	11	12
Bikaner State (*Concld.*)											
Reni Nizamat											
Bhadra ...	678	1	106	8,779	**45,289**	24,364	20,925	37,220	+ 21·7	+ 1·8	67
Churu ...	683	1	93	9,969	**55,528**	28,902	26,626	45,167	+ 22·9	+ ·5	82
Nohar ...	1,505	1	150	11,164	**56,664**	30,535	26,129	39,377	+ 42 09	− 18·0	38
Rajgarh ...	1,000	1	183	10,422	**58,805**	31,466	27,339	47,847	+ 22·9	+ 8·8	59
Reni ...	781	1	95	5,749	**30,083**	15,743	14,340	26,208	+ 14·8	+ 34 7	39
Sujangarh Nizamat											
Dungargarh ...	463	1	90	8,008	**37,549**	19,482	18,067	32,155	+ 16·8	− 1·4	81
Ratangarh ...	396	2	90	10,240	**53,733**	27,595	26,138	44,593	+ 20·5	− 1 7	136
Sardarshahr ...	1,860	1	165	11,060	**56,778**	29,194	27,584	45,242	+ 25 5	− 8·9	31
Sujangarh ...	1,070	2	155	14,522	**72,896**	37,538	35,358	57,631	+ 26 5	− 8.6	69
Suratgarh Nizamat											
Anupgarh ...	1,378	...	148	3,745	**18,883**	10,818	8,065	6,104	+ 209·3	− 49 2	14
Hanumangarh ...	1,087	1	154	12,735	**65,272**	35,749	29,523	43,448	+ 50·2	− 13 4	61
Suratgarh ...	806	1	121	6,623	**32,952**	18,225	14,727	21,091	+ 56·2	− 24·7	41
Bundi State ...	***2,220***	***4***	***809***	***48,335***	***216,722***	***113,101***	***103,621***	***187,068***	+ ***15·9***	− ***14·5***	***98***
Bundi City ...	10	1	...	3,635	**17,991**	9,179	8,812	16,105	+ 11 7	− 17·8	1,799
Baroondhan ...	602	...	198	8,509	**37,088**	19,472	17,616	30,008	+ 23 6	− 13·4	62
Dei ...	429	...	176	9,190	**40,720**	21,381	19,339	35,205	+ 15·7	− 20 3	95
Gaindoli ...	343	1	127	8,397	**37,430**	19,618	17,812	30,903	+ 21·1	− 10·7	109
Hindoli ...	547	...	194	10,220	**45,968**	24,042	21,926	42,124	+ 9 1	− 7·00	84
Patan ...	195	1	82	6,362	**28,658**	14,845	13,813	24,630	+ 16·4	− 20·1	147
Nainwa Kila ...	9	1	...	1,096	**4,726**	2,344	2,382	3,996	+ 18·3	− 19·4	525
Talwas ...	85	...	32	926	**4,141**	2,220	1,921	4,097	+ 1·1	− 11·6	49
Dholpur State ...	***1,221***	***3***	***525***	***54,905***	***254,986***	***140,497***	***114,489***	***230,188***	+ ***10·8***	− ***12·7***	***209***
Dholpur City ..	5	1	...	4,276	**19,586**	10,535	9,051	16,206	+ 20·8	− 18 7	3,917
Bari ...	287	1	110	10,284	**46,550**	25,630	20,920	44,038	+ 5·7	− 15·8	162
Baseri ...	216	...	85	9,554	**41,906**	23,164	18,742	39,801	+ 5·3	− 8·4	194
Gird ...	242	...	148	10,529	**51,004**	28,144	22,860	43,558	+ 17·1	− 13 0	211
Kolari ...	125	...	75	9,037	**43,544**	23,793	19,751	39,858	+ 9·2	− 12·3	348
Rajakhera ...	155	1	75	7,343	**36,808**	20,480	16,328	32,427	+ 13·5	− 11·6	237
Sir Muthra ...	191	...	32	3,882	**15,588**	8,751	6,837	14,300	+ 9·0	− 9 3	82
Dungarpur State ...	***1,447***	***3***	***749***	***46,822***	***227,544***	***114,480***	***113,064***	***189,272***	+ ***20·2***	+ ***18·9***	***158***
Dungarpur Town ...	·4	1	...	1,966	**8,560**	4,418	4,142	7,327	+ 16·8	+ 13·2	21,400
Bara ...	466·6	...	216	10,213	**54,336**	27,396	26,940				117
Chhiasat ...	159	1	88	8,847	**37,765**	18,507	19,258				238
Chorasi ...	508	1	285	13,661	**69,752**	35,189	34,563	181,945	+ 20·3	+ 19·1	188
Tarpod ...	318	...	160	12,635	**57,131**	28,970	28,161				179
Jaipur State ...	***16,682***	***38½***	***5,873***	***566,662***	***2,631,775***	***1,387,067***	***1,244,708***	***2,338,802***	+ ***12·5***	− ***11·3***	***158***
Jaipur City ...	3	1	...	23,774	**144,179**	77,933	66,246	120,207	+ 19 9	− 12·3	48,060
Amber ...	1,191	4	493	45,864	**201,825**	105,126	96,699	183,535	+ 10·0	+ 35·8	170
Dausa ...	1,164	3	736	63,451	**258,546**	135,188	123,358	240,126	+ 7·7	− 25·5	223
Gangapur ...	673	2	241	24,893	**106,748**	56,369	50,379	93,221	+ 14·5	+ 29·3	159
Hindaun ...	735	2	385	38,067	**167,805**	89,986	77,819	152,794	+ 9·8	− 17 5	230
Kotkasim ...	68	...	55	3,584	**16,789**	9,003	7,786	16,281	+ 3·1	− 10 9	247
Malpura ...	1,684	3	373	31,384	**146,806**	77,067	69,739	127,153	+ 15·4	− 6·1	88
Sambhar ...	1,860	1½	448	41,428	**189,662**	99,245	90,417	173,046	+ 9·6	− 22·2	102
Sawai Jaipur ...	1,389	1	810	43,488	**196,663**	104,022	92,641	174,603	+ 12·6	− 63 9	142
Sawai Madhopur ...	2,096	1	571	43,352	**188,895**	99,302	89,593	169,056	+ 11·7	− 18·1	91
Shekhawati ...	8,615	7	439	63,570	**317,870**	170,088	147,782	277,415	+ 14·6	− 4·4	88
Torawati ...	2,204	5	437	63,165	**287,509**	150,411	137,098	260,619	+ 10·3	+ 6·2	131
Khetri Thikana ...		3	292	29,135	**148,606**	77,644	70,962	128,377	+ 15 7	− 4·2	...
Sikar Thikana ...	*	4	433	43,778	**223,509**	116,707	106,802	190,988	+ 17·02	− 4·7	...
Uniara Thikana ...		1	160	7,929	**36,363**	18,976	17,387	31,381	+ 15·9	− 6·9	...

*Area is included in the Nizamats of Shekhawati, Torawati, Malpura and Sawai Madhopur.

PROVINCIAL TABLE I.—Area, Houses and Population of Administrative Units.—*Contd.*

State or District and Administrative Unit (Pargana, Tehsil, Town, etc.).	Approximate area in square miles.	Inhabited towns.	Inhabited villages.	Occupied houses.	POPULATION. 1931. Persons.	Males.	Females.	1921. Both Sexes.	PERCENTAGE OF VARIATION. 1921-31.	1911-21.	Number of persons per square mile in 1931.
1	2	3	4	5	6	7	8	9	10	11	12
Jaisalmer State ...	*16,062*	*1*	*496*	*18,337*	*76,255*	*42,342*	*33,913*	*67,652*	+ *12·7*	− *23·4*	*5*
Jaisalmer Town ...	1	1	...	1,779	**7,120**	3,706	3,414	4,835	+ 47·3	− 34·8	7,120
Bap ...	680	...	24	1,672	**6,669**	3,693	2,976	6,134	+ 8·7	− 28·6	10
Buili ...	700	...	9	356	**1,572**	885	687	1,065	+ 47·6	− 7·9	3
Devikot ...	660	...	26	888	**3,859**	2,174	1,685	4,492	− 14·1	− 20·7	7
Dewa ...	430	...	17	479	**1,872**	1,026	846	1,797	+ 4·2	− 17·8	5
Fatehgarh ...	700	...	39	1,117	**4,767**	2,578	2,189	5,081	− 6·2	− 18·8	7
Jaisalmer ...	1,089	...	51	1,148	**4,484**	2,492	1,992	4,181	+ 7·2	− 17·2	5
Khuiala ...	1,000	...	19	849	**3,640**	2,115	1,525	1,815	+ 100·5	− 40·8	4
Kishangarh ...	400	...	2	200	**851**	515	336	298	+ 190·4	− 66·5	3
Lakha ...	262	...	17	777	**3,558**	2,078	1,480	3,323	+ 7·1	− 21·3	14
Lathi-Nachna ...	1,940	...	35	1,513	**6,409**	3,436	2,973	6,418	...	− 23·4	4
Myajlar ...	800	...	11	590	**2,429**	1,422	1,007	2,122	+ 14·5	− 16·6	4
Nokh ...	2,000	...	69	2,977	**12,935**	7,276	5,659	12,272	+ 5·4	− 26·5	7
Ramgarh ...	400	...	10	596	**2,551**	1,441	1,110	2,041	+ 25·00	− 18·00	7
Sam-Khabha ...	1,700	...	45	1,487	**6,090**	3,378	2,712	5,151	+ 18·2	− 2·2	4
Shahgarh-Ghotru ...	1,600	...	99	809	**3,220**	1,768	1,452	2,594	+ 24·1	− 26·9	3
Sri Mohangarh ...	1,400	...	22	942	**3,526**	1,947	1,579	3,501	+ ·7	− 23·8	3
Tanot ...	800	...	1	158	**703**	412	291	537	+ 30·9	+ 17·8	3
Jhalawar State ...	*810*	*2*	*432*	*23,580*	*107,890*	*56,518*	*51,372*	*96,182*	+ *12·2*	− *·1*	*134*
Jhalrapatan (Chhaoni)	·9	1	...	2,154	**10,442**	5,258	5,184	9,985	+ 4·6	− 13·0	11,602
Awar ...	80	...	44	2,352	**10,848**	5,795	5,053	10,205	+ 6·3	+ 4·8	135
Dag ...	168	...	69	4,276	**19,223**	10,077	9,146	17,575	+ 9·4	− 3·1	114
Gangdhar ...	187	...	112	5,229	**23,965**	12,577	11,388	21,676	+ 10·6	− 2·2	128
Pachpahar ...	204	...	101	5,207	**23,555**	12,564	10,991	19,647	+ 19·9	+ 21·9	115
Patan ...	170·1	1	106	4,362	**19,857**	10,247	9,610	17,094	+ 16·2	− 8·3	117
Karauli State ...	*1,242*	*3*	*374*	*30,938*	*140,525*	*76,729*	*63,796*	*133,730*	+ *5·1*	− *8·8*	*114*
Karauli Town ...	3	1	...	3,800	**19,671**	10,835	8,836	19,579	+ 0·5	− 1·1	6,557
Hazur ...	259	...	101	8,586	**37,089**	20,669	16,420	35,482	+ 4·5	− 18·4	143
Machilpur ...	228	...	81	4,873	**20,656**	11,738	8,918	19,361	+ 6·7	− 4·3	93
Mandrail ...	231	1	52	4,008	**17,331**	9,200	8,131	15,305	+ 13·2	− 17·0	75
Sapotra ...	217	1	82	2,083	**36,730**	19,283	17,447	35,581	+ 3·2	+ 8·7	169
Utgir ...	309	...	58	8,088	**9,048**	5,004	4,044	8,422	+ 7·4	− 29·4	29
Kishangarh State ...	*858*	*3*	*229*	*18,352*	*85,744*	*44,494*	*41,250*	*77,734*	+ *10·3*	− *10·8*	*100*
Kishangarh Town ...	2	1	...	2,374	**11,929**	6,394	5,535	9,452	+ 26·2	− 9·3	5,964
Arain ...	244	...	55	3,608	**16,085**	8,266	7,819	16,391	− 1·9	− 11·9	66
Kishangarh ...	258	...	66	3,904	**18,184**	9,320	8,864	16,768	+ 8·4	− 12·4	70
Rupnagar ...	194	1	47	4,115	**19,191**	10,177	9,014	16,778	+ 14·4	− 15·1	99
Sarwar ...	160	1	61	4,351	**20,355**	10,337	10,018	18,345	+ 10·9	− 4·7	128
Kotah State ...	*5,684*	*4*	*2,525*	*153,688*	*685,804*	*355,056*	*330,748*	*630,060*	+ *8·8*	− *1·4*	*121*
Kotah City ...	4·2	1	...	6,965	**37,876**	20,259	17,617	31,707	+ 19·4	− 3·2	9,469
Aklerah ...	242	...	194	8,229	**36,985**	19,280	17,705	33,200	+ 11·4	+ ·2	153
Antah ...	201	...	76	6,679	**28,678**	14,367	14,311	27,379	+ 4·8	− 2·1	143
Asnawar ...	115	...	82	2,918	**13,588**	7,124	6,464	11,768	+ 15·5	+ 9·1	119
Bakani ...	216	...	188	7,059	**32,962**	17,198	15,764	29,101	+ 13·3	− 1·4	153
Baran ...	204	1	92	10,143	**43,846**	22,433	21,413	40,228	+ 8·9	− ·3	215
Barod ...	158	...	72	4,377	**20,364**	10,401	9,963	19,051	+ 6·9	+ ·8	129
Chechat ...	304	...	135	8,609	**38,083**	19,826	18,257	30,328	+ 25·6	+ ·9	126
Chhipabarod ...	327	...	169	7,870	**35,841**	18,604	17,237	32,681	+ 9·7	− 2·7	110
Digod ...	159	...	73	4,666	**20,250**	10,493	9,757	20,269	− ·1	+ ·7	128
Itawa ...	148	...	60	4,538	**20,217**	10,604	9,613	19,379	+ 4·3	− 7·1	137
Kanwas ...	289	...	105	6,177	**26,741**	13,605	13,136	23,806	+ 12·3	+ 11·1	93
Khanpur ...	358	...	186	10,934	**47,283**	23,969	23,314	44,901	+ 5·3	+ 2·1	133
Kishanganj ...	600	...	158	6,822	**30,511**	15,917	14,594	29,872	+ 2·1	+ 15·6	51
Kunjer ...	330	...	132	10,243	**43,511**	22,288	21,223	42,797	+ 1·7	+ 12·00	132
Ladpura ...	558·8	...	162	11,305	**48,888**	25,739	23,149	42,180	+ 15·9	+ ·9	88
Mangrol ...	179	1	72	6,166	**27,544**	14,194	13,350	25,423	+ 8·3	− 11·3	154
Manohar Thana ...	248	...	181	8,016	**35,135**	18,653	16,482	33,521	+ 4·8	− 4·2	142

PROVINCIAL TABLE I.—AREA, HOUSES AND POPULATION OF ADMINISTRATIVE UNITS.—*Contd.*

State or District and Administrative Unit (Pargana, Tehsil, Town, etc.).	Approximate area in square miles.	Inhabited towns.	Inhabited villages.	Occupied houses.	POPULATION.				PERCENTAGE OF VARIATION.		Number of persons per square mile in 1931.
					1931.			1921.			
					Persons.	Males.	Females.	Both Sexes.	1921-31.	1911-21.	
1	2	3	4	5	6	7	8	9	10	11	12
Kotah State (*Concld.*)											
Sangod ...	197	1	108	6,586	**29,826**	15,111	14,715	27,236	+ 9·5	− 5·6	152
Shahabad ...	590	...	121	5,978	**27,669**	14,385	13,284	27,517	+ ·6	+ ·8	47
Kotris ...	256	...	159	9,468	**40,006**	20,606	19,400	37,716	+ 6·1	− 21·4	157
Kushalgarh Chiefship.	***340***	***1***	***282***	***6,420***	***35,564***	***17,754***	***17,810***	***29,162***	***+ 22·0***	***+ 32·5***	***105***
Kushalgarh Town ...	·85	1	...	804	**3,069**	1,551	1,518	2,731	+ 12·4	+ 5·3	3,611
Dungra ...	53·00	...	66	1,493	**9,341**	4,628	4,713	7,257	+ 28·7		176
Maiyad ...	162·15	...	135	2,831	**15,856**	7,893	7,963	12,867	+ 23·2	+ 36·2	98
Patan ...	124·00	...	81	1,292	**7,298**	3,682	3,616	6,307	+ 15·7		59
Lawa Estate ...	***19***	...	***11***	***608***	***2,790***	***1,445***	***1,345***	***2,262***	***+ 23·3***	***− 11·8***	***147***
Marwar State ...	***35,016***	***25½***	***4,126***	***449,459***	***2,125,982***	***1,109,912***	***1,016,070***	***1,841,642***	***+ 15·4***	***− 10·5***	***61***
Jodhpur City ...	26	1	...	17,205	**94,736**	52,165	42,571	73,480	+ 28·9	− 7·9	3,644
Bali ...	834	1	157	26,302	**114,249**	57,778	56,471	99,005	+ 15·4	− 2·3	137
Bilara ...	792	2	117	16,010	**73,117**	37,632	35,485	60,366	+ 21·1	− 19·6	92
Desuri ...	710	1	146	17,920	**82,242**	41,711	40,531	68,265	+ 20·5	− 1·3	116
Didwana ...	1,136	2	240	23,960	**111,168**	57,801	53,367	88,779	+ 25·2	− 8·7	98
Jalore ...	1,552	1	226	33,712	**149,118**	77,200	71,918	129,631	+ 15·08	− 8·3	96
Jaitaran ...	860	2	154	19,153	**87,516**	44,801	42,715	78,490	+ 11·5	− 21·00	102
Jaswantpura ...	1,360	1	224	25,291	**117,176**	61,734	55,442	100,938	+ 16·08	− 3·5	86
Jodhpur ...	2,870	...	369	29,765	**138,621**	72,817	65,804	116,569	+ 18·9	− 9·9	48
Malani ...	5,670	1	469	34,265	**178,438**	94,741	83,697	162,880	+ 9·6	− 2·3	31
Merta ...	1,616	1	324	27,566	**127,556**	66,628	60,928	113,082	+ 12·8	− 15·5	79
Nagaur ...	2,608	2	306	29,604	**142,796**	73,526	69,270	118,664	+ 20·3	− 16·2	55
Pachbhadra ...	856	2	89	7,008	**31,959**	16,714	15,245	28,584	+ 12·0	− 14·4	37
Pali ...	1,024	1	142	14,275	**63,208**	32,774	30,434	51,891	+ 21·8	− 18·5	62
Parbatsar ...	840	1	201	21,705	**108,874**	56,631	52,243	97,117	+ 12·1	− 7·3	130
Phalodi ...	3,573	3	134	17,973	**85,121**	43,995	41,126	84,061	+ 1·3	− 13·9	24
Sambhar-Marwar ...	560	2	118	15,350	**75,816**	40,284	35,532	67,928	+ 11·6	− 13·9	135
½ Sambhar-Shamlat ...	160	½	6	1,995	**8,520**	4,536	3,984	7,706	+ 10·6	+ 0·8	53
Sanchore ...	1,818	...	231	16,102	**84,337**	44,683	39,654	72,201	+ 16·8	− 11·6	46
Shergarh ...	1,771	...	102	13,030	**63,922**	34,185	29,737	58,044	+ 10·1	− 7·7	36
Sheo ...	2,448	...	68	5,286	**24,814**	13,616	11,198	28,883	− 13·9	− 9·1	10
Siwana ...	760	...	82	10,064	**45,676**	23,568	22,108	37,544	+ 21·6	− 8·1	60
Sojat ...	1,172	1	221	25,918	**117,002**	60,892	56,610	97,634	+ 19·8	− 14·7	100
Mewar State ...	***12,694***	***15***	***8,070***	***334,790***	***1,566,910***	***807,184***	***759,726***	***1,366,980***	***+ 14·6***	***+ 6·7***	***124***
Udaipur City ...	Not available.	1	...	7,809	**44,035**	23,775	20,260	34,789	+ 26·6	+ 4·7	Not available.
Asind ...		...	51	2,810	**12,085**	6,151	5,934	12,898	− 6·3	− 17·6	
Bhilwara ...		2	291	21,152	**95,935**	49,202	46,733	86,560	+ 10·8	...	
Chhoti Sadri ...		1	271½	10,318	**48,625**	25,011	23,614	37,359	+ 30·2	...	
Chitorgarh ...		1	491	22,666	**105,245**	54,361	50,884	93,496	+ 12·6	...	
Deosthan ...		...	120	7,220	**30,777**	15,996	14,781	29,685	+ 3·7	+ 9·1	
Deosthan (Kankroli and Nathdwara) ...		1	62	5,703	**26,852**	13,952	12,900	24,911	+ 7·8	...	
Girwa ...		...	552	25,462	**121,854**	62,563	59,291	104,192	+ 16·9	+ 11·9	
Hurra ...		...	220	11,622	**51,920**	26,932	24,988	44,298	+ 17·2	− 2·8	
Jahazpur ...		1	287	7,089	**60,847**	31,851	28,996	61,367	− ·8	...	
Kapasin ...		1	176	9,922	**45,723**	23,723	22,000	39,191	+ 16·7	...	
Khamnor ...		...	307¼	6,741	**28,722**	14,772	13,950	26,562	+ 8·1	− 4·2	
Kherwara ...		2	786	15,133	**73,998**	38,219	35,779	55,112	+ 34·3	...	
Kumalgarh ...		...	681	14,520	**65,157**	34,023	31,134	56,329	+ 15·7	+ 4·6	
Magra ...		...	478	20,948	**97,234**	48,712	48,522	80,967	+ 20·1	+ 18·1	
Mandalgarh ...		...	333	13,359	**63,471**	32,728	30,743	54,737	+ 15·9	+ 9·6	
Rajnagar ...		...	163	8,948	**41,048**	21,394	19,654	36,386	+ 12·8	+ 25·6	
Rashmi ...		...	125	9,605	**41,785**	21,324	20,461	34,446	+ 21·3	+ 2·6	
Saharan ...		...	330	20,219	**90,356**	46,423	43,933	78,379	+ 15·3	+ 6·4	
Thikanas ...		5	2,228	86,787	**393,054**	201,500	191,554	352,017	+ 11·6	...	
Udaipur ...		...	117	6,762	**28,187**	14,572	13,615	23,299	+ 21·00	+ 31·7	

PROVINCIAL TABLE I.—Area, Houses and Population of Administrative Units.—*Concld.*

State or District and Administrative Unit (Pargana, Tehsil, Town, etc.).		Approximate area in square miles.	Inhabited towns.	Inhabited villages	Occupied houses.	POPULATION. 1931. Persons.	1931. Males.	1931. Females	1921. Both Sexes.	PERCENTAGE OF VARIATION. 1921-31.	1911-21.	Number of persons per square mile in 1931.
1		2	3	4	5	6	7	8	9	10	11	12
Partabgarh State	...	*886*	*1*	*470*	*16,279*	***76,539***	*38,991*	*37,548*	*67,110*	+ *14·1*	+ *7·0*	*87*
Partabgarh Town	...	6	1	...	1,910	**10,845**	5,601	5,244	9,182	+ 18·1	+ 10·2	1,807
Hathunia	...	348	...	198	7,065	**32,536**	16,558	15,978	28,484	+ 14·2	+ 3·3	93
Magra	...	274	...	115	2,090	**9,786**	4,973	4,813	8,840	+ 10 7	+ 28·9	36
Sagthali	...	258	...	162	5,214	**23,372**	11,859	11,518	20,604	+ 13·4	+ 3·3	90
Shahpura State	...	*405*	*1*	*116*	*11,658*	***54,233***	*27,907*	*26,326*	*48,130*	+ *12·7*	+ *1·5*	*134*
Shahpura Town	...	18	1	...	2,181	**9,298**	4,689	4,609	8,296	+ 12·1	+ 4·6	516
Arwar	...	64	...	14	1,516	**6,864**	3,454	3,410	6,396	+ 7·3	− 5·7	107
Dhikola	...	99	...	81	2,286	**10,744**	5,612	5,132	9,752	+ 10·1	+ 3·1	108
Dohria	...	66	...	19	1,536	**7,597**	3,973	3,624	6,009	+ 26·4	+ ·3	115
Kanechan	...	43	...	10	701	**3,321**	1,750	1,571	2,958	+ 12·2	+ 3·9	77
Phulia	...	58	...	16	1,679	**8,061**	4,156	3,905	7,481	+ 7·7	+ 1·1	139
Sangria	...	31	..	6	942	**4,423**	2,258	2,165	4,184	+ 5·7	+ 2·1	142
Shahpura	...	26	...	20	817	**3,925**	2,015	1,910	3,054	+ 28·5	+ 5·5	151
Sirohi State	...	*1,958*	*4*	*409*	*49,450*	***216,528***	*111,675*	*104,853*	*186,639*	+ *16·0*	+ *1·0*	*111*
Sirohi Town	...	{ 44 }	1	...	1,908	**7,463**	3,820	3,643	6,197	+ 20·4	− 6·3	{ 231
Sirohi	...		...	11	594	**2,704**	1,397	1,307	1,487	+ 31·8	+ 15·8	
Abu	...	130	...	11	381	**1,383**	749	634	2,192	− 36·9	+ 47·3	11
Bhakar	...	96	...	23	977	**4,706**	2,461	2,245	3,762	+ 25·1	+ 61·5	49
Barlut	...	208	...	29	5,252	**22,501**	11,479	11,022	20,445	+ 10·05	− 3·1	108
Erinpura	...	1	1	...	359	**1,645**	914	731	2,617	− 37·01	− 13·6	1,645
Madar	...	312	...	57	5,641	**25,672**	13,435	12,237	24,815	+ 3 4	− 2·7	82
Magra	...	200	...	37	5,527	**23,412**	11,818	11,594	21,290	+ 9·9	− 6·6	117
Pamera	...	192	...	62	6,085	**27,088**	13,994	13,094	18,988	+ 42·6	+ ·6	141
Pindwara	...	212	...	48	5,189	**24,743**	12,754	11,989	20,658	+ 19·8	+ 9·3	117
Posaliya	...	239	1	45	6,426	**27,203**	13,812	13,391	24,041	+ 13·1	− 5·9	114
Rohera	...	192	...	39	4,922	**20,763**	10,587	10,176	17,306	+ 20·00	+ 4·5	108
Santhpur	...	132	1	47	6,189	**27,245**	14,455	12,790	22,841	+ 19·2	+ 9·8	206
Tonk State	...	*2,553*	*5*	*1,276*	*71,488*	***317,360***	*164,401*	*152,959*	*287,898*	+ *10·2*	− *5·0*	*125*
Tonk City	...	19	1	...	8,968	**35,798**	18,201	17,597	30,874	+ 17·8	− 10·8	1,884
Aligarh	...	157	...	89	3,848	**16,127**	8,342	7,785	14,300	+ 12·8	− 12·2	103
Chhabra	...	310	1	179	7,912	**34,130**	17,940	16,190	32,529	+ 4·9	− 17·5	110
Nimbahera	...	386	1	183	12,507	**55,890**	28,426	27,464	48,592	+ 15·01	+ 8·7	145
Pirawa	...	252	1	132	7,146	**31,609**	16,491	15,118	28,464	+ 11·05	− 3·1	125
Sironj	...	872	1	428	19,276	**88,782**	46,138	42,644	87,755	+ 1·2	− 1·1	1,029
Tonk	...	557	...	265	11,831	**55,024**	28,863	26,161	45,884	+ 19·9	− 9·5	9

PROVINCIAL TABLE II.

Administrative Units by Religion and Literacy.

EXPLANATORY NOTE.

This Table exhibits for the Administrative Units in each State, figures by sex and literacy for each major religion, the remaining minor religions being amalgamated under the head of "Others". Hindus are further sub-divided into Brahmans, Depressed Classes and Other Hindus.

Total figures for literacy by the age-periods of 0—15, 15—20 and 20 and over are also shown for each unit.

PROVINCIAL TABLE II.—POPULATION OF ADMINISTRATIVE UNITS BY RELIGION AND LITERACY.

STATE OR DISTRICT AND ADMINISTRATIVE UNIT (PARGANA, TEHSIL, TOWN, ETC.).	HINDUS.												JAINS.				SIKHS.			
	Brahmans.				Other Hindus.				Depressed Classes.											
	Number of persons.		Number of literates.		Number of persons.		Number of literates.		Number of persons.		Number of literates.		Number of persons.		Number of literates.		Number of persons.		Number of literates.	
	Males.	Females.	Males.	Females.	Males.	Females.	Males.	Females.	Males.	Females.	Males.	Females.	Males.	Females.	Males.	Females.	Males.	Females.	Males.	Females.
1	2	3	4	5	6	7	8	9	10	11	12	13	14	15	16	17	18	19	20	21
RAJPUTANA ...	***441,990***	***412,585***	***89,403***	***5,412***	***3,782,254***	***3,376,567***	***172,401***	***10,785***	***805,376***	***760,033***	***6,013***	***292***	***146,004***	***154,744***	***75,960***	***4,310***	***24,725***	***16,880***	***1,503***	***196***
Abu District ...	***151***	***82***	***96***	***39***	***1,646***	***1,132***	***270***	***46***	***302***	***185***	***25***	***12***	***10***	***11***	***7***	***3***	***37***	***17***	***18***	***6***
Alwar State ...	***31,297***	***28,279***	***7,070***	***340***	***207,179***	***181,532***	***14,887***	***856***	***51,612***	***49,467***	***184***	***1***	***1,994***	***1,815***	***1,212***	***97***	***21***	***16***	***13***	***4***
Alwar City ...	2,889	2,570	1,580	187	12,522	10,589	3,057	340	1,981	2,067	33	...	500	461	335	50	20	16	12	4
Alwar ...	502	416	116	5	5,981	5,250	491	39	3,113	3,139	5	...	31	29	19	3	1	...	1	...
Ajeraka ...	1,116	1,046	338	3	10,718	9,411	504	1	2,091	1,971	4	...	...	...	...	...	...	...	...	...
Bahror ...	1,914	2,045	586	30	18,464	16,399	1,287	53	2,903	3,042	14	...	27	27	19	3	...	...	...	...
Bansur ...	1,941	1,703	472	14	16,478	13,923	760	14	2,865	2,826	4	...	1	3	1	...	...	...	...	...
Govindgarh ...	409	359	130	6	3,276	2,869	304	14	1,979	1,884	...	...	135	108	76	4	...	...	...	...
Katumbar ...	3,402	2,638	360	13	16,046	13,665	761	36	5,055	4,706	1	...	309	296	168	7	...	...	...	...
Khairthal ...	220	212	76	8	2,945	2,584	412	7	1,880	1,799	2	...	5	3	4	...	...	...	...	...
Kishangarh ...	658	564	226	9	7,366	6,190	561	28	2,186	1,963	6	...	12	13	9	...	...	...	...	...
Lachmangarh ...	1,850	1,550	339	14	14,027	12,437	686	15	3,844	3,751	14	...	276	256	157	9	...	...	...	...
Malakhera ...	1,329	1,194	288	3	10,035	8,745	587	115	2,913	2,616	29	...	31	27	12	...	...	...	...	...
Mandhan ...	1,378	1,511	263	24	9,920	9,190	319	13	1,818	1,946	9	...	8	1	2	...	...	...	...	...
Mandawar ...	1,143	1,017	165	2	8,788	7,218	763	16	2,521	2,304	2	...	46	43	31	2	...	...	...	...
Narayanpur ...	1,352	1,345	242	2	9,196	8,251	350	16	1,703	1,747	1	...	...	...	...	...	...	...	...	...
Partabgarh ...	1,139	1,068	174	3	6,917	6,430	367	7	988	857	...	...	...	...	...	...	...	...	...	...
Rajgarh ...	2,673	2,476	644	20	12,181	11,439	951	52	1,997	1,986	26	1	26	19	21	4	...	...	...	...
Ramgarh ...	404	386	142	5	8,739	8,127	425	18	1,932	1,710	3	...	287	256	175	15	...	...	...	...
Reni ...	1,768	1,550	263	6	12,120	11,168	601	29	2,562	2,459	4	...	113	84	61	...	...	...	...	...
Thana Ghazi ...	2,976	2,714	218	5	7,308	6,633	463	6	1,650	1,571	...	...	25	25	17	...	...	...	...	...
Tijara ...	510	445	163	13	6,626	5,424	513	22	2,392	2,086	25	...	156	158	96	...	...	...	...	...
Tapukrah ...	243	180	46	2	3,862	3,199	162	4	1,636	1,560	...	...	...	...	...	...	...	...	...	...
Circles ...	1,094	879	152	6	5,548	4,722	372	4	1,043	947	...	...	11	6	9	...	...	...	...	...
Nimrana Estate ...	392	461	142	15	3,116	2,724	191	7	560	530	2	...	...	...	...	...	...	...	...	...
Banswara State ...	***4,375***	***5,158***	***1,139***	***96***	***49,717***	***49,843***	***1,236***	***93***	***5,833***	***5,532***	***9***	...	***2,342***	***2,255***	***1,397***	***76***	***4***	***1***	***1***	***1***
Banswara Town ...	685	720	402	67	2,502	2,496	517	45	280	287	1	...	192	178	123	16	4	1	1	1
Khalsa Villages ...	2,421	2,991	497	20	20,795.	20,706	296	14	2,458	2,351	2	...	1,205	1,240	741	39	...	...	...	...
Jagir and other villages ...	1,269	1,447	240	9	26,420	26,641	423	34	3,095	2,894	6	...	945	837	533	21	...	...	...	...

PROVINCIAL TABLE II.—Population of Administrative Units by Religion and Literacy.—*Continued.*

STATE OR DISTRICT AND ADMINISTRATIVE UNIT (PARGANA, TEHSIL, TOWN, ETC.).	MUSLIMS.				CHRISTIANS.				TRIBAL.				OTHERS.				NUMBER LITERATE—						LITERATE IN ENGLISH.	
	Number of persons.		Number of literates.		Number of persons.		Number of literates.		Number of persons.		Number of literates.		Number of persons.		Number of literates.		Aged 0—15.		Aged 15—20.		Aged 20 & over.			
	Males.	Females.	Males.	Females.	Males.	Females.	Males.	Females.	Males.	Females.	Males.	Females.	Males.	Females.	Males.	Females.	Males.	Females.	Males.	Females.	Males.	Females.	Males.	Females.
1	22	23	24	25	26	27	28	29	30	31	32	33	34	35	36	37	38	39	40	41	42	43	44	45
RAJPUTANA ...	*565,962*	*503,363*	*34,340*	*3,144*	*3,107*	*2,671*	*1,782*	*1,278*	*115,420*	*113,672*	*45*	*2*	*190*	*169*	*155*	*115*	*50,864*	*5,626*	*48,270*	*3,903*	*282,468*	*16,005*	*28,209*	*1,686*
Abu District ...	*512*	*288*	*169*	*16*	*84*	*56*	*68*	*36*	...	...	...	...	*11*	*8*	*10*	*8*	*105*	*48*	*88*	*21*	*470*	*97*	*227*	*54*
Alwar State ...	*104,110*	*92,350*	*2,020*	*111*	*48*	*31*	*34*	*21*	...	...	...	...	...	...	...	...	*3,034*	*293*	*3,070*	*245*	*19,316*	*892*	*1,853*	*53*
Alwar City ...	7,637	6,641	901	87	85	22	25	13	...	...	...	...	...	...	...	...	677	141	702	92	4,514	898	1,181	44
Alwar ...	18,892	11,851	82	...	...	...	...	...	...	...	...	...	...	...	...	...	69	11	101	7	544	29	10	...
Ajeraka ...	1,820	1,747	29	...	...	...	...	...	...	...	...	...	...	...	...	...	100	1	104	...	671	3	5	...
Bahror ...	1,200	1,077	79	2	1	...	1	...	...	...	...	...	...	...	...	...	266	16	225	14	1,495	58	41	1
Bansur ...	784	754	29	...	...	...	...	...	...	...	...	...	...	...	...	...	184	7	171	3	961	18	28	...
Govindgarh ...	8,946	8,211	90	6	...	...	...	...	...	...	...	...	...	...	...	...	72	10	66	6	462	14	6	...
Katumbar ...	1,972	1,579	31	2	...	...	...	...	...	...	...	...	...	...	...	...	120	8	149	9	1,052	41	44	...
Khairthal ...	11,486	10,290	94	...	...	...	...	...	...	...	...	...	...	...	...	...	76	2	75	2	437	6	14	1
Kishangarh ...	6,580	5,556	42	...	...	...	...	...	...	...	...	...	...	...	...	...	101	9	75	12	668	16	32	1
Lachmangarh ...	6,052	5,429	62	...	...	...	...	...	...	...	...	...	...	...	...	...	171	5	147	6	940	27	75	1
Malakhera ...	4,286	3,829	27	1	3	3	3	3	...	...	...	...	...	...	...	...	113	9	101	48	727	65	25	1
Mandhan ...	407	518	17	...	...	...	...	...	...	...	...	...	...	...	...	...	85	8	79	6	446	23	14	...
Mandawar ...	4,210	3,789	72	1	...	...	...	...	...	...	...	...	...	...	...	...	162	8	115	3	756	15	26	...
Narayanpur ...	458	438	15	...	...	...	...	...	...	...	...	...	...	...	...	...	66	6	77	4	465	8	9	2
Partabgarh ...	146	116	5	...	...	...	...	...	...	...	...	...	...	...	...	...	45	2	76	...	425	8	4	...
Rajgarh ...	894	769	89	...	3	4	2	3	...	...	...	...	...	...	...	...	257	24	234	10	1,242	46	211	...
Ramgarh ...	11,868	9,882	103	...	...	...	...	...	...	...	...	...	...	...	...	...	108	7	103	6	637	25	26	...
Reni ...	1,017	975	14	1	5	1	2	1	...	...	...	...	...	...	...	...	108	7	117	2	720	28	14	1
Thana Ghazi ...	845	294	20	...	...	...	...	...	...	...	...	...	...	...	...	...	85	4	98	2	585	5	8	...
Tijara ...	11,428	10,395	146	11	...	...	...	...	...	...	...	...	...	...	...	...	108	11	116	9	719	26	41	...
Tapukrah ...	8,862	7,516	88	...	...	...	...	...	...	...	...	...	...	...	...	...	31	...	25	1	190	5	9	...
Circles ...	755	587	27	...	1	1	1	1	...	...	...	...	...	...	...	...	38	...	74	...	449	11	19	1
Nimrana Estate ...	125	107	8	...	...	...	...	...	...	...	...	...	...	...	...	...	42	2	40	3	261	17	11	...
Banswara State ...	*3,300*	*3,210*	*787*	*19*	*98*	*107*	*15*	*23*	*46,313*	*47,017*	*3*	...	*1*	...	*1*	...	*605*	*62*	*588*	*46*	*3,395*	*200*	*133*	*18*
Banswara Town ...	1,382	1,575	308	8	39	44	15	23	56	2	...	...	1	...	1	...	202	32	183	26	978	102	117	18
Khalsa Villages ...	1,067	1,014	258	3	59	63	...	...	15,472	15,765	3	...	...	...	...	...	210	17	226	10	1,356	49	3	...
Jagir & other Villages	851	621	281	8	...	...	...	...	30,785	31,250	...	...	...	...	...	...	193	13	179	10	1,061	49	13	...

PROVINCIAL TABLE II.—Population of Administrative Units by Religion and Literacy.—*Continued.*

STATE OR DISTRICT AND ADMINISTRATIVE UNIT (PARGANA, TEHSIL, TOWN, ETC.).	HINDUS. Brahmans. Number of persons.		Number of literates.		Other Hindus. Number of persons.		Number of literates.		Depressed Classes. Number of persons.		Number of literates.		JAINS. Number of persons.		Number of literates.		SIKHS. Number of persons.		Number of literates.	
	Males.	Females.	Males.	Females.	Males.	Females.	Males.	Females.	Males.	Females.	Males.	Females.	Males.	Females.	Males.	Females.	Males.	Females.	Males.	Females.
1	2	3	4	5	6	7	8	9	10	11	12	13	14	15	16	17	18	19	20	21
Bharatpur State ...	***23,600***	***19,235***	***5,270***	***335***	***136,144***	***111,772***	***12,041***	***730***	***51,534***	***47,438***	***308***	***22***	***1,288***	***1,102***	***831***	***85***	***102***	***55***	***51***	***4***
Bharatpur City ...	2,825	1,926	1,191	162	6,484	4,863	1,796	330	2,405	2,214	88	13	233	202	161	38	27	13	21	1
Bharatpur ...	1,816	1,485	875	10	12,580	10,354	891	31	4,596	4,318	17	1	41	35	22	1	23	12	10	1
Bayana ...	2,844	2,280	461	25	18,537	14,765	1,287	68	7,651	6,947	37	...	113	83	81	1	...	...	...	...
Dig ...	2,281	1,945	532	27	14,580	11,701	1,153	43	4,093	4,347	30	6	161	126	103	10	1	...	1	...
Kaman ...	1,433	1,164	422	20	7,566	6,325	714	36	2,694	2,628	34	...	189	204	123	21	...	...	...	...
Kumher ...	1,902	1,036	364	27	14,455	11,780	1,143	30	4,275	3,986	17	1	67	54	42	2	13	9	6	1
Nadbai ...	2,404	2,126	359	13	14,227	11,765	1,084	33	4,976	4,793	16	...	184	145	96	2	...	...	...	...
Nagar ...	1,431	1,006	235	5	9,092	7,895	749	19	4,141	3,874	5	...	66	59	41	2	2	1	1	...
Pahari ...	445	264	110	6	3,947	3,412	364	9	2,376	2,183	10	...	53	48	37	4	...	...	...	...
Rupbas ...	2,345	1,827	358	12	11,129	9,028	864	42	3,684	3,127	10	...	22	17	17	...	22	13	3	...
Uchain ...	1,214	976	240	1	4,167	3,372	370	20	1,960	1,704	17	...	6	1	4	...	13	6	8	1
Weir ...	3,210	2,651	638	27	19,371	16,512	1,676	69	8,083	7,317	27	1	158	128	104	4	1	1	1	...
Bikaner State ...	***41,625***	***40,042***	***8,808***	***730***	***279,269***	***238,864***	***17,920***	***1,425***	***67,123***	***58,161***	***180***	***11***	***12,479***	***16,294***	***5,522***	***554***	***24,017***	***16,452***	***1,143***	***115***
Bikaner City ...	8,018	7,768	3,618	375	22,262	17,875	4,992	594	3,168	2,606	11	...	3,059	3,898	1,521	177	188	78	81	8
Bikaner Nizamat.																				
Bikaner ...	2,440	2,505	276	15	14,699	13,117	792	27	5,726	5,362	22	...	796	1,110	263	2	3	2	2	...
Lunkaransar ...	1,568	1,360	134	3	9,488	8,049	252	19	1,913	1,809	6	...	305	497	93	6	...	...	...	...
Surpura ...	2,081	2,012	194	...	21,948	19,453	510	20	4,739	4,521	2	...	603	753	171	8	...	...	...	...
Ganganagar Nizamat.																				
Ganganagar ...	818	492	322	28	15,921	11,529	1,177	91	3,492	2,657	20	3	12	9	8	...	4,811	3,283	263	32
Karanpur ...	224	113	97	4	4,101	2,920	342	18	1,608	1,277	...	...	17	10	14	...	5,056	4,056	258	25
Padampur ...	161	134	65	2	6,448	2,545	322	22	1,308	985	7	...	8	3	5	...	3,848	2,132	174	27
Raisingnagar ...	256	154	49	1	4,051	3,049	88	1	899	674	4	...	3	2	...	...	1,929	1,208	57	...
Reni Nizamat.																				
Bhadra ...	1,276	1,147	260	24	17,273	14,596	869	55	3,797	3,411	1	...	148	189	67	14	7	5	...	...
Churu ...	3,235	3,159	889	106	16,369	14,552	1,349	106	3,662	3,577	23	...	761	872	405	83	2	1	2	1

PROVINCIAL TABLE II.—POPULATION OF ADMINISTRATIVE UNITS BY RELIGION AND LITERACY.—*Continued.*

STATE OR DISTRICT AND ADMINISTRATIVE UNIT (PARGANA, TEHSIL, TOWN, ETC).	MUSLIMS.				CHRISTIANS.				TRIBAL.				OTHERS.				NUMBER LITERATE—						LITERATE IN ENGLISH.	
	Number of persons.		Number of literates.		Number of persons.		Number of literates		Number of persons.		Number of literates.		Number of persons.		Number of literates.		Aged 0—15.		Aged 15—20.		Aged 20 and over.			
	Males.	Females.	Males.	Females.	Males.	Females.	Males.	Females.	Males.	Females.	Males.	Females.	Males.	Females.	Males.	Females.	Males.	Females.	Males.	Females.	Males.	Females.	Males.	Females.
1	22	23	24	25	26	27	28	29	30	31	32	33	34	35	36	37	38	39	40	41	42	43	44	45
Bharatpur State ...	***50,308***	***43,746***	***1,975***	***248***	***346***	***279***	***45***	***40***	...	...	...	...	***3***	***2***	***1***	***2***	***3,114***	***357***	***2,563***	***266***	***14,845***	***843***	***1,215***	***67***
Bharatpur City ...	5,055	4,062	788	137	206	157	32	37	...	...	...	...	1	1	...	1	636	158	552	130	2,889	436	849	52
Bharatpur ...	686	513	59	1	3	2	3	2	...	...	...	...	...	...	...	...	204	7	163	7	1,010	33	47	2
Bayana ...	2,456	2,088	140	19	2	...	2	...	...	...	...	...	2	1	1	1	252	32	245	16	1,512	66	75	1
Dig ...	4,125	3,669	163	13	42	37	5	1	...	...	...	...	...	...	...	...	338	23	219	14	1,430	63	69	1
Kaman ...	8,157	7,085	103	11	37	42	...	...	...	...	...	...	...	...	...	...	211	30	168	12	1,017	46	30	2
Kumher ...	1,153	946	75	8	53	41	1	...	...	...	...	...	...	...	...	...	228	28	205	19	1,215	27	36	2
Nadbai ...	1,362	1,282	122	20	1	...	1	...	...	...	...	...	...	...	...	...	268	19	193	11	1,167	47	32	...
Nagar ...	10,376	9,143	167	2	...	...	...	...	...	...	...	...	...	...	...	...	210	11	132	5	856	12	11	...
Pahari ...	12,511	11,116	125	1	...	...	...	...	...	...	...	...	...	...	...	...	67	8	73	3	506	9	2	...
Rupbas ...	1,530	1,345	111	2	...	...	...	...	...	...	...	...	...	...	...	...	175	9	182	15	1,006	32	27	...
Uchain ...	548	483	18	3	2	...	1	...	...	...	...	...	...	...	...	...	109	9	91	3	458	13	15	...
Weir ...	2,349	2,019	104	22	...	...	...	...	...	...	...	...	...	...	...	...	416	88	340	31	1,779	59	22	7
Bikaner State ...	***76,471***	***65,107***	***2,645***	***217***	***160***	***138***	***74***	***53***	...	...	...	...	***9***	***7***	***7***	***4***	***4,919***	***651***	***4,983***	***575***	***26,397***	***1,883***	***3,988***	***147***
Bikaner City ...	9,048	7,810	871	61	86	58	59	41	...	...	...	...	8	7	6	4	1,346	248	1,504	233	8,309	779	1,901	113
Bikaner Nizamat.																								
Bikaner ...	4,393	3,654	68	9	...	...	...	...	...	...	...	...	...	...	...	...	209	8	189	10	1,025	35	63	...
Lunkaransar ...	2,058	1,747	43	3	...	...	...	...	...	...	...	...	...	...	...	...	59	6	60	4	409	21	26	...
Surpura ...	509	428	24	1	...	...	...	...	...	...	...	...	...	...	...	...	47	2	97	5	757	22	14	...
Ganganagar Nizamat.																								
Ganganagar ...	10,719	8,667	196	15	20	23	...	...	...	...	...	...	...	...	...	...	261	25	303	31	1,422	113	427	8
Karanpur ...	5,733	4,751	100	19	28	31	...	...	...	...	...	...	...	...	...	...	67	11	116	15	628	40	120	...
Padampur ...	2,657	2,092	31	4	3	8	1	...	...	...	...	...	...	...	...	...	41	12	84	17	480	26	89	...
Raisingnagar ...	1,317	1,024	46	...	3	2	...	...	...	...	...	...	...	...	...	...	8	1	40	1	196	...	49	2
Reni Nizamat.																								
Bhadra ...	1,863	1,577	74	4	...	...	...	...	...	...	...	...	...	...	...	...	248	23	192	20	831	54	60	3
Churu ...	4,866	4,458	305	24	7	7	4	6	...	...	...	...	...	...	...	...	590	78	417	65	1,970	183	274	...

PROVINCIAL TABLE II.—Population of Administrative Units by Religion and Literacy.—*Continued.*

STATE OR DISTRICT AND ADMINISTRATIVE UNIT (PARGANA, TEHSIL, TOWN, ETC.)	HINDUS.												JAINS.				SIKHS.			
	Brahmans				Other Hindus.				Depressed Classes.											
	Number of persons		Number of literates		Number of persons		Number of literates.		Number of persons		Number of literates.		Number of persons		Number of literates.		Number of persons.		Number of literates	
	Males	Females	Males	Females.	Males	Females	Males.	Females.	Males.	Females.	Males.	Females	Males.	Females.	Males	Females	Males.	Females.	Males.	Females.
1	2	3	4	5	6	7	8	9	10	11	12	13	14	15	16	17	18	19	20	21
Bikaner State.—*Concld.*																				
Reni Nizamat.—Concluded.																				
Nohar ...	2,466	2,154	220	18	20,706	17,932	525	49	4,595	3,612	3	...	115	146	42	8	73	27	...	1
Rajgarh ...	1,923	1,679	268	18	20,873	18,408	1,037	52	5,745	4,426	6	...	518	688	258	17	4	...	...	...
Reni ...	1,939	1,940	169	10	10,300	8,992	550	26	2,154	2,002	1	...	228	276	88	1	...	...	...	...
Sujangarh Nizamat.																				
Dungargarh ...	2,430	2,549	158	13	12,278	11,026	815	17	3,101	2,674	2	...	932	1,233	296	22	5	...	3	...
Ratangarh ...	3,775	5,865	649	15	16,996	14,984	936	50	3,721	3,329	12	1	981	1,411	443	48	3	2	1	...
Sardarshahr ...	4,111	4,341	369	9	17,446	15,791	586	88	3,151	2,907	3	...	1,724	2,268	757	52	1	...	1	...
Sujangarh ...	2,804	3,024	641	46	23,718	21,268	1,318	107	5,953	5,583	16	1	1,997	4,755	936	100	3	...	3	...
Suratgarh Nizamat.																				
Anupgarh ...	128	60	40	3	2,196	1,633	169	2	1,160	645	7	...	2	...	2	...	1,373	870	121	9
Hanumangarh ...	1,040	829	287	29	15,736	12,951	698	48	4,566	3,925	25	3	147	119	72	13	5,481	4,069	143	8
Suratgarh ...	897	757	108	11	10,115	8,194	598	33	2,665	2,179	9	3	123	115	81	3	1,135	719	34	4
Bundi State ...	***8,430***	***8,234***	***1,565***	***94***	***82,996***	***70,431***	***2,369***	***172***	***14,056***	***18,182***	...	...	***2,166***	***1,853***	***920***	***29***	***28***	***17***	***22***	...
Bundi City ...	1,621	1,626	772	73	4,492	4,385	1,138	118	662	605	...	...	398	341	247	18	1	1	1	...
Baroondhan ...	963	922	50	...	15,330	12,173	175	...	2,640	4,143	...	...	184	151	52	...	...	...	...	...
Dei ...	940	940	87	...	17,608	13,852	193	4	1,948	3,870	...	...	469	356	86	1	...	...	...	...
Gaindoli ...	1,174	1,319	311	17	14,236	12,938	205	23	3,433	2,937	...	...	276	250	140	2	...	...	...	...
Hindoli ...	1,090	945	50	...	18,095	15,771	248	2	3,499	3,938	...	...	383	335	146	4	21	14	15	...
Patan ...	2,087	2,143	235	4	10,356	8,730	342	25	1,532	2,154	...	...	158	129	83	4	3	...	3	...
Nainwa Kila ...	354	170	67	...	1,040	1,174	55	...	205	264	...	...	264	276	155	...	3	2	3	...
Talwas ...	201	169	43	...	1,839	1,458	13	...	137	271	...	...	34	15	11	...	...	...	...	...
Dholpur State ...	***16,059***	***11,955***	***2,341***	***138***	***90,185***	***72,421***	***4,734***	***302***	***24,110***	***21,199***	***72***	...	***994***	***805***	***268***	***21***	***160***	***94***	***56***	***15***
Dholpur City ...	1,274	977	635	110	5,433	4,345	1,193	207	681	810	40	...	34	7	29	7	47	33	29	7
Bari ...	2,025	1,484	219	...	16,848	13,501	626	23	4,748	4,120	7	...	6	6	3	1	34	23	4	...
Baseri ...	3,194	2,305	256	6	14,235	11,393	674	18	4,899	4,331	2	...	1	...	1	...	...	...	...	...
Gird ...	2,634	1,905	367	5	19,213	15,635	643	2	5,087	4,200	15	...	238	191	53	1	60	28	12	2
Kolari ...	2,440	1,875	385	3	16,148	13,222	866	17	4,117	3,769	6	...	2	3	2	...	...	...	...	...

PROVINCIAL TABLE II.—POPULATION OF ADMINISTRATIVE UNITS BY RELIGION AND LITERACY.—*Continued.*

STATE OR DISTRICT AND ADMINISTRATIVE UNIT (PARGANA, TEHSIL, TOWN, ETC.).	MUSLIMS.				CHRISTIANS.				TRIBAL.				OTHERS.				NUMBER LITERATE—						LITERATE IN ENGLISH.	
	Number of persons.		Number of literates.		Number of persons.		Number of literates.		Number of persons.		Number of literates.		Number of persons.		Number of literates.		Aged 0—15.		Aged 15—20.		Aged 20 & over			
	Males.	Females.	Males.	Females.	Males.	Females.	Males.	Females.	Males.	Females.	Males.	Females.	Males.	Females.	Males.	Females.	Males.	Females.	Males.	Females.	Males.	Females	Males.	Females.
1	22	23	24	25	26	27	28	29	30	31	32	33	34	35	36	37	38	39	40	41	42	43	44	45
Bikaner State.—*Cld.*																								
Reni Nizamat.—Cld.																								
Nohar ...	2,580	2,358	52	1	...	...	...	...	...	...	...	...	...	...	...	...	124	25	119	15	599	37	37	1
Rajgarh ...	2,408	2,138	90	5	...	...	...	...	...	...	...	...	...	...	...	...	271	26	287	16	1,146	50	132	4
Reni ...	1,122	1,130	18	1	...	...	...	...	...	...	...	...	...	...	...	...	132	10	109	8	585	20	12	...
Sujangarh Nizamat.																								
Dungargarh ...	736	585	86	...	...	...	...	...	...	...	...	...	...	...	...	...	219	13	175	11	966	28	27	2
Ratangarh ...	2,714	2,546	125	3	5	1	5	1	...	...	...	...	...	...	...	...	349	20	307	14	1,515	84	173	1
Sardarshahr ...	2,761	2,277	80	28	...	...	...	...	...	...	...	...	...	...	...	...	205	40	239	32	1,352	100	73	2
Sujangarh ...	2,972	2,724	161	8	1	4	1	1	...	...	...	...	...	...	...	...	394	42	418	42	2,264	179	128	1
Suratgarh Nizamat.																								
Anupgarh ...	5,958	4,857	43	...	1	...	...	...	...	...	...	...	...	...	...	...	26	2	54	3	302	9	85	...
Hanumangarh ...	8,778	7,680	142	17	1	...	1	...	...	...	...	...	...	...	...	...	198	37	198	20	972	61	177	1
Suratgarh ...	3,284	2,754	90	19	5	9	3	4	...	...	...	...	1	...	1	...	125	22	130	18	669	42	112	9
Bundi State ...	***5,398***	***4,894***	***224***	***33***	***21***	***8***	***12***	***5***	***3***	***2***	...	...	***3***	...	***3***	...	***515***	***72***	***545***	***42***	***4,055***	***219***	***244***	***13***
Bundi City ...	1,999	1,902	102	29	...	...	...	...	3	2	...	...	3	...	3	...	243	57	269	27	1,751	154	183	7
Baroondhan ...	355	227	14	...	...	...	...	...	...	...	...	...	...	...	...	...	28	...	84	...	229	...	5	...
Dei ...	416	321	7	1	...	...	...	...	...	...	...	...	...	...	...	...	20	...	28	...	275	6	4	...
Gaindoli ...	478	360	38	...	21	8	12	5	...	...	...	...	...	...	...	...	67	6	85	8	554	33	28	5
Hindoli ...	954	923	5	1	...	...	...	...	...	...	...	...	...	...	...	...	48	1	25	1	391	5	4	...
Patan ...	709	657	38	...	...	...	...	...	...	...	...	...	...	...	...	...	82	8	67	6	552	19	18	1
Nainwa Kila ...	478	496	18	2	...	...	...	...	...	...	...	...	...	...	...	...	24	...	30	...	244	2	2	...
Talwas ...	9	8	2	...	...	...	...	...	...	...	...	...	...	...	...	...	8	...	7	...	59	...	...	...
Dholpur State ...	***8,903***	***7,939***	***764***	***108***	***21***	***42***	***12***	***34***	***64***	***34***	...	...	***1***	...	...	...	***993***	***100***	***1,039***	***108***	***6,215***	***410***	***588***	***45***
Dholpur City ...	3,044	2,837	465	86	21	42	12	34	...	...	...	...	1	...	...	...	256	66	307	88	1,840	302	491	45
Bari ...	1,969	1,836	118	10	...	...	...	...	...	...	...	...	...	...	...	...	99	7	119	7	759	20	34	...
Baseri ...	885	713	88	3	...	...	...	...	...	...	...	...	...	...	...	...	120	3	123	4	728	20	7	...
Gird ...	848	777	22	...	...	...	...	...	64	34	...	...	...	...	...	...	117	1	153	1	842	8	11	...
Kolari ...	1,086	882	40	6	...	...	...	...	...	...	...	...	...	...	...	...	177	5	158	4	969	17	19	...

PROVINCIAL TABLE II.—POPULATION OF ADMINISTRATIVE UNITS BY RELIGION AND LITERACY.—*Continued.*

STATE OR DISTRICT AND ADMINISTRATIVE UNIT (PARGANA, TEHSIL, TOWN, ETC.).	HINDUS.												JAINS.				SIKHS.			
	Brahmans.				Other Hindus.				Depressed Classes.											
	Number of persons.		Number of literates		Number of persons.		Number of literates.		Number of persons.		Number of literates.		Number of persons.		Number of literates.		Number of persons.		Number of literates	
	Males.	Females.	Males.	Females.	Males	Females	Males.	Females.	Males.	Females.	Males.	Females.	Males.	Females.	Males.	Females.	Males.	Females.	Males.	Females.
1	2	3	4	5	6	7	8	9	10	11	12	13	14	15	16	17	18	19	20	21
Dholpur State.—*Concluded.*																				
Rajakhera ...	3,704	2,757	315	9	12,397	9,807	335	14	8,027	2,640	...	...	718	598	180	12	...	...	...	...
Sir Muthra ...	788	612	164	5	5,911	4,518	397	21	1,551	1,329	2	...	...	...	...	...	19	10	11	6
Dungarpur State ...	***5,798***	***7,235***	***1,122***	**80**	***96,256***	***93,591***	***1,621***	**132**	***5,743***	***5,422***	**25**	***1***	***2,836***	***2,965***	***1,684***	**60**	**5**	***4***	**4**	**4**
Dungarpur Town ...	495	499	251	62	2,109	1,818	500	59	204	195	...	...	387	376	275	9	4	4	3	4
Bara ...	675	798	99	3	25,342	24,825	175	20	902	883	5	...	307	347	165	8	...	...	...	...
Chhiasat ...	1,927	2,451	336	6	14,094	14,098	315	8	1,126	1,052	3	...	581	636	372	14	...	...	...	...
Chorasi ...	981	1,818	290	6	30,804	29,960	435	24	1,611	1,601	10	1	377	412	224	14	1	...	1	...
Tarpod ...	1,720	2,234	146	3	23,907	22,890	196	21	1,900	1,691	7	...	1,184	1,194	648	15	...	...	...	...
Jaipur State ...	***142,951***	***135,007***	***25,192***	***1,124***	***909,819***	***798,736***	***45,427***	***2,505***	***204,148***	***192,643***	***1,088***	**94**	***15,518***	***13,974***	***8,536***	**539**	***120***	**69**	**62**	**7**
Jaipur City ...	10,447	9,434	4,380	429	34,575	28,108	6,927	867	5,054	4,746	341	27	3,828	3,414	2,427	291	94	53	47	4
Amber ...	16,184	15,420	1,552	14	69,360	63,045	2,762	58	14,986	14,201	5	...	565	458	259	7	2	2	...	...
Dausa ...	17,410	16,330	1,927	58	90,036	81,242	3,381	178	22,860	21,556	182	1	720	630	406	14	...	...	...	...
Gangapur ...	4,879	4,492	753	47	38,773	33,997	1,468	96	8,715	8,402	82	21	257	240	127	10	8	6	2	1
Hindaun ...	6,651	5,987	1,009	37	59,803	50,328	2,617	88	17,520	16,110	24	1	734	627	396	11	1	...	1	...
Kotkasim ...	630	555	158	12	6,035	4,970	304	2	1,324	1,298	3	...	15	15	7	...	...	...	...	...
Malpura ...	6,156	5,520	1,096	18	50,541	45,822	1,602	29	13,989	13,037	5	...	1,890	1,548	1,052	27	3	...	3	...
Sambhar ...	8,417	8,044	1,718	60	63,850	57,700	2,878	192	17,134	16,021	118	...	2,579	2,278	1,480	54	...	...	...	...
Sawai Jaipur ...	16,342	14,929	1,225	32	63,036	55,102	2,478	111	19,793	19,121	46	1	1,074	917	567	17	1	...	1	...
Sawai Madhopur ...	6,295	5,854	1,202	56	68,779	61,091	2,084	71	15,066	14,514	149	...	1,645	1,416	730	35	...	...	...	...
Shekhawati ...	14,444	13,784	2,958	107	114,813	95,728	6,005	265	21,614	19,450	40	...	287	284	149	33	...	...	...	...
Torawati ...	13,931	14,056	3,320	75	108,515	96,107	6,075	175	20,394	19,738	76	35	428	492	237	13	...	...	...	...
Khetri Thikana ...	6,516	6,404	1,389	67	55,905	49,600	2,647	131	9,081	8,942	12	6	17	21	13	...	9	5	7	1
Sikar Thikana ...	18,572	13,152	2,262	95	72,309	63,688	3,838	222	13,626	12,606	5	...	915	1,063	416	18	2	3	1	1
Uniara Thikana ...	1,077	1,037	234	8	13,499	12,208	366	20	2,992	2,901	...	2	564	471	261	9	...	...	...	...
Jaisalmer State ...	***2,040***	***1,831***	**700**	**24**	***21,675***	***17,387***	***1,048***	***24***	***4,836***	***4,000***	**5**	...	**466**	***451***	**155**	...	**8**	***1***	**6**	...
Jaisalmer Town ...	1,156	1,115	634	24	1,763	1,616	630	22	154	138	1	...	65	99	47	...	2	...	2	...
Bap ...	217	179	14	...	2,446	1,876	28	1	536	491	...	...	...	...	...	...	...	...	...	...

PROVINCIAL TABLE II.—POPULATION OF ADMINISTRATIVE UNITS BY RELIGION AND LITERACY.—*Continued.*

STATE OR DISTRICT AND ADMINISTRATIVE UNIT (PARGANA, TEHSIL, TOWN, ETC.).	MUSLIMS.				CHRISTIANS.				TRIBAL.				OTHERS.				NUMBER LITERATE—						LITERATE IN ENGLISH.	
	Number of persons		Number of literates.		Number of persons.		Number of literates.		Number of persons.		Number of literates.		Number of persons.		Number of literates.		Aged 0—15.		Aged 15—20.		Aged 20 and over.			
	Males.	Females.	Males.	Females.	Males.	Females.	Males.	Females.	Males.	Females.	Males.	Females.	Males.	Females.	Males.	Females.	Males.	Females.	Males.	Females.	Males.	Females.	Males.	Females.
1	22	23	24	25	26	27	28	29	30	31	32	33	34	35	36	37	38	39	40	41	42	43	44	45
Dholpur State.—*Cld.*																								
Rajakhera ...	639	596	31	2	...	...	...	...	...	...	...	...	...	...	...	...	110	12	107	5	644	20	6	...
Sir Muthra ...	482	368	50	1	...	...	...	...	...	...	...	...	...	...	...	...	114	6	77	4	433	23	20	...
Dungarpur State ...	***3,838***	***3,844***	***1,104***	***21***	***4***	***3***	***4***	***1***	...	...	...	...	...	...	...	...	***1,002***	***78***	***767***	***48***	***3,795***	***173***	***149***	***9***
Dungarpur Town.	1,217	1,308	413	12	2	2	2	1	...	...	...	...	...	...	...	...	269	35	199	31	976	81	125	9
Bara ...	170	87	48	...	...	...	...	...	...	...	...	...	...	...	...	...	91	9	84	2	312	20	9	...
Chhiasat ...	779	1,021	240	5	...	...	...	...	...	...	...	...	...	...	...	...	260	12	163	3	843	18	5	...
Chorasi ...	1,413	1,276	332	4	2	1	2	...	...	...	...	...	...	...	...	...	188	14	182	6	924	29	8	...
Tarpod ...	259	152	76	...	...	...	...	...	...	...	...	...	...	...	...	...	194	8	139	6	740	25	2	...
Jaipur State ...	***112,338***	***102,243***	***6,865***	***742***	***795***	***763***	***642***	***479***	***1,349***	***1,250***	***3***	***2***	***29***	***23***	***19***	***13***	***10,570***	***1,118***	***10,427***	***759***	***66,837***	***3,628***	***6,821***	***637***
Jaipur City ...	28,780	20,292	2,800	388	143	186	122	136	4	4	...	...	8	9	4	2	1,993	440	2,053	208	13,011	1,406	3,065	273
Amber ...	4,007	3,548	88	3	...	...	...	...	22	16	...	...	...	...	...	...	463	15	465	9	3,738	58	58	3
Dausa ...	3,792	3,261	373	9	228	214	201	158	142	125	...	...	...	...	...	...	757	83	718	60	4,995	285	665	142
Gangapur ...	3,584	3,109	280	104	142	125	124	95	...	...	...	...	11	8	9	6	421	108	295	51	2,129	221	313	90
Hindaun ...	5,257	4,752	215	22	3	6	3	2	17	9	...	...	...	...	...	...	548	20	486	24	3,231	117	110	5
Kotkasim ...	995	944	33	16	4	4	2	...	...	...	...	...	...	...	...	...	82	4	64	2	361	24	11	...
Malpura ...	3,622	2,872	221	6	1	...	1	...	865	840	1	...	...	...	...	...	419	19	485	10	3,127	51	380	...
Sambhar ...	7,096	6,258	363	30	157	115	130	53	7	5	...	...	5	1	3	1	849	71	724	58	5,126	270	580	60
Sawai Jaipur ...	3,741	2,537	376	12	34	30	26	24	11	5	1	...	...	...	...	...	418	35	545	30	3,752	132	265	28
Sawai Madhopur.	7,497	6,705	207	31	11	8	8	3	7	5	1	2	2	...	...	...	459	35	467	27	3,545	136	126	7
Shekhawati ...	18,919	18,585	569	54	8	...	3	...	8	1	...	...	...	...	...	...	1,176	93	1,324	71	7,224	295	677	9
Torawati ...	7,096	6,673	318	36	11	6	3	...	36	26	...	...	...	...	...	...	1,200	59	1,165	42	7,664	283	130	2
Khetri Thikana ...	6,062	5,921	275	8	58	65	16	5	...	...	...	...	1	4	1	3	855	55	626	26	2,879	140	237	9
Sikar Thikana ...	16,250	16,262	627	18	5	4	3	3	26	23	...	...	2	1	2	1	827	78	954	58	5,873	227	187	9
Uniara Thikana ...	640	579	30	5	...	...	...	...	204	191	...	...	...	...	...	...	108	8	106	8	682	33	17	...
Jaisalmer State ...	***12,502***	***9,614***	***43***	***5***	...	...	...	...	***815***	***629***	...	...	...	...	...	...	***170***	***5***	***248***	***8***	***1,539***	***40***	***74***	...
Jaisalmer Town ...	518	408	36	5	...	...	...	...	48	38	...	...	...	...	...	...	122	5	172	8	1,056	38	65	...
Bap ...	492	421	1	...	...	...	...	...	2	9	...	...	...	...	...	...	1	...	4	...	38	1	1	...

PROVINCIAL TABLE II.—POPULATION OF ADMINISTRATIVE UNITS BY RELIGION AND LITERACY.—*Continued.*

STATE OR DISTRICT AND ADMINISTRATIVE UNIT (PARGANA, TEHSIL, TOWN, ETC.).	HINDUS. Brahmans. Number of persons.		Number of literates.		Other Hindus. Number of persons.		Number of literates.		Depressed Classes. Number of persons.		Number of literates.		JAINS. Number of persons.		Number of literates.		SIKHS. Number of persons.		Number of literates.	
	Males.	Females.	Males.	Females.	Males.	Females.	Males.	Females.	Males.	Females.	Males.	Females.	Males.	Females.	Males.	Females.	Males.	Females.	Males.	Females.
1	2	3	4	5	6	7	8	9	10	11	12	13	14	15	16	17	18	19	20	21
Jaisalmer State—*Concld.*																				
Buili ...	...	...	...	...	425	342	2	...	70	65	...	...	...	...	...	...	...	...	...	...
Devikot ...	44	32	10	...	1,460	1,088	20	...	295	245	1	...	34	28	11	...	...	...	...	...
Dewa ...	10	10	...	...	730	587	8	...	225	210	...	...	...	...	...	...	...	...	...	...
Fatehgarh ...	50	29	9	...	1,523	1,289	64	...	280	270	...	...	94	76	44	...	...	...	...	...
Jaisalmer ...	24	9	1	...	1,467	1,229	18	...	300	290	...	...	24	22	...	...	...	...	...	...
Khuiala ...	1	...	1	...	244	145	8	...	180	137	...	...	...	...	...	...	...	...	...	...
Kishangarh ...	...	...	...	...	8	1	8	...	42	80	...	...	...	...	...	...	...	...	...	...
Lakha ...	121	96	1	...	1,219	834	16	...	249	186	1	...	184	150	46	...	6	1	4	...
Lathi-Nachna ...	71	89	...	...	1,702	1,618	18	...	485	333	...	...	52	69	...	...	...	...	...	...
Myajlar ...	8	3	...	...	749	474	23	...	212	182	...	...	7	4	5	...	...	...	...	...
Nokh ...	311	250	21	...	4,518	3,641	115	...	868	659	...	...	1	2	...	...	...	...	...	...
Ramgarh ...	1	...	1	...	1,061	851	27	1	173	136	...	...	4	1	1	...	...	...	...	...
Sam-Khabha ...	19	17	3	...	1,206	928	28	...	344	279	2	...	...	...	...	...	...	...	...	...
Shahgarh-Ghotru ...	...	...	...	...	124	100	30	...	27	26	...	...	...	...	...	...	...	...	...	...
Sri Mohangarh ...	3	2	3	...	1,022	771	18	...	300	291	...	...	1	...	1	...	...	...	...	...
Tanot ...	4	...	2	...	8	2	2	...	86	82	...	...	...	...	...	...	...	...	...	...
Jhalawar State ...	***3,143***	***2,705***	***1,294***	***194***	***37,915***	***34,093***	***2,921***	***308***	***9,647***	***9,131***	***74***	***1***	***1,390***	***1,240***	***840***	***139***	***15***	***3***	***6***	***1***
Jhalrapatan (Chhaoni) ...	507	480	312	110	2,706	2,598	700	158	415	401	30	...	85	75	70	19	2	3	2	1
Awar ...	193	148	49	1	4,000	3,552	136	1	1,192	997	1	...	250	192	131	4	1	...	...	...
Dag ...	488	370	166	17	6,654	5,802	310	42	2,273	2,273	5	...	305	282	182	22	...	...	...	...
Gangdhar ...	634	537	148	9	8,638	7,805	499	27	2,507	2,362	9	...	264	240	153	8	2	...	1	...
Pachpahar ...	697	582	330	22	8,935	7,808	723	51	1,914	1,843	13	1	204	169	136	18	...	...	...	...
Patan ...	679	588	294	85	6,982	6,533	553	29	1,346	1,255	7	...	282	292	168	68	10	...	3	...
Karauli State ...	***8,120***	***6,725***	***1,612***	***66***	***52,768***	***42,665***	***2,984***	***156***	***11,690***	***10,791***	***5***	***2***	***229***	***219***	***150***	***22***	***1***	...	***1***	...
Karauli Town ...	1,710	1,587	723	49	6,027	4,488	1,205	90	691	687	4	...	172	180	114	20	...	...	...	...
Hazur ...	1,686	1,305	204	6	15,027	11,680	447	7	3,567	3,209	1	...	19	9	8	...	...	...	...	...
Machilpur ...	1,472	1,131	133	1	8,009	5,832	260	4	1,905	1,672	...	...	...	...	...	...	...	...	...	...
Mandrail ...	1,492	1,284	211	8	6,108	5,807	320	9	1,394	1,346	...	...	1	...	1	...	...	...	...	...

PROVINCIAL TABLE II.—Population of Administrative Units by Religion and Literacy.—*Continued.*

STATE OR DISTRICT AND ADMINISTRATIVE UNIT (PARGANA, TEHSIL, TOWN, ETC.).	MUSLIMS.				CHRISTIANS.				TRIBAL.				OTHERS.				NUMBER LITERATE—						LITERATE IN ENGLISH.	
	Number of persons.		Number of literates.		Number of persons		Number of literates.		Number of persons.		Number of literates.		Number of persons.		Number of literates.		Aged 0—15.		Aged 15—20.		Aged 20 and over.			
	Males.	Females.	Males.	Females.	Males.	Females.	Males.	Females.	Males.	Females.	Males.	Females.	Males.	Females.	Males.	Females.	Males.	Females.	Males.	Females.	Males.	Females.	Males.	Females.
1	22	23	24	25	26	27	28	29	30	31	32	33	34	35	36	37	38	39	40	41	42	43	44	45
Jaisalmer State—*Cld*																								
Buili ...	885	274	...	...	...	...	...	...	5	6	...	...	...	...	...	...	...	...	...	...	2	...	...	...
Devikut ...	320	268	...	...	...	...	...	...	21	24	...	...	...	...	...	...	2	...	5	...	35	...	...	...
Dewa ...	61	89	...	...	...	...	...	...	...	...	...	...	...	...	...	...	...	...	...	...	3	...	...	...
Fatehgarh ...	518	445	...	...	...	...	...	...	113	80	...	...	...	...	...	...	9	...	20	...	88	...	5	...
Jaisalmer ...	436	306	1	...	...	...	...	...	181	136	...	...	...	...	...	...	1	...	3	...	16	...	...	...
Khuiala ...	1,646	1,217	1	...	...	...	...	...	44	26	...	...	...	...	...	...	...	...	...	...	5	...	...	...
Kishangarh ...	452	298	...	...	...	...	...	...	18	7	...	...	...	...	...	...	1	...	...	...	2	...	...	...
Lakha ...	280	194	...	...	...	...	...	...	19	19	...	...	...	...	...	...	2	...	6	...	60	...	...	...
Lathi-Nachna ...	1,087	833	...	...	...	...	...	...	89	86	...	...	...	...	...	...	1	...	2	...	15	...	...	...
Myajlar ...	373	295	...	...	...	...	...	...	73	49	...	...	...	...	...	...	1	...	4	...	23	...	1	...
Nokh ...	1,485	1,028	1	...	...	...	...	...	93	79	...	...	...	...	...	...	24	...	19	...	94	...	1	...
Ramgarh ...	154	95	...	...	...	...	...	...	48	27	...	...	...	...	...	...	3	...	3	...	23	1	...	...
Sam-Khabha ...	1,709	1,404	2	...	...	...	...	...	100	84	...	...	...	...	...	...	2	...	2	...	31	...	1	...
Shahgarh-Ghotru ...	1,605	1,322	...	...	...	...	...	...	12	4	...	...	...	...	...	...	...	...	2	...	28	...	...	...
Sri Mohangarh ...	617	510	...	...	...	...	...	...	4	5	...	...	...	...	...	...	1	...	4	...	17	...	...	...
Tanot ...	364	257	1	...	...	...	...	...	...	...	...	...	...	...	...	...	...	...	2	...	3	...	...	...
Jhalawar State ...	***4,377***	***4,181***	***1,157***	***184***	***31***	***19***	***11***	***2***	...	...	...	...	...	...	...	...	***1,268***	***280***	***821***	***121***	***4,214***	***428***	***427***	***12***
Jhalrapatan(Chhaoni	1,539	1,631	415	70	4	1	3	1	...	...	...	...	...	...	...	...	322	118	213	53	1,006	188	220	10
Awar ...	159	164	33	1	...	...	...	...	...	...	...	...	...	...	...	...	91	1	42	2	217	4	3	...
Dag ...	412	419	108	17	...	...	...	...	...	...	...	...	...	...	...	...	162	33	106	17	503	48	1	...
Gangdhar ...	508	426	110	7	24	18	5	1	...	...	...	...	...	...	...	...	186	18	114	7	620	27	20	...
Pachpahar ...	811	599	219	27	3	...	3	...	...	...	...	...	...	...	...	...	258	44	185	18	981	57	72	...
Patan ...	948	942	272	62	...	...	...	...	...	...	...	...	...	...	...	...	249	66	161	24	887	104	111	2
Karauli State ...	***3,914***	***3,387***	***347***	***28***	***7***	***9***	***7***	***4***	...	...	...	...	...	...	...	...	**554**	**44**	**663**	**52**	**3,889**	**182**	**140**	**9**
Karauli Town ...	2,228	1,985	252	28	7	9	7	4	...	...	...	...	...	...	...	...	253	32	809	38	1,743	121	107	8
Hazur ...	370	267	17	...	...	...	...	...	...	...	...	...	...	...	...	...	66	...	82	1	529	12	12	...
Machilpur ...	352	283	24	...	...	...	...	...	...	...	...	...	...	...	...	...	31	...	51	1	335	4	3	...
Mandrail ...	205	194	17	...	...	...	...	...	...	...	...	...	...	...	...	...	73	2	72	2	404	13	8	...

PROVINCIAL TABLE II.—Population of Administrative Units by Religion and Literacy.—*Continued.*

STATE OR DISTRICT AND ADMINISTRATIVE UNIT (PARGANA, TEHSIL, TOWN, ETC.).	HINDUS. Brahmans. Number of persons. Males.	Females.	Number of literates. Males.	Females.	Other Hindus. Number of persons. Males.	Females.	Number of literates. Males.	Females.	Depressed Classes. Number of persons. Males.	Females.	Number of literates. Males.	Females.	JAINS. Number of persons. Males.	Females.	Number of literates. Males.	Females.	SIKHS. Number of persons. Males.	Females.	Number of literates. Males.	Females.
1	2	3	4	5	6	7	8	9	10	11	12	13	14	15	16	17	18	19	20	21
Karauli State.—*Concluded.*																				
Sapotra ...	1,327	1,182	278	2	13,958	12,495	668	43	3,260	3,127	...	2	36	30	26	2	...	...	...	...
Utgir ...	433	286	63	...	3,644	2,913	84	3	873	800	...	...	1	...	1	...	1	...	1	...
Kishangarh State ...	**3,120**	**2,883**	**998**	**59**	**29,005**	**27,000**	**2,361**	**157**	**7,381**	**6,874**	**20**	...	**1,187**	**1,044**	**803**	**67**	**2**	...	**2**	...
Kishangarh Town ...	721	604	438	48	3,358	2,853	991	87	451	419	1	...	379	353	274	54	2	...	2	...
Arain ...	603	575	140	3	5,651	5,451	289	14	1,562	1,389	2	...	245	206	169	3	...	...	...	...
Kishangarh ...	386	421	86	1	6,336	5,980	272	6	1,728	1,702	6	...	142	131	90	1	...	...	...	...
Rupnagar ...	767	723	162	2	6,750	5,907	406	24	2,011	1,810	8	...	164	142	114	3	...	...	...	...
Sarwar ...	643	560	168	5	6,910	6,859	403	26	1,629	1,554	8	...	257	212	156	6	...	...	...	...
Kotah State ...	**19,735**	**16,767**	**7,268**	**746**	**253,954**	**236,111**	**14,551**	**964**	**51,935**	**50,914**	**542**	**25**	**2,759**	**2,435**	**1,664**	**204**	**151**	**122**	**91**	**30**
Kotah City ...	2,622	2,210	1,454	310	9,898	8,041	3,874	329	1,475	1,368	67	2	537	497	371	73	36	27	19	9
Aklerah ...	680	542	161	20	15,124	13,800	361	6	2,647	2,538	26	...	119	137	60	10	1	...	1	...
Antah ...	837	770	249	9	10,383	10,351	515	28	2,090	2,136	11	1	17	13	9	2	1	2	1	1
Asnawar ...	297	239	93	6	5,545	5,005	261	14	1,086	1,050	12	1	18	11	10	1	3	...	3	...
Bakani ...	841	710	298	5	13,177	12,306	566	22	2,086	1,774	8	...	158	121	108	15	2	3	1	2
Baran ...	1,558	1,203	636	78	14,999	14,263	1,529	130	4,104	4,187	45	...	182	174	133	21	7	5	6	2
Barod ...	570	468	209	6	7,252	7,056	449	9	1,722	1,712	14	...	52	32	34	...	1	...	...	...
Chechat ...	1,048	870	245	31	13,829	12,666	708	35	3,360	3,359	82	4	130	105	83	6	2	5	1	...
Chhipabarod ...	728	584	408	38	14,453	13,042	718	63	2,433	2,642	21	2	64	60	43	6	...	...	...	...
Digod ...	672	572	208	8	7,115	6,680	378	81	2,130	2,087	17	...	60	46	32	3	...	...	...	...
Itawa ...	431	335	135	7	7,728	6,961	311	15	1,955	1,954	3	1	94	71	54	2	...	...	...	...
Kanwas ...	696	572	233	12	9,745	9,438	482	11	2,347	2,348	20	...	69	58	41	3	...	...	...	...
Khanpur ...	1,469	1,348	458	21	17,145	17,071	901	26	4,091	3,645	53	1	246	252	134	24	1	...	1	...
Kishanganj ...	474	366	198	12	12,947	11,968	510	23	1,898	1,758	13	...	38	34	24	...	30	16	19	6
Kunjer ...	1,331	1,092	450	25	16,028	15,480	917	30	3,665	3,474	33	3	109	80	59	5	2	...	1	...
Ladpura ...	1,449	1,215	492	73	16,063	14,017	1,096	68	4,412	4,463	44	4	288	244	157	12	60	62	33	10
Mangrol ...	870	841	383	23	9,942	9,248	634	30	1,967	1,974	19	...	85	66	55	2	...	...	1	...
Manohar Thana ...	497	416	141	15	15,662	13,794	346	11	1,345	1,366	21	...	68	46	34	2	1	...	...	...
Sangod ...	1,013	821	298	19	10,394	10,254	533	27	2,397	2,470	14	6	72	47	48	4	...	...	...	...
Shahabad ...	514	433	169	10	11,642	10,817	349	4	1,819	1,712	4	...	64	82	41	...	4	2	4	...
Kotris ...	1,138	1,070	350	12	14,888	13,998	683	52	2,956	2,897	15	...	294	250	184	13	...	...	...	...

PROVINCIAL TABLE II.—Population of Administrative Units by Religion and Literacy.—*Continued.*

STATE OR DISTRICT AND ADMINISTRATIVE UNIT (PARGANA, TEHSIL, TOWN, ETC.).	MUSLIMS.				CHRISTIANS.				TRIBAL.				OTHERS.				NUMBER LITERATE—						LITERATE IN ENGLISH.	
	Number of persons.		Number of literates.		Number of persons.		Number of literates.		Number of persons.		Number of literates.		Number of persons.		Number of literates.		Aged 0—15.		Aged 15—20.		Aged 20 and over.			
	Males.	Females.	Males.	Females.	Males.	Females.	Males.	Females.	Males.	Females.	Males.	Females.	Males.	Females.	Males.	Females.	Males.	Females.	Males	Females.	Males.	Females.	Males.	Females.
1	22	23	24	25	26	27	28	29	30	31	32	33	34	35	36	37	38	39	40	41	42	43	44	45
Karauli State.—*Cld.*																								
Sapotra ...	707	613	29	...	...	...	...	...	...	...	...	...	...	..	...	...	117	10	135	9	749	30	9	1
Utgir ...	52	45	8	...	...	...	...	...	...	...	...	...	...	...	...	...	14	...	14	1	129	2	1	...
Kishangarh State...	**3,467**	**3,130**	**369**	**23**	**8**	**7**	**7**	**6**	**324**	**312**	...	...	...	...	...	...	**624**	**56**	**541**	**38**	**3,395**	**218**	**295**	**7**
Kishangarh Town.	1,477	1,300	206	18	6	6	5	5	...	...	...	...	...	...	...	...	272	48	237	28	1,408	141	272	5
Arain ...	205	198	15	...	...	...	...	...	...	...	...	...	...	...	...	...	81	4	76	1	467	15	6	...
Kishangarh ...	715	666	15	...	...	...	...	...	13	14	...	...	...	...	...	...	59	1	52	1	358	6	3	...
Rupnagar ...	483	481	30	1	2	1	2	1	...	...	...	...	...	...	...	...	93	1	81	1	543	29	4	...
Sarwar ...	587	585	103	4	...	...	...	...	311	298	...	...	...	...	...	...	119	7	95	7	619	27	10	2
Kotah State ...	**24,531**	**22,537**	**3,487**	**327**	**470**	**444**	**284**	**258**	**1,515**	**1,408**	**1**	...	**6**	**10**	**5**	**5**	**4,819**	**739**	**3,800**	**417**	**19,274**	**1,403**	**1,813**	**101**
Kotah City ...	5,599	5,419	756	107	58	50	38	33	34	5	...	...	...	...	...	...	830	224	754	130	3,495	515	948	52
Aklerah ...	709	688	106	17	...	...	...	...	...	...	...	...	...	...	...	...	110	17	97	10	508	26	19	...
Antah ...	998	993	95	9	1	...	1	...	40	46	...	...	...	...	...	...	143	17	118	13	620	20	23	...
Asnawar ...	223	159	40	1	...	...	...	...	2	...	...	...	...	...	...	...	83	2	60	5	276	16	20	...
Bakani ...	984	849	126	9	...	...	...	...	5	1	...	...	...	...	...	...	207	15	145	10	755	28	14	...
Baran ...	1,567	1,481	302	35	4	...	4	...	10	8	...	...	2	2	2	2	482	71	333	40	1,842	157	213	8
Barod ..	773	654	144	4	...	...	...	...	31	41	...	...	...	...	...	...	122	5	122	4	606	10	5	...
Chechat ...	1,242	1,065	242	29	91	80	52	41	124	107	1	...	...	...	...	..	307	58	235	28	872	65	46	4
Chhipabarod ...	856	842	168	14	...	...	...	...	70	67	...	...	...	...	...	...	278	49	176	16	909	58	24	...
Digod ...	479	380	64	5	...	...	...	...	37	42	...	...	...	...	...	...	114	11	86	7	499	29	26	...
Itawa ...	342	253	58	8	...	...	...	...	54	39	...	...	...	...	...	...	80	7	58	4	423	22	14	...
Kanwas ...	584	581	88	7	...	...	...	...	164	139	...	...	...	...	...	...	171	10	108	4	585	19	21	...
Khanpur ...	956	936	107	25	...	...	...	...	61	62	...	...	...	...	...	...	262	43	218	12	1,174	42	19	...
Kishanganj ...	508	480	84	4	22	22	12	11	...	...	...	...	...	...	...	...	153	19	114	10	593	27	29	1
Kunjer ...	917	835	150	9	225	245	139	151	16	17	...	...	...	...	...	...	397	60	232	35	1,130	128	43	4
Ladpura ...	2,738	2,444	391	29	55	39	28	19	672	662	...	...	2	3	2	2	327	52	288	44	1,558	121	257	30
Mangrol ...	1,221	1,131	118	2	...	...	...	...	109	95	...	...	...	...	...	...	188	22	176	12	846	23	19	...
Manohar Thana ...	1,080	860	116	...	...	...	...	...	...	...	...	...	...	...	...	...	111	6	82	6	465	16	10	...
Sangod ...	1,190	1,088	129	7	13	7	9	2	32	28	...	...	...	...	...	...	218	40	145	7	668	18	8	1
Shahabad ...	342	238	69	...	...	...	...	...	...	...	...	...	...	...	...	...	94	2	95	4	447	8	13	...
Kotris ...	1,273	1,211	124	6	1	1	1	1	54	49	...	...	2	5	1	1	147	14	158	16	1,008	55	47	1

PROVINCIAL TABLE II.—POPULATION OF ADMINISTRATIVE UNITS BY RELIGION AND LITERACY.—*Continued.*

STATE OR DISTRICT AND ADMINISTRATIVE UNIT (PARGANA, TEHSIL, TOWN, ETC.)	HINDUS.												JAINS.				SIKHS.			
	Brahmans				Other Hindus.				Depressed Classes.											
	Number of persons		Number of literates		Number of persons		Number of literates.		Number of persons		Number of literates		Number of persons		Number of literates.		Number of persons.		Number of literates.	
	Males.	Females	Males.	Females.	Males	Females	Males.	Females.	Males.	Females	Males.	Females	Males.	Females	Males.	Females	Males.	Females	Males.	Females.
1	2	3	4	5	6	7	8	9	10	11	12	13	14	15	16	17	18	19	20	21
Kushalgarh (Chiefship) ...	**236**	**229**	**165**	**15**	**16,438**	**16,548**	**208**	**18**	**330**	**346**	**5**	...	**297**	**286**	**209**	**18**	...	...	...	...
Kushalgarh Town ...	196	211	139	15	787	775	164	18	50	35	5	...	286	283	202	18	...	...	...	...
Dungra ...	13	11	6	...	4,896	4,493	16	...	153	172	...	...	1	...	...	...	...	...	...	...
Maiyad ...	20	4	14	...	7,647	7,719	16	...	95	109	...	...	3	...	2	...	...	...	...	...
Patan ...	7	3	6	...	3,608	3,561	12	...	32	30	...	...	7	3	5	...	...	...	...	...
Lawa (Estate) ...	**47**	**34**	**21**	**1**	**1,026**	**947**	**20**	**10**	**241**	**251**	...	...	**75**	**60**	**38**	**1**	...	...	...	...
Marwar State ...	**56,150**	**54,020**	**14,951**	**804**	**748,081**	**671,303**	**23,527**	**1,706**	**157,781**	**144,106**	**2,961**	**109**	**52,587**	**61,082**	**28,384**	**1,517**	**17**	**17**	**10**	**7**
Jodhpur City ...	8,155	5,758	3,857	411	24,748	19,557	8,400	772	4,001	3,985	215	20	2,465	2,308	1,591	254	5	7	2	2
Bali ...	1,854	2,145	410	10	38,734	35,517	763	51	8,759	8,025	150	4	5,645	8,146	2,276	80	...	...	...	...
Bilara ...	1,188	1,304	253	17	26,671	25,597	635	162	5,699	4,437	110	3	1,502	1,555	792	88	2	4	2	2
Desuri ...	1,338	1,489	458	23	28,649	26,365	457	25	6,725	6,608	125	4	4,060	5,189	1,765	62	2	...	...	...
Didwana ...	4,863	4,257	967	33	35,341	31,663	1,581	81	7,928	7,552	150	6	1,547	1,989	732	64	...	...	...	...
Jalore ...	1,758	1,683	536	14	52,960	47,770	850	45	13,207	11,492	252	10	7,528	9,471	4,522	123	...	...	...	...
Jaitaran ...	1,452	1,522	387	6	32,445	30,322	273	27	5,890	5,954	121	4	1,655	1,824	1,052	23	1	...	1	...
Jaswantpura ...	4,807	4,264	454	11	42,644	37,711	529	21	8,165	7,137	168	5	4,188	4,742	2,815	35	...	...	...	...
Jodhpur ...	2,720	2,476	559	31	56,235	51,364	914	44	10,292	8,697	220	5	1,538	1,581	709	62	...	...	...	...
Malani ...	2,813	2,020	599	12	68,940	56,142	746	45	11,724	10,937	150	7	3,405	2,963	1,899	32	...	...	...	...
Merta ...	3,950	4,200	556	7	44,677	40,875	809	71	12,788	11,847	241	8	1,809	1,424	746	65	...	...	...	...
Nagaur ...	4,554	4,812	1,063	26	47,487	44,072	1,480	31	11,158	10,067	198	6	2,223	2,088	974	70	1	...	1	...
Pachbhadra ...	684	624	128	4	11,528	9,456	522	5	1,287	2,184	26	3	1,151	1,176	657	10	...	...	...	...
Pali ...	1,443	1,583	241	12	22,278	20,768	709	55	4,568	3,835	92	2	1,783	1,883	978	28	...	...	...	...
Parbatsar ...	2,595	2,982	1,213	28	38,599	34,314	61	63	9,950	9,897	75	6	682	652	347	15	1	...	...	...
Phalodi ...	4,002	4,513	1,059	65	28,143	24,405	689	80	5,602	5,638	105	4	2,030	2,671	845	85	...	...	...	...
Sambhar-Marwar ...	2,648	2,742	785	44	27,079	23,337	1,228	36	6,685	5,820	125	6	1,216	1,203	744	84	4	4	3	2
½ Sambhar-Shamlat ...	323	247	146	...	2,820	2,094	512	57	626	567	40	2	48	36	29	5	...	...	...	...
Sanchore ...	1,823	1,751	116	1	20,567	26,842	304	5	4,992	4,071	98	...	1,485	1,297	904	5	...	...	...	...
Shergarh ...	648	562	75	8	27,466	22,587	543	24	3,303	4,112	26	...	797	731	403	12	...	...	...	...
Sheo ...	225	208	38	...	7,441	6,024	167	...	1,678	1,423	20	...	291	244	184	3	...	...	...	...
Siwana ...	547	528	274	2	16,184	14,681	358	17	3,722	3,307	50	...	2,458	3,089	1,828	21	...	...	...	...
Sojat ...	2,260	2,350	777	39	43,050	40,340	997	39	9,087	7,514	204	4	3,636	4,275	2,092	341	1	2	1	1

PROVINCIAL TABLE II.—POPULATION OF ADMINISTRATIVE UNITS BY RELIGION AND LITERACY.—*Continued.*

STATE OR DISTRICT AND ADMINISTRATIVE UNIT (PARGANA, TEHSIL, TOWN, ETC.).	MUSLIMS.				CHRISTIANS.				TRIBAL.				OTHERS.				NUMBER LITERATE—						LITERATE IN ENGLISH.	
	Number of persons.		Number of literates.		Number of persons		Number of literates.		Number of persons.		Number of literates.		Number of persons		Number of literates		Aged 0—15		Aged 15—20.		Aged 20 and over.			
	Males.	Females.	Males.	Females.	Males.	Females.	Males.	Females.	Males.	Females.	Males.	Females.	Males.	Females.	Males.	Females.	Males.	Females.	Males.	Females.	Males.	Females.	Males.	Females.
1	22	23	24	25	26	27	28	29	30	31	32	33	34	35	36	37	38	39	40	41	42	43	44	45
Kushalgarh (Chiefship) ...	***453***	***401***	***109***	***4***	...	...	...	...	...	...	...	...	...	...	...	...	***117***	***18***	***95***	***10***	***484***	***27***	***80***	...
Kushalgarh Town.	282	214	83	4	...	...	...	...	...	...	...	...	...	...	...	...	111	18	82	10	400	27	78	...
Dungra ...	65	37	14	...	...	...	...	...	...	...	...	...	...	...	...	...	4	...	5	...	27	...	2	...
Maiyad ...	128	131	3	...	...	...	...	...	...	...	...	...	...	...	...	...	2	...	3	...	30	...	4	...
Patan ...	28	19	9	...	...	...	...	...	...	...	...	...	...	...	...	...	...	...	5	...	27	...	1	...
Lawa (Estate) ...	***56***	***53***	***1***	...	...	...	...	...	...	...	...	...	...	...	...	...	***8***	...	***11***	***1***	***61***	***11***	***4***	...
Marwar State ...	***93,234***	***83,629***	***4,873***	**563**	**386**	***300***	**198**	**116**	***1,653***	***1,588***	***29***	...	***23***	***25***	***23***	***19***	***10,438***	***1,016***	***9,865***	**669**	***54,653***	***3,156***	***7,091***	**268**
Jodhpur City ...	12,495	10,744	1,511	252	251	190	156	87	29	...	29	...	21	22	21	17	3,293	491	2,588	308	9,906	1,021	5,810	205
Bali ...	1,229	1,141	172	10	15	8	5	5	1,542	1,489	...	...	...	...	...	...	629	42	490	14	2,657	104	96	2
Bilara ...	2,570	2,588	123	42	...	...	...	...	...	...	...	...	...	...	...	...	271	77	249	29	1,895	208	49	...
Desuri ...	1,034	878	112	9	3	2	2	1	...	...	...	...	...	...	...	...	525	23	443	19	1,951	82	74	...
Didwana ...	8,116	7,897	267	12	...	...	...	...	6	9	...	...	...	...	...	...	368	22	501	27	2,848	147	147	2
Jalore ...	1,752	1,502	86	...	...	...	...	...	...	...	...	...	...	...	...	...	821	35	728	22	4,697	135	34	...
Jaitaran ...	8,358	8,093	158	26	...	...	...	...	...	...	...	...	...	...	...	...	217	20	208	14	1,567	52	68	1
Jaswantpura ...	1,924	1,588	148	8	6	...	6	...	...	...	...	...	...	...	...	...	593	9	509	14	3,018	57	44	...
Jodhpur ...	2,027	1,728	78	9	...	...	...	...	5	8	...	...	...	...	...	...	430	49	279	30	1,771	72	112	1
Malani ...	13,354	11,625	102	22	4	...	4	...	1	10	...	...	...	...	...	...	360	21	462	19	2,678	78	126	1
Merta ...	3,902	3,565	117	97	...	...	...	...	2	17	...	...	...	...	...	...	326	22	345	22	1,798	204	133	8
Nagaur ...	8,028	7,554	524	10	75	82	6	7	...	...	...	...	...	...	...	...	315	81	508	18	3,428	101	134	10
Pachbhadra ...	2,064	1,805	123	6	...	...	...	...	...	...	...	...	...	...	...	...	170	7	178	5	1,118	16	83	...
Pali ...	2,659	2,335	234	1	...	...	...	...	48	30	...	...	...	...	...	...	222	25	277	28	1,755	50	75	2
Parbatsar ...	4,853	4,898	369	17	1	...	1	...	...	...	...	...	...	...	...	...	278	21	233	12	1,560	96	58	1
Phalodi ...	4,213	3,896	55	9	...	...	...	...	5	8	...	...	...	...	...	...	235	23	272	27	2,246	143	72	...
Sambhar-Marwar.	2,648	2,424	250	11	4	2	2	1	...	...	...	...	...	...	...	...	344	20	369	12	2,424	102	120	...
½ Sambhar-Shamlat.	1,208	1,033	94	...	8	5	4	4	3	2	...	...	...	...	...	...	90	15	180	12	555	41	64	4
Sanchore ...	6,816	5,693	58	4	...	...	...	...	...	...	...	...	...	...	...	...	160	7	202	1	1,118	7	33	1
Shergarh ...	1,954	1,725	11	...	...	...	...	...	17	20	...	...	...	...	...	...	88	9	124	4	851	31	9	...
Sheo ...	3,986	3,299	3	...	...	...	...	...	...	...	...	...	...	...	...	...	52	1	49	...	311	2	8	...
Siwana ...	652	500	37	3	3	...	2	...	...	...	...	...	2	3	2	2	250	12	212	7	1,589	26	35	...
Sojat ...	2,392	2,118	221	15	16	11	10	11	...	...	...	...	...	...	...	...	411	34	474	85	3,417	381	212	35

PROVINCIAL TABLE II.—Population of Administrative Units by Religion and Literacy.—*Continued.*

STATE OR DISTRICT AND ADMINISTRATIVE UNIT (PARGANA, TEHSIL, TOWN, ETC.).	HINDUS. Brahmans. Number of persons.		Number of literates.		Other Hindus. Number of persons.		Number of literates.		Depressed Classes. Number of persons.		Number of literates.		JAINS. Number of persons.		Number of literates.		SIKHS. Number of persons.		Number of literates.	
	Males.	Females.	Males.	Females.	Males.	Females.	Males.	Females.	Males.	Females.	Males.	Females.	Males.	Females.	Males.	Females.	Males.	Females.	Males.	Females.
1	2	3	4	5	6	7	8	9	10	11	12	13	14	15	16	17	18	19	20	21
Mewar State ...	**56,046**	**53,554**	**7,083**	**313**	**555,552**	**517,606**	**16,531**	**719**	**84,782**	**84,489**	**238**	**7**	**34,086**	**31,915**	**16,591**	**410**	**17**	**6**	**9**	...
Udaipur City ...	3,076	2,508	1,661	108	10,393	8,797	2,863	153	1,145	1,054	21	1	2,706	2,870	1,675	84	5	3	1	...
Asind ...	746	788	41	1	4,298	4,024	67	...	589	621	...	...	270	247	169	1	...	...	...	...
Bhilwara ...	3,699	3,515	405	27	34,985	33,456	1,500	110	6,047	5,742	17	...	1,459	1,290	778	39	...	...	...	...
Chhoti Sadri ...	1,692	1,507	198	...	18,744	17,855	853	14	2,958	2,936	22	...	703	549	429	5	...	...	...	...
Chitorgarh ...	4,038	3,710	378	11	39,759	37,200	1,094	21	7,056	6,757	28	...	967	879	459	70	...	...	...	...
Deosthan ...	1,264	1,158	178	3	11,951	11,185	362	...	1,720	1,539	6	...	926	864	466	4	...	...	...	...
Deosthan (Kankroli and Nathdwara) ...	2,048	1,817	676	31	9,350	8,566	801	56	1,295	1,317	12	...	661	625	257	3	5	...	3	...
Girwa ...	4,498	4,288	303	2	40,086	37,592	683	26	5,072	5,281	5	...	3,261	3,056	1,581	17	...	...	...	...
Hurra ...	1,780	1,626	208	3	19,465	18,064	682	36	3,383	3,282	8	2	1,267	1,077	637	10	...	...	...	...
Jahazpur ...	1,519	1,540	188	13	23,584	20,952	494	26	4,978	4,981	1	...	597	486	315	4	...	...	...	...
Kapasin ...	1,661	1,520	227	3	17,421	16,078	639	9	2,961	2,921	11	...	742	685	871	6	...	...	...	...
Khamnor ...	1,289	1,331	140	3	11,284	10,521	97	1	1,029	1,045	...	...	1,027	899	485	3	...	...	...	...
Kherwara ...	705	731	156	...	17,654	16,588	359	20	1,166	1,144	2	...	621	606	196	0	...	...	...	...
Kumalgarh ...	2,849	2,714	129	...	24,913	22,560	313	21	2,831	2,516	1	...	2,277	2,397	985	11	...	...	...	...
Magra ...	3,119	3,309	157	1	25,487	24,935	247	11	2,109	2,080	5	...	2,278	2,338	988	9	...	...	...	...
Mandalgarh ...	2,961	2,888	198	8	22,856	21,196	697	28	4,799	4,716	4	...	779	742	403	9	6	3	4	...
Rajnagar ...	2,273	2,334	73	2	15,128	13,760	82	2	2,447	2,228	3	...	1,147	1,043	512	5	...	...	...	...
Rashmi ...	1,710	1,658	218	3	14,980	14,318	599	12	3,178	3,059	10	...	810	777	522	18	...	...	...	...
Saharan ...	3,395	3,253	275	3	32,978	31,316	885	33	6,247	5,896	49	2	2,565	2,303	1,233	26	1	...	1	...
Thikanas ...	10,788	10,520	1,262	96	148,092	137,518	2,992	145	22,966	24,560	88	2	8,684	8,382	4,095	76	...	...	...	...
Udaipur ...	935	949	17	...	12,204	11,246	162	...	806	814	...	...	839	350	85	1	...	...	...	...
Partabgarh State ...	**1,683**	**1,531**	**699**	**38**	**16,736**	**16,047**	**1,582**	**128**	**2,705**	**2,645**	**27**	...	**2,240**	**2,205**	**1,449**	**192**	6	...	**2**	...
Partabgarh Town ...	535	489	313	32	2,426	2,207	647	47	215	179	11	...	1,270	1,327	840	165	4	...	...	...
Hathunia ...	736	696	203	1	9,358	9,005	478	49	1,695	1,647	14	...	438	409	265	7	...	...	...	...
Magra ...	57	54	37	...	532	480	60	2	98	93	...	...	63	54	37	3	...	...	...	...
Sagthali ...	355	292	146	5	4,420	4,355	397	30	697	726	2	...	469	415	307	17	2	...	2	...

PROVINCIAL TABLE II.—Population of Administrative Units by Religion and Literacy.—*Continued.*

STATE OR DISTRICT AND ADMINISTRATIVE UNIT (PARGANA, TEHSIL, TOWN, ETC.).	MUSLIMS. Number of persons. Males.	MUSLIMS. Number of persons. Females.	MUSLIMS. Number of literates. Males.	MUSLIMS. Number of literates. Females.	CHRISTIANS. Number of persons. Males.	CHRISTIANS. Number of persons. Females.	CHRISTIANS. Number of literates. Males.	CHRISTIANS. Number of literates. Females.	TRIBAL. Number of persons. Males.	TRIBAL. Number of persons. Females.	TRIBAL. Number of literates. Males.	TRIBAL. Number of literates. Females.	OTHERS. Number of persons. Males.	OTHERS. Number of persons. Females.	OTHERS. Number of literates. Males.	OTHERS. Number of literates. Females.	NUMBER LITERATE— Aged 0—15. Males.	NUMBER LITERATE— Aged 0—15. Females.	NUMBER LITERATE— Aged 15—20. Males.	NUMBER LITERATE— Aged 15—20. Females.	NUMBER LITERATE— Aged 20 & over. Males.	NUMBER LITERATE— Aged 20 & over. Females.	LITERATE IN ENGLISH. Males.	LITERATE IN ENGLISH. Females.
1	22	23	24	25	26	27	28	29	30	31	32	33	34	35	36	37	38	39	40	41	42	43	44	45
Mewar State ...	***28,346***	***25,487***	***4,146***	***248***	***293***	***186***	***155***	***35***	***48,061***	***46,483***	***6***	...	***1***	...	...	...	***5,004***	***316***	***5,592***	***242***	***34,163***	***1,174***	***1,565***	***44***
Udaipur City ...	5,772	5,216	1,658	45	53	41	36	19	625	271	...	...	...	...	...	...	882	74	999	49	6,034	282	750	27
Asind ...	253	259	10	...	...	...	...	...	...	...	...	...	...	...	...	...	33	...	36	1	218	1	10	...
Bhilwara ...	2,948	2,701	269	34	44	2	43	2	20	28	...	...	...	...	...	...	282	32	400	39	2,390	141	154	3
Chhoti Sadri ...	893	748	182	59	2	2	2	...	19	22	...	...	...	...	...	...	277	21	214	12	1,195	45	58	...
Chitorgarh ...	2,073	1,856	175	4	1	1	...	...	467	481	...	...	...	...	...	...	222	16	270	20	1,637	70	45	...
Deosthan ...	131	90	15	1	...	...	...	...	4	...	...	...	...	...	...	...	118	...	118	1	786	7	5	...
Deosthan (Kankroli and Nathdwara).	598	575	110	27	...	...	...	...	...	...	...	...	...	...	...	...	222	22	232	11	1,405	84	97	1
Girwa ...	1,095	904	143	11	...	...	...	...	8,551	8,240	...	...	...	...	...	...	257	9	294	6	2,164	41	38	...
Hurra ...	1,018	919	79	5	...	...	...	...	18	20	...	...	...	...	...	...	159	9	207	8	1,248	39	29	1
Jahazpur ...	1,127	1,008	107	10	3	...	5	...	43	84	...	...	...	...	...	...	104	12	123	8	883	33	14	...
Kapasin ...	932	844	110	...	...	...	...	...	6	2	...	...	...	...	...	...	147	4	172	2	1,039	12	25	3
Khamnor ...	122	85	82	1	...	...	...	...	71	69	...	...	...	...	...	...	56	2	73	1	575	5	...	...
Kherwara ...	870	572	232	3	69	31	43	6	17,134	16,107	4	...	...	...	...	...	150	6	181	8	711	24	24	2
Kumalgarh ...	272	172	68	3	...	...	...	...	881	775	...	...	...	...	...	...	159	8	192	1	1,145	26	14	...
Magra ...	594	458	102	6	23	19	2	2	15,102	15,388	2	...	...	...	...	...	155	8	200	4	1,148	17	13	...
Mandalgarh ...	1,827	1,198	88	3	...	...	...	...	...	...	...	...	...	...	...	...	120	10	161	9	1,108	24	18	1
Rajnagar ...	404	389	69	...	...	...	...	...	...	...	...	...	...	...	...	...	86	1	89	2	564	6	8	...
Rashmi ...	638	648	52	...	...	...	...	...	8	6	...	...	...	...	...	...	164	9	165	5	1,072	19	9	...
Saharan ...	1,042	986	56	3	18	3	10	2	182	176	...	...	...	...	...	...	354	15	349	12	1,806	42	44	1
Thikanas ...	6,016	5,674	583	33	28	36	2	...	4,930	4,864	...	...	1	...	...	...	964	56	1,109	43	6,899	253	108	4
Udaipur ...	231	205	11	...	57	51	12	4	...	...	...	...	...	...	...	...	93	2	58	...	136	3	112	1
Partabgarh State.	***2,045***	***1,869***	***342***	***14***	***33***	***34***	***11***	***3***	***13,534***	***13,213***	***3***	...	***9***	***4***	***7***	***4***	***578***	***67***	***555***	***66***	***2,989***	***246***	***243***	***7***
Partabgarh Town.	1,055	1,021	224	12	12	10	11	3	75	7	...	...	9	4	7	4	298	49	278	49	1,482	165	199	7
Hathunia ...	668	633	30	...	17	23	...	...	3,646	3,565	1	...	...	...	...	...	129	10	144	6	718	41	20	...
Magra ...	69	51	24	2	...	...	...	...	4,154	4,081	1	...	...	...	...	...	19	1	17	2	123	4	3	...
Sagthali ...	258	164	64	...	4	1	...	...	5,659	5,560	1	...	...	...	...	...	182	7	121	9	666	36	21	...

PROVINCIAL TABLE II.—Population of Administrative Units by Religion and Literacy.—*Continued.*

STATE OR DISTRICT AND ADMINISTRATIVE UNIT (PARGANA, TEHSIL, TOWN, ETC.).	HINDUS. Brahmans. Number of persons. Males.	Females.	Number of literates. Males.	Females.	Other Hindus. Number of persons. Males.	Females.	Number of literates. Males.	Females.	Depressed Classes. Number of persons. Males.	Females.	Number of literates. Males.	Females.	JAINS. Number of persons. Males.	Females.	Number of literates. Males.	Females.	SIKHS. Number of persons. Males.	Females.	Number of literates. Males.	Females.
1	2	3	4	5	6	7	8	9	10	11	12	13	14	15	16	17	18	19	20	21
Shahpura State ...	***1,935***	***1,782***	***487***	***43***	***19,312***	***18,156***	***1,303***	***124***	***4,598***	***4,490***	***16***	...	***757***	***661***	***497***	***43***	...	...	...	...
Shahpura Town ...	428	440	270	40	2,949	2,847	872	109	268	267	6	...	260	249	191	38	...	...	...	...
Arwar ...	226	253	57	2	2,328	2,266	108	7	564	575	2	...	176	158	120	4	...	...	...	...
Dhikola ...	340	299	22	...	3,957	3,641	125	2	1,192	1,106	4	...	48	38	21	...	...	...	...	...
Dohria ...	350	211	59	...	2,733	2,561	43	1	727	729	1	...	120	97	73	1	...	...	...	...
Kanechan ...	88	80	10	...	1,289	1,122	61	...	395	346	...	...	1	...	1	...	...	...	...	...
Phulia ...	233	245	45	1	2,993	2,746	50	4	763	762	2	...	66	53	50	...	...	...	...	...
Sangria ...	185	189	20	...	1,516	1,467	20	1	402	399	1	...	84	56	37	...	...	...	...	...
Shahpura ...	85	65	4	...	1,597	1,506	24	...	302	306	...	...	12	10	4	...	...	...	...	...
Sirohi State ...	***7,655***	***8,030***	***1,289***	***129***	***76,506***	***69,016***	***2,757***	***164***	***16,883***	***15,695***	***182***	***7***	***6,696***	***8,812***	***3,778***	***183***	***8***	***2***	***5***	***1***
Sirohi Town ...	270	226	152	18	2,303	2,170	363	18	402	332	...	...	516	621	360	47	5	1	3	1
Sirohi ...	105	187	11	1	819	743	8	...	342	335	...	...	28	32	16	...	...	...	...	...
Abu ...	37	25	20	4	607	554	20	...	49	27	...	...	39	19	30	...	1	...	...	...
Bhakar ...	...	...	...	...	2,410	2,216	18	...	3	...	...	...	...	...	...	...	...	...	...	...
Barlut ...	1,319	1,402	139	1	6,848	6,172	178	10	2,392	2,211	4	...	793	1,126	443	13	...	...	...	...
Erinpura ...	13	23	13	...	724	535	140	9	86	89	3	...	2	3	2	...	...	...	...	...
Madar ...	810	850	28	3	9,763	8,547	188	10	1,785	1,643	8	2	718	848	396	8	...	...	...	...
Magra ...	1,114	1,258	78	2	7,426	6,595	130	11	2,065	2,175	4	1	1,128	1,495	596	15	...	...	...	...
Pamera ...	1,049	1,108	190	9	9,624	8,817	158	2	2,415	2,166	22	...	725	850	371	3	...	...	...	...
Pindwara ...	974	1,076	82	6	9,095	8,292	168	7	1,690	1,515	11	...	736	908	407	18	...	...	...	...
Posaliya ...	832	814	88	17	9,481	8,581	403	6	2,291	2,152	21	...	1,436	2,065	829	62	...	...	...	...
Rohera ...	832	1,010	176	2	7,696	7,087	158	8	1,456	1,288	7	2	425	708	196	5	...	...	...	...
Santhpur ...	710	556	312	66	9,760	8,757	875	83	1,907	1,762	102	2	155	187	182	12	2	1	2	...
Tonk State ...	***7,794***	***7,267***	***233***	***4***	***100,075***	***91,366***	***2,103***	***46***	***28,106***	***28,072***	***47***	...	***3,608***	***3,260***	***1,025***	***50***	***6***	***4***	***1***	***1***
Tonk City ...	381	862	40	2	5,980	5,608	461	30	1,663	1,718	19	...	406	856	145	18	2	2	...	...
Aligarh ...	393	324	12	...	5,277	4,911	92	...	1,443	1,466	2	...	399	851	102	...	...	...	...	...
Chhabra ...	978	952	41	...	12,980	11,358	232	2	2,442	2,487	2	...	72	77	31	...	1	...	...	...
Nimbahera ...	1,797	1,738	36	1	18,196	17,567	595	8	3,567	3,744	6	...	1,198	1,057	406	16	...	...	...	...
Pirawa ...	891	424	15	...	11,710	10,490	217	1	2,815	2,719	4	...	452	420	126	3	1	1	1	1
Sironj ...	2,497	2,813	65	...	27,090	24,302	305	2	9,684	9,629	3	...	633	609	92	7	2	1	...	...
Tonk ...	1,357	1,159	24	1	18,962	17,135	201	3	6,492	6,309	11	...	448	390	123	6	...	...	...	...

PROVINCIAL TABLE II.—Population of Administrative Units by Religion and Literacy.—*Concluded.*

STATE OR DISTRICT AND ADMINISTRATIVE UNIT (PARGANA, TEHSIL, TOWN, ETC.).	MUSLIMS. Number of persons. Males.	MUSLIMS. Number of persons. Females.	MUSLIMS. Number of literates. Males	MUSLIMS. Number of literates. Females.	CHRISTIANS. Number of persons. Males.	CHRISTIANS. Number of persons. Females.	CHRISTIANS. Number of literates. Males.	CHRISTIANS. Number of literates. Females.	TRIBAL. Number of persons. Males.	TRIBAL. Number of persons. Females.	TRIBAL. Number of literates. Males.	TRIBAL. Number of literates. Females.	OTHERS. Number of persons. Males.	OTHERS. Number of persons. Females.	OTHERS. Number of literates. Males.	OTHERS. Number of literates. Females	NUMBER LITERATE— Aged 0—15. Males.	NUMBER LITERATE— Aged 0—15. Females.	NUMBER LITERATE— Aged 15—20. Males.	NUMBER LITERATE— Aged 15—20. Females	NUMBER LITERATE— Aged 20 and over. Males.	NUMBER LITERATE— Aged 20 and over. Females.	LITERATE IN ENGLISH Males.	LITERATE IN ENGLISH Females.
1	22	23	24	25	26	27	28	29	30	31	32	33	34	35	36	37	38	39	40	41	42	43	44	45
Shahpura State ...	*1,305*	*1,236*	*178*	*3*	...	*1*	...	*1*	...	...	...	...	...	...	...	...	*435*	*68*	*327*	*37*	*1,719*	*109*	*225*	*10*
Shahpura Town ...	799	805	155	3	...	1	...	1	...	...	...	...	...	...	...	...	328	62	202	33	964	96	211	10
Arwar ...	170	158	4	...	...	...	...	...	...	...	...	...	...	...	...	...	37	4	32	2	222	7	5	...
Dhikola ...	75	48	3	...	...	...	...	...	...	...	...	...	...	...	...	...	16	...	17	...	142	2	5	...
Dohria ...	43	26	5	...	...	...	...	...	...	...	...	...	...	...	...	...	18	1	21	...	142	1	1	...
Kanechan ...	27	23	1	...	...	...	...	...	...	...	...	...	...	...	...	...	7	...	10	...	56	...	...	...
Phulia ...	101	99	7	...	...	...	...	...	...	...	...	...	...	...	...	...	23	...	33	2	98	3	2	...
Sangria ...	71	54	3	...	...	...	...	...	...	...	...	...	...	...	...	...	8	1	8	...	70	...	...	...
Shahpura ...	19	23	...	...	...	...	...	...	...	...	...	...	...	...	...	...	8	...	4	...	25	...	1	...
Sirohi State ...	*3,561*	*2,977*	*678*	*105*	*272*	*231*	*192*	*152*	...	...	...	...	*94*	*90*	*79*	*60*	*1,593*	*224*	*1,102*	*104*	*6,265*	*473*	*812*	*174*
Sirohi Town ...	320	291	95	15	4	2	4	1	...	...	...	...	...	...	...	...	194	81	119	13	664	56	99	3
Sirohi ...	12	8	2	...	1	2	1	1	...	...	...	...	...	...	...	...	5	1	13	...	20	1	1	1
Abu ...	16	9	7	5	...	...	...	...	...	...	...	...	...	...	...	...	11	3	10	1	56	5	4	...
Bhakar ...	48	29	1	...	...	...	...	...	...	...	...	...	...	...	...	...	14	...	3	...	2	...	...	...
Barlut ...	127	111	34	...	...	...	...	...	...	...	...	...	...	...	...	...	110	7	105	1	583	16	11	...
Erinpura ...	87	81	24	1	2	...	2	...	...	...	...	...	...	...	...	...	23	4	12	3	149	3	13	1
Madar ...	356	344	45	8	3	5	...	2	...	...	...	...	...	...	...	...	82	11	75	2	458	20	8	2
Magra ...	90	76	8	...	...	...	...	...	...	...	...	...	...	...	...	...	186	6	90	2	581	21	8	...
Pamera ...	181	158	15	2	...	...	...	...	...	...	...	...	...	...	...	...	135	5	109	1	521	10	17	...
Pindwara ...	256	198	50	5	2	...	2	...	...	...	...	...	1	...	...	...	173	11	83	4	464	21	28	1
Posaliya ...	322	279	96	3	...	...	...	...	...	...	...	...	...	...	...	...	272	21	182	13	983	54	29	...
Rohera ...	178	188	32	5	...	...	...	...	...	...	...	...	...	...	...	...	104	6	62	2	403	14	43	...
Santhpur ...	1,568	1,365	269	61	260	222	183	148	...	...	...	...	93	90	79	60	384	118	239	62	1,381	252	551	166
Tonk State ...	*22,993*	*21,241*	*2,057*	*125*	*30*	*13*	*11*	*9*	*1,789*	*1,736*	...	...	...	...	...	...	*399*	*14*	*580*	*28*	*4,498*	*193*	*222*	*11*
Tonk City ...	9,789	9,540	1,133	101	25	12	9	9	5	4	...	...	...	...	...	...	118	8	172	16	1,522	136	155	10
Aligarh ...	898	730	48	...	...	...	...	...	2	3	...	...	...	...	...	...	9	...	21	...	226	...	9	...
Chhabra ...	1,450	1,297	159	...	...	...	...	...	17	19	...	...	...	...	...	...	29	...	43	...	393	2	21	...
Nimbahera ...	2,089	1,804	166	11	5	1	2	...	1,624	1,558	...	...	...	...	...	...	96	2	160	8	955	26	17	...
Pirawa ...	1,084	1,022	141	6	...	...	...	...	88	42	...	...	...	...	...	...	62	...	54	...	888	11	16	1
Sironj ...	6,242	5,735	358	6	...	...	...	...	60	55	...	...	...	...	...	...	68	3	96	2	659	10	2	...
Tonk ...	1,561	1,113	52	1	...	...	...	...	43	55	...	...	...	...	...	...	22	1	34	2	355	8	2	...

PROVINCIAL TABLE III.

Selected Castes by Administrative Units.

EXPLANATORY NOTE.

The castes selected for this Table number in the aggregate 886 persons per mille of the population and are representative of every stratum of society. Individual castes which do not exceed 4 per mille of the total population are Bhat, Charan, Dhed, Grassia, Kaimkhani, Merat, Rawat, Sargara, and Sondhia and these have been selected as being of special or local interest.

The castes shown amount in the aggregate to the following numbers per 1,000 of the total population of each State and District.

Abu	698	Jaipur	927	Lawa	884
Alwar	912	Jaisalmer	686	Marwar	873
Banswara	919	Jhalawar	876	Mewar	900
Bharatpur	895	Karauli	946	Partabgarh	888
Bikaner	788	Kishangarh	831	Shahpura	874
Bundi	897	Kotah	827	Sirohi	899
Dholpur	899	Kushalgarh	939	Tonk	851
Dungarpur	926				

PROVINCIAL TABLE III.—Selected Castes by

Serial Number.	Caste, Tribe, or Race.	Rajputana. Total.	Abu District Total.	Alwar Total.	Alwar: Administrative Unit (Pargana, — Alwar City.	Alwar.	Ajeraka.	Bahror.	Bansur.	Govindgarh.	Katumbar.	Khairthal.
1	2	3	4	5	6	7	8	9	10	11	12	13
1	Ahir ...	182,165	9	71,280	887	686	8,691	18,485	7,091	174	1,415	69
2	Balai ...	218,927	31	5,099	824	32	201	70	202	568	155	...
3	Bambhi ...	162,865	1	...	...	...	...	...	...	...	...	...
4	Bhangi ...	99,083	208	10,494	1,012	452	486	536	421	503	757	513
5	Bhat ...	39,882	26	489	19	...	...	50	3	8	12	...
6	Bhil ...	655,647	900	...	...	...	...	...	...	...	...	...
7	Bishnoi ...	69,873	...	2	...	...	...	...	...	...	2	...
8	Brahman ...	854,634	233	59,576	5,459	918	2,162	3,959	3,644	768	6,040	432
9	Chamar ...	767,263	89	79,556	2,166	5,639	3,268	4,547	4,872	2,797	3,810	3,152
10	Charan ...	35,548	...	273	15	32	1	27	8	...	1	...
11	Dangi ...	50,898	...	...	...	...	...	...	...	...	...	...
12	Daroga ...	177,104	6	5,336	1,064	149	67	187	228	19	262	24
13	Dhakar ...	96,158	...	242	...	...	...	...	...	...	...	...
14	Dhed ...	19,907	9	...	...	...	...	...	...	...	...	...
15	Fakir ...	54,859	...	18,426	572	2,530	336	176	149	1,721	424	1,753
16	Gadaria ...	77,370	3	109	1	...	...	...	4	...	97	...
17	Grassia ...	29,231	27	...	...	...	...	...	...	...	...	...
18	Gujar ...	526,791	4	44,007	876	1,726	523	3,197	7,288	538	2,476	557
19	Jat ...	1,042,153	30	32,844	402	371	4,677	1,021	2,387	23	5,165	666
20	Jogi ...	76,204	2	7,920	148	266	178	847	408	176	488	152
21	Kachhi ...	60,510	...	4	4	...	...	...	...	...	...	...
22	Kaimkhani ...	35,686	...	56	...	...	...	...	...	...	...	...
23	Khati ...	209,937	22	13,474	693	656	726	1,264	632	311	769	614
24	Khatik ...	59,527	...	4,707	394	130	177	150	370	111	384	193
25	Koli ...	90,910	283	10,806	1,724	950	...	...	7	391	1,255	16
26	Kumhar ...	357,751	26	16,771	608	838	551	1,125	1,017	557	1,237	652
27	Kunbi ...	57,815	7	...	...	...	...	...	...	...	...	...
28	Lodha ...	48,503	4	215	...	...	...	...	...	...	152	...
29	Lohar ...	81,070	24	3,248	128	217	8	13	164	230	161	229
30	Mahajan ...	638,820	291	36,442	4,279	1,507	1,207	2,704	1,853	1,015	2,310	1,295
31	Mali ...	369,173	64	29,686	4,586	1,366	197	826	1,988	1,825	3,885	456
32	Meo ...	167,530	...	117,381	789	18,937	1	3	...	11,877	945	7,043
33	Merat ...	3,084	4	...	...	...	...	...	...	...	...	...
34	Mina ...	607,369	11	51,859	1,362	416	700	329	1,423	195	5,604	...
35	Nai ...	166,095	17	11,773	685	518	636	1,065	766	486	645	422
36	Naik ...	62,329	8	737	206	6	...	59	84	14	1	...
37	Patel ...	55,867	...	...	...	...	...	...	...	...	...	...
38	Pathan ...	119,803	135	5,423	2,948	46	81	872	125	209	48	161
39	Purohit ...	45,308	...	168	18	...	...	...	11	...	...	...
40	Raigar ...	130,104	3	1,734	87	...	...	...	...	...	...	...
41	Rajput (Hindu) ...	633,827	178	24,516	1,673	862	638	1,830	2,253	135	2,262	235
42	Rawat ...	27,804	17	52	...	...	...	3	...	...	...	...
43	Rebari ...	135,820	4	798	40	62	...	50	9	...	...	...
44	Sadhu ...	66,597	21	1,693	124	42	70	117	211	56	206	1
45	Sargara ...	31,300	105	...	...	...	...	...	...	...	...	...
46	Sheikh ...	210,499	331	9,386	5,191	45	51	387	97	95	610	148
47	Sirvi ...	53,611	...	...	...	...	...	...	...	...	...	...
48	Sondhia ...	34,257	...	...	...	...	...	...	...	...	...	...
49	Sunar ...	73,455	15	2,597	391	81	171	266	178	98	120	25
50	Teli ...	80,015	17	4,226	227	197	181	386	318	148	314	151

ADMINISTRATIVE UNITS (PERSONS ONLY).—*Continued.*

STATE.

TEHSIL, TOWN, ETC.).

Kishangarh.	Lachmangarh.	Malakhera.	Mandhan.	Mandawar.	Narayanpur.	Partabgarh.	Rajgarh.	Ramgarh.	Reni.	Thana Ghazi.	Tijara	Tapukrah.	Circles.	Nimrana Estate.	SERIAL NUMBER.
14	15	16	17	18	19	20	21	22	23	24	25	26	27	28	1
3,556	1,175	1,187	10,999	4,191	1,053	27	596	5	636	347	4,343	2,612	18	3,037	1
65	77	51	10	166	192	873	184	274	102	1,006	...	...	547	...	2
...	...	...	...	...	...	...	...	...	...	...	...	...	...	...	3
550	839	448	224	457	304	145	360	510	376	159	631	574	129	108	4
55	20	3	...	2	10	25	69	8	195	2	3	...	3	2	5
...	...	...	...	...	...	...	...	...	...	...	...	...	...	...	6
...	...	...	...	...	...	...	...	...	...	...	...	...	...	...	7
1,217	3,400	2,523	2,889	2,160	2,697	2,207	5,149	740	3,318	5,690	955	423	1,973	858	8
3,306	6,624	4,961	3,013	3,968	2,118	260	3,876	2,834	4,487	1,006	3,819	2,456	1,234	846	9
27	6	22	4	2	18	...	74	...	...	2	...	...	34	...	10
...	...	...	...	...	...	...	...	...	...	...	...	...	...	...	11
71	591	358	21	191	373	142	339	5	563	357	43	...	69	193	12
...	...	...	...	...	...	...	143	...	88	...	...	...	11	...	13
...	...	...	...	...	...	...	...	...	...	...	...	...	...	...	14
1,337	1,433	958	39	737	98	30	162	1,930	245	66	2,090	1,460	171	...	15
...	...	3	...	...	...	...	...	1	...	...	...	...	...	3	16
...	...	...	...	...	...	...	...	...	...	...	...	...	...	...	17
1,816	1,876	1,424	50	1,814	3,990	2,966	971	1,192	918	2,266	1,801	2,194	3,887	161	18
2,305	3,853	4,033	369	4,151	1,712	24	111	544	186	320	403	...	90	31	19
153	659	496	404	248	436	782	510	193	568	818	226	3	191	75	20
...	...	...	...	...	...	...	...	...	...	...	...	...	...	...	21
6	...	...	...	4	...	...	...	46	...	...	...	...	...	...	22
562	1,263	639	729	573	584	206	572	869	707	359	553	330	119	274	23
33	316	881	80	211	247	186	241	165	214	248	115	12	180	67	24
31	895	478	...	4	43	871	2,195	159	925	201	67	...	594	...	25
559	1,505	801	725	715	918	553	555	597	832	839	581	354	428	234	26
...	...	...	...	...	...	...	...	...	...	...	...	...	...	...	27
...	59	...	...	...	...	...	...	...	...	...	...	...	...	4	28
150	75	217	58	39	20	158	193	413	79	239	163	194	100	...	29
1,873	1,817	1,339	1,114	1,744	1,214	905	2,061	1,448	1,580	1,107	1,751	836	701	282	30
291	1,642	1,198	108	104	1,910	511	4,228	876	1,254	648	1,240	26	257	264	31
7,713	8,140	5,722	1	3,580	...	...	149	15,089	1,185	...	13,248	12,411	558	...	32
...	...	...	...	...	...	...	...	...	...	...	...	...	...	...	33
20	7,038	2,369	98	480	768	4,567	7,650	409	11,751	3,982	12	...	2,666	...	34
456	686	523	557	620	435	172	489	509	483	398	567	387	149	169	35
17	1	52	44	5	67	75	14	38	...	26	1	49	20	8	36
...	...	...	...	...	...	...	...	...	...	...	...	...	...	...	37
122	158	10	7	125	26	91	330	38	11	96	139	28	219	33	38
3	19	17	85	...	...	...	11	18	41	...	...	...	...	...	39
...	...	5	...	...	474	562	...	...	...	605	...	...	...	1	40
974	2,071	1,511	3,121	623	1,822	361	932	304	1,625	688	138	181	190	587	41
...	5	...	...	...	33	...	...	...	11	...	...	...	...	...	42
...	77	122	...	7	12	28	141	...	102	14	41	...	87	6	43
79	68	108	11	68	42	23	60	11	111	46	78	65	55	46	44
...	...	...	...	...	...	...	...	...	...	...	...	...	...	...	45
223	99	127	12	241	326	56	429	53	8	114	797	2	85	190	46
...	...	...	...	...	...	...	...	...	...	...	...	...	...	...	47
...	...	...	...	...	...	...	...	...	...	...	...	...	...	...	48
116	141	93	91	67	54	85	155	74	77	89	184	18	32	41	49
313	182	219	298	173	171	27	127	182	121	186	270	26	14	...	50

PROVINCIAL TABLE III.—Selected Castes by

Serial Number.	Caste, Tribe, or Race.	Banswara State. Total.	Banswara State. Administrative Unit (Pargana, Tehsil, Town, Etc.). Banswara Town.	Khalsa Villages.	Jagir and other Villages.	Bharatpur. Total.	Bharatpur. Administrative Unit. Bharatpur City.	Bharatpur.
1	2	29	30	31	32	33	34	35
1	Ahir ...	1	1	...	...	3,385	65	316
2	Balai ...	3,183	4	1,408	1,771	1,021	120	54
3	Bambhi ...	12	...	12	...	...	...	...
4	Bhangi ...	527	109	88	330	6,398	694	374
5	Bhat ...	367	7	275	85	509	10	1
6	Bhil ...	144,925	856	53,722	90,347	...	...	...
7	Bishnoi ...	...	...	...	...	...	...	...
8	Brahman ...	9,537	1,409	5,412	2,716	42,837	4,250	8,301
9	Chamar ...	6,161	241	2,759	3,161	79,181	2,078	7,790
10	Charan ...	175	...	120	55	...	...	...
11	Dangi ...	...	...	...	...	...	...	...
12	Daroga ...	2,121	349	182	1,590	553	10	91
13	Dhakar ...	...	...	...	...	4,299	...	...
14	Dhed ...	...	...	...	...	...	...	...
15	Fakir ...	89	43	31	15	9,723	173	240
16	Gadaria ...	1,309	...	323	986	4,678	75	1,304
17	Grassia ...	...	...	...	...	...	...	...
18	Gujar ...	386	6	151	229	40,432	700	1,872
19	Jat ...	5	4	...	1	72,383	1,458	9,625
20	Jogi ...	2,402	7	931	1,464	3,417	64	201
21	Kachhi ...	...	...	...	...	5,306	...	192
22	Kaimkhani ...	...	...	...	...	...	...	...
23	Khati ...	1,266	166	579	521	6,979	253	580
24	Khatik ...	28	20	...	8	2,083	215	85
25	Koli ...	4	...	3	1	...	...	...
26	Kumhar ...	1,605	74	602	929	9,528	396	770
27	Kunbi ...	...	...	...	...	58	51	1
28	Lodha ...	...	...	...	...	5,324	91	849
29	Lohar ...	2,152	221	1,007	924	2,431	135	137
30	Mahajan ...	5,562	1,026	2,634	1,902	22,744	2,975	1,004
31	Mali ...	111	23	56	32	17,389	1,247	890
32	Meo ...	17	16	1	...	46,475	56	14
33	Merat ...	...	...	...	...	...	...	...
34	Mina ...	...	...	...	...	10,844	171	781
35	Nai ...	164	86	87	41	8,254	710	680
36	Naik ...	82	79	3	...	...	...	...
37	Patel ...	14,897	28	8,620	6,249	...	...	...
38	Pathan ...	1,603	659	468	476	3,240	1,758	148
39	Purohit ...	...	...	...	...	...	...	...
40	Raigar ...	...	...	...	...	...	...	...
41	Rajput (Hindu) ...	3,818	337	841	3,140	9,535	525	1,602
42	Rawat ...	...	...	...	...	...	...	...
43	Rebari ...	1,073	6	358	709	321	2	81
44	Sadhu ...	620	81	289	250	3,360	69	432
45	Sargara ...	795	197	260	338	...	...	...
46	Sheikh ...	722	346	81	295	7,822	3,471	142
47	Sirvi ...	...	...	...	...	...	...	...
48	Sondhia ...	...	...	...	...	...	...	...
49	Sunar ...	637	242	240	155	1,272	401	15
50	Teli ...	459	221	93	145	3,958	217	308

ADMINISTRATIVE UNITS (PERSONS ONLY).—*Continued.*

STATE.										
(PARGANA, TEHSIL, TOWN, ETC.).										
Bayana.	Dig.	Kaman.	Kumher.	Nadbai.	Nagar.	Pahari.	Rupbas.	Uchain.	Weir.	SERIAL NUMBER.
36	37	38	39	40	41	42	43	44	45	1
8	141	844	495	52	1,094	352	10	...	8	1
29	18	137	16	2	317	278	...	7	48	2
...	...	...	...	...	...	...	...	...	...	3
393	694	681	405	468	869	891	337	120	472	4
27	103	38	5	288	6	...	6	11	14	5
...	...	...	...	...	...	...	...	...	...	6
...	...	...	...	...	...	...	...	...	...	7
5,076	4,176	2,597	3,538	4,530	2,437	709	4,172	2,190	5,861	8
12,167	7,167	3,874	7,019	8,455	6,333	3,051	5,841	2,972	12,434	9
...	...	...	...	...	...	...	...	...	...	10
...	...	...	...	...	...	...	...	...	...	11
50	6	...	19	...	26	2	307	42	...	12
2,380	...	...	...	...	...	...	35	265	1,619	13
...	...	...	...	...	...	...	...	...	...	14
618	729	1,812	324	378	2,187	2,100	398	160	604	15
73	610	485	980	239	27	58	622	182	23	16
...	...	...	...	...	...	...	...	...	...	17
13,820	4,844	3,083	1,035	864	4,218	1,070	2,625	987	5,314	18
3,403	10,592	1,275	15,200	15,159	2,371	101	2,588	2,163	8,453	19
370	196	169	175	308	302	350	541	65	676	20
738	...	...	...	191	...	...	2,999	1,185	1	21
...	...	...	...	...	...	...	...	...	...	22
743	539	608	643	576	542	642	842	170	891	23
245	254	142	102	261	152	119	166	77	315	24
...	...	...	...	...	...	...	...	...	...	25
879	998	580	968	824	1,321	868	758	260	906	26
5	...	...	...	...	1	...	...	...	...	27
...	883	416	1,074	1	65	185	1,613	147	...	28
251	131	219	197	308	246	276	187	80	264	29
3,066	2,136	1,790	1,425	1,810	1,866	855	1,586	562	3,669	30
832	1,291	1,531	489	1,560	2,511	1,716	23	7	5,292	31
11	3,449	10,751	51	125	14,098	17,919	...	1	...	32
...	...	...	...	...	...	...	...	...	...	33
1,273	184	348	766	1,042	695	153	372	380	4,779	34
866	905	597	729	709	779	657	518	237	917	35
...	...	...	...	...	...	...	...	...	...	36
...	...	...	...	...	...	...	...	...	...	37
308	275	97	91	47	72	65	87	9	283	38
...	...	...	...	...	...	...	...	...	...	39
...	...	...	...	...	...	...	...	...	...	40
902	1,107	1,137	92	127	413	119	2,702	117	692	41
...	...	...	...	...	...	...	...	...	...	32
130	22	...	...	7	...	...	...	...	79	43
388	314	261	316	476	258	87	228	177	404	44
...	...	...	...	...	...	...	...	...	...	45
782	998	462	518	226	250	319	181	1	472	46
...	...	...	...	...	...	...	...	...	...	47
...	...	...	...	...	...	...	...	...	...	58
25	137	45	85	124	78	54	78	29	201	49
556	237	152	426	433	269	139	451	155	615	50

PROVINCIAL TABLE III.—SELECTED CASTES BY

SERIAL NUMBER.	CASTE, TRIBE OR RACE.	Total	BIKANER — ADMINISTRATIVE UNIT (PARGANA,							
			Bikaner City.	Bikaner Nizamat			Ganganagar Nizamat.			
				Bikaner.	Lunkaransar.	Surpura.	Ganganagar.	Karanpur.	Padampur.	Raisingnagar.
1	2	46	47	48	49	50	51	52	53	54
1	Ahir ...	**2,280**	139	300	37	4	406	96	41	44
2	Balai ...	**2,667**	24	13	...	...	12	2	...	...
3	Bambhi ...	**561**	10	...	1	...	7	...	...	...
4	Bhangi ...	**15,087**	1,912	164	62	119	2,535	3,043	1,206	397
5	Bhat ...	**2,386**	289	80	89	124	57	56	17	4
6	Bhil ...	...	...	...	...	...	...	...	...	...
7	Bishnoi ...	**16,415**	73	212	681	6,331	991	126	212	2,321
8	Brahman ...	**81,685**	15,786	4,945	2,928	4,043	1,307	346	295	410
9	Chamar ...	**75,574**	444	4,606	2,299	5,736	3,527	1,363	1,522	964
10	Charan ...	**4,162**	98	1,518	159	667	43	2	1	2
11	Dangi ...	...	...	...	...	...	...	...	...	...
12	Daroga ...	**13,629**	2,181	815	460	1,135	11	8	...	17
13	Dhakar ...	...	...	...	...	...	...	...	...	...
14	Dhed ...	...	...	...	...	...	...	...	...	...
15	Fakir ...	**2,618**	324	5	27	29	31	7	8	...
16	Gadaria ...	**7**	4	...	...	...	...	...	...	...
17	Grassia ...	...	...	...	...	...	...	...	...	...
18	Gujar ...	**2,655**	615	17	5	1	27	36	27	15
19	Jat ...	**215,947**	1,877	6,986	7,988	13,777	12,491	8,837	6,098	4,434
20	Jogi ...	**3,304**	182	128	302	28	199	11	73	28
21	Kachhi ...	**29**	12	...	...	...	17	...	...	...
22	Kaimkhani ...	**9,426**	969	55	59	10	194	79	10	7
23	Khati ...	**24,065**	2,766	1,227	562	1,839	2,147	635	819	383
24	Khatik ...	**889**	13	...	1	12	34	...	2	...
25	Koli ...	**475**	233	165	2	...	44	...	...	...
26	Kumhar ...	**37,901**	1,435	2,211	510	1,761	5,461	912	1,057	597
27	Kunbi ...	**5**	3	...	...	...	...	...	...	...
28	Lodha ...	**17**	9	...	...	5	2	...	...	...
29	Lohar ...	**5,376**	861	266	186	355	421	100	29	45
30	Mahajan ...	**65,192**	12,574	4,435	1,544	3,003	1,385	350	164	169
31	Mali ...	**15,771**	5,480	161	10	32	375	1,029	270	651
32	Meo ...	...	...	...	...	...	...	...	...	...
33	Merat ...	...	...	...	...	...	...	...	...	...
34	Mina ...	**2,069**	65	29	1	25	22	25	10	7
35	Nai ...	**20,260**	1,676	1,447	688	1,405	802	244	242	207
36	Naik ...	**23,882**	1,494	479	1,102	480	3,559	250	739	297
37	Patel ...	**2**	2	...	...	...	...	...	...	...
38	Pathan ...	**2,301**	1,012	114	18	5	79	29	45	30
39	Purohit ...	...	...	...	...	...	...	...	...	...
40	Raigar ...	**5,013**	345	543	180	130	...	...	...	16
41	Rajput (Hindu) ...	**55,510**	4,617	6,095	1,768	8,055	793	244	123	152
42	Rawat ...	...	...	...	...	...	...	...	...	...
43	Rebari ...	**1,378**	8	162	107	186	2	...	7	34
44	Sadhu ...	**5,266**	923	521	138	603	40	28	11	2
45	Sargara ...	**1**	...	...	...	...	...	...	...	...
46	Sheikh ...	**4,995**	2,016	219	50	71	201	46	45	96
47	Sirvi ...	...	...	...	...	...	...	...	...	...
48	Sondhia ...	...	...	...	...	...	...	...	...	...
49	Sunar ...	**11,720**	2,558	465	182	777	346	122	97	108
50	Teli ...	**7,039**	762	276	190	196	586	227	227	67

ADMINISTRATIVE UNITS (PERSONS ONLY).—*Continued.*

STATE .

TEHSIL, TOWN, ETC.).

Reni Nizamat					Sujangarh Nizamat.				Suratgarh Nizamat			
Bhadra.	Churu.	Nohar.	Rajgarh.	Reni.	Dungargarh.	Ratangarh.	Sardarshahr.	Sujangarh.	Anupgarh.	Hanumangarh.	Suratgarh.	SERIAL NUMBER.
55	56	57	58	59	60	61	62	63	64	65	66	1
483	84	20	82	147	9	15	...	124	6	251	42	1
...	26	...	...	...	5	867	...	2,162	...	56	...	2
78	102	15	77	175	7	11	...	36	...	42	...	3
381	366	708	217	131	148	449	331	587	398	1,647	286	4
90	172	195	70	99	84	135	273	112	18	414	58	5
...	...	...	...	...	...	...	...	...	...	...	...	6
64	...	181	64	...	563	3	...	2	239	1,287	3,065	7
2,423	6,894	4,621	3,602	3,879	4,979	7,640	8,452	5,918	188	1,874	1,655	8
4,367	5,504	5,733	6,283	3,140	3,588	5,215	4,338	6,821	1,195	5,913	2,996	9
15	271	122	73	90	49	333	277	400	4	28	10	10
...	...	...	...	...	...	...	...	...	...	...	...	11
193	1,662	700	821	698	458	1,134	1,117	1,899	67	37	216	12
...	...	...	...	...	...	...	...	...	...	...	...	13
...	...	...	...	...	...	...	...	...	...	...	...	14
53	303	128	363	80	95	268	395	426	2	33	41	15
...	...	...	...	...	...	...	...	...	...	3	...	16
...	...	...	...	...	...	...	...	...	...	...	...	17
128	476	23	446	183	18	54	116	279	120	29	40	18
19,800	8,923	21,233	21,645	7,084	10,224	9,481	11,161	13,749	2,468	20,392	7,304	19
156	208	281	204	479	200	187	200	69	4	128	237	20
...	...	...	...	...	...	...	...	...	...	...	...	21
604	2,986	250	458	413	64	914	1,287	734	19	283	31	22
1,554	1,276	1,386	1,466	767	690	1,249	1,355	1,570	245	1,799	830	23
25	167	28	111	31	...	225	49	193	...	3	...	24
...	...	5	...	19	...	...	...	...	...	...	7	25
2,596	1,435	2,130	2,164	1,517	657	2,505	1,382	3,287	611	3,906	1,767	26
...	...	...	...	...	2	...	...	...	...	...	...	27
...	...	...	...	...	...	...	...	...	...	1	...	28
265	454	239	233	207	275	203	366	444	60	218	150	29
2,919	5,269	2,128	3,627	2,375	4,285	5,133	5,616	7,806	146	1,382	882	30
183	2,072	578	305	621	89	1,125	1,209	1,072	95	357	107	31
...	...	...	...	...	...	...	...	...	...	...	...	32
...	...	...	...	...	...	...	...	...	...	...	...	33
41	357	43	531	120	51	264	251	68	62	68	29	34
904	1,453	1,159	1,155	902	1,209	1,477	1,668	1,821	184	1,014	608	35
421	1,510	2,680	778	933	308	1,872	2,355	2,367	225	1,791	742	36
...	...	...	...	...	...	...	...	...	...	...	...	37
61	114	62	147	...	1	58	33	58	50	284	101	38
...	...	...	...	...	...	...	...	...	...	...	...	39
204	387	355	295	207	193	656	417	731	21	145	188	40
809	3,440	1,950	3,452	1,941	2,603	4,898	4,556	7,585	320	987	1,122	41
...	...	...	...	...	...	...	...	...	...	...	...	42
5	9	356	45	10	117	9	118	92	46	11	65	43
34	78	185	82	28	873	356	430	694	6	104	180	44
...	...	...	...	...	1	...	...	...	...	...	...	45
327	641	64	199	47	91	222	43	136	32	312	137	46
...	...	...	...	...	...	...	...	...	...	...	...	47
...	...	...	...	...	...	...	...	...	...	...	...	48
436	842	676	233	242	537	987	1,114	1,276	97	354	276	49
389	951	303	378	233	222	511	338	541	70	365	[illegible]	50

PROVINCIAL TABLE III.—SELECTED CASTES BY

Serial Number.	Caste, Tribe or Race.	BUNDI STATE. Total.	Administrative Unit (Pargana, Tehsil, Town, etc.). Bundi City.	Baroondhan.	Dei.	Gaindoli.	Hindoli.	Patan.	Nainwa Kila.	Talwas.
1	2	67	68	69	70	71	72	73	74	75
1	Ahir ...	938	84	201	167	60	345	6	75	...
2	Balai ...	8,875	213	2,834	595	1,304	1,862	1,929	24	114
3	Bambhi ...	1	...	...	...	1	...	...	...	...
4	Bhangi ...	2,056	273	195	250	423	384	418	60	53
5	Bhat ...	760	16	284	234	76	57	16	68	9
6	Bhil ...	5,495	181	4,033	225	100	844	112	...	...
7	Bishnoi ...	...	...	...	...	...	...	...	...	...
8	Brahman ...	16,664	3,247	1,885	1,880	2,493	2,035	4,230	524	370
9	Chamar ...	18,654	441	1,925	5,575	3,590	4,690	1,441	403	589
10	Charan ...	1,508	68	291	324	279	288	200	24	34
11	Dangi ...	...	...	...	...	...	...	...	...	...
12	Daroga ...	3,019	379	413	522	465	1,094	109	25	12
13	Dhakar ...	6,933	11	1,219	3,185	360	933	1,178	63	4
14	Dhed ...	...	...	...	...	...	...	...	...	...
15	Fakir ...	793	261	60	158	26	83	121	84	...
16	Gadaria ...	...	...	...	...	...	...	...	...	...
17	Grassia ...	...	...	...	...	...	...	...	...	...
18	Gujar ...	27,708	571	6,250	4,225	4,552	8,257	2,969	163	721
19	Jat ...	2,563	27	1,062	829	258	75	160	151	1
20	Jogi ...	809	25	71	227	223	128	118	17	...
21	Kachhi ...	1,318	32	937	171	17	79	71	1	10
22	Kaimkhani ...	...	...	...	...	...	...	...	...	...
23	Khati ...	3,084	269	425	845	456	617	400	54	18
24	Khatik ...	1,536	119	169	204	456	349	170	37	32
25	Koli ...	1,799	296	62	375	551	56	251	185	23
26	Kumhar ...	5,274	219	996	1,024	808	1,014	804	92	317
27	Kunbi ...	6	...	...	...	4	...	2	...	...
28	Lodha ...	538	43	223	17	5	249	1	...	...
29	Lohar ...	1,990	96	191	300	556	891	266	91	99
30	Mahajan ...	8,473	2,125	893	1,280	926	1,762	866	548	73
31	Mali ...	17,394	1,301	2,511	2,319	2,448	5,318	2,651	546	300
32	Meo ...	64	20	9	...	7	...	28	...	...
33	Merat ...	...	...	...	...	...	...	...	...	...
34	Mina ...	33,910	82	4,023	9,087	8,012	6,533	5,362	42	769
35	Nai ...	3,582	284	530	653	812	672	486	97	48
36	Naik ...	849	273	152	131	126	13	154	...	...
37	Patel ...	...	...	...	...	...	...	...	...	...
38	Pathan ...	2,655	712	256	47	220	1,138	147	125	10
39	Purohit ...	...	...	...	...	...	...	...	...	...
40	Raigar ...	805	...	...	421	366	18	...	...	...
41	Rajput (Hindu) ...	5,144	725	751	573	890	1,480	531	82	112
42	Rawat ...	...	...	...	...	...	...	...	...	...
43	Rebari ...	1,181	22	189	1	777	86	15	...	91
44	Sadhu ...	2,663	205	499	633	294	483	382	54	113
45	Sargara ...	...	...	...	...	...	...	...	...	...
46	Sheikh ...	1,060	656	53	31	145	46	81	47	1
47	Sirvi ...	...	...	...	...	...	...	...	...	...
48	Sondhia ...	129	...	125	...	3	...	1	...	...
49	Sunar ...	933	281	197	139	69	171	30	42	4
50	Teli ...	3,288	140	685	560	451	649	327	106	370

Administrative Units (Persons only).—*Continued.*

DHOLPUR STATE.								DUNGARPUR STATE.						
Total.	ADMINISTRATIVE UNIT (PARGANA, TEHSIL, TOWN, ETC.).							Total.	ADMINISTRATIVE UNIT (PARGANA, TEHSIL, TOWN, ETC.).					SERIAL NUMBER.
	Dholpur City.	Bari.	Baseri.	Gird.	Kolari.	Rajakhera.	Sir Muthra.		Dungarpur Town.	Bara.	Chhiasat.	Chorasi.	Tarpod.	
76	77	78	79	80	81	82	83	84	85	86	87	88	89	1
592	319	100	6	87	26	49	5	5	5	...	...	...	...	1
...	...	...	...	...	...	...	...	3,241	53	416	900	570	1,802	2
...	...	...	...	...	...	...	...	8	...	...	...	...	8	3
2,269	401	298	296	403	334	415	122	666	154	12	86	298	116	4
488	16	63	14	80	150	137	28	251	25	1	114	97	14	5
...	...	...	...	...	...	...	...	123,350	453	38,483	12,815	46,681	24,918	6
...	...	...	...	...	...	...	...	...	...	...	...	...	...	7
28,014	2,251	3,459	5,499	4,629	4,815	6,461	1,400	13,033	934	1,478	4,378	2,294	3,954	8
42,405	1,125	8,428	8,824	3,619	7,522	5,174	2,713	6,545	143	1,249	1,126	2,127	1,900	9
...	...	...	...	...	...	...	...	244	...	43	60	47	94	10
...	...	...	...	...	...	...	...	...	...	...	...	...	...	11
5,872	39	57	23	1,566	3,178	965	44	3.040	440	577	412	809	802	12
...	...	...	...	...	...	...	...	...	...	...	...	...	...	13
...	...	...	...	...	...	...	...	...	...	...	...	...	...	14
806	122	160	144	188	181	...	11	149	65	...	19	54	11	15
7,238	633	860	152	1,959	1,244	2,390	...	488	...	...	118	...	370	16
...	...	...	...	...	...	...	...	...	...	...	...	...	...	17
20,752	164	6,489	3,473	6,083	1,268	1,473	1,802	233	...	...	...	233	...	18
2,800	479	167	346	925	736	95	52	...	...	...	...	...	...	19
182	...	10	9	132	...	14	17	2,303	18	598	299	677	711	20
26,517	1,122	4,890	4,015	7,772	7,704	606	408	...	...	...	...	...	...	21
...	...	...	...	...	...	...	...	...	...	...	...	...	...	22
4,285	220	686	793	717	865	754	250	2,062	180	190	614	424	654	23
1,661	102	120	443	431	147	366	52	381	188	16	104	90	33	24
7,847	1,318	1,804	1,224	973	901	1,235	397	...	...	...	...	...	...	25
3,589	294	739	621	588	516	619	212	2,355	97	484	543	500	731	26
...	...	...	...	...	...	...	...	...	...	...	...	...	...	27
10,675	249	296	80	5,121	3,936	992	1	...	...	...	...	...	...	28
279	169	12	83	21	20	...	24	2,835	165	544	595	694	837	29
11,179	1,506	2,056	1,541	1,578	1,972	1,601	925	6,429	1,083	659	1,310	999	2,378	30
108	91	16	...	...	1	...	...	289	52	10	89	68	70	31
9	...	...	...	1	8	...	...	14	13	...	...	...	1	32
...	...	...	...	...	...	...	...	...	...	...	...	...	...	33
10,997	47	3,757	2,903	15	6	6	4,263	...	...	...	...	...	...	34
4,273	446	693	541	793	827	730	243	1,913	112	294	488	433	591	35
50	...	...	50	...	...	...	...	...	...	...	...	...	...	36
...	...	...	...	...	...	...	...	25,131	25	5,486	8,152	4,359	7,109	37
4,608	2,080	1,298	53	304	143	487	243	1,390	761	63	139	322	105	38
...	...	...	...	...	...	...	...	...	...	...	...	...	...	39
...	...	...	...	...	...	...	...	...	...	...	...	...	...	40
20,833	454	4,378	6,843	2,354	3,053	2,565	686	9,924	359	1,044	801	1,259	6,461	41
...	...	...	...	...	...	...	...	...	...	...	...	...	...	42
62	...	4	...	...	3	55	...	1,431	3	191	888	46	353	43
789	17	131	89	223	195	48	86	962	26	175	212	109	440	44
...	...	...	...	...	...	...	...	176	...	...	...	48	138	45
6,101	1,788	1,210	584	438	1,039	596	446	792	578	97	48	56	18	46
...	...	...	...	...	...	...	...	...	...	...	...	...	...	47
...	...	...	...	...	...	...	...	...	...	...	...	...	...	48
960	174	214	170	76	151	99	76	611	224	19	93	96	179	49
3,043	289	569	460	687	296	725	67	515	...	25	182	11	297	50

PROVINCIAL TABLE III.—SELECTED CASTES BY

			JAIPUR					
			ADMINISTRATIVE UNIT					
SERIAL NUMBER	CASTE, TRIBE OR RACE	Total.	Jaipur City.	Amber.	Dausa.	Gangapur.	Hindaun.	Kotkasim.
1	2	90	91	92	93	94	95	96
1	Ahir ...	74,376	1.138	14,638	409	26	188	6,198
2	Balai ...	63,394	1,868	16,660	2,280	337	458	...
3	Bambhi ...	16	...	...	...	...	...	...
4	Bhangi ...	23,517	2,903	1,093	2,709	1,090	1,409	290
5	Bhat ...	4,135	128	278	820	180	134	12
6	Bhil ...	2,218	6	7	...	...	...	...
7	Bishnoi ...	4	...	4	...	...	...	...
8	Brahman ...	277,958	19,881	31,613	33,740	9,871	12,638	1,185
9	Chamar ...	234,442	1,203	762	34,473	13,812	31,576	1,990
10	Charan ...	4,872	64	640	146	...	28	...
11	Dangi ...	...	...	...	...	...	...	...
12	Daroga ...	34,239	1,883	1,880	1,431	275	798	...
13	Dhakar ...	4,436	1	43	1	293	862	...
14	Dhed ...	2	...	...	...	...	...	...
15	Fakir ...	8,977	276	319	369	580	904	...
16	Gadaria ...	282	...	...	41	6	8	...
17	Grassia ...	...	...	...	...	...	...	...
18	Gujar ...	192,542	2,633	11,054	26,025	14,007	19,308	310
19	Jat ...	313,609	1,047	19,628	1,128	1,010	10,424	1,504
20	Jogi ...	24,643	304	2,712	3,778	1,788	3,059	26
21	Kachhi ...	931	1	...	...	...	3	...
22	Kaimkhani ...	16,563	1,232	27	40	8	154	...
23	Khati ...	52,775	2,268	8,998	4,361	1,630	2,606	323
24	Khatik ...	20,817	1,309	1,701	1,670	716	1,018	41
25	Koli ...	38,066	3,106	2,692	12,583	4,198	6,076	34
26	Kumhar ...	92,413	3,797	8,948	5,718	1,794	2,991	297
27	Kunbi ...	199	22	...	...	2	...	...
28	Lodha ...	1,143	317	...	27	82	33	...
29	Lohar ...	7,095	391	277	794	306	369	15
30	Mahajan ...	161,520	17,784	11,549	12,467	5,246	9,010	850
31	Mali ...	136,931	7,499	9,392	19,663	6,282	6,829	374
32	Meo ...	323	5	...	15	1	218	...
33	Merat ...	...	...	...	...	...	...	...
34	Mina ...	260,570	3,050	26,599	59,028	25,247	35,760	124
35	Nai ...	40,212	2,110	2,901	3,236	1,206	2,269	285
36	Naik ...	16,621	1,286	1,055	167	27	31	...
37	Patel ...	55	...	...	...	4	...	...
38	Pathan ...	33,078	10,373	2,566	2,109	1,731	1,663	287
39	Purohit ...	...	...	...	...	...	...	...
40	Raigar ...	54,649	1,750	9,294	4,095	1,491	11	1
41	Rajput (Hindu) ...	113,389	3,776	5,005	7,136	2,916	3,317	130
42	Rawat ...	32	...	...	...	...	...	...
43	Rebari ...	3,094	114	220	203	15	210	...
44	Sadhu ...	11,000	1,169	364	940	709	917	91
45	Sargara ...	...	...	...	...	...	...	...
46	Sheikh ...	90,400	23,196	3,156	2,975	3,059	4,541	1,050
47	Sirvi ...	...	...	...	...	...	...	...
48	Sondhia ...	...	...	...	...	...	...	...
49	Sunar ...	15,149	1,684	648	1,021	432	652	61
50	Teli ...	9,887	608	407	524	409	939	...

ADMINISTRATIVE UNITS (PERSONS ONLY).—*Continued.*

STATE.

(PARGANA, TEHSIL, TOWN, ETC.).

Malpura.	Sambhar.	Sawai Jaipur.	Sawai Madhopur.	Shekhawati.	Torawati.	Khetri Thikana.	Sikar Thikana.	Uniara Thikana.	SERIAL NUMBER.
97	98	99	100	101	102	103	104	105	1
1,180	5,677	4,664	832	5,939	19,820	13,064	607	46	1
8,300	19,079	7,871	511	328	9,604	158	889	551	2
...	...	...	15	...	1	...	...	...	3
1,553	2,030	1,461	2,206	1,948	2,058	861	1,640	271	4
292	508	124	77	280	1,157	34	513	98	5
1,575	82	76	9	68	...	...	...	395	6
...	...	...	...	...	...	...	...	...	7
11,676	16,461	31,271	12,149	28,228	27,987	12,920	26,724	2,114	8
15,616	4,881	15,657	20,228	33,689	18,788	14,617	23,467	4,183	9
862	1,114	151	264	413	203	66	1,364	57	10
...	...	...	...	...	...	...	...	...	11
3,386	4,019	1,817	2,001	6,272	4,811	1,528	8,878	620	12
2,287	...	...	129	2	1	...	...	817	13
...	1	...	1	...	...	...	...	...	14
268	392	231	1,021	2,363	545	927	659	123	15
124	3	4	23	4	...	52	14	3	16
...	...	...	...	...	...	...	...	...	17
16,817	7,843	10,709	22,014	12,001	21,770	19,648	2,807	4,606	18
18,061	38,428	10,229	6,424	69,328	45,144	22,161	57,333	2,765	19
706	837	1,302	3,238	1,645	2,826	1,600	573	249	20
8	...	1	619	9	...	...	...	295	21
103	340	66	41	5,614	...	2,979	5,950	...	22
3,008	3,713	3,737	3,085	8,522	6,054	3,911	5,024	535	23
1,626	2,514	1,546	1,289	2,011	2,363	1,092	1,627	299	24
388	114	3,076	5,186	18	84	6	6	499	25.
4,989	16,841	7,739	4,671	10,608	11,750	4,284	7,304	682	26
68	...	3	68	...	...	...	...	36	27
240	...	869	75	...	...	...	...	...	28
582	707	304	682	1,165	454	179	641	229	29
6,765	11,479	8,154	10,952	22,627	20,180	8,750	14,291	1,416	30
8,329	3,513	9,931	9,744	21,893	17,884	7,540	6,120	2,438	31
45	...	4	5	25	...	5	5	...	32
...	...	...	...	...	...	...	...	...	33
9,238	4,428	28,869	41,848	5,207	11,110	2,977	1,609	5,476	34
2,272	2,821	2,715	2,932	5,800	4,449	2,618	4,046	543	35
736	1,341	301	323	4,312	1,235	1,698	3,828	286	36
1	...	...	2	48	...	...	...	...	37
1,187	3,481	1,591	3,877	1,169	781	1,000	1,033	140	38
...	...	...	...	...	...	...	...	...	39
5,350	7,071	9,476	5,943	2,874	6,288	59	332	614	40
5,583	9,756	5,729	3,747	19,967	20,351	8,149	16,447	1,380	41
...	...	...	...	...	...	32	...	...	42
319	309	272	347	605	138	47	218	77	43
1,710	1,133	657	1,823	608	...	190	324	365	44
...	...	...	...	...	...	...	...	...	45
2,025	5,189	2,178	5,152	12,072	7,189	1,514	16,752	852	46
...	...	...	...	...	...	...	...	...	47
...	...	...	...	...	...	...	...	...	48
533	1,179	501	963	2,719	1,433	764	2,424	135	49
718	836	361	1,555	1,210	678	691	494	407	50

PROVINCIAL TABLE III.—SELECTED CASTES BY

Serial Number.	Caste, Tribe or Race.	Total.	JAISALMER — Administrative Units: Jaisalmer Town.	Bap.	Buili.	Devikot.	Dewa.	Fatehgarh.
1	2	106	107	108	109	110	111	112
1	Ahir ...	...	...	...	...	...	...	...
2	Balai ...	...	...	...	...	...	...	...
3	Bambhi ...	...	...	...	...	...	...	...
4	Bhangi ...	45	42	8	...	...	...	...
5	Bhat ...	17	...	...	...	7	...	1
6	Bhil ...	1,948	163	186	11	64	69	193
7	Bishnoi ...	3,646	21	895	...	...	...	...
8	Brahman ...	3,871	2,271	896	...	76	20	79
9	Chamar ...	1,035	...	...	...	...	...	...
10	Charan ...	723	1	65	...	198	1	314
11	Dangi ...	...	...	...	...	...	...	...
12	Daroga ...	2,371	582	102	4	109	21	212
13	Dhakar ...	...	...	...	...	...	...	...
14	Dhed ...	...	...	...	...	...	...	...
15	Fakir ...	182	28	1	46	...	...	...
16	Gadaria ...	...	...	...	...	...	...	...
17	Grassia ...	...	...	...	...	...	...	...
18	Gujar ...	...	...	...	...	...	...	...
19	Jat ...	430	...	1	...	20	...	...
20	Jogi ...	...	...	...	...	...	...	...
21	Kachhi ...	...	...	...	...	...	...	...
22	Kaimkhani ...	...	...	...	...	...	...	...
23	Khati ...	2,141	51	239	33	160	68	247
24	Khatik ...	2	...	...	...	...	...	...
25	Koli ...	...	...	...	...	...	...	...
26	Kumhar ...	1,534	40	80	78	123	79	195
27	Kunbi ...	...	...	...	...	...	...	...
28	Lodha ...	...	...	...	...	...	...	...
29	Lohar ...	156	28	87	...	...	...	...
30	Mahajan ...	3,823	1,488	138	...	108	19	312
31	Mali ...	647	269	26	...	28	96	46
32	Meo ...	...	...	...	...	...	...	...
33	Merat ...	...	...	...	...	...	...	...
34	Mina ...	1	1	...	...	...	...	...
35	Nai ...	1,038	78	164	19	65	82	110
36	Naik ...	30	11	...	...	...	...	...
37	Patel ...	...	...	...	...	...	...	...
38	Pathan ...	173	114	1	...	21	...	...
39	Purohit ...	...	...	...	...	...	...	...
40	Raigar ...	...	...	...	...	...	...	...
41	Rajput (Hindu) ...	20,068	168	2,082	628	1,613	904	1,169
42	Rawat ...	...	...	...	...	...	...	...
43	Rebari ...	243	...	7	...	26	...	...
44	Sadhu ...	...	...	...	...	...	...	...
45	Sargara ...	...	...	...	...	...	...	...
46	Sheikh ...	8,224	276	779	299	281	99	280
47	Sirvi ...	...	...	...	...	...	...	...
48	Sondhia ...	...	...	...	...	...	...	...
49	Sunar ...	520	175	49	...	4	...	91
50	Teli ...	43	...	29	...	...	...	...

ADMINISTRATIVE UNITS (PERSONS ONLY).—*Continued.*

STATE. (PARGANA, TEHSIL, TOWN, ETC)												
Jaisalmer.	Khuiala.	Kishangarh	Lakha.	Lathi-Nachna.	Myajlar.	Nokh.	Ramgarh.	Sam-Khabha	Shahgarh-Ghotru.	Sri Mohangarh	Tanot.	SERIAL NUMBER.
113	114	115	116	117	118	119	120	121	122	123	124	1
...	...	...	...	...	...	...	...	...	...	...	...	1
...	...	...	...	...	...	...	...	...	...	...	...	2
...	...	...	...	...	...	...	...	...	...	...	...	3
...	...	...	...	...	...	...	...	...	...	...	...	4
...	...	...	...	4	...	2	8	...	...	...	...	5
317	70	20	107	75	122	173	75	184	77	38	4	6
...	...	...	...	347	...	2,382	...	...	...	1	...	7
33	1	...	217	160	11	561	1	36	...	5	4	8
...	...	72	...	...	374	...	...	589	...	...	...	9
7	...	...	61	...	1	75	...	...	...	...	...	10
...	...	...	...	...	...	...	...	...	...	...	...	11
191	14	5	343	146	151	253	24	154	7	53	...	12
...	...	...	...	...	...	...	...	...	...	...	...	13
...	...	...	...	...	...	...	...	...	...	...	...	14
...	6	...	...	...	...	77	1	11	...	17	...	15
...	...	...	...	...	...	...	...	...	...	...	...	16
...	...	...	...	...	...	...	...	...	...	...	...	17
...	...	...	...	...	...	...	...	...	...	...	...	18
10	...	...	1	3	...	322	...	9	...	64	...	19
...	...	...	...	...	...	...	...	...	...	...	...	20
...	...	...	...	...	...	...	...	...	...	...	...	21
...	...	...	...	...	...	...	...	...	...	...	...	22
194	20	...	180	120	34	426	65	197	22	81	...	23
...	...	...	...	...	...	2	...	...	...	...	...	24
...	...	...	...	...	...	...	...	...	...	...	...	25
29	2	...	108	85	3	400	86	212	...	14	...	26
...	...	...	...	...	...	...	...	...	...	...	...	27
...	...	...	...	...	...	...	...	...	...	...	...	28
...	25	...	...	14	5	16	36	...	...	...	...	29
79	2	1	349	806	92	569	44	136	116	64	...	30
10	17	...	7	18	...	102	...	9	...	19	...	31
...	...	...	...	...	...	...	...	...	...	...	...	32
...	...	...	...	...	...	...	...	...	...	...	...	33
...	...	...	...	...	...	...	...	...	...	...	...	34
67	11	...	28	104	14	251	8	39	...	48	...	35
...	...	...	...	12	...	...	...	7	...	...	...	36
...	...	...	...	...	...	...	...	...	...	...	...	37
2	...	...	...	...	...	31	...	...	3	1	...	38
...	...	...	...	...	...	...	...	...	...	...	...	39
...	...	...	...	...	...	...	...	...	...	...	...	40
2,068	276	2	1,135	2,072	907	2,959	1,510	1,304	...	1,270	6	41
...	...	...	...	...	...	...	...	...	...	...	...	42
5	...	...	...	21	...	170	...	...	...	14	...	43
...	...	...	...	...	...	...	...	...	...	...	...	44
...	...	...	...	...	...	...	...	...	...	...	...	45
156	2,082	268	202	968	39	916	165	331	519	511	53	46
...	...	...	...	...	...	...	...	...	...	...	...	47
...	...	...	...	...	...	...	...	...	...	...	...	48
10	...	...	55	27	6	45	35	16	...	7	...	49
...	...	...	...	...	...	14	...	...	...	...	...	50

PROVINCIAL TABLE III.—SELECTED CASTES BY

SERIAL NUMBER.	CASTE, TRIBE OR RACE.	JHALAWAR STATE.						
		Total.	ADMINISTRATIVE UNIT (PARGANA, TEHSIL, TOWN, ETC.).					
			Jhalrapatan (Chhaoni).	Awar.	Dag.	Gangdhar.	Pachpahar.	Patan.
1	2	125	126	127	128	129	130	131
1	Ahir ...	512	57	1	...	15	354	85
2	Balai ...	5,338	78	692	1,651	1,714	857	346
3	Bambhi ...	21	...	1	...	1	17	2
4	Bhangi ...	847	150	55	185	201	115	141
5	Bhat ...	191	7	4	19	97	56	8
6	Bhil ...	3,250	150	82	10	18	849	2,191
7	Bishnoi ...	...	...	...	...	...	...	...
8	Brahman ...	5,848	987	341	808	1,171	1,279	1,267
9	Chamar ...	10,536	542	1,327	2,090	2,065	2,510	2,002
10	Charan ...	255	27	89	16	10	102	61
11	Dangi ...	253	...	...	...	...	15	238
12	Daroga ...	724	344	6	...	242	69	63
13	Dhakar ...	2,038	45	66	9	...	1,021	897
14	Dhed ...	...	...	...	...	...	...	...
15	Fakir ...	364	113	36	33	57	85	40
16	Gadaria ...	11	...	...	...	...	...	11
17	Grassia ...	...	...	...	...	...	...	...
18	Gujar ...	4,807	215	155	138	981	1,553	1,765
19	Jat ...	444	18	11	1	50	264	100
20	Jogi ...	456	...	29	...	50	188	189
21	Kachhi ...	180	...	...	...	...	77	103
22	Kaimkhani ...	...	...	...	...	...	...	...
23	Khati ...	1,611	96	180	294	311	363	367
24	Khatik ...	135	81	29	17	24	15	19
25	Koli ...	224	101	...	1	14	...	108
26	Kumhar ...	2,347	652	220	340	303	465	367
27	Kunbi ...	1,752	...	110	3	14	625	1,000
28	Lodha ...	536	96	147	...	...	20	273
29	Lohar ...	1,305	38	147	250	368	361	141
30	Mahajan ...	4,975	609	471	718	991	1,214	972
31	Mali ...	2,121	476	101	168	140	595	641
32	Meo ...	82	4	...	...	34	33	11
33	Merat ...	...	...	...	...	...	...	...
34	Mina ...	838	40	4	33	98	456	207
35	Nai ...	2,003	268	154	340	510	385	346
36	Naik ...	307	6	71	...	112	107	11
37	Patel ...	...	...	...	...	...	...	...
38	Pathan ...	2,709	1,271	118	350	221	416	333
39	Purohit ...	...	...	...	...	...	...	...
40	Raigar ...	...	...	...	...	...	...	...
41	Rajput (Hindu) ...	3,571	370	133	183	1,110	560	1,215
42	Rawat ...	...	...	...	...	...	...	...
43	Rebari ...	243	4	13	23	63	21	119
44	Sadhu ...	1,535	38	202	294	315	388	298
45	Sargara ...	...	...	...	...	...	...	...
46	Sheikh ...	1,931	779	72	143	219	385	333
47	Sirvi ...	...	...	...	...	...	...	...
48	Sondhia ...	27,179	18	5,109	8,746	8,747	4,524	35
49	Sunar ...	747	77	106	111	147	146	160
50	Teli ...	2,237	179	105	190	468	426	869

ADMINISTRATIVE UNITS (PERSONS ONLY).—*Continued.*

KARAULI STATE.							KISHANGARH STATE.						
Total.	ADMINISTRATIVE UNIT (PARGANA, TEHSIL, TOWN, ETC).						Total.	ADMINISTRATIVE UNIT (PARGANA, TEHSIL, TOWN, ETC).					SERIAL NUMBER.
	Karauli Town.	Hazur.	Machilpur.	Mandrail.	Sapotra.	Utgir.		Kishangarh Town.	Arain.	Kishangarh.	Rupnagar.	Sarwar.	
132	133	134	135	136	137	138	139	140	141	142	143	144	1
15	8	...	...	7	...	...	363	176	9	180	9	39	1
5	...	1	4	...	...	...	4,964	128	797	1,269	2,253	517	2
...	...	...	...	...	...	...	...	...	...	...	...	...	3
1,305	409	194	109	96	410	87	872	146	185	142	289	160	4
410	59	182	52	22	68	27	579	24	75	126	94	260	5
...	...	...	...	...	...	...	773	1	278	37	...	457	6
...	...	...	...	...	...	...	...	...	...	...	...	...	7
14,848	3,250	2,991	2,603	2,776	2,509	719	6,003	1,815	1,178	817	1,490	1,203	8
21,083	918	6,574	3,439	2,615	5,953	1,584	3,443	29	1,316	502	14	1,582	9
...	...	...	...	...	...	...	343	27	13	167	86	50	10
...	...	...	...	...	...	...	...	...	...	...	...	...	11
791	395	47	80	...	807	12	2,347	549	388	487	398	575	12
20	...	17	...	...	3	...	1,076	...	...	...	...	1,076	13
...	...	...	...	...	...	...	...	...	...	...	...	...	14
1,037	211	285	127	63	340	11	428	92	30	123	103	80	15
1	...	...	1	...	...	...	1	1	...	...	...	...	16
...	...	...	...	...	...	...	...	...	...	...	...	...	17
15,164	270	6,171	4,450	828	1,690	1,751	7,269	514	628	2,131	2,088	1,913	18
652	17	429	3	1	198	4	15,529	115	5,636	3,724	4,077	1,977	19
1,741	67	428	264	194	710	78	718	11	294	56	110	247	20
9,824	1,345	5,516	1,128	1,084	394	357	...	...	...	...	...	...	21
...	...	...	...	...	...	...	275	42	3	190	34	6	22
2,091	367	563	231	296	494	140	1,445	138	316	310	227	454	23
585	103	91	68	59	205	59	1,036	174	136	152	368	206	24
4,228	1,425	556	569	329	1,195	154	76	67	2	...	...	7	25
2,921	258	814	462	323	942	122	2,629	151	364	400	845	869	26
3	...	...	...	...	8	...	13	18	...	...	...	...	27
89	89	...	...	...	...	...	...	...	...	...	...	...	28
375	124	71	58	76	33	18	430	87	1	80	109	153	29
7,940	2,429	1,311	760	935	2,239	266	4,871	1,457	866	564	866	1,118	30
1,801	53	26	95	...	1,459	168	4,188	930	331	755	643	1,529	31
...	...	...	...	...	...	...	...	...	...	...	...	...	32
...	...	...	...	...	...	...	100	...	...	100	...	...	33
32,022	355	7,953	2,820	5,239	12,852	2,803	401	38	15	264	43	21	34
1,893	390	413	244	217	530	99	1,293	200	231	233	261	368	35
...	...	...	...	...	...	...	486	34	112	88	127	125	36
...	...	...	...	...	...	...	...	...	...	...	...	...	37
1,748	1,266	40	110	92	223	17	606	473	42	24	21	46	38
...	...	...	...	...	...	...	387	15	80	156	106	30	39
...	...	...	...	...	...	...	4,254	452	474	1,264	1,219	845	40
6,098	866	1,001	1,485	676	1,969	101	3,911	488	684	1,016	925	798	41
...	...	...	...	...	...	...	196	51	...	141	...	4	42
200	82	54	6	39	19	...	274	6	81	89	90	8	43
653	158	229	90	18	146	12	1,653	161	307	495	335	355	44
...	...	...	...	...	...	...	28	11	...	3	14	...	45
1,407	988	41	188	116	66	58	1,213	826	24	164	54	145	46
...	...	...	...	...	...	...	...	...	...	...	...	...	47
...	...	...	...	...	...	...	...	...	...	...	...	...	48
757	393	49	81	98	117	19	539	202	71	32	118	116	49
1,256	194	259	171	149	396	87	571	250	92	22	31	176	50

PROVINCIAL TABLE III.—SELECTED CASTES BY

SERIAL NUMBER.	CASTE, TRIBE, OR RACE.	Total.	KOTAH — ADMINISTRATIVE UNIT											
			Kotah City.	Aklerah.	Antah.	Asnawar.	Bakani.	Baran.	Barod.	Chechat.	Chhipabarod.	Digod.	Itawa.	Kanwas.
1	2	145	146	147	148	149	150	151	152	153	154	155	156	157
1	Ahir ...	**7,531**	92	2	71	43	...	398	424	2,184	318	302	8	271
2	Balai ...	**4,951**	116	38	205	15	395	516	109	500	21	281	807	162
3	Bambhi ...	**250**	...	26	...	45	112	...	...	2	32	...	...	1
4	Bhangi ...	**6,979**	959	178	298	78	186	572	128	233	451	190	140	203
5	Bhat ...	**1,144**	22	11	135	...	148	87	30	31	47	11	52	148
6	Bhil ...	**24,075**	99	2,134	274	2,800	2,605	163	332	1,611	2,048	291	336	929
7	Bishnoi ...	...	...	...	...	...	...	...	...	...	...	...	...	...
8	Brahman ...	**36,507**	4,332	1,222	1,607	536	1,551	2,851	1,038	1,918	1,312	1,244	766	1,268
9	Chamar ...	**83,022**	1,495	4,179	3,606	1,885	2,689	6,965	3,069	5,759	4,010	3,596	3,446	4,009
10	Charan ...	**4,102**	167	365	173	110	410	249	108	155	110	111	142	187
11	Dangi ...	**869**	...	...	...	88	775	...	...	5	1	...	...	...
12	Daroga ...	**3,514**	473	2	169	22	9	199	45	87	109	75	53	79
13	Dhakar ...	**44,778**	92	15	3,292	20	1	3,427	1,719	3,454	4,036	1,299	1,324	2,865
14	Dhed ...	...	...	...	...	...	...	...	...	...	...	...	...	...
15	Fakir ...	**3,106**	338	58	175	7	137	210	134	93	151	130	102	81
16	Gadaria ...	**2,810**	2	370	167	...	...	435	...	...	347	...	...	...
17	Grassia ...	...	...	...	...	...	...	...	...	...	...	...	...	...
18	Gujar ...	**42,357**	692	2,286	1,483	1,446	4,302	1,272	2,821	2,742	1,429	1,428	1,197	1,910
19	Jat ...	**5,198**	111	50	375	111	4	335	37	195	137	267	221	575
20	Jogi ...	**5,581**	44	225	331	63	210	420	235	260	366	241	204	226
21	Kachhi ...	**8,774**	42	303	182	...	869	248	4	237	1,285	8	48	602
22	Kumkhani ...	...	...	...	...	...	...	...	...	...	...	...	...	...
23	Khati ...	**8,508**	428	477	332	141	640	493	280	858	359	318	209	253
24	Khatik ...	**2,797**	129	40	222	29	25	153	171	173	56	154	126	90
25	Koli ...	**9,980**	1,614	48	435	86	7	693	292	375	205	202	921	136
26	Kumhar ...	**14,900**	488	649	824	216	530	1,367	683	759	612	571	638	455
27	Kunbi ...	**1,141**	2	...	...	535	416	8	...	169	...	...	...	...
28	Lodha ...	**25,082**	54	4,434	73	604	5,600	133	...	654	2,336	88	...	8
29	Lohar ...	**6,318**	407	304	341	185	322	361	204	242	277	218	154	321
30	Mahajan ...	**19,740**	2,924	874	684	208	951	1,757	526	1,055	1,122	502	436	475
31	Mali ...	**45,102**	2,159	818	3,898	593	519	5,112	1,233	1,733	1,531	1,672	1,168	2,533
32	Meo ...	**1,492**	5	...	6	2	8	24	1	51	16	...	1	...
33	Merat ...	...	...	...	...	...	...	...	...	...	...	...	...	...
34	Mina ...	**64,680**	421	7,142	2,305	951	539	4,380	2,766	2,921	4,465	2,996	5,445	1,771
35	Nai ...	**10,740**	531	589	543	177	688	683	395	536	639	347	393	368
36	Naik ...	**3,702**	65	2	308	67	10	301	199	108	51	164	182	375
37	Patel ...	**14**	8	...	...	...	...	...	...	...	...	...	...	...
38	Pathan ...	**13,485**	2,500	722	792	175	452	724	473	729	790	371	141	417
39	Purohit ...	...	...	...	...	...	...	...	...	...	...	...	...	...
40	Raigar ...	**44**	...	...	...	...	...	...	...	...	...	...	...	...
41	Rajput (Hindu) ...	**14,646**	1,985	298	501	405	545	518	323	1,269	575	196	173	883
42	Rawat ...	**6,606**	561	...	503	120	309	612	279	421	302	331	58	170
43	Rebari ...	**2,995**	2	14	14	18	16	193	156	416	51	5	37	326
44	Sadhu ...	**7,565**	327	519	276	194	890	365	210	617	434	257	170	332
45	Sargara ...	...	...	...	...	...	...	...	...	...	...	...	...	...
46	Sheikh ...	**9,339**	2,550	108	460	64	246	1,092	165	458	283	86	121	347
47	Sirvi ...	...	...	...	...	...	...	...	...	...	...	...	...	...
48	Sondhia ...	**661**	1	72	...	...	489	...	...	140	1	...	...	...
49	Sunar ...	**3,211**	448	158	125	48	281	225	47	191	114	54	32	77
50	Teli ...	**8,941**	462	548	810	154	502	495	226	685	393	252	184	415

ADMINISTRATIVE UNITS (PERSONS ONLY).—*Continued.*

STATE.									KUSHALGARH (CHIEFSHIP).					LAWA (ESTATE)	
(PARGANA, TEHSIL, TOWN, ETC.).										ADMINISTRATIVE UNITS (PARGANA, TEHSIL, TOWN, ETC.)					
Khanpur.	Kishanganj.	Kunjer.	Ladpura.	Mangrol.	Manohar Thana.	Sangod.	Shahabad.	Kotris.	Total.	Kushalgarh Town.	Dungra.	Maiyad.	Patan.	Total.	SERIAL NUMBER.
158	159	160	161	162	163	164	165	166	167	168	169	170	171	172	1
404	309	361	353	41	4	169	1,678	99	...	...	...	...	...	...	1
165	102	289	753	386	4	188	41	358	**12**	9	...	...	3	**30**	2
1	...	8	23	...	...	...	...	...	**7**	7	...	...	...	**7**	3
574	392	543	434	309	102	336	193	535	**17**	17	...	...	...	**48**	4
22	7	53	226	33	27	28	...	26	**11**	8	...	3	...	...	5
1,574	1	184	3,476	195	4,150	244	310	319	**29,985**	521	8,192	14,620	6,652	...	6
...	...	...	...	...	...	...	...	...	...	...	...	...	...	...	7
2,817	840	2,423	2,667	1,711	913	1,834	948	2,209	**465**	407	24	24	10	**81**	8
5,810	2,744	5,787	6,738	3,197	2,428	3,912	2,977	4,721	**359**	89	198	102	20	**286**	9
328	83	263	505	130	108	160	1	232	**19**	8	...	8	3	**12**	10
...	...	...	...	...	...	...	...	...	...	...	...	...	...	...	11
282	92	130	509	141	8	183	3	844	**298**	202	8	60	19	**170**	12
6,562	2,321	4,906	2,649	1,891	375	2,882	11	1,687	...	...	...	...	...	...	13
...	...	...	...	...	...	...	...	...	...	...	...	...	...	...	14
146	88	151	293	198	144	257	14	199	**9**	6	...	3	...	**13**	15
64	1	522	2	55	611	82	148	4	**40**	3	...	87	...	...	16
...	...	...	...	...	...	...	...	...	...	...	...	...	...	...	17
3,063	2,306	1,570	3,473	1,517	1,332	1,996	148	4,444	**5**	5	...	...	...	**258**	18
655	470	454	487	329	7	332	21	25	...	...	...	...	...	**439**	19
384	191	666	188	305	241	190	97	485	**48**	...	13	35	...	**8**	20
83	1,075	679	817	73	115	256	1,848	1,000	...	...	...	...	...	...	21
...	...	...	...	...	...	...	...	...	...	...	...	...	...	...	22
729	222	656	358	283	423	502	160	387	**15**	10	...	5	...	**38**	23
87	144	165	360	140	16	96	17	899	...	...	...	...	...	**91**	24
190	367	985	610	442	200	328	596	1,298	...	...	...	...	...	**139**	25
979	611	1,073	944	908	405	854	324	1,015	**112**	63	18	26	5	**44**	26
...	2	...	8	...	1	...	...	...	...	...	...	...	...	...	27
7	418	12	451	1	10,255	42	12	...	...	...	...	...	...	...	28
480	213	519	254	154	241	271	553	347	**186**	46	68	54	18	**10**	29
1,218	575	959	1,201	739	445	722	742	1,680	**623**	594	4	3	22	**140**	30
3,303	1,562	2,820	4,679	3,293	639	2,700	114	3,028	**7**	5	...	2	...	**220**	31
22	123	10	184	...	916	17	24	82	...	...	...	...	...	...	32
...	...	...	...	...	...	...	...	...	...	...	...	...	...	...	33
4,125	2,645	5,847	2,795	4,418	1,229	2,353	7	5,159	...	...	...	...	...	**128**	34
941	348	668	527	466	477	486	321	667	**53**	34	9	10	...	**54**	35
332	72	316	358	109	1	524	1	162	...	...	...	...	...	**18**	36
...	...	...	2	...	...	...	...	9	**8**	...	...	1	7	...	37
709	441	848	917	367	303	606	272	727	**204**	60	49	89	6	**20**	38
...	...	...	...	...	...	...	...	...	**7**	7	...	...	...	...	39
...	...	...	...	...	...	...	...	44	...	...	...	...	...	**97**	40
1,615	470	737	1,505	367	208	710	289	1,079	**620**	65	6	193	356	**74**	41
419	47	313	409	152	894	449	78	89	...	...	...	...	...	...	42
540	160	66	313	8	26	77	33	524	...	...	...	...	...	**6**	43
552	221	655	538	311	267	386	123	421	**55**	15	7	21	12	**9**	44
...	...	...	...	...	...	...	...	...	...	...	...	...	...	...	45
385	117	310	331	472	304	309	175	357	**52**	51	1	...	...	**1**	46
...	...	...	...	...	...	...	...	...	...	...	...	...	...	...	47
2	...	3	...	...	3	...	...	...	...	...	...	...	...	...	48
229	48	152	152	119	148	186	231	161	**88**	84	3	...	1	**14**	49
765	373	463	561	340	434	380	446	558	**73**	78	...	...	...	**11**	50

PROVINCIAL TABLE III.—Selected Castes by

Serial Number.	Caste, Tribe or Race.	Total.	MARWAR — Administrative Unit: Jodhpur City.	Bali.	Bilara.	Desuri.	Didwana.	Jalore.	Jaitaran.	Jaswantpura.	Jodhpur.
1	2	173	174	175	176	177	178	179	180	181	182
1	Ahir ...	1,176	17	...	...	2	143	...	3	2	19
2	Balai ...	42,703	...	1,807	2,010	1,651	2,202	2,517	946	1,880	3,215
3	Bambhi ...	158,008	2,206	9,145	4,059	7,064	10,470	14,465	5,236	9,041	11,783
4	Bhangi ...	15,059	1,920	417	684	495	887	926	837	433	804
5	Bhat ...	20,223	175	1,678	857	1,141	1,572	1,176	586	1,747	1,105
6	Bhil ...	46,028	32	2,540	55	378	...	6,751	11	11,821	3,292
7	Bishnoi ...	48,688	119	75	2,498	122	...	13	...	2,862	9,037
8	Brahman ...	110,170	13,913	3,999	2,492	2,827	9,120	3,441	2,974	9,071	5,196
9	Chamar ...	6,224	680	426	225	207	65	515	197	510	144
10	Charan ...	14,003	474	100	498	521	610	542	583	493	1,320
11	Dangi ...	...	...	...	...	...	...	...	...	...	...
12	Daroga ...	52,796	2,981	3,019	1,434	1,540	3,694	3,476	2,574	3,305	3,259
13	Dhakar ...	...	...	...	...	...	...	...	...	...	...
14	Dhed ...	...	...	...	...	...	...	...	...	...	...
15	Fakir ...	3,345	146	10	181	35	771	59	193	21	105
16	Gadaria ...	...	...	...	...	...	...	...	...	...	...
17	Grassia ...	5,022	...	4,888	...	...	...	...	...	...	...
18	Gujar ...	20,890	176	169	466	122	1,399	112	4,231	25	424
19	Jat ...	283,933	1,821	4,555	12,849	1,170	24,678	4,102	4,960	1,238	32,988
20	Jogi ...	6,291	1,551	191	11	101	97	66	612	93	243
21	Kachhi ...	35	...	...	24	...	...	...	...	...	...
22	Kaimkhani ...	8,031	523	90	21	53	4,495	12	33	22	24
23	Khati ...	48,490	986	2,486	1,522	1,368	2,321	4,458	1,440	2,558	2,916
24	Khatik ...	5,552	4	591	282	566	231	38	213	2	214
25	Koli ...	3,586	234	...	...	...	...	...	2	10	7
26	Kumhar ...	87,847	1,904	6,506	3,990	3,721	2,577	8,273	9,250	4,274	4,144
27	Kunbi ...	36,626	4	...	...	...	...	4,403	...	15,728	...
28	Lodha ...	...	...	...	...	...	...	...	...	...	...
29	Lohar ...	20,271	1,107	1,715	719	1,769	473	1,337	747	1,366	1,109
30	Mahajan ...	148,700	9,373	14,202	3,712	9,358	8,746	17,131	3,848	9,082	5,872
31	Mali ...	57,815	6,273	2,053	4,418	1,484	2,352	3,436	4,743	2,210	6,968
32	Meo ...	...	...	...	...	...	...	...	...	...	...
33	Merat ...	2,550	...	11	...	...	...	...	...	...	...
34	Mina ...	22,455	54	9,148	...	1,695	126	7,022	2,589	8	79
35	Nai ...	30,925	1,521	1,367	1,017	1,151	1,975	1,685	1,294	1,555	2,074
36	Naik ...	7,755	568	7	22	7	2,065	7	616	2	...
37	Patel ...	15,015	2	...	11	11	2	4,064	...	8	5,436
38	Pathan ...	13,892	4,387	529	234	895	831	158	349	139	215
39	Purohit ...	44,317	308	3,989	782	4,601	110	10,967	1,184	869	3,371
40	Raigar ...	32,284	752	175	749	145	1,208	80	2,471	138	492
41	Rajput (Hindu) ...	187,874	5,936	9,349	4,200	4,028	10,276	14,988	3,105	10,962	14,985
42	Rawat ...	6,926	206	...	5	212	...	220	6,044	57	...
43	Rebari ...	91,543	282	9,092	2,794	7,015	438	12,836	3,304	12,750	4,584
44	Sadhu ...	2,634	185	842	14	34	27	848	171	...	7
45	Sargara ...	21,598	485	3,652	1,416	2,173	29	3,534	1,858	1,640	813
46	Sheikh ...	44,381	9,867	1,110	570	685	671	1,771	873	588	238
47	Sirvi ...	52,919	...	2,580	4,611	12,951	...	...	6,984	...	182
48	Sondhia ...	...	...	...	...	...	...	...	...	...	...
49	Sunar ...	20,137	1,843	1,515	792	1,124	995	1,419	583	994	1,281
50	Teli ...	7,380	712	3	542	28	477	...	457	...	497

DMINISTRATIVE UNITS (PERSONS ONLY).—*Continued.*

TATE

(PARGANA, TEHSIL, TOWN, ETC.).

Malani.	Merta.	Nagaur.	Pachbhadra.	Pali.	Parbatsar.	Phalodi.	Sambhar-Marwar	Sambhar-Shamlat	Sanchore.	Shergarh.	Sheo.	Siwana.	Sojat.	SERIAL NUMBER.
183	184	185	186	187	188	189	190	191	192	193	194	195	196	1
1	121	295	...	6	4	...	442	66	...	...	...	3	52	1
2,235	8,610	3,004	500	526	8,680	1,507	1,701	55	2,554	2,239	440	2,103	2,821	2
7,978	12,205	9,486	2,181	4,096	10,750	8,068	7,348	501	5,050	4,405	2,468	8,116	6,892	3
224	1,624	1,489	208	829	1,135	233	864	130	195	129	3	203	940	4
469	529	521	111	2,105	1,012	985	123	32	427	457	...	226	3,239	5
8,112	11	85	1,004	644	148	1,576	...	...	4,798	1,456	439	2,705	170	6
5,672	1,218	2,333	829	71	425	9,908	...	...	12,973	475	1	33	24	7
4,833	8,150	9,366	1,308	3,026	5,577	8,515	5,890	570	3,574	1,210	433	1,075	4,610	8
483	74	99	297	265	240	586	208	30	197	218	51	150	357	9
678	714	896	321	614	1,010	855	868	8	781	1,070	945	127	525	10
...	...	...	...	...	...	...	...	...	...	...	...	...	...	11
4,138	3,347	2,381	560	1,881	3,280	1,951	1,850	35	1,740	1,710	852	1,241	3,108	12
...	...	...	...	...	...	...	...	...	...	...	...	...	...	13
...	...	...	...	...	...	...	...	...	...	...	...	...	...	14
59	57	368	61	60	859	74	63	...	41	6	...	...	171	15
...	...	...	...	...	...	...	...	...	...	...	...	...	...	16
...	...	...	...	...	134	...	...	...	...	...	...	...	...	17
67	2,048	842	643	319	3,492	64	3,484	602	...	...	...	56	2,149	18
54,661	34,964	38,254	1,832	670	21,724	7,838	15,810	518	5,082	7,900	2,679	158	3,482	19
9	676	249	18	140	504	9	516	4	3	...	20	8	1,175	20
...	...	...	...	...	...	...	11	...	...	...	...	...	...	21
23	519	1,492	5	2	192	5	416	...	10	2	...	10	82	22
4,300	2,774	3,665	665	1,621	2,679	3,669	1,488	90	1,506	2,710	654	1,349	1,265	23
8	816	248	27	321	500	...	1,091	385	...	...	...	...	565	24
10	110	...	...	...	18	...	4	...	3,101	...	...	9	81	25
5,790	4,506	2,697	1,683	3,131	3,162	1,815	7,646	734	2,549	2,291	797	1,213	5,194	26
3,698	...	...	1,538	...	...	18	...	...	6,819	...	...	3,761	657	27
...	...	...	...	...	...	...	...	...	...	...	...	...	...	28
548	1,108	2,166	179	960	998	591	265	...	881	180	24	292	1,737	29
7,581	5,156	9,883	2,753	4,252	5,445	6,294	4,677	733	2,919	3,238	911	5,654	8,380	30
1,638	2,930	4,182	1,767	853	1,932	1,554	981	276	1,337	1,568	260	1,336	3,264	31
...	...	...	...	...	...	...	...	...	...	...	...	...	...	32
...	...	...	...	...	...	...	...	...	...	...	...	...	...	33
...	27	17	...	1,860	399	...	867	31	...	490	...	85	547	34
2,053	2,118	2,621	593	1,075	1,248	1,712	1,102	70	762	1,024	292	896	1,730	35
28	755	636	...	4	1,196	26	1,186	...	...	...	...	...	630	36
7	...	...	664	4,860	...	...	...	...	...	...	...	455	...	37
481	917	862	4	68	594	283	252	756	2,282	77	1	127	501	38
1,849	325	744	1,996	1,776	1,913	966	144	5	108	1,043	395	4,576	2,351	39
10,569	4,041	4,275	85	487	2,204	226	2,228	426	188	1	...	150	1,244	40
11,865	10,434	11,864	2,674	3,845	10,045	12,288	5,964	219	3,255	21,901	4,927	5,319	5,445	41
...	173	...	...	...	...	...	...	...	...	...	...	...	9	42
6,096	1,405	1,174	940	5,585	1,914	503	522	...	7,763	784	...	4,194	7,568	43
...	27	92	12	12	13	54	27	18	...	2	2	3	799	44
60	467	251	37	1,349	662	...	34	36	...	24	...	791	2,837	45
802	3,971	5,207	700	856	1,264	3,962	2,881	1,080	6,071	720	334	197	568	46
...	11	68	...	3,238	2,731	1,383	...	...	...	...	...	...	18,285	47
...	...	...	...	...	...	...	...	...	...	...	...	...	...	48
1,494	779	1,949	390	748	878	...	586	58	531	515	64	527	1,077	49
434	142	1,918	26	605	463	289	105	21	33	130	31	31	427	50

PROVINCIAL TABLE III.—SELECTED CASTES BY

Serial Number	Caste, Tribe or Race.	Partabgarh State. Total	Partabgarh State. Administrative Units (Pargana, Tehsil, Town, etc.). Partabgarh Town.	Hathuna.	Magra.	Sagthali.	Shahpura State. Total.	Shahpura State. Administrative Units (Pargana, Tehsil, Town, etc.). Shahpura Town.	Arwar.	Dhikola.	Dohria.	Kanechan.	Phulia.	Sangria.	Shahpura.
1	2	219	220	221	222	223	224	225	226	227	228	229	230	231	232
1	Ahir ...	**100**	98	2	...	...	**17**	...	...	...	...	...	...	17	...
2	Balai ...	**1,129**	106	687	12	324	**1,591**	65	242	536	247	101	240	104	56
3	Bambhi ...	**108**	9	96	...	8	...	...	...	...	...	...	...	...	...
4	Bhangi ...	**414**	98	173	13	180	**511**	136	56	61	74	23	108	46	7
5	Bhat ...	**423**	158	181	6	78	**123**	24	13	16	32	...	7	31	...
6	Bhil ...	**29,445**	90	8,955	8,237	12,163	**2,707**	110	272	730	488	272	395	85	355
7	Bishnoi ...	...	...	...	...	...	...	...	...	...	...	...	...	...	...
8	Brahman ...	**3,214**	1,024	1,432	111	647	**3,717**	868	479	639	561	168	478	374	150
9	Chamar ...	**3,562**	92	2,395	166	909	**4,917**	155	580	1,397	858	489	520	411	502
10	Charan ...	**79**	4	58	9	8	**70**	7	1	10	6	18	...	27	1
11	Dangi ...	**853**	...	28	...	825	...	...	...	...	...	...	...	...	...
12	Daroga ...	**1,968**	319	770	184	695	**1,571**	593	318	178	84	51	133	147	67
13	Dhakar ...	**183**	...	...	...	183	**450**	75	4	1	119	...	174	...	77
14	Dhed ...	...	...	...	...	...	...	...	...	...	...	...	...	...	...
15	Fakir ...	**144**	27	114	...	3	**192**	92	31	9	...	...	42	18	...
16	Gadaria ...	**1,678**	14	1,275	13	376	**1,546**	92	1	787	138	16	...	...	512
17	Grassia ...	...	...	...	...	...	...	...	...	...	...	...	...	...	...
18	Gujar ...	**789**	83	397	292	17	**5,179**	267	677	872	504	675	1,197	708	279
19	Jat ...	**213**	55	153	...	5	**4,174**	42	461	1,193	906	176	868	77	456
20	Jogi ...	**1,790**	145	1,026	35	584	**258**	83	18	29	12	...	74	18	24
21	Kachhi ...	...	...	...	...	...	...	...	...	...	...	...	...	...	...
22	Kaimkhani ...	...	...	...	...	...	**537**	326	9	32	26	23	25	71	25
23	Khati ...	**851**	122	491	31	207	**875**	47	114	176	132	48	194	82	82
24	Khatik ...	**205**	67	95	1	42	**703**	425	20	65	20	39	86	46	2
25	Koli ...	**1**	1	...	...	...	**377**	377	...	...	...	...	...	...	...
26	Kumhar ...	**3,320**	123	2,200	18	979	**3,123**	178	436	470	328	430	517	461	303
27	Kunbi ...	**1,604**	3	1,350	2	249	...	...	...	...	...	...	...	...	...
28	Lodha ...	**10**	...	...	...	10	**187**	16	...	7	...	...	63	54	47
29	Lohar ...	**606**	47	300	45	214	**455**	51	50	138	50	49	58	29	30
30	Mahajan ...	**5,176**	3,086	958	129	1,003	**2,906**	1,303	371	270	260	102	354	175	71
31	Mali ...	**583**	162	332	4	85	**2,748**	196	622	760	386	36	466	230	52
32	Meo ...	**139**	16	105	16	2	**4**	2	...	2	...	...	...	...	...
33	Merat ...	...	...	...	...	...	...	...	...	...	...	...	...	...	...
34	Mina ...	**1,448**	65	1,056	1	326	**1,056**	14	...	331	443	...	187	9	72
35	Nai ...	**697**	131	345	13	208	**992**	207	112	176	182	43	114	95	63
36	Naik ...	**165**	2	162	...	1	**724**	137	90	167	68	39	4	58	161
37	Patel ...	...	...	...	...	...	...	...	...	...	...	...	...	...	...
38	Pathan ...	**914**	470	224	28	192	**146**	102	22	11	1	...	7	3	...
39	Purohit ...	...	...	...	...	...	...	...	...	...	...	...	...	...	...
40	Raigar ...	...	...	...	...	...	**1,831**	173	183	263	235	109	619	227	22
41	Rajput (Hindu) ...	**3,362**	266	2,052	58	986	**1,402**	272	241	281	166	106	180	54	102
42	Rawat ...	...	...	...	...	...	**7**	...	...	...	...	5	2	...	...
43	Rebari ...	**44**	...	30	14	...	**267**	4	64	4	...	...	...	121	74
44	Sadhu ...	**19**	11	5	...	3	**878**	133	126	129	209	31	120	67	63
45	Sargara ...	...	...	...	...	...	**12**	...	7	1	...	...	...	4	...
46	Sheikh ...	**1,075**	510	388	67	110	**116**	107	4	2	...	...	1	1	1
47	Sirvi ...	...	...	...	...	...	...	...	...	...	...	...	...	...	...
48	Sondhia ...	...	...	...	...	...	...	...	...	...	...	...	...	...	...
49	Sunar ...	**440**	327	51	6	56	**298**	112	43	36	17	15	37	29	9
50	Teli ...	**1,206**	364	467	31	344	**729**	154	105	119	84	38	137	60	32

ADMINISTRATIVE UNITS (PERSONS ONLY).—*Continued.*

SIROHI STATE.															
	ADMINISTRATIVE UNITS (PARGANA, TEHSIL, TOWN, ETC.).														
Total.	Sirohi Town.	Sirohi.	Abu.	Bhakar.	Barlut.	Erinpura.	Madar.	Magra.	Pamera.	Pindwara.	Posaliya.	Rohera.	Santhpur.	SERIAL NUMBER.
233	234	235	236	237	238	239	240	241	242	243	244	245	246	1
27	2	...	...	...	...	...	...	...	...	1	...	...	24	1
365	...	...	...	...	...	...	1	...	...	5	...	...	359	2
22	1	...	...	...	2	...	...	...	...	...	19	...	...	3
1,290	81	18	9	...	108	58	124	79	105	71	118	60	464	4
2,213	46	98	...	15	142	1	109	214	261	305	187	69	771	5
18,946	403	125	210	737	825	65	3,387	1,420	1,743	1,302	1,137	4,070	3,522	6
15	5	...	...	...	...	...	...	4	...	...	...	...	6	7
15,704	496	382	69	...	2,724	36	1,660	2,367	2,157	2,051	650	1,846	1,266	8
631	78	...	...	...	136	43	1	...	...	123	51	10	189	9
1,005	6	...	8	...	95	...	325	172	68	225	15	49	42	10
...	...	...	...	...	...	...	...	...	...	...	...	...	...	11
3,341	409	63	...	...	535	...	288	591	567	152	487	64	196	12
...	...	...	...	...	...	...	...	...	...	...	...	...	...	13
19,681	229	402	27	3	3,240	52	2,392	3,034	3,441	1,797	2,440	1,727	897	14
60	3	...	...	...	...	...	...	1	...	...	7	4	45	15
12	...	...	...	...	...	3	...	...	...	3	...	...	6	16
16,004	6	...	12	3,765	...	...	102	...	643	4,277	21	1,491	5,687	17
217	1	...	...	...	...	...	1	...	...	84	...	15	116	18
49	2	...	1	...	1	...	...	...	...	8	...	...	37	19
811	44	23	1	...	99	...	153	101	95	104	54	95	42	20
35	...	...	...	...	...	...	...	...	...	...	...	...	85	21
34	...	...	...	...	...	1	...	...	...	12	...	...	21	22
3,312	110	26	5	...	701	14	455	406	381	335	554	240	85	23
166	5	...	...	...	...	...	1	3	10	40	60	4	43	24
6,438	6	3	1	26	...	...	3,112	1	2,777	...	...	1	511	25
12 401	480	314	14	...	1,823	225	697	1,959	1,053	1,202	2,541	1,084	1,009	26
8,727	5	...	1	...	842	...	3,169	977	2,451	303	1	872	106	27
176	...	...	4	...	...	...	...	...	2	8	...	5	157	28
2,653	69	9	2	1	323	10	249	320	429	497	295	248	201	29
17,264	1,139	60	51	4	1,971	119	1,665	2,650	1,690	1,750	3,680	1,800	1,185	30
5,873	320	92	23	...	1,068	1	302	765	631	362	1,047	681	581	31
3	...	...	...	...	...	...	1	...	...	...	2	...	...	32
3	...	...	...	...	...	...	...	...	...	...	...	...	3	33
7,134	347	131	...	...	746	482	...	58	8	1,217	3,537	170	438	34
2,517	106	18	16	...	262	9	333	863	314	295	352	253	196	35
23	...	...	1	...	...	...	...	...	...	...	...	...	22	36
60	...	...	...	...	...	...	...	...	2	...	...	6	52	37
1,263	74	10	4	58	11	39	41	7	58	90	42	48	786	38
4	...	...	...	...	...	...	...	...	...	...	...	...	4	39
149	...	...	...	...	...	...	...	...	...	...	42	1	106	40
15,067	597	247	42	2	1,646	15	1,713	2,220	1,678	1,850	2,508	1,008	1,451	41
5	...	2	...	...	2	...	...	1	...	...	...	...	...	42
18,811	31	335	6	75	1,910	3	2,621	2,009	3,778	2,190	2,708	1,724	1,191	43
110	1	...	...	...	1	...	13	...	18	11	11	38	17	44
6,778	225	166	84	...	864	23	281	949	671	826	1,195	755	790	45
2,578	335	5	17	11	76	123	173	49	145	98	128	180	1,238	46
508	...	...	...	...	...	...	...	...	...	...	7	501	...	47
...	...	...	...	...	...	...	...	...	...	...	...	...	...	48
2,148	249	9	...	...	293	3	141	342	172	237	354	186	177	49
101	6	...	...	...	...	...	...	...	...	27	...	...	68	50

PROVINCIAL TABLE III.—Selected Castes by Administrative Units (Persons only).—*Concluded.*

Serial Number.	Caste, Tribe or Race.	TONK STATE. Total.	Administrative units (Pargana, Tehsil, Town, etc.). Tonk City.	Aligarh.	Chhabra.	Nimbahera.	Pirawa.	Sironj.	Tonk.
1	2	247	248	249	250	251	252	253	254
1	Ahir ...	9,633	194	17	1,306	844	...	5,413	1,859
2	Balai ...	3,709	344	22	1	1,217	1,493	...	632
3	Bambhi ...	348	...	...	2	341	...	5	...
4	Bhangi ...	4,196	484	197	451	350	169	2,129	416
5	Bhat ...	510	12	26	6	92	50	171	153
6	Bhil ...	5,319	8	...	401	3,062	788	353	707
7	Bishnoi ...	...	...	...	...	...	...	...	...
8	Brahman ...	15,061	748	717	1,980	3,586	815	4,810	2,510
9	Chamar ...	40,123	1,761	2,281	4,193	4,891	3,297	14,452	9,748
10	Charan ...	810	...	105	48	511	20	...	126
11	Dangi ...	6,848	2	...	...	1,480	3,953	1,412	1
12	Daroga ...	1,179	15	15	...	819	15	29	286
13	Dhakar ...	5,953	...	442	2,471	2,160	533	...	347
14	Dhed ...	...	...	...	...	...	...	...	...
15	Fakir ...	1,694	144	58	306	223	78	679	206
16	Gadaria ...	3,786	...	...	418	2,609	70	689	...
17	Grassia ...	...	...	...	...	...	...	...	...
18	Gujar ...	16,776	645	1,710	1,476	1,616	1,038	1,760	8,531
19	Jat ...	10,538	57	135	69	2,686	13	127	7,451
20	Jogi ...	1,668	...	188	192	196	90	440	612
21	Kachhi ...	7,275	...	63	568	243	1	6,395	5
22	Kaimkhani ...	295	232	20	...	...	...	...	43
23	Khati ...	5,396	162	185	488	919	699	2,104	844
24	Khatik ...	1,813	494	122	48	444	39	61	610
25	Koli ...	5,632	1,819	81	450	25	14	2,951	292
26	Kumhar ...	6,686	423	346	647	2,005	643	1,489	1,134
27	Kunbi ...	5,100	...	...	4	1,847	1,670	2,063	16
28	Lodha ...	3,760	...	4	2,970	14	32	728	12
29	Lohar ...	2,548	258	116	412	645	256	518	343
30	Mahajan ...	12,030	1,957	823	698	3,316	1,144	2,208	1,889
31	Mali ...	8,179	2,397	1,217	578	742	623	437	2,185
32	Meo ...	912	245	...	12	144	46	118	347
33	Merat ...	...	...	...	...	...	...	...	...
34	Mina ...	18,354	47	4,178	4,289	8,489	57	1,562	4,782
35	Nai ...	5,043	479	219	611	766	667	1,504	797
36	Naik ...	1,543	141	66	39	990	43	...	264
37	Patel ...	...	...	...	...	...	...	...	...
38	Pathan ...	17,790	9,155	558	1,494	1,619	916	3,804	744
39	Purohit ...	...	...	...	...	...	...	...	...
40	Raigar ...	3,264	497	105	...	932	12	19	1,699
41	Rajput (Hindu) ...	10,113	94	109	333	1,614	1,640	5,298	1,025
42	Rawat ...	...	...	...	...	...	...	...	...
43	Rebari ...	347	...	...	14	333	...	...	...
44	Sadhu ...	3,184	40	157	274	1,075	587	595	506
45	Sargara ...	71	...	...	...	71	...	...	...
46	Sheikh ...	8,548	4,244	290	399	595	465	2,130	425
47	Sirvi ...	...	...	...	...	...	...	...	...
48	Sondhia ...	6,250	...	...	...	...	6,250	...	...
49	Sunar ...	1,806	364	72	155	390	254	455	116
50	Teli ...	5,830	648	275	456	1,096	396	2,663	296

PROVINCIAL TABLE IV.

Selected Languages and Dialects by Administrative Units.

EXPLANATORY NOTE.

The languages selected for this Table are Rajasthani, Western Hindi, Bhili and a form of Panjabi spoken in the north of Bikaner. Rajasthani has been further sub-divided into Marwari, Central Eastern and North Eastern Rajasthani and Malvi. The names of dialects are as shown in "The Linguistic Survey of India." These languages and dialects are the Mother tongues of 98·5 per cent. of the enumerated population of the Agency. The Agency totals do not include 113 and 48 speakers of Malvi in Jaipur and Sirohi respectively, nor 4 speakers of Bhili in Jaipur.

Figures for the Abu District have not been shown.

PROVINCIAL TABLE IV.—SELECTED LANGUAGES AND DIALECTS BY

SERIAL NUMBER.	LANGUAGES & DIALECTS.	TOTAL RAJPUTANA.	ALWAR: Total of persons speaking	Alwar City.	Alwar.	Ajerakn.	Bahror.	Bansur.	Govindgarh.	Katumbar.	Khairthal.
1	2	3	4	5	6	7	8	9	10	11	12
	Marwari ...	***5,617,821***	*814*	*61*	...	*12*	*2*	*29*	...	*1*	...
1	Standard ...	2,573,438	166	17	...	...	2	4	...	1	...
2	Marwari-Dhundhari ...	197,277	2	...	...	...	...	...	...	...	...
3	Gorawati ...	7,901	...	...	...	...	...	...	...	...	...
4	Ajmer Dialect ...	256	...	...	...	...	...	...	...	...	...
5	Merwara Dialect ...	4	...	...	...	...	...	...	...	...	...
6	Mewari ...	1,469,477	...	...	...	...	...	...	...	...	...
7	Merwari ...	10,046	...	...	...	...	...	...	...	...	...
8	Sarwari ...	19,154	...	...	...	...	...	...	...	...	...
9	Khairari ...	90,088	...	...	...	...	...	...	...	...	...
10	Godwari ...	17,441	...	...	...	...	...	...	...	...	...
11	Sirohi ...	8,719	...	...	...	...	...	...	...	...	...
12	Deorawati ...	908	...	...	...	...	...	...	...	...	...
13	Marwari-Gujarati ...	20,550	...	...	...	...	...	...	...	...	...
14	Thali ...	56,192	...	...	...	...	...	...	...	...	...
15	Marwari-Sindhi ...	47,786	...	...	...	...	...	...	...	...	...
16	Dhatki ...	121,415	...	...	...	...	...	...	...	...	...
17	Bikaneri ...	81,493	...	...	...	...	...	...	...	...	...
18	Shekhawati ...	701,714	622	44	...	12	...	25	...	...	...
19	Bagri ...	193,962	24	...	...	...	...	...	...	...	...
	Central Eastern Rajasthani ...	***2,157,955***	*29,917*	*6*	...	*1*	*3*	...	...	*13*	...
20	Jaipuri ...	1,021,794	28,073	6	...	1	...	...	...	18	...
21	Torawati ...	264,025	1,644	...	...	...	3	...	...	...	...
22	Kathaira ...	43,943	...	...	...	...	...	...	...	...	...
23	Chaurasi .	34	...	...	...	...	...	...	...	...	...
24	Nagarchal ...	51,633	...	...	...	...	...	...	...	...	...
25	Rajawati ...	80,771	200	...	...	...	...	...	...	...	...
26	Kishangarhi ...	63,614	...	...	...	...	...	...	...	...	...
27	Ajmeri ...	8,393	...	...	...	...	...	...	...	...	...
28	Harauti ...	623,011	...	...	...	...	...	...	...	...	...
29	Sipari ...	737	...	...	...	...	...	...	...	...	...
	North Eastern Rajasthani ...	***478,919***	*393,182*	*3*	*27,120*	*29,900*	*3,801*	*1*	*18,119*	*38,569*	*26,800*
30	Mewati ...	247,293	177,997	2	27,112	...	3	...	18,103	498	25,473
31	Rathi ...	68,135	67,975	1	6	29,900	3,798	...	...	1	1,327
32	Nahera-Mewati ...	66,377	66,374	...	...	...	...	1	4	...	...
33	Kather-Mewati ...	63,398	63,235	...	2	...	...	...	12	38,070	...
34	Ahirwati ...	33,716	17,601	...	...	...	...	...	...	...	...
	Malvi ...	***350,695***	...	...	...	...	...	...	...	...	...
35	Malvi ...	286,894	...	...	...	...	...	...	...	...	...
36	Sondhwari ...	63,801	...	...	...	...	...	...	...	...	...
	Western Hindi ...	***1,719,194***	*325,388*	*47,659*	*16,578*	*3*	*43,280*	*41,248*	*10,054*	*11,070*	*4,575*
37	Bangaru ...	1,402	...	...	...	...	...	...	...	...	...
38	Jatu ...	29	...	...	...	...	...	...	...	...	...
39	Hariani ...	1,471	39	1	...	...	1	1	...	...	1
40	Braj Bhakha or Antarbedi.	340,831	102	...	...	1	...	1	...	1	2
41	Kaumal ...	115,160	...	...	...	...	...	...	...	...	...
42	Dangbhang ...	140,937	...	...	...	...	...	...	...	...	...
43	Urdu ...	103,047	10,281	4,051	1,135	...	28	1	19	...	1,061
44	Hindi ...	1,016,317	314,966	48,607	15,443	2	43,251	41,245	10,085	11,069	3,511
	Bhili ...	***718,730***	...	...	...	...	...	...	...	...	...
45	Girasia ...	19,974	...	...	...	...	...	...	...	...	...
46	Bhilodi ...	60,240	...	...	...	...	...	...	...	...	...
47	Wagdi ..	255,789	...	...	...	...	...	...	...	...	...
48	Bhili ...	382,727	...	...	...	...	...	...	...	...	...
	Panjabi ...	***9,036***	...	...	...	...	...	...	...	...	...
49	Rathi of Bikaner ...	9,036	...	...	...	...	...	...	...	...	...

ADMINISTRATIVE UNITS.

STATE.															
Kishangarh	Lachmangarh	Malakhera.	Mandhan.	Mandawar.	Narayanpur.	Partabgarh.	Rajgarh.	Ramgarh.	Reni.	Thana Ghazi.	Tijara.	Tapukrah.	Circles.	Nimrana Estate.	SERIAL NUMBER.
13	14	15	16	17	18	19	20	21	22	23	24	25	26	27	1
3	***38***	...	***48***	***4***	***263***	***2***	***75***	***215***	***8***	***37***	...	***1***	***8***	***7***	
...	35	...	2	1	7	2	73	...	7	7	...	...	8	...	1
...	...	...	...	...	...	...	1	...	...	1	...	...	...	...	2
...	...	...	...	...	...	...	...	...	...	...	...	...	...	...	3
...	...	...	...	...	...	...	...	...	...	...	...	...	...	...	4
...	...	...	...	...	...	...	...	...	...	...	...	...	...	...	5
...	...	...	...	...	...	...	...	...	...	...	...	...	...	...	6
...	...	...	...	...	...	...	...	...	...	...	...	...	...	...	7
...	...	...	...	...	...	...	...	...	...	...	...	...	...	...	8
...	...	...	...	...	...	...	...	...	...	...	...	...	...	...	9
...	...	...	...	...	...	...	...	...	...	...	...	...	...	...	10
...	...	...	...	...	...	...	...	...	...	...	...	...	...	...	11
...	...	...	...	...	...	...	...	...	...	...	...	...	...	...	12
...	...	...	...	...	...	...	...	...	...	...	...	...	...	...	13
...	...	...	...	...	...	...	...	...	...	...	...	...	...	...	14
...	...	...	...	...	...	...	...	...	...	...	...	...	...	...	15
...	...	...	...	...	...	...	...	...	...	...	...	...	...	...	16
...	...	...	...	...	...	...	...	...	...	...	...	...	...	...	17
...	3	...	26	3	256	...	1	215	1	29	...	...	...	7	18
3	...	...	20	...	...	...	...	...	...	...	...	1	...	...	19
5	...	***1***	...	...	***1,962***	***28***	***26,281***	***2***	***71***	***254***	***2***	...	***1,288***	...	
4	...	1	...	...	243	6	26,280	2	36	191	2	...	1,288	...	20
1	...	...	...	...	1,637	...	...	...	...	3	...	...	...	...	21
...	...	...	...	...	...	...	...	...	...	...	...	...	...	...	22
...	...	...	...	...	...	...	...	...	...	...	...	...	...	...	23
...	...	...	...	...	...	...	...	...	...	...	...	...	...	...	24
...	...	...	...	...	82	22	1	...	35	60	...	...	...	...	25
...	...	...	...	...	...	...	...	...	...	...	...	...	...	...	26
...	...	...	...	...	...	...	...	...	...	...	...	...	...	...	27
...	...	...	...	...	...	...	...	...	...	...	...	...	...	...	28
...	...	...	...	...	...	...	...	...	...	...	...	...	...	...	29
20,722	***10,497***	***6,091***	***24,633***	***7,250***	***21,509***	***9,788***	***171***	***23,400***	***33,512***	***22,994***	***26,603***	***20,735***	***13,921***	***7,043***	
11,171	10,116	6,091	...	6,785	13	...	148	23,369	8,801	16	19,901	18,710	1,683	2	30
661	3	...	24,633	465	119	...	...	7	1	11	...	...	1	7,041	31
...	...	...	...	...	21,374	9,788	4	...	...	22,966	...	...	12,237	...	32
1	378	...	...	...	1	...	19	24	24,710	...	18	...	...	...	33
8,889	...	...	...	...	2	...	...	...	...	1	6,684	2,025	...	...	34
...	...	...	...	...	...	...	...	...	...	...	...	...	...	...	
...	...	...	...	...	...	...	...	...	...	...	...	...	...	...	35
...	...	...	...	...	...	...	...	...	...	...	...	...	...	...	36
10,349	***38,918***	***28,919***	***2,011***	***23,821***	***718***	***7,842***	***7,892***	***9,398***	***210***	***224***	***13,014***	***6,320***	***365***	***920***	
...	...	...	...	...	...	...	...	...	...	...	...	...	...	...	37
...	...	...	...	...	...	...	...	...	...	...	...	...	...	...	38
...	...	...	2	...	33	...	...	...	...	...	...	...	...	...	39
7	4	...	...	2	7	1	20	...	26	29	...	...	...	1	40
...	...	...	...	...	...	...	...	...	...	...	...	...	...	...	41
...	...	...	...	...	...	...	...	...	...	...	...	...	...	...	42
1,213	7	31	...	...	232	...	180	154	22	...	2,147	...	...	...	43
9,129	38,907	28,888	2,009	23,819	446	7,841	7,692	9,244	162	195	10,867	6,320	365	919	44
...	...	...	...	...	...	...	...	...	...	...	...	...	...	...	
...	...	...	...	...	...	...	...	...	...	...	...	...	...	...	45
...	...	...	...	...	...	...	...	...	...	...	...	...	...	...	46
...	...	...	...	...	...	...	...	...	...	...	...	...	...	...	47
...	...	...	...	...	...	...	...	...	...	...	...	...	...	...	48
...	...	...	...	...	...	...	...	...	...	...	...	...	...	...	
...	...	...	...	...	...	...	...	...	...	...	...	...	...	...	49

PROVINCIAL TABLE IV.—Selected Languages and Dialects by

Serial Number.	Languages and Dialects.	Banswara State. Total of persons speaking.	Banswara Town.	Khalsa Villages.	Jagir and other Villages.	Bharatpur Total of persons speaking.	Bharatpur City.	Bharatpur.
1	2	28	29	30	31	32	33	34
	Marwari ...	*1,763*	*270*	*800*	*693*	*632*	*3*	*298*
1	Standard ...	389	76	265	48	631	3	298
2	Marwari-Dhundhari ...	...	...	...	...	1	...	...
3	Gorawati ...	...	...	...	...	...	...	...
4	Ajmer Dialect ...	...	...	...	...	...	...	...
5	Merwara Dialect ...	...	...	...	...	...	...	...
6	Mewari ...	1,374	194	535	645	...	...	...
7	Merwari ...	...	...	...	...	...	...	...
8	Sarwari ...	...	...	...	...	...	...	...
9	Khairari ...	...	...	...	...	...	...	...
10	Godwari ...	...	...	...	...	...	...	...
11	Sirohi ...	...	...	...	...	...	...	...
12	Deorawati ...	...	...	...	...	...	...	...
13	Marwari-Gujarati ...	...	...	...	...	...	...	...
14	Thali ...	...	...	...	...	...	...	...
15	Marwari-Sindhi ...	...	...	...	...	...	...	...
16	Dhatki ...	...	...	...	...	...	...	...
17	Bikaneri ...	...	...	...	...	...	...	...
18	Shekhawati ...	...	...	...	...	...	...	...
19	Bagri ...	...	...	...	...	...	...	...
	Central Eastern Rajasthani ...	*4*	*4*	...	...	*204*	*21*	*1*
20	Jaipuri ...	...	...	...	...	204	21	1
21	Torawati ...	...	...	...	...	...	...	...
22	Kathaira ...	...	...	...	...	...	...	...
23	Chaurasi ...	...	...	...	...	...	...	...
24	Nagarchal ...	...	...	...	...	...	...	...
25	Rajawati ...	...	...	...	...	...	...	...
26	Kishangarhi ...	...	...	...	...	...	...	...
27	Ajmeri ...	...	...	...	...	...	...	...
28	Harauti ...	4	4	...	...	...	...	...
29	Sipari ...	...	...	...	...	...	...	...
	North Eastern Rajasthani ...	...	...	...	...	*64,285*	*17*	*1*
30	Mewati ...	...	...	...	...	64,285	17	1
31	Rathi ...	...	...	...	...	...	...	...
32	Nahera-Mewati ...	...	...	...	...	...	...	...
33	Kather-Mewati ...	...	...	...	...	...	...	...
34	Ahirwati ...	...	...	...	...	...	...	...
	Malvi ...	*1,070*	*336*	*311*	*423*	...	...	...
35	Malvi ...	1,070	336	311	423	...	...	...
36	Sondhwari ...	...	...	...	...	...	...	...
	Western Hindi ...	636	*284*	*244*	*108*	*421,214*	*29,927*	*36,105*
37	Bangaru ...	...	...	...	...	...	...	...
38	Jatu ...	...	...	...	...	...	...	...
39	Hariani ...	...	...	...	...	9	5	1
40	Braj Bhakha or Antarbedi	11	8	1	7	14,172	783	1
41	Kalimal ...	...	...	...	...	...	...	...
42	Dangbhang ...	...	...	...	...	...	...	...
43	Urdu ...	188	128	18	42	12,018	5,812	64
44	Hindi ..	437	153	225	59	395,015	23,377	36,039
	Bhili ...	*220,821*	*9,369*	*86,101*	*125,351*	...	...	...
45	Girasia ...	...	...	...	...	...	...	...
46	Bhilodi ...	4	...	...	4	...	...	...
47	Wagdi ...	125,815	9,311	54,460	62,044	...	...	...
48	Bhili ...	95,002	58	31,641	63,303	...	...	...
	Panjabi ...	...	...	...	...	...	...	...
49	Rathi of Bikaner ...	...	...	...	...	...	...	...

ADMINISTRATIVE UNITS.—*Continued.*

STATE.

Bayana.	Dig.	Kaman.	Kumher.	Nadbai.	Nagar.	Pahari.	Rupbas.	Uchain.	Weir.	SERIAL NUMBER.
35	36	37	38	39	40	41	42	43	44	1
128	***35***	***29***	...	***15***	***3***	***1***	***7***	...	***113***	
128	35	28	...	15	3	1	7	...	113	1
...	...	1	...	...	...	...	...	...	...	2
...	...	...	...	...	...	...	...	...	...	3
...	...	...	...	...	...	...	...	...	...	4
...	...	...	...	...	...	...	...	...	...	5
...	...	...	...	...	...	...	...	...	...	6
...	...	...	...	...	...	...	...	...	...	7
...	...	...	...	...	...	...	...	...	...	8
...	...	...	...	...	...	...	...	...	...	9
...	...	...	...	...	...	...	...	...	...	10
...	...	...	...	...	...	...	...	...	...	11
...	...	...	...	...	...	...	...	...	...	12
...	...	...	...	...	...	...	...	...	...	13
...	...	...	...	...	...	...	...	...	...	14
...	...	...	...	...	...	...	...	...	...	15
...	...	...	...	...	...	...	...	...	...	16
...	...	...	...	...	...	...	...	...	...	17
...	...	...	...	...	...	...	...	...	...	18
...	...	...	...	...	...	...	...	...	...	19
29	***85***	***3***	***9***	***6***	***5***	***1***	***2***	...	***42***	
29	85	3	9	6	5	1	2	...	42	20
...	...	...	...	...	...	...	...	...	...	21
...	...	...	...	...	...	...	...	...	...	22
...	...	...	...	...	...	...	...	...	...	23
...	...	...	...	...	...	...	...	...	...	24
...	...	...	...	...	...	...	...	...	...	25
...	...	...	...	...	...	...	...	...	...	26
...	...	...	...	...	...	...	...	...	...	27
...	...	...	...	...	...	...	...	...	...	28
...	...	...	...	...	...	...	...	...	...	29
2	***3,654***	***14,290***	***25***	***1***	***21,435***	***24,860***	...	...	...	
2	3,654	14,290	25	1	21,435	24,860	...	...	...	30
...	...	...	...	...	...	...	...	...	...	31
...	...	...	...	...	...	...	...	...	...	32
...	...	...	...	...	...	...	...	...	...	33
...	...	...	...	...	...	...	...	...	...	34
...	...	...	...	...	...	...	...	...	...	
...	...	...	...	...	...	...	...	...	...	35
...	...	...	...	...	...	...	...	...	...	36
57,482	***43,867***	***23,133***	***40,309***	***43,233***	***25,638***	***11,488***	***34,045***	***14,374***	***61,613***	
...	...	...	...	...	...	...	...	...	...	37
...	...	...	...	...	...	...	...	...	...	38
...	...	2	...	...	...	1	...	...	...	39
7,054	142	18	6,133	...	2	82	...	...	7	40
...	...	...	...	...	...	...	...	...	...	41
...	...	...	...	...	...	...	...	...	...	42
893	1,404	813	301	1,234	190	538	177	109	483	43
49,535	42,321	22,300	33,875	41,999	25,446	10,867	33,868	14,265	61,123	44
...	...	...	...	...	...	...	...	...	...	
...	...	...	...	...	...	...	...	...	...	45
...	...	...	...	...	...	...	...	...	...	46
...	...	...	...	...	...	...	...	...	...	47
...	...	...	...	...	...	...	...	...	...	48
...	...	...	...	...	...	...	...	...	...	
...	...	...	...	...	...	...	...	...	...	49

PROVINCIAL TABLE IV.—SELECTED LANGUAGES AND DIALECTS BY

SERIAL NUMBER.	LANGUAGES AND DIALECTS.	BIKANER								
				Bikaner Nizamat			Ganganagar Nizamat.			
		Total of persons speaking.	Bikaner City.	Bikaner.	Lunkaransar.	Surpura.	Ganganagar.	Karanpur.	Padampur.	Raisinghnagar.
1	2	45	46	47	48	49	50	51	52	53
	Marwari ...	***785,111***	***79,270***	***48,998***	***26,716***	***56,947***	***25,622***	***3,858***	***9,108***	***8,079***
1	Standard ...	**510,796**	72,920	48,932	26,646	6,491	22,123	3,493	7,870	1,520
2	Marwari-Dhundhari ...	**84**	...	...	2	...	22	...	...	
3	Gorawati ...	...	...	...	...	...	...	...	...	
4	Ajmer Dialect ...	...	...	...	...	...	...	...	...	...
5	Merwara Dialect ...	...	...	...	...	...	...	...	...	...
6	Mewari ...	**127**	84	1	5	7	...	...	...	...
7	Merwari ...	...	...	...	...	...	...	...	...	...
8	Sarwari ...	...	...	...	...	...	...	...	...	...
9	Khairari ...	...	...	...	...	...	...	...	...	...
10	Godwari ...	...	...	...	...	...	...	...	...	...
11	Sirohi ...	...	...	...	...	...	...	...	...	...
12	Deorawati ...	...	...	...	...	...	...	...	...	...
13	Marwari-Gujarati ...	**1**	...	...	...	...	...	...	...	...
14	Thali ...	**1,545**	8	59	...	1,409	66	...	...	...
15	Marwari-Sindhi ...	...	...	...	...	...	...	...	...	...
16	Dhatki ...	...	...	...	...	...	...	...	...	...
17	Bikaneri ...	**78,358**	6,077	2	...	48,923	...	...	...	...
18	Shekhawati ...	**3,661**	117	...	18	108	109	...	226	3[illegible]
19	Bagri ...	**190,539**	64	4	45	9	3,302	365	1,012	6,520
	Central Eastern Rajasthani ...	***2,700***	***266***	***77***	***6***	***15***	***85***	***44***	...	***8***
20	Jaipuri ...	**2,674**	240	77	6	15	85	44	...	8
21	Torawati ...	...	...	...	...	...	...	...	...	...
22	Kathaira ...	**1**	1	...	...	...	...	...	...	...
23	Chaurasi ...	...	...	...	...	...	...	...	...	...
24	Nagarchal ...	...	...	...	...	...	...	...	...	...
25	Rajawati ...	...	...	...	...	...	...	...	...	...
26	Kishangarhi ...	...	...	...	...	...	...	...	...	...
27	Ajmeri ...	**8**	8	...	...	...	...	...	...	...
28	Harauti ...	**17**	17	...	...	...	...	...	...	...
29	Sipari ...	...	...	...	...	...	...	...	...	...
	North Eastern Rajasthani ...	***11***	...	...	...	...	...	...	...	***1***
30	Mewati ...	**10**	...	...	...	...	...	...	...	...
31	Rathi ...	...	...	...	...	...	...	...	...	...
32	Nahera-Mewati ...	...	...	...	...	...	...	...	...	...
33	Kather-Mewati ...	...	...	...	...	...	...	...	...	...
34	Ahirwati ...	**1**	...	...	...	...	...	...	...	1
	Malvi ...	***32***	***19***	...	...	***2***	...	...	...	...
35	Malvi ...	**32**	19	...	...	2	...	...	...	...
36	Sondhwari ...	...	...	...	...	...	...	...	...	...
	Western Hindi ...	***14,248***	***5,171***	***551***	***63***	***13***	***4,525***	***334***	***196***	***125***
37	Bangaru ...	**31**	...	...	...	...	31	...	...	...
38	Jatu ...	**11**	3	...	...	...	...	...	...	...
39	Hariani ...	**1,235**	95	4	42	...	840	21	50	1
40	Braj Bhakha or Antarbedi	**520**	149	...	1	2	202	4	7	6
41	Kalimal ...	...	...	...	...	...	...	...	...	...
42	Dangbhang ...	...	...	...	...	...	...	...	...	...
43	Urdu ...	**1,584**	976	1	12	...	109	176	15	16
44	Hindi ...	**10,867**	3,948	546	8	11	3,848	183	124	102
	Bhili ...	...	...	...	...	...	...	...	...	...
45	Girasia ...	...	...	...	...	...	...	...	...	...
46	Bhilodi ...	...	...	...	...	...	...	...	...	...
47	Wagdi ...	...	...	...	...	...	...	...	...	...
48	Bhili ...	...	...	...	...	...	...	...	...	...
	Panjabi ...	***9,036***	...	***1***	***31***	...	***1,274***	***1,797***	***1,122***	***962***
49	Rathi of Bikaner ...	**9,036**	...	1	31	...	1,274	1,797	1,122	962

ADMINISTRATIVE UNITS.—*Continued.*

STATE.

Reni Nizamat.					Sujangarh Nizamat.				Suratgarh Nizamat.			
Bhadra.	Churu.	Nohar.	Rajgarh.	Reni.	Dungargarh.	Ratangarh.	Sardarshahr.	Sujangarh.	Anupgarh.	Hanumangarh.	Suratgarh.	SERIAL NUMBER.
54	55	56	57	58	59	60	61	62	63	64	65	1
45,003	***54,942***	***55,641***	***58,164***	***30,050***	***37,369***	***53,309***	***56,606***	***70,516***	***4,445***	***34,692***	***25,776***	
292	44,441	3,061	94	6,538	37,334	52,692	50,694	62,025	4,192	34,050	25,388	1
...	...	10	21	...	2	13	14	...	...	...	...	2
...	...	...	...	...	...	...	...	...	...	...	...	3
...	...	...	...	...	...	...	...	...	...	...	...	4
...	...	...	...	...	...	...	...	...	...	...	...	5
...	23	...	...	...	...	...	...	7	...	...	...	6
...	...	...	...	...	...	...	...	...	...	...	...	7
...	...	...	...	...	...	...	...	...	...	...	...	8
...	...	...	...	...	...	...	...	...	...	...	...	9
...	...	...	...	...	...	...	...	...	...	...	...	10
...	...	...	...	...	...	...	...	...	...	...	...	11
...	...	...	...	...	...	...	...	...	...	...	...	12
...	...	1	...	...	...	...	...	...	...	...	...	13
...	...	...	...	...	1	2	...	...	...	...	...	14
...	...	...	...	...	...	...	...	...	...	...	...	15
...	...	...	...	...	...	...	...	...	...	...	...	16
...	9,188	6	...	...	...	...	5,674	8,484	4	...	...	17
...	1,275	33	529	151	30	590	212	...	19	203	2	18
44,711	15	52,530	57,520	23,361	2	12	12	...	230	439	386	19
83	***99***	***3***	***12***	...	***6***	***80***	***9***	***1,878***	***14***	...	***15***	
83	99	3	12	...	6	80	9	1,878	14	...	15	20
...	...	...	...	...	...	...	...	...	...	...	...	21
...	...	...	...	...	...	...	...	...	...	...	...	22
...	...	...	...	...	...	...	...	...	...	...	...	23
...	...	...	...	...	...	...	...	...	...	...	...	24
...	...	...	...	...	...	...	...	...	...	...	...	25
...	...	...	...	...	...	...	...	...	...	...	...	26
...	...	...	...	...	...	...	...	...	...	...	...	27
...	...	...	...	...	...	...	...	...	...	...	...	28
...	...	...	...	...	...	...	...	...	...	...	...	29
...	...	...	***3***	...	...	***5***	...	...	...	***2***	...	
...	...	...	3	...	...	5	...	...	...	2	...	30
...	...	...	...	...	...	...	...	...	...	...	...	31
...	...	...	...	...	...	...	...	...	...	...	...	32
...	...	...	...	...	...	...	...	...	...	...	...	33
...	...	...	...	...	...	...	...	...	...	...	...	34
...	***1***	...	...	...	***10***	...	...	...	...	...	...	
...	1	...	...	...	10	...	...	...	...	...	...	35
...	...	...	...	...	...	...	...	...	...	...	...	36
157	***296***	***529***	***589***	***26***	***30***	***119***	***38***	***172***	***591***	***498***	***225***	
...	...	...	...	...	...	...	...	...	...	...	...	37
...	2	...	...	...	...	2	...	...	1	3	...	38
74	20	24	29	...	...	16	2	6	2	...	9	39
19	...	5	...	5	...	9	8	3	5	79	16	40
...	...	...	...	...	...	...	...	...	...	...	...	41
...	...	...	...	...	...	...	...	...	...	...	...	42
3	102	8	24	3	6	6	21	17	22	21	46	43
61	172	492	536	18	24	86	7	146	561	395	154	44
...	...	...	...	...	...	...	...	...	...	...	...	
...	...	...	...	...	...	...	...			...	...	45
...	...	...	...	...	...	...					...	46
...	...	...	...	...	...	...	...	...	...	...		47
...	...	...	...		...	...		...	...	...	...	48
...	...	***41***	...	...	...	...	...		***2,266***	***1,126***	***416***	
...	...	41	...	...	...	...	...	...	2,266	1,126	416	49

PROVINCIAL TABLE IV.—SELECTED LANGUAGES AND DIALECTS BY

Serial Number.	Languages and Dialects.	Bundi State. Total of persons speaking.	Bundi City.	Baroondhan.	Dei.	Gaindoli.	Hindoli.	Patan.	Nainwa Kila.	Lakheri.
1	2	66	67	68	69	70	71	72	73	74
	Marwari ...	***51,451***	***380***	***4,077***	***773***	***314***	***45,409***	***271***	***227***	...
1	Standard ...	**400**	200	49	6	106	15	24	...	...
2	Marwari-Dhundhari ...	**1,518**	66	143	422	74	442	158	218	...
3	Gorawati ...	...	...	...	...	...	...	...	...	...
4	Ajmer Dialect ...	...	...	...	...	...	...	...	...	...
5	Merwara Dialect ...	...	...	...	...	...	...	...	...	...
6	Mewari ...	**4,788**	75	3,881	23	89	643	70	7	...
7	Merwari ...	...	...	...	...	...	...	...	...	...
8	Sarwari ...	...	...	...	...	...	...	...	...	...
9	Khairari ...	**44,365**	17	4	3	31	44,308	...	2	...
10	Godwari ...	...	...	...	...	...	...	...	...	...
11	Sirohi ...	...	...	...	...	...	...	...	...	...
12	Deorawati ...	**1**	1	...	...	...	...	...	...	...
13	Marwari-Gujarati ...	**4**	4	...	...	...	...	...	...	...
14	Thali ...	...	...	...	...	...	...	...	...	...
15	Marwari-Sindhi ...	...	...	...	...	...	...	...	...	...
16	Dhatki ...	...	...	...	...	...	...	...	...	...
17	Bikaneri ...	...	...	...	...	...	...	...	...	...
18	Shekhawati ...	**375**	17	...	819	14	1	24	...	...
19	Bagri ...	...	...	...	...	...	...	...	...	...
	Central Eastern Rajasthani ...	***161,496***	***16,522***	***32,040***	***39,912***	***35,929***	***222***	***28,247***	***4,483***	***4,141***
20	Jaipuri ...	**708**	4	...	...	567	10	...	127	...
21	Torawati ...	...	...	...	...	...	...	...	...	...
22	Kathaira ...	...	...	...	...	...	...	...	...	...
23	Chaurasi ...	...	...	...	...	...	...	...	...	...
24	Nagarchal ...	**8,914**	7	8	8,895	8	5	1	...	...
25	Rajawati ...	...	...	...	...	...	...	...	...	...
26	Kishangarhi ...	**1**	1	...	...	...	...	...	...	...
27	Ajmeri ...	**17**	17	...	...	...	...	...	...	...
28	Harauti ...	**151,849**	16,486	32,087	31,017	35,359	207	28,246	4,356	4,141
29	Sipari ...	**7**	7	...	...	...	...	...	...	...
	North Eastern Rajasthani ...	***23***	***17***	...	...	...	...	***2***	***4***	...
30	Mewati ...	**23**	17	...	...	...	...	2	4	...
31	Rathi ...	...	...	...	...	...	...	...	...	...
32	Nahera-Mewati ...	...	...	...	...	...	...	...	...	...
33	Kather-Mewati ...	...	...	...	...	...	...	...	...	...
34	Ahirwati ...	...	...	...	...	...	...	...	...	...
	Malvi ...	***255***	***31***	***8***	***1***	***25***	***169***	***19***	***2***	...
35	Malvi ...	**255**	31	8	1	25	169	19	2	...
36	Sondhwari ...	...	...	...	...	...	...	...	...	...
	Western Hindi ...	***1,368***	***236***	***51***	***4***	***933***	***51***	***83***	***10***	...
37	Bangaru ...	...	...	...	...	...	...	...	...	...
38	Jatu ...	...	...	...	...	...	...	...	...	...
39	Hariani ...	...	...	...	...	...	...	...	...	...
40	Braj Bhakha or Antarbedi	**64**	20	...	1	23	4	16	...	...
41	Kalmal ...	...	...	...	...	...	...	...	...	...
42	Dangbhang ...	...	...	...	...	...	...	...	...	...
43	Urdu ...	**276**	147	37	1	43	9	29	10	...
44	Hindi ...	**1,028**	69	14	2	867	38	38	...	...
	Bhili ...	***161***	***134***	***27***	...	...	...	...	...	...
45	Girasia ...	...	...	...	...	...	...	...	...	...
46	Bhilodi ...	...	...	...	...	...	...	...	...	...
47	Wagdi ...	...	...	...	...	...	...	...	...	...
48	Bhili ...	**161**	134	27	...	...	...	...	...	...
	Panjabi ...	...	...	...	...	...	...	...	...	...
49	Rathi of Bikaner ...	...	...	...	...	...	...	...	...	...

DHOLPUR STATE								DUNGARPUR STATE.						
Total of persons speaking.	Dholpur City.	Bari.	Baseri.	Gird.	Kolari.	Rajakhera.	Sir Muthra.	Total of persons speaking.	Dungarpur Town.	Bara.	Chhiasat.	Chorasi.	Tarpod.	SERIAL NUMBER.
75	76	77	78	79	80	81	82	83	84	85	86	87	88	1
413	***20***	***77***	***231***	***1***	***6***	***5***	***73***	***3,128***	***341***	***643***	***656***	***698***	***790***	
213	8	76	95	...	6	5	23	654	32	...	145	474	3	1
...	...	...	...	...	...	...	...	...	...	...	...	...	...	2
...	...	...	...	...	...	...	...	...	...	...	...	...	...	3
...	...	...	...	...	...	...	...	...	...	...	...	...	...	4
...	...	...	...	...	...	...	...	...	...	...	...	...	...	5
...	...	...	...	...	...	...	...	2,474	309	643	511	224	787	6
...	...	...	...	...	...	...	...	...	...	...	...	...	...	7
...	...	...	...	...	...	...	...	...	...	...	...	...	...	8
...	...	...	...	...	...	...	...	...	...	...	...	...	...	9
...	...	...	...	...	...	...	...	...	...	...	...	...	...	10
...	...	...	...	...	...	...	...	...	...	...	...	...	...	11
...	...	...	...	...	...	...	...	...	...	...	...	...	...	12
150	12	1	136	1	...	...	...	...	...	...	...	...	...	13
...	...	...	...	...	...	...	...	...	...	...	...	...	...	14
...	...	...	...	...	...	...	...	...	...	...	...	...	...	15
...	...	...	...	...	...	...	...	...	...	...	...	...	...	16
...	...	...	...	...	...	...	...	...	...	...	...	...	...	17
50	...	...	...	...	...	...	50	...	...	...	...	...	...	18
...	...	...	...	...	...	...	...	...	...	...	...	...	...	19
279	...	***20***	***182***	...	***38***	***4***	***35***	...	...	...	...	...	...	
138	...	5	95	...	...	4	34	...	...	...	...	...	...	20
...	...	...	...	...	...	...	...	...	...	...	...	...	...	21
126	...	...	87	...	38	...	1	...	...	...	...	...	...	22
...	...	...	...	...	...	...	...	...	...	...	...	...	...	23
...	...	...	...	...	...	...	...	...	...	...	...	...	...	24
...	...	...	...	...	...	...	...	...	...	...	...	...	...	25
...	...	...	...	...	...	...	...	...	...	...	...	...	...	26
15	...	15	...	...	...	...	...	...	...	...	...	...	...	27
...	...	...	...	...	...	...	...	...	...	...	...	...	...	28
...	...	...	...	...	...	...	...	...	...	...	...	...	...	29
9	...	...	***2***	***5***	***1***	...	***1***	...	...	...	...	...	...	
9	...	...	2	5	1	...	1	...	...	...	...	...	...	30
...	...	...	...	...	...	...	...	...	...	...	...	...	...	31
...	...	...	...	...	...	...	...	...	...	...	...	...	...	32
...	...	...	...	...	...	...	...	...	...	...	...	...	...	33
...	...	...	...	...	...	...	...	...	...	...	...	...	...	34
...	...	...	...	...	...	...	...	***132***	***43***	...	***3***	***85***	***1***	
...	...	...	...	...	...	...	...	132	43	...	3	85	1	35
...	...	...	...	...	...	...	...	...	...	...	...	...	...	36
251,520	***19,166***	***46,335***	***39,381***	***50,900***	***43,496***	***36,798***	***15,444***	***2,518***	***1,744***	***206***	***75***	***188***	***305***	
...	...	...	...	...	...	...	...	...	...	...	...	...	...	37
...	...	...	...	...	...	...	...	...	...	...	...	...	...	38
...	...	...	...	...	...	...	...	...	...	...	...	...	...	39
241,821	11,183	45,524	39,327	50,278	43,484	36,597	15,428	...	...	...	...	...	...	40
...	...	...	...	...	...	...	...	...	...	...	...	...	...	41
...	...	...	...	...	...	...	...	...	...	...	...	...	...	42
1,709	1,150	514	23	4	9	9	...	14	6	7	...	1	...	43
7,990	6,833	297	31	618	3	192	16	2,504	1,738	199	75	187	305	44
...	...	...	...	...	...	...	...	***219,444***	***6,264***	***53,197***	***36,911***	***67,076***	***55,996***	
...	...	...	...	...	...	...	...	...	...	...	...	...	...	45
...	...	...	...	...	...	...	...	...	...	...	...	...	...	46
...	...	...	...	...	...	...	...	116,155	5,863	16,341	25,164	30,282	38,505	47
...	...	...	...	...	...	...	...	103,289	401	36,856	11,747	36,794	17,491	48
...	...	...	...	...	...	...	...	...	...	...	...	...	...	
...	...	...	...	...	...	...	...	...	...	...	...	...	...	49

PROVINCIAL TABLE IV.—Selected Languages and Dialects by

Serial Number.	Languages and Dialects.	JAIPUR Total of persons speaking	Jaipur City.	Amber.	Dausa.	Gangapur.	Hindaun.	Kotkasim.
1	2	89	90	91	92	93	94	95
	Marwari ...	***931,700***	***1,517***	***449***	***499***	***255***	***662***	***16***
1	Standard ...	**8,183**	640	409	150	219	428	...
2	Marwari-Dhundhari ...	**190,365**	344	5	41	11	...	...
3	Gorawati ...	...	...	...	...	...	...	...
4	Ajmer Dialect ...	**26**	1	...	...	...	...	...
5	Merwara Dialect ...	**2**	...	...	...	...	2	...
6	Mewari ...	**1,009**	48	24	3	19	18	1
7	Merwari ...	**6,308**	2	...	...	...	...	...
8	Sarwari ...	**3**	...	...	...	2	1	...
9	Khairari ...	**43,088**	10	...	2	...	93	...
10	Godwari ...	**85**	60	...	...	...	...	...
11	Sirohi ...	**3**	...	...	...	...	...	...
12	Deorawati ...	...	...	...	...	...	...	...
13	Marwari-Gujarati ...	**108**	...	...	...	...	...	...
14	Thali ...	**8**	...	...	...	...	...	...
15	Marwari-Sindhi ...	...	...	...	...	...	...	...
16	Dhatki ...	...	...	...	...	...	...	...
17	Bikaneri ...	**3,119**	6	5	1	...	...	...
18	Shekhawati ...	**679,388**	403	6	302	4	120	15
19	Bagri ...	**5**	3	...	...	...	...	...
	Central Eastern Rajasthani ...	***1,293,377***	***122,547***	***200,573***	***252,612***	***872***	***31,400***	***45***
20	Jaipuri ...	**862,031**	122,378	199,955	252,267	821	30,800	45
21	Torawati ...	**262,270**	117	572	...	2	6	...
22	Kathaira ...	**43,695**	6	4	1	23	578	...
23	Chaurasi ...	**8**	2	...	...	...	...	...
24	Nagarchal ...	**42,396**	8	...	...	...	...	...
25	Rajawati ...	**80,571**	24	1	337	17	2	...
26	Kishangarhi ...	**34**	...	...	...	...	...	...
27	Ajmeri ...	**1,842**	7	38	6	...	...	...
28	Harauti ...	**522**	10	3	1	9	14	...
29	Sipari ...	**8**	...	...	...	...	...	...
	North Eastern Rajasthani ...	***20,626***	***263***	***502***	***401***	***13***	***149***	***16,297***
30	Mewati ...	**4,334**	98	502	401	12	149	383
31	Rathi ...	**36**	1	...	...	...	...	...
32	Nahera-Mewati ...	**2**	1	...	...	...	...	...
33	Kather-Mewati ...	**163**	158	...	...	...	...	...
34	Ahirwati ...	**16,091**	5	...	...	1	...	15,914
	Malvi ...	...	...	...	...	...	...	...
35	Malvi ...	...	...	...	...	...	...	...
36	Sondhwari ...	...	...	...	...	...	...	...
	Western Hindi ...	***380,761***	***18,193***	***238***	***4,333***	***105,058***	***135,506***	***423***
37	Bangaru ...	...	...	...	...	...	...	...
38	Jatu ...	**17**	...	...	1	6	...	...
39	Hariani ...	**82**	7	1	10	...	...	6
40	Braj Bhakha or Antarbedi	**561**	158	12	144	37	106	...
41	Kalimal ...	**103,575**	67	...	23	102,041	62	...
42	Dangbhang ...	**137,555**	143	80	300	1,025	134,933	...
43	Urdu ...	**20,597**	13,153	41	1,534	556	73	36
44	Hindi ...	**118,374**	4,665	104	2,321	1,398	332	381
	Bhili ...	...	...	...	...	...	...	...
45	Girasia ...	...	...	...	...	...	...	...
46	Bhilodi ...	...	...	...	...	...	...	...
47	Wagdi ...	...	...	...	...	...	...	...
48	Bhili ...	...	...	...	...	...	...	...
	Panjabi ...	...	...	...	...	...	...	...
49	Rathi of Bikaner ...	...	...	...	...	...	...	...

ADMINISTRATIVE UNITS.—*Continued.*

STATE.									
Malpura.	Sambhar.	Sawai Jaipur.	Sawai Madhopur.	Shekhawati.	Torawati.	Khetri Thikana.	Sikar Thikana.	Uniara Thikana.	SERIAL NUMBER.
96	97	98	99	100	101	102	103	104	1
99,512	***135,837***	***1,733***	***159***	***312,595***	***64,648***	***96,131***	***216,742***	***945***	
1,134	...	497	95	1,424	1,117	41	1,851	178	1
55,670	128,215	207	84	17	5,761	...	37	23	2
...	...	...	...	...	...	...	...	...	3
25	...	...	...	...	...	...	...	...	4
...	...	...	...	...	...	...	...	...	5
296	420	12	7	16	32	1	71	41	6
68	6,286	1	...	...	...	1	...	...	7
...	...	...	...	...	...	...	...	...	8
42,288	...	21	...	...	...	...	...	674	9
...	...	...	...	...	25	...	...	...	10
...	...	...	...	...	...	...	8	...	11
...	...	...	...	...	...	...	...	...	12
...	108	...	...	...	...	...	5	...	13
...	...	...	...	...	...	...	8	...	14
...	...	...	...	...	...	...	...	...	15
...	...	...	...	...	...	...	...	...	16
...	113	1	8	584	58	22	2,381	...	17
81	750	994	20	810,604	57,660	96,064	212,386	29	18
...	...	...	...	...	...	2	...	...	19
46,914	***50,714***	***192,410***	***83,531***	***1,600***	***219,563***	***49,941***	***6,174***	***34,481***	
34,439	9,730	192,087	3,226	190	15,160	164	495	279	20
7	118	211	1	1,894	204,398	49,777	5,671	1	21
2,266	40,792	22	...	...	1	...	...	2	22
...	...	4	2	...	...	...	...	...	23
8,361	...	31	17	...	...	...	...	33,979	24
65	...	51	80,048	5	4	...	...	17	25
...	29	...	4	1	...	...	...	...	26
1,728	44	...	2	9	...	...	8	...	27
48	6	4	223	1	...	...	...	203	28
...	...	...	8	...	...	...	...	...	29
7	***46***	***19***	...	***66***	***2,700***	***122***	***32***	***9***	
7	41	17	...	64	2,547	75	32	6	30
...	...	...	...	...	1	34	...	...	31
...	...	...	...	...	1	...	...	...	32
...	5	...	...	...	...	...	...	...	33
...	...	2	...	2	151	13	...	3	34
...	...	...	...	...	...	...	...	...	
...	...	...	...	...	...	...	...	...	35
...	...	...	...	...	...	...	...	...	36
236	***2,607***	***1,826***	***105,006***	***3,385***	***386***	***2,212***	***444***	***908***	
...	...	...	...	...	...	...	...	...	37
...	...	1	8	...	...	...	...	1	38
...	...	...	...	18	33	6	1	...	39
11	25	8	11	6	26	2	9	6	40
...	...	8	1,371	...	...	7	1	...	41
29	50	96	785	2	23	24	11	54	42
71	990	810	2,011	1,343	70	169	98	142	43
125	1,542	1,408	100,820	2,016	234	2,004	324	705	44
...	...	...	...	...	...	...	...	...	
...	...	...	...	...	...	...	...	...	45
...	...	...	...	...	...	...	...	...	46
...	...	...	...	...	...	...	...	...	47
...	...	...	...	...	...	...	...	...	48
...	...	...	...	...	...	...	...	...	
...	...	...	...	...	...	...	...	...	49

PROVINCIAL TABLE IV.—SELECTED LANGUAGES AND DIALECTS BY

		JAISALMER						
Serial Number.	Languages and Dialects.	Total of persons speaking.	Jaisalmer Town.	Bap.	Buili.	Devikot.	Dewa.	Fatehgarh.
1	2	105	106	107	108	109	110	111
	Marwari ...	***72,242***	***7,001***	***6,667***	***1,572***	***3,859***	***1,872***	***4,349***
1	Standard ...	23,254	6,999	802	902	870	...	4,348
2	Marwari-Dhundhari ...	...	...	...	...	...	...	...
3	Gorawati ...	...	...	...	...	...	...	...
4	Ajmer Dialect ...	...	...	...	...	...	...	...
5	Merwara Dialect ...	...	...	...	...	...	...	...
6	Mewari ...	2	...	...	...	...	...	1
7	Merwari ...	...	...	...	...	...	...	...
8	Sarwari ...	...	...	...	...	...	...	...
9	Khairari ...	...	...	...	...	...	...	...
10	Godwari ...	...	...	...	...	...	...	...
11	Sirohi ...	...	...	...	...	...	...	...
12	Deorawati ...	...	...	...	...	...	...	...
13	Marwari-Gujarati ...	...	...	...	...	...	...	...
14	Thali ...	36,216	...	6,865	...	2,989	1,872	...
15	Marwari-Sindhi ...	9,640	...	...	670	...	...	...
16	Dhatki ...	3,128	...	...	...	...	...	...
17	Bikaneri ...	...	...	...	...	...	...	...
18	Shekhawati ...	2	2	...	...	...	...	...
19	Bagri ...	...	...	...	...	...	...	...
	Central Eastern Rajasthani ...	...	...	...	...	...	...	...
20	Jaipuri ...	...	...	...	...	...	...	...
21	Torawati ...	...	...	...	...	...	...	...
22	Kathaira ...	...	...	...	...	...	...	...
23	Chaurasi .	...	...	...	...	...	...	...
24	Nagarchal ...	...	...	...	...	...	...	...
25	Rajawati ...	...	...	...	...	...	...	...
26	Kishangarhi ...	...	...	...	...	...	...	...
27	Ajmeri ...	...	...	...	...	...	...	...
28	Harauti ...	...	...	...	...	...	...	...
29	Sipari ...	...	...	...	...	...	...	...
	North Eastern Rajasthani ...	...	...	...	...	...	...	...
30	Mewati ...	...	...	...	...	...	...	...
31	Rathi ...	...	...	...	...	...	...	...
32	Nahera-Mewati ...	...	...	...	...	...	...	...
33	Kather-Mewati ...	...	...	...	...	...	...	...
34	Ahirwati ...	...	...	...	...	...	...	...
	Malvi ...	*7*	*6*	*1*	...	...	...	...
35	Malvi ...	7	6	1	...	...	...	...
36	Sondhwari ...	...	...	...	...	...	...	...
	Western Hindi ...	*4*	*2*	*1*	...	...	...	*1*
37	Bangaru ...	...	...	...	...	...	...	...
38	Jatu ...	...	...	...	...	...	...	...
39	Hariani ...	...	...	...	...	...	...	...
40	Braj Bhakha or Antarbedi.	3	2	1	...	...	...	...
41	Kalimal ...	...	...	...	...	...	...	...
42	Dangbhang ...	...	...	...	...	...	...	...
43	Urdu ...	1	...	...	...	...	...	1
44	Hindi ...	...	...	...	...	...	...	...
	Bhili ...	*7*	...	...	...	...	...	...
45	Girasia ...	...	...	...	...	...	...	...
46	Bhilodi ...	...	...	...	...	...	...	...
47	Wagdi ..	...	...	...	...	...	...	...
48	Bhili ...	7	...	...	...	...	...	...
	Panjabi ...	...	...	...	...	...	...	...
49	Rathi of Bikaner ...	...	...	...	...	...	...	...

ADMINISTRATIVE UNITS.—*Continued.*

STATE												
Jaisalmer.	Khuiala.	Kishangarh.	Lakha.	Lathi-Nachna.	Myajlar.	Nokh.	Ramgarh.	Sam-Khabha.	Shahgarh-Ghotru.	Sri Mohangarh.	Tanot.	SERIAL NUMBER.
112	113	114	115	116	117	118	119	120	121	122	123	1
4,484	***3,637***	***851***	***3,551***	***6,409***	***2,419***	***12,598***	***2,551***	***6,090***	***116***	***3,513***	***703***	
4,321	15	110	3,551	240	63	2	...	739	110	616	66	1
...	...	...	...	...	...	...	...	...	...	...	...	2
...	...	...	...	...	...	...	...	...	...	...	...	3
...	...	...	...	...	...	...	...	...	...	...	...	4
...	...	...	...	...	...	...	...	...	...	...	...	5
...	...	...	...	...	...	1	...	...	...	...	...	6
...	...	...	...	...	...	...	...	...	...	...	...	7
...	...	...	...	...	...	...	...	...	...	...	...	8
...	...	...	...	...	...	...	...	...	...	...	...	9
...	...	...	...	...	...	...	...	...	...	...	...	10
...	...	...	...	...	...	...	...	...	...	...	...	11
...	...	...	...	...	...	...	...	...	...	...	...	12
...	...	...	...	...	...	...	...	...	...	...	...	13
...	21	...	...	6,169	...	12,595	2,551	1,164	...	2,490	...	14
163	3,601	741	...	...	141	...	...	3,278	6	403	637	15
...	...	...	...	...	2,215	...	...	909	...	4	...	16
...	...	...	...	...	...	...	...	...	...	...	...	17
...	...	...	...	...	...	...	...	...	...	...	...	18
...	...	...	...	...	...	...	...	...	...	...	...	19
...	...	...	...	...	...	...	...	...	...	...	...	
...	...	...	...	...	...	...	...	...	...	...	...	20
...	...	...	...	...	...	...	...	...	...	...	...	21
...	...	...	...	...	...	...	...	...	...	...	...	22
...	...	...	...	...	...	...	...	...	...	...	...	23
...	...	...	...	...	...	...	...	...	...	...	...	24
...	...	...	...	...	...	...	...	...	...	...	...	25
...	...	...	...	...	...	...	...	...	...	...	...	26
...	...	...	...	...	...	...	...	...	...	...	...	27
...	...	...	...	...	...	...	...	...	...	...	...	28
...	...	...	...	...	...	...	...	...	...	...	...	29
...	...	...	...	...	...	...	...	...	...	...	...	
...	...	...	...	...	...	...	...	...	...	...	...	30
...	...	...	...	...	...	...	...	...	...	...	...	31
...	...	...	...	...	...	...	...	...	...	...	...	32
...	...	...	...	...	...	...	...	...	...	...	...	33
...	...	...	...	...	...	...	...	...	...	...	...	34
...	...	...	...	...	...	...	...	...	...	...	...	
...	...	...	...	...	...	...	...	...	...	...	...	35
...	...	...	...	...	...	...	...	...	...	...	...	36
...	...	...	...	...	...	...	...	...	...	...	...	
...	...	...	...	...	...	...	...	...	...	...	...	37
...	...	...	...	...	...	...	...	...	...	...	...	38
...	...	...	...	...	...	...	...	...	...	...	...	39
...	...	...	...	...	...	...	...	...	...	...	...	40
...	...	...	...	...	...	...	...	...	...	...	...	41
...	...	...	...	...	...	...	...	...	...	...	...	42
...	...	...	...	...	...	...	...	...	...	...	...	43
...	...	...	...	...	...	...	...	...	...	...	...	44
...	...	...	...	...	...	...	...	...	7	...	...	
...	...	...	...	...	...	...	...	...	...	...	...	45
...	...	...	...	...	...	...	...	...	...	...	...	46
...	...	...	...	...	...	...	...	...	...	...	...	47
...	...	...	...	...	...	...	...	...	7	...	...	48
...	...	...	...	...	...	...	...	...	...	...	...	
...	...	...	...	...	...	...	...	...	...	...	...	49

PROVINCIAL TABLE IV.—SELECTED LANGUAGES AND DIALECTS BY

Serial Number.	Languages and Dialects.	JHALAWAR STATE. Total of persons speaking.	Jhalrapatan (Chhaoni).	Awar.	Dag.	Gangdhar.	Pachpahar.	Patan.
1	2	124	125	126	127	128	129	130
	Marwari ...	***860***	***25***	***16***	***32***	***51***	***573***	***163***
1	Standard ...	550	4	12	18	33	320	163
2	Marwari-Dhundhari ...	179	20	4	2	...	153	...
3	Gorawati ...	...	...	...	...	...	...	...
4	Ajmer Dialect ...	...	...	...	...	...	...	...
5	Merwara Dialect ...	...	...	...	...	...	...	...
6	Mewari ...	131	1	...	12	18	100	...
7	Merwari ...	...	...	...	...	...	...	...
8	Sarwari ...	...	...	...	...	...	...	...
9	Khairari ...	...	...	...	...	...	...	...
10	Godwari ...	...	...	...	...	...	...	...
11	Sirohi ...	...	...	...	...	...	...	...
12	Deorawati ...	...	...	...	...	...	...	...
13	Marwari-Gujarati ...	...	...	...	...	...	...	...
14	Thali ...	...	...	...	...	...	...	...
15	Marwari-Sindhi ...	...	...	...	...	...	...	...
16	Dhatki ...	...	...	...	...	...	...	...
17	Bikaneri ...	...	...	...	...	...	...	...
18	Shekhawati ...	...	...	...	...	...	...	...
19	Bagri ...	...	...	...	...	...	...	...
	Central Eastern Rajasthani ...	***106***	***4***	***1***	***10***	***34***	***56***	***1***
20	Jaipuri ...	14	...	...	...	14	...	...
21	Torawati ...	...	...	...	...	...	...	...
22	Kathaira ...	...	...	...	...	...	...	...
23	Chaurasi ...	...	...	...	...	...	...	...
24	Nagarchal ...	...	...	...	...	...	...	...
25	Rajawati ...	...	...	...	...	...	...	...
26	Kishangarhi ...	...	...	...	...	...	...	...
27	Ajmeri ...	...	...	...	...	...	...	...
28	Harauti ...	92	4	1	10	20	56	1
29	Sipari ...	...	...	...	...	...	...	...
	North Eastern Rajasthani ...	...	...	...	...	...	...	...
30	Mewati ...	...	...	...	...	...	...	...
31	Rathi ...	...	...	...	...	...	...	...
32	Nahera-Mewati ...	...	...	...	...	...	...	...
33	Kather-Mewati ...	...	...	...	...	...	...	...
34	Ahirwati ...	...	...	...	...	...	...	...
	Malvi ...	***56,624***	***1***	***10,310***	***18,487***	***19,357***	***8,452***	***17***
35	Malvi ...	3,724	1	767	2,894	11	50	1
36	Sondhwari ..	52,900	...	9,543	15,593	19,346	8,402	16
	Western Hindi ...	***48,604***	***10,251***	***515***	***581***	***4,411***	***13,931***	***18,915***
37	Bangaru ...	...	...	...	...	...	...	...
38	Jatu ...	...	...	...	...	...	...	...
39	Hariani ...	...	...	...	...	...	...	...
40	Braj Bhakha or Antarbedi	33	2	...	...	...	30	1
41	Kalimal ...	...	...	...	...	...	...	...
42	Dangbhang ...	...	...	...	...	...	...	...
43	Urdu ...	3,783	2,554	...	452	375	206	196
44	Hindi ..	44,788	7,695	515	129	4,036	13,695	18,718
	Bhili ...	***224***	...	...	...	...	***224***	...
45	Girasia ...	...	...	...	...	...	...	...
46	Bhilodi ...	...	...	...	...	...	...	...
47	Wagdi ...	...	...	...	...	...	...	...
48	Bhili ...	224	...	...	...	...	224	...
	Panjabi ...	...	...	...	...	...	...	...
49	Rathi of Bikaner ...	...	...	...	...	...	...	...

KARAULI STATE.							KISHANGARH STATE.						
Total of persons speaking	Karauli Town.	Hazur.	Machilpur.	Mandrail.	Sapotra.	Utgir.	Total of persons speaking.	Kishangarh Town.	Arain.	Kishangarh.	Rupnagar.	Sarwar.	SERIAL NUMBER.
131	132	133	134	135	136	137	138	139	140	141	142	143	1
551	*145*	*79*	*115*	*180*	*32*	...	*17,899*	*299*	*75*	*145*	*390*	*16,990*	
377	59	9	106	177	26	...	758	203	51	102	314	88	1
48	...	43	5	...	...	...	...	...	...	...	...	...	2
...	...	...	...	...	...	...	...	...	...	...	...	...	3
...	...	...	...	...	...	...	...	...	...	...	...	...	4
1	...	...	1	...	...	...	...	...	...	...	...	...	5
...	...	...	...	...	...	...	690	66	19	41	6	558	6
2	1	1	...	...	...	...	63	...	...	2	61	...	7
...	...	...	...	...	...	...	16,341	...	...	...	...	16,341	8
...	...	...	...	...	...	...	4	...	1	...	...	3	9
...	...	...	...	...	...	...	...	...	...	...	...	...	10
...	...	...	...	...	...	...	...	...	...	...	...	...	11
...	...	...	...	...	...	...	...	...	...	...	...	...	12
94	75	13	...	...	6	...	...	...	...	...	...	...	13
...	...	...	...	...	...	...	...	...	...	...	...	...	14
...	...	...	...	...	...	...	...	...	...	...	...	...	15
...	...	...	...	...	...	...	...	...	...	...	...	...	16
...	...	...	...	...	...	...	2	...	...	...	2	...	17
29	10	13	3	3	...	...	41	30	4	...	7	...	18
...	...	...	...	...	...	...	...	...	...	...	...	...	19
140	*5*	*5*	*82*	*1*	*47*	...	*67,441*	*11,330*	*16,001*	*18,014*	*18,782*	*3,314*	
11	5	4	1	1	...	...	1,596	303	138	82	158	915	20
...	...	...	...	...	...	...	...	...	...	...	...	...	21
61	...	1	17	...	48	...	...	...	...	...	...	...	22
...	...	...	...	...	...	...	...	...	...	...	...	...	23
...	...	...	...	...	...	...	...	...	...	...	...	...	24
...	...	...	...	...	...	...	...	...	...	...	...	...	25
...	...	...	...	...	...	...	63,269	10,921	15,810	17,902	18,619	17	26
...	...	...	...	...	...	...	2,520	102	53	29	4	2,332	27
68	...	...	64	...	4	...	56	4	...	1	1	50	28
...	...	...	...	...	...	...	...	...	...	...	...	...	29
2	*2*	...	...	...	...	...	*48*	*30*	...	...	*1*	*17*	
2	2	...	...	...	...	...	48	30	...	...	1	17	30
...	...	...	...	...	...	...	...	...	...	...	...	...	31
...	...	...	...	...	...	...	...	...	...	...	...	...	32
...	...	...	...	...	...	...	...	...	...	...	...	...	33
...	...	...	...	...	...	...	...	...	...	...	...	...	34
...	...	...	...	...	...	...	*40*	*4*	*4*	*1*	*11*	*20*	
...	...	...	...	...	...	...	40	4	4	1	11	20	35
...	...	...	...	...	...	...	...	...	...	...	...	...	36
139,700	*19,425*	*37,001*	*20,432*	*17,149*	*36,646*	*9,047*	*172*	*131*	*5*	*22*	*8*	*6*	
...	...	...	...	...	...	...	...	...	...	...	...	...	37
...	...	...	...	...	...	...	...	...	...	...	...	...	38
...	...	...	...	...	...	...	...	...	...	...	...	...	39
42,204	20	10	19,883	16,990	...	5,301	54	28	3	22	1	...	40
11,583	165	91	...	12	10,969	346	...	...	...	...	...	...	41
3,379	...	...	...	...	28	3,351	1	...	...	...	...	1	42
3,485	3,428	7	11	27	...	12	1	1	...	...	...	...	43
79,049	15,812	36,893	588	120	25,649	37	116	102	2	...	7	5	44
...	...	...	...	...	...	...	...	...	...	...	...	...	
...	...	...	...	...	...	...	...	...	...	...	...	...	45
...	...	...	...	...	...	...	...	...	...	...	...	...	46
...	...	...	...	...	...	...	...	...	...	...	...	...	47
...	...	...	...	...	...	...	...	...	...	...	...	...	48
...	...	...	...	...	...	...	...	...	...	...	...	...	
...	...	...	...	...	...	...	...	...	...	...	...	...	49

PROVINCIAL TABLE IV.—SELECTED LANGUAGES AND DIALECTS BY

SERIAL NUMBER.	LANGUAGES AND DIALECTS.	KOTAH — Total of persons speaking	Kotah City.	Aklerah.	Antah.	Asnawar.	Bakani.	Baran.	Barod.	Chechat.	Chhipabarod.	Digod.	Itawa.	Kanwas.
1	2	144	145	146	147	148	159	150	151	152	153	154	155	156
	Marwari ...	***8,804***	***1,429***	***47***	***304***	***142***	***21***	***970***	***57***	***820***	***84***	***188***	***109***	***1,141***
1	Standard ...	**4,443**	885	9	11	102	20	622	45	274	9	152	55	852
2	Marwari-Dhundhari ...	**1,972**	180	1	264	89	...	47	12	812	7	20	58	138
3	Gorawati ...	...	...	...	...	...	...	...	...	...	...	...	...	...
4	Ajmer Dialect ...	...	...	...	...	...	...	...	...	...	...	...	...	...
5	Merwara Dialect ...	...	...	...	...	...	...	...	...	...	...	...	...	...
6	Mewari ...	**1,237**	283	86	27	1	1	100	...	222	68	4	1	143
7	Merwari ...	**31**	...	...	...	...	...	...	...	...	...	...	...	...
8	Sarwari ...	...	...	...	...	...	...	...	...	...	...	...	...	...
9	Khairari ...	**46**	8	1	...	...	...	1	...	...	...	4	...	6
10	Godwari ...	...	...	...	...	...	...	...	...	...	...	...	...	...
11	Sirohi ...	...	...	...	...	...	...	...	...	...	...	...	...	...
12	Deorawati ...	...	...	...	...	...	...	...	...	...	...	...	...	...
13	Marwari-Gujarati ...	...	...	...	...	...	...	...	...	...	...	...	...	...
14	Thali ...	...	...	...	...	...	...	...	...	...	...	...	...	...
15	Marwari-Sindhi ...	...	...	...	...	...	...	...	...	...	...	...	...	...
16	Dhatki ...	...	...	...	...	...	...	...	...	...	...	...	...	...
17	Bikaneri ...	**2**	...	...	...	...	...	...	...	...	...	...	...	...
18	Shekhawati ...	**1,073**	678	...	2	...	...	200	...	12	...	8	...	2
19	Bagri ...	...	...	...	...	...	...	...	...	...	...	...	...	...
	Central Eastern Rajasthani ...	***471,579***	***25,334***	***15,068***	***28,131***	***415***	***134***	***33,468***	***20,236***	***1,865***	***32,590***	***19,858***	***19,990***	***24,660***
20	Jaipuri ...	**2,290**	24	4	26	2	1	317	53	371	3	7	11	203
21	Torawati ...	...	...	...	...	...	...	...	...	...	...	...	...	...
22	Kathaira ...	**53**	...	...	...	...	...	53	...	...	...	...	...	...
23	Chaurasi ...	...	...	...	...	...	...	...	...	...	...	...	...	...
24	Nagarchal ...	**133**	...	...	...	...	...	...	2	...	...	...	...	1
25	Rajawati ...	...	...	...	...	...	...	...	...	...	...	...	...	...
26	Kishangarhi ...	**2**	...	...	...	...	...	...	...	...	...	...	...	1
27	Ajmeri ...	**54**	...	...	...	...	...	...	...	3	...	...	...	23
28	Harauti ...	**468,325**	25,297	15,064	28,087	413	133	33,077	20,179	1,491	32,587	19,844	19,939	24,432
29	Sipari ...	**722**	13	...	18	...	...	21	2	...	...	7	40	...
	North Eastern Rajasthani ...	***92***	***4***	...	...	...	***1***	...	...	...	...	...	...	***10***
30	Mewati ...	**92**	4	...	...	...	1	...	...	...	...	...	...	10
31	Rathi ...	...	...	...	...	...	...	...	...	...	...	...	...	...
32	Nahera-Mewati ...	...	...	...	...	...	...	...	...	...	...	...	...	...
33	Kather-Mewati ...	...	...	...	...	...	...	...	...	...	...	...	...	...
34	Ahirwati ...	...	...	...	...	...	...	...	...	...	...	...	...	...
	Malvi ...	***128,963***	***163***	***21,002***	***16***	***11,825***	***32,210***	***51***	***19***	***29,083***	***273***	***18***	***9***	***94***
35	Malvi ...	**128,698**	159	21,001	15	11,825	32,210	51	19	28,855	273	17	9	94
36	Sondhwari ...	**265**	4	1	1	...	...	...	...	228	...	1	...	...
	Western Hindi ...	***72,469***	***9,782***	***856***	***166***	***1,108***	***2[illegible]***	***9,005***	***36***	***6,002***	***2,850***	***162***	***77***	***785***
37	Bangaru ...	**1,371**	88	1	44	...	...	21	13	...	552	77	...	88
38	Jatu ...	...	...	...	...	...	...	...	...	...	...	...	...	...
39	Hariani ...	**1**	...	...	...	...	...	...	...	...	...	...	...	...
40	Braj Bhakha or Antarbedi	**38,565**	1,866	448	51	808	10	1,369	6	620	1,252	21	9	174
41	Kalimal ...	...	...	...	...	...	...	...	...	...	...	...	...	...
42	Dangbhang ...	...	...	...	...	...	...	...	...	...	...	...	...	...
43	Urdu ...	**6,557**	4,489	130	25	45	78	602	1	265	24	11	51	42
44	Hindi ...	**25,975**	3,339	277	46	260	134	7,013	16	5,117	1,022	53	17	581
	Bhili ...	***44***	***5***	...	...	...	...	***39***	...	...	...	...	...	...
45	Girasia ...	...	...	...	...	...	...	...	...	...	...	...	...	...
46	Bhilodi ...	...	...	...	...	...	...	...	...	...	...	...	...	...
47	Wagdi ...	...	...	...	...	...	...	...	...	...	...	...	...	...
48	Bhili ...	**44**	5	...	...	...	...	39	...	...	...	...	...	...
	Panjabi ...	...	...	...	...	...	...	...	...	...	...	...	...	...
49	Rathi of Bikaner ...	...	...	...	...	...	...	...	...	...	...	...	...	...

ADMINISTRATIVE UNITS.—*Continued.*

STATE.									KUSHALGARH (CHIEFSHIP).					LAWA (ESTATE).	
Khanpur.	Kishanganj.	Kunjer.	Ladpura.	Mangrol.	Manohar Thana.	Sangod.	Shahabad.	Kotra.	Total of persons speaking.	Kushalgarh Town.	Dungra.	Maiyad.	Patan.	Total of persons speaking.	SERIAL NUMBER.
157	158	159	160	161	162	163	164	165	166	167	168	169	170	171	1
836	***205***	***270***	***550***	***159***	***477***	***318***	***31***	***646***	***15***	***8***	***1***	***2***	***4***	***15***	
689	98	156	208	5	462	145	80	214	4	...	...	...	4	7	1
122	100	76	187	141	2	137	...	184	...	...	...	...	...	...	2
...	...	...	...	...	...	...	...	...	...	...	...	...	...	...	3
...	...	...	...	...	...	...	...	...	...	...	...	...	...	...	4
...	...	...	...	...	...	...	...	...	...	...	...	...	...	...	5
14	...	16	168	...	3	6	1	198	11	8	1	2	...	3	6
25	6	...	...	...	...	...	...	...	...	...	...	...	...	5	7
...	...	...	...	...	...	...	...	...	...	...	...	...	...	...	8
2	...	...	16	...	...	6	...	7	...	...	...	...	...	...	9
...	...	...	...	...	...	...	...	...	...	...	...	...	...	...	10
...	...	...	...	...	...	...	...	...	...	...	...	...	...	...	11
...	...	...	...	...	...	...	...	...	...	...	...	...	...	...	12
...	...	...	...	...	...	...	...	...	...	...	...	...	...	...	13
...	...	...	...	...	...	...	...	...	...	...	...	...	...	...	14
...	...	...	...	...	...	...	...	...	...	...	...	...	...	...	15
...	...	...	...	...	...	...	...	...	...	...	...	...	...	...	16
...	...	...	...	...	...	...	...	2	...	...	...	...	...	...	17
34	1	22	21	13	10	24	...	46	...	...	...	...	...	...	18
...	...	...	...	...	...	...	...	...	...	...	...	...	...	...	19
45,398	***25,824***	***39,919***	***44,567***	***27,268***	***479***	***27,346***	***212***	***38,817***	...	...	...	...	...	***2,770***	
43	212	225	327	8	1	33	...	419	...	...	...	...	...	2,769	20
...	...	...	...	...	...	...	...	...	...	...	...	...	...	...	21
...	...	...	...	...	...	...	...	...	...	...	...	...	...	...	22
...	...	...	...	...	...	...	...	...	...	...	...	...	...	...	23
...	...	...	42	4	...	...	...	84	...	...	...	...	...	...	24
...	...	...	...	...	...	...	...	...	...	...	...	...	...	...	25
...	...	...	...	...	...	1	...	...	...	...	...	...	...	...	26
5	...	...	4	...	...	...	11	8	...	...	...	...	...	...	27
45,322	25,563	39,669	44,194	27,229	478	27,312	201	37,814	...	...	...	...	...	1	28
28	49	25	...	27	...	...	...	492	...	...	...	...	...	...	29
...	***12***	***1***	...	...	***1***	...	...	***63***	...	...	...	...	...	...	
...	12	1	...	...	1	...	...	63	...	...	...	...	...	...	30
...	...	...	...	...	...	...	...	...	...	...	...	...	...	...	31
...	...	...	...	...	...	...	...	...	...	...	...	...	...	...	32
...	...	...	...	...	...	...	...	...	...	...	...	...	...	...	33
...	...	...	...	...	...	...	...	...	...	...	...	...	...	...	34
292	***209***	***118***	***78***	***10***	***33,403***	***43***	***22***	***25***	***2,474***	***1,638***	***152***	***297***	***387***	...	
272	209	118	72	10	33,408	39	22	25	**2,474**	1,638	152	297	387	...	35
20	...	...	6	...	...	4	...	...	...	...	...	...	...	...	36
689	***4,189***	***3,141***	***2,911***	***67***	***637***	***2,051***	***27,392***	***341***	***838***	***329***	***100***	***343***	***66***	***4***	
146	178	89	124	...	...	...	...	...	...	...	...	...	...	...	37
...	...	...	...	...	...	...	...	...	...	...	...	...	...	...	38
...	1	...	...	...	...	...	...	...	...	...	...	...	...	...	39
211	3,626	180	664	17	155	44	27,071	18	...	...	...	...	...	3	40
...	...	...	...	...	...	...	...	...	...	...	...	...	...	...	41
...	...	...	...	...	...	...	...	...	...	...	...	...	...	...	42
87	218	226	164	7	16	14	16	46	**271**	104	59	106	2	...	43
245	166	2,696	1,959	43	466	1,993	305	277	**567**	225	41	237	64	1	44
...	...	...	...	...	...	...	...	...	***31,085***	***786***	***8,470***	***15,032***	***6,797***	...	
...	...	...	...	...	...	...	...	...	...	...	...	...	...	...	45
...	...	...	...	...	...	...	...	...	**30,608**	518	8,450	14,858	6,787	...	46
...	...	...	...	...	...	...	...	...	**477**	268	20	179	10	...	47
...	...	...	...	...	...	...	...	...	...	...	...	...	...	...	48
...	...	...	...	...	...	...	...	...	...	...	...	...	...	...	
...	...	...	...	...	...	...	...	...	...	...	...	...	...	...	49

PROVINCIAL TABLE IV.—SELECTED LANGUAGES AND DIALECTS BY

SERIAL NUMBER.	LANGUAGES AND DIALECTS.	MARWAR									
		Total of persons speaking.	Jodhpur City.	Bali.	Bilara.	Desuri.	Didwana.	Jalore.	Jaitaran.	Jaswantpura.	Jodhpur.
1	2	172	173	174	175	176	177	178	179	180	181
	Marwari ...	***2,092,869***	***90,392***	***106,971***	***73,071***	***82,133***	***110,795***	***145,553***	***87,358***	***110,824***	***138,470***
1	Standard ...	**1,850,865**	89,624	94,076	73,061	75,327	106,689	144,470	86,976	110,645	138,423
2	Marwari-Dhundhari ...	**2,320**	2	11	6	4	...	2	76	...	...
3	Gorawati ...	**7,777**	...	...	...	...	...	...	...	...	...
4	Ajmer Dialect ...	...	...	...	...	...	...	...	...	...	...
5	Merwara Dialect ...	...	...	...	...	...	...	...	...	...	...
6	Mewari ...	**1,118**	87	847	1	256	1	40	62	...	...
7	Merwari ...	**592**	107	...	...	13	5	7	223	...	...
8	Sarwari ...	...	...	...	...	...	...	...	...	...	...
9	Khairari ...	...	...	...	...	...	...	...	...	...	...
10	Godwari ...	**17,289**	...	10,784	...	6,505	...	...	...	...	...
11	Sirohi ...	**1,854**	6	1,676	...	15	...	129	2	...	...
12	Deorawati ...	**903**	...	...	...	...	...	903	...	...	...
13	Marwari-Gujarati ...	**20,193**	...	...	...	...	...	...	...	165	...
14	Thali ...	**18,423**	...	...	...	...	...	...	...	...	...
15	Marwari-Sindhi ...	**38,146**	6	...	...	...	...	...	...	...	...
16	Dhatki ...	**118,286**	...	...	...	...	...	...	...	...	...
17	Bikaneri ...	...	...	...	...	...	...	...	...	...	...
18	Shekhawati ...	**15,103**	560	77	8	13	4,100	2	19	14	47
19	Bagri ...	...	...	...	...	...	...	...	...	...	...
	Central Eastern Rajasthani ...	***8,191***	***392***	***4***	...	***6***	***299***	...	***95***	...	...
20	Jaipuri ...	**7,629**	293	...	...	5	299	...	5	...	...
21	Torawati ...	...	...	...	...	...	...	...	...	...	...
22	Kathaira ...	...	...	...	...	...	...	...	...	...	...
23	Chaurasi ...	...	...	...	...	...	...	...	...	...	...
24	Nagarchal ...	...	...	...	...	...	...	...	...	...	...
25	Rajawati ...	...	...	...	...	...	...	...	...	...	...
26	Kishangarhi ...	**17**	...	...	...	...	...	...	...	...	...
27	Ajmeri ...	**545**	99	4	...	1	...	...	90	...	...
28	Harauti ...	...	...	...	...	...	...	...	...	...	...
29	Sipari ...	...	...	...	...	...	...	...	...	...	...
	North Eastern Rajasthani ...	***11***	...	...	...	...	...	...	***1***	...	...
30	Mewati ...	**11**	...	...	...	...	...	...	1	...	...
31	Rathi ...	...	...	...	...	...	...	...	...	...	...
32	Nahera-Mewati ...	...	...	...	...	...	...	...	...	...	...
33	Kather-Mewati ...	...	...	...	...	...	...	...	...	...	...
34	Ahirwati ...	...	...	...	...	...	...	...	...	...	...
	Malvi ...	***124***	***69***	...	...	***2***	...	...	***9***	...	***23***
35	Malvi ...	**124**	69	...	...	2	...	...	9	...	23
36	Sondhwari ...	...	...	...	...	...	...	...	...	...	...
	Western Hindi ...	***6,220***	***2,968***	***76***	***28***	***25***	***74***	***27***	***41***	***19***	***91***
37	Bangaru ...	...	...	...	...	...	...	...	...	...	...
38	Jatu ...	...	...	...	...	...	...	...	...	...	...
39	Hariani ...	...	...	...	...	...	...	...	...	...	...
40	Braj Bhakha or Antarbedi	**162**	47	...	...	2	2	2	...	2	7
41	Kalimal ...	...	...	...	...	...	...	...	...	...	...
42	Dangbhang ...	...	...	...	...	...	...	...	...	...	...
43	Urdu ...	**168**	98	...	8	...	7	...	...	...	12
44	Hindi ...	**5,890**	2,823	76	25	23	65	25	41	17	72
	Bhili ...	***16,915***	...	***7,078***	...	...	...	***3,513***	...	***6,324***	...
45	Girasia ...	**4,869**	...	4,869	...	...	...	...	...	...	...
46	Bhilodi ...	**12,046**	...	2,209	...	...	...	3,513	...	6,324	...
47	Wagdi ...	...	...	...	...	...	...	...	...	...	...
48	Bhili ...	...	...	...	...	...	...	...	...	...	...
	Panjabi ...	...	...	...	...	...	...	...	...	...	...
49	Rathi of Bikaner ...	...	...	...	...	...	...	...	...	...	...

Administrative Units.—*Continued.*

STATE

Malani.	Merta.	Nagaur.	Pachbhadra.	Pali.	Parbatsar.	Phalodi.	Sambhar-Marwar.	½Sambhar-Shamlat	Sanchore.	Shergarh.	Sheo.	Siwana.	Sojat.	Serial Number.
182	183	184	185	186	187	188	189	190	191	192	193	194	195	1
178,090	**126,854**	**142,139**	**31,947**	**63,058**	**108,610**	**84,750**	**75,007**	**1,776**	**84,322**	**63,922**	**24,807**	**45,586**	**116,434**	
40,471	125,850	142,081	31,947	62,802	105,462	84,656	58,491	1,773	51,720	45,753	18,342	45,577	116,149	1
...	871	13	...	6	1,766	24	39	...	...	...	...	...	...	2
...	...	...	...	...	372	...	7,405	...	...	...	...	...	...	3
...	...	...	...	...	...	...	...	...	...	...	...	...	...	4
...	...	...	...	...	...	...	...	...	...	...	...	...	...	5
8	2	...	...	32	17	2	19	...	...	...	...	1	243	6
...	24	...	...	149	15	3	3	3	...	...	...	...	40	7
...	...	...	...	...	...	...	...	...	...	...	...	...	...	8
...	...	...	...	...	...	...	...	...	...	...	...	...	...	9
...	...	...	...	...	...	...	...	...	...	...	...	...	...	10
16	...	...	...	7	...	...	...	...	...	...	...	1	2	11
...	...	...	...	...	...	...	...	...	...	...	...	...	...	12
...	...	...	...	...	...	...	...	...	20,028	...	...	...	...	13
254	...	...	...	...	...	...	...	...	...	18,169	...	...	...	14
19,296	...	...	...	...	...	...	...	...	12,459	...	6,378	7	...	15
118,045	...	...	...	...	...	39	...	...	115	...	87	...	...	16
...	...	...	...	...	...	...	...	...	...	...	...	...	...	17
...	107	45	...	62	978	26	9,050	...	...	...	...	...	...	18
...	...	...	...	...	...	...	...	...	...	...	...	...	...	19
...	**4**	**6**	...	**1**	**168**	**35**	**543**	**6,445**	...	...	...	...	**193**	
...	...	...	...	1	69	6	519	6,432	...	...	...	...	...	20
...	...	...	...	...	...	...	...	...	...	...	...	...	...	21
...	...	...	...	...	...	...	...	...	...	...	...	...	...	22
...	...	...	...	...	...	...	...	...	...	...	...	...	...	23
...	...	...	...	...	...	...	...	...	...	...	...	...	...	24
...	...	...	...	...	...	...	...	...	...	...	...	...	...	25
...	...	...	...	...	5	...	6	6	...	...	...	...	...	26
...	4	6	...	...	94	29	18	7	...	...	...	...	193	27
...	...	...	...	...	...	...	...	...	...	...	...	...	...	28
...	...	...	...	...	...	...	...	...	...	...	...	...	...	29
...	**3**	...	...	...	...	...	**7**	...	...	...	...	...	...	
...	3	...	...	...	...	...	7	...	...	...	...	...	...	30
...	...	...	...	...	...	...	...	...	...	...	...	...	...	31
...	...	...	...	...	...	...	...	...	...	...	...	...	...	32
...	...	...	...	...	...	...	...	...	...	...	...	...	...	33
...	...	...	...	...	...	...	...	...	...	...	...	...	...	34
...	**1**	**3**	...	**1**	**8**	...	**8**	...	...	...	...	...	...	
...	1	3	...	1	8	...	8	...	...	...	...	...	...	35
...	...	...	...	...	...	...	...	...	...	...	...	...	...	36
317	**681**	**645**	**6**	**84**	**42**	**318**	**202**	**252**	**14**	...	**7**	**40**	**263**	
...	...	...	...	...	...	...	...	...	...	...	...	...	...	37
...	...	...	...	...	...	...	...	...	...	...	...	...	...	38
...	...	...	...	...	...	...	...	...	...	...	...	...	...	39
11	...	...	...	9	1	...	10	59	...	...	...	2	8	40
...	...	...	...	...	...	...	...	...	...	...	...	...	...	41
...	...	...	...	...	...	...	...	...	...	...	...	...	...	42
10	...	4	...	...	...	...	34	...	...	...	...	...	...	43
296	681	641	6	75	41	318	158	193	14	...	7	38	255	44
...	...	...	...	...	...	...	...	...	...	...	...	...	...	
...	...	...	...	...	...	...	...	...	...	...	...	...	...	45
...	...	...	...	...	...	...	...	...	...	...	...	...	...	46
...	...	...	...	...	...	...	...	...	...	...	...	...	...	47
...	...	...	...	...	...	...	...	...	...	...	...	...	...	48
...	...	...	...	...	...	...	...	...	...	...	...	...	...	
...	...	...	...	...	...	...	...	...	...	...	...	...	...	49

PROVINCIAL TABLE IV—SELECTED LANGUAGES AND DIALECTS BY

SERIAL NUMBER.	LANGUAGES AND DIALECTS.	MEWAR: Total of persons speaking.	Udaipur City	Asind.	Bhilwara.	Chhoti Sadri.	Chitorgarh.	Deosthan	Deosthan (Kankroli and Nathdwara).	Girwa.	Hurra.	Jahazpur.
	2	196	197	198	199	200	201	202	203	204	205	206
	Marwari ...	***1,369,320***	***36,976***	***12,068***	***95,588***	***41,768***	***101,251***	***30,682***	***24,452***	***98,103***	***51,478***	***59,961***
1	Standard ...	**2,494**	177	3	49	246	49	26	108	25	112	44
2	Marwari-Dhundhari ...	**191**	6	...	8	...	1	18	5	...	7	36
3	Gorawati ...	...	...	...	...	...	...	...	...	...	...	...
4	Ajmer Dialect ...	**33**	...	...	...	...	...	...	...	...	...	33
5	Merwara Dialect ...	...	...	...	...	...	...	...	...	...	...	...
6	Mewari ...	**1,354,093**	36,742	12,065	95,513	41,420	101,181	30,630	24,337	98,004	51,324	55,283
7	Merwari ...	**3,012**	6	...	14	1	...	...	...	50	24	5
8	Sarwari ...	**2,798**	...	...	...	...	...	...	...	...	...	2,795
9	Khairari ...	**2,491**	2	...	...	...	...	...	...	14	...	1,747
10	Godwari ...	**39**	...	...	...	6	2	...	...	...	...	...
11	Sirohi ...	**294**	3	...	...	...	...	...	...	...	...	9
12	Deorawati ...	...	...	...	...	...	...	...	...	...	...	...
13	Marwari-Gujarati ...	...	...	...	...	...	...	...	...	...	...	...
14	Thali ...	...	...	...	...	...	...	...	...	...	...	...
15	Marwari-Sindhi ...	...	...	...	...	...	...	...	...	...	...	...
16	Dhatki ...	**1**	...	...	...	...	...	...	...	...	...	...
17	Bikaneri ...	**8**	3	...	1	1	...	...	...	...	...	...
18	Shekhawati ...	**473**	87	...	2	94	15	8	7	10	11	9
19	Bagri ...	**3,393**	...	...	1	...	3	...	...	...	...	...
	Central Eastern Rajasthani ...	***2,507***	***129***	...	***25***	***66***	***19***	***1***	***6***	***5***	***252***	***543***
20	Jaipuri ...	**877**	43	...	10	38	5	1	2	5	13	127
21	Torawati ...	**111**	...	...	...	...	...	...	...	...	...	...
22	Kathaira ...	...	...	...	...	...	...	...	...	...	...	...
23	Chaurasi ...	**4**	...	...	...	...	...	...	...	...	...	...
24	Nagarchal ...	...	...	...	...	...	...	...	...	...	...	...
25	Rajawati ...	...	...	...	...	...	...	...	...	...	...	...
26	Kishangarhi ...	**35**	1	...	...	...	...	...	...	...	1	7
27	Ajmeri ...	**580**	63	...	9	25	5	...	1	...	238	98
28	Harauti ...	**900**	22	...	6	3	9	...	3	...	...	311
29	Sipari ...	...	...	...	...	...	...	...	...	...	...	...
	North Eastern Rajasthani ...	***282***	***41***	...	***19***	***139***	***1***	...	***6***	...	...	***3***
30	Mewati ...	**266**	41	...	4	139	1	...	6	...	...	3
31	Rathi ...	...	...	...	...	...	...	...	...	...	...	...
32	Nahera-Mewati ...	**1**	...	...	...	...	...	...	...	...	...	...
33	Kather-Mewati ...	...	...	...	...	...	...	...	...	...	...	...
34	Ahirwati ...	**15**	...	...	15	...	...	...	...	...	...	...
	Malvi ...	***3,447***	***103***	***4***	***36***	***2,335***	***476***	***23***	***40***	***4***	***2***	***9***
35	Malvi ...	**3,370**	103	4	36	2,335	475	23	40	4	2	9
36	Sondhwari ...	**77**	...	...	...	...	1	...	...	...	...	...
	Western Hindi ...	***8,074***	***1,632***	***4***	***76***	***787***	***420***	***8***	***1,693***	***177***	***181***	***191***
37	Bangaru ...	...	...	...	...	...	...	...	...	...	...	...
38	Jatu ...	...	...	...	...	...	...	...	...	...	...	...
39	Hariani ...	**102**	62	...	...	12	...	...	...	...	...	...
40	Braj Bhakha or Antarbedi.	**2,266**	15	...	...	315	4	...	1,564	174	...	1
41	Kalimal ...	**2**	1	...	1	...	...	...	...	...	...	...
42	Dangbhang ...	...	...	...	...	...	...	...	...	...	...	...
43	Urdu ...	**862**	25	...	32	15	22	...	18	1	1	168
44	Hindi ...	**4,842**	1,529	4	43	445	394	8	111	2	180	22
	Bhili ...	***172,760***	***824***	...	***28***	***3,236***	***2,689***	***25***	***2***	***23,371***	...	...
45	Girasia ...	**246**	...	...	...	...	...	...	...	...	...	...
46	Bhilodi ...	**2,054**	...	...	...	...	698	...	...	...	...	...
47	Wagdi ...	**13,248**	41	...	...	1	1,643	19	1	26	...	...
48	Bhili ...	**157,212**	783	...	28	3,235	348	6	1	23,345	...	...
	Panjabi ...	...	...	...	...	...	...	...	...	...	...	...
49	Rathi of Bikaner ...	...	...	...	...	...	...	...	...	...	...	...

ADMINISTRATIVE UNITS.—*Continued.*

STATE

Kapasin.	Khamnor.	Kherwara.	Kumalgarh.	Magra.	Mandalgarh.	Rajnagar.	Rashmi.	Saharan.	Thikanas.	Udaipur.	SERIAL NUMBER.
207	208	209	210	211	212	213	214	215	216	217	1
45,112	***28,719***	***10,556***	***63,507***	***35,499***	***63,241***	***40,984***	***41,772***	***89,613***	***374,401***	***23,589***	
42	63	196	301	272	9	33	42	97	595	...	1
...	...	1	...	...	...	9	...	16	89	...	2
...	...	...	...	...	...	...	...	...	...	...	3
...	...	...	...	...	...	...	...	...	...	...	4
...	...	...	...	...	...	...	...	...	...	...	5
45,058	28,656	10,138	63,198	35,221	63,225	40,942	41,708	89,228	366,631	23,589	6
...	...	71	...	...	5	...	2	272	2,562	...	7
...	...	1	...	...	...	...	...	...	2	...	8
...	...	4	6	2	...	...	...	...	716	...	9
...	...	...	...	...	...	...	...	...	31	...	10
...	...	140	1	...	...	...	...	...	141	...	11
...	...	...	...	...	...	...	...	...	...	...	12
...	...	...	...	...	...	...	...	...	...	...	13
...	...	...	...	...	...	...	...	...	...	...	14
...	...	...	...	...	...	...	...	...	...	...	15
...	...	...	...	...	...	...	1	...	...	...	16
...	...	...	...	2	1	...	...	...	...	...	17
6	...	5	1	2	1	...	19	...	251	...	18
6	...	...	...	...	...	...	...	...	3,383	...	19
10	...	***5***	***2***	***9***	***47***	...	...	***32***	***1,356***	...	
10	...	1	1	6	27	...	...	23	565	...	20
...	...	...	...	...	...	...	...	...	111	...	21
...	...	...	...	...	...	...	...	...	...	...	22
...	...	...	...	3	...	...	...	...	1	...	23
...	...	...	...	...	...	...	...	...	...	...	24
...	...	...	...	...	...	...	...	...	...	...	25
...	...	...	1	...	3	...	...	...	23	...	26
...	...	3	...	...	11	...	...	9	118	...	27
...	...	1	...	...	6	...	...	...	539	...	28
...	...	...	...	...	...	...	...	...	...	...	29
3	...	***1***	***1***	***5***	...	...	...	***4***	***59***	...	
3	...	1	1	5	...	...	...	4	58	...	30
...	...	...	...	...	...	...	...	...	...	...	31
...	...	...	...	...	...	...	...	...	1	...	32
...	...	...	...	...	...	...	...	...	...	...	33
...	...	...	...	...	...	...	...	...	...	...	34
5	***1***	...	...	***3***	***18***	...	***1***	***36***	***351***	...	
5	1	...	...	3	18	...	1	36	275	...	35
...	...	...	...	...	...	...	...	...	76	...	36
119	...	***626***	***41***	***151***	***4***	***49***	...	***534***	***1,381***	...	
...	...	...	...	...	...	...	...	...	...	...	37
...	...	...	...	...	...	...	...	...	...	...	38
...	...	3	...	18	...	...	...	6	1	...	39
68	...	4	...	11	...	49	...	57	4	...	40
...	...	...	...	...	...	...	...	...	...	...	41
...	...	...	...	...	...	...	...	...	...	...	42
...	...	535	1	...	...	...	...	4	40	...	43
51	...	84	40	122	4	...	...	467	1,336	...	44
...	***2***	***61,546***	***1,435***	***61,301***	...	...	...	***76***	***13,627***	***4,598***	
...	...	51	193	2	...	...	...	...	...	...	45
...	...	6	...	8	...	...	...	...	1,342	...	46
...	...	3,382	...	5,005	...	...	...	15	3,115	...	47
...	2	58,107	1,242	56,286	...	...	...	61	9,170	4,598	48
...	...	...	...	...	...	...	...	...	...	...	
...	...	...	...	...	...	...	...	...	...	...	49

PROVINCIAL TABLE IV.—Selected Languages and Dialects by

Serial Number.	Languages and Dialects.	Partabgarh State. Total of persons speaking.	Partabgarh Town.	Hathunia.	Magra.	Sagthall.	Shahpura State. Total of persons speaking.	Shahpura Town.	Arwar.	Dhikola.	Dohria.	Kanechan.	Phulia.	Sangria.	Shahpura.
1	2	218	219	220	221	222	223	224	225	226	227	228	229	230	231
	Marwari ...	*433*	*156*	*205*	*6*	*66*	*50,795*	*3,713*	*6,401*	*10,569*	*6,945*	*3,131*	*7,218*	*4,009*	*3,809*
1	Standard ...	118	19	65	2	32	108	40	12	15	7	14	1	14	5
2	Marwari-Dhundhari ...	1	...	...	...	1	596	193	18	105	111	1	67	3	98
3	Gorawati ...	...	...	...	...	...	102	36	2	7	15	5	25	12	...
4	Ajmer Dialect ...	...	...	...	...	...	...	...	...	...	...	...	...	...	...
5	Merwara Dialect ...	...	...	...	...	...	...	...	...	...	...	...	...	...	...
6	Mewari ...	253	82	140	3	28	49,901	3,422	6,369	10,379	6,811	3,111	7,125	3,980	3,704
7	Merwari ...	...	...	...	...	...	1	1	...	...	...	...	...	...	...
8	Sarwari ...	...	...	...	...	...	12	6	...	5	1	...	...	...	...
9	Khairari ...	...	...	...	...	...	15	2	...	13	...	...	...	...	...
10	Godwari ...	...	...	...	...	...	...	...	...	...	...	...	...	...	...
11	Sirohi ...	...	...	...	...	...	5	5	...	...	...	...	...	...	...
12	Deorawati ...	...	...	...	...	...	...	...	...	...	...	...	...	...	...
13	Marwari-Gujarati ...	...	...	...	...	...	...	...	...	...	...	...	...	...	...
14	Thali ...	...	...	...	...	...	...	...	...	...	...	...	...	...	...
15	Marwari-Sindhi ...	...	...	...	...	...	...	...	...	...	...	...	...	...	...
16	Dhatki ...	...	...	...	...	...	...	...	...	...	...	...	...	...	...
17	Bikaneri ...	...	...	...	...	...	1	1	...	...	...	...	...	...	...
18	Shekhawati ...	61	55	...	1	5	54	7	...	45	...	...	...	...	2
19	Bagri ...	...	...	...	...	...	...	...	...	...	...	...	...	...	...
	Central Eastern Rajasthani ...	*2*	...	*1*	...	*1*	*3,250*	*426*	*458*	*165*	*646*	*188*	*842*	*412*	*113*
20	Jaipuri ...	...	...	...	...	...	196	55	7	33	36	1	42	13	9
21	Torawati ...	...	...	...	...	...	...	...	...	...	...	...	...	...	...
22	Kathaira ...	...	...	...	...	...	...	...	...	...	...	...	...	...	...
23	Chaurasi ...	...	...	...	...	...	22	13	...	2	4	...	2	...	1
24	Nagarchal ...	...	...	...	...	...	...	...	...	...	...	...	...	...	...
25	Rajawati ...	...	...	...	...	...	...	...	...	...	...	...	...	...	...
26	Kishangarhi ...	...	...	...	...	...	217	20	15	5	28	16	83	16	34
27	Ajmeri ...	1	...	...	...	1	2,744	308	432	120	558	170	709	382	65
28	Harauti ...	1	...	1	...	...	71	30	4	5	20	1	6	1	4
29	Sipari ...	...	...	...	...	...	...	...	...	...	...	...	...	...	...
	North Eastern Rajasthani ...	*15*	*4*	*10*	...	*1*	*14*	*10*	...	...	*4*	...	...	...	...
30	Mewati ...	15	4	10	...	1	14	10	...	...	4	...	...	...	...
31	Rathi ...	...	...	...	...	...	...	...	...	...	...	...	...	...	...
32	Nahera-Mewati ...	...	...	...	...	...	...	...	...	...	...	...	...	...	...
33	Kather-Mewati ...	...	...	...	...	...	...	...	...	...	...	...	...	...	...
34	Ahirwati ...	...	...	...	...	...	...	...	...	...	...	...	...	...	...
	Malvi ...	*45,410*	*8,507*	*23,725*	*1,357*	*11,821*	*79*	*63*	*5*	*6*	*1*	...	...	*1*	*3*
35	Malvi ...	45,410	8,507	23,725	1,357	11,821	61	46	5	5	1	...	...	1	3
36	Sondhwari ...	...	...	...	...	...	18	17	...	1	...	...	...	...	...
	Western Hindi ...	*1,345*	*1,145*	*43*	*75*	*82*	*69*	*61*	*1*	*4*	*1*	*1*	...	...	*1*
37	Bangaru ...	...	...	...	...	...	...	...	...	...	...	...	...	...	...
38	Jatu ...	...	...	...	...	...	...	...	...	...	...	...	...	...	...
39	Hariani ...	...	...	...	...	...	...	...	...	...	...	...	...	...	...
40	Braj Bhakha or Antarbedi	81	80	1	...	...	8	3	...	4	...	...	...	...	1
41	Kalimal ...	...	...	...	...	...	...	...	...	...	...	...	...	...	...
42	Dangbhang ...	...	...	...	...	...	2	2	...	...	...	...	...	...	...
43	Urdu ...	1,095	972	41	19	63	2	2	...	...	...	...	...	...	...
44	Hindi ..	169	93	1	56	19	57	54	1	...	1	1	...	...	...
	Bhili ...	*26,814*	*94*	*7,230*	*8,247*	*11,243*	...	...	...	...	...	...	...	...	...
45	Girasia ...	...	...	...	...	...	...	...	...	...	...	...	...	...	...
46	Bhilodi ...	...	...	...	...	...	...	...	...	...	...	...	...	...	...
47	Wagdi ...	84	25	19	12	28	...	...	...	...	...	...	...	...	...
48	Bhili ...	26,730	69	7,211	8,235	11,215	...	...	...	...	...	...	...	...	...
	Panjabi ...	...	...	...	...	...	...	...	...	...	...	...	...	...	...
49	Rathi of Bikaner ...	...	...	...	...	...	...	...	...	...	...	...	...	...	...

SIROHI STATE.														
Total of persons speaking.	Sirohi Town.	Sirohi.	Abu.	Bhakar.	Barlut.	Erinpura.	Madar.	Magra.	Pamera.	Pindwara.	Posaliya.	Rohera.	Santhpur.	SERIAL NUMBER.
232	233	234	235	236	237	238	239	240	241	242	243	244	245	1
176,518	***6,887***	***2,534***	***1,150***	***123***	***22,030***	***1,324***	***21,663***	***22,129***	***25,360***	***19,233***	***26,181***	***15,336***	***12,568***	
168,431	6,728	2,534	1,150	123	21,838	1,178	21,475	22,129	25,338	18,689	20,446	15,256	11,545	1
...	...	...	...	...	...	...	...	...	...	...	...	...	...	2
22	...	...	...	...	...	...	...	...	...	16	...	1	5	3
197	4	...	...	...	1	14	...	...	...	13	2	6	157	4
1	...	...	...	...	...	...	...	...	...	...	...	1	...	5
460	44	...	...	...	91	2	53	...	...	123	17	46	84	6
32	...	...	...	...	...	...	...	...	...	...	...	...	32	7
...	...	...	...	...	...	...	...	...	...	...	...	...	...	8
...	...	...	...	...	...	...	...	...	...	...	...	...	...	9
28	...	...	...	...	1	...	...	...	...	14	2	11	...	10
6,563	96	...	...	...	84	...	122	...	...	849	5,698	1	218	11
4	...	...	...	...	...	...	...	...	...	...	...	4	...	12
...	...	...	...	...	...	...	...	...	...	...	...	...	...	13
...	...	...	...	...	...	...	...	...	...	...	...	...	...	14
...	...	...	...	...	...	...	...	...	...	...	...	...	...	15
...	...	...	...	...	...	...	...	...	...	...	...	...	...	16
3	2	...	...	...	...	...	...	...	...	...	...	...	1	17
776	13	...	...	...	15	180	13	...	22	29	14	9	531	18
1	...	...	...	...	...	...	...	...	...	...	...	1	...	19
995	***14***	***69***	***4***	...	***3***	***1***	***51***	...	***42***	***88***	***35***	***51***	***637***	
936	13	69	4	...	3	1	51	...	42	88	35	50	580	20
...	...	...	...	...	...	...	...	...	...	...	...	...	...	21
7	1	...	...	...	...	...	...	...	...	...	...	...	6	22
...	...	...	...	...	...	...	...	...	...	...	...	...	...	23
...	...	...	...	...	...	...	...	...	...	...	...	...	...	24
...	...	...	...	...	...	...	...	...	...	...	...	...	...	25
39	...	...	...	...	...	...	...	...	...	...	...	1	38	26
...	...	...	...	...	...	...	...	...	...	...	...	...	...	27
13	...	...	...	...	...	...	...	...	...	...	...	...	13	28
...	...	...	...	...	...	...	...	...	...	...	...	...	...	29
160	***2***	...	***122***	***1***	...	...	...	...	...	***2***	...	***1***	***32***	
28	...	...	...	1	...	...	...	...	...	2	...	...	25	30
124	2	...	122	...	...	...	...	...	...	...	...	...	...	31
...	...	...	...	...	...	...	...	...	...	...	...	...	...	32
...	...	...	...	...	...	...	...	...	...	...	...	...	...	33
8	...	...	...	...	...	...	...	...	...	...	...	1	7	34
...	...	...	...	...	...	...	...	...	...	...	...	...	...	
...	...	...	...	...	...	...	...	...	...	...	...	...	...	35
...	...	...	...	...	...	...	...	...	...	...	...	...	...	36
4,486	***226***	***4***	***51***	***17***	***11***	***250***	***98***	***5***	***60***	***173***	***43***	***113***	***3,435***	
...	...	...	...	...	...	...	...	...	...	...	...	...	...	37
1	...	...	...	...	...	...	...	...	...	...	...	...	1	38
3	1	...	...	...	...	1	...	...	...	...	...	...	1	39
201	9	...	...	...	...	139	...	...	...	1	...	2	50	40
...	...	...	...	...	...	...	...	...	...	...	...	...	...	41
...	...	...	...	...	...	...	...	...	...	...	...	...	...	42
999	15	...	...	6	...	22	32	...	44	47	12	21	800	43
3,282	201	4	51	11	11	88	66	5	16	125	31	90	2,583	44
30,397	***311***	***101***	***5***	***4,488***	***437***	***58***	***2,287***	***1,238***	***1,953***	***5,063***	***890***	***5,192***	***8,374***	
14,859	1	...	...	3,684	...	...	128	...	517	4,143	...	1,224	5,162	45
15,528	310	101	5	804	437	58	2,159	1,238	1,436	910	890	3,968	3,212	46
10	...	...	...	...	...	...	...	...	...	10	...	...	...	47
...	...	...	...	...	...	...	...	...	...	...	...	...	...	48
...	...	...	...	...	...	...	...	...	...	...	...	...	...	
...	...	...	...	...	...	...	...	...	...	...	...	...	...	49

PROVINCIAL TABLE IV.—SELECTED LANGUAGES AND DIALECTS BY ADMINISTRATIVE UNITS.—*Concluded.*

SERIAL NUMBER.	LANGUAGES AND DIALECTS.	TONK STATE.							
		Total of persons speaking.	Tonk City.	Aligarh.	Chhabra.	Nimbahera.	Pirawa.	Sironj.	Tonk
1	2	246	247	248	249	250	251	252	253
	Marwari ...	***52,488***	***73***	...	***27***	***52,174***	***12***	***162***	***40***
1	Standard ...	**597**	69	...	23	385	10	157	3
2	Marwari-Dhundhari ...	...	...	...	...	...	...	...	...
3	Gorawati ...	...	...	...	...	...	...	...	...
4	Ajmer Dialect ...	...	...	...	...	...	...	...	...
5	Merwara Dialect ...	...	...	...	...	...	...	...	...
6	Mewari ...	**51,806**	...	...	4	51,768	2	5	32
7	Merwari ...	...	...	...	...	...	...	...	...
8	Sarwari ...	...	...	...	...	...	...	...	...
9	Khairari ...	**79**	...	...	...	74	...	...	5
10	Godwari ...	...	...	...	...	...	...	...	...
11	Sirohi ...	...	...	...	...	...	...	...	...
12	Deorawati ...	...	...	...	...	...	...	...	...
13	Marwari-Gujarati ...	...	...	...	...	...	...	...	...
14	Thali ...	...	...	...	...	...	...	...	...
15	Marwari-Sindhi ...	...	...	...	...	...	...	...	...
16	Dhatki ...	...	...	...	...	...	...	...	...
17	Bikaneri ...	...	...	...	...	...	...	...	...
18	Shekhawati ...	**6**	4	...	...	2	...	...	...
19	Bagri ...	...	...	...	...	...	...	...	...
	Central Eastern Rajasthani ...	***112,997***	***16,138***	***14,646***	***29,727***	***81***	***8***	...	***52,397***
20	Jaipuri ...	**111,648**	16,138	14,646	28,643	14	1	...	52,206
21	Torawati ...	...	...	...	...	...	...	...	...
22	Kathaira ...	...	...	...	...	...	...	...	...
23	Chaurasi ...	...	...	...	...	...	...	...	...
24	Nagarchal ...	**190**	...	...	...	...	...	...	190
25	Rajawati ...	...	...	...	...	...	...	...	...
26	Kishangarhi ...	...	...	...	...	...	...	...	...
27	Ajmeri ...	**67**	...	...	...	67	...	...	...
28	Harauti ...	**1,092**	...	...	1,084	...	7	...	1
29	Sipari ...	...	...	...	...	...	...	...	...
	North Eastern Rajasthani ...	***159***	...	...	***149***	***10***	...	...	...
30	Mewati ...	**159**	...	...	149	10	...	...	...
31	Rathi ...	...	...	...	...	...	...	...	...
32	Nahera-Mewati ...	...	...	...	...	...	...	...	...
33	Kather-Mewati ...	...	...	...	...	...	...	...	...
34	Ahirwati ...	...	...	...	...	...	...	...	...
	Malvi ...	***112,038***	***4***	...	***1,572***	***109***	***29,553***	***80,799***	***1***
35	Malvi ...	**101,497**	4	...	1,572	109	19,013	80,799	...
36	Sondhwari ...	**10,541**	...	...	...	...	10,540	...	1
	Western Hindi ...	***39,556***	***19,547***	***1,481***	***2,651***	***3,510***	***2,034***	***7,759***	***2,574***
37	Bangaru ...	...	...	...	...	...	...	...	...
38	Jatu ...	...	...	...	...	...	...	...	...
39	Hariani ...	...	...	...	...	...	...	...	...
40	Braj Bhakha or Antarbedi	...	...	...	...	...	...	...	...
41	Kalimal ...	...	...	...	...	...	...	...	...
42	Dangbhang ...	...	...	...	...	...	...	...	...
43	Urdu ...	**39,156**	19,547	1,481	2,651	3,166	2,034	7,703	2,574
44	Hindi ...	**400**	...	...	...	344	...	56	...
	Bhili ...	***58***	...	...	...	...	...	***58***	...
45	Girasia ...	...	...	...	...	...	...	...	...
46	Bhilodi ...	...	...	...	...	...	...	...	...
47	Wagdi ...	...	...	...	...	...	...	...	...
48	Bhili ...	**58**	...	...	...	...	...	58	...
	Panjabi ...	...	...	...	...	...	...	...	...
49	Rathi of Bikaner ...	...	...	...	...	...	...	...	...